FOUR SIDES
OF THE CIRCLE

THE BEATLES' SECOND PHASE, 1970-1974

TERRY WILSON

SUNTE

Four Sides Of The Circle: The Beatles' Second Phase

by Terry Wilson

Copyright © 2022 Terry Wilson

All rights reserved. No portion of this book may be reproduced in any form or by any electronic or mechanical means, including information storage or retrieval systems, without permission in writing from the copyright holder, except for review purposes or as permitted by applicable law.

For permissions contact the author at: terryjwilson2@hotmail.com

Cover photo courtesy of mdjaff/freepik.com

ISBN: 9798845981202 (print)

First edition, 2022

For Archie

Beatles expert, and my unofficial
research assistant.

About the author

Terry Wilson was born in 1968, while Hey Jude was at number 1. He is a freelance writer and journalist, musician, record collector and long-standing Beatles fan. His previous books include *The Secret History Of Crop Circles* (CCCS, 1998) and *Tamla Motown: The Stories Behind The UK Singles* (Cherry Red, 2009). In addition he occasionally writes for music publications and runs several websites on various musical genres of personal interest. He lives in Sussex, England with his wife and son.

Acknowledgements

It's customary in a book like this to include a long list of thank-yous to everyone who helped along the way. In this case, I can't.

This book was written primarily during lock-down, and as such has been a solitary endeavour, researched and written alone – although I thank my wife, Julie, for being here with me throughout, and my son, Archie, for his help and enduring interest. Thanks also to Alec for sending me some useful Harrison literature.

I also must thank the authors and Beatle-ologists who have gone before, whom I have never met but whose research made the creation of this book possible. Many of them are cited in my table of references, and I particularly single out the books by Robert Rodriguez for their encyclopaedic content, and those by Chip Madinger, whose recording sessions research is definitive. And finally Mark Lewisohn, for being inspirational. "Every once in a while, life conjures up a genuine ultimate."

Lastly, I must acknowledge that this book's format owes to the late Ian MacDonald, whose seminal *Revolution In The Head* invented the basic template.

TABLE OF CONTENTS

CREDITS

PREFACE

INTRODUCTION

PART 1: ALL SHINE ON

John Lennon breaks away	7
Sentimental Journey	12
McCartney	24
All Things Must Pass (first phase)	37
Beaucoups Of Blues	58
All Things Must Pass (second phase)	70
Ringo Starr single sessions	89
John Lennon/Plastic Ono Band	91
RAM	108
Ronnie Spector sessions	133
Ascot sessions	135
Imagine	141

PART 2: REALLY THE BORDERLINE

Wild Life	159
Four singles	168
Some Time In New York City	181
Red Rose Speedway (first phase)	198
Red Rose Speedway (second phase)	208

PART 3: TO HELP EACH OTHER

Living In The Material World 225
Paul McCartney screen commissions 239
Ringo 244
Mind Games 259
Band On The Run 276
George Harrison single sessions ....…........ 294
Oldies But Mouldies 295
Jim Keltner Fan Club Hour 308
Paul McCartney single sessions 313
Walls And Bridges 317

PART 4: NOW THE DREAM'S OVER

Goodnight Vienna 337
One Hand Clapping 349
Dark Horse 352
Rock 'N' Roll 366
Wings EMI sessions 380

PART 5: LETTING GO 385

SONG LIST 391

RECORD RELEASES 399

BIBLIOGRAPHY 407

PREFACE

One of the challenges in writing a book like this is the need to find historical accuracy. There are more than enough fallacies in the world of Beatledom to derail even the most dedicated fan, and the post-1969 years are compounded by a comparative lack of research and discussion. I have attempted to present what I believe is a correct body of information, always drawing on original sources where possible – for example, every quotation in this book I have heard with my own ears, or seen on the original printed page in the contemporary music press – nothing is passed on from secondary sources. So although the book you are reading is likely to contain numerous surprises and assertions which may contradict accepted wisdom, the reader can be assured this is the product of proper research, with all the relevant sources provided.

It is sometimes difficult to sort fact from fantasy, especially when the main players – the Beatles themselves – have gone on record with demonstrably inaccurate statements. The Beatles are notoriously unreliable, examples of their memories failing them too numerous to go into, although an example will suffice to make the point: McCartney published his memoir, *The Lyrics*, in 2021, which is as close as we will ever get to an autobiography. On p109 he says he wrote [135] Dear Friend in early 1971, having heard Lennon's words on *John Lennon/Plastic Ono Band*, and 'I was sort of answering him here'. The story appears plausible, Lennon's LP released at the end of 1970, a year before Dear Friend appeared on *Wild Life*, and many readers will think McCartney's given chronology is substantially correct, and that he was *responding to* Lennon. The fact is, Dear Friend appears on a McCartney piano demo recorded before *John Lennon/Plastic Ono Band* was released, and the final version was taped at EMI in July 1971 – before Lennon's [129] How Do You Sleep? had been released, to which it is often wrongly seen as an 'answer'.

This book deals with studio recordings made during the era under review. It does not include live recordings nor home demos, but does contain a good number of unreleased studio tracks, either songs which were not fully realised, or those recorded to near completion but then shelved. In discussing these, a selection process is in play; I do not include *everything* left on the studio floor, and have preferred the recordings I consider the most valuable, complete or interesting. In practise this means original compositions, although in the case of Lennon, several rock and roll cover versions appear; many more remain in the vaults, Lennon usually enjoying jams of old favourites during his album sessions. Some make the cut here, others don't, depending on their quality and significance – although outtakes from his *Rock 'N' Roll* album have tended to feature more heavily, as they form a central part of the project he was working on at the time. We should also qualify our definition of 'unreleased'. For the purposes of this book, it means material not put out during the period, although several – indeed most – of these have since been made available as extras on latter-day album reissues.

Now might be a good point to mention my position on Yoko Ono's releases. As readers will know, she and Lennon worked together on several musical projects, often taking opposite sides of the same 45 and in one case, sharing tracks on an LP. This presents the author with a dilemma – whether to include all of her period work in this survey, whether to only include releases made jointly with Lennon, or whether to disregard them all. On balance, I have taken the third option. This is not born of anti-Yoko bias (which, in point of fact, I don't suffer from; I like her music), but simply a desire to focus on the four solo Beatles. Thus, when we get to their shared releases, Ono's songs – eight in total – are not discussed. I have applied the same principle to those songs recorded by Wings, which were neither written nor sung by McCartney, including Linda's Seaside Woman and Wide Prairie, Denny Laine's I Would Only Smile, and Jimmy McCulloch's Medicine Jar, all of which were recorded contemporaneously with bona-fide group material (although none were released during the time-span of this book).

The songs which do appear are sequenced in order of recording, which is to say, the point at which each track was started in the studio. I have not stuck slavishly to the chronology, so songs recorded in sessions for a specific album will tend to be grouped together to avoid the confusion of jumping from session to session when two unrelated albums are underway concurrently. (As an example: *Sentimental Journey* and *McCartney* were recorded simultaneously in early 1970, but are treated as self-contained sequences, discussed separately from one another.) The fact that it is possible to order the songs in such a manner is due in no small measure to the work of Chip Madinger and Mark Easter, whose *Eight Arms To Hold You* is the standard reference, and contains a fearsome amount of factual information on the solo recording sessions. I recommend it wholeheartedly. We are sometimes seduced by the landmark work of Mark Lewisohn (*The Beatles Recording Sessions*) into thinking it's relatively easy to check when songs were recorded – but in the case of the solo Beatles, we are dealing with sessions in studios all over the world, not all of which kept the same detailed logs as EMI in London. A consequence is that even in spite of Madinger's work, there are some album session dates which remain frustratingly elusive, and in this book I have had to work around the problem as best I could.

Of all the solo Beatles, Harrison kept his session details most closely guarded, there being debate over such fundamentals as the studios he used for some of his 1970s recordings. The situation was exacerbated after he opened his own recording facilities at Friar Park in 1972, there being no openly accessible studio records to consult, assuming there were any in the first place. The most significant gaps in the official record surround the much-celebrated *All Things Must Pass*, where dates are reasonably well known but without listings as to who plays on which tracks. This has been the source of chronic frustration to fans over the years, not even the appearance of an extravagant deluxe album reissue in 2021 able to confirm the full picture – and in fact indicating in the accompanying notes that proper records were never kept. In this instance I defer again to another researcher, Simon Leng, who in his 2003 opus, *The Music Of George Harrison*, published album personnel based on interview material, first-hand testimony and, importantly, the evidence of his own ears, to draw up the first reliable listings. In my book I have used Leng's work as a base line, but unlike in his study, my book presents each track in the order it was recorded. It was one of the delights of the project that when I put Leng's listings into chronological sequence, the details for *All Things Must Pass* fell into place beautifully, starting with Harrison's core band of Eric Clapton, Klaus Voormann, Ringo Starr, Billy Preston and Alan White, gradually developing until the musicians who became Derek and the Dominos started to appear. Then after a break in proceedings in June, the band was formally launched, Derek and the Dominos also becoming Harrison's default studio ensemble from that point on. Subsequent findings, particularly in the excellently researched *All Things Must Pass Away* (Womack and Kruppa, 2021), have allowed me to make the odd refinement, and ultimately, thanks to the foundation work of these and other authors, I am happy to say the details presented here are likely the best available.

Note on release dates: for each recording, the release date given pertains to the first official release of that track in the UK and the US. Tracks may have been issued on LP and single, but the earliest is cited.

Terry Wilson, June 2022

INTRODUCTION

The scene is a rented chalet in Disney World, Florida. The date is 29 December 1974. What's taking place is that former Beatle, John Lennon, is signing a pile of legal documents shipped over to him in the last couple of days from New York, on which are already inked the signatures of each of his erstwhile colleagues, McCartney, Harrison and Starr. Lennon is on the phone to lawyer, Harold Seider, and next to Lennon stands his lover, May Pang, about to photograph him as he puts pen to paper. Why is all this taking place? Because 34-year-old Lennon, who'd started the Beatles in his teens, is adding his name to contracts which will now dissolve the group.

It was a strange thing to happen as late as 1974; so synonymous with the 1960s are the Beatles that to talk of their still existing in the mid-1970s seems absurd. Practically everyone agrees they split at the end of the previous decade – so what was Lennon doing that day in Disney World?

The facts behind the break-up are seldom properly understood, the casual assumption being that the group ceased to exist in the spring of 1970, when McCartney announced they were over. The reality though is rather more complex, there being several layers of truth to what was, in essence, a dissolution *process* which took half a decade to complete. The fact that McCartney was forced to sue the others in 1971 to try to effect a separation is enough to show that behind the neatly delineated popular version, there is more than meets the eye.

The decisive event in April 1970, when the world learned the Beatles were splitting up, was in essence nothing more than over-excited journalism, Fleet Street concocting a headline to cover a slow news day. Lennon had been separated from the group since the previous September, when he declared he wanted out, since which the four had cultivated a public party line on the situation, boiling down to a parroting that yes, they were happy working individually, and that although no new Beatles projects were on the table, it was possible they would work together again if the time was right. (This line, incidentally, held throughout the rest of the 1970s.) McCartney's 'announcement', blazed in news reports throughout the western world, was merely a restatement of same, making the hyperbolic media reaction all the more difficult to understand.[1]

---

[1] McCartney's statement came in the form of a typed press release concerning the making of *McCartney*, a few of the Q&As centring on the current state of the Beatles. His remarks on the album included, 'Not being done with the Beatles means it's just a ▸

With the Beatles' fracture having now blown up in his face, McCartney attempted to explain himself in a interview with Ray Connolly, for the *London Evening Standard*, 11 days later.[2] But history is preserved in headlines, and no amount of protestations would undo what was done, McCartney – whether he liked it or not – going down as the one who there and then ended the band.

What held the Beatles together regardless was a complex of legal ties which arose from their signing an agreement in 1967 to pool their collective revenues. Essentially for tax avoidance they had funnelled their income through a business structure focused on what would soon become Apple, so as to not have to declare it as personal earnings. From there, each could help himself to whatever he wanted, in essence providing equal shares to all four. In the idealism of the day it seemed only right, altruism among comrades of more importance than counting cash. But in the cold light of 1970, the situation was, to say the least, uneasy – the contracts covering solo as well as group projects, and therefore allowing McCartney to take a slice of the proceeds from [3] Instant Karma!, which he had nothing to do with, and Harrison an equal share of *McCartney*, made mostly at home by Paul and Linda – and so on until the agreement expired in 1976. Something, therefore, had to be done, namely a dissolution of the *partnership*, until which time the Beatles would continue to formally exist.

In an ideal world, the four of them would have reached an amicable settlement and gone their individual ways – but after the break-up hit the headlines there was a good deal of rancour in the air, Lennon in particular having formed the view that his old partner had grabbed the news in a cynical attempt to publicise *McCartney*. Thus the three-vs-one situation which had started when Allen Klein became involved in the group's affairs a year earlier, became a schism with battle lines now drawn. This is why McCartney was forced to take the matter to court, the other three having reflexively opposed any suggestion of a settlement. It's another of the paradoxes which surround the affair that McCartney is usually held to be the one most desperate to stay in the band, and yet it was he who insisted they break their ties by issuing his writ, not at face value, the actions of a man who couldn't let go. While he didn't initiate the split – Lennon did – McCartney was at least realistic enough

---

rest', and on the move to solo recording, 'Temporary or permanent? I don't really know'. In essence – he had been working on his own project, and the Beatles might or might not record together in future – hardly a resignation letter. Compare Lennon's comments to David Wigg in February 1970, which didn't make headlines: 'Each Beatle's doing his own thing at the moment... I've no idea if the Beatles will work together again or not.'

[2] Published 21 April 1970: 'My stomach started churning up [when I read the papers]. I never intended the statement to mean, "Paul McCartney quits Beatles".'

to want to move on, despite opposition at every turn from the very individuals usually portrayed as wanting nothing more than for the group to end.

Unlike Harrison, Lennon and Starr, McCartney's priority in the aftermath of the 1971 court case was to set himself up for the coming years by forming a new group. Thus, while the others would repeatedly turn to each other for help, McCartney saw that he had no further need of the Beatles, keeping at his disposal a self-contained band with whom he set about repeating his rags-to-riches musical journey on his own terms. When Wings were taken out for some early low-key dates, they scarcely had enough material to make up a live set, sometimes resorting to repeating a song to fill time – and yet not once did he fall back on his Beatles' catalogue. Likewise when Harrison and Lennon each invited McCartney on stage in the early 1970s, he turned down both offers, precisely on the grounds that he *didn't* want to foster ideas that the Beatles might get back together. This stands in distinct contrast to the supposedly anti-Beatle Harrison, who not only played his old hits in concert but constantly referenced the group in song throughout his career, and at one point was allegedly pushing to reform with Lennon.[3]

The collaborations between Lennon, Harrison and Starr in particular are remarkable however, occasions repeatedly arising where they joined forces – including on one occasion, a three-way studio reunion. Usually they worked in pairs, and of the officially released songs in this book, if one takes McCartney out of the equation then some 25 percent of the output features more than one of them. This is part of the reason why the Beatles cannot truly be said to have separated in 1970, a sense of mutual attraction forever pulling them back together. (It wasn't until 1973-74 that McCartney started involving himself again, initially working with George Martin, then Starr, and then recording informally with Lennon for the first (and only) time in his post-Beatles life.) Moreover, much of the material the individual Beatles were releasing in the first couple of years apart consisted of pre-1970 compositions which could have made it onto a Beatles album, had events turned out differently.[4] In a sense then, the recordings covered in this book are not so much the start of the solo years, as the lingering reverberation of the band – the second phase of the Beatles' long story, spanning another 18 studio albums before the close of 1974.

---

[3] In his famous *Playboy* interview in 1980, Lennon recounted some of the events surrounding the recording of [200] I'm The Greatest in 1973: 'George and Billy Preston started saying, "Let's form a group." I was embarrassed when George kept asking me'. (Golson, p180).

[4] There are at least 23 potential Beatles titles which were issued out individually in 1970 and 1971 alone, a tally sufficient to have made up a couple more Beatles albums: [2]; [22]; [23]; [24]; [26]; [28]; [31]; [33]; [36]; [40]; [43]; [61]; [64]; [65]; [66]; [67]; [90]; [92]; [98]; [124]; [125]; [126]; [131].

Noting the way these early records are infused with the essence of the Beatles, fans have often taken to assembling their own fantasy albums from solo tracks. (Indeed, whole books have been written about it!) While songs like [14] It Don't Come Easy and [125] Give Me Some Truth may not always sit comfortably side-by-side, the intangible sense that this is the *Beatles* in all but name is pervasive, and it's instructive to note that one of the first to compile the early solo work in this way was George Harrison, who according to first-hand accounts, had his own quasi-Beatles album playing in his car.[5]

The fact is, the Beatles were the most talented group of their era and the creative tap didn't turn off overnight. Recording separately, each became his own director, able to shape the music with the minimum of compromise. Consequently, although their output tended to be more conventional at times, great songs were still arriving in abundance, the 18 official studio albums here, released across just five years, encompassing more than 200 individual recordings – to which we can add another 30 or so non-album singles.[6] And the musical standards remained extraordinarily high, Lennon's [130] Imagine, for example, regularly touted as one of the greatest songs of all time, McCartney's [29] Maybe I'm Amazed widely seen as a contender for the best song he *ever* wrote. Harrison's *All Things Must Pass* and its attendant hit, [34] My Sweet Lord, are defining releases, as is McCartney's *Band On The Run* – and Starr's finest achievement, the 1973 album *Ringo*, falls in this period. Looked at from another angle, if we take the period May to October 1973 as an example, we were delivered singles from Lennon: [213] Mind Games; McCartney: [191] Live And Let Die; Harrison: [184] Give Me Love (Give Me Peace On Earth); and Starr: [198] Photograph – all celebrated hits which, if made in the 1960s, would have been remembered as classic Beatles cuts.

Lennon's remark in 1971 that the music they were making individually was better than their group output (for which, he suggested Ono deserved credit for supposedly breaking them up!), was in some senses realistic, and in the case of Harrison and Starr, it's difficult to argue. While the Beatles were still in formal existence in the 1970s, their work stood out, and some of their solo records – *Red Rose Speedway* or *Living In The Material World*, for example – are too often overlooked. In the following pages, we shine a much-needed light on this second half of the Beatles' story – the Beatles Phase II – 1970-1974.

---

[5] Again belying his supposed resentment towards the collective. Thomson, p220, quotes Leon Russell: 'George took me over to Eric Clapton's house one day and on the way he played me what sounded like a series of Beatles songs. He had taken one song out of all their solo records and put them together, and it sounded just like a Beatles record. He thought it was amazing.' (One wonders which specific tracks Harrison selected.)

[6] This compares with a Beatles tally over the preceding five years (ie, 1965-1969, including *Let It Be*) of just seven studio albums and 143 recordings – considerably fewer.

PART 1: ALL SHINE ON

'I think we're much better than we ever were when we were together'

John Lennon, 23 July 1971

John Lennon breaks away:
June 1969 to January 1970

Plastic Ono Band: [1] **GIVE PEACE A CHANCE** (*Lennon, McCartney*)[7]
  Produced by John Lennon, Yoko Ono
  Recorded: 1 Jun 1969, Queen Elizabeth Hotel, Montreal
  UK: 4 Jul 1969 (single A-side)
  US: 7 Jul 1969 (single A-side)
  John Lennon: vocals, guitar; **Tom Smothers**: guitar; **Yoko Ono**, **Timothy Leary**, **Petula Clark**, **Allen Ginsberg**, **Murray The K**, **Derek Taylor**, **André Perry**, **The Radha Krishna Temple** and **various others**: hand claps, percussion, backing vocals

Thrown together in a Canadian hotel room, Give Peace A Chance illustrates Lennon's propensity for distilling solutions to the world's problems in advertising slogans, this one having come to him in conversation with interviewers and journalists during his 'bed-in for peace'. Making best use of some down-time he decided to record it in bed, Derek Taylor dispatched to source some recording equipment and set it up in a roomful of friends and hangers-on. The result is uncompromisingly ragged, lacking a proper melody and employing a series of -isms and name-drops to make up its semi-improvised verses, on the surface getting at nothing in particular. This, though, is to the point, the text deliberately pitched to evoke a sense of nonsense from which the clarity of its chorus slogan bursts into light, simultaneously simplistic and ingenious.

The contrast between the babble and the honesty reflects one of Lennon's key stances, that serious analysis is both elitist and counter-productive. (Months after recording Give Peace A Chance, he was confronted by the *New York Times*' Gloria Emerson, and railed against peace pamphlets 'written by a lot of half-witted intellectuals – and nobody reads them!') In this context the rough-hewn form of Give Peace A Chance, spontaneous and participatory, speaks directly to the world without the detachment which is an unavoidable flip side of sophistication, a straight message delivered in the here-and-now. Whether Lennon's audience, schooled in George Martin's slick productions for the Beatles, was ready for such an unrefined message song was less of a concern than whether Lennon and Ono would be taken seriously at all. A sceptical public, egged on by a scornful media, many of whom turned up for

---

[7] In keeping with their long-standing arrangement, the song was copyrighted jointly with McCartney, who had nothing to do with it; Lennon later remarked he should have registered it as Lennon-Ono instead.

the 'bed-in' curious to see whether Lennon and Ono were about to make love in public, received their peace efforts with more than a pinch of salt, the recent 'bagism' campaign – whatever its idealistic intent – hard to take with a straight face.

As a finished production, Give Peace A Chance scarcely did Lennon justice and was blacklisted by certain Canadian radio stations, not for its political content but on the grounds of poor musicality. Yet as much as any of his more accomplished compositions, the song (to be precise, its title) has gone down as one of Lennon's defining statements, the message more convincing than the utopian All You Need Is Love. The single won over British audiences and would have topped the chart had the Rolling Stones' Honky Tonk Women not lodged itself at number 1 for several weeks in the summer. America, still up to its neck in Vietnam, was less swayed, but Lennon expressed his delight when half a million protestors chanted the song's title on Vietnam Moratorium Day in Washington – one of the reasons Lennon came to be seen as a threat to the US establishment.

In preparing the release Lennon opted to create a new identity: Plastic Ono Band. The genesis of this conceptual group was *Plastic Ono Band 1968*, a Lennon-Ono sculpture constructed from clear Perspex boxes with pieces of audio equipment inside (as depicted on the single's picture sleeve). Developed by Lennon, the idea of an imaginary group which included nobody and everybody appealed to his sense of comedy-idealism, becoming a tag he applied to any team of musicians he happened to work with over the next few years. By releasing it this way, Lennon had symbolically parted ways with the Beatles, proving he could be successfully creative without them. 16 weeks later he revealed he was leaving the group.

Plastic Ono Band: [2] **COLD TURKEY** (*Lennon*)
   Produced by John Lennon, Yoko Ono
   Recorded: 25 Sep 1969, EMI Studios, London; 28 Sep 1969, Trident Studio, London; 29 Sep 1969; 5 Oct 1969, EMI Studios, London[8]
   UK: 24 Oct 1969 (single A-side)
   US: 20 Oct 1969 (single A-side)
   John Lennon: vocals, guitar; **Eric Clapton**: lead guitar; **Klaus Voormann**: bass; **Ringo Starr**: drums

To a lesser or greater extent, Lennon and Ono had formed an intermittent heroin habit though their early time together, something occasionally glimpsed in Lennon's period songs (eg, Happiness Is A Warm Gun). Never quite

---

[8] EMI Studios was re-named Abbey Road Studios in 1976, consequent of the fame it earned from the Beatles' album.

addicts, the two were for a time sufficiently hooked to have to undergo an unpleasant withdrawal process in late August, the experience of which led directly to this song. Lennon had the front to suggest the Beatles record it as sessions for *Abbey Road* were winding down, wanting it out as the group's next single, a proposal inevitably blocked by the others meaning the song had nowhere to go – excepting as a vehicle for Lennon's newly conceived Plastic Ono Band.

Not long after the release of *Abbey Road*, Lennon was invited to appear on stage at the Toronto Rock and Roll Revival Festival, and rapidly rounded up a backing group. And it was while waiting for his flight that he made the profound decision to leave the Beatles and go it alone. (Cold Turkey was among his largely unrehearsed set, and as he hadn't yet memorised the words he needed a clipboard to remind him.) Lennon got back to England on 15 September, days prior to a Beatles business meeting at which he dropped his bombshell on McCartney and Starr (Harrison being absent).

Five days on, he rounded up his group, drafting Starr in to replace Alan White, the inexperienced drummer used in Toronto, and recorded Cold Turkey in EMI's Studio 3. In the event it took several hours and 26 takes to come to nothing, and so the group reconvened at Trident to have another go. The result was now suitably raw as Lennon had intended, rendered so by Clapton's guitar scraping over a chord structure locked uncompromisingly to an obstinate root. And while Starr's flourishes offer the hope of release in the choruses, there is no respite, the song merely collapsing back on itself to go over its internal torment again. The agonised cries which Lennon added alone at EMI, owing a stylistic debt to Ono, predict his work on [80] Mother a year later, although the tagged-on 'Beatles' ending, a backwards guitar section is incongruous.

The release of the single was a minor milestone, although few noticed: the track carried no credit for McCartney. This was Lennon, alone, stepping out of the Beatles and going where his artistic instincts took him. A month later he stuck two fingers to the British establishment by sending his MBE back to Buckingham Palace, his covering letter including in a sarcastic reference to Cold Turkey, undermining an otherwise meaningful action. Cold Turkey remains an uneasy listen, and was duly blocked by some radio stations for its drug references (which Lennon ludicrously tried to deny).

John Lennon with the Plastic Ono Band: [3] **INSTANT KARMA!** (*Lennon*)
Produced by Phil Spector
Recorded: 27 Jan 1970, EMI Studios, London
UK: 6 Feb 1970 (single A-side)
US: 16 Feb 1970 (single A-side)
John Lennon: lead vocals, acoustic guitar, piano, backing vocals; **George Harrison**: electric guitar, piano, backing vocals; **Billy Preston**: Hammond organ, backing vocals; **Klaus Voormann**: bass, electric piano, backing vocals; **Alan White**: drums, piano, backing vocals; **Mal Evans**: chimes, handclaps, backing vocals, tambourine; **Yoko Ono**: backing vocals; **Allen Klein**: backing vocals; **uncredited**: backing vocal chorus

Over the winter of 1969, Lennon and Ono stepped away from the relentless circus which had become their public life and retreated to the seclusion of a small snow-bound cottage in Denmark as guests of Yoko's ex-husband, Tony Cox, custodian of her daughter, Kyoko. Tracked down in spite of their remoteness, the couple was accosted by John Brower and Ritchie Yorke, who made the trek through the snowdrifts to discuss their upcoming free peace festival, which Lennon had hastily said he would support. It was only on seeing their publicity – Free (For One Dollar) John Lennon Peace Festival – that he pulled out, arguing not unreasonably that free meant free. Brower and Yorke had meantime set up a company to handle the festival's affairs – Karma Productions – which caused Lennon to muse on the way the term 'karma' had been so casually appropriated, as if a marketing slogan: karma-as-product, like instant coffee.

Lennon landed back in Britain on 26 January, sleeping off the journey to awaken with a new song, which he hammered out on his upright piano at Tittenhurst Park. Later that day he travelled to Apple and had the song stuck in his head, prompting him to record it then and there. Although not a stable group, the Plastic Ono Band was made up of London-based musicians, all in theory available if needed. (Starr was in the States, promoting his new movie, *The Magic Christian*, opening the door for Alan White again.) To Lennon's disappointment Clapton couldn't make it, so he naturally contacted Harrison, a move which would have long-term ramifications; Harrison happened to be with Phil Spector when he took the call, the veteran producer in London as Allen Klein's guest, and all of them tagged along to EMI's Studio 3 for the fun of it.

Recorded in haste, Instant Karma! was taped in 10 takes starting from scratch with an opening device pulled from Richie Barrett's Some Other Guy (1962). The group's uncertainty is at times tangible (in particular, Klaus Voormann fluffs his bass at 1:01 and again at 2:28) and with the clock ticking, they strive a fraction too hard for a suitably rocking performance, the results having a faint air of stiffness about them. Among so much talent, the saviour of the hour turned out to be the inexperienced Alan White, who'd been developing an innovative drum style with his regular band, Griffin, characterised by unpredictable rhythmical changes. Filling in between verses, his ad-hoc metrical inventions impressed Lennon, who told him to keep them up, and together with his pounding toms (muffled with towels for a more shuffling effect) became the beating heart of the recording.

Striving for scale, Spector had the musicians gather around a couple of pianos to simultaneously bash out the song's distinctive crotchets, but still not satisfied, dispatched Mal Evans to round up volunteers from Hatchetts Playground and Restaurant, a fashionable late haunt on the far side of Mayfair, to provide some clamorous chorus vocals. (This is the point at which the addition of more volume diminishes the impact; the backing voices have the effect of dampening Lennon's rasping lead.) Wrapped up by 3am, Instant Karma! was mixed and declared complete – the fastest work a Beatle had ever done. Coupled up with Yoko's Who Has Seen The Wind? – drawing on a verse by 19th century English poet, Christina Rossetti, and resonant with the imagery of Ono's 1964 book, *Grapefruit* – Instant Karma! was in the shops a little over a week later.

Following the rough [1] Give Peace A Chance, recorded in a crowded hotel room, and the anguished [2] Cold Turkey, relating the traumas of drug abuse, here finally was a straight pop single from Lennon. Underlining its rapid arrival, it was scheduled into BBC TV's *Top Of The Pops* before it had charted, an occasion for which Lennon and Ono filmed a mimed performance at Television Centre in West London, both crop-haired, she crocheting on stage, her eyes bandaged with a sanitary towel, he dressed in denim with a patch reading 'People For Peace' stitched to his arm. Instant Karma! was a turning point for Lennon, Phil Spector having bathed his vocal in 1950s-style reverb, reminiscent of the slap-back echo of Sam Phillips which he'd worshiped as a teen, and so he became a true believer in the producer's craft. Consequently Lennon would shortly ask Spector to rescue the Beatles' dormant *Get Back* album.

RECORD RELEASES

[1] **Give Peace A Chance** / Remember Love [B-side by Yoko Ono]
(UK: 4 Jul 1969, US: 7 Jul 1969)
[2] **Cold Turkey** / Don't Worry Kyoko (Mummy's Only Looking For A Hand In The Snow) [B-side by Yoko Ono]
(UK: 24 Oct 1969, US: 20 Oct 1969)
[3] **Instant Karma!** / Who Has Seen The Wind? [B-side by Yoko Ono]
(UK: 6 Feb 1970, US: 16 Feb 1970)

Sentimental Journey sessions: October 1969 to March 1970

Of the Beatles, Starr was most in need of direction in the second half of 1969. Lennon, McCartney and Harrison were clearly capable of forging careers as individual recording artists, but for their drummer, matters were less clear. Movie acting was becoming an option, his appearance in *Candy* (1968) preceding more recent work on *The Magic Christian*, but the occasional screen role was hardly going to sustain him. Another avenue was contemporary design, Starr having become pally through 1969 with Robin Cruikshank, whose company, Robin Ltd, was at the high end of London fashion when it installed a circular stainless steel fireplace in Starr's Hampstead home. Starr took a keen interest and impressed Cruikshank with several design ideas of his own, the two soon agreeing to work together and taking an empty office on the top floor of Apple's Savile Row building.

Whether he could meanwhile translate his modest singing talents into a full career was questionable, Starr having taken lead on just 11 recordings with the Beatles – roughly one per album. Mulling the situation with George Martin in the wake of *Abbey Road*, he decided to have a go anyway and put a solo album together. Back in 1966 the Beatles had been toying with the idea of recording an album paying homage to their native city, and although it never quite came to pass, there are instances of childhood memories sprinkled throughout the group's subsequent albums. (Lennon and McCartney had both recorded songs about their respective mothers, for example.) These factors were no doubt germinal in Starr's decision to revisit the songs he remembered from his Liverpool upbringing, especially those fondly associated with family gatherings. In support of the idea, the well-connected Martin offered to canvass industry contacts for musical arrangements, looking for a different contributor for each song to keep things interesting – and plans began to firm up in early October. Starr's role was to be lead vocalist; he wouldn't be drumming on the envisaged album, provisionally called *Starrdust*, punning on one of the short-listed songs.

Ringo Starr: [4] **NIGHT AND DAY** (*Porter*)
   Arranged by Chico O'Farrill; Produced by George Martin
   Recorded: 27 Oct 1969, EMI Studios, London
   UK: 27 Mar 1970 (*Sentimental Journey* LP)
   US: 24 Apr 1970 (*Sentimental Journey* LP)
   Ringo Starr: vocals; **George Martin Orchestra**: instrumentation

The first thing recorded for *Starrdust* was Night And Day, an old Cole Porter number which Starr had learned as a child, through his step-father, Harry, who used to sing it around the pubs and clubs of Dingle, usually in the middle of revelling booze-ups. Night And Day was written for the Broadway stage musical, *Gay Divorce*, in 1932 and was a hit for Fred Astaire before gradually becoming a standard – and one of the classics of the genre – in the hands of luminaries like Sinatra and Crosby.

For this new recording, Martin contacted New York-based jazz arranger, Chico O'Farrill, whose long cv included a 1966 album of Beatles covers performed by Count Basie. O'Farrill drew up a manuscript and sent it over to London for Martin to conduct his orchestra through its brassy 'big band' arrangement in EMI's Studio 3. An ambitious option for a first recording, Night And Day's melody spans more than an octave, not on the face of it well-suited to Starr's modest range (Lennon and McCartney had written With A Little Help From My Friends for him across just five notes, to help out), and in this context the results have to be counted a success. Mixed the same day, Starr had the track fully completed and in the can by 10:45 and *Starrdust* was off to a flyer.

Ringo Starr: [5] **STORMY WEATHER** (*Arlen, Koehler*)
    Arranger unknown; Produced by George Martin
    Recorded: 6 Nov 1969, Wessex Sound Studios, London
    UK/US: unreleased
    Ringo Starr: vocals; **George Martin Orchestra**: instrumentation

While *Starrdust* was in its early stages, information on the project was revealed to the music press and a couple of numbers were cited which never appeared, including the old jazz standard, Autumn Leaves, and a Broadway song, I'll Be Seeing You. While it's doubtful either was recorded, one which was attempted was Stormy Weather, taped at Wessex Sound Studios in north London.

Dating to 1933, the song had passed through the hands of countless performers over the years and was a particular favourite of Jim McCartney, who commended its chord changes to his son back in the day. The arranger on Starr's parping brass rendition is not documented and the track seems to have been shelved almost immediately, the singer not troubling to re-do his vocal which comically cracks up in the final line. (Stormy Weather is, in this initial version, the only bona-fide outtake to circulate from *Sentimental Journey*.)

Ringo Starr: [6] **STARDUST** (*Carmichael, Parish*)
  Arranged by Paul McCartney; Produced by George Martin
  Recorded: 7 Nov 1969, Wessex Sound Studios, London; 14 Nov 1969, Trident Studio, London; 28 Nov 1969, EMI Studios, London
  UK: 27 Mar 1970 (*Sentimental Journey* LP)
  US: 24 Apr 1970 (*Sentimental Journey* LP)
  Ringo Starr: vocals; **George Martin Orchestra**: instrumentation

Through the acrimony of the Beatles' final months, the ever-likeable Starr managed to stay on reasonable terms with the others – at least, more so than they did with each other. Realising the LP project would be a pivotal move for Starr, McCartney agreed to score one of the tracks for him. How he managed is the subject of conjecture; since McCartney was unable to read music he would have needed considerable help, and tellingly, George Martin invoiced EMI for the arrangement himself, implying McCartney may have had only a participatory role.

In any respect, the song McCartney accepted was earmarked as the LP's title track, and of all the material in the frame, was the one closest to Starr's heart. Stardust was one of step-father Harry's 'big' turns in Liverpool, which Starr described as having 'incredible memories'.[9] Beyond a natural preference for working with a close collaborator on such an intimate song, McCartney was an astute choice by Starr, having a deep respect for this type of material himself, born of childhood memories listening to the wireless. (Earlier in the year he'd recorded an album with Mary Hopkin containing standards from composers including George Gershwin, Frank Loesser and Irving Berlin.)

Written in 1927 by Hoagy Carmichael and Mitchell Parish, Stardust is considered one of the key American songs of the 20th century, popularised by those such as Louis Armstrong, Nat King Cole, Bing Crosby, and countless others. Despite his long familiarity with the tune, Starr struggled to record a vocal, the first attempts resulting in failure; used to singing it informally, he realised he was not fully cognisant of the correct melody line, and encountered some unexpected intervals in the studio. On one early take, he failed to come in on the right note, and a rejected test mix was done with his voice fading up. Looking for a solution, he also tried singing it drunk, attempting in vain to tap back to the old family knees-ups where he'd first learned it. McCartney's arrangement, twinkling with nostalgic bells, is, in the context of the album, suitably poignant, with hints of Beatles arrangements in McCartney-Martin's orchestration, particularly the swerving cello figures in the final verse, faintly reminiscent of those in Strawberry Fields Forever and I Am The Walrus.

---

[9] Interview conducted by Radio Luxembourg, 11 April 1970. Starr recalled, 'He'd do it everywhere we went. He was really famous for it in the clubs.'

Ringo Starr: [7] **DREAM** (*Mercer*)
   Arranged by George Martin; Produced by George Martin
   Recorded: 14 Nov 1969, Trident Studio, London; 10 Feb 1970, EMI Studios, London
   UK: 27 Mar 1970 (*Sentimental Journey* LP)
   US: 24 Apr 1970 (*Sentimental Journey* LP)
   Ringo Starr: vocals; **George Martin Orchestra**: instrumentation

Having started well, sessions for *Starrdust* were soon running into difficulties. After failing to secure a usable version of [5] Stormy Weather on 6 November, Starr laboured over [6] Stardust the following day, further problems surfacing during the recording of Dream, a George Martin arrangement of a 1943 number from songwriter and co-founder of Capitol Records, Johnny Mercer. (The initial orchestration, recorded at Trident in November, was considered sub-par and had to be partly re-done at EMI on the evening of 10 February.) In truth the choice of song was questionable from the start, Dream an insubstantial composition whose lack of identity is merely underlined by the unusually thin register of Starr's voice, at odds with his characteral persona. That Martin, architect of the recording, was capable of such poor judgement is surprising.

Ringo Starr: [8] **BLUE, TURNING GREY OVER YOU** (*Razaf, Waller*)
   Arranged by Oliver Nelson; Produced by George Martin
   Recorded: 28 Nov 1969; 4 Dec 1969; 24 Feb 1970, EMI Studios, London
   UK: 27 Mar 1970 (*Sentimental Journey* LP)
   US: 24 Apr 1970 (*Sentimental Journey* LP)
   Ringo Starr: vocals; **George Martin Orchestra**: instrumentation

This 'big band' reworking of a pre-War Louis Armstrong hit, recorded in 1930 and issued in Britain on the Parlophone label, was provided by celebrated American saxophonist and band leader, Oliver Nelson. In modernising the antiquated original, Nelson opted for a blazing brass score which was duly recorded at EMI on 28 November, Starr adding his vocal after the band was done. Something wasn't right however, and a week later, arranger and conductor, Johnnie Spence, convened another 17-piece orchestra in Studio 2 for the purposes of overdubbing. (Starr also re-did his vocal that afternoon.)

There *Starrdust* was left to gestate, while Starr was busy through the rest of the month with promotion for *The Magic Christian*, which premiered at the Odeon in Kensington on 11 December. Starr wouldn't return to the album in earnest until the new year, the current track not completed until *another* lead vocal was added, which double-tracked December's. Positioned at the start of the LP's second side, the results sound impressively uncontrived, belying the amount of effort which went into the recording. (It concludes with a jokey ad-lib from Starr.)

Ringo Starr: [9] **LOVE IS A MANY SPLENDOURED THING** (*Fain, Webster*)
Arranged by Quincy Jones; Produced by George Martin
Recorded: 26 Dec 1969, A&M Studios, Hollywood; 14 Jan 1970, Olympic Studios, London; 3 Feb 1970; 5 Feb 1970; 17 Feb 1970; 19 Feb 1970, EMI Studios, London
UK: 27 Mar 1970 (*Sentimental Journey* LP)
US: 24 Apr 1970 (*Sentimental Journey* LP)
Ringo Starr: vocals; **Billy Preston:** piano; **George Martin Orchestra:** instrumentation

Discounting the never-used [5] Stormy Weather, only two songs had been fully completed for Starr's album by the end of 1969, a modest return for several weeks' effort and the expense of repeatedly hiring in orchestras and star-name arrangers. The architect of this latest track was Quincy Jones, one of the few African Americans working in the field, and something of a rising star through the 1960s. According to Martin, Jones was initially bemused by the commission, and needed his arm twisting before accepting.[10]

Working through Boxing Day, Jones prepared a recording at A&M in Los Angeles, to which Starr added his vocal at Olympic three weeks later. Predictably, the results were deemed unsatisfactory, so as soon as Starr returned from the States at the end of the month, he went for a remake. (According to Mark Lewisohn, Quincy Jones conducted the band through this second version, suggesting he'd flown over especially.[11]) That evening, Billy Preston dubbed on a jazzy piano break for the song's instrumental passage, and Starr recorded another lead vocal; and still they weren't satisfied, yet more instrumentation and vocals being dubbed on over the next couple of weeks.

Finally finished on 19 February with the addition of flutes, percussion and a bank of wide-ranging backing singers, the final arrangement flows warmly, offering exactly the sympathetic support Starr's vocals needed. How much the final result owes to Quincy Jones's original orchestration, and how much to Martin's augmentation is unclear, but it's a pity more of the album wasn't done in the same vein; Love Is A Many Splendoured Thing is one of the most satisfying tracks to emerge from these sessions, befitting Starr's genuine affection for the song, which, courtesy of a 78 released in November 1955 by the Four Aces, was one of the first records he'd ever owned.

---

[10] See Martin's comments in *Uncut*, November 2010.
[11] *The Complete Beatles Chronicle* (1996). See entry for 3 Feb 1970. This means the musicianship we hear is by the George Martin Orchestra.

Ringo Starr: [10] **SENTIMENTAL JOURNEY** (*Green, Brown, Homer*)
Arranged by Richard Perry; Produced by George Martin
Recorded: 14 Jan 1970, Olympic Studios, London
UK: 27 Mar 1970 (*Sentimental Journey* LP)
US: 24 Apr 1970 (*Sentimental Journey* LP)
Ringo Starr: vocals; **Richard Perry**: director of instrumentation

Overdubbed at Olympic in the same January session as [9] Love Is A Many Splendoured Thing, the backing track for Sentimental Journey was the work of New Yorker, Richard Perry, who sent his tapes over to London without having yet met up with Starr. (It would, however, start a professional association between the two which would bear more substantial fruit in 1973.) Sentimental Journey, a 1944 number popularised by Doris Day, was chiefly associated in Britain with the end of the War, its lyrics symbolic of the passage back to Blighty for so many veterans. The song therefore carries an exaggerated sense of yearning, particularly relevant to war-ravaged Liverpool, although in Starr's case his birth father, Richy, born 1913, was never conscripted. (25 when war broke out, he was spared call-up by virtue of working in a bakery, a 'reserved occupation'. Had he been drafted, Starr might never have been conceived.)

The recording's most interesting moments arrive in the instrumental break, with George Martin's deployment of a vocoder, a gadget which converts vocals into a robotic electronic buzz, taking the place of a conventional instrument. (One can just make out the lyrics embedded in a signal which sounds vaguely like a slide guitar.) Whether such technical trickery was suited to pre-rock and roll material is another matter.

The song's name and general connection with the past made it a natural choice for the LP title, the unfortunate consequence of which was that it was programmed at the start of side 1, this dour ballad the first thing buyers would hear. Given that Sentimental Journey was now going to usurp [6] Stardust as lead track, a promotional video for the song was shot on Sunday 15 March, on stage at the Talk of the Town on London's Charing Cross Road. Performing the song in suit and comical pink bow tie, and with newly cropped hair – like Lennon, he'd got fed up with having it long – Starr sang live to a specially-mixed backing track, while behind him a platform descended carrying three female singers, one of whom was Doris Troy, currently signed to Apple Records.

Ringo Starr: [11] **HAVE I TOLD YOU LATELY THAT I LOVE YOU?**
(*Wiseman*)
Arranged by Elmer Bernstein; Produced by George Martin
Recorded: 3 Feb 1970, A&M Studios, Hollywood; 9 Feb 1970; 18 Feb 1970, EMI Studios, London
UK: 27 Mar 1970 (*Sentimental Journey* LP)
US: 24 Apr 1970 (*Sentimental Journey* LP)
Ringo Starr: vocals; **Hal Blaine**: drums (?); **Elmer Bernstein**: director of instrumentation

On Monday 26 January, Starr flew to America for the US premiere of *The Magic Christian*, first dropping by NBC Television's studios in Hollywood to film a set of lame sketches for *Rowan & Martin's Laugh-In*. (This is what he was doing while Lennon and Harrison were putting [3] Instant Karma! together in London with Alan White on drums.) The premiere took place at Four Star Theater on Wilshire Boulevard on the Thursday evening, Ringo and Maureen hobnobbing with Hollywood's show-biz cognoscenti, 5,000 miles from home, and a million from the humble Liverpool upbringing which had given impetus to his current LP.

After travelling to meet Elvis in Las Vegas, Ringo and Maureen took a circuitous route back to London, landing home on 2 February. Starr must have known that if *Sentimental Journey* was going to materialise, he would need to knuckle down. Sessions had so far been sporadic, and at most he had half an LP in the can, so the day after getting home he was back at EMI working on [9] Love Is A Many Splendoured Thing, starting the album's second phase which would see it to finality.

As with Quincy Jones's track [9], the current song was prepared at A&M's Hollywood studios, this time by Oscar-winning composer/conductor, Elmer Bernstein. (His previous work included scores for *The Magnificent Seven*, *To Kill A Mockingbird*, and, in 1963, *The Great Escape*.) Working on Have I Told You Lately That I Love You? on 3 February, Bernstein brought his jazz sensibilities to bear, in a sprightly arrangement full of incident, and relying largely on a repertoire of instruments more familiar to pop than classical. (These include electric guitar, piano, keyboards, and a conventional drum kit. Hal Blaine, drummer in LA's Wrecking Crew, recalled having worked on the album, without remembering the specific song. If his memory is correct, it was likely this one.)

Working in EMI's Studio 2 on 9 February, Starr added his first-attempt vocal, provisionally deemed satisfactory and mixed for stereo. Characteristically, he returned nine days later to replace it, this one a keeper. Have I Told You Lately That I Love You? dates to 1944, one of the earliest country music numbers to gain significant success with the American public. It became a hit when Bing Crosby recorded a version in 1949, before being brought to the attention of rock and rollers courtesy of both Elvis and Eddie Cochran. Starr would likely have known all of these versions, which are blown out the park by Bernstein's lively and playful update.

Ringo Starr: [12] **I'M A FOOL TO CARE** (*Daffan*)
Arranged by Klaus Voormann; Produced by George Martin
Recorded: 11 Feb 1970; 17 Feb 1970, EMI Studios, London
UK: 27 Mar 1970 (*Sentimental Journey* LP)
US: 24 Apr 1970 (*Sentimental Journey* LP)
Ringo Starr: vocals; **Billy Preston**: piano; **George Martin Orchestra**: instrumentation

Each of the songs on *Sentimental Journey* held some personal significance for Starr, but unlike the bulk of his selections, I'm A Fool To Care dated from his adulthood, belatedly known to him through the 1954 recording by Les Paul and Mary Ford which he picked up on aged around 20. (The song wasn't given a UK release in 1954, but Starr recalled listening to it on LP, indicating he owned a copy of the 1960 compilation, *Hits Of Les And Mary*.) Arranged for him by close friend, Klaus Voormann, this new version runs faster than its model, a jazzy trumpet solo standing in for Les Paul's guitar licks. The master for the album was a composite of takes 19, 20 and 21, recorded and edited together during the afternoon of 11 February, Starr adding a softly spoken vocal that evening (doing his best to emulate Mary Ford's cool delivery). Six days later, a 15-strong orchestral piece was dubbed on to complete the track.

Ringo Starr: [13] **LET THE REST OF THE WORLD GO BY** (*Ball, Brennan*)
Arranged by Les Reed; Produced by George Martin
Recorded: 12 Feb 1970; 18 Feb 1970, EMI Studios, London
UK: 27 Mar 1970 (*Sentimental Journey* LP)
US: 24 Apr 1970 (*Sentimental Journey* LP)
Ringo Starr: vocals; **George Martin Orchestra**: instrumentation

The ancient Let The Rest Of The World Go By was nominated for inclusion by Starr's mother, Elsie, as a song she remembered harmonising with him for fun when he was a child. She likely learned it from Dick Haymes' 1944 rendition as featured in the movie, *When Irish Eyes Are Smiling*, in which Haymes sings it at piano, backed by a group of gently crooning vocalists.

The commission was given to Les Reed, orchestra leader and composer of several 1960s chart hits including a notable brace for Tom Jones in It's Not Unusual and Delilah. (He also wrote the Applejacks' first single, Tell Me When, bringing the group to the attention of Lennon-McCartney, who provided the follow-up, Like Dreamers Do.) Like Starr, Reed had a childhood connection to Let The Rest Of The World Go By, having played it on his accordion for the entertainment of coach-tripping seasiders when he was 10.

Recording the vocal the way he used to sing it with Elsie, Starr opted for a double-track throughout, allowing him to harmonise with himself. In the context of its childhood associations, and in paying tribute to Elsie through the years, it comes across as one of the sweetest moments on the LP, if not the most musically accomplished.

Ringo Starr: [14] **IT DON'T COME EASY** (*Starkey*)
Produced by George Harrison
Recorded: 18 Feb 1970; 19 Feb 1970, EMI Studios, London; 8 March 1970; 11 March 1970; October 1970, Trident Studio, London
UK: 9 Apr 1971 (single A-side)
US: 16 Apr 1971 (single A-side)
Ringo Starr: vocals, drums; **George Harrison:** guitar; **Pete Ham:** backing vocals; **Tom Evans:** backing vocals; **Stephen Stills:** piano; **Gary Wright:** piano; **Klaus Voormann:** bass; **Ron Cattermole:** saxophone, trumpet; **Mal Evans:** tambourine

During sessions for *Sentimental Journey*, Starr was working on a tune of his own, provisionally titled You Gotta Pay Your Dues and initially running to a mere eight bars. An original composition would have been unsuitable for the album, leading Starr to mull over a 'surprise single' and prompting him to tap up George Harrison for help finishing it. A convenient juncture arose on 18 February, after Starr finished work on [13] Let The Rest Of The World Go By and had Studio 2 free for the evening.

The extent of Harrison's input has been the subject of some uncertainty ever since. Never credited as co-composer, his fingerprints are all over the song, a fact underscored by the existence of session tapes which not only have him on guide vocal, but also reveal a 'Hare Krishna' chorus during the instrumental break. Style-wise, the composition certainly leans more towards Harrison than to Starr, whose two individual copyrights to date, Don't Pass Me By and Octopus's Garden, share a common simplicity of form, both circling around a four-square pattern which comes to rest conventionally on the home key. It Don't Come Easy by contrast is musically elusive, working its way through a sequence which includes an unexpected shift from D to F at the start of its bridge, conforming to the assertive progressions which occur in Harrison's songs. (Compare, for example, the changes in [62] Beware Of Darkness.)

Directing affairs from the studio floor, Harrison guided his colleagues, Stephen Stills and Klaus Voormann, around the song, running them through some 20 takes which were scrapped and re-done the following day. This remake was also ultimately discarded, with another version made at Trident on 8 March, yet more recording following in October, presumably prompted by concurrent work on its eventual B-side, [77] Early 1970. This final session drew the track's elements together at last; a solid punch was delivered by Ron Cattermole's jockeying trumpet blasts, with ingratiating backing vocals contributed by Badfinger's Pete Ham and Tom Evans. Sensitively blended into the mix, these well-judged finishing touches elevate It Don't Come Easy to a commercial proposition, secured by Harrison's attendant arpeggios and a defining wash of cymbal from Starr at the beginning.

Something of a triumph for its creator, it's curious that having recorded this obvious hit, Starr continued to prevaricate. In the context of its protracted birth, the song title itself seems prescient, as if betraying a lack of self-belief on Starr's part. Finally, in April 1971, more than a year after it was started, this debut 45 was unveiled to a receptive public with the attraction of two promotional videos, and promptly sold a million – making its delay all the more mystifying. The eventual success of It Don't Come Easy may have surprised the underdog in Starr, and no doubt raised eyebrows elsewhere in the Beatles' inner circle (its number 4 showing Stateside was on a par with anything Lennon or McCartney had achieved by that stage). Sung by him on stage at the Bangla Desh concert in August 1971 before an adoring crowd (see [140]), It Don't Come Easy was an early high, and is considered by many as one of Starr's most appealing solo recordings.

Ringo Starr: [15] **YOU ALWAYS HURT THE ONE YOU LOVE**
(*Roberts, Fisher*)
Arranged by John Dankworth; Produced by George Martin
Recorded: 25 Feb 1970, De Lane Lea Studios, London; 6 Mar 1970,
   Morgan Studios, London
UK: 27 Mar 1970 (*Sentimental Journey* LP)
US: 24 Apr 1970 (*Sentimental Journey* LP)
Ringo Starr: vocals; **George Martin Orchestra**: instrumentation

A week after starting work on his single, Starr returned to *Sentimental Journey* in a rare session at De Lane Lea, a facility north of The Strand which the Beatles had once used. The assignment was a version of You Always Hurt The One You Love, first recorded by American vocal harmony quartet, the Mills Brothers, in 1944. By comparison to the original, jazz composer John Dankworth's arrangement is blustering, Starr's temptation to emulate the group's velvet vocals unsuited to its hammering drums and brass.

Ringo Starr: [16] **WHISPERING GRASS (DON'T TELL THE TREES)**
(*Fisher, Fisher*)
Arranged by Ron Goodwin; Produced by George Martin
Recorded: 5 Mar 1970, Morgan Studios, London
UK: 27 Mar 1970 (*Sentimental Journey* LP)
US: 24 Apr 1970 (*Sentimental Journey* LP)
Ringo Starr: vocals; **George Martin Orchestra**: instrumentation

With sessions for *Sentimental Journey* nearing completion, Starr continued his tour of London's recording studios, moving to Morgan in out-of-town Willesden for back-to-back sessions. The venue was presumably the choice of his arranger here, Ron Goodwin, who'd grown up in the Willesden area before making a name for himself with a string of successful film scores through the 1960s. Goodwin was on site early on 5 March to conduct a 36-piece orchestra through Whispering Grass, which he'd arranged off the back of a demo made by Starr and George Martin a month earlier.

The song was, like [15] You Always Hurt The One You Love, an oldie co-composed by Doris Fisher, in this case with her songwriter father, Fred, in 1940. Like many, Starr encountered the song via the Ink Spots' version, not in fact the original but made their own after it was first recorded by Erskine Hawkins. Starr had a long-standing love of the song, particularly admiring the line, 'Because you told the blathering trees' – actually written as 'blabbering' but forever mis-heard by Starr who consequently sings it his way. One of the best-recorded numbers on *Sentimental Journey*, Whispering Grass was later nominated by Starr as his favourite from the album.

Quickly finished up, Goodwin departed around lunchtime, handing the studio floor to Maurice Gibb for the album's final recording…

Ringo Starr: [17] **BYE BYE BLACKBIRD** (*Dixon, Henderson*)
Arranged by Maurice Gibb; Produced by George Martin
Recorded: 5 Mar 1970, Morgan Studios, London
UK: 27 Mar 1970 (*Sentimental Journey* LP)
US: 24 Apr 1970 (*Sentimental Journey* LP)
Ringo Starr: vocals; **George Martin Orchestra**: instrumentation

This 1926-vintage song was another of Harry Graves' biggies in the Liverpool clubs, and he might have learned it from any of countless versions he'd picked up over the wireless. Never a UK hit, it had been recorded by artists including Peggy Lee and Dean Martin, but was so ubiquitous that no specific model was necessary. (Another version was made by the Beatles' future publisher, Dick James, and released on Parlophone in 1956, although it's doubtful Starr's family knew of it.)

The backing track was arranged for Starr by Maurice Gibb, who'd done similar duties for his group, the Bee Gees, who the Beatles had crossed paths with via NEMS. The extent to which Gibb took the assignment seriously is open to debate; apart from taking over the orchestra Ron Goodwin left behind, there is evidence that his arrangement was worked out off-the-cuff – he elected to incorporate a prominent banjo part which was only suggested to him the previous evening when he saw a trad jazz band playing in a bar. Since the banjo dominates, he presumably worked out the chart in the studio, there being no time for meaningful pre-planning.

With its cheery disposition, and a happily confident vocal from Starr (double tracked in spots), this familiar old tune might have been better positioned at the end of side 2, thereby reflecting its place in the recording sequence and, through its title, bidding the album a fond farewell. As it transpired, it was sequenced between [16] Whispering Grass and [12] I'm A Fool To Care, where its lightness of mood renders it flimsy against its neighbours.

Sentimental Journey was finished up with final mixing the day after Bye Bye Blackbird was taped. For an album cover, pop photographer, Dick Polak, sought out the place where Starr had grown up. He'd been born in a small terraced house at 9 Madryn Street, and when aged four, his mother Elsie moved them to 10 Admiral Grove, only about 150 yards away, by pushing their possessions in a hand-cart. Between the two houses was the Empress pub on High Park Street, which the family would frequent and where Harry Graves entertained the locals with his songs – and this building, steeped in childhood memories, was selected as the cover image. (From where the photographer stood, he could see Ringo's second home down the lane to the right-hand side and just visible in the photograph. Over his right shoulder he could have seen the narrow entrance to Madryn Street.) To complete the picture, Starr asked Elsie, now 55, for some old photos of the family, which were collaged into place, as if looking out of the pub's windows.

Released to an unprepared public, who'd never heard anything of the sort from an established rock star, *Sentimental Journey* was greeted with some bemusement, but little deserves the near-universal disdain it has since attracted.[12] Admittedly self-indulgent, and oddly retrospective in an era of futuristic rock, *Sentimental Journey* was hampered from the start by the fact that the material, largely drawn from the Great American Songbook, had no

---

[12] Chris Ingham, to take one example, spoke of its 'car crash fascination', proclaiming, 'the lavishness of the backing tracks, the quality of the songs and the foolishness of the singer makes this Ringo's best comedy record' (p143).

meaningful context for those versed in the 1960s pop of *A Hard Day's Night* or *Sgt Pepper*. Viewed as individual recordings, the songs come across as faintly pointless, but seen in the context of Starr's musical schooling, and properly understood as a trove of affectionately remembered souvenirs, the selections on *Sentimental Journey* possess a quaint charm. Decades later it became *de rigueur* for big-name recording acts to mine the depths of American popular song, one of countless stars to indulge, Paul McCartney, who released his set, *Kisses On The Bottom*, in 2010. It happened to include a version of [17] Bye Bye Blackbird, completing a cycle of acceptance 40 years on from Starr's pioneering recordings.

RECORD RELEASES

Sentimental Journey
 (UK: 27 Mar 1970, US: 24 Apr 1970)
 [10] Sentimental Journey / [4] Night And Day / [16] Whispering Grass (Don't Tell The Trees) / [17] Bye Bye Blackbird / [12] I'm A Fool To Care / [6] Stardust / [8] Blue, Turning Grey Over You / [9] Love Is A Many Splendoured Thing / [7] Dream / [15] You Always Hurt The One You Love / [11] Have I Told You Lately That I Love You? / [13] Let The Rest Of The World Go By
[14] **It Don't Come Easy** / [77] **Early 1970**
 (UK: 9 Apr 1971, US: 16 Apr 1971)

McCartney sessions: December 1969 to February 1970

After Lennon announced his departure from the Beatles in 1969, McCartney realised his main purpose in life was slipping away and as a result began a descent into what amounted to a depressive state, in which he began to develop a worrying dependency on scotch. Since he owned a country retreat in Scotland, High Park Farm in Kintyre, he decided to escape the London rat-race and get his head together, and accordingly packed up with Linda and their daughters, Heather and baby Mary, and disappeared from the circuit for a period.

With none of the usual pressures surrounding him, McCartney began to rediscover his musical interests and in due course sketched out some new songs on his acoustic, starting the long process of getting his psychology back on track. After a couple of months in the remote Scottish countryside, and with Christmas looming, McCartney brought his family back to their main home on

London's Cavendish Avenue, still keeping a low profile, but with a sense of coming purpose. He wouldn't fully find himself for some time, but at least had an idea of what to do next; he'd had a four-track tape recorder delivered to his home in September, mounted on casters and parked in the corner of his living room. He'd not yet tried it out, but was now of a mind to see what it could do. With no level meters fitted, the machine was something of an unknown quantity, and when McCartney fired it up, he put the lone microphone in what he thought a suitable spot, and played through a few of his latest songs, marking the start – although he didn't yet realise it – of *McCartney*, and with it, his post-Beatles life.

Paul McCartney: [18] **THE LOVELY LINDA** (*McCartney*)
Produced by Paul McCartney
Recorded: late Dec 1969, 7 Cavendish Avenue, London
UK: 17 Apr 1970 (*McCartney* LP)
US: 20 Apr 1970 (*McCartney* LP)
Paul McCartney: vocals, guitar, bass, percussion

McCartney married his girlfriend, Linda Eastman, on 12 March 1969, at which point he was a highly successful urbanite with the world at his feet, and she therefore couldn't have envisaged how the following months would progress. McCartney's depression and the family's farmhouse exile was especially hard on Linda with a new-born to look after and no real support available in the wilderness of Scotland, this the sternest test their marriage would ever face. Yet there was no denying Linda's loyalty to her new husband, and she stood solidly behind him throughout. Of the handful of songs known from his Scottish sojourn, The Lovely Linda was one which particularly stuck – a romantic, if simple acknowledgement of his wife's support and devotion.

As it happens, The Lovely Linda was not the first song to have been written in her honour. When she was a baby, American composer, Jack Lawrence, named his song, Linda, after her, and it became a significant hit in the 1940s. Linda McCartney would undoubtedly have mentioned this to her husband, and he in turn would likely have investigated it – assuming he didn't know it already. As covered in the popular 1963 version by Jan and Dean, the track includes the vocalised, 'la-la la-la-la l-Linda', which McCartney may have been recalling when sketching out his own lyric.[13]

The Lovely Linda was recorded in the living room, primarily to see how it would come out. (Background noises are evident on the recording, including a prominent squeak near the start, supposedly Linda opening the garden door.)

---

[13] McCartney recorded a version of the Jack Lawrence song in a private session for Linda in 1986. See Perasi, p262.

Happy with the take, McCartney proceeded to overdub a second guitar, bass, and percussion, effected by tapping on the cover of a book. He ended up with a full-length track, incorporating a Spanish section, 'almost mariachi', and in this respect he may have been inspired by Harrison's I Me Mine, which in its original form (as heard in the *Get Back* rehearsals of a year previous) contained a diversion into a flamenco-style passage which was subsequently dropped. If so, that's where the influence ends, there being no further connection between the two songs.

By the time The Lovely Linda was released, it had been pared down to a mere 43 seconds. In its abbreviated form it's a slight affair which breezes contentedly through its only verse, Linda's flowers evoking the swaying daisies of Mother Nature's Son and belying the dark circumstances of its composition (and the fact that it was put together in the middle of winter). As a thank-you to Linda, it was programmed as the opener on *McCartney*, setting the scene for what its author described as an album about 'home, family, love'. Unfortunately it has too much a sense of improvisation about it, underlined by the fact that it concludes with a snigger, as if McCartney recognised it was little more than a throwaway.

Paul McCartney: [19] **THAT WOULD BE SOMETHING** (*McCartney*)
Produced by Paul McCartney
Recorded: late Dec 1969, 7 Cavendish Avenue, London
UK: 17 Apr 1970 (*McCartney* LP)
US: 20 Apr 1970 (*McCartney* LP)
Paul McCartney: vocals, guitar, bass, drums, percussion

Straight after his experimental recording of [18] The Lovely Linda, McCartney pressed record again and ran through another of his Scottish ditties.[14] Not at this stage intended for public consumption, he was happy with essentially two lines of lyric which repeat for two-and-a-half minutes, the falling rain of the second part perhaps hinting at McCartney's pessimistic mood, which The Lovely Linda had obliviated.

As inconsequential as the previous track, That Would Be Something was similarly overdubbed at home, its wiry electric riff fortified with bass guitar. Completing the arrangement, McCartney added tom-tom and cymbal using a drum kit he had lying around the house, bluffing the effect by banging the sticks together and vocalising percussive effects. (Harrison, at least, admired it. On hearing the album he singled out That Would Be Something as 'great'.)

---

[14] It's worth noting that Lewisohn cites this as a song trialled in the 1969 *Get Back* sessions (1996, p309), although this is most likely an editorial error, and no audio evidence is known.

Paul McCartney: [20] **VALENTINE DAY** (*McCartney*)
   Produced by Paul McCartney
   Recorded: late Dec 1969, 7 Cavendish Avenue, London
   UK: 17 Apr 1970 (*McCartney* LP)
   US: 20 Apr 1970 (*McCartney* LP)
   Paul McCartney: vocals, guitar, bass, drums, percussion

Continuing his improvisatory recording, McCartney next ad-libbed an acoustic guitar instrumental into the microphone of his living-room console, literally making it up as he went. Layering instruments in his home-cum-laboratory, he added drums (sounding like the kit was positioned in the next room), bass, and a 'blue' lead guitar, sounding surprisingly like Love's Johnny Echols.

Like much of *McCartney*, the track was properly mixed at EMI in the last week of February, this 100-second jingle christened Valentine Day, perhaps by way of a romantic gesture to Linda. (It was mixed on 22nd, eight days after the occasion.) McCartney later claimed that when they first got together Linda was unaware he played guitar at all, until he demonstrated his talents with some 'blues licks'.

Paul McCartney: [21] **MOMMA MISS AMERICA** (*McCartney*)
   Produced by Paul McCartney
   Recorded: late Dec 1969, 7 Cavendish Avenue, London
   UK: 17 Apr 1970 (*McCartney* LP)
   US: 20 Apr 1970 (*McCartney* LP)
   Paul McCartney: guitar, bass, piano, drums

Two instrumentals attached together, Momma Miss America starts with 1:51 of guitar improvisation originally entitled Rock 'N' Roll Springtime, blocked out with piano chords which move oddly in the stereo picture. A clumsy 'edit' occurs when Rock 'N' Roll Springtime cadences, after which it continues into a lengthy blues guitar piece pitched in a similar vein – McCartney has stated the join was a result of the songs accidentally 'running into one another', indicating inaccurate operation of his home tape recorder.

The usual array of overdubs was added on, this lo-fi exercise in one-man jamming mixed for release at EMI with the piano swept back and forth for fun in its closing moments. Whatever else experiments like this prove, they show McCartney as one of rock's great multi-instrumentalists, able to invent and execute arrangements out of thin air, whenever the mood takes. The song's eventual title is surely another nod to Linda, a native New Yorker who moved to England to be with Paul.

Paul McCartney: [22] **SUICIDE** (*McCartney*)
   Produced by Paul McCartney
   Recorded: Jan 1970 (?), 7 Cavendish Avenue, London;
   UK/US: unreleased
   Paul McCartney: vocals, piano

In 1956, a starry-eyed McCartney began writing tunes on his father's piano in the family parlour, one of them earmarked by the 14-year-old for no less than Frank Sinatra. As a germinal composition it was remarkably accomplished, its music-hall charm informed by his father's stage background, appealing to a budding teenaged writer who did not suspect rock and roll was about to arrive.

During a spell mining some of his very early material in January 1969, McCartney played some of it with Lennon – who clearly recognised the song, despite not having known McCartney when it was first composed. It came up again a year on, when McCartney was playing around with his home tapings, a full three-minute rendition recorded. A curiously jaunty number given its title, Suicide was not ultimately selected for *McCartney*, bar a few seconds' worth, tacked anonymously to the end of [23] Glasses. Its creator returned to the song several times over the years without fully embracing it: another version was made in 1974 for McCartney's unreleased film, *One Hand Clapping* (see [264]), and it was revisited again in 1977, when a studio demo was made and finally sent to an unimpressed Sinatra.

Paul McCartney: [23] **HOT AS SUN-GLASSES** (*McCartney*)
   Produced by Paul McCartney
   Recorded: Jan 1970 (?), 7 Cavendish Avenue, London; Feb 1970,
      Morgan Studios, London
   UK: 17 Apr 1970 (*McCartney* LP)
   US: 20 Apr 1970 (*McCartney* LP)
   Paul McCartney: vocals, guitar, bass, keyboards, drums, percussion, wine glasses

Perhaps prompted by his recent penchant for instrumentals, McCartney turned his attention to this old guitar tune thought up in his teens. Hot as Sun dates to 1959 and, like [22] Suicide, surfaced in the January 1969 *Get Back* sessions, where McCartney ran through the song while vocalising some garbled lyrics. (These were probably made up on the spot, and didn't form part of his original composition, as implied by the fact that he sang 'la, la, la' for much of it.[15]) Taken to Morgan Studios in February, a simplistic contrasting section was added in, newly devised and played by McCartney on organ. He also dubbed on a bass guitar figure, taken from the riff in Elvis's 1956 recording of Don't Be Cruel, thereby pointing back to the period Hot As Sun was first written, and which he'd previously also hacked for The Ballad Of John And Yoko.[16]

After 1:28, the song abruptly switches into Glasses, half a minute of eerily atmospheric *musique concrète*, constructed by McCartney gathering a selection of wine glasses on a table top, strategically measuring water into each one to 'tune' them, then running a fingertip around their rims to produce sustained notes. Using faders, the individual tones were then mixed in and out to create a sound mood. McCartney later claimed the notes were played at random, and while there is a vague structure to the recording, it defies any analysis besides the observation that it's generally rooted in the key of B flat. Edited to Hot As Sun after the event, the sequence gave rise to the happy pun, Sun-Glasses.

Paul McCartney: [24] **JUNK** (*McCartney*)
Produced by Paul McCartney
Recorded: Jan 1970 (?), 7 Cavendish Avenue, London; Feb 1970,
 Morgan Studios, London
UK: 17 Apr 1970 (*McCartney* LP)
US: 20 Apr 1970 (*McCartney* LP)
Paul McCartney: vocals, guitar, bass, piano, xylophone, Mellotron, drums;
Linda McCartney: backing vocals

A familiar ingredient of British popular culture in the late 1960s was an affectionate fascination with the iconography of the past, exemplified by 1920s fashion pastiches and a craze for Edwardian military garb. So far as the Beatles were concerned, *Sgt Pepper* had glanced back to the era of bandstands and brass ensembles, setting the scene in 1947 ('20 years ago'), itself preceded by the childhood-nostalgic vision of a long-gone Penny Lane. Junk rises from the same spring, written at the tail-end of the group's psychedelic phase during their Indian de-tox in early 1968, and indirectly links to Lennon's Being For The Benefit Of Mr Kite, inspired by a poster he chanced upon in an antique shop.

Taking a cue from the British television show, *Steptoe And Son*, Junk

---

[15] Curiously, Tim Rice took up the song in 1980 and added a lyric of his own for a recording by Elaine Page.
[16] Played in 1956 by Bill Black on upright bass. In 1974, Linda purchased Black's original bass and gave it to Paul as a birthday present. (He used it on the 'Threetles' session for Real Love in 1995. See also [287].)

rummages through the bric-a-brac of human existence, sifting the remnants of everyday life.[17] Some of the unwanted objects hint at Britain's not-so-distant War years – military kit, discarded parachutes, candlesticks – McCartney having been born during the conflict and grown up in its immediate aftermath. The song's emotion is therefore not vicarious, the assonant coupling of jubilee and jamboree probably a reference to teenage recollections of the 1957 'Jubilee Jamboree' in which he took part (and which meant he had to miss a debut Quarry Men gig).

Demoed at Kinfauns for possible inclusion on *The White Album*, Junk was not completed. One presumes Lennon disapproved its sentimentality, especially on an album containing the rose-tinted Honey Pie, which he privately resented. On the other hand, it was certainly more characterful than several which did make the double LP, and might in any case have been offered up for *Abbey Road*, although there's no evidence it was.

Reviving the tune in 1970, McCartney recorded Junk twice, neither much more than a provisional demo, although both are better played than the Beatles' 1968 version. When the tapes were taken into Morgan Studios in February for further work, he elected to use both takes, the second preferred for the main track despite being the shorter of the two. It was treated to drums, harmony vocal and a tinkling xylophone, suggestive of a child's play instrument and therefore thematically linked to the song's toyshop charm.

In its finished state, Junk conforms closely to the 1968 demo, retaining the curiously discordant high harmony, and the loose guitar doodle at the end – here, sounding much like the corresponding figures in Simon & Garfunkel's Homeward Bound (1966), which McCartney may have had in mind. That he didn't add a proper solo is partly explained by his decision to play over the longer first take to create a 'singalong' version, where the song becomes grounded with the addition of electric guitar and piano, underscored by a Mellotron for a faux-string effect. When the end arrives, it does so on an unexpectedly final F sharp, leaving the song broken and fading away, like the sepia-tinged junk itself. As issued on *McCartney*, both Junk and Singalong Junk form part of a sequence of musical scraps, sitting between assorted bits and pieces as if on a second-hand shelf. With its sense of yearning regret – even the song's waltz timing is wistfully reminiscent – Junk comes across as one of the most evocative short pieces McCartney ever devised.

---

[17] Set in the junk-filled home of 'dirty old man' Albert Steptoe, the show starred Wilfrid Brambell, who McCartney had worked with in *A Hard Day's Night*. (Hence, the film's running gag that Brambell's character was 'very clean, though'.)

Paul McCartney: [25] **OO YOU** (*McCartney*)
    Produced by Paul McCartney
    Recorded: Jan 1970 (?), 7 Cavendish Avenue, London; Feb 1970,
        Morgan Studios, London
    UK: 17 Apr 1970 (*McCartney* LP)
    US: 20 Apr 1970 (*McCartney* LP)
    Paul McCartney: vocals, guitar, bass, drums, percussion, aerosol can

McCartney was undoubtedly the most stylistically versatile artist of the era, his 1970s catalogue ranging confidently across the genres, music hall to disco, electronica to reggae. Immediately after recording the delicately reflective [24] Junk, he delved into sexual blues territory with this earthy rocker, its tumbling signature riff hinting at Jimi Hendrix's Purple Haze (1967).

    Oo You started life as an instrumental, taped at home with bass right, lead guitar centre. Suffering from tape hiss it was nonetheless taken to Morgan Studios in February as the basis of a new song, McCartney thinking up the lyric, which consisted of what was, to-date, the most meaningless he'd written (eg, 'eat like a hunger') just before leaving the house. At Morgan, the track was overhauled with the addition of a second guitar panned opposite the first, and faded strategically in and out as if to bluff incidental riffs. The job was done hurriedly, with unwanted drop-outs and, according to McCartney's session notes, an aerosol can mixed somewhere into the brew. Retaining its provisional lyrics it obviously wasn't finished when served up to the public on *McCartney*. It's a shame he didn't push himself a little harder, the track containing within itself the germ of a decent up-tempo track.

Paul McCartney: [26] **TEDDY BOY** (*McCartney*)
    Produced by Paul McCartney
    Recorded: Jan 1970 (?), 7 Cavendish Avenue, London; Feb 1970,
        Morgan Studios, London
    UK: 17 Apr 1970 (*McCartney* LP)
    US: 20 Apr 1970 (*McCartney* LP)
    Paul McCartney: vocals, guitar, bass, drums; **Linda McCartney**: backing vocals

Like [24] Junk, Teddy Boy was written in India in 1968 but passed over during the *White Album* sessions to surface with a vengeance during *Get Back*. Perhaps reminded of the song by the group's expressed aim to wind back to their pre-fame days, McCartney ran the others through the 1950s-infused Teddy Boy a number of times without garnering any real interest. (One notable take has Lennon playing a slide guitar throughout, a novelty not explored further.)

    What Lennon thought of the track is not documented, but one wonders if

McCartney was having a dig at him in the lyrics (and whether he suspected as much), Lennon having been the archetypal teddy boy of the Quarry Men when they met. In the song, Teddy Boy's father is an absent soldier, his mother finding herself a new man who Teddy Boy dislikes. Echoes of Lennon seem more than innocent; his mother had a second child by a soldier named Taffy Williams before settling down with John Dykins, who was generally shunned by Lennon. (McCartney would have been aware that his mate 'couldn't stand to see his mother in love with another man'.)

If, indeed, McCartney had Lennon in mind when working out Teddy Boy, he was on thin ice; Lennon was sensitive about his upbringing, particularly since he'd lost his mother when he was 17. That his main involvement in the song was to sabotage its recording by mucking about implies the thought may have crossed his mind. In the event, an extremely provisional Beatles version was submitted by *Get Back*'s original producer, Glyn Johns, for approval as part of a finished LP. After *Get Back* was rejected McCartney had Teddy Boy removed from consideration and kept aside for future use – namely, its inclusion here, on his first solo album.

Despite harkening back to the Quarry Men period, Paul and John jamming Elvis and Little Richard on acoustic guitars, there's no trace of rock and roll in the four-square, bolt-upright chord sequence. Juddering its way from D to F sharp for its third verse, the progression is inventive in McCartney's patent manner, but the results are ungainly and negate any sympathy the lyric might otherwise have conveyed.

Paul McCartney: [27] **KREEN-AKRORE** (*McCartney*)
   Produced by Paul McCartney
   Recorded: 18 Feb 1970, Morgan Studios, London
   UK: 17 Apr 1970 (*McCartney* LP)
   US: 20 Apr 1970 (*McCartney* LP)
   Paul McCartney: vocals, guitar, bass, keyboards, drums, bow-and-arrow;
   Linda McCartney: backing vocals

At some point in February, it occurred to McCartney that the material he'd been accumulating at home might form the basis of an album, so with a view to consolidating what he had, he booked some proper studio time for additional work. At this stage he didn't have enough for a full LP, and decided to keep the ongoing project under wraps; rather than move across to busy EMI, a five-minute walk from home, he ventured out to Morgan Studios where Starr would also work on *Sentimental Journey*, requesting Linda book him in under the pseudonym, Billy Martin. Few, though, would have failed to notice Paul and Linda when they turned up carrying a baby plus armfuls of nappies and toys which ended up strewn across the studio floors.

The first thing McCartney did was take his home-made four-tracks and copy them onto eight-track studio tapes, thus giving space for some necessary overdubs. And in among dubbing and re-mixing, he found time to get a new track down. Kreen-Akrore was inspired by a TV documentary he'd watched the day before, *The Tribe That Hides From Man,* which explored the plight of the Brazilian Kreen Akrore tribe as they tried against the odds to resist encroachment of Western development into their homeland. Taken by the story, McCartney went into the studio with an idea that he would summon the spirit of the Kreen Akrore, and fairly absorbed himself in the process. An exercise in painting a picture in sound, Kreen-Akrore features an audio palette conjuring the mood of the rain forest, unsettling, percussive and with illustrative pointers ranging from stampeding animal noises to a bow-and-arrow. McCartney went so far as to build a bonfire on the floor, apparently to capture the sound of burning, but in the end decided against igniting Morgan Studios and settled for recording the twigs being snapped into pieces.

Cut across with pained electric riffs, symbolising the intrusion of industry over the dark depths of the tribe land, Kreen-Akrore is a showpiece for McCartney-the-musician, his drums and guitar working both with and against one another to create a soundscape which, in its way, is as off-the-chart as almost anything Lennon recorded. Placed at the end of *McCartney* without the necessary context, it merely bemused most listeners.

Paul McCartney: [28] **EVERY NIGHT** (*McCartney*)
Produced by Paul McCartney
Recorded: 22 Feb 1970, EMI Studios, London
UK: 17 Apr 1970 (*McCartney* LP)
US: 20 Apr 1970 (*McCartney* LP)
Paul McCartney: vocals, guitar, bass, drums

Despite his efforts, McCartney didn't yet have a clear hit on his forthcoming album, but did have two particularly strong contenders in reserve. Shifting his work to the familiar surroundings of EMI, he booked in again as Billy Martin, hoping to deter any unwanted visitors by keeping the sessions a secret. The degree to which he succeeded is debatable; Starr was working in Studio 1 on 24 February [8], at the exact time McCartney was in Studio 2 mixing Every Night. Even if they hadn't bumped into each other, their mutual studio acquaintances would surely have mentioned what was afoot.

In any case, sessions began with the recording of a track which McCartney had been toying with for a while, and which he'd briefly tried to develop during the *Get Back* sessions. Unable to make any headway, he fleshed it into a full song in May 1969 while on holiday in Corfu with Linda. Thus, its dark moments expressing a reluctance to get out of bed, and a desire to blank out reality with drink/drugs, were not the product of his recent depression, although they resonate with his mood in early 1970. What he added to them the previous spring, born out of his blossoming love for Linda, was a means of resolution: the uneasy tension of the song's original melody line, pitched on an apprehensive fifth, is discharged by a wish to simply be with her, bringing the verses to a gratified conclusion. The second-best song on *McCartney*, Every Night was entirely his own, and was easily the strongest thing yet recorded for the album.

Paul McCartney: [29] **MAYBE I'M AMAZED** (*McCartney*)
Produced by Paul McCartney
Recorded: 22 Feb 1970, EMI Studios, London
UK: 17 Apr 1970 (*McCartney* LP)
US: 20 Apr 1970 (*McCartney* LP)
Paul McCartney: vocals, guitar, piano, bass, drums

The stand-out number on *McCartney*, Maybe I'm Amazed was begun in 1969, initially as one verse which was gradually added to over the following months. McCartney's hesitation over how to move it forward happened to also fit its theme, a turning over of various aspects of a love he can't come to terms with, trapped in his own internal dialogue and groping in vain for some release. The chord sequence illustrates his preoccupations, beginning on a fade-in exchange between A and D which unexpectedly turns not to the anticipated G, but to a distracted B flat from where it steps obsessively through the 'Circle of Fifths', never finding a way out, repeatedly rushing up the piano keyboard to go through it all again.[18] The sense of McCartney's uncertainty is perceptibly illustrated by a discordant banging on F and F sharp together, making the underlying chord both major and minor at once – like its narrator, puzzled as to which way it should go.

As recorded at EMI, immediately after [28] Every Night, McCartney elected to incorporate a prominent guitar solo, one he couldn't wait to execute, placing it scarcely more than a minute in. Thrilled with his handiwork, he opted to play it a second time towards the song's end, as if showcasing his skills. It must have been in the back of his mind that Harrison would shortly get to hear it; if he thought he might stand to impress his former colleague with such virtuosity, he will certainly have failed. Harrison was constantly antagonised by McCartney's dismissive attitude to his lead guitar playing, and indeed had been allowed only two comparable spotlights on McCartney's

---

[18] The Circle of Fifths is a standardised sequence of chords prevalent in many songs, where the roots step up in fifth intervals – in this case, B flat, F, C, G. Were one to continue (D, A, E etc) it would eventually find its way back to the starting point.

songs since 1967, so was hardly likely to look on with admiration.[19]

Completed in one night, Maybe I'm Amazed was an artistic triumph for McCartney, as strong as practically anything he'd written, and a near-guaranteed number 1 should he have released it on 45 – which he declined to do. Lennon's [3] Instant Karma! had arrived in the UK top 10 the week before Maybe I'm Amazed was recorded, and McCartney would no doubt have known that Harrison played on it – issuing his own track as a single would have put McCartney top of the post-Beatle pecking order, and ordinarily his competitive instinct would have compelled him. So why didn't he? The likely explanation is that in 1970, releasing singles from albums was considered underhand in the UK, seen as selling fans the same songs twice over. Coupled with this was a desire to maintain a low public profile, McCartney still shaken by the separation of the group and sensitive to the perceived hostile treatment he was getting. In no mind to embark on rounds of media appearances, McCartney's reluctance made the non-arrival of Maybe I'm Amazed the most glaring case of a hit-that-never-was in his entire career. (The song did eventually make it onto 45, a live version issued as a trailer to *Wings Over America*, which entered the charts seven years too late.)

With its evasive chord sequence and pining melody line, Maybe I'm Amazed remains one of McCartney's most consistently admired songs, and a manifest highlight of a variable debut album.

Paul McCartney: [30] **MAN WE WAS LONELY** (*McCartney*)
Produced by Paul McCartney
Recorded: 25 Feb 1970, EMI Studios, London
UK: 17 Apr 1970 (*McCartney* LP)
US: 20 Apr 1970 (*McCartney* LP)
Paul McCartney: vocals, guitar, bass, drums; **Linda McCartney**: backing vocals

With 11 songs in the can (discounting [22] Suicide) one more was required to wrap up *McCartney*, the hurriedly prepared Man We Was Lonely recorded and mixed in a marathon final day's work on 25 February. The song started life with just its title, and an accompanying phrase McCartney thought up while lying in bed, which he was particularly pleased with: 'we were hard-pressed to find a smile'. Armed with not much more, he elected to record it for the album, and reserved Studio 2 for the occasion. As he'd done with [25] Oo You, he thought up some more words just prior to leaving home, and Man We Was Lonely was good to go.

---

[19] Back In The USSR and Let It Be. Harrison also soloed on *Abbey Road*'s medley, but as contributions to long musical sequences rather than standard pop constructions.

This final addition to *McCartney* has more personal content than anything else on the album. Originally conceived as an expression of its composer's insecurity, the song turns on its lightly melodic bridge, which like the similarly late additions to [28] Every Night, finds a happy resolution by coming to rest on home and love. (It's fitting that the loneliness of the song title is expressed in the past tense, while the 'we' speaks of present-day unity with Linda, who shares a first-ever vocal with her husband on the track, so that the two are now as one.) The song wears its eventual smile thanks in part to its buoyant country arrangement, effected by McCartney playing his Fender Telecaster with a metal tuning peg from a drum, thereby bluffing the sound of a slide guitar. Finished off with some adventurous panning, Man We Was Lonely is ultimately 'up', ending the sometimes difficult *McCartney* sessions on a prematurely optimistic note.

'Billy Martin' booked one further session at EMI, to hear the whole album back on the evening of 16 March, and was satisfied with the results. Thereafter, a release date was fixed: 17 April.

The LP would now require packaging, the instinctively self-reliant McCartney fortunate in that his wife's main skill lie in photography. Gathering up a pile of her family snapshots he requested his friend, film producer David Puttnam, nominate the best of them. The favoured image, a photo of Paul with baby Mary tucked into his coat, was selected for the front, a shot of a bowl of cherries, emptied and strategically laid out on a white shelf, chosen for the back. Somehow the sides got mixed up so that when printed up the cherries were on the front – confusingly for record buyers, since there was no accompanying text to inform them this new LP was by McCartney.

What happened next is well documented: the long-awaited *Let It Be* movie was suddenly ready for cinematic release, and that meant the associated album would have to come out right away. Since McCartney was boycotting Apple and the Beatles, he was automatically outvoted whenever the other three were in agreement on something, and in respect of *Let It Be*'s timing, they ruled that McCartney's album would have to be held off until June, to avoid the clash. Although there was logic to the decision – the *Let It Be* movie and album were big news and set to be extremely lucrative – McCartney interpreted the postponement as spite, venting his anger on the largely blameless Starr who'd selflessly volunteered to visit him and explain the situation in person. Shocked by McCartney's upset, Starr went back to Apple and persuaded the others to let the original release date stand – which it did.

Unable to face the media scrum it would inevitably attract, McCartney left again for Scotland on the morning of 10 April, having already sent out advance copies with a self-penned Q&A in lieu of a press conference. The contents were routine, mentioning his current domesticity, his break from the group and his uncertainty as to what lay ahead – but somehow Fleet Street contrived to twist his remarks into headline news: *Paul Is Quitting The Beatles!* That he said no such thing didn't stop Harrison, and Lennon in particular, bearing a grudge for years to come, convinced their erstwhile bandmate had deliberately tried to exploit the band's demise for personal gain – promotion of *McCartney*. Quite inaccurately, the ludicrous news reports gave rise to a date in Beatles history – 10 April 1970 – as the point the group split up, and that it was McCartney's doing.

McCartney arrived in the shops on 17 April in its anonymous sleeve, and was greeted with grumbles from an expectant public who'd last heard its creator on the lavishly produced second side of *Abbey Road*. Not anticipating a collection of roughly recorded, largely home-made oddments, some very old, some just improvised, others sounding like instrumental filler, the general consensus was of disappointment. In truth, McCartney didn't help his cause by programming his first three home demos, recorded primarily for the purposes of trying out his recording console, as the lead-off tracks, an error of sequencing he would repeat eighteen months later on *Wild Life*.

Despite everything, enough people bought it to hoist it to the top of the US album charts. Ultimately time has been good to *McCartney*, its estimation having risen steadily in the years since. The album has a carefree lightness about it, belying the tense circumstances of its genesis, and in [29] Maybe I'm Amazed boasts one of the most popular numbers of McCartney's solo career.

RECORD RELEASES

McCartney
(UK: 17 Apr 1970, US: 20 Apr 1970)
[18] The Lovely Linda / [19] That Would Be Something / [20] Valentine Day / [28] Every Night / [23] Hot As Sun-Glasses / [24] Junk / [30] Man We Was Lonely / [25] Oo You / [21] Momma Miss America / [26] Teddy Boy / [24] Singalong Junk / [29] Maybe I'm Amazed / [27] Kreen-Akrore

All Things Must Pass sessions (first phase): May 1970 to June 1970

In mid-1970, Harrison's situation was paradoxical. On the one hand he had built up a steady stockpile of songs he couldn't record with the Beatles, which following their split, might form the start of a solo career. (In tapes from

January 1969 he can be heard discussing this very point with Lennon, who expressed support for Harrison recording the backlogged material alone.) It might have been the case that, away from the group, he was afforded a new freedom – and yet the better part of a year on from Lennon's resignation, he was the only one of the four yet to record anything for himself.

It's characteristic of Harrison's thoughtful approach that he didn't jump straight in. Tempered by insecurity over whether he could succeed as a frontman, a solo artist with a weight of responsibility on his shoulders, his impulses were to size up the situation slowly and pragmatically. Over the winter and spring, Harrison had been far from inactive, involving himself in a range of collaborative projects with other artists – which had the benefit of consolidating a circle of talented friends. Apart from sessions with Billy Preston and Leon Russell, his key move turned out to be a link-up with Delaney and Bonnie, via another increasingly close collaborator, Eric Clapton.

Ostensibly, Harrison was the Beatle least enamoured by concert tours. However his negative attitude to stage performance was coloured by the demands of being in a group whose every public appearance led to pandemonium. A surprise guest on Delaney and Bonnie's December 1969 programme, which took in dates in England, Sweden and Denmark, Harrison was happy to keep a low profile, loitering at the back of the stage and simply enjoying the pleasure of playing again, behind Clapton and the rest of the band – which included Jim Keltner, Carl Radle, Bobby Whitlock, Jim Gordon, Billy Preston, Bobby Keys and Jim Price – all of whom would be called upon when Harrison eventually got down to *All Things Must Pass*. One other bonus was that Harrison got to hang out with Delaney Bramlett, who among other things, gave him some tutoring on slide guitar, which would become a feature of Harrison's style for the rest of his career.[20]

The period was also marked by personal issues which would cast a shadow over the forthcoming album. Harrison's mother, Louise, had become unwell during 1969 and underwent an operation for a brain tumour at the start of 1970. Her condition improved but there was no cure, and Harrison spent the first half of the year intermittently visiting and coming to terms with her imminent death – not the best circumstances in which to launch a solo career. Another unwanted distraction was the release of *Let It Be*, which gave rise to a fresh round of Beatle acrimony when McCartney learned what Phil Spector had done to his songs with direct sanction from Lennon and Harrison. The scars of that particular episode ran deep and would never fully heal.

Towards the end of May, Harrison arranged studio time and made a start

---

[20] Quoted in Thomson (p186), guitarist Dave Mason claims *he* showed Harrison the slide technique at the Croydon show on 7 December, which got him started on 'all that slide guitar stuff'.

on *All Things Must Pass*. He'd decided to offer Phil Spector the production role, in spite of (perhaps partly because of) his recent treatment of McCartney, and the fact that he'd impressed Harrison during the making of [3] Instant Karma! back in January. Proceedings started with Harrison, Voormann and Starr making a set of 15 demo recordings on the Tuesday evening, including 12 songs which would be taken forward during the sessions.[21] Two of the songs are otherwise unavailable and we include them here for the fact that both were recorded in a group arrangement.

George Harrison: [31] **DEHRA DUN** (*Harrison*)
Produced by George Harrison
Recorded: 26 May 1970, EMI Studios, London
UK/US: unreleased
George Harrison: vocals, guitar; **Klaus Voormann**: bass; **Ringo Starr**: drums

Dehra Dun was written in early 1968, during the Beatles' stay at the International Academy of Meditation, located on a cliff top overlooking the Ganges. Harrison set up a music room during his Indian interlude and wrote a number of songs there, including several which were never recorded. One of them concerned a trip the group took to the city of Dehradun, seated in the Doon Valley, 20 or so miles from camp. A reflective survey of the scene, Dehra Dun waxes philosophical on the various paths one can take, framing travellers in search of meaning, including the Beatles themselves, as spiritually impoverished among such divinity: 'beggars in a goldmine'.

As recorded in 1970, Dehra Dun circles around its mantra, recalling the entranced state of its author two years before. The recording was discovered in EMI's tape vaults in 1982, and was subsequently leaked to the public on the so-called John Barrett Tapes, the source of many celebrated Beatles outtakes (including also, [32]; [41]; [52]; [58]; [68]).

George Harrison: [32] **GOING DOWN TO GOLDERS GREEN** (*Harrison*)
Produced by George Harrison
Recorded: 26 May 1970, EMI Studios, London
UK/US: unreleased
George Harrison: vocals, guitar; **Klaus Voormann**: bass; **Ringo Starr**: drums

---

[21] [34]; [35]; [36]; [37]; [39]; [40]; [41]; [43]; [61]; [68]; [63]; [73]. Harrison also captured a solo take of Sour Milk Sea, already 'given away' to Jackie Lomax.

Harrison returns to his musical roots with this archetypal rock and roll song, celebrating a familiar district of north London located away from the northern end of Abbey Road. Harrison was a regular visitor to Golders Green, Apple group Badfinger having for some time lived there in a communal property on Park Avenue, a modest residential street on the edge of Hampstead Heath.

Adapted from Presley's Baby Let's Play House, a number with its own Beatle associations, Harrison swaps the original's pink Cadillac for a more relevant Mercedes Benz. Recorded using the same studio set-up as [31] Dehra Dun, Harrison switching to electric guitar, this fully written track was never destined for *All Things Must Pass*, knocked off for fun as a warm-up for the sessions to come.

24 hours after recording this initial batch of demos, Harrison slipped back to EMI alone to record 15 more, included among them seven songs destined for the album.[22] Taken together, these two sets of preliminary recordings covered every track on *All Things Must Pass*, serving to supply Phil Spector with the reference material he needed for sessions proper, starting the next day.

George Harrison: [33] **WAH-WAH** (*Harrison*)
    Produced by George Harrison, Phil Spector
    Recorded: 28 May 1970; June 1970, EMI Studios, London; Aug/Sep 1970,
        Trident Studio, London
    UK: 30 Nov 1970 (*All Things Must Pass* LP)
    US: 27 Nov 1970 (*All Things Must Pass* LP)
    George Harrison: vocals, backing vocals, guitar; **Eric Clapton**: wah-wah guitar; **Pete Ham**, **Tom Evans**, **Joey Molland** ('Badfinger'): acoustic guitars; **Klaus Voormann**: bass; **Ringo Starr**: drums; **Billy Preston**: keyboards; **Pete Drake**: 'talking steel guitar'; **Gary Brooker**: keyboards; **Bobby Whitlock**: Wurlitzer keyboard; **Jim Price**: trumpet; **Bobby Keys**: saxophone; **Mike Gibbins**: tambourine; **Alan White**: tambourine

Wah-Wah dates to 10 January 1969, the day Harrison walked out of sessions for *Get Back*, the story being that he went home and immediately composed the song, building a double-meaning from wah-wah, both a reference to the guitar effect pedal and to the annoying bickering which had taken place (characterised by Harrison as a 'headache'). Harrison has claimed the song was

---

[22] [33]; [38]; [62]; [67]; [64]; [66]; [65]. The unused eight were Beautiful Girl; Cosmic Empire; Everybody, Nobody; I Don't Want To Do It; Mother Divine; Nowhere To Go; Tell Me What Has Happened To You; and Window, Window. Listed only as Untitled, Beautiful Girl was recorded and released by Harrison in 1976. I Don't Want To Do It was a Dylan composition which Harrison re-recorded in 1984.

written following the famous dispute with McCartney which was filmed and included in *Let It Be*, but this should be weighed against his (and the Beatles' generally) notoriously unreliable recounting of their own history; the movie edit shows events out of sequence, that particular argument having occurred four days beforehand. If the song was indeed written as a direct consequence of Harrison's walk-out, as is usually agreed, it will have been composed in the wake of a decisive clash with *Lennon*, with whom the song is rarely associated.

Why Harrison framed it as a response to friction with McCartney is perhaps explained by the fact that seven weeks before *All Things Must Pass* was begun, McCartney had riled the others with the perceived declaration that he was ending the Beatles. Since the song's genesis marks Harrison's own departure from the group, albeit later withdrawn, the thought that McCartney had just claimed to have resigned for public attention would have given the song a new edge, there being no coincidence that this was the first thing recorded for *All Things Must Pass*. Whoever Harrison had in mind when composing the verses stands dismissed of simply 'being there at the right time'; Harrison must have understood that his career to date rested in no small measure on the dazzling talents of both McCartney *and* Lennon, making such denouncement particularly cutting. There is a possibility too that the song addresses the composer's feeling towards the whole group rather than any specific individual, and in this context it comes across as less deliberately spiteful, although the supposed link to McCartney has stuck.[23] Pointed though the lyrics are, they are not without a mitigating sense of regret, Harrison recalling the camaraderie the group once had, and in an echo of McCartney's The Long And Winding Road, jammed by the Beatles in the days leading up to the fracas, a confession that, in private, he'd been in tears over the situation. (In this respect, Wah-Wah, with its reference to a guitar effect, can be seen as an encumbered sequel to While My Guitar Gently Weeps.)

Wah-Wah expresses its irritation through musical tension, running over an organised progression of major chords rooted in E until it comes to a head on an uncomfortable D7, which Harrison presses home by dwelling there for four complete bars. How Wah-Wah sounded in 1969 is unknown, but there's no mistaking the final riff's resemblance to the similar figure in Delaney and Bonnie's Comin' Home, a December single which Harrison had learned during the concurrent live shows. Bulked out with Phil Spector's blazing arrangement, Eric Clapton handling the requisite wah-wah pedalled guitar, the song is one

---

[23] Asked around now what he thought of the just-released *McCartney*, an uncharitable Harrison opined, 'The arrangements of some of those songs, like [26] Teddy Boy and [24] Junk, with a little more arrangement they could have sounded better.' Since the two tracks nominated were Beatles leftovers; the 'more arrangement' hints at possible versions he might have played on – and by implication, improved.

of the densest on *All Things Must Pass*, its raucous magnitude both an attack and a shout of frustration from a songwriter caught at the crux of two opposite career trajectories. By no means the best thing on the album, the track was of personal importance to Harrison, and one which he used as a suitably attention-grabbing opener at his Concert For Bangla Desh in August 1971. A curious footnote has McCartney – quite possibly the target of Harrison's ire – participating in another live version at the *Concert For George* in 2002.

George Harrison: [34] **MY SWEET LORD** (*Harrison*)
Produced by George Harrison, Phil Spector
Recorded: 28 May 1970; early August, EMI Studios, London; Aug/Sep 1970, Trident Studio, London
UK: 30 Nov 1970 (*All Things Must Pass* LP)
US: 23 Nov 1970 (single A-side)
George Harrison: lead vocals, backing vocals, guitar, swarmandal; **Eric Clapton**: guitar; **Pete Ham**, **Tom Evans**, **Joey Molland** ('Badfinger'): acoustic rhythm guitars; **Klaus Voormann**: bass; **Alan White**: drums; **Jim Gordon**: drums; **Billy Preston**: piano; **Gary Wright**: electric piano; **John Barham**: harmonium; **Ringo Starr**: tambourine; **Mike Gibbins**: tambourine; **unknown**: orchestral parts (arranged by John Barham)

If Something represents the apex of Harrison's writing for the Beatles, My Sweet Lord has similar status in his solo *oeuvre*. Far and away the most successful of his post-Beatles recordings, the song has a long and complex history, with subsequent legal shenanigans adding yet more chapters. Harrison claims to have come up with the song during the Danish leg of his December tour with Delaney and Bonnie, finding the alternating chords by playing around with the terms 'Hallelujah' and 'Hare Krishna'. Recognising its potential, he is said to have sought input from Delaney Bramlett, who together with his backing vocalists, Bonnie Bramlett and Rita Coolidge, contributed further ideas and helped shape it into a song.[24]

Harrison's account, put forward in defence of a subsequent copyright dispute, should be qualified by his other explanation, that he devised it by spinning off Oh Happy Day, a 1969 hit for the Edwin Hawkins Singers which had been deprived of the UK number 1 spot by The Ballad Of John And Yoko. Oh Happy Day was the most overt example of gospel to appear in the pop listings, and shares a similar 'call and response' structure to My Sweet Lord, as

---

[24] Martin Scorsese's 2011 documentary, *George Harrison: Living In The Material World*, includes an archive clip of Billy Preston making the claim that he began the song, not Harrison: 'I went to the piano and I started playing some gospel changes… One of them [Delaney and Bonnie] started, *"Oh my lord…"*.'

well as a broadly matching chord progression. There is probably some truth in both of Harrison's explanations, the second somewhat more persuasive in view of his earlier composition, [64] Hear Me Lord, which provides evidence he could write in the spiritual/religious style without calling for help.

Reluctant to record the track himself for fear of alienating a largely non-religious audience, Harrison initially planned to offer My Sweet Lord to Edwin Hawkins before changing his mind and putting it up for Billy Preston's Apple album, *Encouraging Words* in January 1970, when it was recorded with the Temptations' touring band who happened to be around.[25] The Edwin Hawkins Singers were also in town and were fittingly asked to join the session, the Christian gospel vocalists said to be confused when asked to sing 'Hare Krishna', not knowing what it meant.[26]

Although Harrison had effectively now disposed of the song, Preston's recording remained in the can for several months, which may have been a factor in Harrison's decision to make a version of his own after all. His reading (which includes Billy Preston in the musicians' roster) slows it down, and has the song structure methodically blocked out, lending a more solemn, and suitably prayerful quality. The bedrock of the new arrangement is the track's powerfully circulating acoustic guitar sequence, striding confidently through two alternating shifts: F sharp minor against B, and E against C sharp minor. In an early indication of Phil Spector's instrument-heavy production on *All Things Must Pass*, volume and sonic depth are afforded by having *five* acoustics playing the same chords all at once, the quintet including three members of the Apple group, Badfinger, with the resultant peal mixed across the whole stereo field to make for one super-guitar. No equivalent arrangement exists in the Beatles' catalogue, the decision to use a bank of instrumentation here something thought up by Harrison and Spector without obvious antecedent.

The track was put aside for more than two months until Harrison found a new trademark, and the famous slide guitar section was added at Trident, a studio selected for the album's extensive overdubs due to its multi-track console, more advanced than the hardware at EMI. (In keeping with the general arrangement, the slide riff was conceived for multiple harmonised

---

[25] Harrison confusingly claimed the original version of My Sweet Lord was recorded with the Temptations, and that their drummer, bassist and guitarist play on it. The Temptations, who were purely a vocal outfit, were on tour in the UK in January 1970 with a stage group including Cornelius Grant (guitar), Bill White (bass) and Melvin Brown (drums). Harrison presumably meant these musicians appear uncredited on Preston's track, which was taped at precisely the right time.

[26] My Sweet Lord, and Harrison's religious songs generally, are routinely referred to as gospel. However the African-American idiom has little to do with Harrison's Eastern styles or their chanted mantra elements. Harrison himself was guilty of blurring the distinction at times [64].

guitars before being pared down to just two.) John Barham's orchestral score was also added there, as were the backing vocal parts, Harrison multi-tracking himself endlessly, including lines sung at reduced speed to achieve higher frequency tones when pitch-corrected. These parts infused the track with its most significant ingredient, Harrison liberally mixing his 'Hallelujahs' with, not only 'Hare Krishnas' but also the full text of the Hare Krishna Mantra, plus an entire Vedic chant.[27] Few who later sang along when the record came on the radio noticed these elements, and that was the aim. Harrison's avowed intent was to catch listeners out, seducing them into chanting Hare Krishna before they realised what they were doing, thereby mixing in the spirituality of East and West. Conversely his lines about needing to *see* the Lord are decidedly un-Christian, Harrison reacting against his native Catholicism's doctrine of blind faith under the influence of 19th century Hindu philosopher, Swami Vivekananda: 'If there's a God, let's see Him. If there's a soul, let's perceive it'.[28]

Harrison's magnum opus was finally completed just as Billy Preston's version was issued out to little attention. Harrison's was unveiled at the end of November and rapidly became a hit, riding high in the US charts over Christmas (ironically it landed at number 1 on Boxing Day). Apple accordingly put it out in the UK as well, watching it top the charts again and notch up global sales in the millions. All of which made My Sweet Lord a particularly valuable copyright, a point not lost on Bright Tunes, owners of another song: He's So Fine, a Ronnie Mack composition once recorded by the Chiffons for the Laurie label. Only a modest hit in the UK, it had done its business at home, topping the US singles chart for a month in the spring of 1963, and it's likely therefore that Harrison was familiar with it. (If he wasn't, his producer Phil Spector certainly will have been.) Bright Tunes happened to be in financial straits by 1970, and noting Harrison's global smash was virtually identical in format to He's So Fine, they filed a plagiarism suit in early 1971. (At the same time, American country singer, Jody Miller, issued a new recording of He's So Fine, which mixed in parts of Harrison's guitar sections from My Sweet Lord, played by – of all people – Pete Drake [39]. Harrison viewed the release as a cynical ploy to boost Bright Tunes' case.)

---

[27] The Hare Krishna Mantra had been recorded in its own right by Harrison, with the Radha Krishna Temple (London), and released as an Apple single in 1969. The Vedic chant reads, *Gururbrahmaa, Gururvisnuh/Gururdevo, Mahesvarah/Gurussaakshaat, Param Brahma/Tasmai Shri Gurave Namah*. Translations vary and approximate to 'The Guru is the creator, Lord Brahma. He is Lord Vishnu, the preserver, and Mahesvara, the destroyer. He is the supreme Brahman, to whom I give my prayers.'

[28] Harrison's paraphrasing from an interview by Alan Freeman, 18 October 1974, broadcast on US radio the following year.

Although My Sweet Lord is pitched in E, and He's So Fine in G, the chord progression is a match, notationally, ii-V / I-vi. Set against this is the three-word title phrase of each song, pitched on the same descending triad, and answered with backing vocal interjections. Significantly, Billy Preston's looser recording had enough differences to distinguish it from He's So Fine, not least the bass riff which is a unique feature lending a distinct individuality, and which meant a copyright charge would likely have failed had Bright Tunes thought it worth the expense. Harrison's acoustic arrangement on the other hand serves to almost deliberately expose the song's musical framework, the chords clear and obvious, the notes unambiguously laid out. This was going to be a difficult one to defend.

The lawsuit would go through several twists and turns, and was not fully resolved until well into the 1980s. Initially, Allen Klein put in an offer to purchase Bright Tunes on Harrison's behalf, but the company responded by insisting Harrison surrender to them the lucrative rights to My Sweet Lord, resulting in a stalemate. Matters lie in stasis until 1976, after Bright Tunes entered administration, and when it was due to come to court, Allen Klein, sniffing a payday, purchased Bright Tunes for himself. A lengthy counter case was therefore pursued by Harrison's legal team, which finally succeeded in getting Harrison his full rights when the court granted him a legal option to purchase Bright Tunes from Klein.

The long and torturous history of My Sweet Lord has, to an extent, overshadowed what for Harrison was a spectacular achievement. Those who doubted his chances of making it without the Beatles were comprehensively silenced and Harrison became the first from the group to score a number 1 hit in both the UK and the US. My Sweet Lord is his signature tune, and with its hallmark slide guitar and spiritual message, defines his solo style.

George Harrison: [35] **I'D HAVE YOU ANYTIME** (*Harrison, Dylan*)
Produced by George Harrison, Phil Spector
Recorded: 28 May 1970; 29 May 1970; 4 June 1970, EMI Studios, London; Aug/Sep 1970, Trident Studio, London
UK: 30 Nov 1970 (*All Things Must Pass* LP)
US: 27 Nov 1970 (*All Things Must Pass* LP)
George Harrison: vocals, guitar; **Eric Clapton**: lead guitar; **Klaus Voormann**: bass; **Alan White**: drums; **uncredited**: vibraphone, harmonium

Aside from Lennon and McCartney, the dominant influence on Harrison's songwriting was the Beatles' one-time favourite, Bob Dylan. The group discovered him in early 1964 when Harrison picked up a copy of *The Freewheelin' Bob Dylan*, all four fast becoming fans or, in Lennon's case, a disciple. As the 1960s progressed, Dylan's effect on the Beatles became one of the more pervasive elements of their middle period style – not just in terms of musical delivery but in their understanding of the art and parameters of songwriting, giving them the impetus to delve into much more meaningful lyrical discourse.

Although Dylan and the Beatles had occasionally met during the 1960s, they tended to cross paths vicariously, each following the other with a curious fascination from different continents, aware that apart from being rivals they were also partners in crime. The start of a meaningful meeting of minds was Harrison's visit to Dylan and the Band in the last week of December 1968 when, for the first time, Dylan worked face to face with a Beatle. The fact is, Dylan was entering something of an artistic slump, his last major track, All Along The Watchtower, a year old, and with nothing to rival it on the horizon. Conversely, Harrison was undergoing a significant ascent in his writing, having just released the two finest songs in his growing catalogue in While My Guitar Gently Weeps and Long Long Long – the latter taking inspiration from Dylan's I Shall Be Released, adding another link to the chain.

Convened at Dylan's home near Woodstock, the guitars inevitably came out and Harrison swapped compositional notes with Dylan while jamming. From such interaction, this co-write emerged. Harrison came up with the main section of the song in response to Dylan's curiosity as to how the Beatles found some of their more unusual chords. The sequence Harrison landed on, a run of technically tricky major sevenths from G through B flat and up to C minor is unlike any he'd previously written, and seems to have been a conscious attempt to impress Dylan with his invention around the fretboard. By contrast, Dylan's contribution – the rhythmically ambiguous complementary sections, 'All I have is yours', take a mazy walk around the majors, visiting every natural root except B as if in an attempt to equal Harrison's invention, and serving to pull the song's airy verses back to ground.

I'd Have You Anytime is an anomaly for both writers, not only for its musical allure but also its unconditional confession of romantic love. The closest Dylan had come to this mode of writing was the country-style I'll Be Your Baby Tonight from *John Wesley Harding*, although with its sexual subtext, the earlier song was a more worldly creation. Harrison had written nothing in this vein before. A love song to no-one in particular, the track speaks of the open, honest mood of the session, its narrative spurred not by real-life affairs so much as a desire from both Dylan and Harrison to work in synergy with each other, neither wishing to come up short.

Preserved as a roughly duetted demo, I'd Have You Anytime was left as it stood for some 18 months. Harrison apparently never put the track up for consideration with the Beatles, while Dylan's *Nashville Skyline* appeared in 1969 without it. Even during the extensive *Get Back* sessions, where Harrison repeatedly doodled unreleased Dylan material, the song was completely overlooked, as if being kept back for some other purpose. Was he embarrassed about having such a prestigious collaboration up his sleeve?

Come 1970, and having gotten the strife of the Beatles' difficult final year off his chest with [33] Wah-Wah, Harrison recalled I'd Have You Anytime, laying down the track at EMI with help from Eric Clapton, whose lead guitar alternates between the sedate and the impassioned, incorporating a wealth of bent notes mimicking the slide guitar style heard on much of the album. While Lennon and McCartney were content to work with their respective wives, Harrison surrounded himself with talent – one of the finest guitarists, one of the world's top producers, and, in Dylan, one of the greatest songwriters of the era – and it shows. Swaying on the gentle waft of its relaxed chords, I'd Have You Anytime is a country mile ahead of anything the others had yet recorded, and placed prestigiously at the start of *All Things Must Pass*, ushers in the album with a welcoming warmth. This illustrious collaboration must have drawn at least a tinge of envy from both McCartney and Lennon, if for differing reasons.

George Harrison: [36] **ISN'T IT A PITY** (*Harrison*)
Produced by George Harrison, Phil Spector
Recorded: 29 May 1970; 2 Jun 1970; 3 Jun 1970, EMI Studios, London; Aug/Sep 1970, Apple Studios, London; Aug/Sep 1970, Trident Studio, London
UK: 30 Nov 1970 (*All Things Must Pass* LP)
US: 23 Nov 1970 (single B-side)
Version 1: **George Harrison**: lead vocals, backing vocals, guitar; **Pete Ham**, **Tom Evans**, **Joey Molland** ('Badfinger'): acoustic rhythm guitars; **Klaus Voormann**: bass; **Ringo Starr**: drums; **Tony Ashton**: piano; **Gary Wright**: keyboards; **Billy Preston**: keyboards; **Mike Gibbins**: tambourine; **unknown**: orchestral parts (arranged by John Barham)
Version 2: **George Harrison**: vocals, guitar; **Eric Clapton**: guitar; **Pete Ham**, **Tom Evans**, **Joey Molland** ('Badfinger'): rhythm guitars; **Carl Radle**: bass; **Ringo Starr**: drums; **Tony Ashton**: piano; **Bobby Whitlock**: organ; **Mike Gibbins**: tambourine

According to Mark Lewisohn, Isn't It A Pity was written in 1966 and offered up for *Revolver*.[29] Since its release in 1970, the song has been hailed as one of the best Harrison ever came up with, making its failure to appear in the intervening years mystifying. (It's undoubtedly superior to several Harrison numbers the Beatles *did* record.) Along with a slew of others, it was revisited

---

[29] See note in MacDonald, p345.

during the *Get Back* sessions, although Harrison didn't particularly push for its inclusion, perhaps conscious that it was destined for a solo outing. (He demoed it alone on 25 January 1969 after the group session had ended.)

Harrison recalled the song early in the *All Things Must Pass* sessions, and captured a usable recording at EMI on 2 June, with the standard line-up of Klaus Voormann, Billy Preston and Ringo Starr. But at some point he fancied a second go, this time deploying a couple of Eric Clapton's Dominos, who, during the course of the sessions, gradually became his preferred backing group (see [61]). The timing of the re-make is uncertain. Version 2 was supposedly taped on 3 June, the day after Version 1, but waters were muddied by Harrison's remark in 2000 that the band happened to be jamming the song 'some weeks later', prompting the second recording at that point.[30] Whatever the case, both ended up on the album – unnecessarily, since the original version is obviously the stronger.

The lyric's subject matter – hurt caused by thoughtlessness – resonates with some of Harrison's contemporary material ([33], [66]) so that a connection to the break-up of the Beatles is implied, even if the song pre-dates it. Musically graphic in its composer's patent manner, Isn't It A Pity observes the pain and sorrow via a series of brooding discords expressing the tears and broken hearts – and, in its second verse, contains some of Harrison's more poetic lines, lamenting the sadness. Yet despite its regretful nature the recording is far from morose, and at more than seven minutes, is comfortably the longest on *All Things Must Pass* (discounting the *Apple Jam* [59]).

Part of the song's panorama derives from its extended, circulating fade-out running over three minutes and some 60 bars. An early mix circulates, a little over five and a half minutes, indicating the full-length coda was created with edits, as revealed by the occasional join (eg around 2:20) and minor tempo shift (eg around 3:53). Here, the criticism often levelled at Phil Spector's large-scale arrangements is unjustified, the track's grandeur built on a bedrock of multiple keyboards and guitars, boosted yet further by John Barham's hymn-like orchestral chart (overdubbed at Apple) plus an array of brass instruments, flutes and tympani. At around the time it was scored, Harrison also added his exultant slide guitar passages, conceived at least as far back as 1969, and containing at 2:10 a memorable tritone step from C sharp to G – the 'devil's interval' – tracked by sliding strings for added push. (In the *Get Back* rehearsal of 26 January, Harrison can be heard vocalising these melodic shapes, proving them to have been his conception and not Barham's.)

Harrison went for his Version 2 in a gentler style, suitably sombre and

---

[30] Recollections published in a promotional CD pack accompanying the album's 30th anniversary reissue. The presence in the line-up of Carl Radle and Bobby Whitlock supports this version of events, since neither was in the studio until later in June.

better conveying the heavy heart of its lyric. Effort was expended to achieve a subdued mood with gently prodding piano from Tony Ashton, latterly of Ashton, Gardner and Dyke (and who, among other duties, had played on *Wonderwall Music* in 1967), and Clapton playing through a swimming Leslie cabinet – yet despite being 'wobbled' with ADT phasing, this new take inevitably pales in the shadow of its predecessor, sounding like a preliminary demo. The original version was strong enough to become a hit when coupled with [34] My Sweet Lord and released ahead of the album in the States. Although the other side took the lion's share of plaudits, Isn't It A Pity was listed jointly when the single hit number 1 in December. Forever dwarfed by its spectacularly successful partner track, Isn't It A Pity remains one of Harrison's finest moments.

George Harrison: [37] **I DIG LOVE** (*Harrison*)
Produced by George Harrison, Phil Spector
Recorded: 2 Jun 1970, EMI Studios, London; Aug/Sep 1970,
 Trident Studio, London
UK: 30 Nov 1970 (*All Things Must Pass* LP)
US: 27 Nov 1970 (*All Things Must Pass* LP)
George Harrison: vocals, guitar; **Eric Clapton**: guitar; **Dave Mason**: guitar; **Klaus Voormann**: bass; **Ringo Starr**: drums; **Jim Gordon**: drums; **Bobby Whitlock**: piano; **Gary Wright**: electric piano; **Billy Preston**: organ

The first *new* composition recorded for *All Things Must Pass*, I Dig Love grew from a figure discovered by Harrison while running lazily up and down the bottom two strings of a guitar tuned to an open E. But developed from this initial game, the song, like most riff-based numbers, lacks harmonic interest and is among the least regarded on the album. Its elementary musical structure is mirrored by a lyric consisting of a repetitive, vaguely erotic reference to the era of free love, whose toying variation, 'I love dig', is unamusing and shows little real effort went into it.

The track relies therefore on the comparative strengths of the ensemble performance. Recorded in a slowly throbbing groove, I Dig Love features former Traffic guitarist, Dave Mason, alongside Clapton and Harrison. Mason would go on to become a semi-Domino, the fact that he's playing here in a line-up with pianist, Bobby Whitlock an indication of how the studio team was taking shape. (Whitlock has separately claimed bass on this song was by Carl Radle rather than Klaus Voormann, underlining the uncertainty surrounding the sessions' in-studio details. Jim Gordon's drums, meanwhile, must have been a subsequent overdub on top of Starr since he was not present until later in the project.)

In the end this uninspiring ditty required 20 takes to nail, Phil Spector not content and requesting a late synthesiser addition which was never recorded. This is where his production style differs most sharply from that of George Martin: Spector wanted to add to the mix, where in truth, the song would have been the better for some disciplined trimming down. That it hangs around for a full five minutes only adds to a sense that the album's fourth side, which it sees in, is a fraction more than the available material could reasonably stretch to.

George Harrison: [38] **IF NOT FOR YOU** (*Dylan*)
    Produced by George Harrison, Phil Spector
    Recorded: 4 Jun 1970; 5 Jun 1970, EMI Studios, London; Aug/Sep 1970, Trident Studio, London
    UK: 30 Nov 1970 (*All Things Must Pass* LP)
    US: 27 Nov 1970 (*All Things Must Pass* LP)
    George Harrison: vocals, guitar, harmonica; **Peter Frampton**: guitar; **Klaus Voormann**: bass; **Alan White**: drums; **Gary Wright**: piano; **Billy Preston**: organ; **Ringo Starr**: tambourine; **uncredited**: harmonium

On a visit to New York in the spring of 1970, Harrison dropped in on his friend, Bob Dylan, attending a 1 May session for *New Morning* at Columbia's studio where the two jammed with Dylan's current group of musicians. Recordings from the day exist but are generally unimpressive, and include several ragged and incomplete oldies besides a number of in-development *New Morning* titles, one of them If Not For You.[31] The song was new to Harrison, who had to learn his way around it, something he is said to have done using a slide guitar – incorrectly noted as the earliest recording of his slide work to survive. (He'd recorded slide guitar as far back as 1966, as heard on Strawberry Fields Forever, and briefly on Lovely Rita in 1967.)

If Not For You is an uninhibited love song, supposedly for Dylan's wife, Sara, the like of which he had rarely composed previously. A clear precedent was the romantic [35] I'd Have You Anytime, co-written and therefore indicating an influence from Harrison in Dylan's songs, making this new one a natural choice for the former Beatle to record himself. Dylan was apparently happy for Harrison to claim it, giving him a copy of the session tape to take back to London for reference.

---

[31] Their recording of If Not For You has since had official release, along with Time Passes Slowly and Working On A Guru from the same day, in Dylan's long-running *Bootleg Series*. (Working On A Guru is thought to be a Harrison co-write, although when released it was copyrighted to Dylan alone.) In addition, Robert Rodriguez (2014, p253) has suggested the finished version of Went To See The Gypsy on *New Morning* includes Harrison on guitar, meaning it too originates from this session.

As recorded for *All Things Must Pass*, Harrison added some 'Dylan' harmonica in an arrangement otherwise dominated by Billy Preston's swirling organ section. The slide guitar track was added last, Harrison having developed and extrapolated parts from the May recording to create his signature *obligato*. Thus, when programmed immediately after [61] What Is Life, the track provides a lightness of touch whose country air breezes free from the album's surrounding heftiness.

For Dylan's part, ongoing plans for *New Morning* meant he too wanted the song, and initially the May demo was earmarked for release. Fortunately, Dylan thought better of it, and on 12 August laid down a new recording featuring some amendments including a couple of extra lines and a re-wording in the second verse. Since Dylan's version was released ahead of Harrison's, many listeners assumed the latter had changed it, but in fact Harrison's is original. (Interestingly, when Dylan turned up for The Concert For Bangla Desh the following year (see [140]), the pair duetted the song on stage before the crowds arrived, the lyric and structure conforming to Harrison's recording, not Dylan's.)

The only cover version Harrison made in earnest before 1976, If Not For You stands as testament to his skills as an interpreter, the fact that it was penned by his primary influence, Bob Dylan, satisfying for posterity.

George Harrison: [39] **BALLAD OF SIR FRANKIE CRISP (LET IT ROLL)**
(*Harrison*)
Produced by George Harrison, Phil Spector
Recorded: 4 Jun 1970; 5 Jun 1970, EMI Studios, London; Aug/Sep 1970,
    Trident Studio, London
UK: 30 Nov 1970 (*All Things Must Pass* LP)
US: 27 Nov 1970 (*All Things Must Pass* LP)
George Harrison: vocals, guitar; **Pete Drake**: pedal steel guitar; **Klaus Voormann**: bass; **Alan White**: drums; **Bobby Whitlock**: piano; **Billy Preston**: organ; **Gary Wright**: electric piano

George and Pattie had lived in their bungalow, Kinfauns, for half a decade when they decided it was time to find somewhere more expansive, Harrison's old pal Terry Doran detailed to locate a suitable property for the couple. Friar Park was discovered via an advert in the *Sunday Times* placed by a group of nuns who currently had ownership. Situated in Henley-on-Thames, an affluent Oxfordshire town within reach of central London, the neglected 25-bedroom property rose mysteriously from its overgrown landscaped gardens, and on viewing it, Pattie fell in love. The couple purchased it for £140,000, had the grounds cleaned up and instructed an architect to renovate the building, finally moving in on 12 March 1970.

Harrison too fell in love with his new home, particularly taken by the eccentricity of many of its details. Its first owner, Baronet Sir Frank Crisp, had indulged his sense of humour by incorporating countless odd features including amusingly-captioned follies, lakes with hidden stepping stones, to give the illusion of walking on water, mazes, caves connected by secret tunnels and even a vast replica of the Matterhorn mountain. Friar Park would become one of Harrison's muses, infusing several of his songs (eg [228]), its garden featured on the cover of *All Things Must Pass* and its open spaces used as a setting for the Crackerbox Palace video in 1976, giving viewers a chance to look around. (Harrison also built a recording studio there in 1972, which he would use for much of his subsequent career.)

Nine days after starting work on *All Things Must Pass*, Harrison recorded this new song celebrating his property, pulling in a signature riff and darkly mumbled reference to Sir Frank from one of his unused early demos, Everybody, Nobody (see [32] note). A whistle-stop tour of the grounds, Harrison's text takes us on a graphical 'roll' around the property's many sumptuous features and as if conscious of its potential to be read as a show of new-found material wealth (Harrison was born into a small terrace with an outside toilet), its author threw in an obligatory 'spiritual' reference by name dropping The Inner Light, as inspired by the 48th 'selection' of the 1958 religious anthology, *Lamps Of Fire*. In offering up a visual account of the premises, Harrison's lexicon is unusually rich in colour, conjuring images of 'ye long walks of coole and shades', the maze 'where ye echo lays' quoting Frank Crisp, and, in rejected lines, an 'abode of prancing steeds'.

The 5 June session saw Nashville pedal steel guitar supremo Pete Drake temporarily welcomed into the EMI fold. Flown to London at Harrison's behest, and chauffeured down from the airport, Drake's principal job was to bring a country flavour to the Dylan tribute, [40] Behind That Locked Door, but during a week in and around the studio, he contributed to several other tracks, including this.

One of the highlights of *All Things Must Pass*, Ballad Of Sir Frankie Crisp was too lyrically specific to attract cover versions, something Phil Spector predicted when advising Harrison to change the words. In refusing any dilution of his theme, Harrison may have deprived himself of a commercial hit but succeeded in finishing up a composition seated in his personal biography. Much admired in the intervening years, the song lent a title to Harrison's 2009 career retrospective.

George Harrison: [40] **BEHIND THAT LOCKED DOOR** (*Harrison*)
Produced by George Harrison, Phil Spector
Recorded: 5 Jun 1970; 8 Jun 1970; 3 Jul 1970, EMI Studios, London;
   Aug/Sep 1970, Trident Studio, London
UK: 30 Nov 1970 (*All Things Must Pass* LP)
US: 27 Nov 1970 (*All Things Must Pass* LP)
George Harrison: vocals, guitar; **Pete Drake**: pedal steel guitar;
Klaus Voormann: bass; **Alan White**: drums; **Gary Wright**: piano;
Billy Preston: organ

Harrison's vein of form continued through the first phase of *All Things Must Pass*, this latest recording another to emerge from his association with Bob Dylan ([35], [38]). Recorded by way of homage, Behind That Locked Door was conceived after Harrison had travelled to the Isle of Wight to watch Dylan perform his first live set in three years at the end of August 1969. The Woodstock Festival had been staged a fortnight earlier, but despite living only a matter of miles from the site, Dylan had shown no interest. Instead he brought the Band back to Britain, where they'd last played during his 1966 World Tour.

The subject of considerable advance hype, Dylan's Sunday night appearance was seen as a disappointment to many of the 200,000 at Wootton, near Ryde; those expecting to witness the Dylan of three years previous, belting out electrified and electrifying rock, were instead treated to a set of sedate, country-infused numbers drawing largely on his two most recent albums, *John Wesley Harding* and *Nashville Skyline*. Watching from the side were Lennon, Starr and Harrison, all having shown up a day early to mingle with the group and attend the pre-concert rehearsals (where Harrison gifted Dylan a Gibson Jumbo acoustic guitar).

Observing Dylan from close quarters, Harrison saw him as closed individual who was curbing his emotional and musical self, or at least, keeping his personality in check. With Dylan having been in seclusion since 1966, Harrison felt the urge to coax him from a self-imposed shell, and started Behind That Locked Door the following day. Perhaps reluctant to express his thoughts directly, Harrison's emotionally eloquent lyric comes across as a love song with nothing to betray its specific inspiration, to those not already in the know. In any case, Dylan didn't appear to the rest of the world as someone who needed liberating; were the song not pitched in the second person, Harrison might have been singing about himself, as he stepped from the shadows of Lennon and McCartney in 1969-70.

Recognising the musical style Dylan had embraced on *Nashville Skyline*, Harrison elected to record Behind That Locked Door in a similar arrangement, and called on Pete Drake for some 'country' pedal steel (see [39]). Initially positioned only in the instrumental break, his work was so infectious that Harrison had him play throughout the song. As a former frustrated guitarist in a band with McCartney, Harrison would have been happy to let a good musician flourish, and here, Drake steals the show, his swooping and gliding around the song's riffs simultaneously sympathetic and uplifting.[32]

With its anti-rock arrangement, Behind That Locked Door sits beside [38] If Not For You, offering a contrast to *All Things Must Pass*'s general clamour by seating the album on a Southern farmhouse porch under the stars for a few minutes. Sequenced immediately after [38], the song's Dylan references are implied but not declared, the track concealing its intentions and remaining as private as its subject matter.

George Harrison: [41] **I LIVE FOR YOU** (*Harrison*)
 Produced by George Harrison, Phil Spector
 Recorded: 9 Jun 1970, EMI Studios, London; Aug/Sep 1970,
  Trident Studio, London
 UK/US: unreleased
 George Harrison: vocals, guitar; **Peter Frampton**: guitar; **Pete Drake**: pedal steel guitar; **Klaus Voormann**: bass; **Alan White**: drums; **Bobby Whitlock**: piano

One of the strongest unreleased tracks of the solo Beatles canon, I Live For You was demoed at the start of these sessions but the only known attempt to record it properly is this one, the song having surfaced nowhere else. The circumstances of its writing are unknown, although as a romantic love song, it was presumably composed with Pattie in mind. The arrangement, resting on Bobby Whitlock's sedate crotchet piano, is similar to that of [43] All Things Must Pass, recorded the following day, and happened to come up while Pete Drake was in Studio 3 – his swooping pedal steel figure at the song's hook line, reminiscent of the lead guitar device in the Beatles' I've Got A Feeling, was probably conceived by Harrison. (Another noted participant is Peter Frampton, guitarist in Humble Pie, introduced to Harrison via mutual friend, Terry Doran. See also [38].)

When sessions came to an end a month later, it was clear Harrison had

---

[32] Drake's personality was warmly appreciated. Outtake recordings circulate of Drake impressing the group with his patent 'talking steel guitar' technique in the studio. (The method entails feeding the pedal steel's sound wave into the mouth via a flexible tube, then forming silent words which give the impression that the guitar is speaking.) Consequently, Harrison asked him to add the effect onto the refrain of [33] Wah-Wah. Drake would go on to record cover versions of Behind That Locked Door and [36] Isn't It A Pity, which were issued posthumously.

barely enough material to make up two conventional LPs, filling space with an alternative version of one of the songs. It's odd therefore that this one wasn't finished up and included. It escaped to the public in the 1980s through the John Barrett Tapes (see [31]) and was eventually released officially as a bonus track in the 2001 reissue of *All Things Must Pass*.

George Harrison: [42] **WEDDING BELLS (ARE BREAKING UP THAT OLD GANG OF MINE)** (*Fain, Kahal, Raskin*)
Produced by George Harrison, Phil Spector
Recorded: 9 Jun 1970, EMI Studios, London
UK/US: unreleased
George Harrison: vocals, guitar; **Pete Drake**: pedal steel guitar; **Klaus Voormann**: bass; **Alan White**: drums; **Bobby Whitlock**: piano; **Billy Preston**: organ

This very old number was known to all the Beatles through Gene Vincent's 1956 version for his debut album, *Bluejean Bop!*, which also contained a seminal recording of Ain't She Sweet. Harrison was probably the first to learn it, offering it up in his pre-Quarry Men days to Rory Storm, leader of local group, the Texans, who remained coolly unimpressed with the 14-year-old's talents. 12 years on, it surfaced again during the *All Things Must Pass* sessions, a lack of proper documentation leaving the finer details unknowable. On the evidence of the surviving audio, it was started spontaneously by Harrison, who kicks off alone before the rest of the group gradually join his groove. Given that the range of instruments is broadly similar to that of [41] I Live For You, taped the same day, the personnel can be confirmed with a good degree of reliability.

To Harrison's credit he recalls the lyric well considering there's no evidence he had returned to it in the preceding decade. (Lennon is believed to have handled lead vocals when the Quarry Men performed it in 1960-61.) A song lamenting how romantic love gradually comes between personal friendships, the poignancy of the theme can't have been lost on Harrison who'd seen both Lennon and McCartney form new partnerships over the past couple of years, contributing to the demise of the group's once inviolable unity. McCartney certainly recognised the lyric's relevance; interviewed for *Anthology* in the 1990s, he sang the song's chorus to camera, illustrating his theory of why the Beatles' break-up was unavoidable.

George Harrison: [43] **ALL THINGS MUST PASS** (*Harrison*)
Produced by George Harrison, Phil Spector
Recorded: 10 Jun 1970; Aug/Sep 1970, EMI Studios, London; Aug/Sep 1970, Trident Studio, London
UK: 30 Nov 1970 (*All Things Must Pass* LP)
US: 27 Nov 1970 (*All Things Must Pass* LP)
George Harrison: vocals, guitar; **Eric Clapton**: backing vocals, guitar; **Pete Drake**: pedal steel guitar; **Klaus Voormann**: bass; **Ringo Starr**: drums; **Jim Gordon**: drums; **Bobby Whitlock**: backing vocals, piano; **unknown**: flugelhorn, harmonium, orchestral parts (arranged by John Barham)

Wondering later in life where the inspiration for All Things Must Pass came from, Harrison claimed he couldn't remember, suggesting the song's underlying philosophy was then circulating among 'all kinds of mystics'. While this may have been true, Harrison's cue was almost certainly Timothy Leary's 1966 publication, *Psychedelic Prayers*, in turn based on verse 23 of the classic Chinese text, *Tao Te Ching*, which contained a homage to Lao Tse entitled *All Things Pass*. Harrison must at some point have read Leary's book, so direct is the correspondence, the clincher being that All Things Pass was also the original title of the song.[33]

Harrison is known to have started the track in the wake of his visit to Dylan and the Band in late 1968 (see [35]), visualising it as one for Levon Helm to sing. Although nominally the group's drummer, Helm was also vocalist on several of the Band's hit recordings, including The Weight from *Music From Big Pink*, which had impressed Harrison – so much so that he incorporated its opening acoustic guitar riff into the end section of this new composition. The body of All Things Must Pass though is an ascending guitar run derived from exploring an open E tuning. Beginners in open-tuned guitar invariably find their fingers falling on familiar chord shapes, giving rise to new combinations which can then be rediscovered on a conventionally stringed instrument. Thus, a common run begins on E major, sliding its way up the fretboard in steps to arrive on A, a sequence which crops up in many guitar-written songs – a case in point, McCartney's Here, There And Everywhere, which uses the same progression.[34]

---

[33] Leary's verse reads, 'A sunrise does not last all morning/A cloudburst does not last all day/Nor a sunset all night/All things pass.' Harrison's uncertainty as to the lyric's origins is expressed in the relevant entry of his autobiography.

[34] When recorded for *Revolver*, Here, There And Everywhere was pitched in G. However the fact that McCartney composed it in Lennon's garden means it was written on guitar, then transposed to accommodate the vocal. The same rising sequence occurs in the chorus to McCartney's Getting Better on *Sgt Pepper* and the middle eight of Lennon's >

Having fleshed out a three-verse cycle, Harrison took what he had into sessions for *Get Back* in 1969, where it was worked on extensively by the Beatles in an effort to devise a vocal harmony arrangement. (One idea they tried had Lennon, McCartney and Harrison taking turns to sing lines from the first verse.) It's usually said that the song was 'rejected' by the group, but in fact many hours were expended in an effort to perfect it, McCartney showing considerable interest by putting forward musical ideas, none of which were to Harrison's particular liking. Harrison also had Lennon to thank for 'a mind can blow those clouds away', which was written as 'a wind' before his colleague suggested the change to imply something more cosmic. Yet despite belying the assumption that the group paid little or no attention to Harrison's *Get Back* offerings, the rehearsal versions came to nothing.

In this context, the relevance of Harrison's time Stateside with the Band was pivotal in the break-up of the Beatles. As a performing ensemble, the Band exercised a respectful democracy in which each member was free to write, play or sing, with no dominant presence. (Although Robbie Robertson was sometimes seen as leader, he'd only written four of the 11 tracks on *Big Pink*, and sung just one.) Working in such an environment was artistically liberating for Harrison who was dismayed to find that back in London, he was constantly held to junior status against McCartney and Lennon. His underlying resentment over their attitude meant that when *Get Back* was approaching its conclusion, he effectively withdrew his material from the project, insisting none of his songs be performed in the upcoming live show, and opting to keep All Things Must Pass for himself.

What Harrison planned to do next is not clear. On his 26th birthday in February 1969, he went into EMI alone and recorded an acoustic demo of the track, indicating his thoughts may already have been on a solo release. The next we know of it is from the winter sessions for Billy Preston's *Encouraging Words*, to which Harrison donated this and [34] My Sweet Lord. (Preston knew the song already, having rehearsed it with the Beatles in the Apple basement on 28 January.) In Preston's hands, the song is transformed in the soul styling, incongruously celebratory and bearing little resemblance to Harrison's subsequent version which was undertaken as Pete Drake's presence put him back in mind of Dylan and the Band. Harrison not only decided to record the song while Drake was around, but secured its fame by naming the album after it.

With its cyclical quality, All Things Must Pass speaks of the transitory nature of existence, using the passing of the day as a metaphor for life's inevitable changes. Yet somewhere in the process, Harrison seems to be addressing more immediate concerns, changing tack to confess that his love is

---

Sexy Sadie on the *White Album*.

over and he's about to leave. Framed this way, All Things Must Pass is less a purely philosophical expression and more an ameliorative for someone he's set to separate from. Although it's natural to see Pattie as the subject of these rueful lines, the song's location in time and place suggests more convincingly that Harrison was sending a message to Lennon, McCartney and Starr, reassuring them that, although his time as a Beatle was coming to an end, there would, after all, be Another Day.

All Things Must Pass was the last thing recorded for a while, as Harrison took a break to attend more personal matters.

Beaucoups Of Blues sessions: June 1970

As a life-long country music fan, Starr was particularly pleased to meet up with Nashville musician, Pete Drake, during *All Things Must Pass*. The two became pals after Drake noticed some country tapes in Starr's car, and realising he was an enthusiast, brought up the possibility of making some music together.

Starr, who'd recorded a number of country-styled songs in his Beatle years, was warm to the idea, having mused such a project previously. Yet accustomed to working in the context of the group, Starr imagined a full LP would take several months to make, mildly suggesting a crew of country musicians travel over to London to save him the upheaval. Drake, though, was used to recording in single-take sessions, and pointed out that he'd helped Dylan make *Nashville Skyline* in a matter of days. He ventured he could do likewise with Starr, if a Nashville session could be organised, and Starr was won over, convinced that if he did travel to the States for recording he'd be committing at most a week of his time.

Conceptually, a choice had to be made: whether to pursue the precedent set with *Sentimental Journey*, and record a set of known songs, or opt for original material. In this respect, Drake had the advantage of owning his own label, Stop Records, with a pool of songwriters under contract to his publishing arm, Window Music. Although relying on established material might have offered Starr better odds of scoring a hit, he agreed on the latter course, undoubtedly cajoled by Drake, who will have realised that owning the copyrights to the entire LP would prove lucrative.

With plans firming up, Drake instructed a number of his writers (principally, Stop Records recording artists, Sorrells Pickard, Chuck Howard and Larry Kingston) to prepare some material at once, which resulted in them presenting more songs than were needed. (Although the accepted scenario has them all writing from scratch, given the time constraints, its likely that in at least some cases they dug out material already composed.) And so a week after Drake returned home from his *All Things Must Pass* sojourn, Starr followed him over to Nashville, departing on 22 June. When he landed, Starr unwittingly brought a taste of Beatlemania with him, fiddle player Jim Buchanan nominated to show Starr around the area, which entailed dodging an endless stream of fans loitering about the studios and hotels, trying to catch a glimpse. Unable to throw them off the scent, Buchanan ended up bussing Starr out to a remote farmhouse to escape the clamour.

Beaucoups Of Blues was recorded in town, over an intense three days at Music City Recorders, a modest eight-track facility owned by an investment group which included Elvis's old guitarist, Scotty Moore – who'd once electrified the Beatles with his uncredited work on tracks like That's All Right and Heartbreak Hotel. On the scene too were the King's former backing singers, the Jordanaires, part of a team of more than 20 vocalists and musicians – far more than were truly required; presumably curiosity played its part in drawing them all in, as word of the celebrity session spread. Among the throng was Drake himself, plus Charlie Daniels and Charlie McCoy, all three of whom had played on *Nashville Skyline* the previous year. Used to recording whole albums in as little as a day, the studio team had no difficulty learning their way around the crop of new songs which were taped in back-to-back three-hour sessions, two per day over the Thursday, Friday and Saturday nights.[35]

Ringo Starr: [44] **WOMAN OF THE NIGHT** (*Pickard*)
Produced by Pete Drake
Recorded: 25 Jun 1970, Music City Recorders, Nashville
UK: 25 Sep 1970 (*Beaucoups Of Blues* LP)
US: 28 Sep 1970 (*Beaucoups Of Blues* LP)
Ringo Starr: vocals; **Pete Drake's Session Team**: guitar, drums, fiddle, pedal steel guitar; **Jerry Kennedy**: dobro; **Roy 'Junior' Huskey**: upright bass; **Charlie McCoy**: harmonica; **the Jordanaires**: backing vocals[36]

---

[35] A number of surplus compositions were supposedly recorded, although the notion seems doubtful. Session documentation seems to indicate the full sequence and nothing further is accounted for, bar [52] The Wishing Book and some studio jamming (see [58]).
[36] As with *All Things Must Pass*, the team of musicians on *Beaucoups Of Blues* is known, but no listing of who plays on which track has ever been published (indeed, it's likely these details were never documented). Some instruments have only one candidate musician (for example, Charlie McCoy is the only harmonica player present), and in these cases we can identify them with confidence. In the case of guitars, pedal steel, drums and fiddle, there is more than one possible candidate. Therefore, we credit these instruments collectively to 'Pete Drake's Session Team', which breaks down as >

Getting down to work at 6pm on Thursday 25, the first number captured for *Beaucoups Of Blues* was Woman Of The Night, penned by Jimmy Bazzell under his professional name, Sorrells Pickard. Finding himself suddenly surrounded by so many of Nashville's 'cool cats', a nervous Starr had to be coaxed into letting himself loose at the mike by Pete Drake, watching on from the control room, and did his best to effect a loose country mood.

A platonic love song to a hooker, Woman Of The Night paints an affectionate portrait of someone everyone wants, but nobody cares for. The narrator admires her from a respectful distance, observing as she wanders the local markets looking for business. Sensitively rendered by Starr, the song is vaguely touching, despite its unusual subject matter, rising happily into its standard C major chorus. Neatly delineated by Jerry Kennedy's dobro figures (mixed hard left), the song made for a buoyant start to what were, in truth, somewhat awkward proceedings.

With the first track successfully taken, Starr could start to relax as the group at once turned to the next number.

Ringo Starr: [45] **WITHOUT HER** (*Pickard*)
Produced by Pete Drake
Recorded: 25 Jun 1970, Music City Recorders, Nashville
UK: 25 Sep 1970 (*Beaucoups Of Blues* LP)
US: 28 Sep 1970 (*Beaucoups Of Blues* LP)
Ringo Starr: vocals; **Pete Drake's Session Team**: guitar, drums, fiddle; **Roy 'Junior' Huskey**: upright bass; **the Jordanaires**: backing vocals

A second Sorrells Pickard number, Without Her took up the remainder of the opening day's early session, which was scheduled to wrap up by 9pm. Perhaps selected to appeal to the pop-oriented Starr, the song is the furthest removed from the niche country idiom on the album, and could therefore have made a commercially effective trailer single.

Ticking along on a lightly percussive drum pattern, Without Her is a pleasant affair lamenting a failed love, and in its repeat emphasis on the word 'yesterday', may have been written with a teasing reference to McCartney's song in mind, which shares a similar subject. (Pickard also makes playful use of the double-meaning: 'I'm so weak I just can't stand to be without her'.) Light in mood, the song's melody ranges across exactly one octave, visiting all – and only – the white notes. Custom-made for Starr's range, it is, however, oddly

---

follows: Guitarists: Ringo Starr; Chuck Howard; Charlie Daniels; Dave Kirby; Sorrells Pickard; Jerry Reed; Jerry Shook; Jerry Kennedy; Pedal steel: Ben Keith; Pete Drake; Drums: Ringo Starr; Buddy Harman; DJ Fontana; Fiddle: Jim Buchanan; George Richey; Grover 'Shorty' Lavender.

pitched so as to cause him difficulties reaching down to the bottom C. Why it wasn't bumped up a tone or two is not obvious – the experienced session musicians would have had no concerns with a minor transposition.

The song's composer was an occasional recording artist in his own right and Pete Drake brought him to Stop Records in late 1968. Drake would produce an eponymous album for him in 1972, which included a version of this song (arranged in A), along with [50] $15 Draw.

Ringo Starr: [46] **BEAUCOUPS OF BLUES** (*Rabin*)
Produced by Pete Drake
Recorded: 25 Jun 1970, Music City Recorders, Nashville
UK: 25 Sep 1970 (*Beaucoups Of Blues* LP)
US: 28 Sep 1970 (*Beaucoups Of Blues* LP)
Ringo Starr: vocals; **Pete Drake's Session Team**: guitar, drums, fiddle; **Jerry Kennedy**: dobro; **Roy 'Junior' Huskey**: upright bass; **Charlie McCoy**: harmonica; **the Jordanaires**: backing vocals[37]

Setting a pattern for the three days' work on *Beaucoups Of Blues*, the team took a one-hour break, re-convening at 10pm to capture a trio of songs in the second session. The first recorded track was penned by another Stop Records artist, Buzz Rabin, who'd lived his teenaged years in Louisiana, and in this context is semi-autobiographical, recounting his longing to leave home and see the world. Consequent of Louisiana's French history, Rabin recalled the tendency of locals to use the term 'beaucoups' in conversation, giving him a device to turn his story into a blues in which his dreams fail to materialise. Scored in the model country style, the track features a weaving fiddle and archetypal pedal steel passage, and benefits from one of Starr's best vocal performances, in which he has little difficulty rising above the top C where he'd been capped on [45] Without Her.

Given its title, the song was an obvious choice to name the album after, and was issued on 45 in various parts of the world (but not the UK) in October. Unsuited for the pop listings, it nonetheless made a top showing of 43 in Germany, propelled by its Beatle connection. As a result, Beaucoups Of Blues is the best-remembered track from these sessions, which for most of the participants was the commercial high-point of their careers. As Sorrells Pickard had done with [45] Without Her, Buzz Rabin released his own recording in 1974, on his only album, the Pete Drake-produced *Cross Country Cowboy*.

---

[37] Some sources claim Starr drums on the track.

Ringo Starr: [47] **LOVE DON'T LAST LONG** (*Howard*)
   Produced by Pete Drake
   Recorded: 25 Jun 1970, Music City Recorders, Nashville
   UK: 25 Sep 1970 (*Beaucoups Of Blues* LP)
   US: 28 Sep 1970 (*Beaucoups Of Blues* LP)
   Ringo Starr: vocals; **Pete Drake's Session Team:** guitar, drums, fiddle; **unknown:** piano; **Roy 'Junior' Huskey:** upright bass; **Charlie McCoy:** harmonica; **Buddy Harman:** percussion; **the Jordanaires:** backing vocals

Kentucky rock and roller, Chuck Howard, had been recording material under his own name since 1958, releasing a long run of 45s on a succession of record labels, none of them hits. In 1969 he linked up with Pete Drake and Stop Records, where he issued a cover version of Chuck Berry's The Promised Land, putting him in the frame for the Starr sessions where four of his songs were recorded.

The first of them, Love Don't Last Long, is a desolate depiction of lost romance, its first two verses recounting the story of a pregnant girl and a young lad in trouble with the law, both of whom are abandoned by their parents in their hour of need. Softly arranged by Drake, the recording features a piano track by an unknown musician, not mentioned on the table of credits. (Starr was able to play himself, but given its sometimes articulate and florid style, it's unlikely he was at the keyboard.)

When the album's trailer single, [46] Beaucoups Of Blues/[57] Coochy-Coochy was issued around the world, the Portuguese Parlophone label picked it up and for some reason tagged on Love Don't Last Long as an extra B-side. Perhaps inevitably, Chuck Howard would release his own version of the song on his 1976 album, *Sounds Of Sadness*, along with a recording of [48] Waiting.

Ringo Starr: [48] **WAITING** (*Howard*)
   Produced by Pete Drake
   Recorded: 25 Jun 1970, Music City Recorders, Nashville
   UK: 25 Sep 1970 (*Beaucoups Of Blues* LP)
   US: 28 Sep 1970 (*Beaucoups Of Blues* LP)
   Ringo Starr: vocals; **Pete Drake's Session Team:** guitar, drums, fiddle, pedal steel guitar; **unknown:** piano; **Roy 'Junior' Huskey:** upright bass; **the Jordanaires:** backing vocals

Running past midnight, the first evening's work on the album had already generated four finished tracks, next in line another effort from Chuck Howard. Assuming the song was written especially with Starr in mind, Howard wasn't going easy on him, the first two vocal syllables separated by an interval of a ninth, which Starr handles determinedly.

A second despondent number, Waiting belies Howard's usual rocking style, wallowing in the pain of lost love, told from the perspective of a lonely man hoping his woman will come back. The song was arranged with the same piano accompaniment as the previous number, used here for decorative detail in the second verse. Since the instrument features only in the three Chuck Howard originals ([47], [48], [56]), there is a possibility that Howard himself is the pianist.

All done by 1am, the album had got off to a fine start, Drake living up to his promise that the project could be completed in a few days.

Ringo Starr: [49] **I'D BE TALKING ALL THE TIME** (*Howard, Kingston*)
Produced by Pete Drake
Recorded: 26 Jun 1970, Music City Recorders, Nashville
UK: 25 Sep 1970 (*Beaucoups Of Blues* LP)
US: 28 Sep 1970 (*Beaucoups Of Blues* LP)
Ringo Starr: vocals; **Pete Drake's Session Team**: guitar, drums, fiddle; **Jerry Kennedy**: dobro; **Roy 'Junior' Huskey**: upright bass; **the Jordanaires**: backing vocals

A deceptively cheery song about the torment of romantic failure, I'd Be Talking All The Time was written by Chuck Howard along with yet another of his label mates, Larry Kingston, who'd signed to Stop Records in 1968. The lyric concerns the wealth of words the singer has to express his heartache, but the track lacks any harmonic interest, drifting through a couple of minutes to little effect. At the song's close, Starr name-drops himself before a risible attempt to leap to an octave finish, a fun-sized repeat of the conclusion to With A Little Help From My Friends, which causes his voice to crack. And with that, the first song of this new evening was complete.

Ringo Starr: [50] **$15 DRAW** (*Pickard*)
Produced by Pete Drake
Recorded: 26 Jun 1970, Music City Recorders, Nashville
UK: 25 Sep 1970 (*Beaucoups Of Blues* LP)
US: 28 Sep 1970 (*Beaucoups Of Blues* LP)
Ringo Starr: vocals; **Pete Drake's Session Team**: guitar, drums, fiddle; **Jerry Kennedy**: dobro; **Roy 'Junior' Huskey**: upright bass; **Charlie McCoy**: harmonica; **Buddy Harman**: percussion; **the Jordanaires**: backing vocals

$15 Draw appears to have been built around Starr's happy-go-lucky character, several elements of the lyric conveying parts of his story. The thrust of the song is a communication to his mother back home, reminding her of the adventures he'd had through playing music. In fact, there's more than a hint that Starr had some input into the text; the Uncle Harry of the singer's childhood recalls his musical step-father, Harry Graves, of whom Sorrells Pickard was presumably unaware, while the line that his 'little fingers blistered' reminds us of Starr's exclamation on the *White Album*. The reference in the final verse to Bolton City is curious; no Brit would make such a mistake, but since there's no such place in America, one presumes Pickard was attempting to inject some northern English context, although where he got the location from is anyone's guess.

One of the stronger songs on the album, $15 Draw is very much a Nashville product, Starr buying into its informal 'bumpkin' humour by chucking some comic interjections over Charlie McCoy's bluegrass harmonica and Jerry Reed's hillbilly guitar. All told, this good piece of fun was a lively entry on what was ostensibly a blues record, suitably selected to open the album's second side.

Ringo Starr: [51] **WINE, WOMEN AND LOUD HAPPY SONGS** (*Kingston*)
Produced by Pete Drake
Recorded: 26 Jun 1970, Music City Recorders, Nashville
UK: 25 Sep 1970 (*Beaucoups Of Blues* LP)
US: 28 Sep 1970 (*Beaucoups Of Blues* LP)
Ringo Starr: vocals; **Pete Drake's Session Team**: guitar, drums, fiddle, pedal steel guitar; **Roy 'Junior' Huskey**: upright bass; **the Jordanaires**: backing vocals

The late session on this second day of recording was given over to two numbers, the first this devil-may-care account of life's three basic pleasures set to a country-style waltz. Written by Larry Kingston, the text is pitched in the fall-out of so much indulgence, the song's character dishevelled and hung over, having enjoyed, then lost, all of them. Coming up smiling, he simply intends to do it all again, making the song a celebration of hedonism rather than a statement of regret. Wine, Women And Loud Happy Songs was re-recorded by Larry Kingston in 1975, for Nashville vocalist, Benny Lindsey.

Ringo Starr: [52] **THE WISHING BOOK** (*Adock*)
Produced by Pete Drake
Recorded: 26 Jun 1970, Music City Recorders, Nashville
UK/US: unreleased
Ringo Starr: vocals; **Pete Drake's Session Team**: guitar, drums, fiddle; **Jerry Kennedy**: dobro; **Roy 'Junior' Huskey**: upright bass; **the Jordanaires**: backing vocals

Having got [51] down, the ensemble worked into the night on the album's only reject, The Wishing Book, the plainly rendered story of a girl dissatisfied with her simple country life. Leaving home and family for the bright lights, her main concern seems to be the material wealth she hopes for, her desires including a 'big brass bed', appropriated from Dylan's Lay Lady Lay on *Nashville Skyline*. The song's grief is expressed in the unexpected final verse, where we encounter her spurned lover, the poor boy with dreams of his own.

The Wishing Book was composed by one of Window Music's writers, Johnny Adock, and was later recorded by Stop Records' Len Barrow. With its rousing choruses, it was wrongly arranged for the album, accounting for its ultimate omission, although when an acetate of *Beaucoups Of Blues* was auctioned off in 1992, the prototype disc included the song, indicating it was in the offing until late on. The track escaped to the public via John Barrett's tape copies (see [31]).

Ringo Starr: [53] **FASTEST GROWING HEARTACHE IN THE WEST**
(*Kingston, Dycus*)
Produced by Pete Drake
Recorded: 27 Jun 1970, Music City Recorders, Nashville
UK: 25 Sep 1970 (*Beaucoups Of Blues* LP)
US: 28 Sep 1970 (*Beaucoups Of Blues* LP)
Ringo Starr: vocals; **Pete Drake's Session Team**: guitar, drums, fiddle; **Jerry Kennedy**: dobro; **Roy 'Junior' Huskey**: upright bass; **Buddy Harman**: percussion; **the Jordanaires**: backing vocals

Moving into the third and final day's work, four more songs were needed to finish up the album, the group kicking off at 6pm with Fastest Growing Heartache In The West. One of the most musically satisfying numbers on *Beaucoups Of Blues*, this track was penned by Larry Kingston along with Frank Dycus, a moderately successful guitarist and songwriter signed in 1967 to Pete Drake's Window Music.[38] Dycus was born in Kentucky and moved to California when he was 15, informing the lyrics to Fastest Growing Heartache, which concern a country miss relocating to the West Coast with her man. In the story, the humble girl has her head turned when they get to LA, and starts to look elsewhere for her pleasures – hence the song's bluesy theme.

Among the few session outtakes known, two acoustic guitar rehearsals of the song have emerged, testing out different tempos to that employed on the album, which lands somewhere between both. The guitarist is not identified, but is unlikely to be Starr himself.

---

[38] Kingston and Dycus set up their own publishing company, Empher Music, in 1970.

Ringo Starr: [54] **SILENT HOMECOMING** (*Pickard*)
Produced by Pete Drake
Recorded: 27 Jun 1970, Music City Recorders, Nashville
UK: 25 Sep 1970 (*Beaucoups Of Blues* LP)
US: 28 Sep 1970 (*Beaucoups Of Blues* LP)
Ringo Starr: vocals; **Pete Drake's Session Team**: guitar, drums, fiddle, pedal steel guitar; **Jerry Kennedy**: dobro; **Charlie McCoy**: electric bass; **Buddy Harman**: percussion; **the Jordanaires**: backing vocals

Following nearly a dozen recordings about heartbreak and romantic strife, the next number was the only one to deal with contemporary political issues, Sorrells Pickard offering this tragic tale of a mother waiting for her soldier boy to return from war. Opposition to the Vietnam conflict had continued to grow through 1970, heightened when the US began an invasion of neutral Cambodia in late April. One of several defining moments in the anti-war movement occurred on 4 May, when US soldiers opened fire on a student demonstration in Ohio, killing four unarmed civilians and paralysing another, prompting walkouts and strikes at universities across America. Musically there was no shortage of protest, CSNY rush-releasing a single in June, with the repeat refrain, 'Four dead in Ohio', loudly denouncing the killings.

Against this backdrop Silent Homecoming was written, but the true inspiration is likely to have been an earlier recording, Jimmy Cliff's Vietnam. Although cross-pollination between ska and country music seems, on the face of it unlikely, when Cliff's single was issued in February, Dylan judged it the best protest song of all time, suggesting it was on Pete Drake's radar, at least. What distinguishes Jimmy Cliff's lyric from much of the anti-war genre is the fact that it doesn't delve into the horrors of conflict, or even take a moral position. Rather, it's an individual story of a mother, expecting her son to return home imminently, only to receive a telegram informing her that he'd been killed. The song is, in this context, sympathetic to the military and their families, who were also suffering a profound loss. Pickard's composition covers similar ground, the waiting mother watching as the plane carrying her son lands, only to see instead of his familiar face, a hearse.

Although the song makes the political sharply personal, it also points an insinuating finger at society's values, bringing up the question of children being given toy guns and grenades. The central character of this sad story was one such, unwittingly taught through play that war was a game, and afterwards that he'd simply pack his things away and go home. Placed at the end of *Beaucoups Of Blues*, Silent Homecoming is the album's social allegory, providing a relevance the set would otherwise have lacked. It is also a period piece, its connection to Vietnam locating it among a generation of songs, of which [1] Give Peace A Chance is another example.

Ringo Starr: [55] **LOSER'S LOUNGE** (*Pierce*)
Produced by Pete Drake
Recorded: 27 Jun 1970, Music City Recorders, Nashville
UK: 25 Sep 1970 (*Beaucoups Of Blues* LP)
US: 28 Sep 1970 (*Beaucoups Of Blues* LP)
Ringo Starr: vocals; **Pete Drake's Session Team**: guitar, drums; **Jerry Kennedy**: dobro; **Charlie McCoy**: electric bass; **Charlie McCoy**: harmonica; **Buddy Harman**: percussion; **the Jordanaires**: backing vocals

Not written specifically for Starr, Loser's Lounge was first recorded by Dean Curtis and issued as a Stop Records B-side in 1969. Starr's version ramps it up a notch or two, running faster and filling out the arrangement with percussion, backing vocals and a prominent harmonica from Charlie McCoy, which takes centre stage in the instrumental break.

Bobby Pierce's song was a good choice for Starr. The tale of a lad who can't keep his girl because he's constantly out of cash, it's fertile territory for him to step in and win the day. Sharing some of the flavour of Lennon's I'm A Loser, the song displays no self-pity, and ends on a jocular 'Oh Yeah!', as if emerging triumphant. (The exclamation is probably cribbed from Lulu's Shout, which the Beatles had performed in 1964.)

Ringo Starr: [56] **I WOULDN'T HAVE YOU ANY OTHER WAY** (*Howard*)
Produced by Pete Drake
Recorded: 27 Jun 1970, Music City Recorders, Nashville
UK: 25 Sep 1970 (*Beaucoups Of Blues* LP)
US: 28 Sep 1970 (*Beaucoups Of Blues* LP)
Ringo Starr: vocals; **Jeannie Kendall**: vocals; Pete **Drake's Session Team**: guitar, fiddle, pedal steel guitar; **unknown**: piano; **Roy 'Junior' Huskey**: upright bass; **Buddy Harman**: percussion; **the Jordanaires**: backing vocals

Going into the final session at 10pm, Starr had the album virtually complete, just one more song required. Since the previous recording had been a cover version, there is a hint that the new material may have run dry, which would account for why this track was pitched in E, quite unsuitable for Starr's vocal: he shares singing duties here with 15-year-old Jeannie Kendall, one half of Stop Records vocal act, the Kendalls, consisting of Jeannie and her father, Royce. Since the song is perfectly pitched for her, the suggestion is that it was originally intended as a Kendalls track, written for Royce to sing Starr's part. Whatever the case, that Starr can barely force his register down to the required F sharp in the opening lines works to the track's obvious detriment, and as in [45] Without Her, it's not clear why the musicians didn't simply transpose it – unless, of course, he's singing to a backing track already made for the

Kendalls, which given the lack of drums, is a possibility. (No other track on the album is missing a drum kit.)

A love song about acceptance, I Wouldn't Have You Any Other Way ended sessions for the album proper on a positive note. In all around 16 hours of studio time had been expended, the remainder of this final three-hour booking taken up with jamming, some of which was recorded.

Ringo Starr: [57] **COOCHY-COOCHY** (*Starkey*)
Produced by Pete Drake
Recorded: 27 Jun 1970, Music City Recorders, Nashville
US: 5 Oct 1970 (single B-side)
Ringo Starr: vocals; **Pete Drake's Session Team**: guitar, drums, fiddle; **Jerry Kennedy**: dobro; **Charlie McCoy**: electric bass; **Charlie McCoy**: harmonica; **Buddy Harman**: percussion

Since *Beaucoups Of Blues* wrapped up with time to spare, Starr and the studio musicians were able to indulge themselves into the night, one result being a 28-minute jam on a Starr original named Coochy-Coochy. Musically simplistic, the song adheres to its E major chord throughout, Charlie McCoy providing a monotonous bassline, and an animated overdubbed harmonica solo. Trimmed down for release to a more manageable five minutes, the song fades out while the band is still in full swing, but curiously features a double-tracked lead vocal, indicating it was taken rather more seriously than an idle time-filler.

Despite its basic content – the lyric consists of a few phrases, endlessly repeated – it appears the song was composed in advance and not conjured up on the studio floor. (Starr is known to have written another especially for the occasion, Band Of Steel unrecorded but subsequently given to Texan country star, Guthrie Thomas, for one of his albums.)

Unsuited to the LP, Coochy-Coochy was issued as a flip side to the only trailer single, [46] Beaucoups Of Blues, which never appeared in Britain, making the song a bona-fide rarity in the solo Beatles catalogue until the advent of the CD and associated bonus tracks. With [14] It Don't Come Easy yet to be released, Coochy-Coochy was the first non-Beatles number to bear Starkey's name in the brackets, and only the third full copyright of his career.

Ringo Starr: [58] **NASHVILLE FREAKOUT** (*group improv*)
Produced by Pete Drake
Recorded: 27 Jun 1970, Music City Recorders, Nashville
UK/US: unreleased
Ringo Starr: drums; **Pete Drake's Session Team**: guitars, fiddle; **Jerry Kennedy**: dobro; **Roy 'Junior' Huskey**: upright bass; **Buddy Harman**: percussion; **unknown**: organ, piano

The last thing captured on tape, this 20-minute instrumental sometimes goes by the name, Nashville Jam, and features most, if not all of the session crew. Since Starr doesn't sing, we assume he's at the drum kit, the style sounding much like his. An interesting attempt by the country musicians to approximate rock-blues, the track comes off well, although with its unchanging mood and tempo, quickly starts to lose its attraction. (Officially issued years later on the CD edition of *Beaucoups Of Blues*, it was pared down to a more listenable, but still excessive 6:40.)

All finished by 1pm, the group went on their way, the reels of studio tape subsequently mixed before being sent over to London a week or so later, where the album's final running order was decided. For the LP sleeve, Apple selected a photograph of Starr sitting in the doorway of a farm building belonging to local singer, Tracy Nelson, whose property had been Starr's refuge from curious Nashville fans.

Issued at the end of September, *Beaucoups Of Blues* was greeted by most as an improvement on *Sentimental Journey* but with its country blues flavour, was never destined for major commercial success and a mooted second instalment of similar material didn't appear. For Starr though, the LP represented some sort of artistic vindication, being much truer to his musical values, constituting a record undoubtedly more accomplished than his first.

RECORD RELEASES

Beaucoups Of Blues
   (UK: 25 Sep 1970, US: 28 Sep 1970)
   [46] Beaucoups Of Blues / [47] Love Don't Last Long / [53] Fastest Growing Heartache in the West / [45] Without Her / [44] Woman Of The Night / [49] I'd Be Talking All the Time / [50] $15 Draw / [51] Wine, Women And Loud Happy Songs / [56] I Wouldn't Have You Any Other Way / [55] Loser's Lounge / [48] Waiting / [54] Silent Homecoming

[46] **Beaucoups Of Blues** / [57] **Coochy-Coochy**
   (US: 5 Oct 1970)

All Things Must Pass sessions (second phase): June 1970 to October 1970

George Harrison: [59] THANKS FOR THE PEPPERONI[39]
   Produced by George Harrison, Phil Spector
   Recorded: 18 Jun 1970, EMI Studios, London
   UK: 30 Nov 1970 (*All Things Must Pass* LP)
   US: 27 Nov 1970 (*All Things Must Pass* LP)
   George Harrison: guitar; **Eric Clapton**: guitar; **Dave Mason**: guitar; **Carl Radle**: bass; **Jim Gordon**: drums; **Bobby Whitlock**: piano

After recording [43] All Things Must Pass on 10 June, Harrison took some much-needed time out, with his ailing mother's condition worsening. Meantime, events were developing around him; it was an open secret that of late, Eric Clapton had developed an unhealthy obsession with Pattie Harrison, and had begun writing songs rooted in his unrequited love, along with session pianist, Bobby Whitlock who was living with him at the time in Hurtwood Edge, Clapton's extravagant home on the southern edge of Surrey. Clapton and Whitlock had toured together with Delaney and Bonnie (and Harrison) over the previous winter, along with bassist, Carl Radle, and drummer, Jim Gordon, and all had worked on Clapton's eponymous debut album, about to be released. After Radle and Gordon took up residence with the others at Hurtwood Edge, the impetus to start a new band was irresistible, and along

---

[39] No writing credits were given for this and the following track, although all were copyrighted by Harrisongs. In truth, they were spontaneous group compositions. (The same applies to [70]; [71] and [72].)

with back-up guitarist Dave Mason, they played a debut gig on 14 June, a charity fund-raiser at the Lyceum Theatre in London's West End where they adopted their permanent moniker, Derek and the Dominos. With Harrison's blessing they also took over a day's booking at EMI to record their first tracks, Tell The Truth – with Harrison pitching in on guitar – and Roll It Over, rush-released as a single but withdrawn after they taped a superior version of the former, and realised they could do it better.

In recording *All Things Must Pass*, Harrison had the rare luxury of unlimited studio time, and so he and the Dominos proceeded to indulge in some jams, a couple of which were also recorded. How many instrumentals were attempted across these sessions is unclear, but the best were logged by EMI as Jam 1, Jam 2 etc, before being individually christened with quirky names and issued out as an extra disc under the collective name, *Apple Jam*. A rollicking blues in E, Thanks For The Pepperoni spins off a classic Chuck Berry riff and features rotating lead guitar from Harrison, Mason (who steals the show) and Clapton.[40] Coming to a humorously sudden stop after five and a half minutes, the track is brief compared to some of the other sections of *Apple Jam*, and packs a genuine punch. For a title, Harrison borrowed from counterculture stand-up, Lenny Bruce, whose 1958 live recording, *Religions Inc*, features an imaginary conversation with Pope John XXIII which includes, 'and thanks for the pepperoni'.

George Harrison: [60] **PLUG ME IN**
Produced by George Harrison, Phil Spector
Recorded: 18 Jun 1970, EMI Studios, London
UK: 30 Nov 1970 (*All Things Must Pass* LP)
US: 27 Nov 1970 (*All Things Must Pass* LP)
George Harrison: guitar; **Eric Clapton**: guitar; **Dave Mason**: guitar; **Carl Radle**: bass; **Jim Gordon**: drums; **Bobby Whitlock**: piano

How long Jam 2 lasted in the studio is unknowable, since the released take comes in on a crude edit cutting it down to a little over three minutes. The track was probably taped not long after the previous one, since the instrumentation is identical, and like its predecessor, it's pitched in E. Plug Me In is less formalised and freer in style (its provisional title was Dixieland Rock), featuring a cogent ensemble performance with Jim Gordon firing at the drums and the same exchange of duties on lead guitar, mixed across the stereo space.

---

[40] As analysed by Simon Leng, Harrison (mixed hard right) up to 1:30, Mason (hard left) to 3:00, Clapton (centre) to 4:46, and Harrison again (hard right) for the last minute or so. In the communal spirit of the session, none are left entirely to their own devices when soloing.

George Harrison: [61] **WHAT IS LIFE** (*Harrison*)
Produced by George Harrison, Phil Spector
Recorded: 22 Jun 1970; 23 Jun 1970; 3 Jul 1970; 5 Aug 1970; 8 Aug 1970,
   EMI Studios, London; Aug/Sep 1970, Trident Studio, London
UK: 30 Nov 1970 (*All Things Must Pass* LP)
US: 27 Nov 1970 (*All Things Must Pass* LP)
George Harrison: vocals, guitar; **Eric Clapton**: guitar; **Pete Ham**, **Tom Evans**, **Joey Molland** ('Badfinger'): acoustic rhythm guitars; **Carl Radle**: bass; **Jim Gordon**: drums; **Bobby Whitlock**: piano; **Jim Price**: trumpet; **Bobby Keys**: saxophone; **Mike Gibbins**: tambourine; **unknown**: orchestral parts (arranged by John Barham)

The establishment of Derek and the Dominos in the middle of *All Things Must Pass* would have implications for the rest of these sessions, the group becoming Harrison's *de facto* backing band from here on, giving the remaining songs a heavier, rockier edge than most of the earlier recordings. When Harrison fully returned to work on 22 June to record What Is Life, all of Derek and the Dominos played behind him for the first time. The song they embarked on was another of Harrison's unreleased compositions from 1969, written for Billy Preston on the way to Olympic Studios where sessions for *That's The Way God Planned It* were underway. In the event, Harrison arrived to find Preston already at work and embarrassed by the insubstantial quality of his new song, didn't mention it, and the moment passed. At this point, *Abbey Road* was in process, and Harrison might have offered the song to the Beatles instead, but opted to keep it to himself. It therefore joined the rest of his stockpile, ready for taping come 1970.

Given its already protracted history, it's ironic that What Is Life took multiple dates across two or three months to complete. The first day's work came to nothing, as Harrison didn't like the arrangement, so he went away and devised the descending bass run, giving it an extra hook. The group tried again the next day and secured the basic take at the 11th attempt, Harrison electing to run through the whole thing with an angular fuzz-toned guitar, requiring such concentration he couldn't simultaneously record a vocal – and so the tape gathered dust as an instrumental waiting for something to happen.

All Things Must Pass took another twist at the end of the month when Phil Spector left the sessions, returning to his home in LA. The circumstances are not fully clear, but issues had come to a head due to his unpredictable behaviour, fuelled by constant drinking binges. (According to Harrison, he would indulge in cherry brandies before starting work, and at one point fell to the floor, breaking his arm.) Left to his own devices, Harrison returned to What Is Life in August, dubbing on several new parts including oboe and piccolo trumpet, having in mind the sound achieved on Penny Lane, and thereby incorporating all the major instrument families into the arrangement.

Yet, ever one to vacillate, he decided he didn't like the new instruments either, and had them removed, not sure what to do with it next. Still nominally the album's producer, Spector was sent tapes of the *All Things Must Pass* mixes for his assessment, something he responded to with a long letter giving remarks on every track, and for What Is Life, he recommended the addition of backing vocals – which Harrison proceeded to record at Trident, multi-tracking himself several times to achieve volume, as the soundscape became ever more dense. A lead vocal was then added, and What Is Life was at last ready to go.

The most commercial thing Harrison had yet recorded, the pop-rock flavour of What Is Life made it an obvious choice as a single. Eschewing the gravity which characterised much of the album, it's also the only unqualified love song among a considerable stock of material, something presumably not lost on Pattie. (It's telling that, as sessions for *All Things Must Pass* were winding down, Clapton was in Miami, pouring his heart out to her on vital tracks for *Layla And Other Assorted Love Songs*.) What Is Life was duly released on 7-inch in February, a follow-up to [34] My Sweet Lord in the States and a hit across Europe – but not in the UK, where it was tucked away on My Sweet Lord's B-side. The under-exploited song was eventually spotted by Olivia Newton-John, who took her copy into the British top 20, underlining the fact that Harrison and Apple had missed a trick.

George Harrison: [62] **BEWARE OF DARKNESS** (*Harrison*)
Produced by George Harrison, Phil Spector
Recorded: 22 Jun 1970; 23 Jun 1970, EMI Studios, London; Aug/Sep 1970, Trident Studio, London; Aug/Sep 1970, EMI Studios, London
UK: 30 Nov 1970 (*All Things Must Pass* LP)
US: 27 Nov 1970 (*All Things Must Pass* LP)
George Harrison: lead vocals, backing vocals (?), guitar; **Eric Clapton**: guitar; **Dave Mason**: guitar; **Klaus Voormann**: bass (?); **Carl Radle**: bass; **Ringo Starr**: drums (?); **Jim Gordon**: drums (?); **Bobby Whitlock**: piano; **Gary Wright**: organ; **uncredited**: vibraphone; **unknown**: orchestral parts (arranged by John Barham)

Written a few days before work on *All Things Must Pass* began, Beware Of Darkness dwells on the Hindu conception of light and its relationship to the human soul. The darkness of the song's title refers to a lack of enlightened thought – which in Hindu belief serves to deny divine consciousness – and in asserting that living without spirituality is not our destiny, the lyric comes close to a didactic tract, elevated to a higher purpose by guiding the listener through the shady perils lurking all around.

The full text of Beware Of Darkness was incomplete when Harrison recorded a demo for Phil Spector on 27 May. Lacking an ending for the third verse, Harrison threw in the dummy line 'beware of ABKCO', which if intended as a joke, was a loaded one, implying Harrison was becoming disillusioned with the Beatles' one-time saviour, Allen Klein.[41] When Harrison moved into Friar Park in March, he'd taken with him several Krishna associates who were often heard to mutter, 'Watch out for Maya' (literally, 'that which is not' – see also [270]), and by the time the track was ready for recording, Harrison had made the necessary switch and finished up the verse. (Further private references are incorporated in the lyric, the mention of weeping atlas cedars recalling the trees at Lennon's Tittenhurst Park estate, where the Beatles had posed for their last photographic session the previous August.)

The success of Beware Of Darkness is Harrison's imaginative and impalpable chord sequence, capturing the song's mystical quality by moving around several tonal centres. Often noted is the enigmatic change from a sure-footed opening on G7 to G sharp minor, taking the song along an unexpected pathway, but equally surprising is the drop from C sharp minor to a low D, which, in the song's second verse, arrives in the literal darkness of 'the dead of night' – and from such unusual angularity, Harrison summons a mysteriously flowing piece.

Taped on 22 and 23 June, the group line-up is disputed. According to Harrison's biographer, Simon Leng, Starr appears on drums, but since he left for Nashville on 22nd, it's unlikely to be him – unless there is more to the recording than is known. A better candidate is Jim Gordon, who makes a full complement of Dominos on the track, including Eric Clapton whose Leslie-toned guitar sections provide a sharp edge. (To confuse matters further, the 2021 album reissue quotes Harrison, 'We had two drummers and two bass players', one of whom is named as Klaus Voormann.) One of the most admired songs on *All Things Must Pass*, Beware Of Darkness is Harrison's most deeply philosophical to date, offering a gentle caution belying the album's sometime reputation for brash sonority.

---

[41] ABKCO Industries was Allen Klein's company, to which the Beatles had signed, and which claimed a generous percentage of their earnings. Opposed to Klein's involvement in any of the group's affairs, McCartney was infuriated to find ABKCO's name printed on publicity material for his solo album, taking out adverts at his own expense without the offending logo.

George Harrison: [63] **AWAITING ON YOU ALL** (*Harrison*)
Produced by George Harrison, Phil Spector
Recorded: 22 Jun 1970; 26 Jun 1970, EMI Studios, London; Aug/Sep 1970,
    Trident Studio, London
UK: 30 Nov 1970 (*All Things Must Pass* LP)
US: 27 Nov 1970 (*All Things Must Pass* LP)
George Harrison: vocals, guitar; **Eric Clapton:** guitar; **Carl Radle:** bass; **Klaus Voormann:** bass; **Jim Gordon:** drums; **Jim Price:** trumpet; **Bobby Keys:** saxophone; **unknown:** orchestral parts (arranged by John Barham)

The spiritually-aimed Awaiting On You All came to Harrison through divine intervention, flashing into his mind while he was absent-mindedly cleaning his teeth. Starting with only its hook line, 'You don't need a *something*', Harrison took it to guitar and formalised it, developing a new song by fleshing out a catalogue of ingenious-sounding conclusions in which the fallacies of (other) belief systems are brushed away.

Written in A, the song was raised a whole tone for its studio recording, the introductory riff consisting of a statement of the coming chord repertoire, answered by a diatonic descent on slide guitars – presumably Harrison and Clapton in unison. It seems from the available accounts that the session on 26 June was moved into the bigger Studio 2 for a lengthy evening's work in which the instrumentation was repeatedly changed around before, at take 26, Harrison finally got what he wanted. Consequently struggling under the weight of multiple instruments – not the work of Phil Spector, who'd left the sessions before Harrison's self-directed overdubs were recorded – the track has an overbearing quality, in contrast to its casual conception and ill-suited to conveying its enlightened message. (That Harrison was in a less than holy mood anyway is reflected in the song's opening lines, an apparently unprovoked dig at Lennon.[42])

The thrust of Harrison's lyric is that all that's needed to achieve higher awareness is a simple chant, reciting God's name until a state of heavenly bliss is attained. In this respect, Harrison's influence is from the Japa tradition, wherein a soft-spoken repetition of the Lord's moniker is undertaken in a

---

[42] The lyric, 'You don't need a love-in/You don't need no bed pan' is usually interpreted as a scornful reference to Lennon's 'bed-ins' (see [1]). Harrison's hand-written lyrics, reproduced in his book, *I, Me, Mine*, show the words 'love in' and 'bed pan' to have been written uniquely in block capitals, as if for emphasis. Ostensibly on good terms through 1970, he and Lennon could sometimes be prickly; Lennon dropped in at Friar Park shortly after the release of *All Things Must Pass*, and since Harrison wasn't home, left some unkind remarks about the album with one of the house-guests, which were duly passed on.

suitable setting. (Some Japa practitioners use strings of beads – Japa Mala – to help them count the iterations, 108 being the target.) In other respects, the song displays a kind of multi-faith syncretism, containing evangelical lines on finding Jesus but failing as Harrison delivers the most notorious lyric of career.[43] Dismissing the legitimacy of the Catholic church with reference to its fantastic portfolio of property and investments, Harrison suggests financial markets are of more relevance than any scripture, just four years after Lennon had caused outrage with his 'more popular than Jesus' remark. While Harrison had his point to make, the offending lines were censored by EMI through removal from the album's lyric sheet, while the Vatican issued a public statement playing down the size of its capital stock, to reassure doubting Catholics around the world.

A consequence of its infamy, Awaiting On You All is one of the better known tracks from the album, which Harrison would not back away from, performing it at the Concert For Bangla Desh [140] and delivering an unrehearsed version on acoustic guitar, broadcast on US radio in October 1975. His early demo has also since been made available officially, a reminder of an age when pop stars had something to say about the world they lived in.

George Harrison: [64] **HEAR ME LORD** (*Harrison*)
  Produced by George Harrison, Phil Spector
  Recorded: 23 Jun 1970; 24 Jun 1970; 1 Jul 1970, EMI Studios, London;
    Aug/Sep 1970, Trident Studio, London
  UK: 30 Nov 1970 (*All Things Must Pass* LP)
  US: 27 Nov 1970 (*All Things Must Pass* LP)
  George Harrison: vocals, guitar; **Eric Clapton**: guitar; **Carl Radle**: bass; **Jim Gordon**: drums; **Gary Wright**: piano; **Bobby Whitlock**: organ; **Billy Preston**: keyboards; **Jim Price**: trumpet; **Bobby Keys**: saxophone; **unknown**: orchestral parts (arranged by John Barham)

Continuing a run of recordings based on religious theses, Hear Me Lord was, like [43] All Things Must Pass and [67] Let It Down, a relic of the Beatles' *Get Back* sessions, written on 4-5 January 1969, the group's first weekend off. When Harrison brought it to the others on the Monday morning (announcing, 'I wrote a gospel song at the weekend') it was still incomplete, and had no lyrics in the bridge section. Although it's true the other Beatles paid it little attention, in performances audible on the Nagra Tapes, Harrison seems to be playing it mostly to himself, absorbed in the structure and arrangement while ignoring

---

[43] 'While the Pope owns 51 percent of General Motors/The stock exchange is the only thing he's qualified to quote us.'

the conversations around him.[44] Thus, as with other unused *Get Back* material on *All Things Must Pass*, it's not accurate to say the song was 'rejected' by the Beatles; it was never finished nor proposed for inclusion. Indeed, after its 6 January airing, it was never again mentioned.

17 months on, Harrison recorded a solo demo for Phil Spector, and on this slowly thoughtful recording, the personal quality of the lyric rings true, Harrison pouring out his confessions to the counsel of a fuzz-toned guitar. (Brought up a Catholic, Harrison was taught at an early age that sins needed to be pardoned, hence the opening, 'Forgive me, Lord'.) Regrettably any sense of direct communication with God was obliterated by the patent bawl of the final production, Derek and the Dominos belting it out in an arrangement which in its initial form, ran close to eight minutes. (Gary Wright's piano *obligato* here is particularly effective.) Perhaps feeling the song had been overcooked, Harrison and Spector trimmed back its repeating end section, an exercise in economy which worked to the song's advantage.

With its deep plea for salvation, nothing could effectively follow the serious Hear Me Lord, which was duly positioned at the end of the album proper. As such, it has tended to be overlooked, but interpreted correctly – a musical fusion of religious apprehension and personal longing – its weighty grandeur makes it one of the Harrison's most expressive recordings.

George Harrison: [65] **ART OF DYING** (*Harrison*)
Produced by George Harrison, Phil Spector
Recorded: 23 Jun 1970; 1 Jul 1970, EMI Studios, London; Aug/Sep 1970, Trident Studio, London
UK: 30 Nov 1970 (*All Things Must Pass* LP)
US: 27 Nov 1970 (*All Things Must Pass* LP)
George Harrison: vocals, guitar; **Eric Clapton**: lead guitar; **Carl Radle**: bass; **Jim Gordon**: drums; **Bobby Whitlock**: Hammond organ; **Gary Wright**: electric piano; **Billy Preston**: organ; **Jim Price**: trumpet; **Bobby Keys**: saxophone; **unknown**: orchestral parts (arranged by John Barham)

In interviews from 1969, Harrison remarked that he had a song about reincarnation which he wanted to record, mentioning to a journalist, 'I wrote one called 'The Art Of Dying' three years ago.'[45] That being so, the current track is another very old one, continuing its author's process of working

---

[44] While the Beatles were rehearsing at Twickenham proceedings were being filmed by cameras hooked to mono tape recorders made by Swiss manufacturer, Nagra, which are the source of many hours of bootlegged audio. Hence the term, Nagra Tapes (or Nagra Reels).
[45] *NME*, 20 Sep 1969.

through his backlog with a composition dating to the *Revolver* era. Its vintage corresponds with the growth of Harrison's early interest in Hinduism and a belief in the cycles of the soul, as hinted at in the contemporary I Want To Tell You, in which he pledges to get the girl 'next time around', written as Harrison was working out his spirituality. Yet notwithstanding its connection to Eastern thought, Art Of Dying appears to take its original cue from *Ars Moriendi*, two 15th century European texts on how to move through the process of physical death.[46] A 'heavy' subject even for the mid-1960s, Harrison was aware that he was pushing ahead of his public and consciously ends the lyric with a self-effacing query as to whether what he's said sounds plausible.

The most contemplative thing on *All Things Must Pass*, Art Of Dying was demoed for Phil Spector on acoustic, and at that stage was a despondent number, Harrison possibly mindful of his mother's terminal condition while recording it. When first picked up by the band on 29 May, it was shifted from the original E minor to a more accommodating A minor, giving Harrison's vocal a suitable elevation from the real world. (A teenaged Phil Collins participated in this session, playing congas badly.) Further consideration was given to the arrangement over the following weeks and Harrison then went for this dense re-make, Eric Clapton handling wah-wahed lead guitar against Harrison's fuzz-toned electric. (Clapton's spotlight moment at 2:10 is indulgent but gratifying.) In the end, both takes were short-listed for possible inclusion, the nod given to the later one, which on preliminary album acetates, was positioned as the opening track.

Packed with instruments, Phil Spector's arrangement tends to overpower the personal philosophy from which the song grew. Deeply introspective, the 'Eastern' melody dances its way through a semitonal scheme held inside the boundaries the G major chord, as if imprisoned by material form; no re-birth is allowed, the track drifting away to infinity before a coda is realised. (Perhaps symbolically, Harrison and the group diverted into a wailing rendition of Get Back during the session.)

---

[46] As noted by Womack and Kruppa, p131. *Ars Moriendi* translates from the Latin as The Art Of Dying.

George Harrison: [66] **RUN OF THE MILL** (*Harrison*)
Produced by George Harrison, Phil Spector
Recorded: 24 Jun 1970; 30 Jun 1970; 1 Jul 1970, EMI Studios, London; Aug/Sep 1970, Trident Studio, London
UK: 30 Nov 1970 (*All Things Must Pass* LP)
US: 27 Nov 1970 (*All Things Must Pass* LP)
George Harrison: vocals, guitar; **Carl Radle**: bass; **Jim Gordon**: drums; **Gary Wright**: piano; **Bobby Whitlock**: organ; **Jim Price**: trumpet; **Bobby Keys**: saxophone; **uncredited**: harmonium

The two main currents of *All Things Must Pass*, God and the Beatles, reflect opposite sides of Harrison's state of mind in 1970, the heavenward pull of his spiritual self checked by a lingering, earth-bound rancour over the bitter splitting up of his group – conceptually the light and dark sides of Harrison's world view. While he'd already had a jab at both McCartney [33] and Lennon [63] in song, this latest offering, composed in the aftermath of *Get Back*, is another commentary on the Beatles' break-up, which Harrison later connected specifically with McCartney but which is more generally inclined to a rumination on the failure of all friendships. Harrison impressed himself with the articulation on show here, likening the lyrics to poetry, an assessment which tends to underplay the eloquence of several of his other period compositions.

Given that Run Of The Mill has an unorthodox structure, its many verses never resolving into a chorus, and with no verbal hook to catch the listener, the meaning of its imposed title has been the subject of conjecture. Harrison suggested a play on the northern English expression, 'trouble at t'mill', meaning all is not well, which although making sense contextually ignores the fact that the actual title phrase merely implies something average or commonplace. With Harrison's musical talents routinely under-acknowledged by Lennon and McCartney, it's likely it was meant as ironically self-referential, Run Of The Mill being a particularly compelling creation, which his second wife, Olivia, later nominated as his best.[47]

According to the studio logs, Harrison started work on the track on 29 May in a version apparently scrapped, before revisiting it with Derek and the Dominos in late June for a more decorative arrangement built on descending lead guitar riffs (take 36 circulates). Still not happy he started over again on 1 July, the album version completed at take 61, concluding on the same whole-octave run which Harrison was evidently pleased with since he used it again

---

[47] Thomson, p198. Bobby Whitlock was privy to a private pre-session demonstration of the track by Harrison which incorporated a memorable chord change, 'really unique', which was never recorded (*ibid*).

on Soft Touch in 1978. Coupled with this was a brass chart, overdubbed late on by Jim Price and Bobby Keys and based Harrison's vocalised demonstrations. Singing about the Beatles might have been playing with fire [129] but Run Of The Mill was sufficiently conciliatory that none of his former partners felt the inclination to answer back. The song speaks of the futility of the group's protracted quarrels, and in resisting direct engagement, is both detached and aware, winning the argument without trying.

George Harrison: [67] **LET IT DOWN** (*Harrison*)
    Produced by George Harrison, Phil Spector
    Recorded: 24 Jun 1970, EMI Studios, London; Aug/Sep 1970,
        Trident Studio, London
    UK: 30 Nov 1970 (*All Things Must Pass* LP)
    US: 27 Nov 1970 (*All Things Must Pass* LP)
    George Harrison: vocals, backing vocals, guitar; **Eric Clapton**: backing vocals, guitar; **Bobby Whitlock**: backing vocals, Hammond organ; **Pete Ham**, **Tom Evans**, **Joey Molland** ('Badfinger'): acoustic rhythm guitars; **Carl Radle**: bass; **Jim Gordon**: drums; **Gary Brooker**: piano; **Gary Wright**: organ; **Jim Price**: trumpet; **Bobby Keys**: saxophone; **unknown**: orchestral parts (arranged by John Barham)

One of Harrison's most intimate love songs, Let It Down was written in late 1968 in the long fall-out of his India break. In remaining free from drugs and the worldly temptations of London's rock scene for eight weeks, Harrison was observed to undergo a change in personality through the remainder of the year, Pattie noting how the experience had a depressive effect on his energy levels, causing him to withdraw into deeply meditative states. One consequence of his spiritual quest was a new-found fascination with Krishna, Pattie noting how the Hindu deity was depicted as constantly surrounded by attractive 'young maidens', and imagining that Harrison had started to envisage himself in such a role.[48]

While Harrison's past lack of fidelity was known to, and tolerated by Pattie, an unspoken part of the rock star lifestyle, she reasonably expected him not to bring such things home with him. A line was therefore crossed when, at the end of the year, Harrison began sleeping with a mutual friend, one of Clapton's exes, right under her nose. The situation brought things to a head, and after confronting him on New Year's Day, she packed and left to stay with friends for a period. The following morning, Harrison reported to Twickenham Studios to start work on *Get Back*, and demoed this new song to Lennon first thing.

---

[48] See her autobiography, p122-123.

Given its backdrop, it's difficult to be sure who the attentive lyric is for. Noting the relationship is well-timed, the song hints at a new love while an insecurity lurks beneath the surface, Harrison revealing a desire to keep his passion a secret lest someone should witness it, and expressing uncertainty as to whether her eyes will see him in the same devotional light as his do. In short, the song doesn't *sound* like an overture to a wife of three years, and yet its heartfelt mood is unmistakeable; Harrison couldn't have been so deeply affected by anyone other than Pattie.

As rehearsed during *Get Back*, Let It Down was essentially finished from a compositional point of view but needed a sympathetic arrangement, McCartney's repeating backing vocals exploratory but unusable. By the time the group gave it their undivided attention the sessions were coming to an end, Let It Down joining [43] All Things Must Pass in the remainders pile. It wasn't until the June 1970 session that the song suddenly burst forth, with a clarity not hinted at in the *Get Back* versions. Partly the sheer force of the chorus section owes to the discordant banging of piano from Procol Harum's Gary Brooker, along with Bobby Keys' saxophone, added in a late session and conceived by Phil Spector as a 'screaming madness'. Blazing with trumpets and hammering drums, and firming up from the sensuous major seventh to an unambiguous E, the chorus sections brim with sexual urgency, making for a physical counterpoint to the song's languid, emotive verses.

George Harrison: [68] **OM HARE OM (GOPALA KRISHNA)** (*Harrison*)
Produced by George Harrison, Phil Spector
Recorded: 24 Jun 1970, EMI Studios, London
UK/US: unreleased
George Harrison: vocals, guitar; **Eric Clapton**: guitar; **Carl Radle**: bass; **Jim Gordon**: conga; **Bobby Whitlock**: Hammond organ

This pretty incantation to Krishna, while of Hindustani inspiration, was a recent composition, first heard among Harrison's preliminary album demos. With its light-rock arrangement built around Clapton's Leslie-toned electric, and with standard 'Western' modulations, the song is not drawn directly from the classical Indian tradition (the devotional hymn or *bhajan*), but rather adopts it as a sense of style, repeating a prayerful mantra and concluding with a fast-paced *drut*.

Gopala Krishna – meaning, the infant Lord Krishna – was recorded in the same session as [66] Run Of The Mill and [67] Let It Down, and it is therefore assumed the undocumented musicians are Harrison and the Dominos. Accurately performed by the ensemble, as if rehearsed in advance, it's possible Harrison at this stage had the track short-listed for the album, although it stands in distinct contrast to anything which *was* included. In the event it was put to one side and never heard of again. (With its Sanskrit lyric, it would have been suitable vehicle for the Radha Krishna Temple, had Harrison elected to do any more recording with them.)

George Harrison: [69] **DOWN TO THE RIVER (ROCKING CHAIR JAM)**
(*Harrison*)
Produced by George Harrison, Phil Spector
Recorded: 30 Jun 1970, EMI Studios, London
UK/US: unreleased
George Harrison: vocals, guitar; **Carl Radle**: bass; **Jim Gordon**: drums; **Bobby Whitlock**: piano; **Jim Price**: trumpet

Taped between sessions for [66] Run Of The Mill, Down To The River was a studio improvisation between Harrison and the Dominos, Jim Price evidently around to add some husky trumpet riffs. Ragged and informal, the recording sounds like a *Basement Tapes* leftover, its lolloping gait reminiscent of Please Mrs Henry or You Ain't Going Nowhere. (The similarities are likely unconscious, although the group will undoubtedly have heard Dylan and the Band's unreleased tapes by now, through bootlegs such as *Great White Wonder II*, currently doing the rounds.) Harrison made a new recording of it late in his life which when issued on the posthumous *Brainwashed*, was given the formal name, Rocking Chair In Hawaii – although the 2021 edition of *All Things Must Pass* restores Down To The River as its proper title. Harrison borrowed its novel yodelling elements from Jimmie Rodgers, whose recordings had been a seminal influence in his youth (particularly, Waiting For A Train, which has a matching part).

George Harrison: [70] **OUT OF THE BLUE**
Produced by George Harrison, Phil Spector
Recorded: 2 Jul 1970, EMI Studios, London
UK: 30 Nov 1970 (*All Things Must Pass* LP)
US: 27 Nov 1970 (*All Things Must Pass* LP)
George Harrison: guitar; **Klaus Voormann**: guitar; **Carl Radle**: bass; **Jim Gordon**: drums; **Bobby Whitlock**: piano; **Gary Wright**: organ; **Bobby Keys**: saxophone; **Jim Price**: trumpet; **Al Aronowitz**: unknown instrument (?)

11 minutes of pulsating blues, this instrumental is notable for the sometime prominence of Bobby Keys and Jim Price, Harrison's unsung brass section who were about to be collared by the Rolling Stones for their autumn European tour. The longest of the *Apple Jam* quartet, Out Of The Blue is competently played but tends to lag, its E minor foundation quickly becoming monotonous

for want of any real incident – something the deceleration in pace halfway through only emphasises. (It might have benefited from a fade-out around the seven-minute mark.)

The recording is noted for the alleged presence of US music journalist, Al Aronowitz, said to feature somewhere in the mix, Harrison having first met him on the occasion in August 1964 when he introduced the Beatles to Dylan for the first time. Meanwhile Klaus Voormann handles the lead guitar sections originally credited to Clapton. When *All Things Must Pass* was released, Out Of The Blue was sequenced as the closing track, sitting at the end of side six.

George Harrison: [71] **ALMOST 12 BAR HONKY TONK**
Produced by George Harrison, Phil Spector
Recorded: 3 Jul 1970, EMI Studios, London
UK/US: unreleased
George Harrison: guitar; **Eric Clapton**: guitar; **Carl Radle**: bass; **Jim Gordon**: drums; **Bobby Whitlock**: piano; **Bobby Keys**: saxophone

The most authentically bluesy of the instrumental recordings, Jam 4 was taped the day after [70] Out Of The Blue with, one presumes, Derek and the Dominos handling their regular instruments as normal.[49] Something of a showpiece for Clapton, whose lead motifs are parked on the far left channel, Almost 12 Bar was ultimately discarded, oddly so since this eight-and-a-half minute slow jam in E, while technically not superior to its predecessors, at least offers the interest of a style change and a chance to bulk out the contents of the *Apple Jam* LP which ended up alarmingly brief.

George Harrison: [72] **I REMEMBER JEEP**
Produced by George Harrison, Phil Spector
Recorded: 29 Mar 1969, Olympic Studios, London; 12 May 1969; 3 Jul 1970, EMI Studios, London
UK: 30 Nov 1970 (*All Things Must Pass* LP)
US: 27 Nov 1970 (*All Things Must Pass* LP)
George Harrison: guitar, Moog synthesiser; **Eric Clapton**: lead guitar; **Klaus Voormann**: bass; **Ginger Baker**: drums; **Billy Preston**: organ

This final *Apple Jam* recording is distinct from the rest, having started life more than a year earlier in a pre-session rehearsal for Billy Preston's *That's The Way God Planned It*, which Harrison was set to produce. On 12 May 1969, Harrison dubbed on a Moog synthesiser in a session with Lennon, who wanted the track

---

[49] There is no confirmed list of personnel for this recording, which was unheard until 2021.

for a debut Plastic Ono Band single, provisionally titled Jam Peace. Since Lennon's release never materialised, the tape lay dormant until Harrison was working on the *Apple Jam* suite, whereupon he requisitioned it after the recording of [71] (hinting that he might already have realised Jam 4 was not going to make the album). Readied for *All Things Must Pass*, the original 11-minute instrumental was pared down to eight and re-named in honour of Eric Clapton's Weimaraner hunting dog, which had recently been stolen. (It was eventually reunited with its owner, as evinced by the photo on the cover of Clapton's 1975 album, *There's One in Every Crowd*.)

The decision to release the *Apple Jam* recordings on their own disc was probably taken early on, prototype acetates of the album including it essentially as issued. While the recordings usefully allow a glimpse of some private studio fun, few fans will have failed to notice they were being charged a princely sum for *All Things Must Pass* partly for the privilege of hearing 28 or so minutes of instrumental, and the cost of the requisite packaging (£5 for the set, as against the standard charge of £3.50-£4 for a double album). To date, every reissue has included what, if recorded in the modern era, would have been likely to appear as optional bonus material, and while it's possible to admire the musical virtuosity on display, the jams soon become tiresome and are of interest mainly for their historical significance.

George Harrison: [73] **APPLE SCRUFFS** (*Harrison*)
Produced by George Harrison
Recorded: 25 Jul 1970, EMI Studios, London
UK: 30 Nov 1970 (*All Things Must Pass* LP)
US: 27 Nov 1970 (*All Things Must Pass* LP)
George Harrison: vocals, guitars, harmonica; **Mal Evans**: percussion

The day after the *Apple Jam* sessions concluded, Harrison shot back to Liverpool, news having arrived that his mother, Louise, had taken a turn for the worse. Harrison stayed with her through the next few days, and Louise passed away on 7 July, aged 59. (Harrison was at her bedside when she died, reading from *The Bhagavad Gita*.[50]) This event marked the effective end of the *All Things Must Pass* sessions, which resumed for just one more date – Harrison's solo recording of Apple Scruffs in the last week of the month.

Comforted by the unyielding adoration of his most loyal fans, Harrison sent some love back with this wryly affectionate song, written prior to the start of sessions for the album. The Scruffs – a mostly female gaggle of devotees – would hang around outside the Apple building and other places a Beatle

---

[50] Harrison wrote the tribute [141] Deep Blue shortly before her death. Another period song with associations is Mother Divine, demoed before these album sessions began.

might appear, in the hopes of getting a glimpse or maybe exchanging some words. The Beatles were generally warm to them, Harrison sometimes moved to pop out and give them hot tea if it were particularly cold, and striking up a friendship with one Scruff in particular, Carol Bedford, at least according to her memoirs. (Another story has McCartney singing to them from a bedroom window one evening, his Cavendish Avenue home another of their favourite haunts.)

Apple Scruffs was recorded 'live' in Studio 3 over 18 takes, most of them breaking down, in part because of Harrison's unfamiliarity with the harmonica which he found kept snagging his facial hair. Devoid of bent notes, these passages reveal a lack of expertise on the instrument and yet provide much of the song's spirited character. The last take, running to just 2:30 was deemed suitable, its length extended by half a minute by grafting on a copy of the chorus, with several backing vocal and slide guitar overdubs added to complete the track in a single session. Several Scruffs, including Carol Bedford and Gill Pritchard, were on duty that day at the gates of EMI Studios, Harrison touchingly inviting them inside to hear a playback of 'their' song.

With its affectionate warmth and 'oopsy-dang doo-dang' backing parts, Apple Scruffs offers an antidote to *All Things Must Pass*'s sometimes ponderous sequence of songs, many ruminating on matters of life and death. Arriving at the very end of the project, its recording also served as an entertaining diversion for Harrison, at a time of great personal burden.

George Harrison: [74] **I'LL STILL LOVE YOU** (*Harrison*)
Produced by George Harrison, Phil Spector
Recorded: Aug/Sep 1970, Trident Studio, London
UK/US: unreleased
George Harrison: vocals, guitar; **Carl Radle:** bass; **Jim Gordon:** drums; **Bobby Whitlock:** piano; **Jim Price:** trumpet[51]

A song looking for a home, I'll Still Love You was recorded late-on, according to Chip Madinger and Mark Easter, almost certainly at Trident Studio and therefore during the mixing stage of the album. A reasonably attractive love song built on a circulating bass, the performance is provisional, led by piano and featuring dummy vocals for much of it, despite which the surviving tapes indicate more than 40 attempts were recorded.

With potential for development, the song arrived too late for *All Things Must Pass*, but was not forgotten. Shortly completed and offered to Ronnie

---

[51] The line-up given here is conjecture. There is no known documentation of who plays on the track. However we note the instruments are the same as those used on [69] Down To The River at the end of June.

Spector as I Love You, it was then recorded by Harrison and Cilla Black in 1972 but never appeared. For some reason copyright was registered with the song title as When Every Song Is Sung, but it remained unheard until another version was made for Starr's 1976 album, *Ringo's Rotogravure*, with the title, I'll Still Love You – an episode which resulted in a brief falling out between the two ex-Beatles and threats of litigation.[52]

George Harrison: [75] **IT'S JOHNNY'S BIRTHDAY** (*Harrison, Martin, Coulter*)
Produced by George Harrison
Recorded: 7 Oct 1970, EMI Studios, London
UK: 30 Nov 1970 (*All Things Must Pass* LP)
US: 27 Nov 1970 (*All Things Must Pass* LP)
George Harrison: vocals, guitar; **Mal Evans**: vocal; **Eddie Klein**: vocal

Not conceived as part of *All Things Must Pass*, this very late addition to the running order followed a request sent out to music industry names by Yoko Ono, for recorded greetings to mark the occasion of Lennon's 30th birthday on 9 October. Among those submitted were contributions from Janis Joplin, Donovan, American jazz singer, Blossom Dearie, Ringo Starr [78] and Harrison.[53]

It's Johnny's Birthday was assembled by Harrison using an anonymous fairground tape of the 1968 Cliff Richard hit, Congratulations, found in EMI's audio library. Together with Mal Evans and EMI engineer, Eddie Klein, Harrison overdubbed the recording with vocals and sundry noises including a badly played slide guitar, and speed-adjusted it to make for a jokey greeting which was presented to Lennon on his birthday [89]. Harrison later claimed no knowledge of how it ended up on *All Things Must Pass*, but the fact that it did drew swift attention from the composers of Congratulations, Bill Martin and Phil Coulter, who claimed entitlement to royalties. (Hence their names appear on all bar very early pressings of the album.)

George Harrison: [76] **WOMAN DON'T YOU CRY FOR ME** (*Harrison*)
Produced by George Harrison, Phil Spector
Recorded: 7 Oct 1970, EMI Studios, London
UK/US: unreleased
George Harrison: vocals, dobro, guitar (?)

---

[52] For a potted overview of this little-discussed dispute see Rodriguez, 2014, chapter 2.
[53] Janis Joplin's contribution was made on 26 September, one of the last things she recorded. She died of a heroin overdose on 4 October, before Lennon received the tape.

Another scarcely documented outtake, recorded on the same day as [75], the 1970 version of Woman Don't You Cry For Me was rumoured to exist but remained unheard until the extended album reissue of 2021 unexpectedly delivered it to fans. A Harrison original, the song was written in Sweden during the Delaney and Bonnie tour of December 1969 while he was working on his slide technique. (Harrison later recalled Delaney Bramlett might have given the song its name.) Pitched in open E, the track is an effective exploration of the Delta style, Harrison devising a rootsy lyric drawing on the archetypal 'train blues' with an authentic octave leap in the vocal line. Given that it was likely his first attempt at writing in such a mode the results are impressive, if too removed from the conventions of pop-rock to make it a contender for *All Things Must Pass* – hence why it wasn't taped in the preceding months.

The song was given some late attention, the available recording developed with three instruments all by Harrison and mixed wide for stereo. What he planned to do with it is unknown, and it was left to one side until mid-1976 when he was assembling material for his inaugural Dark Horse album, *Thirty Three & 1/3*, for which purpose it was recovered along with another *All Things Must Pass*-era remnant, Beautiful Girl. By this point the song had undergone some lyrical changes and as recorded, was practically unrecognisable, emerging as a period funk on which Harrison's slide guitar sits somewhat awkwardly. Such are the vagaries of fashion.

At the end of October, the tapes received final production touches in New York, Harrison having flown out with them in order to liaise again with Phil Spector. *All Things Must Pass* was released a few weeks later with Apple labels rendered in 'Krishna' orange, and was an immediate critical triumph, its scope and scale all the more spectacular for the fact that Harrison, previously seen as a junior partner to Lennon and McCartney, was its architect. The first triple album released by a rock artist, the set bursts at the seams, the contents recorded with an expansive and revolving roster of musicians, out of whom Derek and the Dominos coalesced over June. (Their own double album, *Layla And Other Assorted Love Songs* was released more or less simultaneously with *All Things Must Pass*, and is recognised as a career peak for Clapton.)

In the decades since *All Things Must Pass*, its reputation has cooled to some extent, Phil Spector's production having come under criticism for its perceived heavy-handedness. This assessment however ignores the fact that Harrison was directing much of it himself, and many of the arrangements are his own conception, at least in part. Where the album is at times weighty, the sheer presence of its musicality generates a force of its own, and the same can be said for John Barham's string arrangements on nine of the tracks, which seem at times to be realising the promise of Harrison's lyrics and delivering a sort of transcendence. Among its 18 conventional songs are some of Harrison's most admired, and in many cases the towering production and arrangements are the very essence of the tracks, dark, lush and elaborate where needed, light and uncluttered as the music dictates.

Apart from two Beatles-era albums of a non-commercial bent (*Wonderwall Music* (1968); *Electronic Sound* (1969)) this was Harrison's arrival as a solo artist, setting the bar impossibly high for the years to come. Its spiritual/religious themes have tended to dominate discussion over the years, but it can't be avoided that much of the album's contents are coloured by events surrounding the Beatles, starting a never-ending sequence of solo recordings by all four either commenting on the group, or more acutely, one another. There's a political point to be made from the size of the album alone, a public insinuation that McCartney and Lennon had been keeping Harrison down, refusing to allow his abundant music to flourish in a group dynamic which the two controlled. That much of the set was written years before shows Harrison was having to save up his material, although the triple-disc format serves to over-emphasise the point, *All Things Must Pass* in truth suited for around half as much vinyl as it eventually took up.

Irrespective of quibbles over the format and size of the finished product, *All Things Must Pass* is an undisputed pinnacle not just of Harrison's solo career, but any of the Beatles. Containing his most famous recording, [34] My Sweet Lord, it's Harrison's definitive work, and such an outpouring of creative energies it would take him more than two years to gather himself for a follow-up.

RECORD RELEASES

[34] **My Sweet Lord** / [36] **Isn't It A Pity**
   (US: 23 Nov 1970)
All Things Must Pass
   (UK: 30 Nov 1970, US: 27 Nov 1970)
   [35] I'd Have You Anytime / [34] My Sweet Lord / [33] Wah-Wah / [36] Isn't It A Pity (Version One) / [61] What Is Life / [38] If Not For You / [40] Behind That Locked Door / [67] Let It Down / [66] Run Of The Mill / [62] Beware Of Darkness / [73] Apple Scruffs / [39] Ballad Of Sir Frankie Crisp (Let It Roll) / [63] Awaiting On You All / [43] All Things Must Pass / [37] I Dig Love / [65] Art Of Dying / [36] Isn't It A Pity (Version Two) / [64] Hear Me Lord / [70] Out Of The Blue / [75] It's Johnny's Birthday / [60] Plug Me In / [72] I Remember Jeep / [59] Thanks For The Pepperoni

[34] **My Sweet Lord** / [61] **What Is Life**
(UK: 15 Jan 1971)
[61] **What Is Life** / [73] **Apple Scruffs**
(US: 15 Feb 1971)

Ringo Starr single sessions: October 1970

Ringo Starr: [77] **EARLY 1970** (*Starkey*)
   Produced by Ringo Starr
   Recorded: 3 Oct 1970, EMI Studios, London
   UK: 9 Apr 1971 (single B-side)
   US: 16 Apr 1971 (single B-side)
   Ringo Starr: vocals, drums, guitar, dobro, bass, piano; **George Harrison**: guitar, piano; **Klaus Voormann**: bass

This new track from Starr was taped during studio downtime while he was helping Lennon record *John Lennon/Plastic Ono Band*. A devious conspiracy theory surrounds the session, based on the notion that Allen Klein was plotting to undermine any legal case McCartney might have been considering by tricking him into reuniting with the others here, giving rise to a secondary theory that Lennon was in the studio too when Harrison and Starr were at work. Possibly there is a grain of truth somewhere in the rumour, but Lennon was, in point of fact, at home with his feet up.

With a generosity of spirit belying any such duplicity, Starr makes a pitch to each of his mates to come and play music with him again, and follows Harrison's lead in writing a song not *by* but *about* the Beatles. There was no doubting the camaraderie he still had with Harrison, who again helps out.[54] Similarly, he remained on good terms with Lennon, the track recorded during a collaborative album project, Starr throwing in a wink by inserting a 'cookie!' exclamation, having heard Lennon do likewise on [84] Hold On a few days earlier. All of which underscores the alienation of McCartney at this time, which is perhaps why Starr affords him the first verse of this friendly appeal.

Recorded in 13 takes, Early 1970 was arranged in the country style Starr had so enjoyed during his recent time in Nashville, and finds him trying a hand on the dobro while Harrison makes effective use of slide guitar. In fact,

---

[54] After Harrison's death in 2001, his widow, Olivia, came across a hand-written lyric dating from around this time, an unrecorded duet for the two named Hey, Ringo, emphasising their closeness.

Starr's multi-instrumental parts are less an expression of his musical prowess than an acknowledgement of his modest talents, the song's fourth verse an open admission he can hardly play by himself – hence, the demonstrations of his knowingly ham-fisted technique on an array of instruments.

The track, like [14] It Don't Come Easy, was left in the can until the two were finally paired up and issued as a single which went top 5 on both sides of the Atlantic – a striking success for Starr's first mainstream release. By then McCartney had taken the rest of the group through court [112] and succeeded in having a receiver appointed to manage their finances, undermining any prospect of a reconciliation. The song title, switched from the provisional When I Come To Town (Four Knights In Moscow), suggests Starr was attempting to put a date on the sentiments expressed for context, their being so at odds with the reality of the situation by the time it was released.

Ringo Starr: [78] **HAPPY BIRTHDAY JOHN** (*Starkey*)
Produced by Ringo Starr
Recorded: 3 Oct 1970, EMI Studios, London
UK/US: unreleased
Ringo Starr: vocals; **Billy Preston**: keyboards (?); **Klaus Voormann**: bass (?); **George Harrison**, **Stephen Stills**, **'Martin'**, **'Chris' and possibly others**: various instruments and backing vocals

Recorded in the same session as [77] Early 1970, Starr's contribution to Lennon's birthday celebrations consisted of this minute-long vamp on an R&B riff (he likely had Chuck Berry's Johnny B Goode in mind). A bit of drunken revelry – at one point Starr can be heard asking someone if they'd just spilled their drink – the track is extremely ragged with the chorus of vocals oddly out of synchronisation with the chords. Who was present, and who contributed what is not documented, although Preston and Voormann presumably handle their regular instruments and Harrison is said to be involved too. (Starr likely isn't drumming, since his vocals sound as if he's up-front on the studio floor.) One notable participant is Stephen Stills (see also [14]), Starr having recently drummed on his eponymous solo album, made in London over the summer. Never intended for public consumption, Happy Birthday John was presented to Lennon along with [75] on his big day.

RECORD RELEASES

[14] **It Don't Come Easy** / [77] **Early 1970**
(UK: 9 Apr 1971, US: 16 Apr 1971)

John Lennon/Plastic Ono Band sessions: October 1970

John and Yoko had spent the first part of 1970 promoting [3] Instant Karma! and supporting their latest political causes, with Lennon planning to embark on an album project around March. There are indications he already had Phil Spector lined up as producer, something the music press managed to twist into a false story that the two were hard at work in LA when in fact the project had got only as far as Lennon making a few home demos.[55]

Recordings might have started in the spring had an unexpected package not landed on Lennon's doormat: a copy of a just-published book, *The Primal Scream*. Intrigued by its title, which reminded him of Ono's singing style, Lennon was curious enough to flick through the pages, and came upon a series of case studies of patients in Primal Therapy, a psychotherapeutic technique developed by Californian practitioner, Arthur Janov. Recognising himself in the accounts, Lennon came to realise the essence of his underlying unhappiness was the aftermath of a traumatic upbringing, Janov unravelling the way in which repressed emotional pain expresses itself later in life. Moreover, the solutions usually turned to – drugs, religion, success, money – far from being remedies, are merely extensions of the problem, leading Lennon to understand why, while on the face of it he had everything he could want, he couldn't escape his inner demons, his anxiety such that he would sometimes wake in the night with his heart pounding.

Deeply moved by the book, Lennon contacted Janov and enrolled in some sessions, along with Ono. The couple checked in for a month at a clinic near Harley Street, and separately underwent an initial course of therapy, encouraged by Janov to delve into their childhood traumas and re-connect with their early experiences, during which Lennon began expressing his thoughts by writing tracks for *John Lennon/Plastic Ono Band*. (While Lennon was in residence, McCartney phoned him to say he was leaving the Beatles – to which Lennon, who'd quit the group seven months before, responded with an uninterested 'Good luck to yer'.)

At the end of April their treatment was only in its early stages, and to see it through the couple needed to fly to LA, which they did on the last day of the month, not returning to Britain until the autumn, when they would start work on Lennon's first proper solo album.

---

[55] It's doubtful Lennon had enough material to complete a whole album at that stage, although he will have had more songs up his sleeve than is known. Period demos include [85] Isolation; [89] Remember; [119] I'm The Greatest; [126] Oh Yoko!, and extremely early versions of [129] How Do You Sleep? (as Since You Came To Me) and [213] Mind Games (as Make Love Not War).

John Lennon: [79] **MY MUMMY'S DEAD** (*Lennon*)
Produced by John Lennon
Recorded: Summer 1970, Bel Air, California
UK/US: 11 Dec 1970 (*John Lennon/Plastic Ono Band* LP)
John Lennon: vocals, guitar

Lennon spent summer 1970 attending the Primal Institute in LA, effectively cutting himself off from the outside world but publicly speculating that he might move to the States permanently, which would take another year to come good but proved beyond reasonable doubt that he was through with the Beatles. While there, Lennon continued writing songs born from his ongoing Primal sessions, and made several demos using portable tape recording equipment. From these came this bleak track.

Julia Lennon was 26 when she gave birth to John, and by all accounts was ill-suited to motherhood, enjoying the company of men and causing concern among her family when it emerged the infant John was sleeping in her bed, which she was also sharing with her latest partner, John Dykins. Agreeing it was best for Lennon's Aunt Mimi and Uncle George to become his guardians, Julia saw little of her son over the next few years, but when he became a teenager they established a close relationship, Lennon a frequent visitor to her house on Blomfield Road, walking distance from his home on Menlove Avenue. Via an odd sequence of events, Lennon happened to be at Blomfield Road one Tuesday evening in July 1958, while Julia was at Aunt Mimi's discussing his arrangements. Leaving Mimi's to catch a bus home, Julia was run over and killed on Menlove Avenue, right outside Lennon's house, tearing from his life a mother he'd only recently reconnected with. Ever since, Lennon had been unable to come to terms with his cruel loss until, twelve years on, he finally expressed the grief he couldn't admit in the harshly titled My Mummy's Dead.

This brief expression was recorded at the house on Nimes Road which the Lennons were renting during their California stay. (The precise date is not known, but was prior to 28 July, since it was copied onto a compilation cassette that day.) Lo-fi, and brutally to the point, the song has the mood of an infant's nightmare, although with its brevity, Lennon seems to have pictured the general style of a Japanese haiku poem.[56] Although Lennon was 17 when Julia was killed, this deeply personal number was sung as if he was a small child, something Lennon accounted for by explaining the death in the lyric was figurative, referring to the loss of one's parental love, which he'd experienced

---

[56] If this is what he had in mind when writing it, then Ono's presence is clear. Lennon was absorbing a Japanese influence in his life and art through 1970, at one point applying for a Japanese home language course.

when she abandoned him at five. Tacked onto the end of *John Lennon/Plastic Ono Band* it makes for a painful conclusion to a troubled album. (Taking Beatle marketing to remarkable lengths, an alternate take has since been officially released.)

John Lennon: [80] **MOTHER** (*Lennon*)
    Produced by John Lennon, Yoko Ono, Phil Spector
    Recorded: 26 Sep 1970; 27 Sep 1970; 15 Oct 1970; 17 Oct 1970,
        EMI Studios, London
    UK/US: 11 Dec 1970 (*John Lennon/Plastic Ono Band* LP)
    John Lennon: vocals, guitar, piano; **Klaus Voormann**: bass; **Ringo Starr**: drums

When Lennon read *The Primal Scream*, the staunchly honest Mother was one of the first musical results. Abandoned by his father while still a baby, Lennon was effectively then given away by his mother – something he couldn't have comprehended when deposited into a new house with an aunt and uncle, left alone as Julia went home without him. Lennon carried the burden of this estrangement throughout his childhood, imagining himself as an adopted orphan despite the fact that both his biological parents were alive and well, and in contact with the family.

Leafing through *The Primal Scream* 24 years on, Lennon was taken by the personal accounts it contained, one of them the story of 'Phillip', a man by then in his 30s, whose parents had separated when he was small and whose mother left him. His first-hand account reads, in part, 'I screamed... mommy don't go... eventually the time came to tell [father] good-bye.' Lennon later recounted, 'I read the testimonials... I thought, "that's me, that's me"'.[57] Once he'd been through therapy himself, he came to view his early life with complete clarity: 'One of the hardest things is to realise they didn't want you. You're just the result of sex. They didn't want me. That's a fact.'[58]

Drawing on his Primal insights for Mother, Lennon appears also to have had in mind House Of The Rising Sun, which similarly focuses on the narrator's parents, and which Lennon invokes his lyrics.[59] By the time he departed for LA, Lennon had Mother complete, the song unlike anything he'd written previously and captured in full on an early demo recorded Stateside

---

[57] From the 1980 *Playboy* interview, Golson, p103.
[58] Interview with Tariq Ali for *Red Mole*, conducted 12 February 1971.
[59] House Of The Rising Sun contains the lines, 'Mother, tell your children/not to do what I have done', adapted by Lennon in the final verse of Mother. A traditional ballad, it was brought to prominence through Bob Dylan's electrifying recording for his debut album two years before the Animals turned it into a hit.

on electric guitar. 11 days after returning home, Lennon went into EMI with Voormann and Starr, virtually his entire crew for the forthcoming project, to record this defining statement for real.

Lennon groped his way through upwards of 90 takes before he was satisfied, stretching over the ensuing month. Having written the song on guitar, he remained unsure how to arrange it, trying out a version with Starr and Voormann before deciding the approach lacked a cutting edge. Switching to piano, his early attempts had bass and drums pushed to the fore, the piano slowly gathering presence as the number progressed, until after much prevaricating, he completed the track by copying Starr's drum track from the second verse onto the first, abandoning the principle of a gradual build-up and hitting home from the off. The final addition was the grafting on of an English funeral bell, slowed down to a suffocatingly morbid toll, Lennon having heard the effect in a television horror movie he'd seen in LA. (There's no hard evidence Lennon attended his mother's funeral in 1958, though if he hadn't, he would likely have heard the Allerton church bell from across the golf course on Menlove Avenue.)

Recorded with heavy echo, Lennon's vocal is among his most dramatic, particularly in the convulsive end piece, two minutes of anguished pleading sung from the little boy's perspective. Lennon recorded these sections last, having rehearsed them almost daily to get his voice in the right state – a trick he learned from McCartney's efforts on Oh! Darling the previous year. Here, the pain expressed is more fundamental than that heard in the screaming [2] Cold Turkey, whose agonies were, at least, transitory; the upset of Mother was something life-affecting, trailing away into silence with no prospect of comfort, reflecting the hard reality of Lennon's early years. The only resolution he ever found was through Primal Therapy, and here he comes closest to capturing a literal Primal scream on record.

So significant was the track that Lennon arranged to have it issued on single, despite doubts as to its commerciality. In an effort to get some radio play, the opening bells were lopped off although the edit failed to earn the exposure wanted. (Not issued in the UK, the single managed a disappointing 43 on *Billboard*.) One listener who did take note was Barbra Streisand, whose relationship with her own mother had been difficult, and who consequently also recorded it for an unlikely single, released six months after Lennon's.

The key song on *John Lennon/Plastic Ono Band*, and perhaps the most important singular statement of his career, Mother followed Lennon's previous maternal eulogy, the gently forgiving Julia, by a mere two years. One of the earliest songs to emerge under Janov's influence, it was not only the first to be properly taped but was also positioned at the start of the set (which Lennon would later refer to as his 'mother album'), indicating the degree to which he recognised its profundity. It remains his most powerful recording.

John Lennon: [81] **I FOUND OUT** (*Lennon*)
Produced by John Lennon, Yoko Ono, Phil Spector
Recorded: 27 Sep 1970; 7 Oct 1970, EMI Studios, London
UK/US: 11 Dec 1970 (*John Lennon/Plastic Ono Band* LP)
John Lennon: vocals, guitar; **Klaus Voormann**: bass; **Ringo Starr**: drums

Lennon and Ono never did complete their Primal Therapy, which years later gave Janov an excuse for its apparent failure, after Lennon relapsed into a lifecycle of drink and drugs. However when they landed back in England in September 1970 the couple were refreshed and clear-minded, something apparent in the lyric to this song, written in LA and showing a raft of lucid realisations from Lennon. (Sounding like a threat, the song's opening was adapted from a Beatles jam recorded on 26 January 1969 and bootlegged as I Told You Before, twisted into a vocalised version of a guitar riff in which the fingers 'walk' across the fretboard.)

The song itself is a scattergun articulation of Primal insights and bitter sarcasm, throwing targeted jabs at both McCartney and Harrison. The initial draft lyric had the last verse ending on the prominent line, 'I've seen neurosis from Jesus to Paul', which by the time it was recorded at EMI had been moved up and adjusted to the less accusatory 'religion', supposedly a reference to the teenaged adulation the Beatles engendered. Interviewed in New York by journalist, Howard Smith, in December, Lennon attempted to dampen any consequent inter-Beatle conflict by claiming a double-meaning was intended, 'Paul' referring not just to McCartney but also to the Biblical St Paul The Apostle. Harrison also came in for some ire, the lines about Krishna and gurus inspired by Lennon's own misguided attachment to the Maharishi and the Krishna movement generally, but equally reading as if an attack on his colleague's beliefs. In this respect Lennon showed less desire to deny his true intent, expanding on the theme to Smith: 'I wonder how happy George is, or any of the people that are chanting and meditating... this dream of constant joy is bullshit.'[60]

Of a mind to confront all forms of phoniness, Lennon's lyric includes a provocative assertion that Jesus doesn't exist, four years after his relatively benign observation that more teenagers attended Beatles concerts than went to church, remarks which at the time caused a wave of outrage in parts of America. Equally confrontational is the use of 'cock', which he'd originally sung as 'axe' before deciding that such obfuscation was itself part of the bourgeois game he was keen to repudiate, the offending four letters little-

---

[60] Lennon's remarks were made just after *All Things Must Pass* was released. Lennon will therefore have heard Harrison's jibe in [63] Awaiting On You All, although he won't have known the song when he wrote I Found Out.

noticed next to the more overt profanity in [83] Working Class Hero, but enough for EMI to censor them on the album's lyric sheet.

Taken into Abbey Road, the track was executed in appropriately visceral fashion, its primitive non-melody carried on Lennon's fuzz-toned rhythm guitar, mixed down to allow Voormann's bass to lead. A grooving performance, the group extended it by mutating into a version of Gone Gone Gone, an old Carl Perkins B-side remembered from Lennon's Hamburg days, which was faded off the released edit.

John Lennon: [82] **WELL WELL WELL** (*Lennon*)
Produced by John Lennon, Yoko Ono, Phil Spector
Recorded: 27 Sep 1970; 18 Oct 1970, EMI Studios, London
UK/US: 11 Dec 1970 (*John Lennon/Plastic Ono Band* LP)
John Lennon: vocals, guitar; **Klaus Voormann**: bass; **Ringo Starr**: drums

A second exercise in heavy guitar, Well Well Well was recorded immediately after [81] I Found Out and features the same musicianship. Unlike its predecessor the song has no ulterior motive, consisting of an idiosyncratic love song to Ono. If there's any deeper point it centres on women's liberation and the sexual politics of Wilhelm Reich, Lennon's declaration that he could 'eat her' a calculated *double-entendre*. In this context, Starr's pounding bass drum represents the throb of Lennon's infatuation, an urgency merely accentuated in the screaming middle eight.

Completed in October, Well Well Well was presented like the rest of the album's second side in a mix so narrow it was effectively mono. In taking this minimalist approach, Lennon had a willing accomplice in Phil Spector, the two conspiring in the short-lived 'Back to Mono' campaign of the early 1970s. (On the cover of the 1972 Apple reissue of *Phil Spector's Christmas Album*, the producer is pictured with a 'Back to Mono' pin badge in his Santa's beard.)

John Lennon: [83] **WORKING CLASS HERO** (*Lennon*)
Produced by John Lennon, Yoko Ono, Phil Spector
Recorded: 27 Sep 1970; 25 Oct 1970, EMI Studios, London
UK/US: 11 Dec 1970 (*John Lennon/Plastic Ono Band* LP)
John Lennon: vocals, guitar

The third track taped this day was a solo performance of a five-verse dirge railing against the depressing effects of the institutions which control life, Lennon speaking from direct experience. The song title, with its implied reference to class politics, has tended to divert critics from its true intent, a *working class* hero not something Lennon sees in himself, nor something to *become* in the sense of an ambition to strive for, but something to *be*, the self untrammelled by social pressures to appear 'middle class' and therefore more acceptable. Through the 1960s, Lennon had sensed the underlying dishonesty of his own public face, growing increasingly resentful of the way the Beatles had been safely packaged for the sake of distrusting parents. As early as 1963 he was kicking against the process, telling the Queen Mother at the Royal Variety Performance to go and 'rattle her jewellery' in a manner so polite it merely added to the public's affection for him, when backstage the true Lennon had alarmed Brian Epstein by threatening to insert the F-word. By the time he hooked up with Ono in 1968 he was ready to confront 'straight' society with his Revolution sequence, courting the radical left and hinting he was in favour of destroying the existing order, while simultaneously challenging Beatles fans with an avant-garde deconstruction of rock music itself. The British establishment took the bait and busted him for possession of cannabis in October, and when *Two Virgins* was released a few weeks later, Lennon polarised his followers yet further with a public display of nudity which finally severed his association with safe, corporate respectability – exactly what he wanted.

Viewing the tension between conformity and confrontation in a class dimension, Lennon went out of his way to shock, his double-use of the expletive a statement in itself, not merely outlandish for an ex-Beatle, but an honest, uncensored expression of his mindset. (Speaking to *Rolling Stone*'s Jann Wenner in December, Lennon recalled that he'd deliberately avoided the word in the past, which in his new estimation was hypocritical.) In the aftermath of Primal Therapy, Lennon's position had crystallised to the point where he was ready to say what he liked, using the words he liked, with acute clarity.

Starting with the moment of birth, the verses of Working Class Hero progress through the stages of life – home, school, career – laying out the process by which the free spirit of the child is eroded. As a teenager at Quarry Bank High School, Lennon was reported to his Aunt Mimi with the condemning judgement, 'He has too many of the wrong ambitions and his energy is too often misplaced' – a remark which reveals he did have ambition and energy, but of a sort unacceptable to 'the system'; reasoned Lennon, they will hold it against him, even if he is clever – which he was. Dumped out of school at 16, Lennon had no idea what he should do with his life, allowing himself to be steered towards art college for want of anything better, not yet able to comprehend the prospects of a career.

In expressing his experience in song, Lennon took a suitably pared down approach, accompanying himself with just the scrub of an acoustic guitar. Playing and singing together proved challenging, and it took nine attempts to capture a master take on 27 September, only for Lennon to realise he'd accidentally omitted the song's third verse. Accordingly, further recordings were made on 15 October for a drop-in, the studio's engineers trying their best to recapture the ambience of the first version through microphone placement and having Lennon play with the original in his headphones to get a matching mood and tempo. The finished edit consists of the first recording cross-faded with the second around the 1:25 mark, the join achieved almost seamlessly but with a change in dynamics not helped by Lennon inadvertently using the wrong guitar.

Working Class Hero's offending language was sanitised for release in some territories, but the song was banned by almost all major broadcasting channels. In the years which followed it gradually earned respect for its brutal honesty, reaching a wider public when, no doubt to Lennon's satisfaction, it was placed on the B-side of [130] Imagine, a belated single in the UK which resurfaced and topped the charts after his murder in 1980. The term, 'Working Class Hero' has sometimes been applied to Lennon misguidedly as a badge of honour, even used for an official career retrospective CD in 2005. That he had no such pretensions when recording the track has not stopped the title from becoming one of his best-known phrases, unwittingly contorted by later generations from an accusatory polemic into a marketing slogan.

John Lennon: [84] **HOLD ON** (*Lennon*)
Produced by John Lennon, Yoko Ono, Phil Spector
Recorded: 30 Sep 1970, EMI Studios, London
UK/US: 11 Dec 1970 (*John Lennon/Plastic Ono Band* LP)
John Lennon: vocals, guitar; **Klaus Voormann:** bass; **Ringo Starr:** drums

After the caustic recordings of 26 and 27 September, Lennon returned to EMI with this soothing number revealing his sense of vulnerability. The period since his resignation from the Beatles had been fraught with personal difficulties, ranging from media condemnation of his peace campaign, which at times veered towards open ridicule, to a highly publicised court summons under an archaic indecency law, and a continuing undercurrent of opposition to his relationship with Ono, something to which he'd become hypersensitive.[61]

Lennon could have been excused for feeling the world was out to get him, and as if to comfort himself, responded with this song which he'd been toying

---

[61] Back in 1969, Lennon had been approached by a publisher with a request for some drawings, and responded by sketching scenes from his wedding and honeymoon. 'Lithograph' prints of 14 of them ended up forming an exhibition titled Bag One in early 1970, several depicting graphic sexual scenes. Within 24 hours of opening, the exhibition was predictably raided and the drawings confiscated (and, according to one witness, taken back to Scotland Yard police station and pinned to the wall for the amusement of all and sundry).

with since February. Described by its author in terms of a death fear, Hold On was Lennon's experience of living only in the moment, trying to make it through days cocooned with Ono with the emotional distresses inherent in their Primal experiences. Essentially singing to himself, Lennon reprised the line he'd originally used in Revolution ('It's gonna be alright'), to broaden out the message and reassure the world that things will eventually work themselves out.

In one of Lennon's most adept musical performances, Hold On glides on the surface of his guitar, run through a tremolo pedal to achieve a suitably emotional tremble, with his double-tracked lead vocal sent to the extremities of the stereo picture. The final take was captured at the 32nd attempt, not long after an exploratory run-through in a rock arrangement, which fortunately didn't impress the group. Sadly Lennon's sterling studio efforts were let down by a causal mix prepared by Phil McDonald for reference purposes, which Lennon took a shine to when playing back at home, and decided to keep.[62]

Against the toughness of much of the better-known material on *John Lennon/Plastic Ono Band*, Hold On shows the album's other face, the first of a handful of intimate recordings revealing Lennon's sentimental side. With an unlikely optimism, Lennon's exuberant, ad-libbed 'Cookie!' was the result of watching episodes of *Sesame Street* on US public broadcast while eating ice-cream, part of a regression to childhood under Arthur Janov's guidance.

John Lennon: [85] **ISOLATION** (*Lennon*)
    Produced by John Lennon, Yoko Ono, Phil Spector
    Recorded: 6 Oct 1970, EMI Studios, London
    UK/US: 11 Dec 1970 (*John Lennon/Plastic Ono Band* LP)
    John Lennon: vocals, piano, Hammond organ; **Klaus Voormann:** bass;
    Ringo Starr: drums

Initially absent from these sessions, Phil Spector arrived in October to help steer a studio ensemble still led almost entirely by Lennon. Since all the guitar tracks bar [90] were gotten out of the way consecutively, there's a suggestion Lennon was waiting for Spector before recording the remaining piano numbers, his co-producer proficient on the instrument himself as evinced in his performance on [91] Love. On this first track however, it's Lennon at the keyboard, picking out a run on D major, in which the top note of the triad

---

[62] In the album mix, Klaus Voormann's bass is muted, while a couple of minor technical flaws were let through including a fade-in opening (take 32 not having a clean start), and some brief background noise on the vocal track at 1:01. In addition, Starr's hi-hat work is uncertain from 0:47, which could have been patched up had more time been spent.

edges up in a semitonal walk, a device previously encountered in the minor chorus of Hey Bulldog, also played by Lennon.

Isolation was one of the tracks pre-dating Lennon's Primal Therapy, but was finished up in LA. One of the most desolate compositions on the album, Isolation shows him with his defences down, openly admitting his fragility and expressing a sense of hopelessness. With its glassy piano and sustained Hammond notes the track is intensely doomed, although Lennon reveals a residual sense of fight in the song's middle section, where his double-tracked vocal delivers a confrontation to no-one in particular, concluding on a high-flying *fortissimo*. This part, distinct from the rest of the song, was spun from the corresponding section in I Apologize, an old Tamla recording issued as the flip side to Barrett Strong's Money (That's What I Want) in 1959.[63] As with [84] Hold On, Lennon played back a provisional mix and decided he'd got what he wanted, presenting it as the album cut.

John Lennon: [86] **GOD** (*Lennon*)
Produced by John Lennon, Yoko Ono, Phil Spector
Recorded: 7 Oct 1970; 9 Oct 1970; 18 Oct 1970, EMI Studios, London
UK/US: 11 Dec 1970 (*John Lennon/Plastic Ono Band* LP)
John Lennon: vocals, piano; **Billy Preston:** piano; **Klaus Voormann:** bass; **Ringo Starr:** drums

Pieced together from contrasting sections, God is the first example in Lennon's solo catalogue of a song assembled from parts, a technique he had used previously on Happiness Is A Warm Gun. A connection between the two compositions is suggested in that Happiness Is A Warm Gun contains among its elements a classic doo-wop chord sequence, which is also the foundation for the opening part of God – although in his initial Bel Air demo, played on acoustic guitar, the chord voicings are more obviously reminiscent of This Boy.

The initial lines have their origins in a pearl of wisdom offered by the Maharishi in 1968, the thought that time is a concept by which eternity is measured. The phrase must have stuck in Lennon's mind since two years on, when discussing religion with Arthur Janov, he had a moment of insight and declared, 'God is a concept by which we measure our pain'. (Although not particularly concerned with religion, the Primal view of God connects to systems of unreal belief, which the individual uses to avoid facing truth.) The song's central section, Lennon's catalogue of mysticism, dogma and saviours,

---

[63] The original middle eight, written by Smokey Robinson and Berry Gordy, contains the lyric, 'I don't expect you to take me back/after I've caused you so much pain'. Lennon and the other Beatles were known for exploring B-sides in their early days, searching for obscure material to appropriate for their stage shows.

was pieced together and demoed onto cassette on 26 July, starting out with the first four examples which sprang to mind – magic, I Ching, Bible and tarot. Lennon's net was then cast to take in religious figureheads including Buddha and Jesus, roping in the Hindu philosophical traditions of yoga, *The Bhagavad Gita* and chanting of the mantra – areas of thought to which Lennon was a one-time advocate, but which he now declared obsolete. Not directed at Harrison, these lines were a personal repudiation from Lennon, who'd previously announced a rejection of the Maharishi in verse (not only in Sexy Sadie, but in the more accusatory 'Maharishi Song' of 1969, which he never released), which illustrates the opposing trajectories of the two former Beatles' world views in 1970.[64] Besides a rejection of religious/mystical concepts, Lennon also took aim at more familiar targets including political leaders who attracted cult followings, namely Kennedy and Hitler, and at one stage he toyed with adding Churchill to the list. Another idea, probably inspired by Ono, was to include some blank lines so the listener could add his or her personal entries, but Lennon decided not to extend it any further, wary of the song becoming 'like a Christmas card list'.

More shockingly for the rock generation who'd grown up with Lennon as one of their figureheads, he renounced two of his own former idols, Elvis Presley and Bob Dylan, both of whom he'd adopted as guiding figures not just musically but in life. (His late lyrical change from Dylan to Zimmerman was curious; Lennon explained that he'd inserted 'Zimmerman' because the name Dylan was 'bullshit', being a stage persona, although since it was the public character he was rejecting, it would have been the more appropriate choice.) The final line, left hanging on a deafeningly silent suspension, was Lennon's famous declaration that he didn't any more believe in the Beatles, a little over a year after he'd left the group without announcing it. Bringing the shutters down not just on the Beatles, but on the 'dream' of the 1960s, Lennon was addressing his whole generation, consigning the decade to history and looking instead at the new reality of the 1970s.

Lennon took his finished statement into EMI on 7 October, recording it as written, on acoustic guitar. Not feeling he had captured the right atmosphere, a second attempt was made with guitar and piano together, but again failed to achieve the desired effect. The solution was a re-make on just piano, an instrument Lennon was still less than proficient on, therefore calling Billy Preston to join the group two days later, Lennon's birthday, for what became the finished version. Preston's contribution, with its florid fills, is skilfully played but its faint cabaret leanings tend to undermine the direct honesty of

---

[64] Interviewed by Howard Smith shortly after the album's release, Lennon joked that Harrison was planning a cover version of God, reading, 'I *do* believe in..., I *do* believe in...'.

the song, which in the earlier guitar versions was more tangible. Conversely, Starr's drums are his most expressive on the album, forcing home the litany of non-beliefs with a differently styled flourish at the end of every line.

Left to last on *John Lennon/Plastic Ono Band*, the song terminates the album and the halcyon fantasy of the era with a depressing dose of realism, followed only by the grim, if brief, [79] My Mummy's Dead. For Lennon there would be no return to the unreal world of Pepperland and Magical Mystery Tour, leaving the listener in no doubt that so far as he was concerned, the dream was finally and irrefutably over.

John Lennon: [87] **LOST JOHN** (*Trad, arr. Donegan*)
Produced by John Lennon, Yoko Ono, Phil Spector
Recorded: 7 Oct 1970, EMI Studios, London
UK/US: unreleased
John Lennon: vocals, guitar; **Klaus Voormann**: bass; **Ringo Starr**: drums

During the *Plastic Ono Band* sessions, Lennon and his team recorded a number of informal jams, many of them loose versions of rock and roll favourites. Most are partial takes and of only academic interest, and a couple, [148] Honey, Don't and [277] Ain't That A Shame would be better captured later in the decade. Probably the best of them was Lost John, a traditional American tune known in countless variations dating back to the early part of the 20th century which Lennon and the other Beatles learned through Lonnie Donegan's 1956 version, for which the skiffler part-wrote his own lyric.

The song surfaced during the Beatles' *Get Back* sessions when it was jammed on the final morning, Lennon only recalling lyrics to the song's first verse. The same happens here, Lennon running through these lines three times before attempting to ad-lib a humorous new section about being 'spewed' on, which rapidly grinds to a halt. A bit of fun, diversions such as this helped lighten the mood during these sometimes claustrophobic studio dates, Lost John jammed during work on the intense [86] God.

John Lennon: [88] **MYSTERY TRAIN** (*Parker, Phillips*)
Produced by John Lennon, Yoko Ono, Phil Spector
Recorded: Oct 1970, EMI Studios, London
UK/US: unreleased
John Lennon: vocals, guitar; **Klaus Voormann**: bass; **Ringo Starr**: drums

Another rock and roll classic latched onto between formal recordings was this old Elvis A-side which Lennon owned on 78 in his teenage years. The rendition captured here with Voormann and Starr is a slow plod compared to Presley's rockabilly arrangement, pointing in fact to the 1953 version recorded by its composer, Junior Parker, released in the states on the Sun label two years before Elvis covered it. Whether Lennon heard the original, or the similarity in style is coincidental, his knowledge of the song was clearly sketchy, most of his words ad-libbed and bearing at best passing resemblance to the true lyrics. (The nearest match is Lennon's '15 coaches long', one short but close enough.) The song, admired by Lennon and McCartney alike, had been a Quarry Men staple in the late 1950s, as sung by Lennon whose penchant for inventing words to records he couldn't be bothered to transcribe had so amused and impressed his future partner at Woolton Fete in July 1957.

John Lennon: [89] **REMEMBER** (*Lennon*)
Produced by John Lennon, Yoko Ono, Phil Spector
Recorded: 9 Oct 1970; 19 Oct 1970, EMI Studios, London
UK/US: 11 Dec 1970 (*John Lennon/Plastic Ono Band* LP)
John Lennon: vocals, piano; **Klaus Voormann**: bass; **Ringo Starr**: drums

Lennon's 30th birthday started in difficult circumstances when he received a lunchtime visit from his father, Alf (or 'Freddie'). Having not seen him for two years, Lennon's feelings towards his errant dad had been brought into sharp focus by Primal Therapy, so that when the two came face to face in the kitchen of Tittenhurst Park, a furious row erupted, Lennon viciously berating Alf, laying into him for years of neglect, accusing him of cashing in on the Beatles' fame, and, if Alf's account is anything to go by, threatening to kill him and have his body thrown into the sea. Rubbing salt into the wounds, Lennon also informed his father he was taking back the Brighton cottage he'd bought for Alf and his wife to live in.[65] The two Lennons, father and son, would never see each other again.

Having calmed down, Lennon made his way to Abbey Road, ostensibly for the purposes of recording but also as a convenient venue for friends to gather and offer their birthday wishes. Ono had gifted Lennon a 'sensory box' that morning, a novelty object covered in holes to stick fingers into, each offering a different sensation ranging from warm and wet to the mildly painful. Meanwhile Harrison pulled up in his Ferrari and presented his erstwhile colleague with flowers and gifts, including the various musical 'birthday cards' recorded for the occasion, among which were [75] and [78].

Between the fun and pleasantries there was work to be done, and apart from the remake of [86] God, the day's main event was the taping of Remember, which after the bleakness of much of the album to date, offered a

---

[65] Following the encounter, Alf drafted a four-page account of Lennon's tirade, which he deposited with his solicitor, 'to be opened only if I should disappear or die an unnatural death'. The available text can be read in Norman, 2009.

somewhat more buoyant mood, albeit disguising a familiar unease beneath its cheery façade. A collection of half-recalled scenes from Lennon's early childhood, the song invokes family life, forgotten strangers and images glimpsed on movie screens, reading like the pages of a faded scrapbook, unopened for 25 years. There's an unmistakeable sense of sorrow in these verses, the shadow of the album providing sufficient context to realise Lennon's vague recollections are not joyous, despite the forced animation of its piano part. In this respect, the song illustrates the differing outlook of Lennon compared to McCartney, whose 'memories for you and me' were shared in sweetly longing terms in [24] Junk, recorded nine months earlier and also pitched minor.

The main piano figure was devised in July 1969 while the Beatles were working on Something at EMI, originally as part of a long end section which was ultimately binned. Lennon clearly thought the riff of merit and incorporated into another song written around the start of 1970, also discarded.[66] Come October he was able to find a home for the orphaned section in Remember, extending the song as he had with Something by repeating it over several minutes to make an extravagant instrumental coda which was yet again excised for the commercial release, unceremoniously cut off as Lennon ad-libs 'remember the fifth of November' – a quote from a British children's rhyme about the Gunpowder Plot of 1605 where a group of conspirators had sought to blow up London's Houses of Parliament. (Effecting a humorous ending, Lennon grafted on the sound of an explosion to cover the tape edit.)

Captured in 17 takes, the final recording plays to the song's backwards-looking theme by quoting the opening lines of Sam Cooke's [278] Bring It On Home To Me, released in Britain just as the Beatles were cutting their first sides for EMI.[67] Cooke's song was evidently a Beatles favourite, briefly inserted into their live repertoire, with both Lennon and McCartney recording cover versions in the years since.

---

[66] The song goes by the name, Across The Great Water, apparently one of its lyrics. Since it's not in circulation and has only been heard by a select few, it's impossible to evaluate, although its given title reminds us of the Band's Across The Great Divide, released September 1969.

[67] Cooke's lyric reads, 'If you ever change your mind/About leaving, leaving me behind'. Lennon had done a similar trick with both [80] and [85].

John Lennon: [90] **LOOK AT ME** (*Lennon*)
Produced by John Lennon, Yoko Ono, Phil Spector
Recorded: 15 Oct 1970; 17 Oct 1970; 18 Oct 1970, EMI Studios, London
UK/US: 11 Dec 1970 (*John Lennon/Plastic Ono Band* LP)
John Lennon: vocals, guitar

The day after his bruising clash with father Alf, Lennon was at EMI with Starr and Klaus Voormann with nothing specific on the agenda. Warming up with a ragged review of a slew of rock and roll oldies, none up to releasable standard, they proceeded to capture several instrumentals, not pre-meditated but good enough to form the basis of possible songs. From these, via some heavy editing and mixing, the *Yoko Ono/Plastic Ono Band* set was created, once Ono had dubbed on some vocals, to be released in parallel with Lennon's LP. (One of the instrumentals was built up by Lennon and Starr from tape recordings of Harrison playing sitar, making for a three-quarter Beatle track.) Some days later, Lennon slipped back to EMI alone and recorded this deeply self-reflective song.

Look At Me was written in India, and exhibits the same acoustic finger-picking style as Julia, a technique learned from necessity in the remote hills of Rishikesh. Shaped by the solitary process of making music with an unamplified instrument, these songs and others from the period carry a particular introversion, the corollary of which is a detachment from the group interest. (Julia was Lennon's first 'solo' recording as a Beatle, and an intensely personal one.) Written in a moment of emotional honesty, Look At Me arrived during the period Lennon was falling in love with Ono, though he had yet to fully admit it. When Lennon decamped for India in February 1968, he had wanted to take Ono along, but with Cynthia in tow the situation was too awkward. Instead he and Ono flooded each other with secret correspondence, her sending him *Grapefruit*-style messages from her temporary Parisian base (eg, 'If you look up at the sky and see a cloud, it's me sending you love'). Increasingly obsessed, Lennon penned the song with its coded messages drifting back across the continents, 'Oh my love; here I am'. Most tellingly, the bridge section captures a decisive moment as Lennon for the first time turns 'I' into 'we', and no-one else: 'just you and me'. 21 days after his return to London, Lennon and Ono became a couple.

Perhaps judging the text too intimate for a Beatle outing, the song was never in the frame for a group release, Lennon keeping it in reserve for more than two years. Following his Primal Therapy, some of the song's lyrics took on a new slant, the expressions of self-doubt resonating with his re-assessment of his own identity in 1970. Looking to develop it, attempts were made to record the track with Starr drumming, while a separate version was taped with Lennon strumming a steel guitar. None of these innovations proved preferable to the simple honesty of his first conception, and so the song reverted to its original form, Lennon not only singing *to* Ono, but sounding like her too, Look At Me sitting stylistically alongside Remember Love, as if the two of them really were becoming one.

John Lennon: [91] **LOVE** (*Lennon*)
Produced by John Lennon, Yoko Ono, Phil Spector
Recorded: 15 Oct 1970; 19 Oct 1970, EMI Studios, London
UK/US: 11 Dec 1970 (*John Lennon/Plastic Ono Band* LP)
John Lennon: vocals, guitar; **Phil Spector**: piano

Nominally the album's producer, Phil Spector was missing for most of the recording stage, no-one sure where he could be found. Frustrated at not getting his man, Lennon resorted to taking out full-page adverts in the American music press, declaring, 'Phil! John is ready this weekend', which seem to have had the desired effect, Spector reporting to Abbey Road in time to make his presence felt on the studio floor, and in fact, to record this final track as a duet with Lennon.

Written in LA over the summer, Love was intended as a direct paean to Ono. The song derives a sense of soul-bearing honesty from a symmetrical design built on three-word phrases, each opening couplet a mirror reflection of itself, symbolising the two halves which make up what Lennon would characterise as 'Johnandyoko'. The lyric's inspiration may have originated with a newspaper comic strip called *Love Is...* which Lennon, an avid devourer of the printed press, would have seen after its introduction in January 1970.[68]

As demoed in Bel Air, Love was an acoustic guitar number but Lennon considered it worthy of development, testing several arrangement ideas before deciding on its eventual form (as he had with several other album tracks). One try-out had the guitar heavily reverbed, another saw it arranged for piano backed up with bass and drums. Ultimately Lennon opted to meld the guitar and piano versions, thrashing out a final structure with Spector in a live studio session with the tape rolling, running to some 38 attempts during which the producer came up with the song's solo piano introduction. (The released version consisted of the piano intro from take 38 edited to the start of take 37 then faded down for effect.)

Lennon was proud of the results, pointing out its musical strengths to *Rolling Stone* in December, boasting, 'and I'm not even *known* for writing

---

[68] Created by Kim Casali, the 'strip' consisted of a series of single-frame, captioned cartoons of a couple drawn naked, suggestive (to Lennon, at least) of the cover of *Two Virgins*. It ran in the *Los Angeles Times* while Lennon was staying there.

melody!'.[69] Certainly the recording was one of the album's bright spots, considered at length for possible release as a trailer single, before Lennon decided [80] Mother would make a more honest choice. Its commercial viability was therefore open to others, close-harmony MOR group, the Lettermen, taking a version into the US charts, with several more covers closely following, including one from Barbra Streisand for the same album as her version of [80] Mother. (Lennon's own recording was remixed and released on 45 posthumously, making a minor dent in the UK charts in 1982.)

Delicately crafted, Love is one of the most admired tracks of Lennon's solo catalogue, and despite its solemnity, offers a counterpoint to the album's reputed abrasiveness – proof that McCartney had no monopoly on gentle balladry.

Having got the recording phase of *John Lennon/Plastic Ono Band* out of his system, Lennon spent the next few days working on the album mixes with Phil Spector. Its reputation for directness and honesty is not a true reflection of the process, several songs being treated to post-production manipulation, including significant changes to the sequencing on [83] Working Class Hero and [91] Love, as well as the drum loop on [80] Mother. Nonetheless, as an artistic outpouring, the album is remarkable in its openness and purpose. Never a comfortable listen, many of the songs delve into areas of personal turmoil, which whether or not one enjoys them, are difficult not to admire for their sheer honesty.

At the end of October, Lennon and Ono left Britain for New York to work on a couple of art films, *Up Your Legs Forever* and *Fly*. While there, Lennon gave his notorious *Rolling Stone* interview (see Wenner, 1971) in which he let loose on life as a Beatle, declaring the group 'bastards', claiming he had to suffer 'humiliation' to be in the band at all, and comparing McCartney to Engelbert Humperdinck – the first volley in a public slanging match between the two which would endure through 1971.

John Lennon/Plastic Ono Band was released on 11 December, simultaneously with *Yoko Ono/Plastic Ono Band*, in a near-identical sleeve. (The Lennons swapped places for the second photo.) Neither record was a commercial proposition, but while Ono's was never going to be anything other than a niche sale, Lennon's was, in theory, the most important Beatle-related disc of 1970. Broadcasters inevitably blacklisted [83] Working Class Hero, and the [80] Mother single was shunned by radio stations, but Lennon nonetheless declared the album his best-ever work, the equivalent of a one-man *Sgt Pepper*.

---

[69] Wenner, 1971.

It failed to get near the top of the album charts on either side of the Atlantic, but that was not the point; well-received in the music press, gaining near-universal acclaim, it is regarded today as Lennon's finest album, never failing to register with his fans and representing the expression of his true artistic self.

RECORD RELEASES

John Lennon/Plastic Ono Band
  (UK/US: 11 Dec 1970)
  [80] Mother / [84] Hold On / [81] I Found Out / [83] Working Class Hero / [85] Isolation / [89] Remember / [91] Love / [82] Well Well Well / [90] Look At Me / [86] God / [79] My Mummy's Dead
[80] **Mother** / Why [B-side by Yoko Ono]
  (US: 28 Dec 1970)

RAM sessions:
October 1970 to March 1971

While Lennon, Harrison and Starr were all at work through 1970, regularly crossing paths at EMI, McCartney kept his distance, his solo career already in the doldrums following the muted reception given to *McCartney*. Still stewing over the Beatles' unresolved contractual entanglements, he did, at least, accept that the group would never again reform, and made it clear he wanted out of the partnership, at one point turning Beatle fan by dropping a line to the music weekly, *Melody Maker*: 'In order to put out of its misery the limping dog of a news story which has been dragging itself across your pages for the past year, my answer to the question, "will the Beatles get together again?"… is no.' His note was signed off with a drawing of a grinning mouth, a device he would connect to his next album project (see [110]).

The main problem was what to do with his life. Having set up McCartney Productions in early 1969, he prematurely announced plans for a cartoon based on Rupert the Bear, which failed to materialise [103]. At one stage he was approached by Mickie Most for a possible acting role in the bizarre drama movie, *The Second Coming Of Suzanne*, but perhaps not keen to follow Starr into a second-rate screen career, this idea also came to naught. The answer was obvious all along, McCartney doing what he did best by assembling home demos over the summer, including among the 30 or so songs taped, most of the tracks which would make up *RAM*.[70]

---

[70] None of his period demos have circulated but a list of 29 is known, itemising >

With his first album having come under criticism for its sense of homespun improvisation, McCartney resolved that his second would be a fully-formed affair, for which he would require a proper studio band. Yet while he could most likely have tapped up Ringo and Klaus, Billy and possibly Eric, McCartney instead decided to break out of the London circuit completely, and so at the start of October, he and Linda embarked on a five-day cruise across the Atlantic aboard the QE2, intent on finding talent and making a record when they arrived in New York.

Having booked rehearsal space in an attic near Manhattan's Times Square, McCartney put word out that musicians were being sought to record an advertising jingle, something which attracted guitarist David Spinozza to the studio. A couple of days later, McCartney moved down to the basement of the same building, where a much younger drummer, Denny Seiwell, passed his test on a tattered kit, and so with the ruse by then exposed, sessions for *RAM* could proceed. Work was scheduled to start on the morning of Monday 12 October at Columbia's studio in the CBS building on West 57th Street, the first time a Beatle had recorded in New York.[71]

Paul McCartney: [92] **ANOTHER DAY** (*McCartney, McCartney*)
Produced by Paul McCartney
Recorded: 12 Oct 1970, Columbia Studios, New York
UK: 19 Feb 1971 (single A-side)
US: 22 Feb 1971 (single A-side)
Paul McCartney: vocals, guitar, bass, percussion; **Linda McCartney**: backing vocals; **David Spinozza**: guitar; **Denny Seiwell**: drums, percussion

During the 1969 *Get Back* sessions, McCartney was often first on site, whiling away the early part of the morning at the piano waiting for the other Beatles to straggle in. As a result, many McCartney pieces were recorded by the camera crew, including, on 9 January, an early version of Another Day which was already well on the way to completion with two full verses in place.

Ranging through an octave on the diatonic scale, the original composition exudes a carefree lightness, pitched major and typical of McCartney's style, if at odds with its doleful lyrics. A voyeuristic portrait of a young woman bored by her uneventful life, the song fits a pattern of character studies started in earnest in 1966 with Eleanor Rigby, and continued through the despairing

---

the contents of tape reels. It includes every song eventually featured on the album bar [115] Dear Boy, as well as three which would show up on *Wild Life*: [134]; [136]; [137].

[71] Harrison had worked in the same studio with Dylan in May (see [38]), but not recording for release.

runaway in She's Leaving Home. What the story lacked in 1969 was an insight into the person behind the mask, who McCartney now filled out in a minor-key middle eight, describing a 'so sad' home life in which dreams of a loving relationship turn out to be one more let-down.[72]

Missing the minute observation of either Eleanor Rigby or She's Leaving Home, Another Day lacks penetration and is, like its main character, rather devoid of personality, the needless repetition of its contrasting section causing it to drag. McCartney's efforts to enliven things with whoops and cheers merely confuses the issue, lending to the impression that the author himself has no particular concern for her either. Partly the detachment stems from superficial writing, but also from the fact that this was the first thing recorded by the new studio ensemble, taped on day one without their having worked together previously, and consequently rendered somewhat anonymously.

The process established on Another Day set the pattern of work for the forthcoming album, the group typically convening at 9am and rehearsing their way through one specific number until lunch. Proper recordings were taken care of in the afternoons, the team generally knocking off at 5pm, unless later work was required for overdubs. Mixed at A&R on 8 February, Another Day was nominated by studio engineer, Dixon Van Winkle, for McCartney's debut 45, meaning it would not therefore make the album. It turned out to be an astute choice, reaching the upper ends of the singles listing on both sides of the Atlantic, coming within one place of the UK number 1 spot. (The week it hit number 2 it pushed [34] My Sweet Lord down to 3.)

The label's curious writing credit, 'Mr & Mrs McCartney', raised eyebrows within Northern Songs (and its US equivalent, Maclen Music) for the fact that although they were entitled to collect royalties through their contract with Mr McCartney, they had no such arrangement with his wife, and therefore stood to see 50 percent of the song's publishing revenue siphoned off. (Linda's share was to be channelled through a new company named McCartney Inc.) The issue would come back to bite, Northern Songs refusing to believe that Linda, with no history of songwriting, had anything to do with devising this hit single, or for that matter, several other tracks on *RAM* for which she was similarly credited. Given that McCartney composed much of the song before he and Linda were married, much less recording together, her contribution is open to question, although the fact that the middle section was not heard until now supports the possibility that she did have some input. Regardless, Paul – and Linda – finally had a hit single to enjoy, almost two years after Lennon had first done it [1].

---

[72] *The Sound Of Five*, to which the song's character writes, was a 1960s radio show which dished out advice on listeners' personal worries.

Paul McCartney And Wings: [93] **GET ON THE RIGHT THING** (*McCartney*)
   Produced by Paul McCartney
   Recorded: 14 Oct 1970, Columbia Studios, New York
   UK: 4 May 1973 (*Red Rose Speedway* LP)
   US: 30 Apr 1973 (*Red Rose Speedway* LP)
   Paul McCartney: vocals, guitar, bass, piano; **Linda McCartney**: backing vocals; **David Spinozza**: guitar; **Denny Seiwell**: drums

Written over the summer of 1970, Get On The Right Thing was included in the early batch of demo recordings, and was taken over to New York with a vague idea that it was to become an electric guitar showcase. McCartney at one time considered asking Jimi Hendrix to play on the track, his death on 18 September putting paid to any such ideas. In the event, duties were shared between McCartney and Spinozza, neither rising to anything approaching Hendrix's style or standard, and in a nod to mid-period Beatles, the lead part was spooled backwards – home territory for McCartney.

Recorded in a day, Get On The Right Thing was marred by a vocal hiccup when McCartney's headphones became unplugged, his consequent chuckle audible around 1:26. As a result he is said to have lost his place in the lyric sheet, making up words as he proceeded, although any improvised lines are scarcely more provisional than the pre-planned 'your world is as kind as a penny'. With its unusual staircase of rising major chords and thrumming bassline, Get On The Right Thing builds in anticipation towards a climactic chorus, McCartney's lead vocal kicking against banks of backing from Linda. An exciting light-rock production, the track was a highlight of the sessions but judged not to sit comfortably alongside the more relaxed contents of *RAM*, instead being kept aside for a proposed single release in the Autumn of 1971. In the event, McCartney decided to form Wings with a December launch and Get On The Right Thing stalled for a second time. It was finally released to the public in 1973, one of a couple of *RAM* leftovers to make it onto *Red Rose Speedway*.

Paul And Linda McCartney: [94] **3 LEGS** (*McCartney*)
   Produced by Paul McCartney, Linda McCartney
   Recorded: 16 Oct 1970, Columbia Studios, New York; Apr 1971, Sound Recorders Studio, Hollywood
   UK/US: 17 Feb 1971 (*RAM* LP)
   Paul McCartney: vocals, guitar, bass; **Linda McCartney**: backing vocals; **David Spinozza**: guitar; **Denny Seiwell**: drums, tambourine

Supposedly inspired by a drawing from seven-year-old Heather McCartney, A Dog Is Here (as it was originally known) has been the subject of much misinterpretation. Picking up on its tripartite title, theorists have read a Beatles reference into the song, suggesting McCartney had his former bandmates in mind – but if the track has any group connection at all it's through Jimmy McCracklin's 1958 hit, The Walk, a version of which almost made it onto the aborted *Get Back* album in 1969, and which has a similar pattern.[73] This may be why the song particularly appealed to Lennon, who derided *RAM* as 'awful', but expressed an exceptional liking for this one.[74]

As recorded in New York, the basic track was arranged for guitar and piano but oddly lacked bass. Accordingly, McCartney overdubbed his instrument the following April at Sound Recorders in LA. The final mix has Linda's vocals particularly prominent, exposing a mis-quote from Thomas Hardy's *Far From The Madding Crowd* ('maddening'), necessitated by the song's rhythm. 3 Legs was then treated to a promotional video, showing Paul and Linda riding horses around their Kintyre estate, a long way literally and metaphorically from its Manhattan recording session. It was screened on BBC's *Top Of The Pops* in June 1971, despite the track not appearing as a single.

Paul And Linda McCartney: [95] **EAT AT HOME** (*McCartney, McCartney*)
Produced by Paul McCartney, Linda McCartney
Recorded: 16 Oct 1970, Columbia Studios, New York
UK/US: 17 Feb 1971 (*RAM* LP)
Paul McCartney: vocals, bass; **Linda McCartney**: backing vocals; **David Spinozza**: guitar; **Denny Seiwell**: drums

Another track on which Linda claimed a composing share, Eat At Home more plausibly has her input, celebrating the domestic lifestyle the two McCartneys enjoyed, particularly when staying in their farmhouse in Kintyre. Reviewers gleaned an erotic sub-text in the lyric, but other than a reference to eating in bed, there is little to support this – and, indeed, when McCartney effects the sound of a sheep on the word *beeed*, it's in order to underline the song's (for him) homely flavour. As is now more commonly known, Linda had a particular fondness for preparing her own food, something she later made a third career from, giving the song title a literal purpose. (One of her earliest

---

[73] A further influence in McCartney's mind may have been the period just after The Walk was first released. Having finished their school term in July 1958 McCartney and Harrison took off for an adventure in Wales, finding a place to stay in the resort of Harlech. Noticing their host's dog had a limp, Harrison got years of mileage out of a joke he came up with, concerning a woman whose dog had no legs: 'Every morning she'd take it out for a slide' (Lewisohn 2013, p461). Hence, 'My dog he got three legs/your dog he got none'.

[74] *New Musical Express* 8 July 1971.

lead vocals was Cook Of The House, issued by Wings in 1976.)

A shallow rocker built on a blues foundation, Eat At Home's main musical interest comes in its middle eight, a diversion which sounds like a key change but is effected purely by shuffling the order of the chords. In a move he seldom made with Harrison, McCartney afforded David Spinozza not one but *three* guitar solos, none of which are technically accomplished; as he proved with [29] Maybe I'm Amazed, McCartney was capable of better himself, an ironic problem which caused issues in practically every band he ever recorded with.

Favourably received on *RAM*, the song was pulled for a trailer single in most of the world, backed with [110] Smile Away, and enjoyed a degree of commercial success in Europe. Rudimentary in style and bouncing on its guitar bedrock, Eat At Home was current in that it tapped a growing trend for simple three-chord pop-rock, as fashioned through 1971 by acts like Dave Edmunds, T Rex and the early hits of Slade, paving the way in Britain for glam rock; it might therefore have fared better on the UK charts than the eventual choice, [98] The Back Seat Of My Car.

Paul And Linda McCartney: [96] **WHEN THE WIND IS BLOWING**
(*McCartney*)
Produced by Paul McCartney
Recorded: 16 Oct 1970, Columbia Studios, New York
UK/US: unreleased
Paul McCartney: vocals, guitars, bass, percussion; **Linda McCartney**: backing vocals (?)

This gentle instrumental (with scratch vocal) owes its inspiration to Pablo Picasso's 'blue' painting, *The Old Guitarist* (1903), which McCartney saw in Avenue Clinic in St John's Wood while Linda was giving birth to daughter, Mary in August 1969. Picasso's image depicts the frail musician's fingers lined up along the top edge of the fretboard – an impossibility when forming chords, but after scrutinising it for some time McCartney decided the guitarist was playing something with two digits, suggesting to him the idea of writing an entire piece in such a manner – or so he later claimed. Finding some open 'jazz' shapes on the second and fifth frets, McCartney mixed in some further chords capable of being played to match the brief – G6, A7, C major 7 etc – and added a breezy pentatonic melody, evidence of his extravagantly expressive talent which often, as here, displayed remarkable invention while succeeding in meaning very little.

By the time *RAM* was underway, McCartney had in mind an animated Rupert the Bear film (see [103]), and considered When The Wind Is Blowing suitable for inclusion, consequently recording this easy acoustic version on 16 October, in between some much harder material. Wasted when *Rupert* failed to arrive, the song was revived for use on another unfulfilled project, *Cold Cuts*, but remained largely unknown until a 2018 reissue of *Wild Life* finally brought it to the public.[75] McCartney meantime demonstrated it to British audiences during a 1999 interview with Michael Parkinson for BBC television, where he also revealed its back-story.

Wings: [97] **I LIE AROUND** (*McCartney*)
Produced by Paul McCartney
Recorded: 16 Oct 1970; 19 Oct 1970, Columbia Studios, New York;
    Nov 1972, EMI Studios, London (?)
UK: 1 Jun 1973 (single B-side)
US: 18 Jun 1973 (single B-side)
Paul McCartney: vocals, guitar, piano, bass, Mellotron; **Denny Laine**: vocals, guitar; **Linda McCartney**: backing vocals; **Denny Seiwell**: drums, backing vocals; **Hugh McCracken**: guitar (?); **Henry McCullough**: guitar (?), backing vocals; **uncredited**: trumpets

An extant CBS tape box shows this latest McCartney number to have been first recorded on 16 October, alongside [94] 3 Legs and [96] When The Wind Is Blowing. However the officially released version was taped three days later, consequent of guitarist, David Spinozza's, sudden departure from the project, which necessitated a full remake. Initially booked for a four-week stint, Spinozza had become frustrated at the stop-start nature of the early *RAM* recordings, and mindful that he needed to maintain work with his regular industry contacts, kept external bookings while waiting to see if and when McCartney would next need him. Inevitably there came a clash of dates and having committed himself to specific jobs elsewhere, Spinozza advised Linda he couldn't make the next studio session, and was summarily dropped, to be replaced by noted session guitarist, Hugh McCracken.

The new line-up set to work on I Lie Around, expressing of the joys of McCartney's new bucolic lifestyle and a certain philosophical gladness that his old life was no more. Built on a three-chord figure, the song owes a debt to Polythene Pam, particularly in the opening section, block-strummed on acoustic guitar. Whether this was meant as a conscious reference is not clear, but assuming McCartney had the Beatles in mind, I Lie Around laments that he had no option over separating from them and was, after all, relieved to me moving on.

---

[75] In 1974, McCartney was mulling a collection of outtakes and B-sides under the banner *Cold Cuts*. EMI resisted the project due to its inherent lack of commerciality, but it was intermittently revived over the next 13 years, with updated track listings each time. None of them made it to the shops.

Left off *RAM*, I Lie Around was pulled out again in 1972 and spruced up for inclusion on the planned double album release of *Red Rose Speedway*. Several overdubs were added including the sound of convivial chatter at the start and a low brass score, reminiscent of another Beatle oldie, the equally pastoral Mother Nature's Son. Most significantly though, McCartney wiped much of his vocal, leaving it clear for Denny Laine to step up for his first Wings lead.[76]

Having been shelved in 1970, the track was again sidelined when *Red Rose Speedway* was cut back to a single LP in 1973. Too strong to go to waste, it appeared as the flip side to the stand-alone single, [191] Live And Let Die.

Paul And Linda McCartney: [98] **THE BACK SEAT OF MY CAR** (*McCartney*)
Produced by Paul McCartney, Linda McCartney
Recorded: 22 Oct 1970, Columbia Studios, New York; Feb 1971, A&R Studios, New York
UK/US: 17 Feb 1971 (*RAM* LP)
Paul McCartney: vocals, piano, bass; **Linda McCartney**: backing vocals; **Hugh McCracken**: guitar; **Denny Seiwell**: drums; **New York Philharmonic**: orchestration

A highlight of his early solo period, The Back Seat Of My Car was, like [92] Another Day, debuted in one of McCartney's time-killing piano routines during the 1969 *Get Back* rehearsals. Its historical associations are particularly unfortunate in that the session coincided with Harrison's absence from the Beatles following his walk-out days earlier, only McCartney and Starr troubling to turn up to Twickenham on the morning of 14 January. As demoed on that occasion, The Back Seat Of My Car was musically close to complete but lacked any meaningful words, McCartney having thus far only sketched out odd phrases. (His semi-joking 'Gee, it's getting late' was fortunately forgotten.) This rehearsal fragment sheds light on McCartney's composing method, devising the structure of chords and melody first, then landing on words with an appealing sound, to be fleshed out subsequently until the requisite number of bars were filled.

The central theme, two lovers taking a car journey to nowhere, resonates with lines from his period song, Two Of Us, and stems from his and Linda's

---

[76] Laine was a capable singer, having performed with the Moody Blues, including lead vocals on their British number 1, Go Now! (which McCartney subsequently allowed into Wings' stage act). His lead vocals with Wings were understandably infrequent, and when he quit the group in 1980 he took a few such unreleased tracks with him for his solo album, *Japanese Tears*.

liking for long, aimless drives without any idea where they would end up.[77] The underlying feel is one of escape, the couple breaking the ties of everyday life with only 'Daddy' nagging in the back of the female protagonist's thoughts, reminding her of what she *ought* to be doing. (Somewhere in the mix, McCartney seems to have been thinking of Jack Kerouac's 1957 beat novel, *On The Road*, in which the two main characters drive down to Mexico City, leaving their world behind.)

Freely exploring his vocal capabilities, McCartney ranges from the deeply admonishing to a flying ending on an exultant E flat, his musical confidence higher than at any point. The group performance is similarly expansive, running across a raw take in excess of five minutes, which originally included an extended coda with solo guitar sections, uncompromisingly sliced off the album mix. Thinking ahead, McCartney left the song's central bars open for orchestration, which was added in February in an arrangement by George Martin, sent over to the States as a written score to be performed by the New York Philharmonic at A&R Studios. (See also [102]; [106].)

Placed at the end of *RAM*, The Back Seat Of My Car made for an unexpectedly triumphant conclusion, and caught listeners' ears. Accordingly, when [106] Uncle Albert-Admiral Halsey was readied for release as a US trailer single, Apple opted to issue The Back Seat Of My Car in Britain, which despite its promise, limped to a poor 39 in the listings, by far the worst showing of McCartney's career to date. The track nonetheless endures as a fan favourite and an exemplar of what McCartney could achieve when his ambitions were engaged.

Paul And Linda McCartney: [99] **RODE ALL NIGHT** (*McCartney*)
Produced by Paul McCartney
Recorded: 22 Oct 1970, Columbia Studios, New York; 17 Jan 1973,
    EMI Studios, London
UK/US: unreleased
Paul McCartney: vocals, guitar; **Denny Seiwell**: drums

On the afternoon [98] The Back Seat Of My Car was recorded, McCartney and Denny Seiwell spent some time together in the studio, the two musicians having little prior experience working with one another. Sounding like an impromptu jam, Rode All Night was something McCartney already had in

---

[77] In his McCartney-approved biography of 2016, Philip Norman claims the song dates to the period before Paul and Linda were an item, linking it to secret journeys McCartney took with his prior girlfriend, actress, Maggie McGivern. For context though, McCartney dropped McGivern when he hooked up with Linda in late 1968, and as the *Get Back* demo shows, the lyric was written afterwards.

reserve, and as a thematic continuation of the previous track it provided an enjoyable diversion from normal work. After eight frenzied minutes they came to a stop, at which point the studio engineer offered to start recording – McCartney and Seiwell jointly exasperated that their first effort was not captured. Accordingly they had another go, which was preserved on tape.

A repetitive R&B vamp in E, Rode All Night fails to develop, and has the sense of being a song-in-progress. McCartney revisited it in 1977, adding a new contrasting section before giving it to Roger Daltrey for his solo album, *One Of The Boys*, where it appeared under the title, Giddy.

The original session in 1970, besides being a fun experience, helped McCartney and Seiwell gel musically and on a personal level. During proceedings Linda was in the studio, camera in hand, and took a photo of her husband screaming into the microphone, which was included in the *RAM* sleeve collage. (It was used again on the front of *CHOBA B CCCP* in 1998.)

Paul And Linda McCartney: [100] **HEY DIDDLE** (*McCartney, McCartney*)
Produced by Paul McCartney
Recorded: 26 Oct 1970, Columbia Studios, New York; Jul 1974,
    The Sound Shop, Nashville
UK/US: unreleased
Paul McCartney: vocals, guitar, bass; **Linda McCartney**: vocals; **Hugh McCracken**: guitar; **Denny Seiwell**: percussion; **uncredited**: recorders[78]

With its breezy self-contentment, this extended doodle would have slotted nicely onto McCartney's first solo album, and lending to its sense of home production, features percussion on pots and pans. It appears to have been written after *McCartney* since it was demoed over summer 1970, under the working title, She Can't Be Found. As insubstantial as several other *RAM* outtakes, it remained unreleased but was, like [99] Rode All Night, revisited down the line, overdubbed with country instruments in 1974 while McCartney was in Nashville recording [240] Junior's Farm. Thereupon it was short-listed for the *Cold Cuts* album which never appeared [96].

---

[78] The line-up on the original recording is not known precisely, although the regular studio ensemble has been confirmed. It is assumed McCartney played one of the two guitars and dubbed the bass on subsequently.

Paul And Linda McCartney: [101] **A LOVE FOR YOU** (*McCartney*)
Produced by Paul McCartney
Recorded: 26 Oct 1970, Columbia Studios, New York
UK/US: unreleased
Paul McCartney: vocals, bass; **Linda McCartney**: backing vocals; **Hugh McCracken**: guitar; **Denny Seiwell**: drums

Another recording which didn't make the cut, A Love For You was a fully realised attempt at pop-rock which might have been a success had McCartney deemed it worth releasing. That he didn't is surprising, particularly since it was pencilled in as a B-side (to the aborted [93] Get On The Right Thing) only to suffer obsolescence after the formation of Wings. As a band performance, it ranks as one of the most accomplished to come out of the New York sessions, kicking through its verses in McCartney's patent up-beat style, and proving the embryonic ensemble could pack a punch.

Conversely, if there were any doubt the standard of McCartney's lyrics had slackened without Lennon on hand to keep him focused, this song offers a perfect example: to illustrate the point, when the two were composing With A Little Help From My Friends together in 1967, they rejected a line proposed by Cynthia, 'I just feel fine', on the grounds that 'you never use the word "just". It's meaningless. It's a fill-in word'.[79] By way of contrast, McCartney's superficial lines here, 'I really am, I really can, I really do, I really have a love for you' are not so much lazy as an example of the way he'd come to regard them as secondary, his musical instincts driven primarily by melodic and structural form rather than lyrical content.

Well worth a public airing for its highly energised performance, the track was another exhumed for the ill-fated *Cold Cuts* project, after being treated to overdubs from Laurence Juber and Steve Holley in a very late Wings session. Although these efforts came to naught, the recording was attended again as late as 2003 when it was mixed for a remake of the comedy movie, *The In-Laws*, when it was finally issued on the associated soundtrack.

---

[79] Lennon's remark, quoted in Davies, p305.

Paul And Linda McCartney: [102] **LONG HAIRED LADY** (*McCartney, McCartney*)
Produced by Paul McCartney, Linda McCartney
Recorded: 27 Oct 1970, Columbia Studios, New York; Feb 1971, A&R Studios, New York; 7 Apr 1971, Sound Recorders Studio, Hollywood
UK/US: 17 Feb 1971 (*RAM* LP)
Paul McCartney: vocals, bass, keyboards; **Linda McCartney**: backing vocals; **Hugh McCracken**: guitar; **Denny Seiwell**: drums; **New York Philharmonic**: brass

A sequel of sorts to [18] The Lovely Linda, Long Haired Lady was the result of several musical ideas being connected to form a whole, at least some of which, Linda had a hand in writing – developing a love song to herself. Part of McCartney's songwriting craft was his ability to discern how disparate sections could be inter-woven to make something greater than the sum of their parts, a form of 'through-composition' commonly found in classical and opera. The method would become something of a McCartney hallmark in the 1970s, and was pioneered in his Beatles' days, taken to extravagant lengths on *Abbey Road*'s long medley, particularly in You Never Give Me Your Money and the multi-section Carry That Weight-The End.

In the case of Long Haired Lady, three distinct parts are evident, beginning with the vocally slapdash 'Well, well, well', followed by the song's central section, an affectionate tribute to the lady with the 'flashing eyes'. The remaining piece, the lyrically repetitive Love Is Long, was demoed on its own in the summer before the *RAM* sessions started, and was presumably incorporated due to its connection via the word 'long'. (This part, deployed as an extended coda, bears resemblance to the fade of Hey Jude, stepping up through the home triad – and lending to the duration of Long Haired Lady, the lengthiest track on the album.)

Recorded at Columbia, the tapes were overdubbed at A&R with a brassy score provided by George Martin. According to engineer, Eirik Wangberg, during the album's mixing stage at Sound Recorders Studio in March, further vocal harmony parts were recorded to complete the piece; interviewed in 2005, he recalled that when McCartney played the finished track over the studio monitors, he had tears in his eyes.

Paul And Linda McCartney: [103] **SUNSHINE SOMETIME** (*McCartney*)
Produced by Paul McCartney
Recorded: 29 Oct 1970, Columbia Studios, New York
UK/US: unreleased
Paul McCartney: guitar, bass, off-mike vocals; **Linda McCartney**: percussion[80]; **Hugh McCracken**: guitar; **Denny Seiwell**: drums

Around the time his first album was issued, McCartney purchased rights to the Rupert the Bear character which he remembered from childhood story books. His agenda was the making of an animated Rupert film, something he'd been considering since *Yellow Submarine*, and for which he set about composing some new songs. One of them was Sunshine Sometime, demoed over the summer along with [111] Little Lamb Dragonfly, also written especially. The Rupert film did not come to pass and as such, sits with a couple more McCartney movies from the 1970s which were never fully realised, including *The Bruce McMouse Show* and *One Hand Clapping* (see [264]).

Given the song's *raison d'être*, it seems unlikely McCartney ever had it in mind for *RAM*. A gently rolling instrumental, the track is played in the easy listening mode of acoustic lounge music, the hollow click of Denny Seiwell's percussion achieved by tapping on the rim of an African drum. Having no use for it once he decided not to proceed with the film, McCartney left it in the can. (In 1984 an animated short, *Rupert and the Frog Song*, was finally released to cinema, without any of the original compositions.)

Paul McCartney: [104] **OH WOMAN, OH WHY** (*McCartney*)
Produced by Paul McCartney
Recorded: 3 Nov 1970, Columbia Studios, New York
UK: 19 Feb 1971 (single B-side)
US: 22 Feb 1971 (single B-side)
Paul McCartney: vocals, guitar, bass, percussion, gun shots; **Linda McCartney**: backing vocals; **Hugh McCracken**: guitar; **Denny Seiwell**: drums, percussion

Working with US musicians in New York, it's unsurprising to see McCartney pick up an American influence in his songs, Oh Woman, Oh Why starting life as a bluesy group jam with McCracken and Seiwell. In devising a lyric, McCartney draws on the traditions of American country and blues, the woman of the title having him under a spell, despite her cheating ways, turns of phrase

---

[80] The personnel on the track is known, but Linda's role is not clear. Since she had yet to master an instrument, and does not sing, it is assumed she is on the shaker faintly audible in the mix.

he will have absorbed from writers such as Hank Williams and Buck Owens.

Due to its title, the song is often mistaken as an attack on Yoko Ono; that its most striking element is its handgun imagery makes the association particularly uncomfortable in retrospect. By way of illustrating the lyric with sound effects, McCartney went as far as to bring a pistol along, supposedly discharging it in the studio, as heard seven times in the song. (Linda's photographs of him, gun in hand, have been published.) Musical precedents are plentiful, there being no end of seminal songs with gunshots involved – examples including Jimi Hendrix's Hey Joe (1966) where the cheating woman is shot down, or Neil Young's Down By The River (1969), in which he shoots his 'baby', to which we might add Lennon's own 'bang bang, shoot shoot' from 1968. (In his 2021 book, *The Lyrics*, McCartney nominated the traditional Frankie And Johnny as a touch point: 'She pulled out a small .44/And root-e-toot-toot three times she shot/Right through that hardwood door'.)

Delivered in McCartney's screaming voice, last heard to such effect on Oh! Darling, the track benefits from a tight group performance in which the guitars convey an emotional tension, McCartney playing to the song's country links by overdubbing a slide section. Outside his usual range, the song was left off *RAM* but saw release on the B-side of [92] Another Day.

Paul And Linda McCartney: [105] **MONKBERRY MOON DELIGHT**
(*McCartney, McCartney*)
Produced by Paul McCartney, Linda McCartney
Recorded: 5 Nov 1970, Columbia Studios, New York
UK/US: 17 Feb 1971 (*RAM* LP)
Paul McCartney: vocals, bass, piano; **Linda McCartney**: backing vocals; **Hugh McCracken**: guitar; **Denny Seiwell**: drums

Often accused of writing vacuous lyrics, McCartney's early albums are at times marred by songs which, other than displaying musical novelty, have no obvious point. For a writer of his capabilities to record, let alone release, songs such as Monkberry Moon Delight shows a lack of self-evaluation, serving only to feed the critics who had so wounded him when *McCartney* was reviewed.

Inspired by Heather McCartney's habit of referring to milk as 'monk', the song is an exercise in free association, throwing around references to several tomato products in among nonsense about the fantasy milkshake of its title – a musical version of a children's food fight. While there is artistic merit to be had in stream-of-consciousness narratives, practitioners of the calibre of Dylan and Lennon imbued their songs with poetic gravitas, while lyrics such as McCartney's 'I sat in the attic, a piano up my nose' are plain silly. (McCartney's overestimation of his handiwork is shown in his decision to include the text in his 2001 poetical anthology, *Blackbird Singing*.)

Paul And Linda McCartney: [106] **UNCLE ALBERT-ADMIRAL HALSEY**
(*McCartney, McCartney*)
Produced by Paul McCartney, Linda McCartney
Recorded: 6 Nov 1970, Columbia Studios, New York; Feb 1971, A&R
    Studios, New York
UK/US: 17 Feb 1971 (*RAM* LP)
Paul McCartney: vocals, guitar, bass, piano, xylophone; **Linda McCartney**: backing vocals; **Hugh McCracken**: guitar; **Denny Seiwell**: drums; **New York Philharmonic**: synthesiser and orchestration

One of many songs demoed by McCartney over the summer was the part-written We're So Sorry. The song drew from childhood memories of family celebrations with aunties and uncles, of whom Albert Kendall was particularly fondly recalled; one of the clan's characters, uncle Albert would enjoy a drink or three while happily entertaining the family, and, according to McCartney, would sometimes clamber onto a table top so as to 'take the stage'. As the 1960s progressed, McCartney came to realise the happy pleasures of families gathering around pianos to enjoy a communal sing-along were fast becoming a thing of the past, and with them was going the cherished music of old. Ironically, in his role as a Beatle, McCartney was one of the primary forces in the societal shifts which fed the process, hence the apologetic tone of the song.

Another of his song scraps was provisionally titled Hands Across The Water, at this stage little more than a rousing chorus line, but with potential to make a fanfare finale to something. The immediate idea was to connect the two pieces together, and for this purpose McCartney came up with the Admiral Halsey section, which apart from serving as a functional link, also offers a thread of continuity; the sea-faring character was one McCartney could have dreamed up in his Liverpool childhood, watching ships in the Mersey estuary head off 'across the water' to who knew where.

It happens that there existed a real US Admiral Halsey, famous in the War years when McCartney was a baby. (He'd been portrayed in the film, *Tora! Tora! Tora!* in September 1970, which may have brought him to McCartney's attention.) However the song's depiction is based in fantasy, McCartney's Halsey a cartoon authority figure similar in concept to Sergeant Pepper, placed in northern English setting where cups of tea are imbibed with working-class fare (the butter pie – a Lancashire dish of potatoes and onion in pastry). In this light the admiral is more reminiscent of Old Fred the sea captain from the *Yellow Submarine* feature, a make-believe voyager setting off for adventure on the high seas.

Cleverly devised, McCartney's sequence drew some archetypal Beatle touches from George Martin, whose frugal brass score invokes a Liverpudlian Pepperland, with sea birds circling over its 'cast iron shore' in the middle of a downpour (recorded by engineer, Armin Steiner, on the edge of a cliff). The quirky end product was true McCartney, something no other artist could have come up with. Issued as a single in America, it topped the charts – his first such success without the Beatles. It was oddly overlooked in Britain (which preferred [98] The Back Seat Of My Car), despite not only going gold but winning McCartney a Grammy for its arrangement. Finally, he'd done something Harrison had managed but which Lennon hadn't, yet – he proved his commercial clout as a solo artist, allaying insecurities that he might not make it alone.

Paul And Linda McCartney: [107] **TOO MANY PEOPLE** (*McCartney*)
Produced by Paul McCartney, Linda McCartney
Recorded: 10 Nov 1970, Columbia Studios, New York; Jan 1971, A&R Studios, New York
UK/US: 17 Feb 1971 (*RAM* LP)
Paul McCartney: vocals, guitar, guitar, bass; **Linda McCartney**: backing vocals; **Hugh McCracken**: guitar; **Denny Seiwell**: drums, percussion; **uncredited**: brass

Still smarting from his treatment over *Let It Be* and the clash of timing with his own album, McCartney was dismayed through 1970 to realise he'd become the public's fall guy in the break up of the Beatles. And while his physical separation from the others was mostly his own choice, he was nonetheless hurt by the absence of any reconciliatory gestures from them, particularly Lennon, who had dismissed or ignored requests that they come together to end their legal partnership. Seeing Lennon's stance as passively aggressive, there was, reasoned McCartney, a certain hypocrisy in his former partner's championing world peace while entrenching himself in a battle McCartney simply wanted away from.

In Too Many People, McCartney makes his feelings clear, starting by quoting from the song's second line, 'Piece of cake', knowingly pronounced so as to literally tell Lennon to piss off, while the line, 'Too many people preaching practices' was aimed squarely at his ex-partner, McCartney judging Lennon to be 'preaching a little bit about what everyone should do, how they should live their lives'.[81] More damning still, the accusation, 'Yoko took your lucky break and broke it in two' was uncharacteristically direct and guaranteed to make Lennon and Ono bristle, although McCartney ultimately changed his mind about explicitly naming the villain of the piece. This statement, with its Beatlesque double meaning on 'break'/'broke', was intended to convey a regret that the Lennon-McCartney team had split in half,

---

[81] Sleeve notes to *RAM Archive Collection*, 2012.

but with its superior air sounded as if McCartney was implying *he* was to thank for everything, that their joining creative forces was a case of Lennon being fortunate to have him.

This detail highlights a perennial problem in McCartney's couching things in his 'usual veiled manner', several other parts of the song open to interpretation and inviting a reading of references unintended. While there may have been no more to the lyric than McCartney admitted, the comment, 'Too many people going underground', sounds as if aimed at Lennon and Ono's political-art activities, while 'Too many reaching for a piece of cake' could be a reference to the couple secretly consuming chocolate gâteau during their 'bagism' press conference in Vienna in March 1969 (as mentioned in The Ballad Of John And Yoko).

Recorded in a consummate group performance, the song gallops on Denny Seiwell's resourceful drum track, with Hugh McCracken enjoying the freedom of two guitar solos, the second of them heavily fuzzed and showing a dexterity rarely heard elsewhere on *RAM*. Adding to the general animation, percussion sounding like a cowbell (in fact, Seiwell banging the edge of a tom-tom) gives the song a clumping propulsion, the apparent fun being had belying the song's malicious undercurrent.

Whether for its musical potency, or to make sure it got noticed, McCartney programmed it as the lead-off song on the album, and also stuck it on the flip side of the chart-topping [106] Uncle Albert-Admiral Halsey. About as blunt as he could be, most of the references were too cryptically couched for the wider public to register, but on hearing the song, Lennon got the message loud and clear. Relations between the two were deteriorating.

Wings: [108] **LITTLE WOMAN LOVE** (*McCartney, McCartney*)
Produced by Paul McCartney, Linda McCartney
Recorded: 13 Nov 1970, Columbia Studios, New York; 21 Jan 1971,
    A&R Studios, New York; 10 Nov 1971, EMI Studios, London
UK: 12 May 1972 (single B-side)
US: 29 May 1972 (single B-side)
Paul McCartney: vocals, piano; **Linda McCartney**: backing vocals; **Hugh McCracken**: guitar; **Denny Seiwell**: drums, percussion; **Milt Hinton**: double bass

A two-minute jockey through hillbilly blues country, Little Woman Love relies mostly on McCartney's sprightly barrelhouse piano for its vitality. The lyric, into which little thought apparently went, is brisk and faintly patronising, its use of the female diminutive something McCartney would occasionally fall back on when he had nothing else to say ([95]; [226]; [227]); at a time when second-wave feminism was entering mainstream popular culture (Helen

Reddy's I Am Woman becoming something of an anthem in 1972), such apparent condescension left McCartney sounding anachronistic, especially as measured against Lennon's bold stance ([120]; [149]).

Playing up to its country style, McCartney subsequently dubbed on an upright bass, curiously not played himself but by jazz supremo, Milt Hinton, now 61 and plying his trade as a studio session man. Of little import, Little Woman Love was not included on *RAM* but was subject to later overdubs and issued on the back of [165] Mary Had A Little Lamb, billed as a Wings recording.

Paul And Linda McCartney: [109] **HEART OF THE COUNTRY** (*McCartney, McCartney*)
Produced by Paul McCartney, Linda McCartney
Recorded: 16 Nov 1970, Columbia Studios, New York
UK/US: 17 Feb 1971 (*RAM* LP)
Paul McCartney: vocals, guitar, bass; **Linda McCartney**: backing vocals; **Hugh McCracken**: guitar; **Denny Seiwell**: drums

McCartney's homage to life among the sheep and horses of his Scottish homestead, Heart Of The Country's gratified mood sounds like a casual strum-along, when in fact a fair bit of effort went into the track. The song was rehearsed early in the sessions, when David Spinozza was in the group, but no recording was made. McCartney realised that to effect a more casual sound he needed to sing in a lower key, achieved by slackening his guitar strings a whole tone so as to be able to play it through on the same finger shapes. (He made the adjustment carelessly, the chords sounding out of tune throughout.)

Adding to its anti-technological character, Denny Seiwell eschewed his studio kit for a range of found objects including a plastic bin hammered with his bass drum pedal, and a sheet of metal laying around the studio, on which he used his brushes. Matching the song's natural elements, its instrumental break consists of a vocal scat over the guitar solo, lending a faintly jazzy feel to what is otherwise a simple European country ballad – another in a series of songs in which McCartney broadcasts his new-found contentment.

As if to advertise the song's theme, McCartney elected to produce a video film (see also [94]) cobbled together from silent footage of him and Linda relaxing in the Scottish hills and coast of Kintyre. The decision was curious, Heart Of The Country never a contender for single release (although it appeared as a B-side in Britain); an unassuming number, this ode to rural domesticity was positioned at the start of *RAM*'s second side.

Paul And Linda McCartney: [110] **SMILE AWAY** (*McCartney*)
Produced by Paul McCartney, Linda McCartney
Recorded: 16 Nov 1970, Columbia Studios, New York
UK/US: 17 Feb 1971 (*RAM* LP)
Paul McCartney: vocals, bass, keyboard; **Linda McCartney**: backing vocals; **Hugh McCracken**: guitar; **Denny Seiwell**: drums

While reeling from the fall-out of the Beatles' break-up McCartney was keen to maintain a happy public face even when he didn't feel like it, and perfected the art of the insincere expression, according to Denny Seiwell, 'smiling away' while simultaneously communicating a seething mood by glaring with just his eyes.[82] Thus, the exaggerated smile became something of a McCartney motif, as shown in early ideas for *RAM*'s artwork which included billboards depicting cartoon grins with speakers secreted where the nostrils would be, set to blast out tracks from the album. (Earlier in the year, McCartney had written to *Melody Maker* to assure readers the Beatles were not about to re-form, signing off with a sketch of a toothy sneer.)

A piece of three-minute pub rock made from standard chord changes, Smile Away finds McCartney sending up his woes in a semi-comedy lyric, starting with a count-in reminiscent of I Saw Her Standing There from 1963. The track is notable for its bass distortion, obtained by deliberately overloading the console under the weight of multiple takes, some of the basslines electronically processed before being mixed into the general swamp. In a sense, the rasp of the bottom end below an upbeat exterior mirrors the song's underlying concept, although it's doubtful there was any sophisticated theory behind it, the track anticipating the simplistic guitar hits written by Chinn and Chapman for acts like Suzy Quatro and the Sweet in 1973-74.

Paul McCartney And Wings: [111] **LITTLE LAMB DRAGONFLY** (*McCartney*)
Produced by Paul McCartney
Recorded: 19 Nov 1970, Columbia Studios, New York; 1972, Trident Studio, London
UK: 4 May 1973 (*Red Rose Speedway* LP)
US: 30 Apr 1973 (*Red Rose Speedway* LP)
Paul McCartney: vocals, bass; **Linda McCartney**: backing vocals; **Hugh McCracken**: guitar; **Denny Seiwell**: drums, percussion, vocals; **Denny Laine**: backing vocals; **New York Philharmonic**: orchestration

While McCartney's lyrics could often be shallow, he was at times capable of genuine sensitivity, this delicate expression of sorrow for a weak baby lamb

---

[82] Sleeve notes to *RAM Archive Collection*, 2012.

drawing on a true event in which a new-born on a neighbouring farm was brought to Linda to see if she could save its life. The compassion evident in the lyric indicates the seeds of McCartney's vegetarianism (which he converted to in 1975), and concern for animal welfare generally, lay in direct experience, evinced by the fact that he was willing to expend considerable creative and emotional efforts paying tribute to a nameless farm animal.

Having said what he needed to, the song 'Little Lamb' was still far from complete, McCartney falling back on his method of fusing together shorter pieces to create whole songs. In this case, 'Little Lamb' was married up with 'Dragonfly', another sketch depicting a fragile creature glimpsed through McCartney's window, which in his fantasy transforms into the vision of a lost love. Although McCartney would frequently draw on real life for the content of his songs, 'Dragonfly' clearly arises from artistic impulse alone, the scenario in which his lover has left him bearing no relation to actual circumstance.[83] Each section admitting its own form of tenderness, the effect of bringing them together was to elevate the whole, the halves forming a balance such that Little Lamb Dragonfly becomes one of the most impeccable creations of McCartney's solo catalogue.

Having recorded the basic track in November 1970, McCartney made the curious decision not to mix and release it, saving it instead for his vaguely proposed Rupert feature [103] – and thus *RAM* appeared in 1971 without it. On an album coloured by McCartney's experiences of life as a sheep farmer, it's strange that this ode to a new-born lamb was not included; the track would have sat comfortably on the LP, and was obviously stronger than several which were used.[84] Similarly it was overlooked for *Wild Life*, despite another thematic link, finally being revisited and overdubbed for release on *Red Rose Speedway*, two and a half years after its New York recording.

Uncertainty surrounds the dating of events here. At some stage, an understated string section was added, arranged by George Martin, and since he orchestrated other *RAM* tracks in February 1971, it's possible this is when Little Lamb Dragonfly was attended. However the official dates cite unspecified overdubs at some point between March and December 1972, which corresponds with Denny Laine's late vocal additions. Since McCartney worked with George Martin on [191] Live And Let Die in October 1972, it seems probable Little Lamb Dragonfly was completed around the same time, as confirmed by the fact that the final mix was done as late as 8 January 1973.

---

[83] Denny Seiwell is sometimes said to have had a role in the composition, although he has never been officially credited. He too was happily married, to Monique.

[84] This particular reviewer would have left out the opening couplet [107] Too Many People and [94] 3 Legs, and started with [93] Get On The Right Thing followed by Little Lamb Dragonfly, setting the album up in style.

The 1970 recording was McCartney's last at Columbia Studios as he took a winter break to concentrate on other affairs. In all, well over a dozen useable tracks had been recorded, more than enough for a complete album. The main task in the new year would be selection, mixing and overdubbing, and *RAM* would soon be ready to go.

Paul And Linda McCartney: [112] **RAM ON** (*McCartney*)
Produced by Paul McCartney, Linda McCartney
Recorded: 22 Feb 1971, A&R Studios, New York
UK/US: 17 Feb 1971 (*RAM* LP)
Paul McCartney: vocals, piano, Wurlitzer keyboard, ukulele, drums, percussion; **Linda McCartney**: backing vocals

After returning to London in November, McCartney came to realise that if he were to extract himself from the Beatles' joint financial ties, he would have to force the hand of an unco-operative Harrison, and, in particular, Lennon, who so far had shown nothing but contempt for McCartney's approaches. As far back as June, McCartney had written to Allen Klein through his legal advisor, Lee Eastman, demanding the Beatles' contracts be dissolved, Klein not even troubling to respond – the very act of having to communicate with Lennon via third-party representatives underlining the dire situation which had come to pass. With friendships close to breaking down completely, McCartney found himself more isolated than ever when a December meeting with Harrison ended in acrimony. Seemingly unable to have even a constructive discussion about the problem, let alone come to a resolution, McCartney began to seriously muse the prospect of taking the matter to court to effect a proper separation of interests. It was a decision he was loath to take, an 'unholy act' forced on him through others' intransigence, and so in the run-up to Christmas a writ was issued in which McCartney sought to have the group's income-pooling arrangements terminated, and to have Klein formally removed from his position as the Beatles' manager, since McCartney did not consent to his appointment in the first place. In taking the issue to court, McCartney was obliged to directly name Lennon, Harrison and Starr as defendants, and on the last day of the month, a preliminary session was held to consider the merits of the application and set a schedule for full proceedings in the new year. The history books therefore show that McCartney, who everyone assumed had announced he was exiting the Beatles in April, was now suing to formally end the group – as if the entire impasse was of his doing.

To make matters worse, around now the first half of Lennon's *Rolling Stone* interview landed, his scathing remarks about McCartney there for all to see, prompting an incensed Linda to write to her husband's former colleague appealing to him to disengage from open warfare.[85] This time Lennon did reply, his characteristically stinging letter accusing Linda of having a 'perverted mind', and claiming that far from resenting McCartney, he in fact felt sorry for him. Meanwhile McCartney's public reaction to the *Rolling Stone* article was to purchase advertising space in the music press to run full-page photos of a couple wrapped in bed clothes, captioned only with the words 'Happy Xmas'. With the man sporting round glasses and a bulbous plastic nose, the woman disguised in a 'Wimpy' mask (a character from *Popeye*) which made her appear like a Japanese geisha, the image looked unmistakeably like an insulting caricature of John and Yoko, sarcastically reprising their 'War Is Over' ads from the previous December.[86] Such was the state of Beatle affairs in early 1971.

On the morning of 19 February, the day McCartney's debut single was released [92], proceedings began in London, set to run over 11 days. Not willing to stomach any more conflict, McCartney packed up and left town, heading back to New York with Linda to concentrate on finishing *RAM* while events at home unfolded without him. This time his venue was A&R Studios on 7th Avenue, a facility opened in 1967 by Jack Arnold and record producer, Phil Ramone, who was set to oversee the recording of George Martin's orchestral scores.

During his time in New York, McCartney had taken to carrying a ukulele around with him, sometimes surprising cab drivers by spontaneously bursting into song with it. From such light-hearted moments he found a new tune, its title an outgrowth of his decision to name his pending album *RAM*.[87] Ram On toys with a stage name McCartney had invented in 1960, when each of the Beatles temporarily adopted a *nom de plume* for their Scottish tour behind Johnny Gentle (he'd opted for Paul Ramon for no other reason than it sounded French and, to him, sophisticated) but he was likely reminded of it due to the presence here of Phil Ramone.[88]

The first time McCartney used a ukulele in a studio, Ram On endured for

---

[85] The new edition's cover date was 21 January 1971, but it went on sale on 16 December.

[86] The anonymous masked couple was Paul and Linda dressed up for Halloween, but readers had no clue as to who was behind it. The photo was presumably taken innocently; its public distribution in such a manner is hard to read as anything other than deliberate provocation.

[87] McCartney's explanation was that the word 'ram' had several appealing connotations, suggesting purpose and masculinity. It's curious that back in February 1970, a single called Ram You Hard was released by Leo Graham under the headline-grabbing pseudonym, John Lennon and the Bleechers.

[88] The other Beatles had come up with Carl Harrison (after Carl Perkins), Stuart de Staël (after French artist, Nicolas de Staël) and, less flamboyantly, Johnny Lennon.

close to three minutes before a spontaneous lurch into a provisional 'Who's that coming round that corner' brought it to an end. (This fragment would later resurface in [157] Big Barn Bed.) Essentially just one line repeated over and over, it was the most simplistic tune to make it onto *RAM*, McCartney attempting to give it some much-needed substance by dubbing on several instruments including a novel Wurlitzer electric piano. In the end he faded the song down some way before the finish, slotting it into side one of the album and using the offcut as a link between [102] Long Haired Lady and [98] The Back Seat Of My Car.

Paul And Linda McCartney: [113] **NOW HEAR THIS SONG OF MINE**
(*McCartney*)
Produced by Paul McCartney
Recorded: 22 Feb 1971, A&R Studios, New York
UK/US: unreleased
Paul McCartney: vocals, piano, bass drum, hand claps, tambourine, organ;
Linda McCartney: backing vocals, hand claps[89]

Believed to have been recorded on the same day as [112] Ram On, this ragged jingle was put together to help promote *RAM*, under supervision of studio engineer, Eirik Wangberg. Led by McCartney on piano, the song is elementary but fun, and was taped three times in different styles: a standard piano version in G; an extended, slow singalong in A; and an up-beat 'barroom' rendition in C. Together they account for around a minute and a half of studio tape.

When *RAM* was due for release, McCartney considered 'Now Hear This' as an advertising slogan, but changed his mind. The song was used however, inserted in multiple repeating sections into a promotional disc called *Brung To Ewe By*, placed between mock interviews with the McCartneys where it was adorned with sheep noises and sound effects. (The track has never been officially released; 1000 copies of *Brung To Ewe By* were manufactured and issued to radio stations, now valuable collectors' items.)

Paul And Linda McCartney: [114] **GREAT COCK AND SEAGULL RACE**
(*McCartney*)
Produced by Paul McCartney
Recorded: 23 Feb 1971, A&R Studios, New York
UK/US: unreleased
Paul McCartney: guitar, bass, drums, piano, electric piano; **Linda McCartney**: percussion (?)

---

[89] Performer credits are presumed. No official list has been published.

An R&B instrumental in A, Great Cock And Seagull Race appears to be a solo McCartney recording, drummer Denny Seiwell having confirmed that he missed the session, despite later receiving an official credit. Of no particular merit, the track is vaguely reminiscent of Harrison's [72] I Remember Jeep, but without the style. Unsure what to do with it, McCartney let it rest before pulling it out for a radio broadcast to promote *Wild Life*, for which he dubbed on some bird noises including a rooster, recalling the start of Good Morning Good Morning.

Paul And Linda McCartney: [115] **DEAR BOY** (*McCartney, McCartney*)
Produced by Paul McCartney, Linda McCartney
Recorded: 1 Mar 1971; 9 Mar 1971; 10 Mar 1971; 12 Mar 1971; 7 Apr 1971, Sound Recorders Studio, Hollywood
UK/US: 17 Feb 1971 (*RAM* LP)
Paul McCartney: vocals, guitar, bass, piano, percussion; **Linda McCartney**: backing vocals; **Denny Seiwell**: drums, percussion; **Paul Beaver**: synthesiser; **Philip Davis**: synthesiser; **Jim Guercio**: backing vocals

The last thing recorded for *RAM*, Dear Boy was written in Scotland, McCartney taking a circuitous route in expressing his love for Linda by aiming a lyric at her ex. Linda had met and married Mel See in the early 1960s, giving birth to Heather in December 1962 before the relationship broke down, leading to divorce three years later.[90] From McCartney's perspective, See had let a great woman slip through his fingers, hence the song's goading tone, balanced by McCartney's realisation that he was fortunate to have found her when he did, Linda providing the loyal support he needed through 1970.

The track was recorded over a series of late dates at Sound Recorders in Hollywood, McCartney taking great pains over the much-admired harmony arrangement, in which Linda, while being adored in song, was drilled mercilessly to get her vocal lines just-so. While in the Beatles, McCartney could rely on the musical instincts of Lennon and Harrison for support, and the classical expertise of George Martin for direction, but in Linda he had a relatively inexperienced collaborator, part of the reason producer, Jim Guercio, was asked to help out. The results warranted the effort, Linda earning her stripes with a vocal dove-tailing seamlessly with McCartney's, lending the track a lavish harmonic fluency – by far her most accomplished contribution to date. Mixed in wide, mid-60s-style stereo, the final track runs a little over two

---

[90] See's actual name was Joseph, and since he lived in Tucson, Arizona, the Get Back character, 'Jo Jo' is sometimes thought to be based on him. However the composing evidence on the 1969 Nagra Tapes suggests otherwise, McCartney finding the name and location separately, by trial and error.

minutes, a miniature glimpse of McCartney at his most compelling, just in time to make the album.

After the *RAM* sessions wrapped up, McCartney enlisted Eirik Wangberg to oversee mixing, something the studio engineer paid great attention to, feeling a weight of responsibility on his shoulders and working in subdued studio lighting to concentrate the mood. With McCartney only interested in giving after-the-event approval on individual tracks, Wangberg had the luxury of directing much of the album's running order and creating the necessary sequencing and cross-fades so that by the time McCartney heard it back in its entirety, he did so with a degree of freshness. Of the tracks left on the cutting-room floor, not all were wasted, a number of them turning up on subsequent albums and B-sides over the ensuing couple of years (ie, [93]; [97]; [108]; [111]).

On 12 March, Justice Stamp delivered his ruling in McCartney's case and although widely reported as having come down in favour, in fact deferred a decision indefinitely, leaving the Beatles' joint agreements intact and legally binding. However in the secondary matter of Allen Klein's status as the Beatles' manager, it was ruled that McCartney's rights had been breached by having to suffer unwanted representation. And so while Klein was entitled to – and indeed did – continue to represent Lennon, Harrison and Starr as individual clients, he was relieved of responsibility for the group's collective affairs, replaced by a court-appointed receiver to handle business ongoing, much to the disgust of the other former group members.

So far as *RAM* was concerned, McCartney elected to design the sleeve himself, assembling photo collages and adorning the borders with garish patterns drawn in felt-tipped pen. The centrepiece of the front cover was Linda's snap of McCartney wrestling with one of his sheep, but not missing the opportunity to direct further jabs at his erstwhile colleagues, McCartney also incorporated the Halloween photo of himself and Linda which he'd distributed to the media in December [112], to guarantee fans were in on the joke. More pointedly, the album art included an image of a beetle screwing another beetle – the subtlety of which was lost on no-one – and to underline the message, the photo was included twice: four beetles in all.

Buoyed by having gained ground in his legal dispute, McCartney had reason to be optimistic about *RAM*'s prospects as it was readied for release. Apart from a number of striking new songs, he'd by now scored a hit with [92] Another Day, and in Linda, seemed to have unlocked a latent talent for both performing and helping write hit material, the subsequent rumblings of malcontent from Northern Songs over her due share of the royalties at this stage largely an irrelevance. Less irrelevant was the critical savaging dished out by the music press, something McCartney was wholly unprepared for, *Rolling Stone* leading the charge in their 8 July edition in which Jon Landau ludicrously denounced the album as 'the nadir in the decomposition of sixties rock'.

Bruised but not defeated, McCartney stood by *RAM* to the extent that in June he went into EMI to re-record the entire set as a suite of instrumental lounge music, arranged by Richard Hewson. (Unreleased in its day, it appeared to little fanfare in 1977 under the fictional identity of Percy 'Thrills' Thrillington, pressed for the UK on the quaintly named Regal Zonophone label.) Like *McCartney* before it, *RAM* may have been a critical failure but was a commercial hit, making the top of the album charts in the UK, and peaking at 2 in America. Re-evaluated over the ensuing decades, *RAM* has gradually come to be recognised as one of his strongest solo releases.

RECORD RELEASES

[92] **Another Day** / [104] **Oh Woman, Oh Why**
(UK: 19 Feb 1971, US: 22 Feb 1971)
RAM
(UK/US: 17 May 1971)
[107] Too Many People / [94] 3 Legs / [112] Ram On / [115] Dear Boy / [106] Uncle Albert-Admiral Halsey / [110] Smile Away / [109] Heart Of The Country / [105] Monkberry Moon Delight / [95] Eat At Home / [102] Long Haired Lady / [112] Ram On (Reprise) / [98] The Back Seat Of My Car
[106] **Uncle Albert-Admiral Halsey** / [107] **Too Many People**
(US: 2 Aug 1971)
[98] **The Back Seat Of My Car** / [109] **Heart Of The Country**
(UK: 13 Aug 1971)

Ronnie Spector sessions: February 1971

Fans of Phil Spector's productions for acts like the Teddy Bears and the Crystals, the Beatles welcomed one of his flagship girl groups, the Ronettes, to join their 1966 US tour. Having met the Beatles previously, lead singer, Ronnie – by then Phil's lover – had provoked jealousy when Lennon took an obvious shine to her, and in consequence Phil had her removed from the stage act, ensuring she didn't get to perform those famous gigs. Although Ronnie's singing career more or less ended there, Spector maintained a desire to see her reach individual stardom, and one or two late 1960s recordings ensued before his presence at Apple resulted in an obvious move: she was offered a recording contract, with Harrison especially keen to work with her.

The sessions were intended to generate an album of new songs, chief among them, [116] Try Some Buy Some, written especially. In the event Ronnie tired of the project, perceiving the songs as below par, and there ended her hopes of a career revival. Try Some Buy Some was put out regardless, backed with an ad-hoc studio jam led by Phil Spector, who ordered some Indian food before taking to the piano to belt out the dreadful Tandoori Chicken, which she gamely sang. She left behind a small pile of unfinished tapes, two of which would later be pressed into service as Harrison tracks. [91]

George Harrison: [116] **TRY SOME BUY SOME** (*Harrison*)
    Produced by George Harrison, Phil Spector
    Recorded: Feb 1971, EMI Studios, London; late 1972-early 73,
        Apple Studios, London
    UK: 22 Jun 1973 (*Living In The Material World* LP)
    US: 30 May 1973 (*Living In The Material World* LP)
    George Harrison: vocals, guitars; **Klaus Voormann**: bass; **Gary Wright**: electric piano; **Jim Gordon**: drums; **uncredited**: mandolins

When she landed in England, Ronnie Spector was not sure what lie in wait and when taken into EMI the day after her arrival, didn't initially recognise the bearded George Harrison, assuming him to be one of the studio staff. With the necessary introductions done, she was treated to a first hearing of Try Some Buy Some, a custom-made track recorded by Harrison and Spector, just needing her vocal on top. Duly completed, it was released as an Apple single in April 1971 to little interest, and few fans purchased it.

The recording might then have been forgotten had Lennon not cribbed the arrangement for [144] Happy Xmas (War Is Over), which reminded Harrison that he still had Spector's tapes in the vaults, which he went and retrieved with a view to making his own version. His decision to re-use the original backing track was problematic in that it was pitched in B flat, on the low side for Ronnie Spector, but high for Harrison who had to audibly reach up to find the notes. In truth he would have been better starting from scratch, the underlying composition attractive for its descending chords, discovered by Harrison when trying to play an electric organ without knowing his way around it. Caked in sickly mandolins, the emphasis put on getting arrangement right shows how comparatively little attention was paid to the lyric, which, if about anything,

---

[91] Besides Try Some Buy Some, outtakes include a version of Harrison's later single, You. Also recorded were [74] I'll Still Love You, Phil Spector's I Love Him Like I Love My Very Life, and Toni Wine's Lovely La-De-Day, which was nearly completed.

appears to be a celebration of love as a cure for drug addiction. Lennon clearly liked it, as did David Bowie who later covered it, but despite two official outings, Try Some Buy Some never reached its true potential.

Ascot sessions: February 1971

John Lennon: [117] **IT'S SO HARD** (*Lennon*)
Produced by John Lennon, Yoko Ono, Phil Spector
Recorded: 11 Feb 1971, Ascot Sound Studios, Berkshire; 4 Jul 1971; 5 Jul 1971, Record Plant, New York
UK: 8 Oct 1971 (*Imagine* LP)
US: 7 Sep 1971 (*Imagine* LP)
John Lennon: vocals, guitar, piano; **Klaus Voormann**: bass; **Jim Gordon**: drums, tambourine; **King Curtis**: saxophone; **the Flux Fiddlers**: strings

Lennon and Ono bought their Tittenhurst Park mansion in 1969, which while offering extravagant space, was several miles out of London, forcing Lennon to journey into the city for work. A notoriously bad driver who'd smashed up his Austin Maxi 18 months previously, he preferred to be chauffeured in his Rolls Royce, adding a further layer of inconvenience, and so after recording *John Lennon/Plastic Ono Band* at EMI he resolved to have a professional studio built in his home – a move each of his fellow ex-Beatles would also make in the following few years. Christened Ascot Sound, the facility was installed in what was once a small private chapel complete with pipe organ, and boasted an eight-track console, on a par with what Abbey Road could offer, EMI having made the step-up from four-track recording only as recently as 1969.

On 11 February, with no specific project in mind, Lennon took Klaus Voormann and Dominos drummer, Jim Gordon, down to the studio for the first time to put it through its paces. First on the agenda was this tough 12-bar blues, an exposition of life's travails which continued the raw guitar expression of [2] Cold Turkey and [81] I Found Out. (Lennon's devious streak comes to the fore in the middle eight, where we learn his real interest in 'going down', thereby also revealing the *double-entendre* of the song's title.)

Exploring the possibilities of eight-track recording at his leisure, Lennon took the unusual step of playing an orthodox guitar solo in the song's instrumental section, doubling it and panning it to the extremes, echoing the exploratory work McCartney had done on his own home equipment. After he decided to use It's So Hard on *Imagine*, Lennon elected to round off its abrasive edges with strings and a saxophone section, recorded in New York in July. For the session he called on King Curtis, a respected old hand who'd supported the Beatles on their 1965 US tour, and who was on home turf with the song's 12-bar structure, contributing a stirring sax backing in a couple of takes. Unsure at first what he wanted, Lennon had Curtis play riffs throughout, Phil Spector directed to fade the instrument in and out of the final mix as required. The result gives It's So Hard an American urban quality, appropriately so, since by the time it was released, Lennon was a New Yorker.

John Lennon: [118] **WELL!** (*Ward*)[92]
Produced by John Lennon
Recorded: 11 Feb 1971; 16 Feb 1971, Ascot Sound Studios, Berkshire
UK/US: unreleased
John Lennon: vocals, guitar; **Klaus Voormann**: bass; **Jim Gordon**: drums; **Jim Keltner**: percussion; **Bobby Keys**: saxophone

Originally recorded by doo-wop outfit, the Olympics, this song appeared in Britain in 1958 on the HMV label, a B-side to the 78, Western Movies. It caught Lennon's attention and was taken into the Beatles' early stage act where it remained until 1962. It seems to have popped back into his mind following the recording of [117] It's So Hard, with which it shares a similarly rudimentary blues structure, besides also being pitched in A. Accordingly the three-piece group at Ascot ran through a swaggering version, notable for Lennon's use of heavily wah-wahed lead guitar. Reportedly with Ono's 38th birthday in mind (on 18 February), he recorded a second version a few days later, reciprocating the gesture she'd made to him on his 30th [75]. The re-make, running to some six minutes, featured Bobby Keys' saxophone, setting a stylistic tone which presumably inspired the later overdubs on [117] and [121].

John Lennon: [119] **I'M THE GREATEST** (*Lennon*)
Produced by John Lennon
Recorded: 11 Feb 1971, Ascot Sound Studios, Berkshire
UK/US: unreleased
John Lennon: vocals, piano; **Klaus Voormann**: bass; **Jim Gordon**: drums

When Muhammad Ali defeated Sonny Liston in 1963 he famously declared himself 'The Greatest', giving rise to a catchphrase which, seven years on, inspired a semi-autobiographical lyric from Lennon. Pre-dating his Primal

---

[92] The song title has morphed over the years. Lennon recorded a version on stage with Frank Zappa in June 1971, released as Well (Baby Please Don't Go). The same song was later issued on Lennon retrospectives as just Baby Please Don't Go. This may not have been accidental; Lennon already had a song called [82] Well Well Well.

Therapy, the song casts a more positive light on his early years than the material on *John Lennon/Plastic Ono Band*, initial drafts recalling his mother's approval and encouragement of him. (Julia took a genuine interest in the Quarry Men and taught the teenaged Lennon songs on her banjo.) Although his experiences under Janov would permanently alter his outlook, he didn't discard the song after bidding Julia's memory goodbye in [80] Mother; rather, he extrapolated the lyrics, bringing in approving mention of Ono in the third verse. A tentative studio arrangement was captured in the first session at Ascot, which owes something of its make-up to Mean Mr. Mustard. Uncertain how it would be received should he go public with such apparent self-adulation, Lennon set the song aside until the advent of Starr's 1973 album, *Ringo*, when it was dusted off and updated once again (see [200]).

John Lennon: [120] **POWER TO THE PEOPLE** (*Lennon*)
Produced by John Lennon, Yoko Ono, Phil Spector
Recorded: 15 Feb 1971, Ascot Sound Studios, Berkshire; 22 Feb 1971,
    EMI Studios, London[93]
UK: 8 Mar 1971 (single A-side)
US: 22 Mar 1971 (single A-side)
John Lennon: vocals, piano; **Klaus Voormann**: bass; **Jim Gordon**: drums; **Bobby Keys**: saxophone; **Rosetta Hightower and choir**: backing vocals

Lennon's intermittent dalliances with the New Left have as their genesis the release of Revolution in 1968, in which, speaking from his privileged position as a Beatle, he offered considered advice on what the global movement was doing wrong. Understandably he drew flak from the very people he wanted to engage, condemned for his perceived abstraction from the real world. Raked over the coals in the pages of *The Black Dwarf*, a newspaper tied to the International Marxist Group, Lennon was characterised as representative of 'big business' (ie, Apple), with Revolution ridiculed as 'no more revolutionary than Mrs Dale's Diary'.[94] Marking the first time Lennon had entered into anything resembling a debate with the far left, his response ran in the 10 January 1969 edition, where he stuck to his guns on opposition to physical

---

[93] The date of the overdub session is not confirmed, although generally accepted to have been done at EMI. Madinger and Raile do not provide details but note a mix of the track was done at EMI on 22 February, which is presumably when the choir was recorded. When *Imagine – The Ultimate Edition* was issued in 2018 it gave the date of the backing track as 22 January, with the overdubs on 15 February. However Lennon was in the States on 22 January, so this cannot be correct.

[94] *The Black Dwarf*, 27 October 1968. Mrs Dale's Diary was a BBC radio drama about middle-class life in the London suburbs.

destruction: 'You smash it – and I'll build around it'.

Increasingly political in his public life, by the end of 1969 Lennon was vocally supporting Michael X and his Black House commune in north London, HQ of the Racial Adjustment Action Society, while also championing single-issue campaigns such as that of James Hanratty, executed for murder in 1962 on what many considered to be flimsy evidence. (At the 1969 UNICEF gig, heard on bonus LP with *Some Time In New York City*, Yoko can be heard openly accusing the British state of murdering Hanratty.[95])

Although his Primal Therapy interlude had swallowed up much of 1970, taking Lennon off the circuit, he didn't lose his political senses and in 1971 began to re-engage with the radical left. In February he invited activists Robin Blackburn and *The Black Dwarf*'s former editor, Tariq Ali, now running the revolutionary paper *Red Mole*, into Tittenhurst Park, granting them an extensive interview where, over the next two hours, he did his best to impress them with his political credentials, claiming to read the left-wing *Morning Star* and deliberating on how capitalism could best be destroyed. Clearly his nagging stance on 'destruction' (ie, violence) remained unresolved, stuck as he was for an answer to whether 'popular violence' to overthrow oppression could be justified. ('You can't take power without a struggle', he puzzled, in opposition to Ono's more hopeful comment that music can be the catalyst for a non-violent uprising.) The most revealing parts of the discourse though were Lennon's open espousal of feminist politics, something he learned through Ono and which set him ahead of the mainstream in the movement: 'How can you talk about power to the people unless you realise "the people" is *both* sexes?'

Galvanised by the exchange, and no doubt flattered that his political views were being taken so seriously, Lennon decided it was time for an update to Revolution, and during the following day came through with Power To The People, at once singing it down the phone to Tariq Ali. Using as its foundation stone the most obvious of slogans, the song begins with a restatement of the first line of Revolution, as if to announce this is intended to be heard as a sequel, but here, rather than proceeding to argue over the tactics of the left, Lennon is uncritical in his encouragement for revolt here and now. Conceived as an anthem for those engaged in struggle, pitched for chanting on the barricades, the rallying cry of the song's chorus was, Lennon later conceded, the result of 'wanting to be loved by Tariq Ali and his ilk'.[96] Not that the intent wasn't genuine; what differentiates it from traditional 'red' marching ballads is

---

[95] Sincere though the Lennons were, their often poor judgement served to fuel their detractors, as when Michael X was convicted of a 1972 murder and hanged. (Hanratty was also confirmed to have committed murder when DNA testing became available.)
[96] His retrospective explanation in the 1980 *Playboy* interview. See Golson, 1981.

the detail of Lennon's verses, in which he expands on the feminist points which had come up during his interview. (The line, 'A million women working for nothing' was a re-think of the original 'workers working', challenging the traditional domestic role of the married female from a Marxist perspective, she getting no break from her labours, nor a salary.)

With his new studio at hand, Lennon was typically impatient to get the track down and recorded it straight away, calling again on Bobby Keys for saxophone embellishment. Wrapped up in a few takes, the resultant track is suitably rousing in style, the subsequent overdubbing of stamping feet not invoking the lifting of weary spirits, a cliché of leftist battle hymns, but sounding out a purposeful taking to the streets. What stopped Lennon getting it in the shops at once was EMI's reaction to the slated B-side, Ono's Open Your Box, UK MD Philip Brodie finding the lyrics unpalatable ('box' being US slang for vagina). As a consequence the release was put back from the planned 5 March so Lennon and Ono could prepare a cleaned up mix, the single therefore appearing in the racks late, though as it turned out, on the same morning *Red Mole* arrived carrying Lennon's interview. (Perhaps keen to avoid a repeat of the problem with its flip side, Capitol in America deployed Touch Me from *Yoko Ono/Plastic Ono Band* instead.)

Issued in a picture cover, Power To The People depicted Lennon with militant clenched fist, sporting a Japanese police helmet. When it landed it became a modest hit, marking the arrival of Lennon the Revolutionary, thereby acting as precursor to his next-but-one album, *Some Time In New York City*. Its March release ensured it made the UK top 30 listings alongside singles by each of the other ex-Beatles one year after the group's final hit; the chart published on 17 April had them side-by-side, their musical offerings disparate and showing their divergent artistic interests: Lennon the political spokesman, McCartney with his character study [92], Harrison espousing a religious view [34] and Starr happy with a good pop song [14].

John Lennon: [121] **I DON'T WANT TO BE A SOLDIER** (*Lennon*)
Produced by John Lennon, Yoko Ono, Phil Spector
Recorded: 16 Feb 1971; 18 Feb 1971 (?); 24 May 1971, Ascot Sound Studios, Berkshire; 5 Jul 1971, Record Plant, New York
UK: 8 Oct 1971 (*Imagine* LP)
US: 7 Sep 1971 (*Imagine* LP)
John Lennon: vocals, guitar; **George Harrison**: electric slide guitar; **Joey Molland**: guitar; **Tom Evans**: guitar; **Klaus Voormann**: bass; **Jim Keltner**: drums; **Nicky Hopkins**: electric piano; **John Barham**: piano; **King Curtis**: saxophone; **Mike Pinder**: tambourine

Lennon had been toying with early drafts of this, his first anti-war song since [1] Give Peace A Chance, since late 1970, but it wasn't until the days following his interview with Tariq Ali and Robin Blackburn [120] that he crystallised his thoughts and recorded it. Loose in the style of an informal jam, the first draft had little to it apart from its opening line, and an impressive groove based on a see-sawing two-chord pattern which was sadly dropped along the way. Pleased though with what he had, Lennon developed some lyrics spinning off 'soldier', coming up with the obvious 'sailor' which set him on a path down the children's rhyme, Tinker, Tailor, from which he constructed the rest of the song.[97] Sparing with his lyrics, Lennon added little else of substance and forced to close each line with a rhyme for 'die', ended up with some odd couplets (eg, the poor man, 'fly').

By the time *Imagine* was underway Lennon had a tougher approach in mind and re-made the basic track in eight takes, Jim Keltner on drums and a couple of guitarists from Badfinger effectively inviting themselves to the party, while Moody Blues keyboardist, Mike Pinder, was on hand to shake a tambourine. Having raised the pitch from G to A, Lennon had Harrison dub on an acidic lead guitar, probably in the days immediately following the basic take, but didn't see through his threat to add sound effects including a motorcycle and a recording of a toilet flushing. Final touches were done in New York, where, in the same session as [117] It's So Hard, he had King Curtis record a double-tracked saxophone break, which turned out to be one of the sax man's final dates; Curtis was stabbed in a street confrontation on 13 August and died.

Added to *Imagine*, this ponderous track closed side 1 after Lennon had initially considered it for the opening cut; an over-indulgence at more than six minutes, Harrison later opined correctly that it should have been trimmed down.[98] It would have been a telling choice for the B-side of [120] Power To The People, had Lennon and Ono not been committed to sharing their sides equally. As it is, the track gives *Imagine* a sombre dimension harkening back to *John Lennon/Plastic Ono Band* and, despite its personal tone, is the most overtly political number on the set.

The week spent recording at Ascot had been largely unfocused but resulted in the creation of a batch of useful studio recordings, some just promising jams, a

---

[97] The rhyme, typically used by children as a counting game, differs in Britain and America. The version Lennon knew reads, 'tinker, tailor, soldier, sailor, rich man, poor man, beggar man, thief'. (The Rutles later used some of its words in Goose-Step Mama, their parody of Some Other Guy.)

[98] Interview published in *Record Mirror*, 18 December 1971.

couple destined for *Imagine* and one of them Lennon's forthcoming single. Having proved the studio's worth, Lennon now decided his next album could be made here, the first time he would record at length outside of EMI.

Sessions for *Imagine* would have to wait, however, Lennon and Ono for the moment preoccupied with trying to locate Ono's daughter, Kyoko, who had fallen out of touch in recent months, and who, so far as Ono was concerned, was missing. In an effort to track her down, John and Yoko headed off to France, and then on a tip-off to Spain and on to Majorca, where they located Kyoko, taking her back to their hotel. Her father, Tony Cox, understandably panicked and informed the local police who promptly arrested Lennon and Ono, and for a while, threatened to bring serious kidnapping charges. In the end Ono appeared in the dock in Majorca but nothing came of it and the Lennons understood that if they were ever to be reunited with Kyoko, they would have to file for legal custody. And there the matter was left, at least for now. By the time dust settled on this frantic episode, Power To The People was on its way out of the charts, and Lennon was ready to start his next recording project.

RECORD RELEASES

[120] **Power To The People** / Open Your Box [B-side by Yoko Ono] (UK: 8 Mar 1971)

[120] **Power To The People** / Touch Me [B-side by Yoko Ono] (US: 22 Mar 1971)

Imagine sessions: May 1971

Back at home after his European chase, Lennon was ready to commence work on the follow-up to *John Lennon/Plastic Ono Band*, with what was becoming a regular circle of musicians. So far as new songs were concerned, he had around half a dozen in the frame, and a few more which dated back to the late-Beatles era, now ripe for completion. (As with his previous long player, Ono was due her own set with Lennon's not inconsiderable help, to be released concurrently by Apple as a partner album.) Convened at Ascot on Saturday 22 May, the group was first tasked with helping Lennon get a non-album track recorded, the *Imagine* sessions therefore starting with his latest campaign song.

John Lennon: [122] **GOD SAVE US** (*Lennon, Ono*)
   Produced by John Lennon, Yoko Ono, Phil Spector
   Recorded: 22 May 1971, Ascot Sound Studios, Berkshire; 9 Jun 1971,
      EMI Studios, London
   UK/US: unreleased
   John Lennon: vocals, guitar; **Klaus Voormann**: bass; **Nicky Hopkins**: piano; **Jim Keltner**: drums; **Jim Horn**: Baritone saxophone; **Bobby Keys**: saxophone

A by-product of Lennon's new radicalism, God Save Us was written on 13 April after he was contacted by journalist, Stan Demidjuk, to help raise funds for the Friends of Oz group. *Oz* was a current underground magazine whose editors had landed themselves in court on charges of Conspiracy to Corrupt Public Morals, following the publication of issue 28 in early 1971, which went a step too far with its 'School Kids Issue', the association of children with nudity, profanity and overt sexual content leading the police to raid their offices, a move seen by *Oz* supporters as state censorship.[99]

Deciding the best help would be to release a single, Lennon devised a song and taped a rough demo the same day, under the provisional title, God Save Oz (with dummy lyrics, including the playground line, 'pick your nose and eat it too'). Not wanting to headline, Lennon planned to make a proper recording with a different lead vocalist, a slapdash 'crowd version' consequently taped a few days later with hippie musician, 'Magic' Michael Cousins at the mike, backed up by a crowd of *Oz* supporters and staffers, including an 18-year-old Charles Shaar Murray, who'd helped edit the offending magazine. Unhappy with the results, the recording was scrapped, Lennon resolving to capture another more disciplined version.

Though not released at the time, the new take taped on 22 May was Lennon's own, recorded with his regular team and featuring his vocal track. What he intended to do with it is not known, but when he left the UK on 1 June, the tape sat gathering dust with no realistic prospect that it might be released. To the rescue came Mal Evans, who had recently been advocating for unknown vocalist, Bill Elliott, and had the singer replace Lennon's lead at EMI.[100] With the Elastic Oz Band moniker attached, this revised version hit the

---

[99] Calculated to offend, the title 'School Kids Issue' was a reference to the fact that issue 28 had been edited by a group of teenagers. Among them were a couple of 15-year-old girls, one of them pictured in the magazine in school uniform under the caption, 'Jail Bait of the Month'.

[100] Elliott was member of a group named Half Breed, who Evans had tried to get signed to Apple in 1970. He and bandmate, Bobby Purvis, would break away and form Splinter, who were subsequently signed by Harrison to his Dark Horse label.

shops in July, issued by Apple and with no mention of Lennon except in the label credits.

John Lennon: [123] **DO THE OZ** (*Lennon, Ono*)
   Produced by John Lennon, Yoko Ono, Phil Spector
   Recorded: 22 May 1971, Ascot Sound Studios, Berkshire
   UK/US: unreleased
   John Lennon: vocals, guitar; **Yoko Ono**: vocals; **Klaus Voormann**: bass; **Nicky Hopkins**: electric piano; **Jim Keltner**: drums; **Dave Coxhill**: saxophone; **Geoff Driscoll**: saxophone; **Phil Kenzie**: saxophone

Needing a B-side, the band quickly concocted Do The Oz, a dragging jam on E flat notable for the presence of Ono on backing vocals. Its lyric consists of an invitation to dance, Lennon's directions based on the words of the Hokey Cokey and intended to be performed lying down. Unreleased in his own discography, the recording was put out as an Elastic Oz Band track, as intended. No sooner had the single appeared than Judge Michael Argyle delivered his inevitable guilty verdict in the *Oz* trials, the carefully selected charge of Conspiracy to Corrupt Public Morals carrying a possible life sentence for defendants, Richard Neville, Jim Anderson and Felix Dennis. (In a contemporary pirate radio interview, Lennon described the situation as 'disgusting fascism' and branded Judge Argyle 'an old wanker'.[101]) In the event custodial sentences were imposed but overturned on appeal – not before all three had been incarcerated and had their heads shaved. Ultimately, the legal episode caused a great deal more outrage than *Oz* magazine ever had, plus a blaze of publicity, one effect being that the barely-known title saw its circulation briefly leap to 80,000.

John Lennon: [124] **JEALOUS GUY** (*Lennon*)
   Produced by John Lennon, Yoko Ono, Phil Spector
   Recorded: 24 May 1971; 29 May 1971, Ascot Sound Studios, Berkshire;
      4 Jul 1971, Record Plant, New York
   UK: 8 Oct 1971 (*Imagine* LP)
   US: 7 Sep 1971 (*Imagine* LP)
   John Lennon: vocals, guitar, whistling; **Joey Molland**: guitar; **Tom Evans**: guitar; **Klaus Voormann**: bass; **Jim Keltner**: drums; **Nicky Hopkins**: piano; **John Barham**: harmonium; **the Flux Fiddlers**: strings; **Alan White**: vibraphone; **Mike Pinder**: tambourine

---

[101] Interview broadcast on Radio Free London, 14 July 1971.

Written in the cool mountain air of India in 1968, Lennon's meditative Child Of Nature was inspired by the same Maharishi lecture which gave McCartney the impetus for Mother Nature's Son. When the Beatles got back to England the two songs were demoed at Harrison's bungalow for the *White Album*, but only McCartney's made the cut. Possibly they were deemed too alike to sit comfortably together, but the compositional strengths of Child Of Nature were such that Lennon tried it out again during the *Get Back* rehearsals.

Recorded once more in a clutch of private demos in late 1970, the song was still in its original form, but soon thereafter Lennon transformed it with a new set of lyrics stripping out its scenic imagery and instead confessing his personal fragility. (Traces of the original can be found in the revised text, Lennon still 'dreaming', and admitting he's 'just' the character of the song title.) At first glance the new draft concerns Lennon's relationship with Ono, the vulnerability admitted in the fear of being unloved speaking of Lennon's doubts over the relationship. On the other hand, the generally unromantic mood of the song, not to mention its long memory ('dreaming of the past') more convincingly implies the reference point as McCartney, a reply in kind to the regretful Two Of Us from *Let It Be*. McCartney certainly thought so, claiming in a later interview that Lennon once told him as much.[102]

Sessions for *Imagine* got properly underway on the Monday after the *Oz* recordings, with this reinvented number top of Lennon's agenda. A busy session, there was one too many drummers in the packed Ascot studio, Alan White happening to have a vibraphone outside in his car, which he brought in and set up in the adjoining toilet cubicle as an excuse to play the session. (Mike Pinder had the opposite problem, his Mellotron refusing to work, landing him on tambourine duties.) The result though is anything but cluttered, and after Lennon dubbed a vocal on (with a rare whistled section), he'd created his most openly accessible solo track to date. What remained to be done was a strings overdub, executed in New York on Independence Day by musicians from the New York Philharmonic, affectionately dubbed the Flux Fiddlers by Lennon.

Venturing closer to standard pop than anything Lennon had recorded since the mid-1960s, Jealous Guy set the bar for the coming sessions, only the strength of the album's title track preventing it being selected for a hit single. Immediately after Lennon's death in 1980 a tribute version was issued by British group, Roxy Music, which underlined the song's universal appeal by topping the UK charts, prompting EMI to attempt to cash in with a 45 release of Lennon's original a few years on.

---

[102] *Playgirl*, February 1985: 'He wrote "I'm Just A Jealous Guy" and he said that the song was about me.'

John Lennon: [125] **GIVE ME SOME TRUTH** (*Lennon*)
Produced by John Lennon, Yoko Ono, Phil Spector
Recorded: 25 May 1971; 28 May 1971, Ascot Sound Studios, Berkshire;
    4 Jul 1971, Record Plant, New York
UK: 8 Oct 1971 (*Imagine* LP)
US: 7 Sep 1971 (*Imagine* LP)
John Lennon: vocals, guitar; **George Harrison**: electric slide guitar; **Andy Davis**: guitar; **Rod Lynton**: guitar; **Klaus Voormann**: bass; **Nicky Hopkins**: electric piano; **John Barham**: piano; **Alan White**: drums

In its finished state the provocative Give Me Some Truth hardly seems the product of spiritual transcendence, but since Lennon included it among his Indian compositions in a 1968 list, it was started in that period. The spark for the song may have been Lennon's disillusion with the Maharishi shortly before he walked out of Rishikesh, supported by the fact that when it resurfaced in the 1969 *Get Back* tapes, it was hardly yet developed. As heard among the 3 January recordings, Lennon is uncertain where to take it, reminding McCartney of his own 'hangman bit', presumably an independently written part set to be inserted, which might have brought it towards a co-write had it been pursued.

Since Lennon revisited the song after his discourse with Tariq Ali on 12 February [120], his current politicisation must have inspired him to complete it, so that by the time the *Imagine* sessions started it was ready to record. For the session more musician friends were hovering around Ascot, the recording featuring the usual crew plus guitarists, Rod Lynton and Andy Davis, the latter a member of up-and-coming rock band, Stackridge. Captured in just four takes, the song was then treated to a vocal overdub for its technically tricky lyric, and a suitably fervent slide guitar solo from George Harrison, who joined the resident throng the following day.

What marks Give Me Some Truth as a stand-out number is its bitter, quick-fire delivery in which Lennon lays into all he sees as objectionable, from slippery politicians to insincere journalists and, courtesy of his Ono-inspired enlightenment, male chauvinists. Owing a stylistic debt to Dylan, whose mid-1960s songs were frequently packed with fast-paced lyrics providing rhythm, Give Me Some Truth was ripe for dissection by Lennon 'pseuds' trying to glean specifics from such effusive outpourings.[103] While the phrase Tricky Dicky persuaded American listeners Lennon was making a topical reference to Richard Nixon, his use of the Mother Hubbard appellation was thrown at *all* politicians who claimed to have no funds when public needs were pressing.

---

[103] Dylan precedents include All I Really Want To Do, Subterranean Homesick Blues, It's Alright, Ma (I'm Only Bleeding), etc.

And while 'hypocritics' is a classic *portmanteau* aimed at his and Ono's enemies in the music press, the description of Lennon's adversaries as 'short-haired' illustrates the culture change in Western society during the 1960s; eight years earlier, such an observation on personal style would have come across as neutral or even approving, but in 1971 spoke accusingly of society's 'straights', distrusted for their conformity to obsolete standards.

Lennon later talked of *Imagine* as being a 'sugar-coated' record, its content sweetened for public consumption, but the bile on display in Give Me Some Truth is without parallel in his cannon. Programmed at the start of side 2, Give Me Some Truth proved Lennon, having started to move on from his Primal experiences, had lost none of his edge.

John Lennon: [126] **OH YOKO!** (*Lennon*)
Produced by John Lennon, Yoko Ono, Phil Spector
Recorded: 25 May 1971, Ascot Sound Studios, Berkshire
UK: 8 Oct 1971 (*Imagine* LP)
US: 7 Sep 1971 (*Imagine* LP)
John Lennon: vocals, guitar, harmonica; **Phil Spector**: backing vocals; **Andy Davis**: guitar; **Rod Lynton**: guitar; **Klaus Voormann**: bass; **Nicky Hopkins**: piano; **Alan White**: drums

After Lennon and Ono became a couple they rarely left each other's side, living and working together continuously, a mutual sense of wholeness arising from their being in each other's company. Entirely obsessed, Lennon went so far as to tell the world they were effectively now one person and should be addressed as such, creating for them a fused identity and legally changing his middle name to Ono. (Consumed by the relationship, when Lennon filled out a Q&A sheet for a journalist in 1969, he answered virtually every question with the same word: Q. What is your favourite colour? A. Yoko – and so on.) Such was the couple's single-mindedness that when they began their Primal Therapy, Janov sensed they were dependent on one another and insisted they separate for a few days, the longest they had ever been apart, which Lennon later admitted was a struggle.

It's no surprise then that Lennon elected to commemorate his hour-by-hour devotion in song, Oh Yoko! dating to the very start of their relationship and therefore pre-dating McCartney's equivalent, [18] The Lovely Linda. Video tape of Lennon and Ono in the spring of 1969 shows the song being sung interchangeably as Oh Yoko! and Oh John!, depending who was doing the singing, although there's no dispute that Lennon wrote it. (He mentioned to an *NME* reporter at around that time that he'd written something for Ono, provided she changed the name – no doubt this one.) As love songs go, Oh Yoko! is plainly sincere, avoiding the sweet sentimentality of the typical adoring vignette. Played in a busker's style, with Nicky Hopkins' piano dancing merrily in the background, the recording carries a sense of relaxed enjoyment, prompting Lennon to take his old Beatles harmonica off the shelf for a rare outing. Capped off with vocal harmonies from Phil Spector (billed along with Lennon as 'The J&P Duo'), the track saw out the album on an uplifting note, and was mooted for possible release on 45. Slightly shy about its sentiment, Lennon argued it was too personal for the pop charts, leaving it as one of his most fondly admired album cuts.

John Lennon: [127] **HOW?** (*Lennon*)
Produced by John Lennon, Yoko Ono, Phil Spector
Recorded: 25 May 1971; 29 May 1971, Ascot Sound Studios, Berkshire;
 4 Jul 1971, Record Plant, New York
UK: 8 Oct 1971 (*Imagine* LP)
US: 7 Sep 1971 (*Imagine* LP)
John Lennon: vocals, piano; **Klaus Voormann**: bass; **Nicky Hopkins**: electric piano; **Alan White**: drums; **the Flux Fiddlers**: strings

The third track recorded in an exceptionally productive day, How? dates to the period Lennon spent in California at the Primal Institute [79], and as such is infused with insights gained through therapy. Taken at face value, his series of rhetorical questions makes little sense in the context of Lennon's wealth and fame, and he came under criticism for expressing what were heard as self-pitying woes. But understood through the prism of Primal theory, the lyric's meaning becomes clear, Lennon's remarks converging on his own inability to think and to feel, having been emotionally deprived in early life.

Plucked from the pages of *The Primal Scream*, Lennon's ruminations conform to the experiences of typical Primal patients, 'How can I give love, when love is something I ain't never had?' more or less summarising sections of the book and paraphrasing the way such processes perpetuate from parent to child: '*They* can't give because *they*'ve never been given to.'[104] From such bleak reflections came this delicate piano piece, stuttering uncertainly in its phrasing and tumbling sadly down the scales until, solemnly, Lennon finds his answer: 'Oh no'/'Ono'.

As arranged for *Imagine*, How? displays little of the starkness evident on *John Lennon/Plastic Ono Band*, its mood softened with a sympathetic string overdub which gives it heart. Understated between the headline-making [129] How Do You Sleep? and the jaunty [126] Oh Yoko!, How? is a miniaturised self-portrait, framed in vulnerability and reminding the world that despite the trappings of stardom, Lennon was, at core, an ordinary human.

---

[104] Interview with Tariq Ali, 12 February 1971.

John Lennon: [128] **CRIPPLED INSIDE** (*Lennon*)
  Produced by John Lennon, Yoko Ono, Phil Spector
  Recorded: 26 May 1971, Ascot Sound Studios, Berkshire
  UK: 8 Oct 1971 (*Imagine* LP)
  US: 7 Sep 1971 (*Imagine* LP)
  John Lennon: vocals, guitar; **George Harrison**: dobro; **Ted Turner**: guitar; **Rod Lynton**: guitar; **Klaus Voormann**: upright bass; **Steve Brendell**: upright bass; **Nicky Hopkins**: piano; **Alan White**: drums

This recording marks the arrival of Harrison among the ever-expanding troupe of musicians at Lennon's home studio, also now including Ted Turner of fledgling rock band, Wishbone Ash, and (why not?) a member of Apple's office staff, Steve Brendell, helping out on bass. As if that were not enough, 26 May also saw the addition of a camera crew into the cramped setting, hired to capture proceedings for a possible documentary Lennon had in mind to accompany the eventual album release, having not, apparently, been dissuaded by his experiences with the long and arduous *Let It Be* movie project.

The first task at hand was the recording of Crippled Inside, another song rooted in Lennon's Primal Therapy, and an account of how neurosis inevitably reveals itself. (Janov's theory holds that the outwardly normal individual is often merely presenting a socially acceptable face, attempting to conceal a deep-seated need.) Some listeners took the lyric as an attack on McCartney, and while lines like 'You can comb your hair and look quite cute' may give the idea credence, it is at odds with objectively pitched lyrics such as 'You can judge me by the colour of my skin'.

Recorded in 17 takes, the track is arranged in the informal quasi-rockabilly vein, Harrison's bluesy dobro adding a country mood with Nicky Hopkins' bar-room piano afforded a second solo towards the end. In truth the song's influences are varied, Crippled Inside a melting pot of ideas which owes part of its melody to the vocal scatting previously heard in Dig A Pony. The most obvious borrowing though comes in the song's middle eight, copied straight from Black Dog, a traditional American tune adapted in 1963 by Koerner, Ray And Glover for their US Elektra album, *Lots More Blues, Rags And Hollers* and jammed by the Beatles in January 1969; Lennon's debt is slyly revealed in his lyric, verbal references to cats and dogs giving the game away. Lennon's habitual appropriation of elements of other songs like this was asking for trouble, and he by now had a lawsuit hanging over him courtesy of Big Seven Music Corp, who filed a copyright claim in December 1970 based on a line he'd previously taken from Chuck Berry's You Can't Catch Me – see [236].

Signing off with an ironic music-hall finale, Crippled Inside seems to offer a cheery smile, a wave to the crowd after a winning performance. However the acting metaphor is apt, the apparent optimism a mask for the emotional troubles concealed within, the song reflecting its theme by adopting a false persona.

John Lennon: [129] **HOW DO YOU SLEEP?** (*Lennon*)
Produced by John Lennon, Yoko Ono, Phil Spector
Recorded: 26 May 1971, Ascot Sound Studios, Berkshire; 4 Jul 1971, Record Plant, New York
UK: 8 Oct 1971 (*Imagine* LP)
US: 7 Sep 1971 (*Imagine* LP)
John Lennon: vocals, guitar; **George Harrison**: electric slide guitar; **Klaus Voormann**: bass; **Nicky Hopkins**: electric piano; **Alan White**: drums; **the Flux Fiddlers**: strings

With McCartney's lawsuit having come down vaguely in his favour back in March – or, at least, not having been ruled against – feelings between him and Lennon were at an all-time low, Lennon galled by his failure to emerge as victor. While the dust began to settle through April, the arrival of *RAM* in mid-May re-ignited Lennon's anger through what he saw as a succession of digs against him sprinkled among the lyrics. But while it was true that the opening cut, [107] Too Many People, was aimed at him and Ono, Lennon's enraged state caused him to read far more into the album than was ever intended. [98] The Back Seat Of My Car was singled out for the line, 'We believe that we can't be wrong', [115] Dear Boy was obviously another patronising put-down (in fact it had nothing to do with Lennon, being directed at Linda's former husband), and [94] 3 Legs had to be a comment on the other ex-Beatles, right? Lennon resolved at once to even the score, and nine days after *RAM* was released, was in his studio recording How Do You Sleep?, describing it as a 'reciprocal song' (ie, revenge).[105]

Part of How Do You Sleep?'s spite stems from the fact that Lennon had not composed himself, the lyric being thrown together in the heat of the moment. The song's genesis can be traced to early 1970, when under the working title, Since You Came To Me, Lennon recorded a dummy version with just the opening line in place, the rest blocked out with lyrics from Chuck Berry's Rock And Roll Music.[106] Its conversion into an anti-McCartney tirade was done in 1971 in the studio with Ono and Allen Klein, who had a considerable grudge of his own against McCartney, over his loss of the Beatles'

---

[105] Interview broadcast on WABC Radio, New York, on the day *Imagine* was released.
[106] According to Lennon, 'I started writing it in 1969, and the line, "So Sergeant Pepper took you by surprise..." was written about two years before anything happened.' (Interview published in *Cash Box*, 11 December 1971.)

management role. Egging each other on, Lennon, Klein and Ono gleefully started throwing around lines, greatly amusing themselves while trying to outdo one another with anti-McCartney witticisms. Some of the song's rejected lines were particularly nasty, one of them ridiculing McCartney's 'Little Richard' singing style, dropped for being just too cruel. Another, Lennon's rejoinder to the accusation that McCartney's only decent composition had been Yesterday – 'You probably pinched that anyway' – vetoed by Klein in case he was sued. (The replacement lyric, 'Since you've gone you're just Another Day', was Klein's admittedly droll substitute.)

An unpleasant listen, the song's invective was clearly out of proportion to McCartney's perceived digs on *RAM*, and during its gestation in Ascot Sound, Starr was present and said to be increasingly uncomfortable as each successive line was devised, his appeals to Lennon to pull back falling mostly on deaf ears. Several of the assembled musicians were also uneasy about the track, Lennon having each of them read through the final lyric draft before consenting to play on it. One who appears to have voiced no concerns was George Harrison, who had registered his own resentment in song a year earlier [33], and pitched in with one of his most effective slide guitar solos to date, as if rising to the occasion. (Lennon later praised it as the best Harrison had ever done.) Regardless, his very presence on the recording suffices to confirm his support for Lennon's stance, something he subsequently sought to bluff his way out of with the 'explanation', 'People don't really understand'.[107]

Drawing on the song's opening reference to *Sgt Pepper*, How Do You Sleep? commences with the room's ambient sounds prior to the band starting up. From there it proceeds with a mix so narrow it approximates mono, concentrating its force, arrow-like, in a single direction, only the addition of the late string overdubs widening the sound stage in any appreciable way. When McCartney heard it he must have been dismayed, Harrison's consummate accompaniment on the track rubbing salt into already open wounds. Ever the diplomat, McCartney adopted a philosophical public face, and criticised it in only the mildest terms as 'silly'. Many of the song's criticisms were obviously unfounded, not least its title, McCartney having said and done nothing to lose sleep over. In fact, there are compliments to be gleaned if one deconstructs the accusations, Lennon referencing McCartney's good looks with a tinge of envy and commending him for Yesterday; but none of this will have offered McCartney much comfort at the time.

Following its release the song gained instant notoriety, and when Lennon was feeling more amicable he sought to play down his nastiness, phoning McCartney in apologetic tone in mid-October. He later claimed the song wasn't about McCartney at all, and was autobiographical, which while

---

[107] Interview in *Record Mirror*, 16 October 1971.

superficially of no credence, might contain a germ of truth, Lennon perhaps subconsciously including sentiments which were more applicable to his own situation than his old partner's. (The line, 'Jump when your mama tell you anything' was supposed to imply McCartney was being controlled by Linda, when most observers would cast him in a dominant role. Lennon, on the other hand, was far more under the spell of his wife than McCartney ever was.) Ultimately, Lennon – who had disposed of the Beatles in [86] God, and would subsequently attack Dylan in Serve Yourself – was of a character to set about those he disagreed with in the most disproportionate manner, How Do You Sleep? one of the most overt cases of his going too far and repenting at his leisure. It's to McCartney's lasting credit that he did not respond in kind, the legacy of How Do You Sleep? a black mark on Lennon's reputation far greater than any damage done to his erstwhile colleague's.

John Lennon: [130] **IMAGINE** (*Lennon*)
    Produced by John Lennon, Yoko Ono, Phil Spector
    Recorded: 27 May 1971, Ascot Sound Studios, Berkshire; 4 Jul 1971,
        Record Plant, New York
    UK: 8 Oct 1971 (*Imagine* LP)
    US: 7 Sep 1971 (*Imagine* LP)
    John Lennon: vocals, piano; **Klaus Voormann**: bass; **Alan White**: drums; **the Flux Fiddlers**: strings

Recorded a day after the toxic [129] How Do You Sleep?, Imagine shows the other Lennon, the side posterity prefers to recall. The origins of this signature song are filled with uncertainty, there being several component influences in coalescence. Musically, the C major piano progression is simplistically methodical, reflecting Lennon's lack of prowess on the instrument, the up-down chord change consisting merely of a shift of fingers over to the next available white notes. Ono later described watching Lennon devise the song on his bedroom Steinway early in 1971, but whether consciously or not, the pattern he discovered exactly matches another song: That's My Life (My Love And My Home), co-written and recorded in 1965 by Lennon's father, Alf, and released under the name Freddie Lennon. Although Lennon Jr never mentioned his father's song in the context of Imagine, the progression is so alike that coincidence seems beyond the realms of chance.

So far as the much-quoted lyric goes, Lennon later claimed at least part was inspired by a book on Christian prayer, handed to him by civil rights activist, Dick Gregory. Given his root-and-branch denunciation of religion in [86] God a few months earlier, this would be a curious point of reference but, according to Lennon, motivated him to compose lines concerning a world absent of sacred doctrine, 'Without this my-god-is-bigger-than-your-god thing'. From the known evidence, this part of the lyric came first with the remainder shaped to fit around the same structure.[108]

Notwithstanding these formative elements, Lennon's artistic self was stimulated by Ono's 1964 book, *Grapefruit*, which was reprinted in May 1970 and contained a succession of inspiring propositions such as 'Imagine one thousand suns in the sky at the same time. Let them shine for one hour'. Another of them, 'Imagine the clouds dripping. Dig a hole in your garden to put them in', was reproduced on the back of the *Imagine* album cover, having been penned by Ono in spring 1963, around the time Lennon, unknown to her and three and a half thousand miles away, was recording I'll Get You with its opening line, 'Imagine I'm in love with you'.[109] Years later, Lennon conceded his debt to Ono, as he had with [1] Give Peace A Chance, and her name was eventually appended to the copyright courtesy of the poetry which Lennon rather crudely summed up as series of 'imagine this, imagine that' pieces.

Beyond the song's structural ingredients, the lyrical undercurrent is a softened espousal of Marxist doctrines, later characterised as a musical expression of the *Communist Manifesto*. While the song and the book have little in common, there's no denying that Imagine advocates several positions fundamental to Marxism, from the rejection of church and its associated mysticism, to the dissolution of nation states and the unity of peoples. But while the utopian vision of a world free from war and national boundaries sounds like a quixotic ideal, the lines for which Lennon would be eternally derided come in the final verse, a suggestion of life without possessions.

Picked up by everyone from political opponents to cynical rock journalists for his perceived hypocrisy, Lennon having recorded the song from the opulence of his capacious mansion, the scorn it attracted is misplaced. What Lennon was getting at was not that individuals should surrender their personal belongings, but that ownership of private capital should be devolved to 'the people' – Marxism an attempt to restructure the economy, rather than an individual code of conduct. But however one interprets Lennon's sentiments, the political bedrock of Imagine has been little grasped since its release, the song's dreaming tones diverting from its revolutionary core. Thus, there appeared no contradiction when the song was later endorsed by the

---

[108] Hand-written lyrics are known from April 1971, when Lennon and Ono were in Majorca on the trail of Kyoko Cox. Whereas the second and third verses show corrections and discarded lines ('No-one need even be hungry' / 'It really could be true'), the opening verse is indicated only by the note, 'Imagine there's no heaven etc', implying it was already complete and memorised.

[109] The coincidences continue. Lennon's book of verse, *In His Own Write*, was published in 1964 and contained the poem, *The Fat Budgie*, with its couplet, 'Imagine all the people, laughing till they're sick'.

United Nations (while imagining no countries, one presumes).

That Lennon opted to hold the song back until the *Imagine* sessions were almost finished indicates a reservation over the song's idealistic sentiment, despite a realisation that he'd come up with a classic. Completed in one long daytime session, Lennon initially demoed it for his musicians on upright piano, Phil Spector at once suggesting they try it on the white baby grand which Lennon had purchased as a gift for Ono on her 38th birthday. However the instrument was stuck in their 'white room', where the acoustics proved unworkable, and so they returned to the studio and devised a group arrangement dominated by John Barham's harmonium and Nicky Hopkins' electric keyboard. While the new version benefited from additional melodic touches, it also created an incongruent droning atmosphere and at this point it was decided to revert to a simple, piano-based approach, Alan White having the brainwave that his drums hold off until the second verse, effectively completing the blueprint. Five weeks later it was orchestrated in New York by Torrie Zito along with several other *Imagine* tracks, and Lennon's most celebrated anthem was complete.

An obvious hit-in-waiting, Imagine might have made a bigger splash had Lennon not been reticent about its release. Although it was put out in America, where it reached the top 10, it wasn't issued in Britain, fans having to hear it on LP until 1975 when, finally, it came out as a single in support of the *Shaved Fish* compilation. (It belatedly spent a month at number 1, in the shocking aftermath of Lennon's murder, its exposure helped by the famous video sequence.) In spite of the sometimes critical disdain it has attracted, and the fact that its romantic score tends to subvert the simplicity of its piano-led message, Imagine remains one of the key recordings of its era, frequently listed at the top end of 'best-ever song' polls and voted in a 2001 British television survey, the greatest number 1 single of all time, two places ahead of Hey Jude.

John Lennon: [131] **OH MY LOVE** (*Lennon, Ono*)
Produced by John Lennon, Yoko Ono, Phil Spector
Recorded: 28 May 1971, Ascot Sound Studios, Berkshire
UK: 8 Oct 1971 (*Imagine* LP)
US: 7 Sep 1971 (*Imagine* LP)
John Lennon: vocals, piano; **George Harrison**: guitar; **Klaus Voormann**: bass; **Nicky Hopkins**: electric piano; **Alan White**: tingsha

Not long after John and Yoko became a couple they conceived a baby due in the first part of 1969. Unfortunately Ono was to suffer a miscarriage at the end of November, which left them both heartbroken, and in the traumatic aftermath she composed a moving poem to her lost child which began, 'John, my love, for the first time in my life, my heart is wide open'. In private tapes made by the couple in their Kenwood home, Lennon attempted to set it to music on his acoustic guitar, in the process creating the melody of Oh My Love from its opening lines. Although the song might, in theory, have developed from there into a potential Beatles offering (were it not too personally upsetting) it was apparently taken no further until 1971 when it reappeared with a new set of lyrics.

Having come out the other side of Primal Therapy, Lennon's replacement verses are a lucid depiction of spiritual clarity, his perceptions cleansed and rejuvenated by his experiences.[110] Whether Ono had any input into the reworking is unclear, but the gentle references to wind and sky show at least an influence (compare the lyrics of the Ono-inspired Because), and since her original verse was the starting point, the co-copyright is justified – although Lennon had to explain himself before the credits were formally assigned, on the heels of several songs on *RAM* which had been jointly attributed to Paul and Linda McCartney.

The last of the *Imagine* songs taken into the studio, Oh My Love is an extremely delicate recording, Harrison's softly picked guitar figures flowing into Nicky Hopkins' electric piano and tracking Lennon's vocal with bone-china fragility. The suggested use of a dobro would have cluttered the soundscape, Oh My Love a spell-binding affair, ornamented only by the clear ring of a Buddhist tingsha, a cymbal used in Tibetan prayer. In exercising such restraint, Lennon proves the idiom that less is sometimes more, Oh My Love emerging as one of the most flawless pieces of his career.

With *Imagine* more or less finished, Lennon was aware he'd created a strong album, and at his leisure turned to a series of peripheral projects to accompany the set, making for something of a multi-media package. Among other things he had the album mixed in cutting-edge quadraphonic, and worked alongside Ono on her partner album, *Fly*, to be released around the same time. His chief interest though was the making of a set of short film clips to accompany each track, a prototype for the pop video but on an album scale, an idea the Beatles had toyed with during the early stages of *Sgt Pepper* before losing interest. But in charge of his own destiny, Lennon was able to direct the project to completion, much of the footage shot at Tittenhurst Park and showing such surreal images as he and Ono playing chess on an all-white set (one of her 1970 art exhibits) and at random moments eating the pieces. Another sequence showed Lennon miming to [130] Imagine on Ono's white baby grand.

---

[110] His description of his post-Primal senses awakening corresponds with other patient reports, for example, 'Everything is sharp and clear now. I'm smelling smells I never knew existed... colours have come alive for me' (Janov, p166).

What still needed to be done was overdubbing of strings and brass, undertaken at Record Plant while the Lennons were in New York. By now they were flitting back and forth across the Atlantic with frequency, staying in hotels with Lennon depending on a never-ending series of temporary visas, his 1968 drugs conviction preventing him from taking up longer term residency. But this time his visit would prove decisive; staying in Manhattan's bohemian quarter, Greenwich Village, in the space of one week the Lennons consorted with a succession of influential figures which would pull them in permanently. Lennon was quickly introduced to countercultural political activist, Abbie Hoffman, founder of the Yippie movement, and his colleague, Jerry Rubin, and around the same time came across hippie street musician, David Peel, whose provocative political songs and open advocacy of marijuana appealed to the rebel in Lennon. Then on 6 June, he found himself on stage with Frank Zappa at New York's Fillmore East venue on Second Avenue, for an impromptu half-hour session which was recorded and later packaged as bonus material with *Some Time In New York City*. Little wonder Lennon felt he'd discovered a home-from-home, hanging out with like-minded creatives like Zappa and Andy Warhol, the pull of Greenwich Village irresistible after the sedate surroundings of Tittenhurst Park.

Imagine landed in America on 7 September, housed in a sleeve shot by Ono, depicting Lennon with clouds drifting across his mind. (The original idea of placing clouds in just his eyes came out somewhat macabre.) Underlining the bad blood between him and McCartney [129], Lennon deviously included a photograph of himself grappling with a pig, shot during the making of the *Imagine* movie sequences, and openly ridiculing the cover of *RAM*. (Due to legal quibbles over the album credits, there was a delay with the British release which arrived a month late, by which time it had already been certified Gold in the States.)

The record was received with enthusiasm in the music press, gradually earning its status as one of the great albums of its era. Reviewing *Imagine* in the week of its US release, *Billboard* declared Lennon a British Bob Dylan, its mixture of politics, poetry and guile winning over audiences with its assured production, more accessible than *John Lennon/Plastic Ono Band* and for most, head and shoulders above *RAM*. Its sequence of ten songs shows Lennon at his most creative, strong on melody where *Plastic Ono Band* had been abrasive, warm where its predecessor had been stark. Partly this was the result of Lennon having widened out his circle, musicians of the calibre of King Curtis and Badfinger joining the fold alongside 50 percent of the Beatles, making for a team effort which would shine through the ensuing years. Yet beneath its surface, *Imagine* has moments as deeply cutting as any Lennon album, from the angry [125] Give Me Some Truth to the searing [121] I Don't Want to Be a Soldier, and in [129] How Do You Sleep?, one of his most biting texts. Lennon being Lennon, his sharp character tended to be tolerated as one aspect of his overall personal magnetism, respected as much for his outspokenness as for his commitment to honesty. In this respect Lennon was right to point out that *Imagine* was simply *Plastic Ono Band* with sugar on top ('for conservatives'), while the album topped the popular charts around the world. As it turned out, it would be the only set he ever recorded at Ascot Sound Studios, and his last in England. Lennon and Ono, from here, would head Stateside for good.

RECORD RELEASES

Imagine
 (UK: 8 Oct 1971, US: 7 Sep 1971)
 [130] Imagine / [128] Crippled Inside / [124] Jealous Guy / [117] It's So Hard / [121] I Don't Want To Be A Soldier / [125] Give Me Some Truth / [131] Oh My Love / [129] How Do You Sleep? / [127] How? / [126] Oh Yoko!

[130] **Imagine** / [117] **It's So Hard**
 (US: 11 Oct 1971)

PART 2: REALLY THE BORDERLINE

'I don't care if people don't like it...'

Paul McCartney, 7 December 1971

Wild Life sessions:
July 1971

The critical pasting given to *RAM* left McCartney somewhat despondent over mid-1971, both of his post-Beatles albums having now drawn flak from the music press, belying their commercial success. *RAM* had been a turning point in that McCartney had worked at length with a team of non-Beatle musicians for the first time, suggesting his future might lie with the creation of a permanent band – which would give him fresh impetus, besides also supporting his argument that the Beatles, and their contractual bonds, were obsolete. The idea was not without qualification; absorbing himself into a collective was in some ways retrograde, running the risk his credibility might be diluted next to the independence of Lennon and Harrison, besides which he'd be bucking a popular trend for individual singer-songwriters, several of whom rose to prominence in the late 1960s and opening part of the 1970s.[111]

What swung it was McCartney's dream of performing live again, the idea hinging on a vague plan to relive his Quarry Men days, starting from scratch, playing the halls, then gradually working his way up to become world-beating. The problem was, without wishing to recruit any star names to the group he was relying on unknowns with little hope that he'd stumble across anyone with a fraction of the musical nous or stage presence of a Lennon or a Harrison. His first thoughts turned to the little-noted session men he'd employed on *RAM*, Hugh McCracken and Denny Seiwell, and although McCracken declined the offer, Seiwell was a provisional 'yes'. But the key recruit turned out to be Denny Laine, known to McCartney since mid-1963 when his first band, Denny and the Diplomats, had appeared on the same bill as the Beatles. One more role needed to be filled, someone to handle keyboards, and for this assignment McCartney looked no further than Linda, inexperienced though she was, and unsure she could handle the brief.

The idea of starting a band from scratch had a romantic appeal, but was at odds with the reality of life for a long-famous pop star approaching 30. For one thing, Linda was heavily pregnant with Stella, and besides McCartney needing to be constantly at her side, new bandmates Laine and Seiwell were without any income stream, forcing McCartney to employ them on a £70 weekly wage. Nonetheless, an enthusiastic McCartney rehearsed them all in one of his farm outbuildings, then promptly booked them into EMI the following Saturday to record their first album – an echo of events in 1963, when the Beatles had done

---

[111] Leading the way were Neil Young, Neil Diamond, Don McLean, Elton John, Leonard Cohen, Gilbert O'Sullivan, Van Morrison, etc. Another, James Taylor, had his career break on Apple Records in 1968, with McCartney's help.

the same at a similarly frantic pace. Reflecting the McCartneys' rustic existence, simplicity was the order of the day, the group afforded none of the familiar show-biz trappings, and put to work immediately with all the spontaneity that would engender – rough features included.[112] In truth, McCartney's haste had got the better of him, this fledgling outfit having at most a few days to make an entire LP, with only half a dozen songs available. Regardless, for the first time since 1957, McCartney had himself a new band – and for him, they were on their way to the toppermost.

Wings: [132] **BIP BOP** (*McCartney, McCartney*)
Produced by Paul McCartney, Linda McCartney
Recorded: 24 Jul 1971; 2 Oct 1971, EMI Studios, London
UK/US: 7 Dec 1971 (*Wild Life* LP)
Paul McCartney: vocals, guitar, bass; **Linda McCartney**: vocals, percussion; **Denny Laine**: guitar; **Denny Seiwell**: drums, percussion

The first thing recorded for *Wild Life*, the much maligned Bip Bop started as a casual riff found by playing around on the bottom string of an acoustic, to which McCartney added semi-meaningless vocal sounds to entertain his daughter, Mary, coming up to her second birthday. Halfway between a blues lick and a nursery rhyme, but effective as neither, Bip Bop is as bereft of meaning as anything McCartney ever released, one of the clangers of his career. Apparently pleased with it, he also taped a brief solo guitar rendition which was dropped discreetly between [134] I Am Your Singer and [137] Tomorrow as a link track, although in the years since, he has effectively disowned the song.

Wings: [133] **LOVE IS STRANGE** (*Baker, Smith*)
Produced by Paul McCartney, Linda McCartney
Recorded: 24 Jul 1971; 3 Oct 1971, EMI Studios, London
UK/US: 7 Dec 1971 (*Wild Life* LP)
Paul McCartney: vocals, bass; **Linda McCartney**: vocals, keyboards; **Denny Laine**: guitar, backing vocals; **Denny Seiwell**: drums, percussion

With little of substance to work with, the band naturally relaxed by jamming their way through this opening session. One of their efforts was recorded: a five-minute run around a chord pattern familiar from Buddy Holly's Words Of Love. Performed in a loose reggae style, the influence here is from Linda, who'd awakened McCartney's interest in the genre by playing him some of her

---

[112] The rehearsal space was a converted barn christened Rude Studio, 'rude' in this sense meaning rudimentary.

records in Scotland. Not initially sure what he had, McCartney named the instrumental Half Past Ten until he noticed a similarity to Love Is Strange, an old Bo Diddley number copyrighted in his wife's name, Ethel Smith, and recorded by US R&B act, Mickey & Sylvia in 1956.[113]

During early October, Paul, Linda and Laine added their vocals, arranged as a three-part harmony which comes out curiously flat, despite McCartney's efforts to inject some excitement. Stylistically out of kilter with the rest of the material, Love Is Strange was nominated as a stand-alone single, for which an edit was prepared and a catalogue number assigned, only to be scrapped at the 11th hour. With *Wild Life* chronically short of songs, it ended up there instead, McCartney's first non-original since *Help!*.

Wings: [134] **I AM YOUR SINGER** (*McCartney, McCartney*)
Produced by Paul McCartney, Linda McCartney
Recorded: 24 Jul 1971; 29 Jul 1971, EMI Studios, London
UK/US: 7 Dec 1971 (*Wild Life* LP)
Paul McCartney: vocals, bass, electric piano, recorders (?); **Linda McCartney**: keyboards, vocals; **Denny Laine**: guitar; **Denny Seiwell**: drums, percussion

The first full vocal duet between Paul and Linda, I Am Your Singer reads as if written especially for the occasion. In fact it dates to the pre-*RAM* era, noted among a list of unheard demos McCartney recorded in 1970, long before he decided to form a group with her – if conceived for two voices, it precedes their decision to record together.

A sparse arrangement relying on Seiwell's thumping bass drum and Laine's heavily reverbed guitar, I Am Your Singer is sketchily performed, as if the group has not yet fully worked it through – a quality not helped by McCartney's decision to release a rough mix prepared by studio engineer, Alan Parsons. Appealing nonetheless for its bluff air of homeliness, the song features an inventive musical structure, its main chord run nudging downwards in semitones in search of its home E. With a ranging melody positioned over the top, the song was a challenge for the novice in Linda, which she makes a fair attempt at, her often derided solo sections mechanical next to McCartney's but finding all the right notes and meshing endearingly with her husband's in the song's bridges. In a throwback to The Fool On The Hill, McCartney dubbed on a recorder solo where the guitar break would normally sit, Denny Laine presumably wondering what he was brought into

---

[113] The song was originally copyrighted to Smith alone. The UK edition of *Wild Life* gave the credit as Baker-Smith, while the US edition gave Smith-Baker-Robinson. (Baker and Robinson are the respective surnames of Mickey & Sylvia.)

the band for. When Wings took the song on tour in 1972, McCartney handled the lead vocal alone, Linda perched behind her electric keyboard shaking a pair of maracas.

Wings: [135] **DEAR FRIEND** (*McCartney, McCartney*)
Produced by Paul McCartney, Linda McCartney
Recorded: 24 Jul 1971; 16 Oct 1971, EMI Studios, London
UK/US: 7 Dec 1971 (*Wild Life* LP)
Paul McCartney: vocals, bass, piano, vibraphone; **Denny Seiwell**: drums

Of the material lined up for this first day's work on *Wild Life*, the main event was Dear Friend, by far the most personal song McCartney had available, and one he opted to record almost alone. In the context of his musical sparring with Lennon ([107]; [129]) it's easy to read this rueful statement as an olive branch after the acrimony of the past 18 months. Indeed, in his later years the revisionist in McCartney sought to paint it as just such a gesture, 'after John had slagged me off in public... I wrote Dear Friend, saying, in effect, let's lay the guns down'.[114] But the facts do not bear him out: Dear Friend was written in 1970, long before their antagonisms spilled into the open, and was recorded for *Wild Life* six weeks before McCartney heard [129] How Do You Sleep? on the *Imagine* album.[115]

With Lennon nonetheless in his thoughts, McCartney's song is reflective, pitched in a regretful minor key and in mood and intent, a meaningful comparison can be made with [124] Jealous Guy, which McCartney was about to hear as a confessional from his former partner. In any case, that McCartney was by now over his post-Beatles resentment is revealed by his choice of arranger, the same Richard Hewson who had scored The Long And Winding Road a little over a year earlier, at the behest of Phil Spector and Allen Klein. Booked for an orchestral overdub on 16 October, Hewson was detailed to make the strings on Dear Friend sound distant and low-key, McCartney perhaps holding some residual fears that he might have a repeat overblown arrangement on his hands.

In McCartney's prevailing style, the lyrics of Dear Friend are cryptic and indirect, the rhetorical enquiry, 'what's the time?' having no point on literal terms. Yet there's no doubting the emotion in the heart of the song, its echoing

---

[114] Quote from an interview by Mark Lewisohn published in McCartney's official fan magazine, *Club Sandwich*, Winter 1994.
[115] McCartney did consider writing a 'reply' to [129] How Do You Sleep?, getting only as far as a title: Quite Well, Thank You. Another song, the up-tempo Best Friend, was a feature of Wings' live act in 1972, but was never taken into the studio, so far as is known. It's likely unrelated, though often linked to Dear Friend through its title.

musical suspensions sombre and portentous, its constantly falling piano figures yearning for resolution. McCartney has admitted an emotional reaction to hearing it played back, its close association with his old comrade in the years since Lennon's murder adding a further dimension to its depiction of personal loss. Lennon never remarked on the track, perhaps embarrassed by it, but it's significant that after throwing messages back and forth on their records, this was the last time McCartney and he communicated with each other in such a manner.

Wings: [136] **SOME PEOPLE NEVER KNOW** (*McCartney, McCartney*)
Produced by Paul McCartney, Linda McCartney
Recorded: 25 Jul 1971, EMI Studios, London
UK/US: 7 Dec 1971 (*Wild Life* LP)
Paul McCartney: vocals, guitar, bass, piano, percussion; **Linda McCartney**: backing vocals, keyboards; **Denny Laine**: guitar, backing vocals; **Denny Seiwell**: drums, percussion

Its opening chords based on a guitar technique in which a standard A major is modified with hammer-ons, Some People Never Know refutes the often touted idea that *Wild Life* was thrown together carelessly, its multi-instrumental arrangement and intuitive musical sequence one of the most interesting of McCartney's early catalogue. Developing from its initial riff, the song switches to E, from where it proceeds to fall bar-on-bar down the scales to land back to where it started, the progression followed along by McCartney's vocal line, holding each chord's root note for the entire run. Behind him is Linda, tracking his every step in parallel thirds, a subtle addition which disguises the song's methodical foundation, making Some People Never Know the most cleverly crafted on the album.

Like several tracks on *Wild Life*, the song was written the year before in the undercurrent of the Beatles' split, which may have informed some of its lyrics, particularly the outspoken middle eight in which McCartney opines on rights and wrongs. Released next to [135] Dear Friend, the song's subtext has been overlooked but one wonders if Lennon picked up on these lines, having previously read a personal message into the similarly worded 'we believe that we can't be wrong' in [98] The Back Seat Of My Car. If this part of the lyric does concern Lennon it is, like Dear Friend, passive in tone ('I know I was wrong'), evidence that McCartney, while not shy of fighting his corner when he needed to, wanted reconciliation with Lennon all along.

The basic track was laid down in a single take, which was subsequently indulged with an array of additional instrumentation including harmonium, presumably played by Linda. It's not known how percussion duties were divided out, but among several novel ingredients was the guiro, a hollow wooden bulb with grooves cut into its surface to be rasped with a stick, audible in the closing section. A final touch from Seiwell is the 'whirly tube' which McCartney is said to have found in a shop on Oxford Street, consisting of a plastic pipe swung in the air to produce a whistling sound, which abruptly changes pitch when a certain velocity is reached.

Resourceful as it is, Some People Never Know was in truth a four-minute song, deliberately extended to take up six and a half with a shift into a faux-instrumental passage in which McCartney's voice is mixed down, to remain just audible behind the banked backing vocals. He knew that in *Wild Life* he was short of songs, resorting to such tricks to stretch out the material, but Some People Never Know remains a highlight of the album.

Wings: [137] **TOMORROW** (*McCartney, McCartney*)
Produced by Paul McCartney, Linda McCartney
Recorded: 26 Jul 1971, EMI Studios, London
UK/US: 7 Dec 1971 (*Wild Life* LP)
Paul McCartney: vocals, guitar, piano; **Linda McCartney**: backing vocals;
Denny Laine: backing vocals, bass; **Denny Seiwell**: drums

On the Monday, two days after work on *Wild Life* began, McCartney and the group wrapped up their final recordings. For a band which had never worked together, carrying a keyboard player who'd never even been in a group, the results were encouraging, their collective sound noticeably improving as the sessions went by. It's a pity proceedings came to a finish when they did, this day's work the best yet; had they continued in the same vein, they would undoubtedly have generated a strong debut.

Composed in 1970 and demoed before *RAM* was recorded, Tomorrow was written with a plan in mind, musically as well as thematically holding a mirror to Yesterday. Whereas McCartney's 1965 classic had dwelt on the pain of a lost love, Tomorrow looks positively at a found one, McCartney's vision of sitting in the countryside with his girl an idealised depiction of life with Linda. For a chord sequence, allowing for the transposition to D, Tomorrow employs the same progression as Yesterday throughout its first line, switching to the relative minor of Yesterday's major in the second – the same idea but used to radically different effect such that the correspondence is virtually unnoticeable.

According to Denny Seiwell, pianist on the track was McCartney himself, Denny Laine taking over on bass. That being the case, McCartney's guitar must have been overdubbed subsequently, defining the tumbling run down to the song's middle eight against the album's most beguiling three-part harmony section. The whole thing rounded off with the indulgence of an extended coda in 6/8, *this* is what McCartney's new group could achieve when they were on their game, the song earning grudging admiration even from

Wild Life's most vocal critics. (McCartney later referred to it as a song 'only freaks or connoisseurs know'.[116])

Wings: [138] **MUMBO** (*McCartney, McCartney*)
Produced by Paul McCartney, Linda McCartney
Recorded: 26 Jul 1971; 2 Oct 1971, EMI Studios, London
UK/US: 7 Dec 1971 (*Wild Life* LP)
Paul McCartney: vocals, bass; **Linda McCartney**: keyboards; **Denny Laine**: guitar; **Denny Seiwell**: drums, tambourine (?)

Another studio jam [133], Mumbo started as an instrumental when, after around five minutes, the group locked into a solid groove which engineer, Tony Clark, decided was worth capturing – hitting the record button just as McCartney called out to him to do just that (hence the ungainly tape glitch which starts the album). Getting into the moment, McCartney's 'vocal' consists of a spontaneous dummy lyrics, a technique used to facilitate subsequent writing by exploring the sound of suggested words. That he didn't finish it, and served up his garbled phrases on the final album, was a decision for which he would forever be condemned.

McCartney sought to save face by claiming to enjoy its 'wackiness', comparing it to the much-travelled Louie Louie, but in truth it was a lazy effort. As he'd done with [132] Bip Bop, McCartney went back to the studio alone and recorded a brief second version running less than a minute, which he positioned anonymously after the album's final track, and which cuts off with an ugly tape edit, ending the record where it began.

Wings: [139] **WILD LIFE** (*McCartney, McCartney*)
Produced by Paul McCartney, Linda McCartney
Recorded: 26 Jul 1971, EMI Studios, London
UK/US: 7 Dec 1971 (*Wild Life* LP)
Paul McCartney: vocals, guitar, bass; **Linda McCartney**: backing vocals, keyboards; **Denny Laine**: backing vocals, guitar; **Denny Seiwell**: backing vocals, drums

McCartney found himself at a loose end in November 1966, travelling around France and Spain for a period before deciding on a whim to fly to Kenya with Mal Evans for a safari trip. There he toured Amboseli Game Reserve, a national park in the shadow of Mount Kilimanjaro, where elephants roam and visitors are kept under instruction not to interfere with them and to allow them priority over motor vehicles. Accordingly, McCartney noticed signs stating,

---

[116] *Rolling Stone*, 31 January 1974.

'Animals have the right of way', which struck him for its implied meaning, placing nature above transitory human wants. Although there's no evidence he came back and wrote a song about it in 1966, the thought stuck with him so that by 1971, it gave rise to this title track.[117]

Commencing with a prelude seeming to set it in the key of C, the song unexpectedly lands on the minor chord, the start of an unrelenting and unresolved cycle to F major and back. Set to a waltz timing in 6/8, Wild Life makes a foundation of Linda's time-keeping keyboard, on which the rest of the instrumentation is hung. More virtuosic is McCartney's sharply angular lead guitar, darting between and under the vocals, and adding to the song's sense of urgency – reflecting the issue it purports to represent. (McCartney claimed Wild Life was the first song he'd done which was 'saying something', a message to the world.)

If the vocal track is any measure of his sincerity, McCartney was fully engaged, his performance potent and committed, ranging through octave steps and pregnant with anguish until at 4:22 he almost loses control. (Musicologist, Adrian Allan, describes a technique of 'word-painting', drawing attention to the pushed delivery of 'hard' (at 1:37), and the abrupt block at the word 'stop' (2:45), McCartney illustrating language in sounds.) How much of this drama comes from true emotion is open to debate; for a song supposedly addressing a question close to his heart, it's odd that he should choose to make a joke of it ('aminals'), and he can be heard chuckling at 1:28, as if momentarily slipping out of character. Either way, the track – all six and a half minutes of if – is the work of a band exploring its possibilities, and a recording with which McCartney was justifiably pleased.

McCartney's sense of optimism over his new group was promptly deflated when the album received its first reviews. Received with even more derision than *RAM*, the LP drew some brutal notices which in no small way undermined its commercial potential, one notorious assessment declaring McCartney a 'spent force', the album consisting of 'third-rate suburban pop'. *NME* judged his music to be 'at a absolute nadir', while the esteemed *Rolling Stone* called the album 'vacuous, flaccid, impotent, trivial and unaffecting'. What, one might ponder, had McCartney done to deserve *this*? Asked for a reaction in mid-December, he put on a philosophical face, describing hostile reviews as 'a headache of your business career' – but in truth, he was

---

[117] *Revolver*'s suggested title, *Beatles On Safari*, was mooted long before McCartney's trip. There was, however, one benefit to the group: on the flight home, McCartney conceived the idea for *Sgt Pepper's Lonely Hearts Club Band*.

hurting.[118] To add to his woes he now had a lawsuit to deal with, Northern Songs and their US counterpart, Maclen Music, suing for $1 million over the writing credits on [92] Another Day, the same attribution which had just been applied to all the original tracks on *Wild Life*. (Linda's publishing was now being handled by Kidney Punch Music, a pointedly named company set up as part of MPL.)

Some of the less vindictive reviewers speculated that McCartney had released a rough and ready album for effect, and there was some truth in this. McCartney was committed all along to a no-frills approach, *Wild Life* intended as an honest first effort for an unknown outfit – their equivalent of *Please Please Me*. In the event it came out more akin to Glyn Johns' unreleased *Get Back*, a quasi-live studio set roughly recorded and dubiously edited; *Wild Life*, with its style changes and air of improvisation, sounds like a session bootleg. The fact is, McCartney had blundered in making an album so impatiently, the group under-rehearsed and forced to stretch an insufficient stock of songs across two long sides, a liberty not even imaginative sequencing would disguise. (Side 1 was hopefully programmed to showcase danceable tracks, side 2 smoochy ballads.) But the principle reason for its poor reception was the choice of opening tracks, one of the worst such examples in music history. Hampered by a paucity of viable options, there was little alternative but to use the made-up [138] Mumbo at the start, so it wouldn't collapse the sequence of proper songs, but following it with the frivolous [132] Bip Bop running into the golden oldie which was [133] Love Is Strange, most listeners were alienated before they'd got through half a side.

Those who stuck with it were rewarded with a succession of admirable tracks, side 2 one of the most consistent sequences of McCartney's solo career. Had he waited, and recorded another three or four tracks in the same vein, he might have come up with a modest classic. History shows the record was given all too few fair hearings, and it remains the most reflexively trashed album McCartney ever released. When reissued in the 1980s, it appeared on EMI's budget imprint, Fame, the equivalent of tossing it into the bargain bins. Seldom has a pop album with several genuine highlights suffered such unrelenting dismissal.

---

[118] Interview for WCBS of New York, 15 December 1971.

RECORD RELEASES

Wild Life
   (UK/US: 7 Dec 1971)
   [138] Mumbo / [132] Bip Bop / [133] Love Is Strange / [139] Wild Life /
   [136] Some People Never Know / [134] I Am Your Singer / [137] Tomorrow
   / [135] Dear Friend

Four singles: July 1971 to February 1972

Mid-1971 was time of varying fortunes for the individual Beatles. While Lennon recorded an album widely seen as his best ever, McCartney had one about to be greeted as his worst; Harrison and Starr meantime had no albums in the offing at all, each busy with other projects. Instead, fans were offered a run of variable non-album singles, one from each ex-Beatle, and all in the form of campaigns for one thing or another.

A week after the *Wild Life* sessions McCartney announced to the media that he'd formed a band, but the news came at an awkward time, Linda about to give birth to Stella, leaving the couple – and the group – away from the public eye for a while. In September Linda was admitted to King's College Hospital in inner-London, requiring an emergency Caesarean, McCartney waiting outside the theatre and praying she'd come through. And there, sitting on the floor of the hospital corridor, he had a momentary vision of a winged angel, just as Stella was being born on 13 September.

It was not until October that the *Wild Life* tapes were finally attended, mixed and overdubbed for release. Then there was the matter of what to call the band; one fan wrote to McCartney suggesting the Dazzlers, while Turpentine was another close contender. But remembering his experience outside the operating theatre in September, McCartney came up with Wings of Angels – before settling on just Wings. The band was officially launched with a Monday-night bash at the Empire Ballroom in London's Leicester Square, *Melody Maker* gleefully covering the star-studded event and carrying a photo of the group on its front cover. Next on McCartney's agenda was to take Wings out on the road.

Lennon's trajectory was markedly different in the second part of the year. Their private life still dominated by the quest to locate and win custody of Ono's daughter, Kyoko, much of the Lennons' summer was taken up by the chase, and a succession of court hearings which took them as far as the US Virgin Islands. Awarded legal custody in August, Ono was still not reunited with Kyoko by the time Tony Cox persuaded a Texas judge to assert his court's precedence over the Virgin Islands court, and grant him permanent custody instead. The Lennons were not present for the decisive ruling, and although endless further hearings and judgments took place through 1972, the cause was lost and Ono would not see her daughter again until she was grown.

When Lennon set off for New York on 12 August, he didn't realise he would never set foot in Britain again. Taking up rooms near the top of Manhattan's 20-storey St Regis Hotel, Lennon became a permanent US resident, despite the fact that he was, at that point, on one more temporary visa, good only until 30 November. Meantime, in an echo of McCartney's move, Lennon was plotting the start of a new band – Jim Keltner, Klaus Voormann, Nicky Hopkins, Phil Spector (on rhythm guitar!) and Eric Clapton, if he would agree, all lined up to join John and Yoko for a December world tour.[119] That it never came to pass was partly down to Lennon not having a clear idea of where his future lie, his eventual meeting with local rockers, Elephant's Memory, negating any need for Keltner, Voormann *et al*, but also cementing him in the New York scene.

As for Starr, his early attempts at forging a solo recording career were by now receding into the past, although the long-awaited release of [14] It Don't Come Easy in April reminded fans he was still around. He and Maureen had celebrated the birth of their third child, Lee, in November 1970, contributing to Starr's temporary withdrawal from public life, while his interests focused increasingly on his interior design business. Having started up in 1969, he and partner Robin Cruikshank were making a stir with their imaginative and expensive seats, shelving units and hi-fi stands, their celebrated Rolls Royce coffee table, constructed from two radiator grills joined by a stainless steel panel, one of Starr's ideas. Commissioned to design disco interiors for Cunard, and receiving a prestigious exhibit at Liberty's, Robin Ltd was renamed Ringo Or Robin Ltd – ROR for short – and put itself well and truly on the map by the end of 1971, grabbing the attention of London's rich and trendy.

Successful though the business was, Starr was at heart a performer. With a dearth of recording projects on the go and looking to get his acting career back on track, he accepted roles in a couple of unusual new films. The first, the now forgotten *200 Motels*, was a surrealist Frank Zappa-Tony Palmer vehicle centred on the libidinous adventures of a touring rock band with all the madness which surrounds it, Starr cast as Larry the Dwarf, who is somehow, simultaneously, also Zappa. (Much of the script seems to have been made up as they went.) The other was the odd but somewhat more viable *Blindman*, a spaghetti western shot in Spain, casting Starr as a Mexican bandit in his most

---

[119] Lennon outlined his plans in an interview with David Wigg for BBC Radio 1, 25 October 1971.

impressive role yet, and it was this project which drew him back to the recording studio in August.[120]

Harrison's life through 1971 had been on a relatively even keel, and although he'd released no new music since *All Things Must Pass*, he was busy in the studio nonetheless, working on a succession of recording projects friends and colleagues. Besides playing half of Lennon's *Imagine*, and helping Ronnie Spector with her planned comeback [116], he hadn't forgotten his pal, Billy Preston, pitching in with guitar on his new album, *I Wrote A Simple Song*. Another project he committed to was production of Badfinger's third album, *Straight Up*. The Apple group had never made the breakthrough their talents promised, and when their latest recordings were blocked from release by Klein, Harrison stepped up to salvage them. But only a few songs in, he was also pulled away, production reins passing instead to Todd Rundgren.

What drew Harrison was the humanitarian disaster unfolding in Bangladesh. Embroiled in a savage war with the western region of Pakistan, the fledgling state of Bangladesh in the east was fighting for its survival, literally millions of people displaced and mostly fleeing across the border into India, where woefully inadequate resources could not sustain them. Ravi Shankar, born in what was now the Bangladesh region and with members of his own family caught up in events, showed Harrison some of the emerging news reports, and put forward the idea of staging a concert to raise money for assistance.

George Harrison: [140] **BANGLA-DESH** (*Harrison*)
  Produced by George Harrison, Phil Spector
  Recorded: 4 Jul 1971 (?), 5 Jul 1971 (?), 10 Jul 1971 (?), Record Plant,
    Los Angeles
  UK: 30 Jul 1971 (single A-side)
  US: 28 Jul 1971 (single A-side)
  George Harrison: vocals, guitar; **Klaus Voormann**: bass; **Billy Preston**: keyboards; **Leon Russell**: piano; **Ringo Starr**: drums; **Jim Keltner**: drums; **Jim Horn**: saxophones[121]

When Harrison was alerted to the Bangladesh crisis he happened to be in LA working on Shankar's Apple-sponsored documentary, *Raga*. Initially uncertain

---

[120] One of the producers of *Blindman* was Allen Klein. Starr's character was named Candy, unrelated to his earlier film, *Candy*, which was a vaguely psychedelic comedy.
[121] The session was done in a hurry and there is no definitive list of who plays. Simon Leng gives this line-up but Madinger and Easter suggest Eric Clapton and Bobby Keys may have also been involved. The recording date too may not be accurate, but if wrong, is very close.

how to organise a star concert, they began by getting a list of names to persuade to turn out for free. The notion of pop stars playing purely for charity was not new, Shankar having himself appeared for free at the 1967 Monterey Pop Festival alongside Jefferson Airplane, the Who, the Grateful Dead, Jimi Hendrix, Otis Redding and others, but in 1971 such a venture was still novel and needed to be thought through. Harrison and Shankar immediately put themselves on the performers' list and decided meantime to release a single each to raise more money. (This too was innovative, if not unprecedented; Lennon's recent [122] God Save Us was about to appear in aid of the *Oz* campaign, but so far as charity goes, these two discs are recognised as the first of their kind.)

Shankar's effort, a three-track EP titled *Joi Bangla* ('Victory To Bengal'), was swiftly produced by Harrison and issued on Apple. Harrison's own effort was sketched out 'in 10 minutes' and taken into the studio to be licked into shape by a troupe of musicians, a couple of whom – Jim Horn and Jim Keltner – would become regulars on his future sessions. (Thus, Harrison's first full recording Stateside took place at Record Plant's Los Angeles studio, informally Record Plant West, while a few days prior Lennon had done the *Imagine* overdubs at Record Plant East, New York.) Of necessity prepared in haste, the song's up-beat pop style sat awkwardly with the seriousness of the issue at hand, Leon Russell offering the wise idea that it should start in a more sensitive tone, something Harrison obliged with a sombre introductory section recapping the circumstances.

As a piece of music, Bangla-Desh is lyrically to-the-point but melodically dour, its main interest one of Harrison's characteristically assertive chord switches ('I've never *seen* such distress'). The principle musicality comes from a couple of Harrison's new boys, Horn's saxophone sections and Russell's restless piano effectively leading the band. Measuring any such virtuosity is to miss the point though, this recording a practical move to publicise both the issue and the forthcoming concert, rather than to create a memorable pop tune.

The event was staged at Madison Square Garden on 1 August, initial ticket sales so overwhelming that a second show was promptly scheduled for earlier the same day. Billed ambiguously as featuring Harrison 'And Friends', it was never certain in advance who would appear – big-name invite, Bob Dylan, unconfirmed literally until the moment he stepped onto the stage. Staff and equipment from Record Plant were dispatched to make recordings for a subsequent album edition, the show also filmed for lucrative cinema release.

Wowing the stage that day were Dylan, Billy Preston, Eric Clapton, members of Badfinger and several other artists, all drawn from Harrison's current circle. One familiar face was Starr, who had his moment in the spotlight, but conspicuous by their absence were Lennon and McCartney, both of whom had been rumoured as surprise guests. Harrison did invite them both, Lennon reputedly 50/50 on whether to attend, but in the end too preoccupied with the ongoing hunt for Kyoko, and, if some of the accounts are accurate, rowing with Harrison over whether Yoko could join him on stage. McCartney on the other hand demurred on the basis that such an appearance would have generated unwanted and distracting headlines about the group coming back together.[122] Ironically, Harrison was almost a no-show himself, his plane getting caught in a violent storm on the way to the venue, nearly resulting in a crash. (The unscathed Harrison later opined that his chanting the names of Hindu gods prevented a disaster.)

In the end Harrison's efforts raised substantial sums despite the insistence of tax authorities that they have their cut, much to Harrison's disgust. After the concert ended, Harrison considered taking the show on tour, a thought which although came to nothing, inspired others. A separate London concert was staged in September, featuring Mott The Hoople, the Faces, the Who, and several acts of note, while Dylan's old partner, Joan Baez, released her own single, Song Of Bangladesh, in 1972. In the ensuing years, the all-star charity record/concert has become a familiar event; one such in 1979 was organised by McCartney in aid of victims in the war in Kampuchea, while the biggest of the lot, the Live Aid event of 1985, drew McCartney back to the live stage once again, amid the usual swirling rumours of a Beatles reunion. In this way, the legacy of Harrison and Shankar's groundwork in 1971 has reverberated down the years.

George Harrison: [141] **DEEP BLUE** (*Harrison*)
    Produced by George Harrison, Phil Spector
    Recorded: 4 Jul 1971 (?); 5 Jul 1971 (?), Record Plant, Los Angeles
    UK: 30 Jul 1971 (single B-side)
    US: 28 Jul 1971 (single B-side)
    George Harrison: vocals, guitar, dobro; **Klaus Voormann**: bass; **Jim Keltner**: drums

The flip side of [140] Bangla-Desh was written in an 'atmosphere of doom' between Harrison's visits to his sick mother's bedside as she lie in hospital.[123] Devised one exhausted morning during the making of *All Things Must Pass*, the studio details are vague and some commentators have suggested it was taped during those 1970 album sessions. There is no evidence for this,

---

[122] See McCartney's interview in *Melody Maker*, 20 November 1971. Allen Klein subsequently spread a rumour that McCartney had unsuccessfully tried to coerce Harrison into agreeing to terminate the Beatles' partnership as a condition of his appearance.
[123] *I, Me, Mine*, p212.

however, the more likely occasion being the studio date for its associated A-side, the first time Harrison had recorded for his own ends in almost a year.

Sung over a repeating guitar riff, Deep Blue betrays in its lack of transition the fatigue Harrison was experiencing when he wrote it. Superficially bright, the song contains what Harrison described as the smell and sense of helplessness encountered in medical wards. While his own impressions of the track were no doubt coloured by personal associations, there's no missing the dolour concealed between the song's lines, his want for comprehension of life's 'repetition' a reference to the Hindu concept of a rebirth cycle.

Recorded sparsely, Voormann's dotted bass pattern fits the track's downcast current, Harrison adding a bluesy element with his dobro, mixed centre and lending credence to the recording's vintage; Harrison started using the instrument on sessions in 1971, including Lennon's [128] Crippled Inside, recorded six weeks earlier. A singularly significant track, Deep Blue follows both Julia and Let It Be among the Beatles' tributes to their respective mothers. Since Harrison had no album project on the horizon, its only outlet was this B-side, where it gained its reputation as a 'lost' track until the CD era brought it back to a mass audience as a bonus cut on *Living In The Material World*.

Ringo Starr: [142] **BLINDMAN** (*Starkey*)
Produced by Ringo Starr, Klaus Voormann
Recorded: 18 Aug 1971; 19 Aug 1971, Apple Studios, London
UK: 17 Mar 1972 (single B-side)
US: 20 Mar 1972 (single B-side)
Ringo Starr: vocals, drums; **Pete Ham**: guitar (?); **Klaus Voormann**: bass (?); **uncredited**: percussion/sound effects

Enthused by his appearance in Ferdinando Baldi's *Blindman*, shot on the same part of the Spanish coast where five years earlier Lennon had made *How I Won The War*, Starr agreed to write the movie's soundtrack, compositional inexperience notwithstanding. The first thing he came up with, designed to serve as a theme song and single to publicise the movie, was this effort, which seems to have been drafted on location. Something of a slow drone, Blindman was ill-suited for chart success, but as a vehicle for a spaghetti western is suitably authentic, its lyric casting an observing eye over the film's plot in which fifty women, hired as mail-order brides, are abducted by bandits. Atmospherically arranged, Starr's double-tracked vocal is effectively pitched against the ominous thump of a distant kettle drum, while extensive use of the guiro invokes the rattlesnakes of Mexico.

The track is said to have been recorded at Apple in August 1971, but there is doubt over the precise details. Apple Studios was covered in scaffolding through the summer while the facility was being overhauled for its official opening at the end of September. Therefore, unless Starr was working among the building contractors and engineering staff, it was either recorded later, or at a different location entirely. In any case, when Starr presented his work to the film's producers, he was disappointed to learn they weren't impressed and wouldn't be using it – and with that went Starr's hopes of scoring the rest of the movie. Instead, the commission went to Italian film composer, Stelvio Cipriani, and *Blindman* premiered in Rome in November absent any hit song to push it. With the recording completed, Starr sat on Blindman until the eventual release of [143] Back Off Boogaloo in 1972, where it served as a B-side.

Ringo Starr: [143] **BACK OFF BOOGALOO** (*Starkey*)
Produced by George Harrison
Recorded: Sep 1971 (?), Apple Studios, London (?)
UK: 17 Mar 1972 (single A-side)
US: 20 Mar 1972 (single A-side)
Ringo Starr: vocals, drums, percussion; **George Harrison**: slide guitar, acoustic guitar; **Gary Wright**: piano; **Klaus Voormann**: bass, saxophone; **Madeline Bell**, **Lesley Duncan**, **Jean Gilbert**: backing vocals

This Starr original – according to the label – began life one Sunday morning after a dinner with Britain's latest pop sensation, Marc Bolan, its title and main hook based on one of Bolan's pet sayings. Seemingly 'written' in his sleep, Starr awoke with the song already formed before scrabbling around the house for a working tape recorder to catch it before it passed from memory. Later that day he happened to have his television tuned to ITV's football highlights show, *The Big Match*, overhearing pundit, Jimmy Hill, describe a goal as 'tasty' – from which the song's middle eight was promptly concocted. (Starr inserted 'wasted' as a rhyme, considering it a 'wicked word'.[124]) With the track some distance from completion, Starr fell back again on Harrison to knock it into shape, making Back Off Boogaloo another co-write not openly acknowledged. As with its eventual B-side [142], recording details are vague, Madinger and Easter suggesting a possible window in March 1971, other commentators plumping for September, which seems more likely given Starr's working patterns through the year. Either way, he had time to offer it to Cilla Black first, who turned her nose up, cheekily requesting a first option on [198] Photograph instead.

Starting on a snare drum tattoo, Back Off Boogaloo marches through its four-square riff somewhat monotonously, Starr leading with a double-tracked

---

[124] Interview for BBC Radio 1, *Scene And Heard*, 13 March 1972. *The Big Match* covered the current football league season, which kicked off on 14 August 1971, giving the song an approximate vintage.

vocal line smoothed off with a chorus of female singers including Blue Mink's Madeline Bell. Untidy fun, the track makes the most of its thin substance thanks largely to the enthusiasm of Harrison, his trademark slide riffs echoing Starr in octaves, signed off with a string of hammering piano sevenths copied over from [67] Let It Down.

Given its simplistic and generally unchanging structure, the song was well received, slotting effortlessly into the burgeoning glam rock mode, thereby leading to speculation that Bolan himself had helped write it, which on the strength of the available evidence is fallacious. (Bolan's style-defining hits to date consisted of the shimmering and similarly repetitive Ride A White Swan, Hot Love and Get It On, the last of these topping the charts around the time Back Off Boogaloo was written.) Another enduring rumour had Starr aiming a dig at McCartney in the lyrics, the lines, 'Wake up, meat head/don't pretend that you are dead' and 'Everything you try to do/you know it sure sounds wasted' open to interpretation by over-analytical fans, particularly in the light of Starr's recently expressed disappointment with the contents of *McCartney* and *RAM*.

In an effort to wring a hit from it, Starr filmed a promotional video clip in the gardens of Lennon's vacant Tittenhurst Park mansion, its comedy gothic-horror theme reflected in the single's artwork, an incongruous black and white photo of a monster smoking an oversized cigarette. It's not clear why it took six months to release, but any concerns that Starr's popularity might have waned in the extended aftermath of [14] It Don't Come Easy were unfounded; this long-awaited follow-up proved his most successful UK hit, coming within a whisker of topping the chart. Thus embedded in his *oeuvre* it lent itself to a re-make in 1980, recorded during the week of Lennon's death and poignantly serving as a scrapbook onto which were stuck multiple Beatles lyrics. Starr released a third version in 2017 where, Free As A Bird-style, Jeff Lynne helped make a hybrid recording using the original demo tapes, with Harrison posthumously noted alongside his old pal in the brackets.

John & Yoko and the Plastic Ono Band: [144] **HAPPY XMAS (WAR IS OVER)** (*Ono, Lennon*)
Produced by John Lennon, Yoko Ono, Phil Spector
Recorded: 28 Oct 1971; 31 Oct 1971, Record Plant, New York
UK: 24 Nov 1972 (single A-side)
US: 6 Dec 1971 (single A-side)
John Lennon: vocals, guitar; **Yoko Ono**: vocals; **Hugh McCracken**: guitar; **Chris Osbourne**: guitar; **Teddy Irwin**: guitar; **Bob Fries**: guitar; **Stuart Scharf**: guitar; **Nicky Hopkins**: piano, chimes, glockenspiel; **unknown**: bass; **Jim Keltner**: drums, sleigh bells; **May Pang**: backing vocals; **Harlem Community Choir**: backing vocals

Towards the end of 1970, Lennon and Ono made some home recordings at their Tittenhurst piano, apparently in festive mood since part of them included a long ad-lib centred on the words, 'Merry Christmas'. As a whole the tape displays Lennon's erratic humour in the same way as the earlier Beatles Christmas recordings, which had themselves included several seasonal ditties, as well as the fully formed Christmas Time Is Here Again in 1967. Lennon's 1970 skit must have lingered on his mind since one morning the following July, he and Ono decided to put a proper Christmas single together, writing the basis of this new number more or less on the spot. Lennon later spoke of his original intention being to supplant White Christmas as the definitive Yuletide song, and while this may have been a factor, it's more likely he conceptualised it as a vehicle to permanently embed his peace message in the hearts of the general public, the connection of his anti-war slogan with a Christmas anthem a natural fit. (Lennon and Ono's 1969 poster campaign had appended a Christmas greeting to the headline, War Is Over!)

It was to the single's ultimate detriment that Lennon and Ono didn't act on the idea at once, distracted as they were by other matters. The main creative work Lennon did after moving to the States on 12 August consisted of shooting movie footage with Ono, including the making of *Clock*, a visual representation of a timepiece running for one hour, behind which Lennon played a medley of Buddy Holly songs. He didn't get around to recording Happy Xmas (War Is Over) until the end of October, on the late side for a pre-Christmas release in an era when singles had to *climb* the charts.

Credited as by Ono first, Lennon second, the song they came up with was a variation on the traditional On Top Of Old Smokey, which may have suggested itself through the lyrics about snow cover.[125] Lennon might have

---

[125] The resemblance is emphasised by singing alternate lines from the two songs: 'On top of Old Smokey'/'And a happy New Year'. Lennon was taped singing On Top Of Old Smokey on his 31st birthday, 19 days before Happy Xmas (War Is Over) was recorded.

heard Tom Glazier's 1963 adaptation, On Top Of Spaghetti, recorded with a children's backing chorus similar to the arrangement he would himself use, although the basic run is so ubiquitous that, if he didn't devise it from scratch, one of several other models might have been in mind. (One is Stewball, as re-arranged by Peter, Paul and Mary in 1963. Spector on the other hand nominated I Love How You Love Me, which he'd produced for the Paris Sisters in 1961, as a point of reference.)

Lennon's provisional band was invited to form the studio group for the session on 28 October but since Klaus Voormann didn't show, one of the multiple session guitarists deputised on bass, among their ranks one Hugh McCracken, who until recently had been McCartney's man, almost becoming a founder member of Wings over the summer. (Lennon was apparently unaware of McCracken's recent history until the session was already underway. Fortunately, when he found out, he saw the funny side.) Also named among the sprawling credits was 21-year-old May Pang, an employee of ABKCO whom the Lennons had acquired as a do-all assistant.

In generating a Christmassy arrangement, Spector fell back on his experience producing *A Christmas Gift For You* in 1963, when he arranged a slew of festive classics for his roster of girl groups.[126] Going to town on this new production, he mixed standard instruments with chimes and sleigh bells and even a glockenspiel, throwing everything into the mix, Christmas-pudding style. The song's fingerprint though was Lennon's idea, a request that Spector reproduce the mandolin effect from Harrison and Ronnie Spector's recent [116] Try Some Buy Some. (Without a mandolin to hand, Spector directed the bank of guitarists to bluff it, which they managed to surprisingly good effect with the rapid use of plectrums.) A couple of days later the track was completed with the addition of a choir of 30 children from a local community organisation, assembled to sing the anti-war chant which Lennon chalked up for them on a blackboard, and with this in mind, the Lennons finished by dubbing on whispered greetings to each of their own children at the start, Kyoko and Julian, sounding oddly as if they were saying their own names.

For a B-side the usual pattern was followed with the inclusion of one of Ono's originals, the attractive and suitably Christmas-flavoured Listen, The Snow Is Falling, a song she'd had since 1968. (Like its A-side, it carried a familiar-sounding melody, close to the Bee Gees' Massachusetts (1967) although the similarity was a coincidence.) The recording was made the

---

[126] Acts including the Ronettes and the Crystals handled material of the calibre of Frosty The Snowman, Rudolph The Red-Nosed Reindeer, Winter Wonderland and so on. *A Christmas Gift For You* was reissued on Apple in 1972, repackaged as *Phil Spector's Christmas Album*.

following night with the same set-up of musicians, except that by now Voormann had arrived to contribute a bassline, the whole thing rounded off with wintry sound effects from Record Plant's tape library stock.

By the time the single was mixed, manufactured and shipped, there were only two chart return days left before Christmas, not enough for it make a splash, although its failure to crack Top 40 *Billboard* was a disappointment – a situation not overcome even by its appearance on novel green vinyl. (That [130] Imagine was still on chart and selling well didn't help either.) In Britain the situation was worse, the release blocked completely following the intervention of Northern Songs, who were threatening legal action over the claim that Ono was the A-side's co-writer. It eventually made the shops in time for Christmas 1972, where it had some commercial success, becoming a perennial favourite which would regularly return to the charts over the holiday period. (Besides the coloured vinyl, the label too was eye-catching, featuring a succession of images of Lennon's face mutating into Ono's, a sequence originally created by photographer, Ian Macmillan, for a contemporary art exhibition by Ono.)

Despite the complications surrounding its release, the unwarranted delay in the UK and its poor chart return in America, Lennon had come up with one of his most famous recordings. The plain simplicity of its peace slogan has made this, his fifth custom-made solo 45, an enduring statement, the dying fade of 'war is over' echoing through the years following his murder.

Wings: [145] **GIVE IRELAND BACK TO THE IRISH** (*McCartney, McCartney*)
Produced by Paul McCartney, Linda McCartney
Recorded: 1 Feb 1972, EMI Studios, London
UK: 25 Feb 1972 (single A-side/B-side)
US: 28 Feb 1972 (single A-side/B-side)
Paul McCartney: vocals, bass, guitar, penny whistle; **Linda McCartney**: backing vocals, electric piano; **Denny Laine**: backing vocals, guitar; **Henry McCullough**: guitar; **Denny Seiwell**: drums; **uncredited**: handclaps

Following the critical bashing meted out to *Wild Life*, and its struggle to register meaningful sales, McCartney headed into 1972 with plans to put Wings on the map. When the proposed January release of [133] Love Is Strange / [134] I Am Your Singer was cancelled, McCartney's attention turned to getting the group in front of the fans, something he'd genuinely missed since the Beatles retired from stage performance in 1966. One issue to be resolved was the handling of guitar duties. While McCartney could use overdubs in the studio, in a live setting he'd be on bass with Laine on rhythm, leaving Wings without a lead man. For this reason, at Laine's suggestion, McCartney put a call out to Irishman, Henry McCullough, a skilled professional without a band of his own, whose bluesy style (hoped Laine) had the potential to steer Wings away from the lighter end of the pop spectrum. McCullough accepted McCartney's offer, and the £70 wage which came with it, and Wings were now a five-piece ready to go out and entertain.

At the same time political events suddenly flared in Northern Ireland, temporarily diverting McCartney's attention. On 30 January, at a protest against Britain's imprisonment of hundreds of suspects, marchers found themselves in violent clashes with the British Army, who elected to fire live rounds into the crowd, killing 13 people and wounding as many again. When McCartney heard the news he was shocked enough that on awakening the following morning, he went to his piano and quickly wrote a song to capture his feelings. 24 hours later he was at EMI with Wings, recording a sloganeering single with a haste which would have impressed Lennon.

As with most 'message' songs, the main purpose of Give Ireland Back To The Irish lives in its lyrics. It's no surprise therefore that song and arrangement are basic, the only memorable element being McCartney's excited octave-wide vocal jump into the second chorus. With speed of the essence, Wings rocked their way through the track before creating a second, instrumental 'version' for a B-side, an idea prompted by the reggae singles the McCartney's had been listening to through 1971 [133] and effected by he and McCullough playing solos over the original's backing track. (Although McCartney had recordings in the can from previous sessions which he could have used, the move had the advantage that should DJs seek to avoid playing the A-side for its political content, they wouldn't be able to flip it without at least reading out the title.) Some sources say the track was then mixed at Island Studios in Notting Hill, others (including Denny Laine) claiming the work was done at Apple, a premises McCartney apparently hadn't visited for two years.

Unavoidably controversial, the recording was quickly presented to an unimpressed Joseph Lockwood, who advised McCartney EMI wouldn't release it, and that it would inevitably be banned. McCartney got his way and once the single was cleared for release, copies were sent out to the media – eliciting the expected reaction. (The BBC banned it from their weekly *Top Of The Pops* television show, calling it only 'A song by a group called Wings' when reading out the chart placings.) Forced to explain himself, McCartney did an interview for ABC television and offered that his intent was a critique of his own government's actions: 'I'm British. The song's written from a British point of view'. As it happens he was also of Irish stock although he appears not to have known this for sure: 'I've probably got some Irish background'.[127]

---

[127] McCartney was interviewed at Cavendish Avenue in February 1972. Unless he did private research in the intervening years, he would only have learned his ancestry via Mark Lewisohn's *Tune In* in 2013, which established that he was descended from Irish >

Give Ireland Back To The Irish was issued with a custom label covered with green shamrocks, McCartney's most overt political statement in song. It predictably topped the charts in the Irish Republic.

Although the four former Beatles were moving in different directions by 1972, a sense of gravity found them forever circling back into each other's orbits, as illustrated by these four non-album singles. Lennon's was based on a Harrison arrangement; Harrison's featured Starr on drums; Starr's was written with Harrison and thought to be about McCartney; and McCartney's – with its political sloganeering – was in a style set by Lennon. Although no longer together, the four could not seem to exist on separate terms, and at Madison Square Garden in August there was briefly a framework by which they might have performed together. As it was, two did, and the others at least considered it, both of them now planning to go back on the road separately. Endless media speculation that a reunion was on the cards seemed to be underscored by the fact that all four were actively pursuing their performing careers, events such as Bangladesh hinting that there was at least a possibility that they might at some point join forces again. It wasn't apparent at the time that only half an album would be forthcoming from any of them over the next year.

RECORD RELEASES

Harrison: [140] **Bangla-Desh** / [141] **Deep Blue**
    (UK: 30 Jul 1971, US: 28 Jul 1971)
Lennon: [144] **Happy Xmas (War Is Over)** / Listen, The Snow Is Falling
    [B-side by Yoko Ono]
    (US: 6 Dec 1971)
McCartney [with Wings]: [145] **Give Ireland Back To The Irish** / [145] **Give Ireland Back To The Irish (Version)**
    (UK: 25 Feb 1972, US: 28 Feb 1972)
Starr: [143] **Back Off Boogaloo** / [142] **Blindman**
    (UK: 17 Mar 1972, US: 20 Mar 1972)
Lennon: [144] **Happy Xmas (War Is Over)** / Listen, The Snow Is Falling
    [B-side by Yoko Ono]
    (UK: 24 Nov 1972)

Protestants on his father's side, Irish Catholics on his mother's.

Some Time In New York City sessions: February 1972 to March 1972

Once it became apparent to Lennon and Ono they were in New York for the long-haul, remaining holed up in the St Regis Hotel was no longer practical. Accordingly they began scouting for a home to rent, chancing on an apartment owned by the Lovin' Spoonful's Joe Butler, a modest-looking house on Bank Street in Greenwich Village which behind its unremarkable façade contained a vast bedroom with spiral staircase and a bed constructed from old church pews. Delighted with their find, the Lennons moved in on 1 November. (A photo of the house was included on the back cover of *Some Time In New York City*.)

At this juncture, Lennon's relationship with McCartney was as strained as ever, something not helped by the fallout of *Imagine*, and in particular, [129] How Do You Sleep?, which McCartney heard in October. Fighting in the public eye was guaranteed to stir the interest of journalists, and inevitably the counter-shots were felt when *Melody Maker* elected to headline a recent interview with McCartney, *Why Lennon Is Uncool*, their 20 November edition picked up in New York and provoking a fresh volley from Lennon. In the habit of sounding off in print, he had laid into George Martin over the summer after the producer discussed the Beatles in a long interview for the magazine, to say nothing of his tirade in *The Village Voice* in August, aimed at a correspondent named Harold Carlton, who had written in criticising the Lennons' recent films. Lennon's reply began, 'To Shithouse Carlton – listen you tight mouthed English shit liberal...' and went downhill from there. The response to McCartney's piece was similarly outraged and after berating him at length, Lennon rounded off with a triumphant, 'If we're not cool, WHAT DOES THAT MAKE YOU?'[128]

In the face of such hostilities, it's surprising that the open slanging match between the two suddenly came to an amicable end. On 7 December, Lennon acquired a tape reel dub of the recent Beatles bootleg, *Yellow Matter Custard*, carrying 14 of the group's BBC radio performances from 1963. Wrongly believing he'd stumbled across the long-unheard Decca audition tape, Lennon excitedly ran off a copy for McCartney and sent it over to Scotland. Spotting the opening he'd been waiting for, McCartney was in New York within days,

---

[128] Lennon wrote to *Melody Maker* on 24 November. His remark, 'Wanna put your photo on the label like uncool John and Yoko, do ya? (Ain't ya got no shame!)', suggests he'd seen a pre-release copy of *Wild Life* where Paul and Linda's faces were featured instead of the usual apple design – as had been the case with Lennon on *Imagine* and Ono on *Fly*. (It's odd therefore that Lennon didn't also remark on the album cover photo, which bore close resemblance to that of *John Lennon/Plastic Ono Band*.)

visiting Lennon's new home with several press cuttings which he laid out, explaining away the many fabricated anti-Lennon quotes the media had published in his name. Lennon chose to believe him, and so on 15 December, the two made an unlikely peace pact, agreeing not to attack each other again in public, which they both stuck to.[129] McCartney would see more of Lennon over the following weeks, their friendship soon back on an even keel after two years of often bitter friction.

For the US-based Lennon, McCartney was increasingly part of a life he'd left behind as the Beatles began to recede into the distance, his attentions concentrated instead on his immediate future. Lennon's musical direction at the close of 1971 was being shaped by the radical contacts he made when he first settled in New York. Chief among them was David Peel, a local performer who plied his trade in the open street, offering free entertainment for anyone who'd listen, with a quasi-skiffle style which particularly appealed to Lennon. Many of his songs were as outspoken and provocative as any Lennon would come up with, filled with political and social polemics guaranteed to affront the status quo. Particularly amused by Peel's The Pope Smokes Dope, Lennon wasted little time getting him into Record Plant to record an album, sorting him out with a recording agreement through Apple. Peel had something else going for him – he had a ragtag backing outfit by the name the Lower East Side – and Lennon needed a band.

Lennon made sporadic appearances with Peel and his group in late 1971, mostly in support of this or that cause, his political sensibilities sharpened by his association with Jerry Rubin, whose 1970 book, *DO IT!: Scenarios Of The Revolution*, Lennon devoured. Through a string of campaign events Lennon began to expose his latest songs to the public, each of them politically loaded manna to New York's radical underground. (At one point a live album was reputed to be in the pipeline, Lennon and Peel having recorded a couple of their recent stage appearances, although the idea fizzled out when the tapes were listened back and found to be below par.) Lapping up his growing stature as figurehead of a social movement, Lennon announced in December that he, Peel and Rubin were to launch a performing outfit named the Rock Liberation Front, their aim to travel the world agitating with any local activists they would find along the way, and playing free music wherever they ended up – a whimsical idea, the appeal of which also gradually faded. In truth Lennon found Peel's group wanting, and after being tipped off by Jerry Rubin that the unsigned rock band, Elephant's Memory, were rehearsing a couple of blocks from Lennon's Bank Street home, decided they offered better prospects. The group was impressively hard-rocking, reminding Lennon of the

---

[129] Lennon's fullest account of this decisive meeting was in an interview for *The Joe Blow Show* on Dutch radio, broadcast 7 January 1972.

Hamburg-era Beatles, Ono also taking a liking to them when she realised Plastic Ono-Elephant's Memory would have the acronym, Poem. Jamming with them through the night in the first days of 1972, Lennon decided they were to become his band, and accordingly, Apple had another new artist on its books.[130]

The Plastic Ono-Elephant's Memory combo was unveiled in public during mid-February when a week's worth of *The Mike Douglas Show* aired, Lennon and Ono acting as co-hosts for the duration and taking the opportunity to play a few songs.[131] With special guests including Jerry Rubin and Black Panther activist, Bobby Seale, the shows did not go unnoticed, Lennon by now attracting the unwanted attentions of the US state, who for some time had been monitoring his activities. Tagged for surveillance by the FBI, and believing his phone was being tapped, Lennon sensed that his political activism was ruffling feathers in high places, a suspicion confirmed when his routine request for a visa extension was denied and he was ordered to leave the country by mid-March. Up for the fight, his next move was to take Elephant's Memory into the studio and make a new album rounding up his latest numbers, bent on continuing his high-profile agitations, or, as he saw it, challenging the apathy he detected in America's youth. What followed was by far his most politically outspoken statement, setting him on a direct collision course with the authorities.

John And Yoko/Plastic Ono Band: [146] **SUNDAY BLOODY SUNDAY**
(*Lennon, Ono*)
Produced by John Lennon, Yoko Ono, Phil Spector
Recorded: 12 Feb 1972, Record Plant, New York
UK: 15 Sep 1972 (*Some Time In New York City* LP)
US: 12 Jun 1972 (*Some Time In New York City* LP)
John Lennon: vocals; **Yoko Ono**: backing vocals; **Wayne (Tex) Gabriel**: guitar; **Gary Van Scyoc**: bass; **Stan Bronstein**: saxophone; **Richard Frank Jr**: drums, percussion; **Jim Keltner**: drums, percussion[132]

---

[130] To help negotiate the deal, drummer, Rick Frank, hired John Eastman, McCartney's representative in his suit against Lennon, Klein and the others in 1971.
[131] Performances during the week included [117] It's So Hard, [130] Imagine, and the as-yet unrecorded [154] The Luck Of The Irish. Another highlight was an appearance by Chuck Berry on day three, who along with Lennon and Elephant's Memory, blasted through versions of Memphis, Tennessee and Johnny B Goode.
[132] Elephant's Memory drummer, Richard Frank, and session man, Jim Keltner, are jointly credited throughout this album. Since it's not possible to be certain which did what on each track, they receive joint billing in this book. Keltner's presence was never explained, but implies Lennon was not entirely happy with Frank's style. (The two drummers played side-by-side kits at Lennon's One To One concert in August.)

Written in reaction to the Bloody Sunday killings in Northern Ireland, this new Lennon number was recorded 11 days after McCartney's corresponding protest [145], at a time when Lennon had the Irish issue on his mind (he'd written [154] The Luck Of The Irish over the winter). In the immediate aftermath of the shootings, Lennon had shown his support for the Irish Republican movement by attending a demonstration rally on the streets of New York and appears to have written this song over the following week, since he performed The Luck Of The Irish for the assembled crowds, but not this more pointedly relevant number.

Given its immediacy, Sunday Bloody Sunday was the first choice of track at Record Plant, Lennon and Elephant's Memory getting their teeth into it before Phil Spector's arrival. As a vehicle for settling the group in it was a sensible choice, consisting mostly of a rhythmic stomp through the key of E major in which the assembled musicians could settle into a groove, finding symbiosis with Lennon. Drum-heavy and charging through its verses with Stan Bronstein's leading sax, the recording constitutes an aural attack matching the acerbic mood of its lyric, which hangs on a series of suspensions modelled on those in Come Together, zeroing in on such lines as, 'Keep Ireland for the Irish, put the English back to sea' – essentially the same conclusion McCartney had come to, but with added venom.[133]

Shooting from the hip, Lennon's lyric decries the 'Anglo pigs and Scotties', declaring, 'It's those mothers' time to burn', underlining the instability of his world-view in which, a few weeks earlier, he'd announced, 'Let's stop all the fight/war is over' [144]. Lennon's current support for the IRA, flagged by his parading a banner at a London demonstration the previous August, had been fuelled largely by his association with *Red Mole* (see [120]), and while often held up as an example of rank hypocrisy, should be qualified by the fact that the IRA had not yet started terror attacks in Great Britain. Challenged over his apparent contradictions after the album came out, Lennon sought to explain himself: 'If two people [sic] are fighting, I'm probably going to be on one side or the other,' which while making a degree of logical sense, is far removed from his earlier unqualified utopianism.[134] Sunday Bloody Sunday remains a forceful recording, Lennon's leanings for the cause such that in some parts he effects an Irish accent. Accordingly, having said his piece he donated the song's royalties to 'the civil rights movement', leaving behind a full-tilt lyric which would divide opinion for decades to come.

---

[133] Besides the musical reference to Come Together, the song borrows another 'Beatle' element, the false ending previously heard on Strawberry Fields Forever and Helter Skelter.
[134] Interview published in the US bi-monthly music paper, *Rock*, 14 August 1972.

John Lennon/Elephant's Memory: [147] **ROLL OVER BEETHOVEN** (*Berry*)
  Produced by John Lennon
  Recorded: 12 Feb 1972, Record Plant, New York
  UK/US: unreleased
  John Lennon: vocals, guitar; **Wayne (Tex) Gabriel**: guitar; **Gary Van Scyoc**: bass; **Adam Ippolito**: piano; **Stan Bronstein**: saxophone; **Richard Frank Jr**: drums, percussion; **Jim Keltner**: drums, percussion

Used to playing with specially assembled teams of studio musicians, Lennon had not experienced the thrill of rocking with a fully charged band since his touring days, jamming with Elephant's Memory putting him in mind of the Beatles in their Cavern Club heyday. So it was only natural that after getting the serious business out of the way [146], Lennon steered them towards the rock and roll classics on which he'd learned his trade.

Chuck Berry's Roll Over Beethoven had been in the Beatles' repertoire since 1958, and courtesy of its inclusion on *With The Beatles* (*The Beatles' Second Album* in North America) was widely known. It's inconceivable then that Elephant's Memory weren't familiar with it, yet when Lennon burst into the famous opening riff, the band broke down, Lennon having to identify the track and even shout out the occasional chord. Nerves could have played a part; bassist, Gary Van Scyoc was particularly out of his zone, making wrong changes on what is a fairly orthodox rock/blues progression. Likewise, when the instrumental break arrives, Lennon calls to Tex Gabriel for a solo which doesn't come, Lennon taking over himself.

Ignoring such lapses, the performance is spontaneous and exciting and captures a moment in time, one of several oldies jams from these sessions worthy of preservation. How the studio was set up is not known; Ono appears to have been present, since Lennon complains she's too loud in his headphones, but there are presumably no other microphones plugged in as none of the group can be heard singing behind him. (Reflecting Elephant's Memory's uncertainty over the chord changes, Lennon doesn't know half the lyrics, the song having been Harrison's number in the Beatles.)

John Lennon/Elephant's Memory: [148] **HONEY, DON'T** (*Perkins*)
  Produced by John Lennon
  Recorded: 12 Feb 1972, Record Plant, New York
  UK/US: unreleased
  John Lennon: vocals, guitar; **Wayne (Tex) Gabriel**: guitar; **Gary Van Scyoc**: bass; **Adam Ippolito**: organ; **Stan Bronstein**: saxophone; **Richard Frank Jr**: drums, percussion; **Jim Keltner**: drums, percussion

A Carl Perkins oldie which the Beatles used to belt out in Hamburg and Liverpool, Honey, Don't made its way into their official EMI discography when it was recorded for *Beatles For Sale* in 1964. On the occasion, lead vocal was handed to Starr for his feature slot but in truth the Beatles' arrangement belonged to Lennon. (He sang it on British radio a full year earlier, as preserved on the 1994 collection, *Live At The BBC*, and also jammed it with the tape rolling during sessions for *Plastic Ono Band*.) Here, Elephant's Memory are more assured than on [147] Roll Over Beethoven, dropping out at appropriate moments and swinging to the correct rhythm, although Lennon still has to teach them the unusual E/C chord changes in the middle section. As enjoyable as the previous jam, this warts-and-all run through of a number close to Lennon's heart has him revelling in rock and roll, pure and uncomplicated. (All four Beatles were life-long fans of Carl Perkins, Starr selecting the same track as a knowing tribute to Harrison at the 2002 *Concert For George* at the Royal Albert Hall.)

John And Yoko/Plastic Ono Band: [149] **WOMAN IS THE NIGGER OF THE WORLD** (*Lennon, Ono*)
Produced by John Lennon, Yoko Ono, Phil Spector
Recorded: 16 Feb 1972; 22 Feb 1972; 18 Mar 1972, Record Plant, New York
UK: 15 Sep 1972 (*Some Time In New York City* LP)
US: 24 Apr 1972 (single A-side)
John Lennon: vocals, guitar; **Wayne (Tex) Gabriel**: guitar; **Gary Van Scyoc**: bass; **Adam Ippolito**: piano; **Stan Bronstein**: saxophone; **Richard Frank Jr**: drums, percussion; **Jim Keltner**: drums, percussion; **Invisible Strings**: orchestration

The only track on *Some Time In New York City* dating to the Beatles era, Woman Is The Nigger Of The World started life in the spring of 1969, around the time Lennon and Ono married. Its roots lie in an interview the couple did for *Nova*, a London-based women's magazine with a political slant, which published it in their March edition. Asked by journalist, Irma Kurtz, about his ancestry, Lennon came out with one of his typically unpremeditated declarations: 'I believe in reincarnation. I believe that I have been black, been a Jew, been a woman; but even as a woman you can make it,' at which point, Ono, sitting by his side, interjected, 'Woman is the nigger of the world'. Probably her remark would have been forgotten had the editors of *Nova* not elected to print it on the cover beneath a picture of Lennon and Ono, which apart from anything else, kept it in Lennon's mind. A comment Ono made in the middle of a Lennon dialogue, there seemed to be no prior history to the phrase which was born of spontaneous thought, although scholars have since pointed to a similar quote in Zora Neale Hurston's 'Harlem Renaissance' classic, *Their Eyes Were Watching*

God (1937), which deals with feminism in the context of black slavery, and therefore brings the two strands of the eventual song together.[135]

When first written, Lennon's focus was on the power of the title phrase, against which he used the imagery of the slave to depict woman's perceived role in personal relationships. It was not until Lennon's radicalisation in late 1971 that he firmed it up, shoe-horning in the cumbersome, 'If you don't believe me, take a look at the one you're with' – a direct message back to the male-dominated left and a reminder of the sentiment expressed in [120] Power To The People. Around this time Lennon also came across the pamphlet, *The Re-Conquest Of Ireland* by republican leader, James Connolly, who famously equated the male worker with a slave whose wife was therefore a slave twice over – which suited Lennon's metaphor and was used to complete the lyric.[136] (Lennon demoed Woman Is The Nigger Of The World on Boxing Day 1971, along with the otherwise unknown Man Is Half Of Woman (Woman Is Half Of Man), built on another quote, this time from Gandhi. Had Lennon pursued that song instead, he would have avoided much controversy.)

What Lennon took into the studio on 16 February was a text he knew would inflame and accordingly he threw himself into the recording, which in its unedited version ranges across a full five minutes to conclude with the most intensely troubling section, the menacing repeat, 'We make her paint her face and dance', Ron Frangipane's angular strings invoking the nightmarish vision of a voodoo ceremony. That the recording was made behind closed doors by a tough New York bar band with not a female in sight didn't apparently faze Lennon, who far from pleading from the woman's side, in fact addressed society's male-dominated bastions with a challenge pitched directly to *them*, an argument put man-to-man.

Accusatory, belligerent, outspoken, the track was undeniably potent in Lennon's singular manner, yet his main problem was getting the song some exposure, its use of the forbidden N-word no small matter. Scheduled for release in the States on 24 April, backed with Ono's parallel Sisters, O Sisters, his first obstacle was having Apple pay for promotion, American office manager, Peter Bennett, declaring he wanted nothing to do with it. (A UK issue was blocked due to an ongoing dispute over Ono's inclusion in Lennon's current copyrights (see also [144]).) Lennon put considerable personal effort into making the song a hit by calling up US radio shows to encourage a fair hearing, apologetically explaining to one live broadcaster, 'I'm really upset if

---

[135] In which the character, Nanny, reflects on the white man ordering a black slave to pick up his baggage, only for the slave to pass it to a woman to carry: 'De nigger woman is de mule uh de world'.

[136] Connolly: 'The worker is the slave of capitalist society, the female worker is the slave of that slave.'

any of the black people take it badly, because it's meant as no insult. It's really meant in all sincerity'.[137] Meanwhile he took out a full-page advert in the music press, quoting black politician, Ron Dellums, with a lengthy definition of the word by which he concluded, 'You don't have to be black to be a nigger in this society'.[138]

Such efforts in damage limitation had little effect as the single, inevitably starved of airplay, limped in and then out of the lower reaches of the charts. Defiantly, Lennon and Ono took Elephant's Memory onto ABC's *Dick Cavett Show* to perform it for the cameras, an appearance which gave Lennon the opportunity to state his defence, a full reading out of Ron Dellums' earlier statement attracting applause from the studio audience who at least understood the perspective. In truth reaction to the song was not uniformly negative, and after the broadcast several hundred complaints were made – not about the song, but about the fact that Cavett had been forced to apologise for it. In August the Lennons were further vindicated when the pressure group, the National Organisation For Women, recognised the 'Positive Image Of Women' on both sides of the single. Emboldened, Lennon and Ono performed the song again at their One To One concert at Madison Square Garden at the end of the month.

Undoubtedly the negative responses were a consequence of Lennon's blunder in expressing the issue of women's subjugation via a highly offensive racial slur. Moreover the inclusion of such a derogatory term – no matter if well intentioned – detracted from the message, the song standing fundamentally against discrimination and yet upsetting many who heard it, serving merely to divert the subject. Seen for what it is – an expression of support for women's liberation – the track has a small place in history, being the first open statement on gender equality from a major recording artist. (Helen Reddy's Grammy-winning I Am Woman was recorded in 1971, but Lennon's concept pre-dates it by two years.) Despite the controversy, Woman Is The Nigger Of The World made it onto Lennon's 1975 singles collection, *Shaved Fish*, ensuring that, for better or for worse, it would not be airbrushed from his career discography.

---

[137] The call was to KDAY-AM of Santa Monica on 20 April – cited in Madinger and Raile, p318.
[138] The notice ran in *Billboard*'s 6 May edition.

John Lennon/Elephant's Memory: [150] **SEND ME SOME LOVIN'** (*Price, Marascalco*)
Produced by John Lennon
Recorded: 16 Feb 1972, Record Plant, New York
UK/US: unreleased
John Lennon: vocals, guitar; **Wayne (Tex) Gabriel**: guitar; **Gary Van Scyoc**: bass; **Adam Ippolito**: piano; **Stan Bronstein**: saxophone; **Richard Frank Jr**: drums, percussion; **Jim Keltner**: drums, percussion

After Lennon got hold of a copy of Little Richard's [238] Lucille in 1957 (the UK issue appearing on a London label 78) he discovered on its B-side a track which would become one of his favourites: Send Me Some Lovin', written by John Marascalco and Leo Price. Widely taken up, including a version by another of Lennon's key influences, the Crickets, it naturally became a staple of the Beatles' early stage repertoire, as performed for several years in Liverpool and Hamburg.

Jammed late-night at Record Plant, Lennon and Elephant's Memory handle the song with affection, pianist, Adam Ippolito, replicating Richards' tinkling ivories, Stan Bronstein letting loose with a sax section ahead of anything on the original. Not knowing the ending, Lennon calls them to a halt after two and a half minutes. He'd return to the track during sessions for *Rock 'N' Roll* in 1974 [278].

John Lennon/Elephant's Memory: [151] **HONEY HUSH** (*Turner*)
Produced by John Lennon
Recorded: 16 Feb 1972, Record Plant, New York
UK/US: unreleased
John Lennon: vocals, guitar; **Wayne (Tex) Gabriel**: guitar; **Gary Van Scyoc**: bass; **Adam Ippolito**: piano; **Stan Bronstein**: saxophone; **Richard Frank Jr**: drums, percussion; **Jim Keltner**: drums, percussion

The degree to which Lennon truly bought into the many causes he championed has been the subject of scepticism, his flirting with the IRA [146] causing some to question the strength of his professed commitment to non-violence. In a similar way, his recording of the current song on the same evening as the pro-feminist [149] Woman Is The Nigger Of The World reveals an unresolved tension between the idealist in him and the reality of his world, shaped during a working-class Liverpool upbringing in which he witnessed women as house workers, in the service of, and dependent on, men. That Lennon could lurch from lamenting, 'When she's young we kill her will to be free' to the threatening, 'Stop all that yackety-yack, I don't want no talking back' inside a single session tends to undermine the credibility he was striving for. In fairness, Lennon was drawn to rock and roll songs for their *feel* rather than their lyrical content, and it's by no means certain he gave any thought to the meaning behind the original text, of which he recalls little here. (Lennon's musical senses were neatly delineated in an interview for WHRW-FM over the summer, where he explained his outlook: 'I think it's quite fair to just groove on the music without paying any attention to the words. Rock and roll is basically the overall *thing*.')

Written by 'Big' Joe Turner in 1953 – the copyright being given to his wife precisely so that she would have her own income stream – Honey Hush most likely came to Lennon's knowledge via the 1957 release from by Johnny Burnette on the Vogue label, another in a stream of B-sides mined by the early Beatles for obscure gems. 30 years on McCartney took the song back to the Cavern Club stage, following its inclusion on his 1999 album, *Run Devil Run*.

John And Yoko/Plastic Ono Band: [152] **ANGELA** (*Lennon, Ono*)
Produced by John Lennon, Yoko Ono, Phil Spector
Recorded: 23 Feb 1972; 18 Mar 1972, Record Plant, New York
UK: 15 Sep 1972 (*Some Time In New York City* LP)
US: 12 Jun 1972 (*Some Time In New York City* LP)
John Lennon: vocals, guitar; **Yoko Ono**: vocals; **Wayne (Tex) Gabriel**: guitar; **Gary Van Scyoc**: bass; **Adam Ippolito**: organ; **Stan Bronstein**: saxophone; **Richard Frank Jr**: drums, percussion; **Jim Keltner**: drums, percussion; **Invisible Strings**: orchestration

Started in New York in October 1971, this latest offering began as the tale of 'JJ', a possibly real but unidentified female who couldn't get sex at a party. Seeking to shape it into something less specific, Lennon transformed the initial lyric into another of his quasi-utopian tracts philosophising on 'People' not getting what they need, and this is how the song sat as late as December, when he received a request to write something in support of Angela Davis, a political activist jailed in October 1970 for her connections to a botched courtroom siege in which four people had been shot and killed.

Something of a *cause celebre* among black and left-wing activists, her case drew attention for the fact that, although charged with first degree murder, she hadn't been present in the court, hadn't shot anybody and was uninvolved except inasmuch as she owned the guns which had been used. With Davis's card marked as an anti-establishment trouble-maker, pre-judged by President Nixon as a 'dangerous terrorist', she was initially kept in solitary confinement, contributing to widespread public sympathy for her cause, which among other things, prompted Jagger and Richards to write Sweet Black Angel, portraying her as a 'gal in chains'.

Reviving 'People' for the job, Lennon and Ono drafted a third set of lyrics about this 'political prisoner', in which Ono's presence looms large, the final song probably close to a 50-50 co-write. (The line, 'There's a wind that never dies', is pulled directly from a piece she wrote in January 1966, *To The Wesleyan People*.) The fact that her input was pivotal is underscored by the song's general sensitivity, in which 'sister' is deprived of equality, and the fact that Ono effectively takes lead vocal, Lennon following her in low, parallel octaves. With his softly picked guitar, derived from the patterns on Dear Prudence, and Ron Frangipane's gently drifting strings, Angela is comfortably the least challenging listen on *Some Time In New York City*, illustrating that Elephant's Memory, for all their hard approach, were capable of subtlety of expression when called for – Adam Ippolito's organ solo particularly atmospheric and sounding like the Band's Garth Hudson. (The most melodic number on Elephant's Memory's 1972 Apple album, Wind Ridge, is considerably rougher hewn than what's on display here.)

Angela Davis was tried in May and found not guilty, her release effected on 4 June, days before the song was issued on *Some Time In New York City*, rendering it instantly obsolete. Such are the perils of recording topical material.

John And Yoko/Plastic Ono Band: [153] **NEW YORK CITY** (*Lennon*)
Produced by John Lennon, Yoko Ono, Phil Spector
Recorded: 8 Mar 1972, Record Plant, New York
UK: 15 Sep 1972 (*Some Time In New York City* LP)
US: 12 Jun 1972 (*Some Time In New York City* LP)
John Lennon: vocals, guitar; **Wayne (Tex) Gabriel**: guitar; **Gary Van Scyoc**: bass; **Adam Ippolito**: piano; **Stan Bronstein**: saxophone; **Richard Frank Jr**: drums, percussion; **Jim Keltner**: drums, percussion

Yoko Ono had known New York City since she moved there as a 20-year-old in 1953, but for Lennon it represented something of a promised land. Declaring it 'the Rome of today. Like a 'together' Liverpool', he quickly became smitten, and of a nature to throw himself in at the deep end, at once commemorated his latest infatuation in song.[139] New York City takes a Lennon's-eye look around the place, drawing in the sights and sounds of his first few months' residency, in which he manages to make a rhyme of the street corner with Ono's name. (The first draft used the better-fitting, but unauthentic name, Doris Horner.)

Lennon started writing the song almost as soon as he arrived, multiple additions and changes occurring over the latter part of 1971, tracing out new events as they happened. By the time he demoed it in December he'd worked in his meetings with David Peel and Jerry Rubin, referencing also his Fillmore East gig with Frank Zappa and his appearance at the Apollo on 17 December

---

[139] Interview with Ray Coleman, cited in Blaney, p109.

for the Attica State Benefit Concert (see [155]). Since he didn't join forces with Elephant's Memory until the start of 1972, these lines must have been added last, bringing the song up to date for its March recording.

A barrage of a performance, New York City has been heralded as Lennon's best of the era, its rollicking energy captured live on the studio floor in 14 takes. A sequel of sorts to his earlier 'diary' song, The Ballad Of John And Yoko, New York City provides a suitably newsy title track, acting as an antidote to the rest of the album's political posturing for listeners not warm to Lennon's radical positions, besides also heralding his adoptive status as a New Yorker, home for the rest of his life.

John And Yoko/Plastic Ono Band: [154] **THE LUCK OF THE IRISH**
(*Lennon, Ono*)
Produced by John Lennon, Yoko Ono, Phil Spector
Recorded: 9 Mar 1972; 18 Mar 1972, Record Plant, New York
UK: 15 Sep 1972 (*Some Time In New York City* LP)
US: 12 Jun 1972 (*Some Time In New York City* LP)
John Lennon: vocals, guitar; **Yoko Ono**: vocals; **Wayne (Tex) Gabriel**: guitar; **Gary Van Scyoc**: bass; **Adam Ippolito**: piano; **Stan Bronstein**: flute; **Richard Frank Jr**: drums, percussion; **Jim Keltner**: drums, percussion; **Invisible Strings**: orchestration

Written in November 1971, The Luck Of The Irish reflects Lennon's awareness of the political situation several months before the Bloody Sunday killings [146]. Playing ironically on a hackneyed phrase in which the Irish are held to enjoy good fortune, Lennon rakes over the history of the island, remarking on how, back in Liverpool, the story is recounted of 'a thousand years of torture and hunger', a reference in part to the Irish Potato Famine of the 1840s, an event pivotal in the rise of the independence movement. Unknown to Lennon, his Liverpool ancestry (researched in recent times by Mark Lewisohn) began with an Irishman named James Lennon, John's great grandfather, fleeing the hardship to eventually settle in Liverpool's Saltney Street, where the family took root. (He might have guessed his lineage in any case, Lennon being an Anglicised form of the Irish name, O'Leannain. In rehearsals for the song, Lennon joked Yoko also had an Irish name: O'No.)

Not held in check, Lennon's lyrics have a tendency to overstate the position, his draft line that the Irish were sorry they were even born changed to the no less outrageous claim that they would rather be English. It's overtly clear where Lennon's sympathies lie as he blasts the British 'bastards' for raping Ireland and committing 'genocide', quoting Bob Dylan along the way for good measure, a broadside only partly tempered by the calm of Ono's contrasting passages, which have attracted unending scorn. Of Japanese-

American background, Ono lacked the cultural and historical knowledge of Ireland to grasp the politics, accounting for the excessive naivety her verses display – the childishly picturesque references to shamrocks, Galway Bay and the Blarney Stone were intended to conjure an ideal, a vision of a happy Ireland projected onto the world. (That the cynical Lennon went along with such romanticised reverie is more surprising than Ono's presumption to write about a society of which she knew so little.)

This song of two extreme perspectives was toured during Lennon's current spate of live appearances, first heard in December at the John Sinclair Freedom Rally before being taped twice for US television and then performed live in front of a crowd of protesters in New York in the days following Bloody Sunday. When sessions for *Some Time In New York City* were underway in March, it occurred to Lennon that to fill out the album he would have to capture versions of this and the two other songs he'd been hawking around, [155]; [156], taking all three into the studio for proper recording on 9-10 March. Adorned with Stan Bronstein's celtic flute passages and scored with Ron Frangipane's 'Invisible Strings', The Luck Of The Irish was earmarked for a single but pulled in favour of [149] Woman Is The Nigger Of The World.

John And Yoko/Plastic Ono Band: [155] **ATTICA STATE** (*Lennon, Ono*)
Produced by John Lennon, Yoko Ono, Phil Spector
Recorded: 10 Mar 1972, Record Plant, New York
UK: 15 Sep 1972 (*Some Time In New York City* LP)
US: 12 Jun 1972 (*Some Time In New York City* LP)
John Lennon: vocals, guitar; **Yoko Ono**: vocals; **Wayne (Tex) Gabriel**: guitar; **Gary Van Scyoc**: bass; **Adam Ippolito**: organ; **Stan Bronstein**: saxophone; **Richard Frank Jr**: drums, percussion; **Jim Keltner**: drums, percussion

Lennon's response to the September riot at Attica Correctional Facility, in which 38 were shot and killed, began as an improvised chant at his birthday party on 9 October. Appalled by the reckless way the riot had been handled, authorities filling the prison with tear gas before shooting into the smoke and hitting anyone who happened to be in the way – including nine members of their own staff – Lennon quickly worked his initial idea into a proper song, falling back on an old trick by pulling a pentatonic vocal melody from a 'walking' guitar riff (*cf* the introduction to [81] I Found Out). Lyrically true to form, Lennon takes an extreme stance, characterising prisoners as seekers of truth and calling for their judges to be incarcerated in their place, something he'd picked up from Jerry Rubin's *DO IT!: Scenarios Of The Revolution*.[140] In

---

[140] 'The first Yippie act when we take power will be to open the jails. Free the prisoners >

truth, elements of the song hold a more qualified position, expressing sympathy for guards as well as prisoners, the line, '43 poor widowed wives' taking into account the entire final toll – something he took pains to point out when rounded on by an angry audience member when he sang it on *The David Frost Show* in December. Nonetheless, the song's assertion that all prisoners are victims hardly stood up to scrutiny, Frost's challenge that there are some people who need to be restrained for the protection of others answered only with the vague, 'I'm not sure about that'. Making allowances for Lennon's lack of objectivity, Attica State has at its core a concern for 'people in jail who aren't violent, who don't kill', its sentiments warmly received by the amassed crowd at the Attica State Benefit at Harlem's Apollo Theater on 17 December, where Lennon and Ono performed the song in their 10-minute appearance.

As recorded in the studio, Lennon and Ono tackle the vocal in unison, as they had on [152] Angela, abandoning their initial plan to sing alternate lines probably because of Ono's chronic problem with the song's timing. Behind them, Elephant's Memory put in one of the sharpest performances on the album, Stan Bronstein's pulsing sax holding the tempo against Adam Ippolito's electric organ, rich with bluesy sevenths, and Tex Gabriel's piercing slide guitar. Epitomising 1972 Lennon, the track stands as an effective monument to his political phase, constituting with hindsight an historical time capsule, in and of its day.

As a sobering footnote, Lennon's assassin, Mark Chapman, was sent to Attica State prison in 1981, his intermittent eligibility for parole in the intervening years routinely objected by Ono, decades after she sang, 'Free the prisoners' with Lennon. Times change.

John And Yoko/Plastic Ono Band: [156] **JOHN SINCLAIR** (*Lennon*)
Produced by John Lennon, Yoko Ono, Phil Spector
Recorded: 10 Mar 1972, Record Plant, New York
UK: 15 Sep 1972 (*Some Time In New York City* LP)
US: 12 Jun 1972 (*Some Time In New York City* LP)
John Lennon: vocals, dobro; **Wayne (Tex) Gabriel**: guitar; **Gary Van Scyoc**: bass; **Richard Frank Jr**: drums, percussion; **Jim Keltner**: drums, percussion

The last addition to *Some Time In New York City*, this 'topical' song was long out of date by the time of its recording on 10 March. John Sinclair had been a particularly prominent figure in the US counterculture, one-time manager of the band, MC5, and founder of the White Panthers, a partner organisation to the Black Panthers, of whom Angela Davis had been a member [152]. An open

---

and jail the judges!' (Rubin, p160).

advocate of rock and roll, dope-smoking and free love, Sinclair had for some time been in the sights of the US government who 'busted' him for possession of marijuana several times in the mid-1960s. In a wide-sweeping dawn raid in Michigan at the start of 1967, he was picked up again and accused of having handed two joints to an undercover female cop the previous month, beginning the start of a lengthy legal battle which was finally ruled in July 1969 – Sinclair was found guilty of possession and sentenced to a jail term of between nine and a half and ten years, a draconian punishment widely seen as politically motivated.

The case drew considerable publicity, Abbie Hoffman making headlines by invading the stage at Woodstock weeks later to address the crowds on Sinclair's behalf, before being thrown off by Pete Townshend. At this point, Sinclair believed his sentence was too obviously unjust to stand and launched appeals in the expectation he would soon secure his release, but as his solitary confinement dragged into 1971 he asked supporters on the outside to take up the cause, one result of which was the writing of a poem, *The Entrapment Of John Sinclair* by Ed Sanders, which Lennon and Ono came across, arousing their interest. Thus, when The John Sinclair Freedom Rally was organised in Ann Arbor, Michigan, Lennon was invited to play, writing the song (provisionally, Ten For Two) for the occasion.

Staged on Friday 10 December, the 15,000-strong gathering drew appearances from several 'names' including Stevie Wonder and Phil Ochs, the main event being Lennon and Ono's taking to the stage in the early hours, where this new number was performed for the first time. Apparently spooked by the show of mass support for Sinclair, the authorities acted swiftly, the Michigan Supreme Court freeing him as soon as they convened on the Monday, Lennon hearing the news later that day and speaking down the phone from Record Plant East to an elated Sinclair, who claimed not to even know why he'd been released. Three days on, Lennon was booked to appear on *The David Frost Show* and elected to play the song regardless, celebrating the victory and recounting Sinclair's story for the benefit of the studio audience.

Come March, Lennon's conundrum was whether to let the song go, its subject matter already history, or commemorate the episode by recording it for the album, which he opted to do. Carried mainly on a messy slide-dobro blues riff, the final track is arranged largely as written, for busking with David Peel, little additional work having been done on it. Elephant's Memory take a back seat on the track which, with its bold sloganeering and irritating repetitions is the least musically accomplished on the album, yet when considered as a product of the moment, earns its place. Lennon's insinuating, 'was he jailed for what he done, or representing everyone?' strikes at on the heart of the issue: the state's misuse of laws governing the relatively innocuous practise of smoking dope.

Lennon himself was about to become the subject of similar, threatened for the next few years with no less a measure than deportation on the pretext that he'd been convicted of merely *possessing* cannabis in London back in 1968. Whether this was the true motivation for the US government's push to remove him is measured against that fact that, at the John Sinclair Rally, Lennon was under surveillance by the FBI, agents transcribing the lyrics to John Sinclair which were duly added to their growing files. Reminding listeners that Sinclair's treatment was not unique, the album version of the song included as a late addition, 'They got old Lee Otis, too', a reference to the case of Lee Otis Johnson, a student leader currently serving an amazing 30 years for passing a joint to another undercover police officer. Johnson also happened to be an outspoken political activist, the pattern of state abuse of marijuana legislation to take opponents out of circulation obvious enough, at least to Lennon.[141]

Some Time In New York City was wrapped up with string overdubs on 18 March and mixed on 20th – Lennon and Ono's third wedding anniversary – but had to wait until June for release, and September in the UK. Packaged in a mock up of *The New York Times*, the album defines Lennon's era, its political activism neatly captured in a sleeve signalling the focus on current affairs, its journalistic song lyrics aptly presented as newspaper coverage.[142] As for the contents – a grab bag of slogans, political opinion and topical reportage – judgement of its merits has been split since first hearing. While *Melody Maker* in its 10 June edition declared the album a masterpiece, most notices were less kind, *Rolling Stone*'s review 10 days later judging the lyrics as 'witless doggerel'. Lennon's songs were nothing if not brave, his decision to loudly challenge the status quo on every topic which came his way, from single issues [152] to society at large [149], something he was unfaltering on, believing in his heart that he was right on all counts. The trouble was, if listeners didn't like the message, they would tend not to like the songs.

Where *Some Time In New York City* struggles is the forced manner of writing, outside of Lennon's idiom where much of his work since 1966 had been deeply self-referential and born of spontaneous inspiration. Here, working on a list of topics, he lacked his usual creative impulse, pushing out

---

[141] He was asked why he was facing deportation by journalist, Geraldo Rivera, on 18 April. The reply: 'The official reason is that I was bust in England for pot. The real reason is because I'm a peacenik. The real reason is our politics.'

[142] The idea was not new, US copies of Harrison's [140] Bangla-Desh and adverts for Lennon's own [122] God Save Us having carried collages of press cuttings in 1971. By unfortunate coincidence, Jethro Tull's new album, *Thick As A Brick*, appeared in May using the same idea, just weeks ahead of *Some Time In New York City*.

commentary to order as external forces demanded. Thus there is a strained quality to much of the content, the inner artist silenced in the service of the politics. Ono's contributions on the other hand show a growing maturity, particularly her Born In A Prison with its harmony chorus (one of three self-penned numbers to make the cut). The album is ultimately a joint work, Ono's songs interspersed, and where possible sequenced against Lennon's to make pairs (Born In A Prison, for example, following [155] Attica State). Added to this is the input of Elephant's Memory, an often overlooked outfit whose brand of hard-edged rock and roll seeps into every corner of the set, hectoring and challenging the listener in the same way Lennon's lyrics tend to confront. In [153] New York City, they turn out a genuinely rousing performance, while the album's trailer single, [149] Woman Is The Nigger Of The World – despite its title – is one of the most forceful recordings of Lennon's New York phase.

Through late 1971 and into 1972, Lennon had also been toying with the release of a disc of live recordings, at one point announcing the imminent arrival of *London Air And New York Wind*, which failed to materialise. In the event the tapes were readied and packaged as a bonus LP with *Some Time In New York City*, making it into a double album. Containing audio of the December 1969 UNICEF gig with Harrison (who consequently appears in the cover photos) and Lennon's unannounced set with Frank Zappa at the Fillmore East in June 1971, this supposedly free record added largely unwanted bulk, bumping up the price and contributing to the album's poor showing on the charts.

Ongoing disputes over the songwriting credits on *Some Time In New York City* were responsible for delays, so that by the time it was issued out in Britain, its contents were even less current. Lennon's problems mounted when his visa applications failed and he found himself in a tussle to remain in the States at all, one consequence of which was his inability to do paid work – which apart from anything else, ended his plans to resume touring – although he was permitted to play for nothing, as evinced through 1972 charity appearances at The Jerry Lewis Muscular Dystrophy Telethon, and, most significantly, the One To One concert at Madison Square Garden on 30 August in aid of Willowbrook House school for disabled children, the last time he would play a full set before a live audience. Nervous about headlining and having patched things up with McCartney the previous December, Lennon invited Wings to appear on the same bill, the band having by then played two or three dozen gigs of their own.[143] 'Busted' on 10 August for possession of marijuana, McCartney's freedom to enter the States was also now under

---

[143] Madinger and Raile quote a McCartney interview with Ray Connolly from 2 December 1972: 'A few months ago John asked us to do a concert with him at Madison Square Garden and it's a pity now that we didn't do it.'

constraint, the absurd application of drugs laws effecting twin pressures which undermined the possibility of Lennon and McCartney playing together again.

The One To One appearance has Lennon and Ono commanding their audience with selections from *Some Time In New York City* plus choice oldies including [2] Cold Turkey and Come Together. Radical in military garb and battle helmet, this performance represents the high watermark of Lennon's political period, imagery of him rocking the crowds preserved through the eventual release of the live footage (*Live In New York City*, 1986). Had events not unfolded in reverse order it would have made a far stronger partner set to the studio album than the actual live disc which, for all its historical importance, served only to undercut the overall integrity of what has become Lennon's least popular post-Beatles release.

RECORD RELEASES

[149] **Woman Is the Nigger Of The World** / Sisters, O Sisters
[B-side by Yoko Ono]
(US: 24 Apr 1972)
Some Time In New York City
(UK: 15 Sep 1972, US: 12 Jun 1972)
[149] Woman Is the Nigger Of The World / [155] Attica State / [153] New York City / [146] Sunday Bloody Sunday / [154] The Luck Of The Irish / [156] John Sinclair / [152] Angela
[Yoko Ono tracks: Sisters, O Sisters / Born In A Prison / We're All Water. Also contains a bonus disc of live recordings.]

Red Rose Speedway sessions (first phase): March 1972

Having got the distraction of [145] Give Ireland Back To The Irish out the way, McCartney's focus for 1972 was getting Wings up in front of live audiences, plans for a low-key tour of the UK quickly generating momentum. In the spirit of homespun making do, the only advance planning was the acquisition of a hire van to get them around, which over the space of a fortnight, snaked Wings up and down the UK, cold calling at university campuses nominated along the way. First in Nottingham, then York, up to Newcastle and back down via Wales, McCartney's entourage pulled up, checked the student facilities could accommodate them, and unloaded their gear, charging 40p or 50p a head for each performance, the proceeds collected in cash and divided up in the back of the van where Laine, McCullough and Seiwell were each handed a fistful of loose change and crumpled pound notes as if in an amateur band.

Enjoying getting back to his roots, McCartney's experience on the University Tour was uniquely invigorating, putting him in contact once again with his public – the fulfilment of an impulse he'd had since at least 1969.[144] For the rest of Wings the project was of less obvious merit, complicated by the fact that Linda had never done a gig in her life, nerves getting the better of her on at least one occasion when she forgot how to play. What the tour did achieve was the road-testing of several numbers the fledgling band would incorporate into their sets longer term, including a clutch of originals as yet unrecorded and in line for the group's second album, to be recorded at Olympic Studios with Glyn Johns at the controls.

Paul McCartney And Wings: [157] **BIG BARN BED** (*McCartney*)
Produced by Paul McCartney
Recorded: 6 Mar 1972, Olympic Studios, London
UK: 4 May 1973 (*Red Rose Speedway* LP)
US: 30 Apr 1973 (*Red Rose Speedway* LP)
Paul McCartney: vocals, piano, bass; **Linda McCartney**: backing vocals; **Denny Laine**: guitar, backing vocals; **Henry McCullough**: guitar, backing vocals; **Denny Seiwell**: drums

Meeting at Olympic on 6 March, Wings embarked on their first album as a five-piece confident that under direction of Glyn Johns, they would be able to hone their developing sound into a set worthy of McCartney's name. Their lead man had a point to prove, after all, the harsh critical reaction to *Wild Life* followed by a ban and new round of condemnation over [145] Give Ireland Back To The Irish still raw in his mind – yet almost at once Wings settled into a routine of lazy jamming, using up studio time and expensive magnetic tape on McCartney's habitual doodles – the first of which was Big Barn Bed.

Not one to let a musical offcut go to waste, the song was built on a snippet previously heard at the end of [112] Ram On's reprise, developed with skewed reference to McCartney's farmhouse. Why so much significance was attached to a song whose only point of interest was the *non-sequitur* 'leaping armadillo' is a mystery, but it was used as opener to both *Red Rose Speedway* and the 1973 television special, *James Paul McCartney* [192]. 30 years on, Henry McCullough re-recorded the track by himself, bringing out its hidden blues elements – although no amount of production could cover up the song's empty content.

---

[144] McCartney later described how in the meeting where Lennon quit the Beatles in September that year, he'd suggested, '...this idea of playing surprise one-night stands in unlikely places... just letting a hundred or so people in the village hall, so to speak' (Madinger and Raile, p147).

Paul McCartney And Wings: [158] **WHEN THE NIGHT** (*McCartney*)
  Produced by Paul McCartney
  Recorded: 7 Mar 1972, Olympic Studios, London
  UK: 4 May 1973 (*Red Rose Speedway* LP)
  US: 30 Apr 1973 (*Red Rose Speedway* LP)
  Paul McCartney: vocals, piano, bass, kazoo; **Linda McCartney**: electric piano, Moog (?), backing vocals; **Denny Laine**: guitar, backing vocals; **Henry McCullough**: guitar, backing vocals; **Denny Seiwell**: drums, backing vocals

Having more or less wasted their first session, Wings knuckled down the following day with this logically constructed ballad founded on a tussle between major and minor chords. Starting with a step down the bottom keys of Linda's keyboard, the song tumbles dejectedly into its opening A minor, only to muster itself in the fifth bar for an unexpectedly reassuring cadence on C major, where it happily comes to rest – or so it seems, since it then collapses to go around again. Set in the unusual tempo of a regular 8/8, When The Night was recorded in a coolly dispassionate mood, its jazzy undercurrent owing to Denny Seiwell's ticking hi-hat, enlivened by the thwack of a snare on the fourth quaver of each bar. For a solo, McCartney demonstrated what he wanted to McCullough by humming through a kazoo, the guitarist obliging by overdubbing a lead section following the notes as directed – the final mix retaining both.

A genuine team effort, the eventual track brings every member of Wings to the microphone for a neatly organised backing vocal arrangement. Although the song may owe its origins to [282] Stand by Me, whose opening words are borrowed, the influence is the clipped girl-group sound of the early 1960s, each 'answering' section defined in the gaps between the main lyrics, a technique McCartney learned with Lennon and Harrison in Hamburg and Liverpool on songs like Please Mr Postman and Boys. Worked out by the musical craftsman in him, When The Night is McCartney's most fully realised creation since [111] Little Lamb Dragonfly and the most seductive recording on the album, deserving of the effort expended by the group.

Paul McCartney And Wings: [159] **THE MESS** (*McCartney*)
  Produced by Paul McCartney
  Recorded: 8 Mar 1972, Olympic Studios, London
  UK/US: unreleased
  Paul McCartney: vocals, bass; **Linda McCartney**: electric piano; **Denny Laine**: guitar; **Henry McCullough**: guitar; **Denny Seiwell**: drums, percussion (?)

Thought to take inspiration from the Band's The Shape I'm In, released in October 1970, The Mess I'm In (as it was originally known) dates to the start of 1972, having been developed by Wings in February sessions anticipating their University Tour. The track was taken into Olympic and recorded for the album, but over the coming summer Wings would go back on the road and perform it in a series of European shows, by which time The Mess became tighter and faster, incorporating backing vocals and more incisive lead guitar breaks from McCullough and Laine.

As it happened, one of the gigs was professionally recorded and the superior stage performance was accordingly substituted into the provisional running order for *Red Rose Speedway* – at that point scheduled as a double LP. Having selected it for the final cut, the subsequent stripping back of *Red Rose Speedway* to a single disc meant something had to give, the live recording one of the casualties – unfortunately so, since it carries an attack lacking from the rest of the album. Too good to be disposed of it was employed instead as a B-side to [178] My Love, while the original studio version was permanently shelved.

The first recording, though stilted against the freer live arrangement, has its own attractions, Linda in particular pitching in with some concise keyboard sections in unison with McCullough's lead riffs, and a churchy suspended section at 3:44. Ostensibly built on a blues structure, the song shifts erratically through a series of discrete parts, spaces for solo spots allowing McCullough to show off a range of lead styles before the whole rocking construct comes to an abrupt close on a playfully restful major seventh.

Paul McCartney And Wings: [160] **SINGLE PIGEON** (*McCartney*)
Produced by Paul McCartney
Recorded: 9 Mar 1972, Olympic Studios, London; 29 Jan 1973,
    EMI Studios, London
UK: 4 May 1973 (*Red Rose Speedway* LP)
US: 30 Apr 1973 (*Red Rose Speedway* LP)
Paul McCartney: vocals, piano; **Linda McCartney**: backing vocals; **Henry McCullough**: guitar; **Denny Seiwell**: bass; **Denny Laine**: drums; **uncredited**: brass

Behind a public face of uninterrupted marital bliss, the relationship between Mr and Mrs McCartney had the usual ups and downs typical of any long-term relationship. The autobiographical text of Single Pigeon, which lurks behind its avian character, records an early Sunday fall-out in which McCartney finds himself walking alone along the side of the canal which cuts across the northern edge of London's Regent's Park, more or less at the end of his road in St John's Wood. Set minor, this brief song has the feel of a gloomy morning after, McCartney observing the solitary birds dotted around the open spaces and projecting his sorrows in the sadly falling, 'Did she turf you out in the cold morning rain'. Turning on a major triad, 'I'm a lot like you', the composition suddenly takes wing and flies, like the birds seen through the park railings, McCartney's patent inclusion of major-minor contrasts used to succinctly convey his feelings.

This reflective thing was arranged for piano, the 9 March session seeing Denny Seiwell deputise on bass, and if the official credits are correct, Denny Laine at the drums. When *Red Rose Speedway* was being prepared for release, a brass section was dubbed over the last 20 seconds, trailing away to nothing and adding a further sense of unresolved despondency.

Paul McCartney And Wings: [161] **TRAGEDY** (*Burch, Nelson*)
Produced by Paul McCartney
Recorded: 13 Mar 1972, Olympic Studios, London; 28 Jan 1973,
   EMI Studios, London
UK/US: unreleased
Paul McCartney: vocals, bass; **Linda McCartney**: backing vocals; **Denny Laine**: guitar, backing vocals (?); **Henry McCullough**: guitar; **Denny Seiwell**: drums; **uncredited**: sitar, vibraphone

A hit in 1959 for Thomas Wayne with the DeLons, the wistfully romantic Tragedy was an obscure choice for McCartney; he may have heard of Wayne's death in a traffic accident in August 1971, making the song – title and all – a means of paying tribute. The lullaby arrangement, with its warm major sevenths and soft harmonies, successfully conjures a sense of nostalgia in which one can 'see' the glowing valves of a 1950s wireless set – though it old-time mood scarcely suited a fledgling band just finding its way as a live act.

Recorded in March 1972, the arrangement is pitched so low McCartney struggles to make the bottom notes, suggesting it may have been taped with a view to having Linda or Denny Laine sing it. Laid to rest for the better part of a year it was recovered and overdubbed with vibes and an incongruous sitar which eschews Indian scales to fill the role of lead guitar, after which the track was scheduled for *Red Rose Speedway* then culled at the 11th hour. McCartney purchased the Bluff City Music copyrights in the mid-1970s, adding the song to his early music publishing portfolio.

Paul McCartney And Wings: [162] **MAMA'S LITTLE GIRL** (*McCartney*)
Produced by Paul McCartney
Recorded: 14 Mar 1972, Olympic Studios, London; 17 Nov 1972,
    EMI Studios, London
UK/US: unreleased
Paul McCartney: vocals, guitar, bass (?), drums, percussion (?); **Linda McCartney**: backing vocals, tambourine; **Denny Laine**: bass (?), backing vocals; **Henry McCullough**: guitar (?); **Denny Seiwell**: percussion; **Heather McCartney**: backing vocals

Another of McCartney's paeans to family life, Mama's Little Girl lovingly watches over one of his three daughters, probably Heather who was the eldest by some years (having turned nine in December) and was asked to sing 'like a skylark' on the recording. The song's air of domestic contentment and pastoral calm places it alongside [18] The Lovely Linda and [109] Heart Of The Country in McCartney's *oeuvre*, the latest in a sequence of acoustic productions which wouldn't have sounded out of place next to Blackbird or Mother Nature's Son. (Indeed, McCartney may have had Beatles songs on his mind when drafting it, since the lyric recycles a line from Things We Said Today.)

More than a throwaway, the song was caught somewhere between charming and self-indulgent, eventually losing its place on *Red Rose Speedway* when the album was stripped down to a single LP. Overdubbed in 1980, it was scheduled for the latest incarnation of *Cold Cuts* (see [96]), but didn't escape until 1990 when McCartney released Put It There, a tribute to his late father whose generational connection made it an apt choice for the B-side. The disc carried the credit, Paul McCartney & Wings, bucking a habit of blurring group and solo work.

Paul McCartney And Wings: [163] **LOUP (1ST INDIAN ON THE MOON)** (*McCartney*)
Produced by Paul McCartney
Recorded: 15 Mar 1972, Olympic Studios, London
UK: 4 May 1973 (*Red Rose Speedway* LP)
US: 30 Apr 1973 (*Red Rose Speedway* LP)
Paul McCartney: guitar, bass, Moog, backing vocals; **Linda McCartney**: organ, backing vocals; **Denny Laine**: guitar, backing vocals; **Henry McCullough**: guitar, backing vocals; **Denny Seiwell**: drums, percussion, backing vocals

Often thought to have been inspired by Pink Floyd, who were recording *Dark Side Of The Moon* at EMI during 1972, Loup was taped at Olympic several months before those sessions started, precluding any direct link. In fact, although the track bears resemblance to some of Pink Floyd's recent albums, it has more in common with their experimental early work such as the multi-section Interstellar Overdrive from *The Piper At The Gates Of Dawn* (1967). McCartney, though, has consistently played down any connection, insisting that Loup was just 'a bit of fun... pretty experimental' rather than a premeditated attempt to break into prog-rock territory.[145]

Unearthly and mysterious, this droning sequence in A minor is as far removed from Wings' patent style as anything they would ever record, its breathy sonics exploring the textures and minute dynamics of the instrumental palette. Equally elusive is the song's title, loup being French for wolf, although what that has to do with the music – let alone with Indians on the lunar surface – is anyone's guess. Such material, shorn of lyrical content and lost in the depths of its own form, may be better presented on exploratory albums than rubbing shoulders with [160] Single Pigeon and [172] One More Kiss, but from a musician's point of view, the recording can only have been a rewarding project. If nothing else it shows McCartney's endless enquiry into the possibilities of musical creation in all its various styles.

Paul McCartney And Wings: [164] **THANK YOU DARLING** (*McCartney*)
Produced by Paul McCartney
Recorded: 23 Mar 1972, Olympic Studios, London
UK/US: unreleased
Paul McCartney: vocals, bass, kazoo; **Linda McCartney**: backing vocals;
Denny Laine: guitar; **Henry McCullough**: guitar; **Denny Seiwell**: drums

When McCartney was at a loose end he had a tendency to while away his talents on music hall comedy numbers, of which Thank You Darling is a prime example. Sounding like an unplanned studio invention (with a possible distant link to Thank You Girl), the track was brought into Olympic after being performed in the February live sets – making its squandering arrangement here all the more puzzling. Yet despite affecting silly voices and blowing the instrumental gaps with an absurd kazoo fill (the instrument having been lying around since [158] When The Night), there are signs that McCartney expended some time on getting the production right, going so far as to record separate vocal tracks (which can be heard overlapping at 1:34). A patent waste of effort, the track could not have been a serious contender for release as it stood, adding to the frustrations of engineer and would-be producer, Glyn Johns, who found himself having to indulge McCartney's whims at length when twaddle like this surfaced. Fresh from having produced the Eagles'

---

[145] Interview published on paulmccartney.com, 26 Nov 2018. The fact that the track and Floyd's album would share the word Moon is similarly coincidental.

eponymous debut album, and with his recent commissions including heavyweight projects for the Who and the Faces, Johns' tolerance was starting to wear thin and would shortly snap.

Wings: [165] **MARY HAD A LITTLE LAMB** (*McCartney. McCartney*)
Produced by Paul McCartney, Linda McCartney
Recorded: 27 Mar 1972, Olympic Studios, London
UK: 12 May 1972 (single A-side)
US: 29 May 1972 (single A-side)
Paul McCartney: vocals, bass (?), piano, percussion, recorder (?); **Linda McCartney**: vocals, percussion (?), Moog (?); **Denny Laine**: guitar, bass (?), backing vocals; **Henry McCullough**: guitar, mandolin, backing vocals; **Denny Seiwell**: drums, percussion, recorder (?), xylophone (?), backing vocals; **Heather McCartney**: backing vocals; **Mary McCartney**: backing vocals

For many a low point in McCartney's discography, Mary Had A Little Lamb was issued as a non-album single to follow-up [145] Give Ireland Back To The Irish, leading to speculation that he was responding to his BBC ban by serving up the most mindlessly inoffensive material imaginable. In fact the song was written earlier, and has as its genesis the fun McCartney had singing it to his two-year-old daughter, Mary, who enjoyed it for the simple reason that it contained her name. (McCartney may also have liked the coincidence with [111] Little Lamb Dragonfly.)

Written in the 19th century, its nursery-rhyme lyric contains several sections not normally recited, and in realising this McCartney developed the fanciful notion that the public might be interested to hear the whole thing – thus, Wings were obliged to record and release the track despite the fact that no-one other than McCartney had a good word to say for it. Naturally melodic, McCartney's octave-wide accompaniment ranges freely around the verses, only deviating from its diatonic major scale for a harmonically adventurous *ritardando* towards the finish, the track's most effective ingredient. With his wife and kids joining in for fun (Heather can be heard chattering in the background during the first chorus), the track caused many who heard it to cringe; this from the man who had written some of the finest music of the modern era.

Set on making it a hit, McCartney had several promotional clips shot and unveiled it to pre-pubescent Britain on BBC television's *The Basil Brush Show*, apparently undecided whether he wanted to be a rock star or a children's entertainer. In truth he was trying to be both at once, which may have worked better for his variety credentials than his musical reputation. What Lennon would have thought of the track, had it been presented to the Beatles, one can only wonder (his own current single, [149] Woman Is The Nigger Of The World, could hardly have stood in greater contrast). For release it was paired up with the *RAM* leftover, [108] Little Woman Love, McCartney taking solace from the fact that he at least got a chart hit out of it. He was later pleased to hear that Pete Townshend's three-year-old daughter, Emma, was a fan of the song – perhaps missing the point that Townshend himself avoided saying that *he* liked it. As for the effect it had on the other members of Wings, it undoubtedly caused tensions, McCartney's decision to release it at all when he had [178] My Love up his sleeve, the biggest singular misjudgement of his career.

Fed up with spending his time under McCartney's demanding eye, recording what he considered sub-standard material, Glyn Johns reached the point that while the group was busy rehearsing, he was often up in the control room reading the paper and generally ignoring them. Realising he'd stopped even running the tape, the group called him down for a conference on the studio floor where Wings were bluntly informed that – McCartney or no McCartney – most of their music was not worth the effort. Obviously an impasse had been reached which could have only one outcome – the resignation of Johns from the project, which meant in effect, the departure of Wings from Olympic Studios – Johns' home patch. In Johns' defence, Wings had so far recorded nine complete tracks, of which the only substantial fruit was [158] When The Night and [159] The Mess, a paltry return for almost a month's work.

The breakdown of sessions had the effect of stalling the entire album, which turned out to be a blessing in disguise for not only did it put the brakes on what might have become another critical failure of a release, it allowed McCartney to turn his attention to getting Wings on the road for some better organised gigs. He'd intended to tour properly since the group first came together, purchasing a disused open-top Bristol bus from a dealer in Norfolk towards the end of 1971. The idea was to load up the kids and the group and take off on an adventure, for which he asked a Carnaby Street boutique owner to have the bus painted in *Yellow Submarine*-style cartoons. And so on 7 July they all departed, destination France, for the start of a six-week tour around northern Europe playing a series of low-key concert venues, sufficiently off-Broadway to constitute a dress rehearsal for the real thing: a British tour to be arranged in the near future.

The 'Wings Over Europe' experience turned out to be memorable for a variety of reasons, some good and some not so good. The fun the ensemble will have had trundling from town to town, sunning themselves on the open top deck of a psychedelic tour bus was offset by the group's financial arrangements in which Laine, Seiwell and McCullough were kept on their regular weekly wage – and while McCartney willingly paid for travel and hotels, the recreational life they inevitably indulged in over a month and a half meant that by the time the tour wound up, they had nothing left. Laine, meantime, had every reason to remember the tour fondly: after the second night's show at Juan-les-Pins on the south coast of France, he met then began a relationship with Joanne LaPatrie – Jo Jo – who later became his wife.

The choice of stage material was curious, conspicuously omitting any of McCartney's Beatles songs but including spotlight moments for Linda, Denny Laine and Henry McCullough – a gesture which smacked of tokenism considering their songs were all grouped together in the middle of the sets, as if forming something of an interlude. (Linda sang her own Seaside Woman, pre-performance nerves so great that before the opening night she broke down in tears.) Having thus blooded his team, McCartney also intended to release footage of some of the tour as part of a film project dubbed *The Bruce McMouse Show*, interspersing it with cartoon animation of a mouse who lived under the concert stage – another of his whimsical ideas which, like *Rupert*, was never seen through. A venture of mixed fortunes, Wings Over Europe is most remembered for a notorious 'bust' in Gothenburg on 10 August, when the McCartneys were arrested and accused of trafficking drugs after police found a packet of marijuana which had been posted to them. Although they managed to negotiate a swift release, and saw out the final two weeks of the tour, McCartney's card had been marked so that apart from anything else, he would now inevitably be denied entry to the States should he wish to go – which meant that even had he been of a mind to reunite with Lennon at the One To One concert at Madison Square Garden on 30th, he wouldn't have been able to.

Wings Over Europe concluded on 25 August in Berlin, a three-week rest and recuperation needed before, tight from 26 live engagements, Wings resumed work on *Red Rose Speedway*, moving to the more comfortable setting of Abbey Road.

Red Rose Speedway sessions (second phase): September 1972 to January 1973

Wings: [166] **C MOON** (*McCartney, McCartney*)
  Produced by Paul McCartney
  Recorded: 2 Sep 1972, Morgan Studios, London
  UK: 1 Dec 1972 (single A-side)
  US: 4 Dec 1972 (single B-side)
  Paul McCartney: vocals, piano, cornet; **Linda McCartney**: backing vocals, percussion; **Denny Laine**: bass, backing vocals; **Henry McCullough**: drums; **Denny Seiwell**: cornet, xylophone; **Heather McCartney**: backing vocals; **Mary McCartney**: backing vocals

The first thing recorded by Wings on their return from Europe was this pop-reggae number taped in a singular session at Morgan and never intended for the album. Why this track was given priority is unclear, particularly since the group had not played it on tour and had a much stronger offering waiting in line [169]. The song's impetus derived from McCartney's mulling the lyric to Wooly Bully, a 1965 reggae-infused novelty for Sam the Sham and the Pharaohs, particularly the line, 'Let's not be L7' (the final two digits side-by-side appearing to form a square, ergo, uncool). The hip counterpart McCartney came up with was a crescent moon opposite a letter C to make a circular 'cool'.[146]

McCartney seems to have been playing off Wooly Bully in devising his semi-nonsense lyric, the original characters Hatty and Matty contorted into Bobby and Patty, a couple living in sin whose clandestine relationship is unfortunately not explored in a verse ending only with a rhetorical, 'What's it all about?'. But the most obvious borrowing is the style of execution, its reggae rhythm absorbed by McCartney who considered no musical genre outside of his scope, and in common with much of the general public at the time was pursuing his ongoing interest in Jamaican music.[147] In this context, the version

---

[146] McCartney had the moon in his thoughts during the era, having already recorded [105] Monkberry Moon Delight and [163] Loup (1st Indian On The Moon). Wings were currently playing Elvis's Blue Moon Of Kentucky in their stage sets. L7 is also a postal district in Liverpool, covering part of the city centre close to where the Cavern is situated (c/w Starr's 2008 album, *Liverpool 8*).

[147] See also [133] Love Is Strange. Linda was an influencing factor, helping him discover reggae singles during a trip to Jamaica in December 1971, including Peter Tosh's Maga Dog, which was a particular favourite. (On a visit to Tony's Record Store in Kingston, the couple were amused to find a 45 called Poison Pressure by Byron Lee and the Dragonaires, which had Lennon-McCartney as the claimed composers. Another >

of C Moon glimpsed in *One Hand Clapping* (see [264]) is closer to the song's original conception.

Exceptionally fluent in his musicality, McCartney's verses display an openness of melody, sweeping over their four chords with freedom – a quality not apparent after the transition to the bouncing kiddie-pop of the hook lines in which Denny Seiwell tinkles a xylophone and McCartney's kids again sing along ([162]; [165]). This constant tendency to waste his musical talents on cutesy triteness was a source of chronic frustration to McCartney fans in the 1970s, fatuous lyrics often casually inserted where careful thought would have steered many of his period songs into much more credible territory, this particular example including 'I'd never get to heaven if I filled my head with glue' – not to mention a vocalised question to his studio engineer after McCartney missed his cue, which was preserved on the master tape for no reason. (Quite what the song was getting at when lamenting the older generation's misunderstanding of its singer is uncertain, McCartney a father of three just past his 30th birthday. Possibly he was singing from the child's perspective.)

With musicians swapping instruments, rhythm guitarist on bass, lead guitarist on drums, drummer playing the cornet, C Moon was an entertaining project for the group, who took the song more seriously in subsequent live performance where its reggae roots are paid due respect. Anticipating a ban on [169] Hi, Hi, Hi when released in December, McCartney astutely made C Moon its double A-side in the UK, ensuring enough radio exposure to lift the single into the top 5.

Wings: [167] **HOLD ME TIGHT** (*McCartney*)
Produced by Paul McCartney
Recorded: 15 Sep 1972, EMI Studios, London
UK: 4 May 1973 (*Red Rose Speedway* LP)
US: 30 Apr 1973 (*Red Rose Speedway* LP)
Paul McCartney: vocals, piano, bass; **Linda McCartney**: backing vocals; **Denny Laine**: guitar, backing vocals; **Henry McCullough**: guitar, backing vocals; **Denny Seiwell**: drums, backing vocals

Struck by Glyn Johns' critique back in March, that Wings' songs weren't worth recording, McCartney set about a more ambitious plan, thinking he could recreate the masterful *Abbey Road* medley from a set of unused songs. The sequence on side 2 of *Red Rose Speedway* began as a suite of three ([175] Power

---

purchase was Buttercup, principally for the fact that the artist was named Winston Scotland.) While in Jamaica, Linda composed her reggae-styled Seaside Woman, recorded by Wings for her only solo single (as Suzy and the Red Stripes, 1977).

Cut having not yet been appended), brought to the studio ready-assembled for the group to record as a single piece.[148] Unable to capture a viable take, they decided to attempt the individual tracks in order then edit them together, the first to be tackled this light rocker which shares its title with one of McCartney's earliest songs, recorded in 1963 for *With The Beatles*.

Starting on A, the song's uneasy first verse teases its way up to D in a succession of semitonal steps, the narrowest changes available. It then embarks on an astonishing journey back around the entire 'Circle of Fifths' (see [29]), stepping through some 11 changes before arriving back on A for verse 2, one of the most remarkable musical sequences McCartney ever came up with. One minute in, the song bursts into a surprisingly cheerful restatement of itself led by Denny Laine's acoustic dancing around the scales until, having nowhere left to go, it pulls up on a high suspended E, poised to dissolve into [168] Lazy Dynamite.

Paul McCartney And Wings: [168] **LAZY DYNAMTIE** (*McCartney*)
Produced by Paul McCartney
Recorded: 16 Sep 1972, EMI Studios, London
UK: 4 May 1973 (*Red Rose Speedway* LP)
US: 30 Apr 1973 (*Red Rose Speedway* LP)
Paul McCartney: vocals, piano, Mellotron, bass; **Linda McCartney**: backing vocals; **Denny Laine**: harmonica; **Henry McCullough**: guitar; **Denny Seiwell**: drums, percussion (?)

Continuing work on the planned medley, McCartney turned his attention to the oddly titled Lazy Dynamite, a tale of guarded love whose imploring quality derives from two elongated bridge sections, positioned so as to form the centrepiece of the song. Dwelling on the implied pleading of the minor key, McCartney's exhortation to his loved one to open her heart reveals an emotional engagement missing from the rest of the medley, with a consolation found in the wide vocal steps towards the relief of its E major hook. Subsumed into the song sequence, Lazy Dynamite has often been overlooked in McCartney's canon, bracketed between lesser weights, but in its nuanced style is among the most attractive products of these sessions.

Archetypal of Wings' style for the rest of the 1970s, the guitar solos played by McCullough were probably McCartney's idea (at least in principle), flying airily above the backing track. As the song approaches its conclusion, McCullough switches to a block chord sequence, running through each natural major from G up to E, forcing the necessary shift to A for [174] Hands Of Love, of which McCartney sings a few bars to prepare the listener.

---

[148] According to studio engineer, John Leckie (see Perasi, p96).

At this point, the recording of the medley was put on hold while studio time was devoted to making the group's next single. They would return to complete it a fortnight later.

Wings: [169] **HI, HI, HI** (*McCartney, McCartney*)
Produced by Paul McCartney
Recorded: 18 Sep 1972; 19 Sep 1972, 20 Sep 1972; EMI Studios, London
UK: 1 Dec 1972 (single A-side)
US: 4 Dec 1972 (single A-side)
Paul McCartney: vocals, guitar, bass; **Linda McCartney**: organ, backing vocals; **Denny Laine**: guitar, backing vocals; **Henry McCullough**: guitar; **Denny Seiwell**: drums, cowbell

During Wings' University Tour it was glaringly apparent the group had insufficient material to fill out a concert set, forcing them to perform tracks such as [159] The Mess and [145] Give Ireland Back To The Irish twice. Clearly they needed additional songs for their more ambitious European outing, forcing McCartney to come up with a clutch of new numbers, the most promising of which was the rocker, Hi, Hi, Hi.[149]

Written in Benidorm, Hi, Hi, Hi was the product of McCartney's lustful mood and not, as is often assumed, a mocking reaction to his drugs bust in Gothenburg, which it precedes. A puerile statement of libidinous intent towards some young lady, the song all too explicitly expands on the Beatles' Why Don't We Do It In The Road, besides carrying a similar 'blues' chord pattern and appropriately pounding arrangement. Purposely designed as a straight rocker, the song was deployed as a closer to the stage show, sending the crowds off on a literal high, McCartney correctly recognising its commercial potential and pencilling it in for the group's third 45.

Initially played in a hammering R&B arrangement with archetypal guitar solos, the song was licked into shape over three night sessions at EMI, McCartney at pains to get the instruments and backing vocals just right. Despite having taken it on the road and performed it live more than two dozen times, the group struggled to find the magical ingredients McCartney demanded, a satisfactory master only captured at the 61st attempt. Part of his pedantic search for an exact feel entailed hooking his bass up to one of the studio speakers to alter its frequencies, while Henry McCullough made the most of the opportunity to exhibit his skills on the slide guitar in a series of overdubs compensating for the fact that his solo spots had been dropped.

---

[149] The European tour also saw the debut of [176] 1882, [264] Soily and Best Friend, none of which made it to vinyl. (A live performance of Soily, taped in 1976, was officially released on *Wings Over America*.)

Whether such protracted efforts were warranted on what in truth, was something of a comedy number, is a matter only McCartney could judge.

Released at the start of December, Hi, Hi, Hi was received exactly as anticipated – with a broadcasting ban for its sexual content and drugs references. While McCartney made a token gesture of protesting all innocence, claiming his lyrics had been mis-heard, much of the song's most provocative content went unnoticed including his pronunciation of 'my funky little mama' in which the 'n' was knowingly omitted – not to mention a tell-tale buzzing noise immediately following the wielding of his 'body gun'. (As late as 2021, McCartney was still denying much of this, claiming in *The Lyrics* that 'body gun' was mis-heard from 'polygon', as derived from Alfred Jarry's *Ubu Cocu*.) Yet in spite of courting yet more controversy, Hi, Hi, Hi was Wings' first genuine commercial success, making the top 10 on both sides of the Atlantic – something McCartney had not managed since his first solo release [92] almost two years earlier. As such it represents a meaningful marker in his post-Beatles fortunes.

Paul McCartney And Wings: [170] **COUNTRY DREAMER** (*McCartney*)
Produced by Paul McCartney
Recorded: 26 Sep 1972, EMI Studios, London
UK: 26 Oct 1973 (single B-side)
US: 12 Nov 1973 (single B-side)
Paul McCartney: vocals, guitar, piano, percussion (?); **Linda McCartney**: backing vocals; **Denny Laine**: bass, backing vocals; **Henry McCullough**: pedal steel guitar; **Denny Seiwell**: drums

With ironic timing, in the middle of sessions for [169] Hi, Hi, Hi, McCartney suffered an unwelcome distraction when, on 19 September, an over-zealous police officer, aware of his recent drugs bust in Sweden, took it upon himself to snoop around McCartney's Scottish farmhouse. Hoping to find some incriminating substances he got lucky, identifying five marijuana plants growing in McCartney's greenhouse, and an arrest and charge of growing and possessing duly followed. McCartney tried to defend himself with the unconvincing claim that he'd been posted some anonymous seeds and was curious enough to find out what they were by planting them, which he later recounted to news cameras with a faint smile, '…and they came up illegal'. Amusing it may have been for the moment, but another court case would now follow with the theoretical possibility of jail and McCartney's chances of having free passage across international boundaries even further jeopardised.

As if to escape these troubles, his next date at EMI was given over to this tranquil vision of afternoons whiled away in the hills and meadows around Kintyre, written during the time of the similarly idyllic [109] Heart Of The

Country. (McCartney's *RAM*-era demo is not in circulation but is said to include insect noises, a throwback to the chirping crickets on Sun King.) Inspired by his fondness for Hank Williams, whom the Beatles admired in their early days, McCartney arranged the song for pedal steel, an assignment for which Henry McCullough was put to the test on the first time he'd played the instrument.[150] Hank Williams' self-penned songs included Honky Tonk Blues, which was in Lennon's early stage act, and the better-known Jambalaya (On The Bayou), which might have particularly appealed to McCartney for its nonsensical-sounding lyrics; that the song served as inspiration is suggested by the appropriation of the 'Southern' phrase, 'me oh my'.[151] McCartney's most successful attempt at the country music idiom thus far, the track captures a moment of rural repose, the happy mood of Country Dreamer a pleasing addition to *Red Rose Speedway* where it was initially partnered next to [157] Big Barn Bed. It was removed at the last moment to remain in limbo until the release of the homesick [222] Helen Wheels when it was selected for a B-side, after the Carpenters had meantime taken a recording of Jambalaya into the UK charts.

Paul McCartney And Wings: [171] **NIGHT OUT** (*McCartney*)
    Produced by Paul McCartney
    Recorded: 28 Sep 1972, EMI Studios, London
    UK/US: unreleased
    Paul McCartney: vocals, bass; **Linda McCartney**: organ, backing vocals, percussion (?); **Denny Laine**: vocals, guitar; **Henry McCullough**: guitar; **Denny Seiwell**: drums[152]

Devoid of lyrics, this edgy guitar rocker was at one point threatening to serve as the opener to *Red Rose Speedway*, repeating a pattern set by [138] Mumbo on the group's previous album. McCartney's evaluation of the track appears to have been in flux, since this would-be curtain-raiser was dropped completely by the time the final running order was decided, and having thus been jettisoned, was kept in reserve for the occasionally revived *Cold Cuts* project [96], but was ultimately unheard until 2018.

Blazing through two and a half tense minutes, the song's agitated mood better captures McCartney's state of mind in the fall-out of his latest bust than

---

[150] According to Denny Seiwell, interviewed in Perasi, p85.
[151] The words to Jambalaya were not invented, although McCartney may have been unfamiliar with terms such as bayou (a marshy lake), filé gumbo (a dish popular in Louisiana), or Fontaineaux (a Cajun surname).
[152] The personnel on Night Out has never been confirmed and these credits are based on aural evidence only. Mixes with additional (much later) overdubs also circulate.

[170] Country Dreamer, recorded two days before. An unresolved battle between the keys of A and B, Night Out's main feature is its twin lead guitar, presumably Laine versus McCullough, but all of the band weighs in, Seiwell maintaining a solid four-square beat behind McCartney's frenzied exclamations. Absent any further development, the thrill of the song's energy soon fades, leaving the aftertaste of a promising idea abandoned too quickly.

Paul McCartney And Wings: [172] **ONE MORE KISS** (*McCartney*)
Produced by Paul McCartney
Recorded: 29 Sep 1972; 30 Sep 1972, EMI Studios, London
UK: 4 May 1973 (*Red Rose Speedway* LP)
US: 30 Apr 1973 (*Red Rose Speedway* LP)
Paul McCartney: vocals, guitar; **Linda McCartney**: electric harpsichord; **Denny Laine**: bass; **Henry McCullough**: guitar; **Denny Seiwell**: drums

The last of McCartney's overt homages to home and family, One More Kiss grew from something daughter Mary said when tiring of her father's over-affection. Minded of the thematic link, he used as a starting point a melodic phrase from [12] I'm A Fool To Care, fashioning a short scenario in which he's departing in the aftermath of a row, begging a final embrace before he goes. Surprisingly, this relatively simple guitar tune took Wings some 85 takes to complete, many of them no doubt accounted for by efforts to nail a double-tracked slide guitar, mixed to either side of the stereo picture and giving the song what McCartney considered to be a 'country and western' character. A musical curiosity, One More Kiss moves around a series of enigmatic minor chords for its chorus, only finding the longed-for resolution to G major with its verse. Pretty in execution and with its sentimentality held in check, it's among the more attractive examples of McCartney's delicate quasi-acoustic style.

Paul McCartney And Wings: [173] **BRIDGE ON THE RIVER SUITE** (*McCartney*)
Produced by Paul McCartney
Recorded: 29 Sep 1972, EMI Studios, London; Nov 1973, Studios Pathé Marconi, Paris; 11 Jul 1974, The Sound Shop, Nashville
UK/US: unreleased
Paul McCartney: guitar, bass; **Linda McCartney**: synthesiser; **Denny Laine**: guitar; **Jimmy McCulloch**: guitar; **Thaddeus Richard**: saxophone; **Bill Puitt**: saxophone; **Norman Ray**: baritone saxophone; **George Tidwell**: trumpet; **Barry McDonald**: trumpet; **Dale Quillen**: trombone; **Davey Lutton**: drums

During the first session for [172] One More Kiss on 29 September, McCartney performed a 'five minute guitar thing' on the studio floor, which engineer, Alan Parsons, chose to record.[153] Taking a shine to it, Parsons edited and mixed it in his own time and offered the finished tape to McCartney, whereupon it became something of a white elephant, its composer unclear what to do with it. He took the tapes to Paris in mid-November 1973 (revisiting the studio where Can't Buy Me Love had been recorded), when among exploratory work for a possible album by Linda, further instrumentation was dubbed on. Still the song lacked an outlet until, come 1974, McCartney decided to record one of his father's old compositions in Nashville, a lively instrumental named Walking In The Park With Eloise, which provided an opportunity to add more to Bridge On The River Suite (see also [240]). Thus completed, the track ended up far removed from its original inspiration, the finger-picked guitar largely buried beneath brass and drums. Transformed into a sauntering jazz number, it was never in the frame for release on a Wings record but was issued out by EMI on the flip side of Walking In The Park With Eloise, concealed beneath the moniker, the Country Hams.

Paul McCartney And Wings: [174] **HANDS OF LOVE** (*McCartney*)
Produced by Paul McCartney
Recorded: 1 Oct 1972, EMI Studios, London
UK: 4 May 1973 (*Red Rose Speedway* LP)
US: 30 Apr 1973 (*Red Rose Speedway* LP)
Paul McCartney: vocals, guitar, ocarina; **Linda McCartney**: backing vocals; **Denny Laine**: guitar; **Henry McCullough**: percussion; **Denny Seiwell**: drums, percussion

While his recent arrest and the making of Wings' next single had kept McCartney's mind occupied through September, his would-be showpiece for *Red Rose Speedway* – the side 2 medley – was gathering dust, half-complete. Eventually attention turned to finishing up the sequence, starting with this slight acoustic piece in which McCartney falls into the hands – not arms – of love. Despite its somewhat juvenile quality, some work went into the recording of Hands Of Love, drums and bass in particular treated to electronic processing to alter the tones, McCartney incorporating too an ocarina, a flute-like instrument shaped like a bulb. Any such attentions were trivialised by McCartney's jesting vocal imitations, which apart from filling the bars which might have been given over to a guitar solo at 0:44, become a chorus of parping and tooting Wings at 1:28.

---

[153] See Madinger and Easter, p178. Parson does not clarify whether the piece was improvised.

Paul McCartney And Wings: [175] **POWER CUT** (*McCartney*)
Produced by Paul McCartney
Recorded: 3 Oct 1972; 4 Oct 1972, EMI Studios, London
UK: 4 May 1973 (*Red Rose Speedway* LP)
US: 30 Apr 1973 (*Red Rose Speedway* LP)
Paul McCartney: vocals, bass, piano, celesta, Mellotron; **Linda McCartney**: electric piano; **Denny Laine**: guitar, backing vocals; **Henry McCullough**: guitar, backing vocals; **Denny Seiwell**: drums

Power Cut obliquely references a period of industrial turmoil in which electricity supplies were rationed due to a strike by Britain's coal miners – a situation which had posed a threat to Wings' University Tour, staged in the middle of the February crisis. While McCartney's lyric is not in any sense a political commentary it picks up on the currency of the phrase, albeit developed into a metaphor for the breakdown of a relationship. Its conclusive theme made it an apt album closer, for which it was recorded across a couple of days at EMI in October, its accentuated off-beats tapping into the reggae style McCartney was currently enjoying ([133]; [166]).

As presented on *Red Rose Speedway*, Power Cut concludes the medley but was obviously written as an independent piece, capable of standing on its own terms (and at 3:53 is comfortably the longest of the mini-set). McCartney though viewed the medley as a whole from the outset, each component track recorded in the correct sequence, with a running thread in which the keys of A and C predominate. (Power Cut concludes on the repeating chord of A major, in mood and key ready to blend back into the start of [167] Hold Me Tight, so that in theory the sequence could go around again, and forever.) The 11-minute suite was compiled on 16 January, and knowing where he was going, McCartney dubbed a set of lead guitars over this final song's coda, restating the melodic hooks from the preceding sections. Since these parts are not extemporised there is no stylistic clue as to who plays them, but if McCartney was intent on recapping the roundhouse finale of The End, as is widely supposed, they will have been delegated to Laine and McCullough, alongside McCartney himself. Novelties aside, the medley pales next to that of *Abbey Road*, not in terms of the raw compositions, which are hardly inferior to fare such as Polythene Pam, but inasmuch as they lack incision, needing Lennon's sharp attitude and Harrison's poised guitar phases to bring them out. As well as any post-Beatles work, the *Red Rose Speedway* medley exposes what McCartney missed from his former partners, sorely wanting for Lennon's fuzz-toned rhythm and goading harmonies to push it to the edge.

An afterthought: 5 October 1972, the day after Power Cut was recorded, was the 10th anniversary of the Beatles' first single, Love Me Do. The occasion passed without commemoration.

Paul McCartney And Wings: [176] **1882** (*McCartney*)
Produced by Paul McCartney
Recorded: 13 Nov 1972, EMI Studios, London
UK/US: unreleased
Paul McCartney: vocals, bass; **Linda McCartney**: keyboards, backing vocals; **Denny Laine**: guitar; **Henry McCullough**: guitar; **Denny Seiwell**: drums

Written on piano in 1970, this post-Dickensian tale of a servant boy stealing a loaf of bread from his master was an unlikely inclusion in Wings' summer tour of Europe, pulled out to help fill the group's thin repertoire. Given the song's vintage its content is surprisingly focused, McCartney setting out a story of crime and punishment across three verses, its fictionalised account drawing on the severity of juvenile sentencing in Victorian Britain; the song's mood is captured in the arrangement, a sombre waltz in A minor running for nearly seven minutes, sarcastically introduced by McCartney as, 'to celebrate'.

Having taken it on the road McCartney seemed set on releasing the song to the wider public, preparing a live recording from the 24 August show in Berlin during a lengthy mixing session on 11 November. For some reason he was unhappy and started again with this full studio version two days later, essentially reproducing the stage recording note-for-note. Neither was released in the day, the song only known to collectors through live bootlegs until both versions were eventually issued in an extended-format *Red Rose Speedway*.

Paul McCartney And Wings: [177] **JAZZ STREET** (*McCartney*)
Produced by Paul McCartney
Recorded: 27 Nov 1972, AIR Studios, London
UK/US: unreleased
Paul McCartney: bass, piano (?); **Linda McCartney**: percussion (?); **Denny Laine**: guitar; **Henry McCullough**: guitar; **Denny Seiwell**: drums

Wings issued their third non-album single on 1 December ([169] / [166]), ahead of *Red Rose Speedway* which was by now running so late it was set to miss the lucrative pre-Christmas market.[154] In truth, despite sessions having endured for most of 1972, McCartney didn't have enough material for his double LP, the proposal to include two live recordings and a version of Denny Laine's I Would Only Smile transparently over-stretching his hand.

Taped at George Martin's AIR Studios on Oxford Circus, the freewheeling Jazz Street gave the band a rare opportunity to express their ensemble skills,

---

[154] The UK release of the single came within a week of Lennon's belated [144] Happy Xmas (War Is Over), the two appearing together in the top 10.

McCartney momentarily standing down from his *de facto* directorship to allow Laine, Seiwell and McCullough a free hand. They spent a considerable effort trying to get it into shape, McCartney dubbing on some backwards-spooled acoustic guitar and revelling in the studio's panning controls which end up distracting through frantic swiping back and forth. If an exercise to help complete the album, this lengthy instrumental proved futile, not destined for inclusion and merely using up studio time. While moderately engaging to hear, this eight-minute improvisation in E was essentially more filler for an album already featuring the instrumental [163] Loup, and consequently it went unreleased until 2018 when it was finally unveiled in a more manageable five-minute edit.

Paul McCartney And Wings: [178] **MY LOVE** (*McCartney*)
    Produced by Paul McCartney
    Recorded: 26 Jan 1973; 27 Jan 1973, AIR Studios, London
    UK: 23 Mar 1973 (single A-side)
    US: 9 Apr 1973 (single A-side)
    Paul McCartney: vocals, electric piano; **Linda McCartney**: backing vocals; **Denny Laine**: bass, backing vocals; **Henry McCullough**: guitar; **Denny Seiwell**: drums, tambourine (?); **uncredited**: orchestration (directed by Richard Hewson)

The jewel in *Red Rose Speedway*'s crown, My Love has an uncertain origin, several sources claiming it was written in the late Beatles period, or, according to McCartney, 'in the early days' of his relationship with Linda.[155] Taken literally this indicates late 1968, yet there is no evidence of the song's existence prior to 1972 when it suddenly arrives on Wings' radar. McCartney's remark, on which the datings are based, was made from a distance of almost a third of a century, and it seems plausible that his 'early days' was intended to mean metaphorically 'early *years*', thereby pointing back to 1972 which accords with the known evidence.

    Further question marks attach to the recording session, identified by Madinger and Easter as 26-27 January 1973 at AIR. This should be weighed against the 2018 edition of *Red Rose Speedway* which claims the track was recorded at EMI, which is credible but contradicts the research. Moreover, the existence of an acetate disc containing a prototype of the album from December, with My Love included in the listing – before it was recorded – indicates there is more to the matter than is understood. Possibly two studio versions were made, one at each location, or conceivably, the acetate contained a stage performance from the summer European tour.

---

[155] Interview for *Billboard*, 16 March 2001.

The real mystery surrounding My Love is why McCartney left it until last, having kept the song to one side while Wings spent time on relative trivialities such as [164] Thank You Darling and [171] Night Out. As a composition, the song was essentially complete as early as February 1972 when it was included the 'ICA rehearsals', a video-taped warm-up for the University Tour in which Linda contributes some of the most inept and off-key backing vocals she ever performed. It was then unveiled to the public on stage, with Linda's superfluous sections still intact but about to be dropped for good.

In anticipation of the long-awaited session in the last weekend of January, McCartney commissioned Richard Hewson to write a score, cramming an orchestra into the studio alongside Wings for a 'live' recording – incomprehensibly bucking the standard practice of recording the strings in a separate session. Unlikely as it seems, Wings and the classical section – all 50 of them – performed as a vast ensemble, McCartney at keyboards, Laine filling in on the increasingly familiar electric bass, knowing that one individual slip from any of them would require all to go again from the top, with the meter running on dozens of expensive virtuosi. According to those present, they got as high as take 20 before they were satisfied, by which time the classical musicians were said to be fed up with the assignment, repeating technically flawless performances more times than they were used to.

Despite the abundance of skilled professionals, the most outstanding musicianship on show was Henry McCullough's, his much-admired guitar solo the outpouring of a gnawing frustration in which he'd too often been restricted to playing lines supplied to him by McCartney. In concert he had yet to come up with anything decent for My Love, but resolving now to assert himself he asked outright if he could make something up on the spot. Understandably concerned about the live nature of the session, McCartney's nervousness had its roots in his own experience when, during his first Quarry Men gig at 15 he fluffed a solo spot in front of an audience, leaving scars of embarrassment he couldn't get past, never playing lead on stage again. The only guitarist he'd worked with at length since was Harrison, a notorious struggler when it came to improvisation, yet McCullough rose to the occasion with a searing piece striding across two octaves of self-devised melody, his most memorable contribution to Wings' discography. Ironically he ended up making a rod for his own back, McCartney subsequently insisting he stick to the same solo in every live performance, arguing it's what the audience wanted, thereby reigning McCullough's talents back in – the price the guitarist paid for a moment of creative inspiration.

My Love stands as the boldest of McCartney's ballads since The Long And Winding Road, its novel opening on a sustained A falling under the romantic spell of B flat, as it seduces the accompanying chord into a warm major seventh, McCartney's opening on the word 'and' stressing this isn't a new feeling, but a love already running deep. With his vocal stepping along the F scale, the song's key remains elusive until it finds a final, emphatic cadence on the word 'good', an effect dramatically underscored by the song's arch coda, in which McCartney truly does find a conclusion. Whereas his previous love songs to Linda had often tended towards superficiality, My Love carries with it an air of authority, a statement which, behind its undeniably schmaltzy façade, *means something*.

An obvious choice for a single, My Love went to the top of the US charts, heralding the start of McCartney's popular resurgence and attracting a steady stream of cover versions. With it came a twist on the group's identity, the labels naming McCartney as well as the band – putting paid to any thoughts that Wings might, after all, develop a group democracy. For McCartney, this was very much *his* moment to shine, My Love later cited by its author as his favourite among Wings' 100 or so releases.

On 8 March, McCartney's court case for growing cannabis, which had been hanging over him since September (see [170]) was finally settled, the outcome effectively nothing more than a slap on the wrist. During the same period, the seemingly never-ending work on the double *Red Rose Speedway* took a decisive turn when McCartney presented his efforts to EMI only to meet with objections from the company who, in fairness, had watched most of Wings' releases to date struggle in the market place.[156] The circumstances of its cutting down to a single disc are unclear, the consensus being that EMI forced the issue, but according to Philip Norman, the impetus may have come from Henry McCullough.[157] If so, he saw to it that bandmate, Denny Laine, would be denied a release of his I Would Only Smile, on an album which ended up promoting McCartney to such an extent it could have passed for a solo effort.

From McCartney's perspective he'd been working towards a double album for a year, observing in the meantime Yoko Ono release her second two-LP set in a row with *Approximately Infinite Universe*, and on a label he was joint director of. Yet his own ambitions were blocked, which with the benefit of hindsight, worked for the better, *Red Rose Speedway* in danger otherwise of attracting a further savaging for what would have emerged as an inconsistent collection of bits and pieces, several of them self-indulgent and one track, Seaside Woman, written by his wife. The cover featured McCartney alone, a portrait of him feigning surprise while holding a rose in his mouth, in front of

---

[156] The double album offered to EMI consisted of [171]; [93]; [170]; [157]; [178] / [160]; [158]; Seaside Woman (Linda McCartney); [97]; [159] (live) / Best Friend (live); [163]; [167]; [168]; [174]; [175] / [162]; I Would Only Smile (Denny Laine); [172]; [161]; [111].
[157] 2016, p458.

a motorcycle flown to London from the States just for the sake of the photo. Carrying a plush illustrated book, and a greeting to Stevie Wonder embossed in Braille, the packaging of *Red Rose Speedway* was completed with an ad for the newly conceived Wings 'Fun' Club together with a band logo – something Harrison, Lennon and Starr all noticed with amusement.

When it appeared in late spring, *Red Rose Speedway* was cautiously welcomed, the usual perspective that this was an improvement on *Wild Life* taken as a sign McCartney was finding his feet. Despite the insipid nature of some of the material recorded, the insertion of the side 2 medley and of [178] My Love, plus two of the stronger remnants from *RAM* in [93] and [111], meant McCartney somehow managed to pull an album out the bag which at the time was reckoned his best since the end of the Beatles.

Over the winter, an unauthorised box set of Beatle recordings (group and solo) had been doing the rounds in America, titled *Alpha Omega* and brazenly advertised on television. EMI were swift to respond with court action, and in April put out their own offerings, the two double albums *1962-1966* and *1967-1970*, the first time the Beatles' discography had been officially compiled in such a way. The albums proved spectacular sellers and offered the strongest competition to *Red Rose Speedway*, which followed them into the shops by only a couple of weeks. Representing some sort of vindication, *Red Rose Speedway* toppled *1967-1970* from the summit of the *Billboard* album chart, a symbolic moment in which the real solo McCartney finally seemed to have arrived.

RECORD RELEASES

[165] **Mary Had A Little Lamb** / [108] **Little Woman Love**
(UK: 12 May 1972, US: 29 May 1972)
[169] **Hi, Hi, Hi** / [166] **C Moon**
(UK: 1 Dec 1972, US: 4 Dec 1972)
[178] **My Love** / [159] **The Mess**
(UK: 23 Mar 1973, US: 9 Apr 1973)
Red Rose Speedway
(UK: 4 May 1973, US: 30 Apr 1973)
[157] Big Barn Bed / [178] My Love / [93] Get On The Right Thing / [172] One More Kiss / [111] Little Lamb Dragonfly / [160] Single Pigeon / [158] When The Night / [163] Loup (1st Indian On The Moon) / Medley: [167] Hold Me Tight-[168] Lazy Dynamite-[174] Hands Of Love-[175] Power Cut

PART 3: TO HELP EACH OTHER

'I hear there's a track going on.
Is it okay if I come down?'

George Harrison, 13 March 1973

Living In The Material World sessions: October 1972 to March 1973

Spotting Harrison on the music scene of 1972 was a rare thing, his time largely consumed by various tasks surrounding the *Concert For Bangla Desh* project, which kept him occupied through the first part of the year. Having got the soundtrack album out at the end of 1971, Harrison was dismayed to learn the professionally shot footage was below the standard he had hoped for, leading to months of work editing and preparing the documentary film which premiered in New York in late March, an event attended by Lennon who might have appeared in it, had he been minded to perform. (A secondary issue distracting Harrison was the inflexible manoeuvring of tax authorities who managed to lock up much of the revenue which ought to have been flowing into the relief fund.) Then, over the summer, Harrison elected to follow Lennon's lead and have his own recording facilities installed at his home. Friar Park Studios, Henley-on-Thames, usually referred to by the ungainly acronym, FPSHOT, was completed in October and boasted a 16-track console installed on the building's second floor.

These album sessions, which started around that time, were characterised by a lack of proper organisation underlined by the fact that Phil Spector, who was supposed to be directing affairs, was unable to get his act together through a haze of non-stop cherry brandies, leaving Harrison to produce it largely – if not entirely – by himself. Officially *Living In The Material World* was taped at Apple, which if correct makes it the only solo Beatle album recorded there. However there is much residual uncertainty and Klaus Voormann has claimed it was in fact made at FPSHOT – which is easy enough to accept given that Harrison's brand new home studio would otherwise have stood pointlessly empty while he travelled back and forth to London, not a particularly persuasive notion.[158] The absence of any publicly available studio paperwork (if it ever existed) leaves the matter frustratingly unresolved, and with this caveat we nominate Apple as the location in the following pages, in accordance with Madinger and Easter. Unlike with *All Things Must Pass*, Harrison was able to keep a tight circle of musicians throughout the project, maintaining a core band in Gary Wright, Nicky Hopkins, Jim Keltner and Klaus Voormann, with best estimates that work began in October 1972 and concluded around March 1973, when Harrison left the UK on other matters.

---

[158] Voormann was interviewed circa 2002 by Simon Leng (p126): 'On the record it says it was cut at Apple, but it was done at his house'. Graeme Thomson (p240) accepts this, while noting the overdubs were done at 'Savile Row' (ie, Apple) (p242).

George Harrison: [179] **SUE ME, SUE YOU BLUES** (*Harrison*)
Produced by George Harrison
Recorded: Oct 1972-Mar 1973, Apple Studios, London[159]
UK: 22 Jun 1973 (*Living In The Material World* LP)
US: 30 May 1973 (*Living In The Material World* LP)
George Harrison: vocals, guitar, dobro; **Nicky Hopkins**: piano; **Gary Wright**: electric piano; **Klaus Voormann**: bass; **Jim Keltner**: drums

The legal circus which surrounded the Beatles' split became something of a running joke within the music business, an endless stream of litigation following the four of them around for several years. Matters began to sour as early as 1969 when McCartney appointed the legal firm, Eastman and Eastman, sending them into business meetings against Allen Klein and the rest of the group in long-running tussles over finances, ownership of Northern Songs and the Beatles' royalty rate from EMI. Elsewhere, Harrison was facing court action over [34] My Sweet Lord, and Lennon over Come Together, and with ATV-Northern-Maclen next threatening both McCartney and Lennon in early 1971 over claims that Linda and Yoko respectively had been helping them write their songs, relations reached their nadir when McCartney openly sued Harrison, Lennon and Starr – to the point where, as one satire later suggested, any of them could have inadvertently sued themselves and not realised.[160] In this context Harrison wrote Sue Me, Sue You Blues, presenting the never-ending legal battles as a square dance in which four partners circle to music, swapping positions as they proceed.

Given its bitter outlook, it's no surprise the song came through in the Delta blues style, Harrison first recording his woes in a remarkable slide guitar demo, probably during the difficult first months of 1971. Given to Oklahoma rock-blues guitarist, Jesse Ed Davis, after the two had played together at the Concert For Bangla Desh, it was recorded and released as a single on the Atco label in January 1972, slipping out largely unnoticed, at least by Beatles fans, leaving the door open for a recording by Harrison himself a year or so later. By the time of the *Living In The Material World* sessions, Harrison had inserted an extra verse referencing money held in escrow, no doubt still smarting over McCartney's partial victory in which a receiver had assumed control of the

---

[159] As recording dates for the album tracks are unknown, we present them in the order they were written, which can be established to a fair degree of accuracy with reference to Harrison's autobiography.
[160] The Rutles (1978) parodied this aspect of the Beatles' story, joking their final recording, *Let It Rot*, was released as a film, an album and a lawsuit. In a sense, McCartney *had* sued himself, his 1971 action citing Beatles & Co, of which he was co-owner, as the primary defendant.

Beatles' joint finances. Dominated by Harrison's slide sections, played on a dobro, the track benefits from Nicky Hopkins' dancing piano trills and Gary Wright's Wurlitzer keyboard passages, which make for a second instrumental break towards the end, but despite such efforts it fails to elevate itself from the underlying self-sorrow of its conception.

Its eventual release coincided with the expiry of Allen Klein's management contract, whereupon he issued a fresh writ against Lennon for unpaid loans, which Lennon, Harrison and Starr reacted to with a writ of their own, leading Klein to counter-sue McCartney, with whom he had no direct dealings – and so the legal merry-go-round continued.

George Harrison: [180] **WHO CAN SEE IT** (*Harrison*)
Produced by George Harrison
Recorded: Oct 1972-Mar 1973, Apple Studios, London; Feb 1972,
    Apple Studios, London (?)
UK: 22 Jun 1973 (*Living In The Material World* LP)
US: 30 May 1973 (*Living In The Material World* LP)
George Harrison: vocals, guitar; **Nicky Hopkins**: piano; **Gary Wright**: keyboards; **Klaus Voormann**: bass; **Ringo Starr**: drums; **Jim Keltner**: drums; **uncredited**: orchestra, brass, choir

As hinted at by his decision to record [179] Sue Me, Sue You Blues, Harrison was far from over his Beatle past through 1972, constantly making reference to the group in song as if trying to expunge something from his system. This number, like its predecessor, dates to the lull between *All Things Must Pass* and the Concert For Bangla Desh, and finds Harrison on the defensive, justifying himself to his public in spite of the great commercial success which had so far failed to convince him that he'd emerged in his own right. It's one of the paradoxes of Harrison's life that the pull of his spirituality was countered by an equally overpowering concern with worldly ego, the current song's pressing home of his need to be recognised a case in point. In *Rolling Stone* (19 December 1974), Harrison declared, in deference to Who Can See It, 'My life belongs to me,' before realising his mistake: 'It actually doesn't. It belongs to Him. My life belongs to the Lord Krishna and there's my dog collar to prove it.'

Musically Who Can See It plays around with its rhythms, inserting then dropping half-beats as it progresses, as if trying to subvert any sense of balance. The effect is to accentuate the underlying tension, Harrison's pleading to be given his independent dues paid off by a concession to the group, his lead guitar (played on the low strings) running through a swimming Leslie speaker as deployed frequently on the Beatles' final albums. Perhaps seeking to reinvent himself, Harrison imagined the vocal sung by Roy Orbison whose style he emulates, rising sternly through the build-up to the chorus to find an exultant plateau in which he seems to finally reach his true level. Overlaid in February with a score by John Barham, placed low in the mix, Who Can See It manages to transverse its emotional burdens, coming across as one of the album's highlights – a notable triumph of arrangement and delivery.

George Harrison: [181] **MISS O'DELL** (*Harrison*)
Produced by George Harrison
Recorded: Oct 1972-Mar 1973, Apple Studios, London
UK: 25 May 1973 (single B-side)
US: 7 May 1973 (single B-side)
George Harrison: vocals, guitar, harmonica; **Klaus Voormann**: bass; **Jim Keltner**: drums, cowbell, percussion

Written on sabbatical in Los Angeles during April 1971, Miss O'Dell takes the form of a memo sent back to Chris O'Dell, an old friend of the Harrisons who'd lived at Friar Park for a while and was currently working at Peter Asher's Apple office. Something of a ramble, the lyric wanders from thoughts of war in Bangladesh to pollution in LA and the fact that Harrison's record player seemed to have broken down, his sense of boredom cooped up in a rented Malibu beach house all too apparent.

Sections of the song bear distinct resemblance to Lon and Derrek Van Eaton's Without The Lord, a track from their contemporary Apple album, *Brother* (where it is programmed immediately before the Harrison-produced Sweet Music). Which song influenced which is a matter for conjecture, the release sequence suggesting Harrison borrowed from the Van Eatons – but Miss O'Dell was written before the duo arrived at Apple, indicating the reverse, unless Harrison's song underwent changes down the line. Another recognisable influence is Dylan, whose It's All Over Now, Baby Blue (1965) serves as a close template for the verses and presumably suggested the use of a harmonica.

In the studio Harrison mixed up his words around the minute mark, chuckling off the mistake and continuing to a finish, at which point he was reminded of the perfectionist McCartney – who would have been annoyed at such a blunder – and jokingly recalled his pal's old phone number, Garston 6922. Ostensibly a spoiled take, Harrison ran through the song again but in the event opted to release the 'comic' version as the B-side to [184] Give Me Love (Give Me Peace On Earth) in May. From a professional point of view the recording was a lapse, but fans enjoyed the sound of Harrison laughing again.

George Harrison: [182] **BE HERE NOW** (*Harrison*)
Produced by George Harrison
Recorded: Oct 1972-Mar 1973, Apple Studios, London
UK: 22 Jun 1973 (*Living In The Material World* LP)
US: 30 May 1973 (*Living In The Material World* LP)
George Harrison: vocals, guitar, tambura (?); **Gary Wright**: keyboards; **Nicky Hopkins**: piano; **Klaus Voormann**: upright bass

Unhappy with the isolation of his Malibu base [181], Harrison quickly found some new digs in Nichols Canyon, a residential area in the Hollywood Hills which apart from providing more nightlife, was a stone's throw from Record Plant West where he and Ravi Shankar were working on the film, *Raga*. The achingly beautiful Be Here Now came to him in bed one night, Harrison drifting in a semi-dream state, channelling the spirit of Shankar and the Indian traditions which were absorbing his days.[161] Sleepily meandering through its scales, Be Here Now is both exotic and meditative, an uncanny fusion of Western and Eastern music in which one can smell the incense and hear the distant tinkling of bells carried on a gentle Himalayan breeze.

Underscored by a softly droning tambura, the recording marks a return to Harrison's quasi-Indian style, the first time he'd explored such territory in his solo career, notwithstanding the unreleased [31] Dehra Dun and [68] Om Hare Om (Gopala Krishna). Recognising its natural qualities, Klaus Voormann elected to perform his bass part on an acoustic upright, using the old technique of setting up in the lavatory to achieve a suitable resonance off the walls, which he later commemorated in an artwork given to Harrison.

The soul of the song rises from the philosophy of Ram Dass, who had just published his spiritual story, *Be Here Now*, containing tales of travels in India imbibing LSD and searching for meaning. Something of a countercultural 'bible', *Be Here Now* offers a philosophy of disengagement with the passage of time by dwelling entirely in the present, a technique of emancipation which in the hands of Western youth often leant merely to not bothering with the consequences of one's actions.[162] Harrison's musical distillation was accordingly received as a repudiation of his Beatle self, and there may be something in such a reading – although Harrison was expressing a core belief which he would restate years later in the song, Flying Hour: 'The past it is gone/The future may not be at all'.

---

[161] The song has something of the flavour of Gurur Bramha, one of the tracks Shankar was working on.

[162] The book's title phrase comes from the narrator's discussion with his guide, Bhagavan Das: 'We'd be sitting somewhere and I'd say, "Did I ever tell you about the time that Tim and I..." and he'd say, "Don't think about the past. Just be here now".'

Capturing a place where time stands still, Be Here Now is the album's purest creation, its atmosphere of enlightenment shrouded in mystery reflecting the yin-yang of life's eternal dualism, four minutes in which Harrison managed to transcend the physical world and touch a universal truth.

George Harrison: [183] **THE DAY THE WORLD GETS 'ROUND** (*Harrison*)
Produced by George Harrison
Recorded: Oct 1972-Mar 1973, Apple Studios, London
UK: 22 Jun 1973 (*Living In The Material World* LP)
US: 30 May 1973 (*Living In The Material World* LP)
George Harrison: vocals, guitar; **Nicky Hopkins**: piano; **Gary Wright**: organ; **Klaus Voormann**: bass; **Jim Keltner**: drums; **Ringo Starr**: drums

The situation in Bangladesh pulled Harrison's psyche in two directions at once, optimism that he could help counter-balanced by a resentment over the lack of government action to resolve things, which in Harrison's eyes was merely a question of having the will to act. Thus the altruism surrounding the two concerts, which had seen prominent musicians give up their time for free and masses of audience members rally to the cause, was tempered by a despair for humanity whose destructive side had led to the crisis in the first place. After the concerts closed on the Sunday night, and the after-show party had subsided, Harrison remained in New York and in the emotional come-down wrote the current song, reflecting on affairs and wondering why responsibility for trying to alleviate suffering should rest so heavily on his own shoulders.

Harrison has come in for much criticism for the lyric, the usual angle being that he was taking a holier-than-though stance, his observation that there are too few following a righteous path interpreted as a claim of moral superiority. However there is no such adversarial sentiment in the song, which is observing the world passively, Harrison setting his thoughts to the most gentle of melodies and even including a pun in the title – which while offering no levity, does at least show his mood to have been compassionate. The song's most pointed lines come in the tough middle section, where he sits up and points a finger, 'If you're the destructive kind/I don't want to be like you' – a paraphrase of the position expressed by Lennon in Revolution.

Harrison's efforts to work for the wider good turned out to be more of a burden than he anticipated, largely vindicating his judgement. Soon circled by record company lawyers arguing over the concert recording rights and royalties, Harrison was angered to learn Allen Klein had failed to properly register the shows for charitable status, a technicality exploited by the tax system which in the case of the US meant the government, while not only selling arms to the combatants, was also profiting from the relief effort. In this way the sense of futility underpinning The Day The World Gets 'Round was fairly realistic after all, a sad assessment of human nature encapsulated in Harrison's guitar harmonics, landing on the song's title phrase like teardrops.

George Harrison: [184] **GIVE ME LOVE (GIVE ME PEACE ON EARTH)**
(*Harrison*)
Produced by George Harrison
Recorded: Oct 1972-Mar 1973, Apple Studios, London
UK: 25 May 1973 (single A-side)
US: 7 May 1973 (single A-side)
George Harrison: vocals, guitar; **Nicky Hopkins**: piano; **Gary Wright**: organ; **Klaus Voormann**: bass; **Jim Keltner**: drums

Harrison's second-biggest hit came to him as a prayer, the words arriving spontaneously, accounting for its lyrical brevity and – by his standards – unusually light content. Translated into the pop format, the sacred inspiration is buried beneath a surface shining with guitars but reveals itself in the content, Harrison's imploring line, 'Keep me free from birth' an expression of the Hindu *moksha*, a release from *samsara*, the endlessly repeating cycle of physical death and rebirth. Thus, the apparent universality, in which its pleas for peace on Earth have seen it compared to [1] Give Peace A Chance, are internalised – not a calling to the world at large so much as an expression of Harrison's hope for his own existence during this transitory life.

With its looping slide guitar, double tracked and self-harmonising, this was the most easily accessible recording on *Living In The Material World*, its pleasingly unforced arrangement sweetened by Nicky Hopkins' piano figures, presumably his own idea and borrowed from Bob Dylan's I Want You (*Blonde On Blonde*, 1966). A natural choice of single, it was issued ahead of the album, and did its main business in the States where on 30 June, it knocked McCartney [178] off the number 1 spot, no doubt to Harrison's delight.[163] A commercial coup, two years after the disappointing [140] Bangla-Desh, Give Me Love reminded the world that Harrison was still around and capable of producing high-quality music.

---

[163] My Love was relegated to number 2, while at number 3 was Harrison's close friend, Billy Preston, whose Will It Go Round In Circles assumed top spot the following week.

George Harrison: [185] **THE LORD LOVES THE ONE (THAT LOVES THE LORD)** (*Harrison*)
Produced by George Harrison
Recorded: Oct 1972-Mar 1973, Apple Studios, London
UK: 22 Jun 1973 (*Living In The Material World* LP)
US: 30 May 1973 (*Living In The Material World* LP)
George Harrison: vocals, guitar; **Nicky Hopkins**: piano; **Gary Wright**: keyboards; **Klaus Voormann**: bass; **Jim Horn**: saxophone; **Jim Keltner**: drums, shaker (?); **Ringo Starr**: drums; **Zakir Hussein**: tabla

Harrison's religious absorption was deepening through 1971 and 1972, his studious attention to Hindu philosophy leading him to seek direct tuition from AC Bhaktivedanta Swami Prabhupada, head of the international Krishna movement, for hours-long discourses at Friar Park, some of which were tape-recorded. From such sessions Harrison was inspired to write The Lord Loves The One, musing the life-long efforts spent acquiring money and status, only to lose them again in the inevitability of death – with a flimsy dig along the way at politicians 'acting like big girls'. Harrison's address reflects on his personal situation and the superficiality of 'fame and fortune', the lyric's judgemental quality essentially a public self-analysis revolving around the principles of karmic law and speaking of a deep-seated belief in an eternal truth hiding beneath the human ego.[164] Harrison's devotion to the Krishna movement was genuine, exemplified during these recording sessions by his purchasing of Piggott's Manor, an extravagant Hertfordshire estate which he donated to the temple after they'd outgrown their London base. (It was subsequently renamed Bhaktivedanta Manor.)

Musically the recording has been admired for its punch, Starr present to contribute a second drum section and with a classic Harrison solo towards the close. Originally recorded with a guide vocal, Harrison returned to capture a proper performance but in the end decided to run both voices together, making for a novel faux-harmony through parts of the song. In this respect he may have been inspired by one-time hero, Marvin Gaye, whose What's Going On single had been released to the UK in mid-1971, featuring the same effect throughout.

---

[164] His terse summary of the song's subject matter was stated in conversation with Prabhupada at Henley on 22 August 1973.

George Harrison: [186] **LIVING IN THE MATERIAL WORLD** (*Harrison*)
Produced by George Harrison
Recorded: Oct 1972, Apple Studios, London
UK: 22 Jun 1973 (*Living In The Material World* LP)
US: 30 May 1973 (*Living In The Material World* LP)
George Harrison: vocals, guitar, tambura (?); **Nicky Hopkins:** piano; **Gary Wright:** Hammond organ; **Klaus Voormann:** saxophone, bass; **Jim Horn:** saxophone, flute, recorders; **Ringo Starr:** drums; **Jim Keltner:** drums, percussion; **Zakir Hussein:** tabla

As with the previous song, Living In The Material World has its origins in deep conversations with Prabhupada about the Hindu understanding of reality and release from the reincarnation cycle, and essentially re-states parts of *The Bhagavad Gita*. A six-verse, semi-autobiographical review, the lyric hinges on the idea that 'we are not these bodies', the existence of the physical plane relegating the human form to a vessel in which the real self is travelling: 'Use my body like a car/taking me both near and far'. Written in the late summer of 1971 (and probably the first thing to be recorded) Living In The Material World represents more than just a song, capturing Harrison's outlook on life – and as such provides an apt title for the album.

What lifts the track from another religious oration is its humour, Harrison explaining his position with a smile, as if to close friends. Listener attention naturally focuses on the naming of each fellow Beatle in a wry comment on worldly success, Harrison even asking 'Richy' to add a signature drum fill just after his name is heard. Full of such light moments, including a flute flourish from Jim Horn following mention of Krishna, and an ironic 'showbiz' finish, the track manages to not take itself seriously, Harrison sufficiently aware that delivering a lecture on vinyl was likely to alienate at least part of his target audience.

Where the song breaks from its earthly bonds is in the contrasting section, nominally the middle eight, where Harrison momentarily ascends to the 'Spiritual Sky', that place where in Vedic thought, Lord Krishna dwells, and to which the human spirit seeks to manifest.[165] Initially unsure how to record these sections, Harrison left the requisite number of bars blank, later returning to dub on a tabla played by Zakir Hussein, the son of Ravi Shankar's friend and colleague, Alla Rakah, and a droning string instrument, uncredited but probably a sitar or tambura, which Harrison likely handled himself.

Having lent its title to the LP, Living In The Material World has become

---

[165] Spiritual Sky was used as the name of a record label which re-issued the Harrison-produced Apple album, *The Radha Krsna Temple*, at around the same time. Re-titled *Goddess Of Fortune*, it was given away to passers by on the London streets.

one of Harrison's key recordings after which he named a benevolent organisation set up in 1973 to support artistic endeavours and philosophical exploration. As such it has indirectly become one of his defining songs, the title phrase pulled into service again in 2011 when Martin Scorsese produced an Emmy Award-winning documentary surveying Harrison's life, an accolade out of proportion to its musical merits, but which emphasises the importance of the track in encapsulating his slant on human existence.

George Harrison: [187] **THAT IS ALL** (*Harrison*)
Produced by George Harrison
Recorded: Oct 1972-Mar 1973, Apple Studios, London
UK: 22 Jun 1973 (*Living In The Material World* LP)
US: 30 May 1973 (*Living In The Material World* LP)
George Harrison: vocals, guitar; **Nicky Hopkins**: piano; **Gary Wright**: harpsichord; **Klaus Voormann**: bass; **Jim Keltner**: drums; **uncredited**: orchestration (arranged by John Barham)

Probably written on piano, this regretful ballad, which shares its upward chromatic steps with Lennon's [85] Isolation, was fully worked out as an instrumental before Harrison added a lyric born from the strains of his eight-year relationship with Pattie, one of their problems Harrison's inability or refusal to articulate his thoughts. Speaking of their breakdown years later, Pattie recalled Harrison's intransigence, her husband distant and frequently lost in meditation: 'If you talked to him you didn't know whether you would get an answer in the middle of his chanting.'[166] As if an attempt to account for his remoteness, the lyric's hopeful plea that silence often means more than mere talk, while unlikely to convince Pattie, at least indicates Harrison had thoughts of saving the marriage. Yet within a year they were having affairs with close friends behind one another's back, leading to their inevitable separation in 1974 (see [268]).

Recorded in a placid, bass-high arrangement, Harrison lifting to the top of his vocal register, That Is All is a disarming affair, the only signs of fight coming in his Leslie-toned guitar solo which in its brevity is as emotionally closed as Harrison himself. Overdubbed late in the sessions by John Barham, the song was adorned with harpsichord, strings and an angelic choir, oddly reminiscent of the arrangement on The Long And Winding Road but mixed low so as to not overpower a song which, in the final assessment, remains a deeply personal statement.

With its conclusive-sounding title, That Is All was placed at the end of the

---

[166] *Wonderful Tonight*, p181-182. The middle eight here expresses the same frustrations as I Want To Tell You, written just after the two had married in 1966.

album, closing it with an unusually introverted half-cadence – a reflective finish to a set rooted in Harrison's inner thoughts. Catching the ear for its melodicism the track was immediately picked up by Andy Williams for a cover version, the American crooner no doubt hoping he'd stumbled on another Something. For his album, *Solitaire*, Williams employed some familiar names – Jim Keltner, Nicky Hopkins, Klaus Voormann and others close to Harrison – Harry Nilsson's later attempt at the track featuring much the same line-up again – the constantly circulating session musicians drifting from job to job through the 1970s while Harrison's life and loves moved on.

George Harrison: [188] **SO SAD** (*Harrison*)
    Produced by George Harrison
    Recorded: Oct 1972-Mar 1973, Apple Studios, London; Aug-Sep 1974,
        Friar Park Studios, Henley-on-Thames; 30 Oct 1974, A&M Studios,
        Hollywood
    UK: 20 Dec 1974 (*Dark Horse* LP)
    US: 9 Dec 1974 (*Dark Horse* LP)
    George Harrison: vocals, guitars 'and the other things'; **Nicky Hopkins**: keyboards; **Willie Weeks**: bass; **Ringo Starr**: drums; **Jim Keltner**: drums

Written in New York during 1972, So Sad is pitched in the third person but like [187] That Is All, conveys the emotional distance between Harrison and his wife. Lyrically the song recalls the Everly Brothers' 1960 hit, So Sad (To Watch Good Love Go Bad), a song Harrison had admired at the time and which likely prompted him to formally register his own title as So Sad (No Love Of His Own).[167]

The song's recording history is drawn-out and sketchy, the officially acknowledged presence of Starr, Hopkins and Keltner, convincing evidence it was taped during sessions for *Living In The Material World*. However it was not issued out at that stage, and instead Harrison gave it to Ten Years After vocalist, Alvin Lee, for his 1973 album, *On The Road To Freedom*, where the mood is slower and consequently more pensive, and to which Harrison, under the feeble pseudonym, Hari Georgeson, contributes a dobro line. It wasn't until after he and Pattie separated that Harrison elected to finish up his own version, first dubbing on a bass guitar played by Willie Weeks, then hurriedly adding his coarse vocal track in Hollywood on the eve of his 1974 North American Tour. (Perhaps as a consequence of the protracted timescale, the given album credits are vague, Harrison claiming only to have played some

---

[167] Lewisohn (2013, p743) reports the existence of Harrison's hand-written lyrics to So Sad (To Watch Good Love Go Bad) circa 1960, suggesting it may have been in the Beatles' sets.

unspecified parts, which seemingly include a range of guitars and percussion.)

An airy creation, So Sad starts and ends with a descending run down the major scale, falling from an unstable F and probably developed from the similar device in [66] Run Of The Mill, with which it shares a sense of loss. Harrison's chord structure though succeeds in rising above defeat, gathering its energies on a run into a chorus swaying up and down a repeating three-chord pattern with an ironic smile. A pleasing addition to *Dark Horse* at the end of 1974, it's a pity Harrison opted not to release it on *Living In The Material World*, which would have benefited from the song's light touch.

George Harrison: [189] **THE LIGHT THAT HAS LIGHTED THE WORLD**
(*Harrison*)
Produced by George Harrison
Recorded: Oct 1972-Mar 1973, Apple Studios, London
UK: 22 Jun 1973 (*Living In The Material World* LP)
US: 30 May 1973 (*Living In The Material World* LP)
George Harrison: vocals, guitar; **Nicky Hopkins**: piano; **Gary Wright**: organ; **Klaus Voormann**: bass; **Jim Keltner**: drums

This curiously pained ballad was conceived in the autumn of 1972 as a vehicle for Harrison's old friend, Cilla Black, while they were working on [74] I'll Still Love You. Reckoning she might need a B-side, he tried to conjure something of relevance to Black, who'd lived on Liverpool's notorious Scottie Road, and mindful of the stereotypical 'northern' attitude that those who move on in life are betrayers of kith and kin, devised the song's opening couplet. After sessions broke down Harrison decided to finish it up for himself – and to judge by the lyric's unusually vexed tone, needed to get something off his chest.

Critics have tended to interpret the lyric's antagonism as a reference to Harrison's Beatle past, yet the dialogue focuses more on differing states of mind than on his career history. The thrust of the text, that he was suffering the slings and arrows of jealousy, has a faintly unpleasant air about it as if the writer were pouring scorn on those not on his spiritual plane, and thus after 10 lines of politely expressed irritation he gets to the point – that his adversaries 'down in a hole' are failing to perceive the supreme lord Brahman, who in Hindu texts is the source of all light which illuminates the world. (See also [62] Beware Of Darkness.)

Built on a classic descending bassline, the track's major-key foundation promises more than it delivers, the dour vocal for the main part jockeying between two notes and failing to offer the uplift hinted at in its title. What liberates it as a recording is the addition of Nicky Hopkins' breezy piano, which transcends Harrison's weariness to take a lead role, his solo at 1:22 the most enjoyable passage on the album. (Such was Harrison's respect for the pianist that between sessions for *Living In The Material World*, he and Voormann helped out with Hopkins' solo album, *The Tin Man Was a Dreamer*, released in 1973 to warm reviews.) For some reason, when Harrison's album was moving towards completion, *The Light That Has Lighted The World* was pencilled as its title, an idea which was fortunately dropped since the song's judgemental slant meant it needed no emphasis.

George Harrison: [190] **DON'T LET ME WAIT TOO LONG** (*Harrison*)
Produced by George Harrison
Recorded: Oct 1972-Mar 1973, Apple Studios, London
UK: 22 Jun 1973 (*Living In The Material World* LP)
US: 30 May 1973 (*Living In The Material World* LP)
George Harrison: vocals, guitar; **Nicky Hopkins**: piano; **Gary Wright**: electric piano, harpsichord; **Klaus Voormann**: bass; **Jim Keltner**: drums, castanets; **Ringo Starr**: drums

After the laborious [189] The Light That Has Lightened The World, Harrison's final contribution was this sprightly three-minute pop number celebrating the salvation of his woman's love. Launching directly into its chorus, the song's lightness of mood and subject matter is sufficiently out of keeping with the rest of the collection that Harrison was obviously writing in character, customising for himself a potential chart hit. The only place his true musical self is revealed is in the gear change from F to C sharp during the song's verse, a trademark shift which provides a mood contrast, preventing the song from lapsing into frivolity.

At some point in the new year Harrison applied his slide guitar overdubs to the backing track, oddly refusing a solo during the central instrumental break. Thus readied, any thoughts of releasing the song on 45 had to wait until [184] Give Me Love (Give Me Peace On Earth) was out the way. Capitol-Apple eventually scheduled it for 24 September, the same day as [198] Photograph, but presumably seeking to avoid the clash, Don't Let Me Wait Too Long was indefinitely postponed. Whatever the rationale Harrison was deprived of another chart success on the back of [184].

Harrison celebrated his birthday on 25 February 1973, after which all four ex-Beatles had passed into their thirties. In an era when pop music was considered almost entirely a young man's game, this was uncharted territory, the major artists of the 1960s now entering a period of maturity exemplified by the Rolling Stones' transitional *Goat's Head Soup*, and Dylan's comeback starting with the *Pat Garrett And Billy The Kid* soundtrack, both recorded concurrently with *Living In The Material World*. Harrison's advancing years had seen his musical output deepen in introspection, which at times gave the impression he was carrying a sense of obligation, the usual line that he was unhappy as a public figure belied by the fact that he chose to continue pursuing a high-profile recording career.

The gloominess lurking beneath many of the songs on *Living In The Material World* stems from a spiritual perspective whose flip side was a negativity towards the world around him, bringing the failings of friends and politicians into increasingly sharp relief. That he chose to comment in song was, if nothing else, emotionally honest, the inclusion on the album of four slow and 'heavy' tracts in [180] Who Can See It; [183] The Day The World Gets 'Round; [187] That Is All and [189] The Light That Has Lighted The World evidence of Harrison's emphasis on self-expression. What seemed lost in the process was Harrison-the-guitarist, whose free-flowing sections on *All Things Must Pass* are scarcely reprised here. With the exception of his lead contributions to [184] Give Me Love and [185] The Lord Loves The One, there is little memorable in his playing, musical space too frequently conceded to keyboards and, in the case of the title track, a losing battle against dominant saxophone.

The packaging of the set was taken no less lightly, the front cover carrying a Kirlian photograph of Harrison's right hand surrounded by an aura, in the palm of which was a Hindu charm, with the corresponding image on the back pointedly showing him holding a silver dollar instead. Extravagantly presented in gatefold sleeve with printed lyrics and artwork reproduced from *The Bhagavad Gita*, the main photography continued to contrast the spiritual and the material, Harrison's ironic recreation of *The Last Supper* shot in the grounds of a Hollywood mansion with Starr pictured among the 'apostles'. Where he did have some fun was in the footnotes, Harrison having spotted McCartney's plugging of the Wings Fun Club on the back of *Red Rose Speedway*, and parodying it with the absurd Jim Keltner Fan Club, complete with corresponding winged logo, for details of which fans were invited to send a 'stamped undressed elephant' to 5112 Hollywood Boulevard, the address of Leon Russell's Shelter record label. (Although initially flattered, Keltner later complained of receiving crank letters from fans, which were somehow passed on to him.)

Living In The Material World might have arrived sooner, had it not been for release congestion which saw McCartney's album issued in April along with the two Beatles compilations, *1962-1966* and *1967-1970*. Modestly promoted, it was nonetheless a commercial triumph and on 23 June, toppled *Red Rose Speedway* from the summit of the *Billboard* album charts, seven days before [184] Give Me Love (Give Me Peace On Earth) did the same to [178] My Love in the singles listing – a remarkable double achievement. *Living In The Material*

World was well-received in its day, cited by *Rolling Stone* as a classic, but which in the years since has all but disappeared in the public's awareness, to become what Simon Leng succinctly described as, 'a million-plus seller that gets nary a mention'.[168] For Harrison, after the extravagance of his epic triple set two and a half years earlier, then the commercially sprawling *Bangla Desh* project, it also marked the start of a standard release schedule which would see him through the rest of the 1970s.

RECORD RELEASES

[184] **Give Me Love (Give Me Peace On Earth)** / [181] **Miss O'Dell**
(UK: 25 May 1973, US: 7 May 1973)
Living In The Material World
(UK: 22 Jun 1973, US: 30 May 1973)
[184] Give Me Love (Give Me Peace On Earth) / [179] Sue Me, Sue You Blues / [189] The Light That Has Lighted The World / [190] Don't Let Me Wait Too Long / [180] Who Can See It / [186] Living In The Material World / [185] The Lord Loves The One (That Loves The Lord) / [182] Be Here Now / [116] Try Some Buy Some / [183] The Day The World Gets 'Round / [187] That Is All

Paul McCartney screen commissions: October 1972 to April 1973

During the period in which *Red Rose Speedway* was finished then readied for release, the ever-restless McCartney had three further commissions, each pushing new artistic territory and all linked to television or film productions. Thus, over the winter of 1972 running into 1973, he came up with a small cache of new material destined not for standard Wings projects but for screen broadcast, each highly variable in style and with the benefit of a hit single among them.

---

[168] Leng, p124.

Wings: [191] **LIVE AND LET DIE** (*McCartney*)
Produced by George Martin
Recorded: 19 Oct 1972; 20 Oct 1972, AIR Studios, London
UK: 1 Jun 1973 (single A-side)
US: 18 Jun 1973 (single A-side)
Paul McCartney: vocals, piano; **Linda McCartney**: keyboards, backing vocals; **Denny Laine**: bass, backing vocals; **Henry McCullough**: guitar; **Denny Seiwell**: drums, percussion (?); **Ray Cooper**: percussion, duck whistle; **George Martin Orchestra**: instrumentation

At some point in 1972, former head of Apple, Ron Kass, contacted McCartney with a proposal that he compose a theme song for the next James Bond movie, scratching an itch McCartney had since at least 1966, when with George Martin, he'd scored *The Family Way*, a Roy Boulting drama about the strife of a couple of newly weds. McCartney was possibly familiar with the storyline to *Live And Let Die*, having claimed to have read Ian Fleming's 1954 novel several years earlier, and set about putting something together probably in late summer, after the European tour was over.[169] His first task was re-acquainting himself with the book, zipping his way through a copy and noting that unlike other Bond capers, this one was set largely in New York and Jamaica – suggesting musical styles he could tap into, particularly the insertion of a short reggae part penned by Linda.[170]

With the song taking form, McCartney invited George Martin to his home to go through it and devise some orchestral sections, the first time the two had directly collaborated in three years. Martin himself had a solid history in the movies, and aside from working on Beatles films, his cv included the soundtrack to *Goldfinger*, which in 1964 started a policy of having noted singing stars record the main Bond theme – in that case, Shirley Bassey vocalising a number penned regular composer, John Barry. Keen on the project, and the idea of reuniting with McCartney, Martin's thoughts turned to the cinematic format for an arrangement switching action from scene to scene with all guns blazing, a process conveniently facilitated by McCartney's collage

---

[169] Interviewed by Larry Kane on 20 August 1964, McCartney mentioned, 'Last tour in Australia [ie, earlier that summer] we just read every James Bond book out... we were just talking "James Bond" for the whole tour'. (Interview transcript in *Mojo*, '1000 Days Of Beatlemania' (part 1, 2002), p137.) There were 12 Bond titles on the market by that point however, and it's possible they didn't read all of them.

[170] McCartney might also have taken note of a conversation between Bond and the character, Captain Dexter, in chapter 4: 'Our policy with Mr Big is live and let live'. Interestingly, in the story Bond and Dexter met at the St Regis Hotel, where Lennon lived when he first arrived in New York.

technique of splicing together separate musical components.

What they ended up with was a miniature movie in sound, carrying the tension-release of a murder plot as its opening verse creeps to the top of the melody, a pregnant pause, and a dramatic crash down to the word 'die' – followed by a frantic musical chase around the major scales. Here, Martin's arrangement is at its most powerful, brass and kettledrums hammering home the dramatisation with urgent changes of pace, as heard in such pieces as Grieg's *Peer Gynt Suite No. 1*, with which the classically trained producer would have been well acquainted. Taking refuge on swooning cellos suggesting a breezy Caribbean beach, before trailing away on a cliff-edge polychord in which one can almost see the credits rolling, the track packs into its three minutes more visualisation than practically anything in popular song, all the more remarkable for the fact that it was recorded in a live performance by orchestra and band together, in the same way as [178] My Love.[171]

Released in parallel with the film, each publicising the other, the recording could hardly fail, not only scoring McCartney a second major hit in weeks, but earning him a prestigious Oscar nomination at the 46th Academy Awards. On the heels of My Love, this robust new hit was the most exciting thing he had released in years, sending out a signal to fans and critics: McCartney was back on form, and for added spice, the new single had George Martin's name on it.

James Paul McCartney: [192] **GOTTA SING, GOTTA DANCE** (*McCartney*)
Produced by Paul McCartney
Recorded: Mar 1973, EMI-MGM Elstree Studios, Hertfordshire
UK/US: unreleased
Paul McCartney: vocals, piano; **uncredited:** brass, orchestration, backing vocals, sound effects

With Northern Songs and Maclen Music locked in a legal battle with the McCartneys over Linda's claim to co-authorship of several 1971 releases (see [92]), an amicable solution was reached when Sir Lew Grade, head of parent company ATV, brokered a deal. Aware that Lennon-McCartney's contract with Northern was due to expire on 10 January, he proposed a new arrangement between ATV and McCartney Music to co-publish all solo material, with compensation for alleged historical losses met with the creation of a television spectacular, drawing lucrative advertising revenue.

---

[171] After recording the band alone, as a safety measure, Martin ushered the 38 classical musicians in, only to find the studio acoustics couldn't contain them all. His solution, as creative as many of his works with the Beatles, was to send half of them into the next studio, synch two multi-track recorders together, and then mix the results back onto a single tape.

From McCartney's side the deal proved constructive – he and Linda got to keep the lion's share of the disputed royalties which had already accrued, plus a chance to promote McCartney and his music, particularly the pending *Red Rose Speedway*. (And thereafter, the hitherto prolific Linda mysteriously stopped composing.) McCartney had been mulling just such a television project since 1970, and was given free rein to put the show together himself, an arguably foolhardy concession from Grade given that McCartney's track record in this respect consisted solely of the critical failure, *Magical Mystery Tour*.

With the project turning over in his mind, McCartney and Wings flew out to the quirky and opulent La Mamounia hotel in Morocco, where plans started to take shape amid the sun and associated refreshments, which may have been a factor in McCartney's imagination running away with him. Several ideas verged on the ludicrous, including a routine in which he planned to impersonate Diana Ross, and another in which he turned up in a Liverpool pub to mix it with the ordinary folk, enjoying a singalong with Linda among brimming beer glasses and overflowing ashtrays. While such elements were poorly conceived, the 50-minute extravaganza had several genuine highlights among a stream of song performances, including a first hearing of [191] Live And Let Die, and, for US viewers only, a brand new composition: [224] Bluebird.

Gotta Sing, Gotta Dance was one which might have been better left on the drawing board along with the Diana Ross drag sequence. The number, a big '1940s' show tune with choreographed routine, was written for 1960s fashion icon, Twiggy, as the title number of a proposed movie which she never made. Putting it to use here, McCartney was filmed jigging through a tap-dance in gold platform shoes and garish pink mourning suit, surrounded by formations of synchronised dancers. Bafflingly irrelevant to most viewers, this section of the show exposed McCartney's desire to appeal to every conceivable demographic, further distancing rock-based fans who might have hoped to see more of Wings in full flight. As with the *Red Rose Speedway* cover design, the program title – *James Paul McCartney* – had the effect of airbrushing the group out of the picture, despite their compliance which entailed such ignominies as performing [165] Mary Had A Little Lamb in a field of sheep and being injured by an exploding piano. (In the sequence for [178] My Love, all of Wings bar McCartney were literally kept in the dark, there being only one spotlight in use.) At the end of *James Paul McCartney*, the camera shot withdraws into a fish-eye lens, symbolically so as it was never aired again.

Paul McCartney And Wings: [193] **ZOO GANG** (*McCartney*)
  Produced by Paul McCartney
  Recorded: 25 Apr 1973, EMI Studios, London; Nov 1973, Studios Pathé
    Marconi, Paris
  UK: 28 Jun 1974 (single B-side)
  Paul McCartney: bass, keyboards, accordion; **Linda McCartney**:
  percussion; **Denny Laine**: guitar; **Henry McCullough**: guitar; **Denny
  Seiwell**: drums

McCartney's new publishing deal with ATV opened the door to further collaborative projects, the first of which was an invitation to pen a theme tune for the planned television drama, *The Zoo Gang*. McCartney had some previous when it came to writing television themes, past efforts including Step Inside Love in 1967 for *Cilla*, and the brassy Thingumybob in 1968, both of which were adventurous outings on which he spent some considerable effort. In the case of Zoo Gang he knocked off a perfunctory instrumental – although to his credit went to the trouble of dubbing on an accordion in Paris, a nod to the programme's French setting.

The TV show, based on a 1971 book by Paul Gallico, ran to six episodes covering the escapades of five crime-busting former French Resistance fighters with zoological code names (Tiger, Elephant and so on), their mission to con the conmen and pinch the money for good causes. McCartney's theme song was essentially a keyboard riff repeating across a minute or so, tightly performed and carrying an energetic bassline – and in the context of television themes generally, was as strong, and as disposable, as most. To garner publicity for the programme Sir Lew wanted it out as a single, but so far below A-side standard was it that no such release was feasible. Instead, songwriter Tony Hillier was booked to make a copy with a session team going by the name Jungle Juice, who issued their version as a 45 in May, by which time the series had ended its run. McCartney slipped out his original on the back of the UK edition of [221] Band On The Run a year on, easily his most forgettable B-side. Neither version was made available in the States.

RECORD RELEASES

[191] **Live And Let Die** / [97] **I Lie Around**
  (UK: 1 Jun 1973, US: 18 Jun 1973)
[221] **Band On The Run** / [193] **Zoo Gang**
  (UK: 28 Jun 1974)

Ringo sessions:
March 1973 to July 1973

While the release of [143] Back Off Boogaloo had kept Starr's name current through 1972, in musical terms he was at a quiet ebb, having recorded next to nothing since *Beaucoups Of Blues* in mid-1970. Through 1972 he had pursued his interest in movie making, a thus-far patchy acting career reaching its peak when he accepted a part in the Claude Whatham production, *That'll Be The Day*, the story of a couple of 1950s Teddy Boys whose lives consisted mostly of drinking and having one-night stands, mirroring Starr's own teenaged years to such an extent that he was essentially playing himself. Sensing an opportunity lie in screen productions Starr took the vacant position of Head of Apple Films, eyeing up a couple of movies for musical pals, the first fruit of which was *Born To Boogie*, a concert film featuring T Rex in which Starr makes a passing appearance with Elton John. His next film, riding the rock-star vantiy merry-go-round, was the comedy-horror, *Son Of Dracula* in which he appeared as Merlin alongside Nilsson (his new friend and drinking buddy), Keith Moon, John Bonham and others – a riotous, if expensive indulgence which lay unseen until April 1974.

While these productions gave him something to do, demand for his talents remained mostly on the rock circuit, Starr turning up on a series of albums by friends and colleagues, early work with Leon Russell and Stephen Stills followed by an appearance on Peter Frampton's *Wind of Change* and projects with both BB King and Howlin' Wolf, the latter as part of a set of 'super sessions'. His main friend and collaborator, Harrison, also guested with him on albums by Lon and Derrek Van Eaton and Bobby Keys, Starr enjoying the role of session man which had the advantage that he didn't need to commit to lengthy and laborious recording projects, just turning his hand to the kit as and when an opportunity arose. One key album he was involved in was Nilsson's *Son Of Schmilsson*, recorded at Trident in the first half of 1972 and setting in train a sequence of events which would eventually take Starr back into the studio on his own terms: *Son Of Schmilsson* was produced by Richard Perry, who'd crossed Starr's path on *Sentimental Journey* [10] and a subsequent Bobby Hatfield project, and it was suggested Perry and Starr make a new album together. (By 1973, Perry's stock had risen considerably, his *No Secrets* by Carly Simon having topped the US charts for a month.)

Starr's thoughts were initially on a 'world album' in which each track was recorded in a different location, an interesting idea scrapped when the logistics of it dawned on him. In the event, the *Ringo* album fell into place almost by itself, starting with the announcement that both Starr and Nilsson were in the running for Grammys in early 1973, which prompted their joint appearance at the ceremony in Nashville.[172] Realising he was back where he'd made *Beaucoups Of Blues* two and a half years earlier, Starr decided the time was right to attempt some new recordings, calling up Richard Perry to see if he was still interested, the producer suggesting they convene instead in LA, where an informal circle of top musicians was on hand.[173] Perry swiftly booked Sunset Sound Studios in Hollywood, and put word around that Starr was heading in – and thus, without meaning to, they started the ball rolling on what became Starr's first standard pop album.

Ringo Starr: [194] **HAVE YOU SEEN MY BABY** (*Newman*)
  Produced by Richard Perry
  Recorded: 5 Mar 1973; 15 May 1973, Sunset Sound Studios, Los Angeles;
    11 Jul 1973, Producer's Workshop, Los Angeles; unknown date,
    A&M Studios, Hollywood
  UK: 9 Nov 1973 (*Ringo* LP)
  US: 31 Oct 1973 (*Ringo* LP)
  Ringo Starr: vocals, drums; **Marc Bolan**: guitar; **James Booker**: piano;
  Klaus Voormann: bass; **Jim Keltner**: drums; **Milt Holland**: percussion;
  Tom Scott: saxophone

Arriving at Sunset Sound with no clear plans, Starr and his crew warmed up with long jams giving rise to a couple of covers, [195] You're Sixteen following this track, picked up from Randy Newman's second album, *12 Songs* (1970). If Starr wasn't familiar with Newman's work from the outset, he will have been introduced to it via Harry Nilsson, a committed fan who released *Nilsson Sings Newman* a couple of years earlier. (Newman had previously helped arrange a version of the same song for Fats Domino, a follow-up to his extraordinary cover of Everybody's Got Something To Hide Except Me And My Monkey.)

A standard mid-tempo rocker, Have You Seen My Baby follows the dalliances of some milkman-fancying strumpet, casting the singer as a cheerful failure in love, thus suiting Starr's public persona. As performed by the session team, his version follows Newman's template fairly closely until, two and a

---

[172] Starr and Nilsson both won awards, Starr accepting for Album Of The Year, *The Concert For Bangla Desh*, while Nilsson bagged Best Male Pop Vocal Performance for his cover of Badfinger's Without You. They also presented Best R&B Vocal Performance together to Billy Paul, in his absence.

[173] Perry had at his disposal the Wrecking Crew, a large, loosely defined aggregation of musicians who recorded between them hundreds of hits without formal credit. Among their ranks, and recruited to help on *Ringo*, were Jim Keltner, percussionist, Milt Holland, brass men, Jim Horn and Chuck Findley, and conductor/arranger, Jack Nitzsche.

half minutes in, New Orleans pianist, James Booker, steps forth with a barrelhouse section not present in the original, adding an ear-catching ingredient to an otherwise routine recording. As the album was being mixed for release, the track was overdubbed at the Producer's Workshop with sax from Tom Scott before Starr collared his friend, Marc Bolan, to 'glam' it up with some Telegram Sam-styled guitar riffs in an undocumented session at A&M in Hollywood.

Ringo Starr: [195] **YOU'RE SIXTEEN** (*Sherman, Sherman*)
   Produced by Richard Perry
   Recorded: 5 Mar 1973; 6 Mar 1973, Sunset Sound Studios, Los Angeles;
      Apr 1973, Apple Studios, London
   UK: 9 Nov 1973 (*Ringo* LP)
   US: 31 Oct 1973 (*Ringo* LP)
   Ringo Starr: vocals, drums; **Paul McCartney**: 'mouth sax'; **Jimmy Calvert**: guitar; **Vini Poncia**: guitar; **Nicky Hopkins**: piano; **Klaus Voormann**: bass; **Harry Nilsson**: backing vocals; **Jim Keltner**: drums

When Perry agreed to pursue the recording project with Starr his mind turned to suitable material, and having in his possession a demo containing a modern arrangement of You're Sixteen, written by the Sherman Brothers and first recorded in 1960 by Johnny Burnette, recognised it as a viable contender. A reasonably big hit in its day, the song had been forgotten though the 1960s, but Starr liked it enough to agree to a remake of this 'good old rocker' in an age when a 33-year-old man expressing his desires for a 16-year-old girl caused no apparent outrage.[174]

An enjoyable exercise, the recording captures the band in buoyant form, led by Nicky Hopkins' gambolling piano (sounding like an upright but in fact a Bechstein grand) which makes the most of the original's drum rhythm by formalising it into a riff, similar to that heard in the Foundations' 1968 hit, Build Me Up Buttercup, which may have been in his mind. Further fun was had with Harry Nilsson's camp multi-tracked backing vocals, added the next day, while Starr can be heard spontaneously launching into Clarence 'Frogman' Henry's celebrated (I Don't Know Why) But I Do in the song's fade-out. The finishing touches were added in an all-night session in London, during work on [203] Six O'Clock, in which McCartney went to lengths to effect a vocal saxophone solo by singing through a processing unit with fuzz tone, which merely ended up making him sound like a kazoo.

By good fortune, between the recording sessions and the release of *Ringo*,

---

[174] Starr's fond recollection of the song was expressed in a BBC Radio 1 interview for Brian Matthew, broadcast 7 April 1974.

the original version of You're Sixteen turned up in the blockbusting move, *American Graffiti*, bringing it to a new audience. Thus, the track had a leg-up when issued as the second single from *Ringo*, which duly lodged itself at the top of the US charts in January 1974, its infectious high spirits adding to Starr's temporary position as the most popular ex-Beatle. Richard Perry rated it as the best performance of Starr's career.[175]

Ringo Starr: [196] **OH MY MY** (*Starkey, Poncia*)
  Produced by Richard Perry
  Recorded: 6 Mar 1973; 7 Mar 1973; 14 Mar 1973; 12 May 1973, Sunset
    Sound Studios, Los Angeles
  UK: 9 Nov 1973 (*Ringo* LP)
  US: 31 Oct 1973 (*Ringo* LP)
  Ringo Starr: vocals, drums; **Billy Preston**: organ, piano; **Jimmy Calvert**: guitar; **Klaus Voormann**: bass; **Jim Keltner**: drums; **Tom Scott**: saxophone; **Jim Horn**: brass; **Vini Poncia**: backing vocals; **Martha Reeves**: backing vocals; **Merry Clayton**: backing vocals; **uncredited 'friends'**: backing vocals

Of the many positive developments from the *Ringo* sessions, possibly the most notable was the meeting of minds between Starr and Vini Poncia, the latter a long-time associate of Richard Perry who'd also been in Phil Spector's circle, having co-written material for the Ronettes in the 1960s. Having come together in LA, Starr and Poncia realised a shared problem – part-written songs they didn't know how to complete, or, as Starr put it, 'I had an intro, and he had an intro, so I finished his song off and he finished mine'.[176] Probably the initiative on this particular number was Poncia's, its unorthodox melody exploring the underlying chords, adventurous as compared to Starr's previous efforts. (The duo's other joint effort, [197] Devil Woman, carries by contrast Starr's unchanging, 'flat' style and four-square format, flagging it as largely his.)

A droll account of a visit to the doctor's surgery, Oh My My attempts to extract the most from its light-hearted lyric with a celebratory arrangement, Voormann's bassline bouncing across the octaves and characterised by some upbeat slide notes. Much of the track's energy comes from the enthusiastic input of its two guest divas, Merry Clayton, whose modest claim to fame was the original recording of The Shoop Shoop Song in 1963, and Martha Reeves, Motown's former darling who was left behind when the company moved to

---

[175] Perry, 2020.
[176] Radio 1 interview, broadcast 7 April 1974.

LA in 1972.[177] Whether by coincidence or in homage to Reeves, Jim Keltner's triple-time shuffle reflects directly the production touch of Motown's Holland-Dozier-Holland team, as heard in classic cuts such as Reach Out I'll Be There and You Keep Me Hanging On, which in all other respects are recordings from a different planet. In an effort to milk the commercial success of [198] Photograph and [195] You're Sixteen, Apple selected Oh My My as a third US single, rewarding Starr with another top 5 hit. With no equivalent in the UK, the song had to wait until January 1976 for an outing, trailering Starr's compilation, *Blast From Your Past*, the last album Apple issued.

Ringo Starr: [197] **DEVIL WOMAN** (*Starkey, Poncia*)
Produced by Richard Perry
Recorded: 8 Mar 1973; 12 May 1973, Sunset Sound Studios, Los Angeles;
    11 Jul 1973, Producer's Workshop, Los Angeles
UK: 9 Nov 1973 (*Ringo* LP)
US: 31 Oct 1973 (*Ringo* LP)
Ringo Starr: vocals, drums; **Jimmy Calvert**: guitar; **Tom Hensley**: piano; **Klaus Voormann**: bass, backing vocals; **Jim Keltner**: drums; **Tom Scott**: saxophone; **Chuck Findley**: brass; **Milt Holland**: percussion; **Richard Perry**: backing vocals

A partner track to [196] Oh My My, Devil Woman was a second Starr-Poncia creation, built on a vaguely similar foundation – although its lack of harmonic movement and almost complete absence of melody soon wears thin. Up for the job, the assembled musicians give of their best, noted session man, Tom Hensley contributing a honky-tonk piano section and Jim Keltner indulging himself with a routine 13-second drum solo partway through. Most striking is a searing fuzz-toned guitar solo from Jimmy Calvert, a former bandmate of Vini Poncia during their years in the Trade Winds, and the late addition of blazing brass overdubs courtesy of the Wrecking Crew's Tom Scott and Chuck Findley. In truth they were flogging a dead horse, Devil Woman barely worth their not inconsiderable talents. Lyrically the song is an odd assortment of drama and poor taste, Starr oscillating between stated desires to 'get her in bed' and 'beat her up'. That he names his tormentor 'Sexy Sadie' only adds to the song's lack of direction, Lennon's original character being the Maharishi by another name.

---

[177] In a failed attempt to reinvent her career, Reeves followed up this session by recording a whole album with Richard Perry, issued on MCA in 1974.

Ringo Starr: [198] **PHOTOGRAPH** (*Starkey, Harrison*)
Produced by Richard Perry
Recorded: 9 Mar 1973, Sunset Sound Studios, Los Angeles; 29 Jun 1973, Warner Brothers Studio, Burbank, California
UK: 19 Oct 1973 (single A-side)
US: 24 Sep 1973 (single A-side)
Ringo Starr: vocals, drums; **George Harrison**: guitar, backing vocals; **Vini Poncia**: guitar; **Jimmy Calvert**: guitar; **Nicky Hopkins**: piano; **Klaus Voormann**: bass; **Bobby Keys**: saxophone; **Jim Keltner**: drums; **Lon Van Eaton**: percussion; **Derrek Van Eaton**: percussion; **uncredited**: orchestra, chorus (arranged by Jack Nitzsche)

Written in May 1971 in southern France, Photograph was born of a moment in which the criss-crossing paths of the ex-Beatles happened to be overlapping. The four had each been invited to the Saint-Tropez wedding of Mick Jagger and Bianca Pérez-Mora Macias on 12 May, an event which Starr and McCartney attended, meeting one another cordially for the first time since the fractious court case in February, which had momentarily turned them against each other [112]. Lennon, not deigning to join the throng, was in the region anyway to attend the Cannes Film Festival, where his movies, *Fly* and *Apotheosis* were being screened, and thus sensing the opportunity for some partying, Starr chartered a vast three-decked yacht, *The Marala*, for the duration, with an open invitation to guests. Harrison meanwhile had travelled over with a view to watching the Monaco Grand Prix on 23 May, and by chance Starr bumped into a holidaying Cilla Black, she and Harrison, along with Marc Bolan, joining Starr for an idyllic evening aboard *The Marala* on the French Riviera.

Concocted on the yacht, Photograph seems to have been begun by Starr, although who did what is lost in the clouds of time with Black's recollection holding the assembled revellers all helped out: 'everyone on board was chipping in with words and lines'.[178] Ultimately copyrighted by Starr and Harrison together – a rare occasion when two ex-Beatles share credits – the song was inexplicably left on the shelf, despite Starr's concurrent success with [14] It Don't Come Easy, to which it would have made an opportune follow-up. When Starr met up with Perry in Nashville he had the song in mind at once and played it to his impressed producer in the hotel suite, effectively short-listing it for the coming sessions, so when Harrison turned up at Sunset Sound on 9 March they were ready to nail this long-overdue track.[179]

---

[178] p217. Black also claims Harrison (not Starr) was writing it for her, but that Starr intervened to claim it. (Black eventually recorded a version in 2003, for *Beginnings*.)

[179] The session also reunited them with Lon and Derrek Van Eaton, whose Apple >

Light years ahead of [197] Devil Woman, Photograph shows Harrison's distinctive hand in its construction, Starr's basic three-chord foundation enlivened by the playful push and pull of the timing, with a technical fluidity beyond anything he had composed by himself. The contrasting passages too are essentially Harrisonesque, landing with a trademark detour to G sharp for an introspective minor sequence, complete with strategic gap for an instrumental riff. (The same style of collaborative writing between the two had been on show during the *Get Back* sessions on 26 January 1969, when Starr's lumpen prodding of the piano keyboard in an effort to 'find' Octopus's Garden was overheard by an interested Harrison, who talked him through some chord changes and developed a middle eight, lifting the song several notches and revealing a surprisingly strong synergy between the two composers of which too few examples exist.)

Draped with Harrison's backing vocals, lightening Starr's bass tones, and lifted by a soaring orchestral score overdubbed on 29 June, Photograph was by far the most engaging thing he had yet recorded, Harrison's galvanising presence on the studio floor described by producer Perry as casting 'a certain magic' over proceedings. (So persuasive was the performance that Nicky Hopkins' mis-strikes of his piano keys in the fade-out were allowed through.) Selected as a single, the first thing released from these sessions, Photograph arrived with a humorous promotional video filmed, like that of [143] Back Off Boogaloo, in the grounds of Tittenhurst Park, Starr having by then purchased it from Lennon. Spectacularly successful, the 45 put Starr at the top of the US charts, rapidly becoming one of his most admired recordings. (Starr re-recorded it in 2017 for *Give More Love*, alongside new versions of Don't Pass Me By and [143].)

Ringo Starr: [199] **STEP LIGHTLY** (*Starkey*)
  Produced by Richard Perry
  Recorded: 9 Mar 1973, Sunset Sound Studios, Los Angeles; Apr 1973,
    EMI Studios, London; 10 Jul 1973, Sound Labs Studio, Los Angeles
  UK: 9 Nov 1973 (*Ringo* LP)
  US: 31 Oct 1973 (*Ringo* LP)
Ringo Starr: vocals, drums, tap shoes; **Steve Cropper**: guitar; **Nicky Hopkins**: electric piano; **Jimmy Calvert**: guitar; **Klaus Voormann**: bass; **uncredited**: clarinets (arranged by Tom Scott)

---

album they had both played on. As was the case with Martha Reeves (see [196]) the Van Eatons' meeting with Richard Perry spawned an album, *Who Do You Out Do* (sic) for A&M.

Recorded on the same day as the uplifting [198] Photograph, this Starr original continued an impressive roll of honour, featuring on this occasion famed guitarist, Steve Cropper, latterly of Booker T & the MGs, and thereby justifying Richard Perry's decision to stage the sessions in LA. A lightly bouncing dance tune, made quaint with clarinets approximating the style of an old-time brass band, the song tips a nod to the concept trumpeted on the LP cover – a *Pepper*-esque show with Starr as star. The soundscape was completed during a visit to London at the start of April to record [203] Six O'Clock, with the sound of Starr tap-dancing drunk on the floor of EMI Studios.[180] Something of a novelty, the recording was deployed as a B-side to [196] Oh My My when it was released in the US.

Ringo Starr: [200] **I'M THE GREATEST** (*Lennon*)
Produced by Richard Perry
Recorded: 13 Mar 1973; 14 Mar 1973, Sunset Sound Studios, Los Angeles
UK: 9 Nov 1973 (*Ringo* LP)
US: 31 Oct 1973 (*Ringo* LP)
Ringo Starr: vocals, drums; **John Lennon**: piano, backing vocals; **George Harrison**: guitar; **Billy Preston**: organ; **Klaus Voormann**: bass

By stroke of luck, just as Harrison and Starr were in LA working on [198] Photograph, Lennon was also in town to submit evidence in the ongoing tussle with Maclen-Northern over his song copyrights. The three soon realised they were in each other's vicinity and with current Beatle business to discuss – namely the pending dissolution of their management arrangements with Allen Klein and the release of *1962-1966* and *1967-1970* – took the opportunity to meet up, socially and around the table. Inevitably learning that Harrison had been helping Starr with his sessions, and not one to be outdone, Lennon offered the same, taking into Sunset Sound a leftover song (see [119]) which he considered an ideal gift for his good friend.

As Lennon had written I'm The Greatest for himself with lyrics concerning his own past, adjustments were required, Lennon and Ono getting down to a partial re-write for which she takes credit for the family-centric third verse. Lennon's personal touch is revealed in the song's new middle eight, referencing *Sgt Pepper* and [143] Back Off Boogaloo, plus a line from his poem, *The Fat Budgie* (1964), whose words had curiously also shown up in [130] Imagine.[181]

---

[180] Sometimes mistaken for someone playing spoons, the percussive effect was revealed in a 1974 BBC radio interview with Brian Matthew: 'I tap-danced holding a mike stand, as I was a bit merry at the time.'

[181] The poem reads, in part, 'I love him more than daddie, and I'm only thirty two' – a >

Lennon showcased the song to Starr and Perry at the piano, the first time either had heard what was obviously a strong prospect. In the studio was Klaus Voormann but not enough musicians for a proper recording, making what happened next extremely timely. Working on the song's closing section, Richard Perry was interrupted by the phone – the caller one Mal Evans, on behalf of Harrison, who'd got wind of the session and fancied coming along. 20 minutes later he slipped into the studio via the back door, guitar and amplifier in hand, and simply joined in with the others. And suddenly, for the first time since 1969, he, Lennon and Starr found themselves together on the studio floor.

By Starr's recollection, the significance of this moment was unspoken among the main participants: 'We were just looking at each other and smiling because the three of us were together.'[182] Richard Perry described a 'fantastic energy' to the session, 'You could tell they were excited', which is probably a fair reflection of the mood.[183] More elated was the local media, who'd twigged what was afoot at Sunset Sound, a journalist from the KMET radio station calling the studio directly to hear the facts for himself, while TV and newspaper reporters gathered in the parking lot outside. News soon rippled around the world, the longed-for Beatles reunion supposedly about to become a reality, just four days passing before the British music press announced extravagantly, 'The Beatles have teamed up for recording purposes'.[184] The reality was that a lone album cut had been made in a one-off session, and one of the former bandmates wasn't even in the country – but with a gnawing sense of nostalgia and a dream that the Beatles might live again, hearts, however briefly, were willing to rule heads.[185]

The 13 March session would reverberate with Beatles fans for years to come, solidifying in legend as the occasion on which the magic was fleetingly rekindled. In its immediate aftermath, Billy Preston slipped into the studio to add some keyboard parts to the track, including embellishment to the long, repeating fade-out reprising Harrison's riff from [37] I Dig Love, which provided for an emphatic closing passage. Taking note of the lyric's reference to Billy Shears and looking to capture something of the atmosphere of *Sgt*

---

convenient rhyme for 'Boogaloo'.
[182] BBC Radio 1 broadcast, 4 July 1974.
[183] Interview in *Melody Maker*, 31 March 1973, pp 8-9.
[184] *Melody Maker*, 17 March 1973.
[185] The fantasy of a four-way reunion would never be relinquished. McCartney's absence from the session is still ascribed solely to the fact he was facing travel restrictions courtesy of his two drugs busts in 1972 [170], but in truth there was no pre-planning to these events, and so he could never have been asked along, even had all parties been willing.

Pepper, Richard Perry decided to use this section as a canvas on which to place sounds of audience approbation, and approached EMI – with Beatle endorsement – for a copy of the tapes containing the applause heard on that album's title track. Happily EMI consented, shipping over a four-track copy of the *Sgt Pepper's Lonely Hearts Club Band* master tape, which was mixed in by Perry to complete the picture.

A remarkable episode, the creation of this track brought a realisation that these sessions, which had begun speculatively, were now consolidating into an album's worth of strong recordings, almost all of them originals. The dust would settle on 13 March. Lennon would fly back to New York, Harrison would return his attention to work with Ravi Shankar, and Starr would exit Sunset Sound a couple of days on with nine new tracks under his belt. With composition by Lennon, and three Beatles in participation, I'm The Greatest was the period's defining moment, the track inevitably selected as the opening cut on *Ringo*, even if on musical terms, [198] Photograph would have been the superior choice.

Ringo Starr: [201] **SUNSHINE LIFE FOR ME (SAIL AWAY RAYMOND)**
(*Harrison*)
Produced by Richard Perry
Recorded: 15 Mar 1973, Sunset Sound Studios, Los Angeles
UK: 9 Nov 1973 (*Ringo* LP)
US: 31 Oct 1973 (*Ringo* LP)
Ringo Starr: vocals, drums, percussion; **George Harrison**: guitar, backing vocals; **Robbie Robertson**: guitar; **Levon Helm**: mandolin; **Garth Hudson**: accordion; **Rick Danko**: fiddles; **David Bromberg**: fiddles, banjo; **Klaus Voormann**: upright bass; **Vini Poncia**: backing vocals

Harrison's second contribution to *Ringo* dates from 1971, written during an Easter visit to Donovan, then living at the large estate of Castlemartin in Ireland's County Kildare. Penned in the fall-out of the Beatles' court case, the song expresses a longing to escape the group's burdens for freedom in some far-off idyll – in this context a sequel to Here Comes The Sun, written in similar circumstances in 1969. (The title incorporates a reference to Raymond Skilling, one of Allen Klein's appointed lawyers from top London law firm, Clifford-Turner.) Harrison found the song by exploring an open tuning on his 12-string acoustic, having in mind the folk tradition, although its pentatonic roots emerge as more of a modern sea shanty. At least part derives form the much-travelled folk tune, Sail Away Ladies, which to judge by the arrangement means he had in mind the 1920s recording by Nashville banjo player, Uncle Dave Macon (whose middle name was, coincidentally, Harrison).

For the recording a call was made to Robbie Robertson who rounded up four fifths of the Band, currently in LA working on their covers album, *Moondog Matinee*, again proving the benefits of close proximity.[186] Multi-instrumentalists all, they reprised the fiddle-mandolin arrangement heard on Rag Mama Rag (*The Band*, 1969), with support from another of the circle's some-time collaborators, singer-songwriter, David Bromberg. Thus developed, Sunshine Life For Me ended up so distantly removed from its initial subject – McCartney's depressing London lawsuit – that it fitted effortlessly into the good-time *Ringo*, the passing of two years providing enough distance for Harrison's woes to have receded over the horizon, as the lyric promises.

Ringo Starr: [202] **YOU AND ME (BABE)** (*Harrison, Evans*)
 Produced by Richard Perry
 Recorded: Mar 1973; 12 May 1973, Sunset Sound Studios, Los Angeles;
  29 Jun 1973, Warner Brothers Studio, Burbank, California; 10 Jul 1973;
  11 Jul 1973, Producer's Workshop, Los Angeles
 UK: 9 Nov 1973 (*Ringo* LP)
 US: 31 Oct 1973 (*Ringo* LP)
 Ringo Starr: vocals, drums; **George Harrison**: guitar; **Vini Poncia**: acoustic guitar; **Nicky Hopkins**: electric piano; **Klaus Voormann**: bass; **Milt Holland**: marimba; **uncredited**: brass (arranged by Tom Scott); **uncredited**: strings (arranged by Jack Nitzsche)

After the Beatles stopped touring in 1966, Mal Evans' position as roadie gradually settled into one of all-round personal aide, reliably on hand whenever any of them needed something. His responsibilities not relinquished after they split up, he was in Hollywood with Harrison during the *Ringo* sessions carrying a work-in-progress version of the current track, a romanticised account of a date in which the subject is also, somehow, performing from the stage.[187] Shaped up with Harrison, the song was taken into Sunset Sound just as sessions were winding down, and suggested to Richard Perry a 'Memphis groove' until Harrison claimed the centre ground

---

[186] One of the Band was absent – Richard Manuel currently struggling with alcohol misuse and declining to join the others.
[187] Aside from attending to the Beatles, Evans dabbled in a music career himself, trying his hand at record production and artist management, as well as songwriting. His near-misses included contributions to Fixing A Hole, for which he was allegedly promised a slice of the royalties which never came, and co-authorship of the Splinter track, Lonely Man, which almost appeared as an Apple single. (By the mid-1970s he had his own publishing company, Malcontent Music.) Interviewed by Ken Doyle for Californian radio station, KCSN-FM, in December 1975, Evans discussed his songwriting, emphasising he was primarily a lyricist, and that "I play very bad guitar. Three chords".

with a guitar section including patterns reminiscent of Starr's [14] It Don't Come Easy and some functional, if well admired slide solos. Overdubbed in May, Tom Scott's brass chart played into the format, its riffs drawing on Badfinger's Day After Day, which Harrison had produced in 1971.

While contributing a vocal, Starr recognised this was probably the last thing he would record at Sunset Sound, and spontaneously launched into a list of thank-yous to each of his main collaborators, including by name, Lennon, Harrison and McCartney.[188] Thus destined to end the show with a cheery wave, You And Me (Babe) was initially cross-faded to [197] Devil Woman before being separated again and presented as a stand-alone track, a happy, all-inclusive finale to a set of recordings made in the open spirit of camaraderie.

Ringo Starr: [203] **SIX O'CLOCK** (*McCartney, McCartney*)
Produced by Richard Perry
Recorded: 2 Apr 1973, Apple Studios, London; Apr 1973,
 EMI Studios, London
UK: 9 Nov 1973 (*Ringo* LP)
US: 31 Oct 1973 (*Ringo* LP)
Ringo Starr: vocals, drums; **Paul McCartney**: piano, synthesiser, backing vocals; **Linda McCartney**: backing vocals; **Vini Poncia**: guitar, percussion; **Klaus Voormann**: bass; **uncredited**: strings, flutes (arranged by Paul McCartney)

According to Starr, McCartney's involvement in the *Ringo* project stemmed from a sense of loyalty to his old bandmate, after Lennon and Harrison had both participated: 'I didn't want to leave Paul out, so I phoned him'.[189] However a different version has been put forward by Richard Perry, who flew to England with Starr after the session for [202] You And Me (Babe), having been fortuitously commissioned for the sound work on *James Paul McCartney*, about to go into production. According to his memoirs, Perry himself seized the initiative: 'The next day, I approached Paul McCartney about writing a song for Ringo's album. "Give me a deadline," he said. "I work best under pressure."' – after which he composed Six O'Clock. Which of the two versions is correct cannot be certain but Starr's account is evidently more plausible given that Perry is unlikely to have approached McCartney of his own volition – but either way, arrangements were made and McCartney promptly

---

[188] Since McCartney had yet to contribute anything to *Ringo*, his name check was presumably included in anticipation of the coming London session for [203].
[189] BBC radio interview with Brian Matthew, broadcast 7 April 1974. Assuming Starr called McCartney from LA, this would explain the advance credit.

presented the fruits of his labours by playing Six O'Clock down the phone to Perry a few days later.

A morose depiction of a struggling romance, this new track bears the hallmarks of personal experience, like [160] Single Pigeon, hinting at late-night conflict between Paul and Linda, although as taken up by Starr, any contact with the background story is negated. Thus Six O'Clock lacks meaning, its sad lyric treated to a pleasantly bobbing piano rhythm and a novel mini-Moog keyboard effect, which conveys nothing of its troubled origins.

The basic track was recorded at Apple, Klaus Voormann also back from the States to handle bass to McCartney's keyboards, after which Perry played some of the earlier session tapes to the assembled personnel, prompting McCartney to dub his 'mouth sax' onto [195] You're Sixteen. Over the following few days arrangements were written for the strings overdubs for Six O'Clock at McCartney's home in St John's Wood, after which it was finished up in a gruelling nine-hour session at EMI, which appropriately finished at 6am. Having kept themselves going through the night with a steady supply of booze, Starr decided to send his driver out at dawn to source some tap shoes, which were duly found, allowing him to also apply the finishing additions to [199] Step Lightly as he danced around one of the Abbey Road microphones.

By all accounts an enjoyable night's work, Six O'Clock represented an achievement for Starr in edging McCartney back into the collective fold, as one of the main barriers, Allen Klein, was departing the scene. The first time McCartney had collaborated with any of the ex-Beatles in more than three years, the session was in context as remarkable a happening as that of [200] I'm The Greatest, and was similarly the result of happenstance, the confluence of Starr, McCartney and Richard Perry's work patterns bringing them all briefly together in one place. For *Ringo* it meant McCartney's name would be proudly added alongside the others, allowing the four ex-Beatles' to appear shoulder to shoulder again, in spirit, if not in body.

Ringo Starr: [204] **DOWN AND OUT** (*Starkey*)
    Produced by George Harrison, Richard Perry
    Recorded: Oct 1972-Mar 1973, Apple Studios, London (?); May 1973,
        Sunset Sound Studios, Los Angeles (?)
    UK: 19 Oct 1973 (single B-side)
    US: 24 Sep 1973 (single B-side)
    Ringo Starr: vocals, drums; **George Harrison**: guitar; **Gary Wright**: keyboards; **Klaus Voormann**: bass; **uncredited**: brass (arranged by Richard Perry)[190]

---

[190] The musicianship on the track is unconfirmed, the listing above based on several sources. Some (eg Clayson, p244) nominate Gary Brooker as pianist. Official credits >

An odd-man-out on *Ringo* and something of a puzzle, Down And Out was older than the rest, having been started by Starr at some unknown juncture, probably during sessions for *Living In The Material World*. (If correct this would place the backing track concurrent with Harrison-Starr's first exploratory work on [198] Photograph, and explains the production credits on the release.) Whatever existed on tape was added to the stockpile in May when Richard Perry worked it into releasable shape at Sunset Sound, despite having 10 other tracks already available.

Built on a standard blues foundation, Down And Out is, like [197] Devil Woman, melodically constrained with a vocal line locked monotonously to the fifth note of the chord. With a rolling bassline from Voormann replicating the part heard in Dizzy Miss Lizzy, the track's relatively sedate pace cancels out any corresponding excitement, Perry's efforts in beefing it up consisting mostly of the addition of a dotted brass section, and on the evidence of the audio, a spot repair to Starr's singing at 2:23 which sounds as if he vocalised it himself. Most interesting are the twin instrumental breaks, a rocking blues passage from Gary Wright's piano followed by 12 bars of swoopingly heckling lead guitar from Harrison. Not needed on the album, Down And Out appeared on the B-side of [198] Photograph, a deployment which may have been its purpose all along.

The tapes for *Ringo* were polished up in a series of sporadic dates over the late spring and summer, when string and brass additions were captured, the final session taking place on 11 July. What had started as a vague idea to secure a few tracks had turned under its own momentum into a set of celebrated recordings which Starr would remember fondly as his 'accidental album'. The cordial atmosphere of its creation revealed the esteem in which the other ex-Beatles still held Starr, their generous contributions born of a desire to help, friendships rekindled in and out of the studio, something not unnoticed in the music press. As reunion rumours did their inevitable rounds, three of the four were as close as at any point since the Beatles separated, openly enjoying one another's company; Lennon, Harrison and Starr were spotted together at a celebrity-packed Hollywood fund-raiser on 7 April, two days before their joint attendance of a party in the home of Capitol's president, Bhaskar Menon, at which Harrison delighted revellers with selections from *Living In The Material World*.

Getting *Ringo* into the shops turned out to be an onerous task, the decision to house the disc in an extravagantly illustrated package with custom artwork

---

given on a CD reissue list only Starr and Harrison, and are obviously incomplete.

delaying it further. What might have been a summer release ended up dragging through the autumn after Klaus Voormann accepted a commission for a set of inked illustrations for each of the 10 songs, to be carried inside a 24-page book of lyrics. The record sleeve too was a creative endeavour, Richard Perry 'discovering' American artist, Tim Bruckner, and bringing him over to England to draw some illustrations featuring the musicians heard on the record. His selected sketch shows Starr on stage, the balcony behind him packed with a crowd of faces, happily (if accidentally) reminiscent of the throng on *Sgt Pepper* – many of them recognisable – Marc Bolan, Billy Preston, Harry Nilsson etc – and together at the centre, to emphasise the point, Lennon, McCartney and Harrison. Reflecting the congenial mood of the album, a wealth of in-jokes was secreted in the artwork, including Starr as Merlin from the as-yet unreleased *Son Of Dracula*, 'the Blue Nun' taken from bottles of the German wine frequently quaffed during the sessions, and at the top of the front cover, running around a green apple, the words, *Duit On Mon Dei*, an old Beatle gag taking a humorous slant on the motto of the British monarchy.[191]

The celebratory mood of *Ringo*, with its Beatle flavour and *Pepper* references, couldn't resolve the perennial problem of what Starr was to do with his life, the publication of five new copyrights scarcely pointing towards a future career as a songwriter. Having seen the termination of his EMI-linked music publisher, Startling Music, and the end of management by Allen Klein, Starr sought to organise his professional affairs in the project's wake, first by creating Richoroony Ltd to publish his new material, then by appointing former Apple executive, Hilary Gerrard, to represent him, thereby setting himself up with a framework for the coming years.

Ringo landed towards the end of 1973, six months after Starr had won plaudits for his role in *That'll Be The Day*, his stock now at an all-time high. Universally recognised as the best record he ever made, the album was also – like *Sentimental Journey* and *Beaucoups Of Blues* – ground-breaking; no major artist had recorded a set of tracks supplied by and performed with a roster of famous guests, let alone those of the stature found on *Ringo*. (Such a landmark was it in Starr's cannon, that when he launched Ring O'Records in 1975, its first release was an instrumental cover version of the entire set, by synthesiser pioneer, David Hentschel.) Its arrival gave Starr the credibility he needed after the less-than-ecstatic reactions to his previous two albums, and in carrying a pair of number 1 singles, placed him at the top of the ex-Beatle hierarchy, before the arrival of *Band On The Run* restored the normal order of things.

---

[191] A play on *Dieu et Mon Droit*, the joke was Derek Taylor's, first printed in a 1968 newsletter circulated among Apple staff, with another royal motto, *Honi Soit Qui Mal Y Pense*, modified to include the name, Mal Evans. When RCA refused to let Harry Nilsson call his 1975 album *God's Greatest Hits*, he changed it to *Duit On Mon Dei*.

RECORD RELEASES

[198] **Photograph** / [204] **Down And Out**
(UK: 19 Oct 1973, US: 24 Sep 1973)
Ringo
(UK: 9 Nov 1973, US: 31 Oct 1973)
[200] I'm The Greatest / [194] Have You Seen My Baby / [198] Photograph / [201] Sunshine Life For Me (Sail Away Raymond) / [195] You're Sixteen / [196] Oh My My / [199] Step Lightly / [203] Six O'Clock / [197] Devil Woman / [202] You And Me (Babe)
[195] **You're Sixteen** / [197] **Devil Woman**
(UK: 8 Feb 1974, US: 3 Dec 1973)
[196] **Oh My My** / [199] **Step Lightly**
(US: 18 Feb 1974)

Mind Games sessions: August 1973

Around the time Lennon was hanging out with Starr and Harrison in LA, he was coming and going from New York where he and Ono were scouting a permanent place to live, having by now rented their temporary Bank Street home for a year and a half. At the start of April they settled on an apartment on the seventh floor of the Dakota building, immediately next to Central Park at the eastern end of West 72nd, which they assumed possession of around 1 May (not before calling on the services of a medium to see if there were any unwanted spirit guests lurking about).

Events coincided with a lean spell in Lennon's career, only occasional production for others punctuating the long year between the completion of *Some Time In New York City* and the LA session for [200] I'm The Greatest. Ono's recording activity had meantime taken the opposite trajectory, with a flowering of creativity resulting in some of the best music she would ever record. Prior to the Dakota move, she released *Approximately Infinite Universe*, her second double album in little over a year, all of it self-written and about to be followed up by a third, only late instruction from EMI limiting this latest set to a single disc. In the same period Lennon had released just seven songs, five of them written jointly with her. Partly his artistic malaise was down to the personal pressure he was under in 1973; still being monitored by the FBI, who he was convinced had his house bugged and his phone tapped, Lennon was continuously under the oppressive threat of deportation, his legal cat-and-mouse with US Immigration showing no signs of abating any time soon. On top of this was the residual criticism surrounding *Some Time In New York City*, Lennon's lengthy absence from the recording studio a result of the first hard knock to his confidence since his breakthrough in 1963.

Ono's next recording project, *Feeling The Space*, was scheduled to start in June at Record Plant East, for which she assembled a team of session musicians built around the core quartet of Ken Ascher, Gordon Edwards, Jim Keltner and David Spinozza, the last of these a lead guitarist who, unknown to the Lennons, had on his cv a clutch of songs recorded with McCartney, including [92] Another Day. Lennon's keen interest in Ono's work saw him play on a couple of late tracks, Woman Power and She Hits Back, giving him a taste for recording again, and accordingly he retained Ono's band when *Feeling The Space* came to an end, starting work on his own album the following day.

John Lennon: [205] **I KNOW (I KNOW)** (*Lennon*)
Produced by John Lennon
Recorded: 1 Aug 1973, Record Plant, New York
UK: 16 Nov 1973 (*Mind Games* LP)
US: 5 Nov 1973 (*Mind Games* LP)
John Lennon: vocals, guitar; **David Spinozza**: guitar; **Ken Ascher**: keyboards; **Gordon Edwards**: bass; **Jim Keltner**: drums

Having lived in each other's pockets for half a decade, the stresses and strains of lives entwined had taken a toll on Lennon and Ono. For two artists to subsume themselves into a round-the-clock partnership entailed an element of self-sacrifice, neither of them able to function independently, a restriction felt more acutely by Lennon who by instinct kicked against stability. Of a nature to act on impulse, Lennon's behaviour became increasingly problematic to the comparatively centred Ono, reaching a crisis point when they attended a party together at Jerry Rubin's house on 7 November 1972, Lennon giving Ono a humiliating dressing down in front of everyone before unashamedly taking a female guest into the next room and sleeping with her. The marriage survived but damage was done, Ono and Lennon continuing to drift apart through the following months, as evinced by her emergence as an individual recording artist, flagged on 20 May by a debut live gig without her husband.

Written during Lennon's inactive period, I Know (I Know) admits his role in their current disjuncture and offers Ono an explicit apology – a curious way for Lennon to attempt to repair his relationship, given that he might have just talked to her. In a sense his confessing regret from the remoteness of the recording studio underlines the problem, Lennon seemingly unable to articulate his feelings in person: 'I never could speak my mind', as also, unintentionally, hinted at by the song's title – a hurried way of closing down dialogue. (In his 1980 *Playboy* interview, Lennon was asked about the song and in similarly evasive fashion offered only, 'Just a piece of nothing'.[192]) In the reassuring line, 'I love you more than yesterday', there's little doubt that his words were meant for Ono, although his inclusion of a McCartney song title, followed by a phrase from Getting Better, gave sufficient fodder for Beatle sleuths to decode a message from John to Paul.

The song was demoed, essentially fully formed, over the early summer 1973 among a pile of home tapes which included four other tracks recorded during the *Mind Games* sessions.[193] Built on a softly picked guitar phrase, a close approximation of the corresponding part in I've Got A Feeling, attention to detail was required in an arrangement which magnified every imperfection. Thus, Jim Keltner's oddly conceived drum patterns in the quieter passages give the unwanted effect of background noise, Lennon's double-tracked lead vocal sometimes noticeably uncertain and out of synch with itself.

Looping around its chords, I Know (I Know) features an unusually – for Lennon – orthodox progression leading to a perfect cadence, an assuredly resolute 'ending' missing from the song's eventual coda in which the phrase, 'no more crying' instead repeats itself until fading away on an ambiguously hanging F sharp minor, depicting both Lennon's hopes and fears in one succinct moment.

John Lennon: [206] **TIGHT A$** (*Lennon*)
Produced by John Lennon
Recorded: 1 Aug 1973; 5 Aug 1973; 13-14 Aug 1973, Record Plant, New York
UK: 16 Nov 1973 (*Mind Games* LP)
US: 5 Nov 1973 (*Mind Games* LP)
John Lennon: vocals, guitar; **David Spinozza**: guitar; **'Sneaky Pete' Kleinow**: pedal steel guitar; **Ken Ascher**: keyboards; **Gordon Edwards**: bass; **Jim Keltner**: drums

Having got the pressing stuff out of his system ([205]), next on Lennon's agenda was this comforting eight-bar rocker, a throw-back to his rock and roll roots included just for the fun of it. Pitched roughly in the style of Chuck Berry, the track was characterised by Lennon as a 'Tex-Mex', something he may have had in mind when writing it although the conventional rock arrangement tends to obscure such influences.[194] Stepping away from the

---

[192] Golson, p181.
[193] Specifically, [206]; [207]; [208]; [211]. In the same period, Lennon also recorded preliminary versions of the later-recorded [247] Nobody Loves You (When You're Down and Out); [249] Steel And Glass; and [235] Here We Go Again.
[194] Golson, p180. Tex-Mex or Tejano music originated in Texas and is a loosely defined >

emotional current of the previous track, Tight A$ carries a knowingly worldly lyric, playing with drug references and innuendo, and most likely for no other reason than to acknowledge its American flavour, Lennon used a couple of dollar signs in the title (one of which was dropped on release) leaving the listener unsure whether he was singing about money or sex. Probably both.

Not content with the results from the first day's session, Lennon came back to it the following Monday and at the sixth attempt captured a performance with sufficient attack, featuring two solos from each of David Spinozza and country rocker, 'Sneaky Pete' Kleinow, the whole thing running close to five minutes. Trimmed down for the album, the released version is an edit of four parts sequenced seamlessly together, thereby leaving some of Spinozza's soloing on the cutting-room floor. The full take circulates on bootlegs.

John Lennon: [207] **ROCK & ROLL PEOPLE** (*Lennon*)
Produced by John Lennon
Recorded: 1 Aug 1973; 4 Aug 1973, Record Plant, New York
UK/US: unreleased
John Lennon: vocals, guitar; **David Spinozza**: guitar; **Ken Ascher**: piano; **Gordon Edwards**: bass; **Jim Keltner**: drums

This first day's work saw the resurrection of a Lennon stomper in a similar vein to [206] Tight A$, providing another opportunity for the band to flex their collective muscle. Rock & Roll People was written on piano in late 1970, around the time *John Lennon/Plastic Ono Band* was underway, and in contemporary home demos was styled as a slow blues. Basic in construction, the stop-time pattern vaguely resembles the similarly uncompromised Yer Blues, whose mother/father couplet was reframed with insinuating word play: 'My father was a mother–'. Taken up again in 1973 the track needed to find its own identity, this 1950s arrangement fitting a lyric which obliquely references rock stardom but fails to provide a suitable focus. Lennon clearly thought it had something going for it since he re-recorded it a few days later through numerous takes, none judged worthy of release, making a rare case of Lennon setting aside an original composition.

The track wasn't lost to history; after rock-blues guitarist, Johnny Winter, expressed a wish to record something by Lennon, his manager Steve Paul made the necessary enquiries and was offered this leftover. Winter's high-octane version, with a few lyrical refinements, appeared as the lead track to his 1974 album, *John Dawson Winter III*. Six years after Lennon's death, Ono elected

---

blend of US country and Spanish styles, often incorporating traditional instruments such as accordion.

John Lennon: [208] **INTUITION** (*Lennon*)
   Produced by John Lennon
   Recorded: 2 Aug 1973; 11 Aug 1973; 13-14 Aug 1973, Record Plant,
      New York
   UK: 16 Nov 1973 (*Mind Games* LP)
   US: 5 Nov 1973 (*Mind Games* LP)
   John Lennon: vocals, guitar; **David Spinozza**: guitar; **'Sneaky Pete' Kleinow**: pedal steel guitar; **Ken Ascher**: keyboards; **Michael Brecker**: saxophone; **Gordon Edwards**: bass; **Jim Keltner**: drums

Written in 1973, Intuition is an outwardly confident celebration of life and music, essentially restating Lennon's post-Primal view of the world, as heard to greater length on the more sombre *John Lennon/Plastic Ono Band*. When he emerged from therapy in 1970, Lennon was disburdened of the paradigms which had previously controlled his life, openly renouncing the mystics and gurus he'd once relied on, in songs such as [81] I Found Out and [86] God, in which he distilled his new-found perspective: 'I just believe in me'. This new song treads similar ground, rejecting the fallacies of superstition in favour of his own instincts, and it's telling that in a composing tape, recorded prior to the album sessions, he dropped in several lines from God, as if to illustrate the point.

   How much of this positive slant arose from genuine emotion, and how much was a conscious attempt at self-affirmation is uncertain, the track at odds with the tone of much of the album which, when expressing inner feelings, reveals a Lennon struggling to come to terms with the passing years. The fact that his early piano demo metamorphosed into the crochet chords from McCartney's [22] Suicide hints that behind its sunny exterior, shadows lurk. (The word 'suicide' also turns up in the opening lines of Intuition, suggesting Lennon was free-associating.) Opening the second half of *Mind Games*, Intuition embodies the duality of Lennon's current situation, presenting an unconvincingly happy face in which cracks are visible.

John Lennon: [209] **BRING ON THE LUCIE (FREDA PEEPLE)** (*Lennon*)
Produced by John Lennon
Recorded: 2 Aug 1973; 5 Aug 1973; 13-14 Aug 1973; 16 Aug 1973, Record Plant, New York
UK: 16 Nov 1973 (*Mind Games* LP)
US: 5 Nov 1973 (*Mind Games* LP)
John Lennon: vocals, guitar; **'Sneaky Pete' Kleinow**: pedal steel guitar; **Gordon Edwards**: bass; **Jim Keltner**: drums; **Rick Marotta**: drums; **Something Different**: backing vocals[195]

Free The People, as it was originally known, was started in late 1971 at the height of Lennon's political radicalism, which it survived. Composed on Lennon's new dobro (which debuted on [156]), the song started out with its slowly swinging chorus, owing a debt to Lou Reed's Sweet Jane from the Velvet Underground's *Loaded* (1970), which has essentially the same structure.[196] Not considered among the issue-specific material on *Some Time In New York City*, there was little substance to the song bar a sloganeering refrain which remained in mothballs for 18 months, when it was extended with a series of accusatory verses, which thanks to timing, tended to be read as an indictment of the Nixon administration, currently under pressure from the Watergate exposures.

Lennon's first attempt at recording it resulted in a gentle bass-high arrangement dominated by Gordon Edwards and 'Sneaky Pete' Kleinow, which while competently executed lacked the bite demanded by its subject matter. Lennon seems to have realised as much, undermining the first recording with a succession of jokey vocal inflections, including a spot of Dylan mimicking at 2:03. Inevitably returning for a tighter take three days later, Lennon re-cast the track with a harder edge, which improved its credentials but remained insipid by his standards. (Elephant's Memory would have done it more justice.)

Given Lennon was facing deportation through 1973 (see [217]) his decision to add these newly written verses was brave, the dangers of further upsetting those in high places not deterring him from saying his piece. Sneering at governments in general for 'jerking one another off', and comparing them to the devil, Lennon's lyric was scarcely likely to win him friends, although the lack of any particular political focus rendered his message rather blunt. This

---

[195] Something Different was the collective name given to Lennon's backing vocalists, session singers, Jocelyn Brown, Diane Coakley, Kathy Mull and Christine Wiltshire.

[196] Sweet Jane starts with the line, 'Standin' on the corner', which recurs in Lennon's [153] New York City, written around the same time as Bring On The Lucie, indicating Lennon was hip to it.

may have been a factor in Lennon shelving the song's original name in favour of the non-specific Bring On The Lucie, which if it means anything at all, alludes only to Lucy In The Sky. (The odd title led to US copies carrying the mis-spelling, 'Freeda'.)

John Lennon: [210] **YOU ARE HERE** (*Lennon*)
   Produced by John Lennon
   Recorded: 3 Aug 1973; 13-14 Aug 1973; 16 Aug 1973, Record Plant,
      New York
   UK: 16 Nov 1973 (*Mind Games* LP)
   US: 5 Nov 1973 (*Mind Games* LP)
   John Lennon: vocals, guitar; **David Spinozza:** guitar; **'Sneaky Pete' Kleinow:** pedal steel guitar; **Ken Ascher:** keyboards; **Gordon Edwards:** bass; **Jim Keltner:** drums, steel drum (?); **Something Different:** backing vocals

Asked in 1980 what the current composition represented, Lennon offered the curious explanation, 'a Latinesque song in a ballad tradition'.[197] While its quasi-Hawaiian style draws on Spanish and Portuguese influences, which may have been what Lennon was getting at, the song has its origins in *You Are Here (To Yoko From John, With Love)*, Lennon's Ono-inspired art exhibition staged in London in July 1968 which made the title phrase something of a slogan, printed on T-shirts and on one of the exhibits, written in tiny letters at the centre of a large, blank canvas.

Its first deployment in song came after Lennon met Harry Nilsson during the *White Album* sessions, and each challenged the other to come up with something bearing the three words. While Nilsson finished his song and recorded it in Hollywood on 1 July 1968 (coincidentally the day the exhibition opened), there's no sign Lennon started work on his in 1968, the first evidence of this overture to Ono dating from these 1973 sessions, which happened to occur at a time when the marriage needed more than a new tune to ease its troubles. A pitch to her romantic side, this tranquil piece wonders at the improbability of their having found one another, separated as they were by several thousand miles until, in Lennon's mind, fate intervened. Happily invoking Japanese imagery (the Land of the Rising Sun is also the Land of Surprising Sun), and borrowing from Rudyard Kipling's *The Ballad of East and West*, the song eschews Lennon's usual pragmatism/cynicism for a dream picture, resting on the faint hope that the staunchly realistic Ono might be seduced by such whimsy.[198] That she wasn't is proven by the fact that, five

---

[197] Golson, p181.

[198] Kipling: 'East is East, and West is West, and never the twain shall meet' (1889). >

weeks after the track was finished, Lennon was on a plane to LA without her.

Recorded over six takes, You Are Here clocked in around the five-minute mark before Lennon's decision to excise the second verse contrasting Japanese temples with English village greens. After 'Sneaky Pete' re-did his double-tracked pedal steel it was deemed ready, a South Sea excursion floating away across gently undulating Pacific waves. The irony was that Lennon and Ono's marriage was similarly adrift, this passively thoughtful appeal conspicuously missing the vital urgency which had once driven the same, obsessed man to write I Want You (She's So Heavy).

John Lennon: [211] **MEAT CITY** (*Lennon*)
Produced by John Lennon
Recorded: 3 Aug 1973; 11 Aug 1973, Record Plant, New York
UK: 9 Nov 1973 (single B-side)
US: 5 Nov 1973 (single B-side)
John Lennon: vocals, guitar; **David Spinozza:** guitar; **Ken Ascher:** keyboards; **Michael Brecker:** saxophone; **Gordon Edwards:** bass; **Jim Keltner:** drums; **Rick Marotta:** drums

The last of Lennon's period rockers, Meat City was, like much of the impersonal content of *Mind Games*, a song with a long gestation period, having been started prior to *Some Time In New York City*. It began as a rhythmically irregular guitar vamp drawing on the 1961 hit, Quarter To Three, by Gary U.S. Bonds, lines from which turn up in a home demo recorded in 1971 at Lennon's Bank Street apartment.[199] By the time it was recorded Lennon had ensconced himself in New York, his lyric revisions taking an acquired view of life in the Big Apple, and whereas [153] New York City, his previous song for his adopted home, had revelled in the bustle of its street culture, Meat City takes a less roseate view, casting around a neon-tinged world of hustlers, freaks and seedy fast food joints. (Much of the narrative alludes to Kentucky Fried Chicken's current advertising slogan, 'Finger-lickin' Good'.) Lennon's shotgun imagery draws much of its sleazy character from the influence of his new Marxist friends, finding revulsion in American-style consumerism which seeps

---

Lennon's re-wording brings East and West together. He'd been musing this idea for at least 18 months, since he remarked on his marriage on *The Mike Douglas Show*, recorded 27 January 1972, 'Mark Twain (*sic*) was wrong, you know. East and West met'.

[199] People were dancin' like they were mad/It was the swingingest band they had ever had.' Perhaps conscious of the fall-out from the similar steal in Come Together (see [236]), only a trace of this was retained: 'People were jumping like there's no tomorrow'. Quarter To Three had been a favourite of Lennon, sung by him in the Beatles' early stage shows.

out between the song's lines, ticked off with a *de rigueur* thumbs up for Mao's China which Lennon resolves to visit in order to weigh things up for himself.[200]

A firestorm of a song, Meat City encapsulates the confusion of the inner-city in a barrage of dirty noise, driven by Lennon's fuzz-tone rhythm guitar, his echo-drenched voice sounding as if emanating from the bottom of some side street. Recorded in 18 takes, the track was treated to post-production effects, atypical for 1970s Lennon and drawing on his experiences working with George Martin. Chief among them are three reverse-spooled drop-ins, the first of which revealed a cryptic message to those able to decipher it when spinning their 7-inch singles backwards, studio engineer, Roy Cicala: 'Check the album'. Attentive listeners noted a slight difference at this point in the album mix, revealing a rather less subtle message regarding a 'pig', likely referencing fighting the police – a parting shot from Lennon underscoring the song's confrontational subtext.

John Lennon: [212] **ONLY PEOPLE** (*Lennon*)
Produced by John Lennon
Recorded: 3 Aug 1973; 11 Aug 1973; 16 Aug 1973, Record Plant, New York
UK: 16 Nov 1973 (*Mind Games* LP)
US: 5 Nov 1973 (*Mind Games* LP)
John Lennon: vocals, guitar; **David Spinozza**: guitar; **Ken Ascher**: keyboards; **Michael Brecker**: saxophone; **Gordon Edwards**: bass; **Jim Keltner**: drums, percussion (?); **Something Different**: backing vocals

A rallying call to the 'switched on' generation, Only People has its origins in a succinct phrase by Ono: 'Only people can change the world', which Lennon took and adapted for the lyric.[201] But where his inspiration fired, he also seems to have run dry almost at once, the song ending up as a string of generalisations with no real insight, one of the most banal happening to be a nod to Dylan: 'Bake the cake and eat it too'. Partly this is accounted for by complacency; addressing those who had sought to bring about a new society in the 1960s, he was preaching to the converted and had little need to come up with anything convincing. Instead he fell back on a superficially cheery

---

[200] In an interview carried by the music paper, *Record Mirror* (29 April 1972), Lennon stated a desire to meet Mao in person and build bridges through rock concerts: 'I shall go to China. I will take the opportunity to try to see Mao... I want to take a rock band,' to which Ono appended, 'Not only musicians but with people like Jerry Rubin.'

[201] It's been noted that 18 months earlier, when the couple hosted *The Mike Douglas Show*, Lennon declared, 'Only people can save the world', leading some to assume the original thought was his. The programme was recorded 27 January 1972, the same episode in which Lennon also unwittingly enunciated the idea behind [210] You Are Here.

advertising pitch, likened by Andrew Grant Jackson to the 1971 jingle, I'd Like To Buy The World A Coke, which carries a similar melody line.[202]

Later judged a failure by Lennon, the song's cause wasn't helped by a studio group who far from pushing a united political front, set it to a pointlessly bouncy middle-of-the-road arrangement, negating any sense of gravitas. 19 takes were attempted, the 18th of which was selected as the master, overdubbed with soulful harmonies from Something Different and laid to rest halfway through the second side of *Mind Games*.

John Lennon: [213] **MIND GAMES** (*Lennon*)
Produced by John Lennon
Recorded: 4 Aug 1973; 10 Aug 1973, Record Plant, New York
UK: 9 Nov 1973 (single A-side)
US: 5 Nov 1973 (single A-side)
John Lennon: vocals, guitar, clavichord; **David Spinozza**: guitar; **Ken Ascher**: Mellotron; **Gordon Edwards**: bass; **Jim Keltner**: drums

Lennon came up with the basis of this, a contender for his best post-*Imagine* recording, towards the end of 1969, starting out with the lead phrase, 'make love, not war'. Its vintage accounts for the 1960s idealism, although even by the fading months of the decade such sentiment was becoming *passé*, explaining its excusing rejoinder, 'I know you've heard it before', and probably also accounting for its laying undeveloped for three and a half years. Lennon only revisited it after being sent a copy of the book, *Mind Games: The Guide To Inner Space* by Robert Masters and Jean Houston, a four-part manual on deepening one's inner awareness, which made a significant enough impression that he began weaving phrases from its text into Make Love Not War – in spite of its recurring references to Hindu trances and the sacred Om, a form of mysticism supposedly repudiated in Primal Therapy (see [86]).

Folding his thoughts into lyrics, Lennon managed to create a mosaic of references, a sort-of poetical impressionism capturing the flavour of the book's lexicon swirled with elements from a range of inspirations.[203] While certain

---

[202] *Still The Greatest* (2012). Since that tune was quickly re-written as the utopian I'd Like To Teach The World To Sing, it's plausible Lennon was making direct reference.

[203] Interviewed by Elliot Mintz for ABC TV in November 1973, Lennon claimed, 'The lyrics have nothing to do with the book'. However it's possible to trace numerous touch-points, for example from page 208, 'the search for this Holy Grail… that stone has been the life-long objective' manifests in song as, 'the search for the grail… the stones of your mind'. Lennon also claimed to have written an introduction for the already-published book, although his piece never appeared in subsequent editions. Possibly he sent something unsolicited to the authors.

parts of the lyric are therefore of the moment, most scan back across years, the phrase Absolute Elsewhere deriving from the name of a high-end cushion shop in Chelsea, owned by actor, Michael Crawford, Lennon's co-star in *How I Won The War*, and 'Yes is the answer' referencing the occasion on 7 November 1966 when Lennon and Ono first met at her London art exhibit, *Unfinished Paintings*. Ultimately a collage, the lyric to Mind Games thereby shows a reversion to Lennon's 1960s mode in which the 'random', free-form constructs of songs like Across The Universe and Dig A Pony make a reappearance, the whole thing tinged by Procol Harum's grandiose A Whiter Shade Of Pale, which had fascinated Lennon in the summer of 1967, and which similarly carries a slow, circulating chord structure over a descending bassline. (Played by Gordon Edwards, the line in Mind Games steps down the scale methodically in plain whole bars, an economy of style which the musically exuberant McCartney would never have contained.)

Imaginatively arranged, with 'orchestration' effected by Mellotron and clavichord, the recording session was particularly enjoyable, Jim Keltner rising to the occasion with a series of spontaneous fills and the band as a whole flying confidently through a middle eight conceived by Lennon as 'reggae', which he later recalled was a new idiom for them.[204] Finished up with a double-tracked lead vocal fed to opposite extremes of the stereo spectrum, Mind Games was by far the most successful product of these August sessions, and an obvious choice of single which despite its modest placing, marked his first appearance in the *Billboard* top 40 for two years.

John Lennon: [214] **OUT THE BLUE** (*Lennon*)
   Produced by John Lennon
   Recorded: 4 Aug 1973; 13-14 Aug 1973; 16 Aug 1973; 3 Sep 1973, Record Plant, New York
   UK: 16 Nov 1973 (*Mind Games* LP)
   US: 5 Nov 1973 (*Mind Games* LP)
   John Lennon: vocals, guitar; **David Spinozza:** guitar; **'Sneaky Pete' Kleinow:** pedal steel guitar; **Ken Ascher:** piano; **Gordon Edwards:** bass; **Jim Keltner:** drums; **Something Different:** backing vocals

With the high creativity of [213] Mind Games carrying them, Lennon and the band pressed ahead on the same session with this, a plaintive ballad which by its close becomes unexpectedly exultant, thanks largely to a wordless backing section from Something Different which almost succeeds in achieving

---

[204] Lennon was interviewed by Andy Peebles for the BBC, two days before his death: 'It's basically a reggae middle eight if you listen to it. But it was hard telling these [American session musicians], they didn't know what reggae was.'

transcendence. The net output from this Saturday's work, two of the most attractive recordings of Lennon's 1970s *oeuvre*, managed to rescue what he must have realised was threatening to become a stinker of a follow-up to *Some Time In New York City*, which instead stood to reaffirm his standing as a *song*writer now the politics were largely out of his system.[205]

Written for Ono, Out The Blue was pieced together not long before its recording, indicating that at this stage Lennon was still badly in need of his wife, so much so that his lyric borders on desperation.[206] While his characterisation of the relationship as 'two minds, one destiny' was a fairly standard expression of devotion, 'I was born just to get to you', bypassing the listener and addressing Ono directly, finds Lennon anticipating the emotional turmoil he was about to face with their impending separation, pouring his heart out in a hopeless attempt to win her back. The fact was, Lennon needed Ono far more than she needed him, the fracturing of their marriage largely a result of his wayward behaviour, leading her to, as he later confessed, kick him out of their home – thereby casting him adrift from the only stable element in his life. That the song mattered to him as a personal communication is signalled by the fact that, until late on, he intended to name the album after it.

The song's most prominent line, comparing Ono's arrival to the appearance of a UFO, while on one level risible, is in fact a reasonable analogy for him to have made, Ono seeming to have landed in his world unexpectedly, from some far-off place. (Lennon would famously see a UFO over New York during their time apart, an apparition perhaps of Ono watching down on him.) Enlivened with Ken Ascher's piano frills, probably modelled on Sexy Sadie (originally played by McCartney) which caries the same characteristic step from G to F sharp 7, Out The Blue avoids any sense of self-pity, an ostensibly optimistic counterpoint to some of the despondency in evidence elsewhere on the album.

---

[205] Commenting with hindsight on his radical phase in a *Rolling Stone* interview in 1975, (cover date, 5 June), a reformed Lennon wryly observed, 'I basically feel that I'm a poet [but] you get into that bit where you can't talk about trees, 'cause, y'know, y'gotta talk about corruption on 54th Street.'

[206] A scrap of notepaper retrieved from Lennon's bin is reproduced in *The John Lennon Letters* (Davies, 2012) and catches the genesis of the lyric in a few sketchy phrases scribbled in red ink: 'Life/knife... Born get to you... Anyway I survived... – Wife... Born to be with you'. Other details on the sheet demonstrate this was noted down in mid-1973.

John Lennon: [215] **AISUMASEN (I'M SORRY)** (*Lennon*)
Produced by John Lennon
Recorded: 5 Aug 1973; 13-14 Aug 1973, Record Plant, New York
UK: 16 Nov 1973 (*Mind Games* LP)
US: 5 Nov 1973 (*Mind Games* LP)
John Lennon: vocals, guitar; **David Spinozza**: guitar; **'Sneaky Pete' Kleinow**: pedal steel guitar; **Ken Ascher**: piano; **Gordon Edwards**: bass; **Jim Keltner**: drums, percussion (?)

A low-tempo counterpoint to [214] Out The Blue, this palliation to Ono grew from a sketch Lennon had lying around since 1971, provisionally titled Call My Name. Written as a gesture of emotional support the song rested on the refrain, 'I'll ease your pain' but by the time Lennon took it off the shelf for *Mind Games* he was in need of a crutch himself, thereby contorting the hook line into a similar-sounding Japanese apology.[207] Lennon had tried to familiarise himself with Ono's language in 1970 (see [79]), but his inclusion of three Japanese terms in the current song smacks of a deliberate concession to meet her on her own territory. (Sanpaku, mentioned in the third verse, literally meaning 'three whites', refers to a condition of the human eye in which the sclera becomes visible below the bottom of the iris, sometimes seen in Japan as a portent of illness or doom.)

Pitched in a gloomy 6/8, Aisumasen too openly expresses Lennon's blues, its tiredness not lifted by David Spinozza's scorching guitar solo, positioned as a closer and sounding in style much like Pink Floyd's David Gilmour.[208] While Lennon's lyric extends a sympathetic hand to Ono, the line, 'it's hard enough I know, just to feel your own pain' more forgiving than the uncompromising statement in [81] I Found Out, finds Lennon not knowing what to do; never in his career had he sounded so defeated.

---

[207] Aisumasen is a mistake for ai-sumimasen, often spoken as 'suimasen', which translates either as 'I'm sorry' or 'excuse me'.
[208] Spinozza is said to have been attempting the sound of Harrison's lead in Octopus's Garden.

John Lennon: [216] **ONE DAY (AT A TIME)** (*Lennon*)
  Produced by John Lennon
  Recorded: 5 Aug 1973; 11 Aug 1973; 13-14 Aug 1973; 16 Aug 1973,
    Record Plant, New York
  UK: 16 Nov 1973 (*Mind Games* LP)
  US: 5 Nov 1973 (*Mind Games* LP)
  John Lennon: vocals, guitar; **David Spinozza**: guitar; **'Sneaky Pete' Kleinow**: pedal steel guitar; **Ken Ascher**: keyboards; **Gordon Edwards**: bass; **Michael Brecker**: saxophone; **Jim Keltner**: drums; **Something Different**: backing vocals

The last in a series of soul-searching ballads, One Day (At A Time) concludes the *Mind Games* sessions where they began [205], with Lennon musing on Ono and trying to reason a way through. Delivered in airy falsetto (Ono's suggestion) to overcome difficulties in the pitching, the vocal was decided on during six days of after-the-event overdubbing onto take 19. Remarkably the track's lightness of touch survived an arrangement policy in which Lennon threw the kitchen sink at it, adding in saxophone, pedal steel and a prominent backing section from Something Different, which apart from anything else served to bury Ken Ascher's keyboard patterning, particularly in the instrumental break.

Lennon's survival strategy in this difficult period, 'one day at a time' expresses a commitment to living in the present, as he'd done in the equally tough period following his Primal Therapy (see [84]). Desperation pitched as a lullaby, the song both reveals and obscures, Lennon's philosophical slant in which he and Ono are complementary parts of a universal whole too verbally forced to entirely convince (and ending up apiculturally challenged.) Like several of his period outpourings ([205]; [214]; [215]), the song doesn't cadence, floating off mysteriously into the void – probably a pattern Lennon was unconscious of during the sessions but which reveals an uncertainty as to what the future may hold.

John Lennon: [217] **NUTOPIAN INTERNATIONAL ANTHEM** (*Lennon*)
  UK: 16 Nov 1973 (*Mind Games* LP)
  US: 6 Nov 1973 (*Mind Games* LP)

The creation of Nutopia, an imaginary land open to all the world's population, began as one of Ono's conceptual 'works', some years before matters in Lennon's deportation case came to a head. In the early part of 1973 the latest of his temporary US visas expired, resulting in a ruling on 23 March that he leave the country within 60 days. The situation was complicated by the fact that Ono had technical custody of her estranged daughter Kyoko, on condition that should they be reunited the child would be brought up in the States. Thus, Ono was put in the impossible position of remaining with her husband – and leaving the country – or choosing to stay for her daughter and becoming separated from Lennon, adding a further layer of outrage to what was already looking like a farcical deportation case. The Lennons' response was typically creative, and aimed at mobilising public sympathy: the time had come to declare Nutopia.

Electing to issue a jointly signed statement, the Lennons delivered their announcement on April Fool's Day, drawing the media's attention in advance of a press conference the following morning in which the two read out their formal declaration in unison before the world's microphones.[209] Essentially a make-believe place without laws (other than 'cosmic'), Nutopia was defined only in the mind, a state of absolute neutrality, its flag a plain white handkerchief and citizenship requiring nothing more than knowledge of its existence.[210] The Lennons even provided an address for the Nutopian embassy, 1 White Street, which on the face of it appeared merely another abstract invention but was in fact a real premises in New York occupied by the Guerrilla Art Group, co-founded in the late 1960s by Belgian radical, Jean Toche, whose cause was to provoke the art world through 'happenings' designed to subvert its perceived commercialisation.[211] Known primarily to Ono through her work on the New York arts scene, Toche was involved on the fringes of Fluxus, one of whose main strategies was the use of humour to affect perception – thus, the concept of Nutopia was delivered with a punchline: Lennon was seeking UN recognition of his status as Nutopian ambassador, and thereby claimed diplomatic immunity from deportation. Taken as a legal argument the proposition was absurd, but Lennon succeeded in making a point so that by the end of the month there existed a National Committee For John And Yoko, rousing support from unlikely sources such as the usually

---

[209] 'We announce the birth of a conceptual country, Nutopia. Citizenship of the country can be obtained by declaration of your awareness of Nutopia. Nutopia has no land, no boundaries, no passports, only people. Nutopia has no laws other than cosmic. All people of Nutopia are ambassadors of the country. As two ambassadors of Nutopia, we ask for diplomatic immunity and recognition in the United Nations of our country and its people.'

[210] Interviewed by Danny Schechter for WBCN Boston on 3 June, Lennon explained, 'The country, if it has no land, [means] nothing to fight for', reminding the interviewer of the lyric to [130] Imagine.

[211] One of Toche's most famous stunts involved spraying animal blood around the entrance lobby of Manhattan's Museum of Modern Art. On another occasion he participated in a public burning of the US flag, precisely to challenge the authorities' application of state law, resulting in him being sentenced as one of the so-called Judson 3 whose cause was supported by Lennon and Ono in 1971.

apolitical New Yorker, Neil Sedaka, whose The Immigrant championed Lennon's side.

Given Nutopia's ultra-neutralist policy, its anthem consisted of an indefinable few seconds of silence positioned at the end of side 1 of *Mind Games*, while its manifesto, Lennon and Ono's April statement, was printed in full on the album's inner sleeve. In keeping with the wry humour underlying the campaign, Nutopia's national seal was designed as an illustration of an aquatic seal perching a yin and yang symbol on its nose, commemorated in a sign fixed to Lennon and Ono's Dakota kitchen door. Back in the real world, further formal appeals were lodged by Lennon's lawyers, his residency continuing to hang in the balance while his physical presence in the States dragged into its third year.

Lennon finished up his first solo set for two years, provisionally titled *Out The Blue*, with a series of mixing sessions running into early September. During this period, Ono made a pivotal decision concerning her troubled marriage and resolved to separate from him, a move effected by informing Lennon that he had to leave, Ono recognising that, like her, he needed distance from a relationship which had become stifling – at least for a while. The danger for Ono was that should Lennon discover a sense of liberation without his wife, his inevitable infidelities could result in her losing him for good.

She therefore took the extraordinary decision, in an era of social sexual liberation, to find him a new partner, both to keep his libido in check and to keep him on a long lead. The girl she selected was May Pang, a 22-year-old assistant Ono had recently taken on from ABKCO, and who currently worked for her in the Lennons' Dakota apartment. By all accounts Ono gently sounded Pang out to test her feelings, the young assistant at first reluctant to agree but won over when Lennon, understanding he'd been given the green light by Ono, came on strong to her, taking her into the recording studio and talking his way into her apartment; and from Pang's side, at least this was going to be an adventure.[212]

Lennon and May Pang began their affair in New York during August, but the situation was hardly liberating for any of them given their close proximity to Ono. Accordingly, she suggested the couple leave town completely, giving her the space she craved and allowing Lennon to get – whatever it was – out of his system. The destination agreed on was LA, home to a vibrant music scene and about as far away as possible. Thus, less than five months after moving into his new marital home, Lennon left Ono and the Dakota with Pang,

---

[212] For her account of the period, see Pang and Edwards, p61-77.

boarding a flight to the opposite end of the country on 22 September, marking the start of his 'lost weekend'.

Mind Games was released at the start of November in parallel with *Feeling The Space*, and came housed in a jacket of Lennon's making, depicting him walking away from Ono like a lost soul, carrying his hand luggage. Ono's only credit on the package was for 'space', her own current album title making the same point.[213] Basically recorded in just five days, Lennon's record, for someone of his character, was remarkably unremarkable, treading a cautious path partly explained by the lingering backlash to *Some Time In New York City*. And while Lennon's decision to retain Ono's band for the project was expedient, they were never *his* (Jim Keltner excepted), and lacked the grit to bring his music out of itself. The fact is Ono needed her musical rough edges smoothing off but Lennon didn't, *Mind Games* a frustratingly conservative recording with Lennon's nagging relationship strife casting a shadow over proceedings. (His production decisions too were at times ill-judged, ranging from the incongruity of an orchestrated section in the street-campaigning [212] Only People to the intrusion of an unfamiliar singing troupe in intimate material such as [216] One Day (At A Time).[214])

Settling in the new surroundings of Los Angeles, Lennon and Pang spent their early weeks exploring the local nightlife and socialising with fellow rock stars, including a first meeting with Elton John. In no time at all, Lennon was embarking on his next musical project, an album of rock and roll oldies to be recorded with Phil Spector, sessions for which commenced just 25 days after Lennon had hit town.

RECORD RELEASES

[213] **Mind Games** / [211] **Meat City**
(UK: 9 Nov 1973, US: 29 Oct 1973)

Mind Games
(UK: 16 Nov 1973, US: 5 Nov 1973)
[213] Mind Games / [206] Tight A$ / [215] Aisumasen (I'm Sorry) / [216] One Day (At A Time) / [209] Bring On The Lucie (Freda Peeple) / [217] Nutopian International Anthem / [208] Intuition / [214] Out The Blue / [212] Only People / [205] I Know (I Know) / [210] You Are Here / [211] Meat City

---

[213] Ono's influence is manifest in Lennon's application of a red *Gago-in* in the bottom corner of his album sleeve, an old Japanese method of signing artworks with carved, personalised handstamps. His reads, 'Like a cloud, beautiful sound'.

[214] Lennon's diagnosis of the album's shortcomings, expressed in a 1980 interview for the *LA Times*: 'No clarity of vision'.

Band On The Run sessions:
August 1973 to October 1973

The day after the UK screening of *James Paul McCartney* ([192]), with its poor reviews hanging in the air, Wings embarked on the next phase of McCartney's plan to retrace his Beatle career. Wings' first UK tour, ostensibly in promotion of *Red Rose Speedway*, was set to run in two phases between May and July, and offered a prime chance to break them as a live act, exactly a decade after the Beatles had conquered Britain. The ensuing 20 performances saw the group snake across the country, starting in Bristol, down to Bournemouth's Winter Gardens where the Beatles had played in 1963, up to Sheffield City Hall where they'd long ago supported Helen Shapiro, and north again to the Newcastle venue they'd rocked during their 1963 Autumn Tour. This was the first time a Beatle had played the circuit since 1965, and in scenes reminiscent of Beatlemania, the gig at Green's Playhouse in Glasgow on 24 May was met by a frenzy of eager fans who had to be held in check by police marshals. Poignantly, McCartney's itinerary included two performances in Liverpool at the same Empire Theatre the Beatles had performed every year from 1962 to 1965, shows which in 1973 drew his family out to watch, as they'd done in the early days.[215] This, for McCartney, represented a homecoming literally and figuratively, his wowing of legions of adoring fans constituting a kind of rehabilitation after three years in the comparative wilderness.

Looking to strike while the iron was hot, McCartney swiftly drew up plans for his next project, rehearsing Wings through a series of pre-sessions for what would become *Band On The Run* at his Scottish studio, meanwhile writing a clutch of new songs. The album was to be recorded abroad in some sunny clime, McCartney recalling that when Harrison was preparing his soundtrack to the film *Wonderwall* in 1967, he decamped for EMI's studios in Bombay. Knowing the company had facilities across the world McCartney pictured a pleasantly relaxing locale where he could enjoy some recreational down time while soaking up the local music, his final choice coming down to a toss-up between Brazil and Nigeria.

Former Cream drummer, Ginger Baker, happened to be currently based in the Nigerian coastal town of Lagos and over the past couple of years had built

---

[215] Both shows were on 18 May, nine days prior to the closure of the Cavern Club – something McCartney seemed indifferent to at the time. The Cavern was bulldozed and a car park built on the site. It was later reconstructed and reopened as a live venue in 1984, McCartney finally returning to its stage in 1999.

his own studio, ARC (Associated Recording Company) which opened its doors in January 1973. Excellently equipped with 1,000 square feet of studio space and a 16-track console, it was probably Africa's most advanced facility in its day and a considerable attraction for McCartney, who had a representative scope out the place before agreeing to record *Band On The Run* there. (Baker was also pals with Denny Laine, having been in a band with him a couple of years earlier.) Unfortunately, just as plans were crystallising, a critical disagreement flared up between McCartney and Henry McCullough, the guitarist, already disgruntled over his being stuck on a basic weekly wage, walking out after McCartney tried to make him play a solo the way *he* wanted it. And with Baker's ARC studio booked, the loss of his lead guitarist threatened to put a dampener on things, Denny Seiwell urging McCartney to postpone the project until a replacement could be secured and bedded in. That McCartney refused to wait was part of the reason Seiwell too threw in the towel, calling up the night before departure to announce he wasn't coming, and Wings suddenly were down to three and in danger of dissolving.

Defiantly, McCartney, Linda, the kids and Denny Laine boarded their flight to Nigeria's Ikeja airport on 9 August armed with their rehearsal tapes and determined to turn them into an album. Since the new material had already been worked through, there would be no need to devise group arrangements, just tighten up and develop what was already there. But what greeted them on landing was far removed from the tropical idyll McCartney had hoped for – no exotic paradise, Lagos was an impoverished, cholera-ridden city which the current rainy season had turned into a muddy pit where human bodies could be spotted laying in the roads. The entourage (Wings, engineer, Geoff Emerick, and a couple of roadies – likely Ian Horne and Trevor Jones) was welcomed to Lagos by Ginger Baker who recognised that such a prestigious project would put ARC firmly on the industry map and so organised three houses for them to stay in, with staff and a couple of cars laid on.[216] Baker had the band's equipment delivered to ARC, and everything looked set for what promised to be an adventurous set of sessions over the following few weeks.

---

[216] In his entertaining memoir, *Hellraiser* (2010), Baker claimed EMI were unable to arrange a visa for McCartney and so he used the booking at ARC as a means of levering the Home Office.

Paul McCartney And Wings: [218] **MAMUNIA** (*McCartney*)
Produced by Paul McCartney
Recorded: Aug-Sep 1973, EMI Studios, Apapa, Lagos; Oct 1973,
   AIR Studios, London
UK: 7 Dec 1973 (*Band On The Run* LP)
US: 5 Dec 1973 (*Band On The Run* LP)
Paul McCartney: vocals, guitar, bass, percussion; **Linda McCartney**: Moog synthesiser, backing vocals; **Denny Laine**: guitar, backing vocals, percussion; **Ian Horne** or **Trevor Jones** (?): bass drum

If Ginger Baker was pleased to have McCartney record his next album at ARC, his joy was short-lived. Less than pleased with the opening of ARC, which offered direct competition, EMI were in unco-operative mood and joined forces with Decca to deny ARC use of their mutual record pressing facilities, forcing Baker to have his discs manufactured in England and shipped back across, eroding his margins.[217] Thus, it was not out of character when they reminded McCartney soon after arrival that he was an EMI artist and they therefore required him to abandon ARC and move to their own studio in the coastal district of Apapa at the other end of town.

The move incensed Baker and his colleagues, among them the influential Nigerian musician, Fela Kuti, with whom Baker had worked and recorded extensively over the previous couple of years. The morning after McCartney shifted base Kuti turned up at EMI's studio on Wharf Road with a mob of angry friends, intent on halting proceedings. Added to the friction was Kuti's not unreasonable assumption that McCartney had arrived in Lagos to exploit the local musical styles, which he and Baker reckoned would be the next big thing. (Kuti still bore a grudge against South African trumpeter, Hugh Maeskela, who'd visited Nigeria before travelling to America and enjoying commercial success.) McCartney's reassurances that he had no such intention, plus the promise that he'd go back to ARC record something before he was done, helped defuse the situation, and with Baker acting as intermediary, they soon smoothed things over and became friends.[218]

---

[217] Baker also claimed, in chapter 18 of his autobiography, he was collared by EMI's overseas MD, who advised him in no uncertain terms: 'We're going to screw you. You can't build a studio here – this is EMI territory and you've got to get that into your head.'
[218] Kuti ran the Lagos nightclub, the Shrine, and invited McCartney over to watch his band, Africa 70, which proved to be a deeply moving experience. Before McCartney left Lagos, he was gifted a copy of Kuti's album, *Shakara* (not yet available in Britain), which he generously publicised, taking it with him to play on Kenny Everett's radio show on 24 November.

These tensions added to the generally problematic environment McCartney was in. He was further dismayed to find himself caught in the middle of the oppressive monsoon season, which in Southern Nigeria stretches roughly between March and November. Fittingly, the first thing recorded there was the rain-soaked Mamunia, taped in the middle of a violent deluge, its lyrics putting a brave face on the circumstances. Mamunia takes its name from the Moroccan hotel Wings had stayed in at the start of the year ([192]), the placid musicality of its chorus indicating it started life as a lazy acoustic sketch. By contrast the verses, logically expanding on why precipitation is good, seem to have been written in Los Angeles to judge by their reference points, likely during the mixing stage of *RAM*. (McCartney may have recalled the occasion Armin Steiner ventured up a cliff-top to make a recording of a thunderstorm [106].) Reminded of Mamunia when he saw the word again, written on a house sign in Lagos, both parts of the eventual song were in McCartney's mind at once, and if not already joined together, they were now. (The supposition that the two sections were written separately is supported by the fact that they are in different keys.)

Thoughtfully arranged, with a tidy counterpoint vocal from Laine in its latter passages, Mamunia's strong card is its Moog solo, recorded by Linda in November in the dry comfort of London's AIR Studios, commencing with a walk up the entire A major scale before slipping into a smoothly gliding dance around the home key. Initially selected by Capitol as the flip side to [226] Jet, the song was soon after earmarked for possible A-side exposure and so swapped out for the UK choice, [225] Let Me Roll It, making early US pressings collectors' items. (A Mamunia single never did materialise.)

Paul McCartney And Wings: [219] **MRS. VANDEBILT** (*McCartney*)
   Produced by Paul McCartney
   Recorded: Aug-Sep 1973, EMI Studios, Apapa, Lagos; Oct 1973,
      AIR Studios, London
   UK: 7 Dec 1973 (*Band On The Run* LP)
   US: 5 Dec 1973 (*Band On The Run* LP)
   Paul McCartney: vocals, guitar, bass, drums, percussion; **Linda McCartney**: electric piano, backing vocals, percussion (?); **Denny Laine**: guitar, backing vocals, percussion (?); **Howie Casey**: saxophone

EMI's recording studio had only recently been recipient of a portable recording console, and with its generally shambolic condition turned out to be scarcely fit for purpose. (McCartney later recounted how, on first visit, he was amazed to find a team of workers hand-pressing records in a back-room, ankle-deep in water.) His engineer, Geoff Emerick, discovered the recording equipment consisted mostly of a few cardboard boxes containing cheap and faulty microphones, and with help from the on-site studio chief named Monday, and his assistant, Innocence, had to oversee a minor reconstruction, a local team press-ganged to build some internal sound screens. Emerick managed to cobble together a functional studio floor, and among the hammering rain and equipment failures, pressed ahead, the predicament they were in sharply delineated during the recording of Mrs. Vandebilt when the studio lost power partway through proceedings, forcing the group to rely on a noisy generator which threatened to spoil the audio (and gave a new twist to the song's opening line).

Ironically, among so much privation, the subject of this new track was a millionaire socialite, Gloria Vanderbilt, part of what was once the richest family in America. McCartney claimed to know practically nothing of her life and circumstances but recognised the name as belonging to someone of wealth, and so, despite a minor mis-spelling, elected to commemorate her in song as 'a figure of authority'.[219] McCartney may not have known Vanderbilt personally but plausibly crossed paths with the family, one of the clan, John P Hammond, having made a name for himself as a guitarist working with the likes of Clapton, Hendrix and the Band, while Gloria was renowned in her own right for work in theatre and fashion. That McCartney should opt to record this Spanish-tinged rock song, whose verses deal with escaping the forced obligations of mixing with high society, is understandable given his commitment to leading a simple rural life, the only weakening of his affirmative outlook revealed in the deflating, 'What's the use of anything?'.

Likely written over the summer, Mrs. Vandebilt shows echoes of [158] When The Night in its composition, the opening phrase, 'When your light…' corresponding to the first lyrics of the earlier song, also pitched in A minor. Mrs. Vandebilt is entirely contemporary, however, and includes in its recording the only overtly African references on Band On The Run – the loosely whooping commotion dubbed over its final bars conjuring the noise of a tropical rainforest, and specific mention of the jungle in the song's introductory chant, based on a children's rhyme which McCartney would have known from his youth.[220]

A catchy hit in Europe and Australia, Mrs. Vandebilt features a sax riff from Howie Casey, brought into AIR for the autumn overdubs by arranger, Tony Visconti, who'd used him on recent sessions with T Rex. Casey brought

---

[219] According to McCartney, the secondary character Mrs Washington 'represents the political capital of America' (2021, p485).
[220] These lines originated as a running gag on 'Cheeky' Charlie Chester's wireless show of the late 1940s: 'Down in the jungle, living in a tent/Better than a prefab – no rent!'. Prefabs were (supposedly) temporary constructions made from prefabricated concrete sections, widely built to address Britain's post-war housing shortage.

with him an air of familiarity, having been an old associate of McCartney from Liverpool and Hamburg, when playing sax for Derry and the Seniors.

Paul McCartney And Wings: [220] **NO WORDS** (*McCartney, Laine*)
Produced by Paul McCartney
Recorded: Aug-Sep 1973, EMI Studios, Apapa, Lagos; Oct 1973, AIR Studios, London
UK: 7 Dec 1973 (*Band On The Run* LP)
US: 5 Dec 1973 (*Band On The Run* LP)
Paul McCartney: vocals, guitar, bass, drums, percussion (?); **Linda McCartney**: vocals, keyboards, percussion (?); **Denny Laine**: vocals, guitar; **Trevor Jones**: backing vocals; **Ian Horne**: backing vocals; **Beaux Arts Orchestra**: strings (arranged by Tony Visconti)

A talented multi-instrumentalist, Denny Laine was one of a number of musicians who down the years found themselves overshadowed in McCartney's company, only Lennon ever standing as a true artistic equal. As a songwriter, Laine had shown early promise in co-composing several tracks for the Moody Blues, a couple of which were chart hits, although his subsequent solo success quickly petered out. At a loose end in the early 1970s, Laine fancied another stab at individual stardom, embarking on a new album project which was underway when he got the call to join Wings, a development which might have put the project in permanent stasis. The sudden appearance of one of his old compositions in the UK top 20, Say You Don't Mind, in a 1972 cover version by Colin Blunstone, may have come as a surprise, but served to encourage Laine to complete his solo LP, something McCartney reportedly supported. The entirely self-composed *Ahh Laine!* saw release in November 1973 more or less concurrently with *Band On The Run*, McCartney's concession in letting it through particularly generous given the timing, Laine paying his dues by sporting a Wings T-shirt on the front cover.[221]

Perhaps as acknowledgement of his loyalty in sticking with Wings when the rest of the group fell away, McCartney consented to collaborate on No Words, a track Laine had available for some time. What McCartney brought to the composition is not entirely certain, musicologist, Adrian Allan, having it on authority that his principal contribution was the insertion of the song's uber-

---

[221] Laine later wrote two songs for Wings, Time To Hide (1976) and Again And Again And Again (1979), besides co-writing seven with McCartney, including Mull Of Kintyre, Britain's all-time best-selling single in its day. When he left the group he took with him three unused compositions: Send Me The Heart; Weep For Love; and the *Red Rose Speedway* reject, I Would Only Smile, all for his *Japanese Tears* album.

falsetto contrasting section, 'Your burning love'.[222] While these eight bars have McCartney's fingerprints on them, particularly in the acute climb of the solo vocal line, the underlying chords are Laine's, matching those in the existing verses. In fact, McCartney has nominated lyrical additions elsewhere as his – particularly, 'It's only me, I love you', something Lennon once said to him in the middle of a row.

So irrepressible is McCartney's work that he emerges as the dominant force, singing throughout, and in the second verse switching his harmony to a high line, thereby moving to the front. The hot and bluesy lead guitar in the song's closing section is his too, although his key contribution, a vital drum section with frizzling hi-hats, is mixed so low as to lose its impact. (The drumming was presumably buried because of a blunder at 0:59, causing McCartney to stop completely and regain himself – the inadvertent drop-out effective in highlighting what there is of a lyrical hook. The irony is, had events in Lagos taken a different turn, McCartney would have had one of the best drummers in the business at his disposal: Ginger Baker.)

Brought back to London, No Words was treated to a string quartet arrangement by Tony Visconti, recorded at AIR Studios by hired musicians working under the name the Beaux Arts Orchestra. Meshing with McCartney's lead guitar and thereby reminiscent of early ELO (particularly their 1972 hit, 10538 Overture) these parts pull through a distant thread from George Martin's arrangements for the Beatles, an additional 'brass' section effected on Linda's keyboard in the middle eight[223]; with the drum track repaired and mixed so as to emphasise its dynamics, the recording, which tends to slip under the radar somewhat, would nevertheless emerge as one of the stand-out tracks on *Band On The Run*.

---

[222] 2019, p79.

[223] Once referred to by Lennon as 'Son of Beatles', the Electric Light Orchestra was founded in 1970 as a project to extrapolate the integration of classical music into pop on albums such as *Sgt Pepper*. McCartney can hardly have failed to notice ELO's version of Roll Over Beethoven in the British charts earlier in 1973. It's also worth observing that Denny Laine, after exiting the Moody Blues in 1966, was part of the proto-ELO outfit, Electric String Band, having previously been in a group with Bev Bevan.

Paul McCartney And Wings: [221] **BAND ON THE RUN** (*McCartney*)
   Produced by Paul McCartney
   Recorded: Aug-Sep 1973, EMI Studios, Apapa, Lagos; Oct 1973,
      AIR Studios, London
   UK: 7 Dec 1973 (*Band On The Run* LP)
   US: 5 Dec 1973 (*Band On The Run* LP)
   Paul McCartney: vocals, guitar, keyboards, bass, drums; **Linda McCartney**: Moog synthesiser, backing vocals; **Denny Laine**: guitar, backing vocals; **Beaux Arts Orchestra**: strings (arranged by Tony Visconti)

Wings' accommodation in Lagos consisted of a few houses near Ikeja airport, separate from one another but close enough to be within walking distance. McCartney had been warned of the risks of street crime, but regardless decided to stroll back from Laine's one night carrying some valuables, including camera equipment and tapes. Inevitably he and Linda were set upon by a gang of muggers, who made off with everything they had, which apart from leaving them shaken, deprived McCartney of his album demos, forcing him to recall the rest of his songs from memory.[224]

Coupled with the stresses and strains which dogged the project from the start, this event proved something of a tipping point for McCartney, who succumbed to a health episode in which he collapsed in the studio, struggling for breath before losing consciousness completely. After a frantic Linda managed to get him to hospital, doctors diagnosed only a trivial complaint, a 'bronchial spasm' probably caused by too much smoking. An enthusiastic partaker of marijuana, who'd been busted twice in the past year, McCartney had no doubt over-indulged in the local produce, whose potency was unexpected, an explanation which didn't stop him from being deeply concerned for his own welfare – thus adding another layer of strife to the sessions.[225]

Given the circumstances, thoughts of escape must have held a certain attraction for McCartney who put together this combination of song parts sequenced so as to evoke a feeling of liberation. Band On The Run is made up of three distinct pieces recorded in two sections, the first, the relaxed sounding 'Stuck inside these four walls' adjoining and ushering in the key statement, written off a remark made by Harrison in one of the Beatles' long-winded

---

[224] McCartney had preserved his demos on cassettes, which were never recovered and are presumed lost. The robbery partly accounts for the lack of album outtakes in circulation.

[225] Interviewed by podcaster, Marc Maron, in August 2018, McCartney recalled the Nigerian grass: 'It was stronger than anything I'd ever had. I don't know if there was something [else] in it.'

business meetings of the late 1960s: 'If we ever get out of here'. In this context the song bears comparison to You Never Give Me Your Money, similarly assembled from fragments and written against the backdrop of Apple's unravelling. (This bridging part, sung in McCartney's deep voice, is a parallel to the 'Out of college' section in the 1969 track, representing a fleeing from financial burdens and a return to the simplicity of ordinary life.)

The song's second half, an extravagant coda expressing the thrill of freedom, was recorded in a separate session and grafted on at a later date. Luca Perasi considers this to have been taped back in London, reckoning there to be audio evidence in the quality of the sound, but this should be countered by the fact that when McCartney travelled home, he brought with him tape boxes marked 'Band On The Run (1st Part)' and 'Band On The Run (2nd Part)', and since this final segment is the only place the song title occurs, it must have formed part of the sequence while he was in Lagos.[226] What McCartney had in mind was a band of renegades – not a musical group, as is often inferred – standing on the wrong side of the law, a concept crystallised by his own criminalisation for possessing drugs in 1972. Part nonsense and part autobiography, this three-minute song-within-a-song celebrates a joyful flight from authority, happily name-dropping a character from McCartney's childhood, the voyager, Sailor Sam from the Rupert stories which he had so enjoyed [103].

Returning with his two tapes, McCartney had a problem which naturally fell to his arranger, Tony Visconti to solve – namely that section one concludes on a dispirited E minor, with section two following on an upbeat C major running at a different tempo, needing some sort of join. The solution was to divert into a five-bar orchestral link which required some 50 classical musicians and an inordinate amount of time to get right, but which expressively summons the breaking of bonds. (The concluding piece, with its consequent sense of liberation, arrives on a bold 12-string acoustic which, when taken into Wings' live act in 1975, allowed Laine to play a visually striking Ibanez dual-necked guitar, so as not to have to switch instruments mid-performance.)

As adventurous a statement as post-Beatle McCartney had yet made, Band On The Run gave its album a name and garnered strong interest among those who heard it. Interviewed for BBC Radio 1's *Rock Week* in November – before the LP had been released – McCartney was asked if he intended to issue the track as a single, to which he answered in the negative.[227] Apart from

---

[226] For Perasi's comments, see 2013, p104.
[227] 11 November 1973, interviewed by Paul Gambaccini. McCartney: 'I think probably the best thing to do is leave the album as it is and then think of another single, completely different thing.'

McCartney's inherent reluctance to pull 45s from his albums, one barrier was the track's play-time, the medley of sections running to an indulgent five minutes-plus. Not wanting to miss out on a hit, Capitol resolved the problem by creating a truncated edit, trimming off a quarter of its length for radio. Thus, despite McCartney's misgivings, its release as a single became an inevitability, once the similarly purloined [226] Jet had run its course on the charts.

Band On The Run remains one of McCartney's most popular tracks, its fusing of elements the latest in a line of 'through-composed' mini-suites which contain among them some of his most impressive works ([98]; [102]; [106]; [191] etc). Issued out in the States in April, it topped the *Billboard* charts, leading EMI-UK to follow suit with their own edition which almost repeated the feat (despite an odd choice of flip side: [193]). Worthy of commemoration, a video sequence was belatedly issued, prepared unofficially in the 1970s by fan, Michael Coulson from a lengthy montage of Beatles photographs including Lennon in his *Pepper* suit and Harrison mixing it with the Maharishi – an odd visual accompaniment to a Wings song. In 1996, Denny Laine recorded a bland version of his own for the semi-retrospective *Wings At The Sound Of Denny Laine* (1996), if nothing else, an indication of the song's enduing popularity.

Paul McCartney And Wings: [222] **HELEN WHEELS** (*McCartney*)
  Produced by Paul McCartney
  Recorded: Aug-Sep 1973, EMI Studios, Apapa, Lagos; Oct 1973,
     AIR Studios, London
  UK: 26 Oct 1973 (single A-side)
  US: 12 Nov 1973 (single A-side)
  Paul McCartney: vocals, guitar, bass, drums; **Linda McCartney**: Moog synthesiser, backing vocals; **Denny Laine**: guitar, backing vocals

4000 miles from home, McCartney sought comfort in this spirited track, reminding him of his now familiar drives down to London from his farm in Kintyre. Conceived as a UK equivalent to the classic road song, Route 66, the lyric takes in the major towns and cities along the M6, with droll references to the 'Kendal Freeway' and a line about Carlisle, spinning off Bobby Troup's original, 'Oklahoma city is mighty pretty'.[228] (There's also an in-joke – the borrowing of a lyric about Sailor Sam from the as-yet unreleased [221] Band On The Run.)

Built almost entirely on the A chord, Helen Wheels is the most straightforward product of these sessions, driving through its verses with a sense of

---

[228] The song stops by, in order, Glasgow, Carlisle, Kendal, Liverpool, Birmingham and finally heads for London, roughly tracing the route of the motorway.

immediacy – something accentuated by its fashionable glam rock arrangement, making it a natural choice for the next single. Issued ahead of the LP, the track dipped into the US top 10 on 12 January, aided by a promo video which brought McCartney back together with *Let It Be* director, Michael Lindsay-Hogg. Before the single's success, Capitol had already arranged to squeeze it onto the US edition of *Band On The Run* against McCartney's wishes, sequencing it between [220] No Words and [223] Picasso's Last Words (Drink To Me), an intrusion on the correct running order anticipating a cash-in.

Paul McCartney And Wings: [223] **PICASSO'S LAST WORDS (DRINK TO ME)** (*McCartney*)
Produced by Paul McCartney
Recorded: Aug-Sep 1973, ARC Studios, Ikeja, Lagos; Oct 1973, AIR Studios, London
UK: 7 Dec 1973 (*Band On The Run* LP)
US: 5 Dec 1973 (*Band On The Run* LP)
Paul McCartney: vocals, guitar, electric piano, bass, drums, percussion; **Linda McCartney**: backing vocals, percussion; **Denny Laine**: vocals, guitar, percussion; **Ginger Baker**: percussion; **Beaux Arts Orchestra**: strings, brass; **Pierre Denis Le Sève**: French narration; **uncredited**: percussion

Holidaying in Jamaica in the break between *James Paul McCartney* [192] and the start of Wings' UK tour, McCartney found himself wandering Montego Bay and chanced upon a film shoot. Blagging an 'in', he found himself on the set of the forthcoming classic *Papillon* starring Dustin Hoffman, with whom he struck up a friendship, leading to an invite to dinner and, with McCartney picking up a guitar, a conversation about songwriting. Goading his guest, Hoffmann offered McCartney a magazine article on the recently deceased Pablo Picasso, inviting him to show off his skills on the spot – and working from the page, McCartney promptly came up with the basis of the current song – to Hoffmann's reported fascination and delight.[229]

When it came to record the track, one of the most complex on *Band On The*

---

[229] Picasso died on 8 April 1973. The article, *Pablo Picasso's Last Days and Final Journey*, appeared in *Time*, 23 April: 'Later that evening Picasso and his wife Jacqueline entertained friends for dinner. Picasso was in high spirits. "Drink to me; drink to my health," he urged, pouring wine into the glass of his Cannes lawyer and friend, Armand Antebi. "You know I can't drink any more." At 11:30 he rose from the table and announced: "And now I must go back to work."… before he went to bed, he painted until 3 a.m.' (Picasso died from a heart attack the following morning, waking at 11:30 but unable to rise from his bed.)

Run, McCartney elected to honour his promise to Ginger Baker (see [218]) and make use of the 16-track facilities at ARC. Initially undertaking a straight run-through, McCartney realised what he wanted was an equivalent of Picasso's painting style, which was effected by recording and re-recording several fragmented sections for later re-assembly – in McCartney's mind a form of musical cubism. Thus guided by a central idea, a set of assorted passages was prepared, each varying in tone with, in one place, Baker and his crew pitching in on makeshift percussion using gravel-filled tins. Thrown onto the audio canvass were components of both [226] Jet and [219] Mrs. Vandebilt, taking an angled perspective on other sections of the album, and, starting around the 3:44 mark, a chorus of 'drunken' revellers depicting Picasso's final hours.

What state the tapes were in when McCartney brought them back to London in September is unknowable since the track was then edited together and extensively overdubbed at AIR, including the addition of several heavily orchestrated passages which couldn't have been prepared to any great extent in Lagos. Chief among these are the two 'French' sections, scored by Tony Visconti's in stylistic imitation of American musician/composer, Jack Nitzsche, known for his work with Phil Spector and the Rolling Stones, and featuring the speaking voice of Pierre Denis Le Sève, host of BBC French Service's *Le Flash Touriste*.[230]

Constructed from pieces, the final collage ran to almost six minutes, its cohesion remarkable given that its chief designer, McCartney, was untutored.[231] Understanding that Picasso's method was to probe a pathway intuitively, changing and scrapping parts he didn't like as he progressed, McCartney's synaesthetic expression of painting in sound is not only engaging sport but a fitting tribute to its subject, from one artist to another. McCartney's personality shows through the song's 'northern' elements, the double-tracked bassoon solo which he took pains to oversee resembling the theme to the working-class television drama, *Coronation Street*, and the central role played throughout by his bass guitar, linking the sections with a running thread. Where McCartney's liking for whimsical musical diversions has sometimes led to ghastly miscalculations of style, here his reaching outside of the conventional song form must be counted a success.

---

[230] A Spaniard by birth, Picasso had spent most of his life in France. Le Sève's narration, consisting of promotional recordings for a series of French tourist guides, was used without his knowledge.

[231] There are eight identifiable passages, consisting of (1) standard song opening; (2) starting around 1:34, the first of the 'French interludes'; (3) the ticking orchestral [226] 'Jet'; (4) 'orchestral' restatement of the song's main hook lines; (5) from 3:38, the 'drunken chorus'; (6) second 'French interlude'; (7) orchestral passage; (8) starting at 5:00, coda section based on the chant from [219] Mrs. Vandebilt.

Paul McCartney And Wings: [224] **BLUEBIRD** (*McCartney*)
Produced by Paul McCartney
Recorded: Aug-Sep 1973, EMI Studios, Apapa, Lagos; Oct 1973,
   AIR Studios, London
UK: 7 Dec 1973 (*Band On The Run* LP)
US: 5 Dec 1973 (*Band On The Run* LP)
Paul McCartney: vocals, guitar, bass, percussion (?); **Linda McCartney**: backing vocals; **Denny Laine**: guitar, backing vocals; **Howie Casey**: saxophone; **Remi Kabaka**: drum, percussion

Written during his Jamaican vacation of December 1971, the soothing Bluebird is one of McCartney's most harmonically enigmatic songs, its 'Dorian' verse vaguely medieval and commencing on a remote C, sharpening the third of the underlying chord which is simultaneously flattened by the guitar arriving in G minor. Avoiding a resolution, McCartney's bass proceeds to fall to F in the third bar, rather than rising to the expected G sharp, leaving song's direction ambiguous, thereby portraying the free range of the bluebird's flight before a cadence on the refrain brings it to ground.

More than a guitarist's game, much of the song's harmonic play stems from the placing of the vocals in which Linda has a key role, her warming high major sevenths in the chorus flitting above McCartney's tenor. Here, the song's romantic qualities are revealed, the bluebird itself an ancient and ubiquitous symbol of happiness which McCartney transforms into the physical embodiment of love.[232] Appropriately, then, its first acoustic outing on *James Paul McCartney* in March [192] had just Paul and Linda singing it together, eye-to-eye, its cute attachment to a performance of Blackbird a pleasing musical sequence inexplicably edited out of the UK screening. (McCartney seems to have puzzled over the pitching of the song, debuting it on *James Paul McCartney* in D (on a guitar tuned a whole tone up), before recording it, here, in E flat then shifting it to F for stage performances.)

When taken into the studio, its distinctive percussion was added courtesy of Remi Kabaka, a drummer who had once been in Ginger Baker's Air Force alongside Denny Laine, and who happened to hail from Lagos. His presence gives the track its quixotic air, guiro, wood blocks and paired cowbells lifting

---

[232] The legendary Bluebird of Happiness is mentioned in the *Yellow Submarine* script and has been invoked in song countless times. The British war tune, (There'll Be Bluebirds Over) The White Cliffs Of Dover (which includes an allusion to freedom, as does McCartney's verse) might have been lurking somewhere in the back of his mind, while the Phil Spector-produced Zip-A-Dee Doo-Dah (1962) includes the line, 'Mr Bluebird's on my shoulder' which McCartney would casually sing in his 1984 movie, *Give My Regards To Broad Street*.

into the air with an animated spirit of abandon. Most noted though is Howie Casey's sax solo, his first attempt capturing a natural if hesitant movement around the song's evasive chord structure, which takes flight as it progresses.[233] As fanciful in its way as [160] Single Pigeon, albeit more subtly put, Bluebird's innocence and open idealisation may have caused a degree of embarrassment to McCartney, his assertion that 'I'm a bluebird' answered with a debunking 'yeah, yeah, yeah', pointing back to She Loves You and suggesting a level of self-consciousness.

Paul McCartney And Wings: [225] **LET ME ROLL IT** (*McCartney*)
Produced by Paul McCartney
Recorded: Aug-Sep 1973, EMI Studios, Apapa, Lagos; Oct 1973, AIR Studios, London
UK: 7 Dec 1973 (*Band On The Run* LP)
US: 5 Dec 1973 (*Band On The Run* LP)
Paul McCartney: vocals, guitar, bass, drums; **Linda McCartney**: backing vocals, organ; **Denny Laine**: backing vocals, guitar

Devised at McCartney's home in Scotland, sitting in the sun 'plonking on a guitar', the 6/8 Let Me Roll It is constructed from a terse repeating riff, which McCartney visualised as a stuttering effort to express an emotion. Written with the top two strings sounding simultaneously, McCartney double-tracked the harmonised riff in Lagos, allowing for sharper definition, its cutting resonance effected by running the signal via a vocal PA speaker. Disproportionately pleased with the results ('searing... a rare beauty'), he can only have been miffed when he realised that when Wings performed it live, lead duties would have to be delegated to Denny Laine while McCartney remained on bass.[234]

Despite reprising a line from [35] I'd Have You Anytime, the lyric centres on the art of constructing marijuana joints, carrying with it an erotic sub-text and allusion to 'self-loving' in its opening verse. Reflecting the track's mutinous subject matter, McCartney soaked his vocals in a caustic echo, giving the soundscape a penetration drawing comparison with some of Lennon's biting early solo work ([2]; [81]; [82]). At 4:23 a curious thing happens: the bass/drum track momentarily repeats itself, something ascribed by Geoff Emerick as a bad edit.[235] Whether the result of accident or design, this too was incorporated into the live arrangement, giving the band a convenient point to bring the song to a juddering conclusion.

---

[233] Casey protested he could do better, and McCartney allowed him a couple more takes before selecting the first regardless.
[234] For McCartney's comments, see 2021, p421.
[235] Emerick, p352.

Paul McCartney And Wings: [226] **JET** (*McCartney*)
Produced by Paul McCartney
Recorded: 3 Oct 1973, AIR Studios, London
UK: 7 Dec 1973 (*Band On The Run* LP)
US: 5 Dec 1973 (*Band On The Run* LP)
Paul McCartney: vocals, guitar, bass, drums, piano; **Linda McCartney**: backing vocals, Moog synthesiser; **Denny Laine**: backing vocals, guitar; **Howie Casey**: tenor saxophone; **unknown**: alto saxophone; **Beaux Arts Orchestra**: strings (arranged by Tony Visconti)

McCartney and his entourage wrapped up their Nigerian visit in the second half of September, bidding their hosts farewell with a beach party before flying back to London on 22nd. McCartney brought with him the bulk of what would become *Band On The Run*, and while the exercise had been a fruitful one, it was not something he would want to repeat – although moving to foreign climes elsewhere for recording projects became common practice for Wings.[236] Counting [222] Helen Wheels, eight tracks were in the works, McCartney moving into George Martin's AIR studios in October to finish them up, and also to record the couple more he needed to make for a full album.

First to be attempted was Jet, which, like [225] Let Me Roll It, was written in Kintyre, McCartney whiling away a summer's afternoon alone with his guitar around the ruins of an old hillfort (probably Dun Skeig, 20 miles north of his farm). For more than 30 years McCartney maintained the song's main figure, Jet, was a Labrador puppy, leading commentators to draw a parallel with his older Beatles song, Martha My Dear; however in a 2010 interview for British television he revealed the true subject was a black pony which the McCartneys kept as a pet.[237] That issue aside, the cast of characters is vaguely defined, the sergeant major apparently an amalgam of several authority figures, with Linda's father Lee looming largest, and the make-believe 'mater' a subconscious summoning of 'the ghost of my real mother'.[238] (Most problematic is the 'little lady suffragette', McCartney's unintended put-down awkwardly followed by a promotional campaign for the song featuring a

---

[236] [240] Junior's Farm / [239] Sally G would be recorded in Nashville, *Venus And Mars* in New Orleans and *London Town* in the Virgin Islands.

[237] Example: 'One of our dogs had just had a litter of black pups and one of them we'd named Jet, and this little dog was coming around and playing at me, and kind of gnawing at my guitar and stuff. So I just started making this song up about Jet' (interview 7 February 1974, with Jay Stone for KSLQ-FM radio, Missouri). Most assumed confusion in his 2010 revision, until his autobiographical *The Lyrics* (2021) confirmed the facts. His early evasion might have stemmed from a fear of showing off his affluence in admitting keeping a pony.

[238] McCartney, 2021, p379.

topless woman with the word 'Jet' written on her breasts, in service of the slogan, 'Expose it!'.)

One of McCartney's most commercial recordings, Jet bristles with ear-catching gimmicks spread across what, at heart, is a rudimentary structure. (Much of the song rests on a pounding A chord, its only novelty a gentle uplift to B major 7 after the second line.) The recording is built atop a droning low note on Linda's Moog keyboard, whose texture was fortuitously coarsened by the fact that the magnetic tape in use was suffering from oxidisation, compelling Geoff Emerick to generate a safe copy to work from. Linda's presence is also pivotal in the song's third verse, in which her lead solo replicates the main melody line with a flourish at its end, while her and Laine's flowing backing vocals generate some of the track's most melodic ingredients. Peppered with sensational flashes from a 'chick-chick' guitar to a series of James Brown-style vocal exclamations, and a title bellowed from the bottom of McCartney's stomach, Jet is easily the most exciting listen on *Band On The Run*, rounded off with two saxophones joining forces for a brassy *ritardando* finale swept over a span of 12 whole tones.[239]

If not the best thing Wings had yet recorded, then certainly the most sparkling, Jet was an obvious contender for single release, something Capitol was keen to push once US radio had cottoned onto the track. Thus, it became only the second McCartney single to be pulled from an already-released album, sharing the UK top 10 in March with Starr's [195] You're Sixteen.

Paul McCartney And Wings: [227] **NINETEEN HUNDRED AND EIGHTY FIVE** (*McCartney*)
Produced by Paul McCartney
Recorded: Oct 1973, AIR Studios, London
UK: 7 Dec 1973 (*Band On The Run* LP)
US: 5 Dec 1973 (*Band On The Run* LP)
Paul McCartney: vocals, guitar, bass, piano, keyboards, drums, percussion (?); **Linda McCartney**: backing vocals, keyboards, percussion (?); **Denny Laine**: backing vocals, guitar, percussion (?); **Beaux Arts Orchestra**: strings/brass (arranged by Tony Visconti)

Although minor, Nineteen Hundred And Eighty Five provided an emphatic ending for *Band On The Run*, climaxing on a series of squalling iterations of the song's main chord run. The track is thought to have been made entirely in London – the last thing recorded for the album – since the repeating piano

---

[239] Howie Casey could not reach the top notes on his tenor sax, one of Tony Visconti's session players filling in on alto, with Casey taking over seamlessly as the melody got within range.

figure is central to the arrangement, there being no piano available in Lagos.[240]

The song began with its opening couplet, the second line (and eventual song title) not a reference to Orwell but merely a catchy rhyme for 'alive'. From there, McCartney extrapolated one of the most unusual love songs of his career, set in the then-distant future and pledging allegiance only to his present-time muse. (Luca Perasi suggests the bulk of the lyric was written on the day of recording, which would explain the underdeveloped premise.[241]) A tense affair, the song's dense banks of instrumentation suddenly give way at 1:36 to the first of two heavenly-angelic choral passages mourning the coming apocalypse, ahead of a crescendoing instrumental coda seeming to sum up the whole album in two succinct minutes. Its triumphant conclusion on an authoritative C major serves to prepare a surprise return to the album's opening track [221], with eight bars from its final chorus grafted on to guide the listener back to the start, as if imploring them to go through it all again.

It's notable that when McCartney returned from Lagos, he made no effort to reconvene Wings nor to seek a great deal of musical assistance before ploughing on with the sessions. The fact was, so far as studio recording was concerned he didn't need a band around him, being more than capable of handling all instruments and vocals himself, as evinced here on the strongest album he ever made, and which required only the comforting support of Linda and Denny Laine to help it along. The blunt truth was he could do better than any of the musicians he'd so far worked with, and unfettered by the need to consider and placate a team of extras, his creativity was free to blossom and his songs take shape the way *he* wanted them to.

The only area in which McCartney required external help was in the formal writing of the album's classical sections, for which Tony Visconti was afforded just three days before recording over a single hectic date at AIR Studios with the 50 musicians who made up the Beaux Arts Orchestra, overseen by US conductor, David Katz. The final mixing stage took place at Kingsway Studio in London's Holborn and at EMI, with the album complete and ready for pressing by the second week of November. All that remained was the creation of an LP cover, for which Linda suggested the impressive image of a gang of runaways caught in a prison searchlight. Thus, half a dozen famous faces were recruited for a photo shoot at the Osterley Park estate in west London, proceedings of which were also filmed for posterity.

Band On The Run became McCartney's fifth and final album for Apple,

---

[240] Definitive session dates are not available, even McCartney's official sleeve credits providing only a vague (and factually incorrect) Lagos/London for everything.
[241] Perasi, p115.

released at the start of December. Favourably reviewed, its contents at first came as a relief to legions of fans jaded by Wings' sometimes insubstantial efforts of the previous two years. Here at last was an album with no sentimental throwaways about domestic bliss and none of the children's ditties which had alienated much of his adult audience. *Band On The Run* was the *real* McCartney, its achievement all the more remarkable for the testing circumstances in which it was created.

The US edition of *Band On The Run* carried in its grooves three hit singles at a time when the industry was shifting from the traditional separation of 45s to a general principle of issuing them straight from current LPs. The album's performance on *Billboard* shows why; issued when [222] Helen Wheels was climbing the top 20, it peaked at a relatively modest 7, until [226] Jet began its ascent of the listings in February, after which it was propelled to the summit of the LP chart. Hovering around the top 10 into June, it returned to top spot on the day [221] Band On The Run did the same on its own chart, and was still there in July – and number 1 in Britain as late as September, a full 10 months after release, the trailer singles keeping it afloat throughout 1974.

Its critical and commercial success provided for McCartney a long-awaited sense that he could stand tall as an artist on his own terms, having taken three long years to land an album worthy of comparison with Harrison and Lennon's 1970 debuts. As a result of its landmark status, and due in part to the absence of any musical silliness, it has tended to be overrated in the years since its release, its cast of cover stars alone prompting absurd comparisons with *Sgt Pepper*. That said, *Band On The Run* is seen as the highpoint of a long career, the only Wings album to truly stand the test of time.

RECORD RELEASES

[222] **Helen Wheels** / [170] **Country Dreamer**
  (UK: 26 Oct 1973, US: 12 Nov 1973)
Band On The Run
  (UK: 7 Dec 1973, US: 5 Dec 1973)
  [221] Band On The Run / [226] Jet / [224] Bluebird / [219] Mrs. Vandebilt / [225] Let Me Roll It / [218] Mamunia / [220] No Words / [223] Picasso's Last Words (Drink To Me) / [227] Nineteen Hundred And Eighty Five
  US copies add [222] Helen Wheels between [220] and [223].
[226] **Jet** / [218] **Mamunia**
  (US: 28 Jan 1974)
[226] **Jet** / [225] **Let Me Roll It**
  (UK: 15 Feb 1974, US: 18 Feb 1974)

[221] **Band On The Run** / [227] **Nineteen Hundred And Eighty-Five**
(US: 8 Apr 1974)
[221] **Band On The Run** / [193] **Zoo Gang**
(UK: 28 Jun 1974)

George Harrison single sessions: November 1973

George Harrison: [228] **DING DONG** (*Harrison*)
Produced by George Harrison
Recorded: Nov 1973, Aug/Sep 1974, Friar Park Studios,
Henley-on-Thames[242]
UK: 6 Dec 1974 (single A-side)
US: 9 Dec 1974 (*Dark Horse* LP)
George Harrison: vocals, guitar, organ, clavinet, percussion; **Ron Wood**: electric guitar; **Alvin Lee**: electric guitar; **Mick Jones**: acoustic guitar; **Gary Wright**: piano; **Klaus Voormann**: bass; **Ringo Starr**: drums; **Jim Keltner**: drums; **Tom Scott**: saxophone; **uncredited**: female choir

After the release of *Living In The Material World*, Harrison's studio work consisted mainly of collaborations with friends and colleagues, one of the most notable, Splinter's debut album, *The Place I Love*, which would eventually come out on Dark Horse Records. Harrison's only self-intended effort was the backing track for this single, a knowing attempt to cash in on the seasonal market which in the wake of Lennon's [144] Happy Xmas (War Is Over) was becoming standard practice for mainstream British acts, and which Harrison lends a new slant on by celebrating the turn of the new year.

Ding Dong was written in a few minutes – unsurprisingly, given its simplistic melody and the fact that none of the lyric was original, taken entirely from verses inscribed on the walls of Friar Park by its former owner; the song's main section is from Alfred, Lord Tennyson's 1850 poem, *Ring Out, Wild Bells*, while the contrasting passage was copied verbatim from the side of one of the estate's out buildings. With passing chords apparently borrowed from Hey Jude, and the inclusion of the Westminster Chimes, soon to reappear in McCartney's hit single, Let 'Em In, the song's implied references to Beatledom are underscored by a promotional video in which Harrison dons

---

[242] Sessions at Harrison's home studio are invariably weak on specific dates due to a lack of published records. Madinger and Easter point to November 1973 for the backing track, based on circumstantial evidence. Simon Leng concurs.

various pieces of familiar attire, tracing his years in the group.[243]

Not completed until 1974, when *Dark Horse* was underway, the song betrays a deterioration in Harrison's voice which would also mar the album. Given the large array of musicians on the track, including Starr, its possible some overdubs were added in the months prior to the vocal session, Harrison doing his best to effect a contemporary 'glam' sound, emulating the 1973 Christmas hits for Wizzard and Slade which had proved the viability of the formula. Unfortunately for Harrison, his own effort limped only into the lower reaches of the charts, a forgettable hit which sits awkwardly at the start of the LP's distinctly non-festive second side.

RECORD RELEASES

[228] **Ding Dong** / [273] **I Don't Care Anymore**
(UK: 6 Dec 1974)
[228] **Ding Dong; Ding Dong** / [266] **Hari's On Tour (Express)**
(US: 23 Dec 1974)

Oldies But Mouldies sessions: October 1973 to December 1973

Arriving in LA in late 1973 with only May Pang for company, Lennon wasted little time establishing a social circle for himself. Beyond the reach of Ono's curbing influence, just weeks into his so-called lost weekend Lennon was formulating plans for a set of recordings with one of his mates and another of rock's wild boys, Phil Spector, once he'd cajoled the producer into taking part. The catalyst for this new project was the long, lingering copyright case over Lennon's adoption of a few words from Chuck Berry's [236] You Can't Catch Me in 1969, the rights to which had been acquired at some point by Morris Levy's publishing concern, Big Seven Music Corp. Fed up with the litigation hanging over him, Lennon instructed his legal team to settle out of court, leading to an agreement that he would record versions of three of Big Seven's

---

[243] The promo film shows Harrison in Hamburg-style leather followed by collarless Beatle suit, his *Sgt Pepper* outfit, and finally a 1968-style kaftan while holding Eric Clapton's red Gibson as played on While My Guitar Gently Weeps. The clip also includes a private joke in which Harrison lowers a pirate flag at Friar Park, hoisting in its place one bearing an Om sign – reversing something Pattie had done when she first learned of Harrison's affair with Maureen Starr (see [256]). By the time the footage was taken, Harrison had split with Pattie and was seeing Olivia Arias, the flag change thereby signalling goodbye to his wife.

songs for his next album – an extraordinarily handsome compensation deal for a minor infringement which had cost Levy nothing in the first place.

Once Lennon had agreed, the project took on a momentum of its own, expanding to a whole album's worth of rock and roll classics, reaffirming his musical roots and in his mind, casting him back to the status of Liverpool teenager. Many of the short-listed songs included those he'd performed in the Quarry Men, some of special personal significance, all of them representing a kind of liberation through regression. Spector was, therefore, an appropriate choice of producer, rising from the same scene as architect of several period recordings which the early Beatles had all adored – the main trouble being his insistence on controlling every aspect of the process, with Lennon acting only as a hired vocalist.

With the provisional title, *Oldies But Mouldies*, playing on Lennon's Beatles past (against Spector's more resolute choice, *Back To Mono*) the sessions were arranged in a haze of excitement, word quickly spreading around LA's tight circle of musicians that Spector was hiring for sessions at Hollywood's A&M Studios. As a result, and consequent of the producer's preference for packing his tracks with multiple instruments playing in unison, the studio floor quickly became the scene of mass gatherings, an unsuspecting Lennon amazed each night to see a succession of noted names, familiar faces from the Wrecking Crew and the occasional musical legend wander in and casually take their place among the crowd, which would typically number up to two dozen on a single track.

To Spector's credit he put his own unique touch into all of these songs, resisting simple re-makes and modernising them for the 1970s, thereby attracting criticism for the sometimes frustrating results. (Given the short notice he was on, it's likely some, if not all of the arrangements were devised in the studio.) Had Lennon had the presence of mind to recognise what was happening he might have called a stop to such over-indulgence, his would-be reliving of some simple teenaged fun bloated out of all proportion by the sheer bulk of his own celebrity and a seemingly bottomless budget, coupled with a steady flow of drink and drugs guaranteed to compromise the process. Ono's voice from the far end of a long telephone connection was not enough to put a brake on Lennon's excesses, nor stop proceedings from getting out of hand very quickly, as the ensuing weeks would all too clearly prove.[244]

---

[244] According to May Pang's memoir, Ono was in constant contact, telephoning Lennon multiple times every day and trying in vain to dissuade him from the current venture.

John Lennon: [229] **BONY MORONIE** (*Williams*)
Produced by Phil Spector
Recorded: 17 Oct 1973, A&M Studios, Hollywood; 6 Oct 1974, Record Plant, New York
UK: 21 Feb 1975 (*Rock 'N' Roll* LP)
US: 17 Feb 1975 (*Rock 'N' Roll* LP)
John Lennon: vocals, guitar; **Jesse Ed Davis**: guitar; **Jim Calvert**: guitar; **Larry Carlton**: guitar; **Steve Cropper**: guitar; **Ronald Kossajda**: guitar; **Phil Spector**: piano (?); **Leon Russell**: keyboards (?); **Ray Neapolitan**: bass; **Barry Mann**: brass; **Jeff Barry**: brass; **Jim Horn**: saxophone; **Jackie Kelso**: saxophone; **Chuck Findley**: trumpet; **Hal Blaine**: drums; **Jim Keltner**: drums; **Steven Forman**: percussion

The long, arduous project which would eventually turn into Lennon's swansong album began on 17 October, the first night's gathering including Steve Cropper of Booker T & the MGs (see also [199]), Leon Russell, Brill Building legends, Barry Mann and Jeff Barry, and several other stellar names, each reading off a sheet of musical instructions while Lennon stood and watched with curiosity. These sessions were to be very much Spector's, his idiosyncratic methods consisting of drilling each section of the band through take after take while the rest of the throng killed time waiting their turn. With no ensemble performance to listen back to, the musicians scarcely knew what they were aiming for but after several hours (during which Joni Mitchell wandered in and started telling Spector he was doing it wrong) Lennon finally got to hear the results, adding his double-tracked vocal, which he dedicated to May Pang, at 3am.

Selected by Lennon for the fact that he'd played it in front of his mother way back in 1958, Bony Moronie was originally a hit for Larry Williams, issued out in America on the Hollywood-based Speciality label then brought to Liverpool through the London imprint. Spector's re-arrangement robs it of its vitality, sharpening it by a semitone but slowing the rhythm to a distorted plod which Lennon's impassioned voice goes partway towards remedying. (In this respect, Spector inadvertently approached the glam rock style of bands like Slade, currently taking the UK by storm but likely unknown to him.[245]) To accommodate the reduction in tempo the sax break had to be excised, regrettably denying the track some breathing space.

---

[245] On the day this was recorded, Slade were number 2 in the UK with their ninth successive hit, the similarly paced My Friend Stan. They never cracked the US top 40.

John Lennon: [230] **BE MY BABY** (*Spector, Barry, Greenwich*)
Produced by Phil Spector
Recorded: 18 Oct 1973, A&M Studios, Hollywood; 7 Oct 1974 (?), Record Plant, New York
UK/US: unreleased
John Lennon: vocals, guitar; **Jesse Ed Davis**: guitar; **Jim Calvert**: guitar; **Steve Cropper**: guitar; **Ronald Kossajda**: guitar; **Phil Spector**: piano (?); **Ray Neapolitan**: bass; **Barry Mann**: brass; **Jeff Barry**: brass; **Jim Horn**: saxophone; **Jackie Kelso**: saxophone; **Nino Tempo**: saxophone; **Chuck Findley**: trumpet; **Hal Blaine**: drums; **Jim Keltner**: drums; **Steven Forman**: percussion

Having had a moderately successful first night [229] Lennon and the collective met up again the following day to work on one of Phil Spector's signature pieces, the old Ronettes tune from 1963 which had given the group their first hit. (Spector's co-writer, Jeff Barry, features as a session musician on this remake.) As he had with the preceding track, Spector's brainwave was to slow the tempo considerably, transforming the archetypal girl-group sound into a weighty ballad with Lennon's airy falsetto floating detachedly above. Spector's idea to re-arrange his material this way might have been suggested by one of his Brill Building colleagues, Carole King, whose low-tempo re-recording of the Shirelles hit, Will You Love Me Tomorrow, caught the ear on *Tapestry* (1971). Unfortunately, in comparison to King's gentle, intimate re-interpretation, Spector's was a sloppy effort, running raggedly past the six-minute mark until Lennon, by then shouting and swearing, calls the group to a stop. Here, just one day in, the sessions were audibly starting to slide, Lennon clearly the worse for alcohol with his emotion-laden pleas, 'I need you', shortly before the end, exposing a desperation over his recent separation from Ono. A year later, when *Rock 'N' Roll* was being readied for release, Lennon had the track skilfully edited into more manageable shape, but it remained officially unreleased until 1998, circulating meantime on the *Roots* LP issued in 1975 without proper authorisation.

John Lennon: [231] **ANGEL BABY** (*Ponci*)
Produced by Phil Spector
Recorded: 20 Oct 1973, A&M Studios, Hollywood
UK/US: unreleased
John Lennon: vocals, guitar; **Jesse Ed Davis**: guitar; **Jim Calvert**: guitar; **Ronald Kossajda**: guitar; **Art Munson**: guitar; **Phil Spector**: piano (?); **Ray Neapolitan**: bass; **Barry Mann**: brass; **Jeff Barry**: brass; **Jim Horn**: saxophone; **Jackie Kelso**: saxophone; **Nina Tempo**: saxophone; **Chuck Findley**: trumpet; **Hal Blaine**: drums; **Jim Keltner**: drums; **Steven Forman**: percussion

Having over-indulged on the evening of 18 October [230], Lennon cancelled his session the following day, returning instead for this Saturday recording of Rosie and the Originals' debut single, part-written and sung in 1960 by California schoolgirl, Rosie Hamlin.[246] A firm favourite of Lennon throughout his life, the song was oddly never performed by the Beatles, and didn't eventually make the cut for *Rock 'N' Roll* either, its omission all the more surprising for the fact that this rendition, blasted out by more than a dozen of America's top session men, leaves the original standing for sheer presence. (Hamlin had recorded her sweetly innocent version in a converted aircraft hanger.)

Set to a classic 1950s waltz, Angel Baby finds Lennon at the top of his register, paying his respectful dues to 'Rosie, wherever she may be', in a moment of genuine warmth which scarcely hinted at the havoc about to unfold. While Spector knocked back his customary bottle of Courvoisier, Lennon and Jesse Ed Davis hit the vodka, the catalyst for a heavy drinking session among the band, who were growing increasingly restless from the protracted hours taken to record a single track again and again. While Spector tried in vain to impose some order on the session, arguments began to arise and at length Lennon's inebriation turned to violence, a punch-up with Davis leading to his being wrestled into the back of a car and driven home, trapped upside-down on the floor with his feet against the window, sobbing for Yoko. Deposited at his borrowed apartment, he proceeded to smash the place up and had to be tied down for his own good, alarming May Pang who'd never seen him in such a rage. And here, if it wasn't obvious already, *Oldies But Mouldies* started to look like a disaster in the making, Lennon's supposed freedom from the restraints of married life more than could cope with.

---

[246] The song began as a poem written by Hamlin for her boyfriend. Since she was only 15 at the time, the copyright was assigned entirely to group member, David Ponci.

John Lennon: [232] **SWEET LITTLE SIXTEEN** (*Berry*)
Produced by Phil Spector
Recorded: 22 Oct 1973, A&M Studios, Hollywood
UK: 21 Feb 1975 (*Rock 'N' Roll* LP)
US: 17 Feb 1975 (*Rock 'N' Roll* LP)
John Lennon: vocals, guitar; **Jesse Ed Davis**: guitar; **Jim Calvert**: guitar; **Ronald Kossajda**: guitar; **Art Munson**: guitar; **Phil Spector**: piano (?); **Dr John**: keyboards; **Ray Neapolitan**: bass; **Barry Mann**: brass; **Jeff Barry**: brass; **Anthony Terran**: trumpet; **Gene Cipriano**: brass/saxophone; **Nino Tempo**: saxophone; **Hal Blaine**: drums; **Jim Keltner**: drums; **Jim Gordon**: drums; **Steven Forman**: percussion

Unsurprisingly, following the mayhem of 20 October, no recording was done the following day, Lennon sleeping off his weekend hangover to surface again on the Monday as if nothing had happened. Making his way to A&M, he noticed Phil Spector walk in dressed in his usual flamboyant style and carrying a black eye, the consequence of a run-in with a female make-up artist he'd managed to upset the night before. Among such fractious circumstances Lennon sought solace in this old Chuck Berry number, one he'd been playing since 1958 and which the Beatles recorded a couple of times.[247] An archetypal 16-bar progression, Berry's original was issued in Britain on the London label in March 1958, and had a significant impact on both Lennon and McCartney (who learned some of his drumming style from Fred Below's breaks) although according to Mark Lewisohn, the group based their arrangement on Eddie Cochran's.[248]

Any deference to the early recordings is undetectable in this new arrangement swinging on a slow brass riff. Lennon does an admirable turn at the mike, his throaty vocal by far the most rousing element, but notwithstanding his obvious passion for the material, the recording follows the rest of the sessions to-date in being lumbering and overweight. Part of the problem is the unnecessarily voluminous cast of characters, which on this occasion included Malcolm John Rebennack Jr, AKA Dr John, among its swollen ranks, all of which is at odds with the youthful, of-the-moment spirit of 1950s rock and roll. May Pang later recalled the undisciplined way in which star names saw the sessions as an invitation to drop by and party: 'Every night there was somebody else coming in – it was like a free for all: Joni Mitchell,

---

[247] The earliest group recording was made offline at Hamburg's Star Club at the end of 1962. They subsequently taped it in a BBC session in July 1963.
[248] Lewisohn 2013, p598. Cochran didn't release a recording of the song but the Beatles (or at least, Lennon) heard him perform it in Liverpool in early 1960.

Warren Beatty, David Geffen, Cher...'.[249] This evening, visitors included Elton John with whom Lennon was building a close friendship, leading to a couple of professional collaborations in the mid-1970s (see [245]).

John Lennon: [233] **JUST BECAUSE** (*Price*)
Produced by Phil Spector
Recorded: 24 Oct 1973, A&M Studios, Hollywood; 6 Oct 1974, Record Plant, New York
UK: 21 Feb 1975 (*Rock 'N' Roll* LP)
US: 17 Feb 1975 (*Rock 'N' Roll* LP)
John Lennon: vocals, guitar; **Jesse Ed Davis**: guitar; **Jim Calvert**: guitar; **Art Munson**: guitar; **David Cohen**: guitar; **Louie Shelton**: guitar; **Phil Spector**: piano (?); **Dr John**: keyboards; **Michael Lang**: keyboards; **Bob Glaub**: bass; **Ray Neapolitan**: bass; **Jeff Barry**: brass; **Nino Tempo**: saxophone; **Conte Candoli**: trumpet; **Bob Hardaway**: woodwind; **Hal Blaine**: drums; **Jim Keltner**: drums; **Jim Gordon**: drums; **Steven Forman**: percussion

May Pang turned 23 on 24 October, an occasion marked by Lennon's gift of a new car followed by lunch at Tiny Naylor's restaurant on Sunset Boulevard, across the way from A&M. In the adventure of her life, she then went with Lennon and Elton John to a film shoot which on the evidence of the studio session later that day, was the start of a protracted alcohol binge, Lennon in no fit state to record come evening but determined to do so anyway. (Elton John is not credited on the resultant track, but tagged along to A&M, to judge by Lennon and Spector's recorded banter.)

The task at hand was a version of Just Because, a 1957 R&B hit for singer-songwriter, Lloyd Price, to which Lennon was oblivious. Spector's choice, Lennon had to be swiftly shown how it went before recording one of the most third-rate sessions of his career, in which he managed to slur and stagger his way through a six-minute rendition while lecherously expressing what he'd like to do to some of the females who happened to be in the room. That his performance, which incorporated a drunken request for 'a little cocaine', was recorded in front of May Pang – on her birthday, too – betrays how little regard Lennon had for her, the idea that she might be embarrassed or offended by his antics apparently not crossing his mind.

Left in the can for a year, Just Because was considered salvageable by Lennon who in readying the *Rock 'N' Roll* album for release in 1974, took Spector's backing track and overdubbed a clean new vocal. Still not knowing the song by rote, he needed the rare original 45 to obtain the lyrics, May Pang

---

[249] *Mojo* July 2001.

placing a call to friend and record collector, Dave Morrell, to source a copy and bring it down to the studio.[250] As re-done that night, the recovered track extended to five and a half minutes with Lennon ad-libbing a 'goodnight from Record Plant East, New York', which he later suggested was a subconscious farewell to the world, at the effective conclusion of his 12-year recording career.[251] (The final album edit was faded down prior to Lennon's name-checking [258] Goodnight Vienna then sending his greetings to 'Ringo, Paul, George, how are you?', indicating the more positive frame of mind he was in a year after the dismal first session.)

John Lennon: [234] **TO KNOW HER, IS TO LOVE HER** (*Spector*)
Produced by Phil Spector
Recorded: 28 Nov 1973, A&M Studios, Hollywood
UK/US: unreleased
John Lennon: vocals, guitar; **Jesse Ed Davis**: guitar; **Jim Calvert**: guitar; **Art Munson**: guitar; **David Cohen**: guitar; **Ronald Kossajda**: guitar; **Michael Hazelwood**: guitar; **Phil Spector**: piano (?); **Michael Lang**: keyboards; **Andy Thomas**: keyboards (?); **Michael Melvoin**: keyboards; **Ray Neapolitan**: bass; **Bob Glaub**: bass; **Conte Candoli**: trumpet; **Donald Menza**: saxophone; **Nino Tempo**: saxophone; **Plas Johnson**: saxophone; **Jeff Barry**: brass; **Hal Blaine**: drums; **Jim Keltner**: drums; **Frank Capp**: drums; **Steven Forman**: percussion; **Gary Coleman**: percussion

After the session for [233] generated an entirely unusable recording, Lennon and Spector took a month off and weighed up how far they'd got – which wasn't very. The fact was, their five 'finished' tracks were scarcely the stuff of a successful album and hardly warranted the expansive and expensive raft of musicians employed, neither Lennon nor Spector having been able to bring any sense of cohesion to the project so far. At his lowest ebb through the end of October, Lennon's drinking was causing enough concern among his associates that studio engineer, Roy Cicala, placed a call to Ono in New York and convinced her to travel to LA in the hope that her presence would help steady the ship.

Ono had spent much of the time since Lennon's departure pursuing her own musical career, rehearsing then performing in New York with the 'Plastic Ono Super Band', a set-up comprised of essentially the same group as had

---

[250] Morrell recounted the occasion in an interview with Mark Lewisohn for the podcast, *Fabcast*, in November 2016.

[251] Lennon's remarks on the implied meaning, made in a 1980 interview with *Los Angeles Times* journalist, Robert Hilburn, are belied by the fact that when *Rock 'N' Roll* was released he had a never-recorded follow-up album on the drawing board.

played on both *Feeling The Space* and *Mind Games*. (It included David Spinozza on guitar, with whom Ono was becoming increasingly close.) Summoned to Lennon's side, she booked into the Beverley Hills Hotel, but after a week of meetings with her estranged husband, flew home, leaving him as lost and helpless as before. (One bright moment during her stay was the 5 November release of the Lennons' two albums, landing side-by-side the same morning like they had in the good days.) Whether by consequence of Ono's trip, or as a strategic move to support his immigration battles (the perceived end of his marriage to an American would undermine his claim to US residency), he also broke off with May Pang, a separation within a separation which achieved nothing and lasted all of three weeks.

Lennon and Spector eventually rallied their energies and reconvened to capture a gender-corrected version of To Know Him, Is To Love Him, one of Spector's cherished compositions from 1958, based on a phrase carved on his father's grave. His original recording with the Teddy Bears, on which he sang, topped the American charts and hit number 2 in Britain, getting noticed by the fledgling Beatles who absorbed it into their repertoire and recorded it a couple of times.[252] That this re-make's two chief architects were struggling for inspiration is apparent in the decision – again – to remodel the song at a markedly slower pace, turning the already sedate original into a funereal plodder, cast in 4/4 time against the Teddy Bears' 6/8, with superfluous extra bars inserted between the main vocal lines, putting the song to sleep. (Lennon's inert delivery was possibly suggested by the Beatles' earlier arrangement, in which McCartney and Harrison's backing sections sustain the second word, 'to *kno—ow*'.) The most exciting moments, which go some way towards alleviating the lethargy, are Lennon's, his occasionally guttural explosions hinting he was reaching from the heart across the 3,000-mile divide separating him from Ono. The track never did make it onto *Rock 'N' Roll*, but was put out posthumously on 1986's *Menlove Avenue* along with the other session scraps, [231]; [235] and [237].

---

[252] Extant versions include the Decca audition take of January 1962 and a better-known BBC session from July 1963. Like [232] Sweet Little Sixteen it also turns up in the primitive Hamburg tapes.

John Lennon: [235] **HERE WE GO AGAIN** (*Lennon, Spector*)
Produced by Phil Spector
Recorded: 3 Dec 1973, Record Plant, Los Angeles; 7 Oct 1974 (?), Record Plant, New York
UK/US: unreleased
John Lennon: vocals, guitar; **Jesse Ed Davis**: guitar; **Jim Calvert**: guitar; **Art Munson**: guitar; **David Cohen**: guitar; **Michael Hazelwood**: guitar; **William Perry**: guitar (?); **Phil Spector**: piano (?); **Michael Omartian**: keyboards; **Michael Wofford**: keyboards; **Ray Neapolitan**: bass; **Bob Glaub**: bass; **Nino Tempo**: saxophone; **Donald Menza**: saxophone; **Anthony Terran**: trumpet; **Jackie Kelso**: saxophone; **Jeff Barry**: brass; **Barry Mann**: brass; **Hal Blaine**: drums; **Jim Keltner**: drums; **Frank Capp**: drums; **Steven Forman**: percussion; **Gary Coleman**: percussion

Speaking to KABC-TV's *Eyewitness News* while these sessions were in progress, Lennon mentioned the album's retrospective working title, *Oldies But Mouldies*, 'but I seem to be writing a few [new] songs'.[253] What he'd come up with is not clear, although Madinger and Raile note that copyrights were registered on 3 December for [247] Nobody Loves You (When You're Down and Out) and [252] Beef Jerky, both presumably new and to be formally recorded the following summer. The only original to surface from the *Oldies But Mouldies* period was the current track, uniquely registered as the joint product of Lennon-Spector.[254]

Here We Go Again reveals the discomfort of the period through its world-weary title, and in Lennon's adopting a vocal delivery casting back to the troubled [80] Mother, whose screams he threatens to replicate. Unhappy flavour excepted, this new composition bears little stylistic resemblance to the oldies it was recorded between, its eerily atmospheric opening bars lapsing into a mildly jazzy run oscillating between F sharp minor and A major, trapped uncertainly between positivity and negativity; even the transition to a robust D is undercut by a lyric which sounds like self-reflection: "Round and 'round we go/where it's going, nobody knows'.

By the time of its studio recording, Lennon, Spector and the crew had been evicted from A&M by a management who'd witnessed night after night of uncontrollable revelry, drinking and general disorder which at times had spilled out to the car park. The solution for Lennon was to move to the other side of Santa Monica Boulevard to Record Plant West, where Spector had once

---

[253] Interview by Elliot Mintz, circa 29 October 1973.
[254] A second Lennon-Spector track is believed to have been written around the same time, Mucho Mungo, which Lennon recorded with Nilsson in 1974. Spector's name does not appear in the official copyright however.

worked with Harrison on [140] Bangla-Desh. As events of the following days would show, the switch of venue signalled no let up in the wild behaviour, making the song's title particularly apposite.

John Lennon: [236] **YOU CAN'T CATCH ME** (*Berry*)
    Produced by Phil Spector
    Recorded: 3 Dec 1973, Record Plant, Los Angeles; 11 Jul 1974, Record Plant, New York
    UK: 21 Feb 1975 (*Rock 'N' Roll* LP)
    US: 17 Feb 1975 (*Rock 'N' Roll* LP)
    John Lennon: vocals, guitar; **Jesse Ed Davis**: guitar; **Jim Calvert**: guitar; **David Cohen**: guitar; **Ronald Kossajda**: guitar; **Michael Hazelwood**: guitar; **William Perry**: guitar (?); **Phil Spector**: piano (?); **Michael Wofford**: keyboards; **Thomas Hensley**: keyboards; **Ray Neapolitan**: bass; **Bob Glaub**: bass; **Jeff Barry**: brass; **Bobby Keys**: brass; **Barry Mann**: brass; **Ronnie Lang**: saxophone; **Nino Tempo**: saxophone; **Conte Candoli**: trumpet; **Hal Blaine**: drums; **Jim Keltner**: drums; **Steven Forman**: percussion; **Gary Coleman**: percussion; **Alan Estes**: percussion; **Dick Hieronymus**: unknown

The song which indirectly gave rise to Lennon's *Rock 'N' Roll* album, You Can't Catch Me contains in its second verse, the lines, 'Here come a flat-top, he was moving up with me'. Thus when *Abbey Road* came out, the opening cut containing 'Here come old flat-top, he come grooving up slowly' was clearly derivative, attracting the attention of the original copyright holder, Morris Levy, who in December 1970 initiated legal action against Apple Records, Northern Songs and Maclen Music, incumbent on Lennon to sort things out. In truth the two songs shared just half a dozen words, the 'steal' no more significant than, for example, the middle eight of [85] Isolation – although in this case the fall-out would endure for half a decade.[255]

In agreeing to compensate Levy, Lennon consented to record three of his songs, You Can't Catch Me among them, dispatched at Record Plant on the same day as [235] Here We Go Again. Originally recorded by Chuck Berry and

---

[255] Lennon was a veteran pilferer of phrases from songs he admired. [85] Isolation borrowed from I Apologize by Barrett Strong, and other examples are legion, including the opening line of Run For Your Life (c/w Presley's Baby Let's Play House); the opening two lines of Sexy Sadie (c/w the Miracles' I've Been Good To You); 'Yes I'm Lonely, wanna die' from Yer Blues (c/w Presley's Heartbreak Hotel); the refrain of [211] Meat City (c/w Gary U.S. Bonds' Quarter To Three) and so on. Usually, as here, he tweaked them to suit. (Cheekily, Lennon included a brief quotation from Jimmy McCracklin's The Walk in the middle of this recording of You Can't Catch Me.)

issued as his second UK 45 in February 1957, the track was oddly never performed by the Beatles, who'd otherwise covered Berry prolifically.[256] And although Berry was author of the song, he wasn't the owner of the rights and hadn't been involved in the legal action initiated by Levy. Thus, when Lennon met him on *The Mike Douglas Show* in February 1972, there was no ill-feeling and the two happily ran through a couple of vintage hits together.

An early pioneer who wrote his own material, Berry's recording has a spirited enthusiasm to it, a quality missing from Lennon's re-make which implies the arrangement was modelled to bring it closer in style to Come Together. (Notably, Lennon changes the verb in the line, 'he was moving up with me', to 'grooving'.) The recording's weight was further added to when the decision was made in a 1974 overdub session in New York, to copy the opening verse and chorus back into the song a second time, an edit which extended it by almost a minute, pushing double the playing time of Berry's classic original.

John Lennon: [237] **MY BABY LEFT ME** (*Crudup*)
 Produced by Phil Spector
 Recorded: 14 Dec 1973, Record Plant, Los Angeles; 7 Oct 1974 (?), Record Plant, New York
 UK/US: unreleased
 John Lennon: vocals, guitar; **Jesse Ed Davis**: guitar; **Jim Calvert**: guitar; **David Cohen**: guitar; **Michael Hazelwood**: guitar; **Ronald Kossajda**: guitar; **William Perry**: guitar (?); **Phil Spector**: piano (?); **Michael Wofford**: keyboards; **Thomas Hensley**: keyboards; **Bob Glaub**: bass; **Ray Neapolitan**: bass; **Jeff Barry**: brass; **Barry Mann**: brass; **Bobby Keys**: brass; **Conte Candoli**: trumpet; **Nino Tempo**: saxophone; **Matty Matlock**: saxophone; **William Perkins**: saxophone; **Hal Blaine**: drums; **Jim Keltner**: drums; **Frank Capp**: drums; **Terry Gibbs**: vibraphone; **Steven Forman**: percussion; **uncredited**: female vocal section

Work on *Oldies But Mouldies* had endured off and on for two months, generating nine songs of varying quality which approached the tally needed for an LP. (Industry practice in the States would have permitted five per side; British record buyers tended to expect more.) That the album had come as far as this was something of a fluke, Lennon's emotional turmoil coupled with

---

[256] Beatles recordings of nine Chuck Berry songs have been officially released at one time or another: Carol; I Got To Find My Baby; I'm Talking About You; Johnny B Goode; Memphis, Tennessee; Rock And Roll Music; [147] Roll Over Beethoven; [232] Sweet Little Sixteen; and Too Much Monkey Business. Additionally, the 1962 Star Club Tapes include a live performance of Little Queenie.

Spector's Courvoisier-fuelled erraticism (worsened by his own break-up with wife Ronnie) an unstable foundation for such an ambitious project, which here involved the hire and direction of 22 musicians and a bank of singers. Signs that the end was near were apparent three days prior to the recording of the aptly named My Baby Left Me, when on the day May Pang resumed her affair with Lennon, Spector discharged his gun in the studio building during a bout of horseplay involving Mal Evans. It didn't dawn on Lennon until the next day that his producer was carrying live ammunition, something which hardly fazed him when the two met for this final date, Lennon showing his contrastingly less dangerous side by chasing Spector around the studio floor in a drunken cake fight.

The pre-rock and roll My Baby Left Me was the work of Mississippi-born blues man, Arthur 'Big Boy' Crudup, whose version was issued in the States on RCA Victor in early 1951. It achieved far greater exposure in 1956 when Elvis issued a recording as the flip side to his US number 1, I Want You, I Need You, I Love You – Elvis having been enough of a fan that he'd covered Crudup's That's All Right for his debut release in 1954. A long-time admirer of the track, Lennon had sung it informally a number of times before the opportunity arose here to capture a proper studio recording.

Jokingly starting with the same exclamation as on [211] Meat City (itself probably suggested by the opening to Gene Vincent's [283] Be-Bop-A-Lula), Lennon's version was – to judge by the studio ambience – made in a celebratory atmosphere, as if the whole thing was recorded as a live ensemble performance. Straight from Spector's box of tricks, the female backing singers, with their ironic call and response sections, make a novel addition to Lennon's gravel-toned vocal, the track coming off as one of the more enjoyable listens, suggesting that had the whole set been recorded in the same loose way, it might have been more satisfying.[257] Oddly, on release of Rock 'N' Roll in 1975, My Baby Left Me was omitted from the listing, only appearing in the 1980s on the outtakes collection, Menlove Avenue, where it was erroneously billed as Since My Baby Left Me, the album compilers thereby unable to identify and append the writer's name. (See [118] for a similar confusion.)

This laboured album was still theoretically underway through the rest of December, although no further recordings were done. Following the shooting incident on 11th, the project's locus changed again, play-back listenings taking place at Gold Star, Spector's old haunt on Santa Monica Boulevard. The next recording date, booked for 4 January, resulted in a no-show and from there,

---

[257] The female vocalists are unidentified but likely include Darlene Love, formerly with Spector's group, the Blossoms.

the sessions fell into stagnation, Spector distracted by the more immediate pressures of his divorce and a custody battle for his adopted children. Having thus petered out, any hopes Lennon had of completing the album ended when Spector was involved in a serious car accident around the end of February, terminating his interest – and since he had paid for the recordings, he had the tapes and wouldn't give them back, leaving Lennon empty-handed, a disappointing conclusion to what was meant as an enjoyable, back-to-roots adventure.

Jim Keltner Fan Club Hour: March 1974

Jim Keltner Fan Club Hour: [238] **LUCILLE** (*Penniman, Collins*)
  Produced by unnamed staff
  Recorded: 28 Mar 1974, Record Plant, Los Angeles
  UK/US: unreleased
  John Lennon: vocals, guitar; **Paul McCartney**: vocals, drums; **Harry Nilsson**: vocals; **Jesse Ed Davis**: guitar; **Stevie Wonder**: electric piano; **Linda McCartney**: keyboards; **Ed Freeman**: bass; **Bobby Keys**: saxophone; **May Pang**: tambourine[258]

If Lennon's disassociation from Phil Spector offered the daylight he needed to get his life in Los Angeles on an even footing, the fact that his social circle consisted primarily of hard drinking pals merely resulted in more of the same. On 12 January a trip to see Ann Peebles at Hollywood's Troubadour club with Jesse Ed Davis and Jim Keltner descended into chaos when they got roaring drunk, Lennon drawing attention to himself by spending much of the evening with a sanitary towel stuck to his forehead. Later, at the home of Lennon's legal adviser, Harold Seider, an unruly party ensued where Lennon smashed Davis over the head with a Coke bottle, his partner, Patti Daley, screaming so frantically that he'd been killed that neighbours called the police. A few weeks later another notorious incident occurred as Lennon and Nilsson became out of control at a Smothers Brothers show at the same venue, shouting and heckling to the point where their table was overturned, and as Lennon and Nilsson started to fight one another, the club's management had little option but to forcibly eject them both.

In the period, Lennon found himself increasingly in the company of Starr, the drummer having similarly felt the pull of LA when his troubled domestic

---

[258] Pang claims Danny Kortchmar was also involved (Pang and Edwards, p209).

life started to weary him. Although it was good for Lennon to have a friendly face around, Starr's liking for drink, coupled with an emerging friendship with rock reveller, Keith Moon, merely added a couple more names to the list of hell raisers and so the circus continued. Reflecting the general lack of purpose, and a pervasive sense of laziness about these rich, famous musicians, there began a series of recreational studio jams, typically late-night gatherings which on different occasions had drawn the likes of Harrison and Starr along. These events, irregular though they were, had been collectively dubbed the Jim Keltner Fan Club Hour, referencing a dig at McCartney carried on the packaging of both *Living In The Material World* and *Ringo*. Now living among the crowd, Lennon had started to tag along, finding the process of jamming with everyone and anyone a viable escape from his daily troubles and sometimes giving him the chance to do something constructive. One such session, held on Sunday 24 March, had seen Mick Jagger drop by, whereupon Lennon produced his impromptu recording of Too Many Cooks (Spoil The Soup), a 1969 hit for 100 Proof Aged In Soul, and a product of the ex-Motown Holland-Dozier-Holland team.[259]

Pondering how to fill his time, Lennon recalled an idea to produce an album for Nilsson, who agreed it would be good to do *something* with their days rather than waste them on drinking binges, and so the two started to draw up plans. Lennon decided it would be easier to keep the project on track if he had the musicians together in one place, and so rented a $5,000-a-month house on Pacific Coast Highway which was to become home to them all. Lennon and Pang took the master bedroom, Starr a small outbuilding, with Nilsson, Voormann and various others piling in on 27 March, the day before the first session, booked at Record Plant's Studio A.

Meanwhile, on the other side of the Atlantic, McCartney had of late been mulling the impasse of being unable to get the other Beatles to agree to nullify their joint contracts, the open-ended court ruling of 1971 still nowhere near resolved. In late 1973 he contacted the others in an attempt to arrange a four-way meeting, but although Lennon showed an interest, Harrison and Starr didn't, and the closest they came to thrashing out a settlement was a five-day summit among their legal advisers, held in New York in mid-February, which got nowhere, reportedly as a result of Lennon's excessive demands.

While Lennon's life was characterised by lethargy, and an absence of direction, McCartney had the opposite problem, launching into yet another of the side projects which punctuate his busy 1970s. The occasion this time was

---

[259] Representing a typical Jim Keltner Fan Club line-up, the track (released in 2007) features Al Kooper, Jesse Ed Davis, Bobby Keys, Harry Nilsson, Trevor Lawrence, Danny Kortchmar and Jack Bruce. Lennon does not play, and neither does Bill Wyman, who is said to have been present.

the recording of *McGear* at Strawberry Studios in Greater Manchester, running from January into February. Ostensibly his brother Mike's second solo album, the set in fact has more to do with McCartney, who wrote or co-wrote nine of the ten tracks besides playing an extensive array of instruments and adding his distinctive vocals. Significantly, the set of session men employed included Denny Laine and some names new to the McCartney fold: guitarist, Jimmy McCulloch and drummer, Gerry Conway, each of whom was invited to help re-form Wings in the following weeks.[260] Unsurprisingly, McCartney fans have adopted the record as an unofficial Wings release, although to the wider public it slipped out unnoticed.

McCartney himself was by now at the peak of his post-Beatles popularity, invited to attend the 16th annual Grammy Awards in Hollywood on 2 March, where [191] Live And Let Die was in the running for Best Pop Performance.[261] Having been blocked from entering the States, consequent of his two 1972 busts (see [170]), he was permitted to travel over when a probationary visa was granted, and heading for Los Angeles, knew he'd be within reach of Lennon. They'd not seen each other for a couple of years, but as sessions for Nilsson's album were getting underway, with business to attend as well as a friendship to rekindle, McCartney knew where to find him.

On 28 March, day one of *Pussy Cats* (under its provisional title, *Strange Pussies*), Lennon, Nilsson and several others tracked a dense remake of Dylan's Subterranean Homesick Blues, with Starr on drums alongside Jim Keltner. The session petered out late in the evening and by midnight only a few die-hards were left along with Lennon and Nilsson, another Jim Keltner Fan Club Hour seemingly about to take place – when in walked Paul McCartney, sporting a new bushy moustache and soul patch beard. In May Pang's account, after exchanging perfunctory small talk McCartney spotted Starr's empty kit and took the opportunity to seat himself for some action, Linda following his lead by heading for the keyboards. In compliant mood, Lennon went along with it, picking up his guitar, and with a couple of others pitching in, ran through an unrecorded version of Midnight Special, the traditional song which long-ago the Beatles had picked up via Lonnie Donegan's 1958 recording. Enjoying the experience, Lennon requested the control room staff start rolling tape, and meantime the assembled musicians began to assess what they had by way of a group line-up, record producer, Ed Freeman, eagerly volunteering himself as

---

[260] Confirmed in an interview with Jay Stone for KSLQ-FM on 7 February. In the event, Conway declined his offer, having already committed to a touring schedule (he can consequently be heard on Cat Stevens' live album, *Saturnight*).

[261] It lost out to Neither One Of Us (Wants To Be The First To Say Goodbye) by Gladys Knight and the Pips. It won in the category, Best Arrangement Accompanying Vocalists, but the recipient was George Martin.

bassist (which, to judge by his subsequent performance was not his first instrument). Someone among them also knew Stevie Wonder was working in the adjacent studio and nipped through to collar him, his entrance into Studio A captured on the available tape.[262]

From what we hear, the next five minutes were spent on aimless warm-ups, the make-shift band clearly nervous in the company of both Lennon and McCartney; at one stage Lennon calls for song suggestions from the floor only to be met with complete silence, no-one daring to respond – as per his later remark that, 'There was 50 [sic] other people playing, and they were all just watching me and Paul'.[263] (His stipulation that they play material 'no later than '63' should be heard as 'no Beatles songs'.) The group got their act together when Wonder led a keyboard jam on electric piano, wandering through chord changes which don't make for a recognisable song until Lennon arrives out of nowhere, with a blood-curdling scream: *Lucille!* – and the band instantly lock into the old Little Richard hit, which McCartney used to sing in the Beatles' early repertoire. (Lennon here shows he can more than match his old partner for sheer attack, with the most throat-stripping vocal he ever recorded. Even McCartney can barely stay with him.)

Raggedly spontaneous, this six-minute interpretation has Lennon front, McCartney at the kit with a vocal mike, and Wonder on electric Piano, taking centre stage in the multiple instrumental breaks. Lennon's lead remains exhilarating throughout, although he only recalls the words to one verse which he sings over and over, McCartney dutifully harmonising a low part and giving the impression he was desperate to stand alongside Lennon in the middle of the floor. (Ironically, had Starr not decided to leave early, he'd have claimed the drum kit and McCartney almost certainly would have assumed bass guitar, his rightful position.)

Musically the performance is nowhere close to the potential of its stellar cast, coming over as rough, disorganised and sonically unsteady, caused in no small measure by the recording crew's constant attempts to adjust and correct the microphone feeds, which do little more than undermine the soundscape, and which about three minutes in, cause the loss of McCartney's drums from the tape. (Bobby Keys' sax can just be heard wailing away somewhere in the distance.) It hardly matters, the pure magic of hearing Lennon and McCartney belting a song together in the 1970s making up for any technical shortcomings.

---

[262] Wonder had drifted to LA in the early 1970s when Motown upped sticks from Detroit and settled on the West Coast. Aged just 23, he was currently making his reputation as one of the world's foremost recording artists, his lauded *Innervisions* about to be followed up with the critically acclaimed *Fulfillingness' First Finale*.

[263] Interview with Bob Harris for BBC Television's *Old Grey Whistle Test*, 21 February 1975.

It's usually assumed that Lennon was drunk or stoned or both, but measured by the recording he is lucid throughout, leading the group and giving directions; in fact, his casual enquiry at the end of the performance, 'Where's all that drink they always have in this place', indicates that having been in the studio all evening, he's not yet touched a drop, and certainly he doesn't *sound* like someone the worse for several hours' indulgence.

The rest of the session is frustratingly incomplete in the surviving recording, Lennon repeatedly berating the studio staff for taking things 'seriously' – ie, trying too hard to get the levels right and causing problems in his headphones. (The staff in the booth are not known, but at one stage Lennon addresses one of them as Gary.) There follows a run of protracted false-starts on [282] Stand By Me, which at the fourth attempt promises to be *great*, Lennon and McCartney in vintage synergy, answering each other's vocals until Lennon's mike drops out, terminating any chance we have to appreciate the performance. From there Lennon can just be made out, a long way off mike, but the only clear vocals now are backing sections from McCartney, plus Nilsson, who suddenly dominates. Had the studio crew been on their game, the tape would have been a genuine treasure; as it is, it tends to be regarded by fans with a mix of curiosity and dismissal, an *ersatz* Beatle reunion worth only a footnote.

The following day Lennon didn't surface until lunchtime and when he did, McCartney was already at his Pacific Coast Highway base, paying a social visit. Starr was also there, as photos from the afternoon show, three quarters of the Beatles relaxing happily together in the sunshine as they hadn't for years. How long McCartney stayed in the area, and what they got up to, is yet to be told although it seems he was around for several days since he and Lennon are known to have gone to a Captain Beefheart gig together at the Whiskey a Go Go on Sunset Strip on 3 April, door staff ridiculously following orders by turning them away, since they had no formal invite. And that's the last which is publicly known of McCartney's visit, Lennon thereafter resuming work on Nilsson's album, and McCartney heading back to Britain with Linda.

Details of what had unfolded on 28 March remained private until into the 1980s, and were generally unknown to Beatles fans for many more years. Lennon mentioned the session in passing in a couple of contemporary interviews but it was not until the publication of May Pang's memoir in 1983 that meaningful details came to light.[264] In 1992 the session tape finally leaked with the release of *A Toot And A Snore In '74*, a bootleg which had little by way

---

[264] In an interview with Jim Ladd for LA radio on 10 October 1974, broadcast by KMET-FM, Lennon revealed, 'We had a jam session together in West Coast. It was the first time we'd been in a studio together.' He later divulged the same to Bob Harris for *Old Grey Whistle Test*, but little notice was taken.

of supporting information and disappointed many, given the thrilling names listed on the front cover. In truth, it's a weak recording as judged dispassionately, half an hour of mostly unlistenable studio noise and poorly balanced audio. Viewed from its correct historical perspective though, it remains a priceless artefact; there is nothing in solo Beatles history to match the wonderful, terrible recordings made that night, John and Paul – the Nerk Twins – jamming on Little Richard like they had at the Cavern and the Star Club an age ago.

Paul McCartney single sessions: July 1974

Having attempted to re-form Wings in 1974, McCartney managed to cover off one vacancy when ex-Thunderclap Newman guitarist, Jimmy McCulloch, was recruited following his work on *McGear* (see [238]). But the drum seat remained unoccupied after Gerry Conway turned down his corresponding offer, a brooding McCartney electing to hold open auditions, as he had in the build-up to *RAM*, staged at London's Albery Theatre near Covent Garden in April. The event attracted some 50 hopefuls, one of whom was former Jimi Hendrix Experience drummer, Mitch Mitchell, who might have been a shoe-in were it not for the fact that he was famous in his own right, and therefore likely to resist McCartney's micro-management. (McCartney had a fractious encounter with Ginger Baker in 1973, which might have been in the back of his mind.) Instead the job went to Geoff Britton, a little-known drummer from the capital who apart from being a non-smoking tee-totaller, unlikely to participate in the recreational side of being in a band, was diametrically opposite his volatile new colleague, Jimmy McCulloch, with whom he was expected to gel. Wise to the issue, McCartney booked the group for a working holiday in Nashville starting 6 June, where besides getting to know one another, they could also rehearse ahead of a possible tour, although to judge by events, McCartney also planned to do some studio work, since he took with him several unfinished tapes to work on. Linda's father, Lee Eastman, put them in touch with Buddy Killen, who ran The Sound Shop studio on Nashville's Music Row, providing a suitable city venue to record between bouts of horse riding and taking in the extensive countryside around the ranch belonging to Curly Putman, one of the songwriters contracted to Killen's Tree Publishing concern, who agreed to put them up.

Paul McCartney And Wings: [239] **SALLY G** (*McCartney*)
Produced by Paul McCartney
Recorded: 9 Jul 1974, The Sound Shop, Nashville
UK: 25 Oct 1974 (single B-side)
US: 4 Nov 1974 (single B-side)
Paul McCartney: vocals, guitar, bass; **Linda McCartney**: vocals, melodium (?); **Denny Laine**: vocals; **Jimmy McCulloch**: guitar; **Geoff Britton**: drums; **Lloyd Green**: pedal steel guitar, dobro; **Johnny Gimble**: violin; **Bob Wills**: violin[265]

During a month relaxing around Nashville, Wings took the opportunity to absorb the local country music, befriending the likes of Floyd Cramer and Chet Atkins and watching Dolly Parton in concert.[266] One evening took them to Printer's Alley, the neon strip of nightclubs and jazz bars which included noted live venues including Hugh X Lewis Country Club, Captain's Table and Skull's Rainbow Room, where McCartney watched local stage singer, Diane Gaffney, being especially struck by her performance of Tangled Mind, originally recorded in 1957 by Canadian country star, Hank Snow. Galvanised, McCartney is said to have found a piano in a back room where he promptly wrote a song commemorating the moment, the subsequent lyric switch from Diane G to Sally G possibly effected to avoid any legal action she might take for use of her real name.

So as not to lose the intangible spirit of his surroundings, McCartney opted to record this new song at once over a late evening session at The Sound Shop. Playing on its country origins, McCartney abandoned piano for an acoustic guitar arrangement, the rest of the group finding their way around this style exercise before the addition of native instrumentation from a few of Nashville's session men including noted steel guitarist, Lloyd Green, for verisimilitude. With no musical style outside his scope, McCartney's adoption of the country form is pulled off with fluency, the track's weaving guitars and pedal steel licks authentic and easy compared to the earlier [170] Country Dreamer, contrived by Wings with no outside help. Tucked away on a B-side, Sally G might have passed the public by but became popular with music stations, its listing on the country charts less surprising than its arrival in the *Billboard* top 40, after Apple issued it again as a double-sided promotional disc. (British chart protocol made it ineligible for listing in its own right, any sales it attracted being automatically counted towards the A-side, [240] Junior's Farm.)

---

[265] Some sources additionally cite bluegrass fiddle player, Vassar Clements, as a participant.

[266] Parton was currently riding high. Two days after Wings arrived, her original recording of I Will Always Love You hit number 1 in the *Billboard* country music chart.

Paul McCartney And Wings: [240] **JUNIOR'S FARM** (*McCartney*)
Produced by Paul McCartney
Recorded: Jul 1974, The Sound Shop, Nashville
UK: 25 Oct 1974 (single A-side)
US: 4 Nov 1974 (single A-side)
Paul McCartney: vocals, bass; **Linda McCartney**: keyboards, vocals; **Denny Laine**: guitar, vocals; **Jimmy McCulloch**: guitar; **Geoff Britton**: drums

With The Sound Shop at his disposal, McCartney and his new-look group had several opportunities for recording, which apart from securing [239] Sally G, generated an oddly variable pile of material, including a take of Denny Laine's country-infused Send Me The Heart and one of McCartney's most celebrated off-shoots, Walking In The Park With Eloise, a bouncing instrumental concocted by his father decades earlier.[267] The last thing recorded was Junior's Farm, like Sally G, newly composed, but drawing on unfinished parts McCartney had written earlier in the year.[268] In any case, the inspiration for the song was manifold, including elements of McCartney's love of reclusion on his own country farm, and paying tribute in its title and hook to Curly Putman Jr, via (supposedly) Bob Dylan.[269]

Whatever he had in mind, the lyric comes through as obscure, combining real-life points of reference (the gee-gees relate to his and Linda's horse riding escapes; the retail price rises to the recent financial crash and consequent inflation), with fantasy/surrealism in the form of a poker-playing sea lion juxtaposed with Oliver Hardy. Concerning nothing in particular, the lines wherein a bag of cement is purchased for the president's sake, presumably to bury him, were subsequently dropped from the concert arrangement, Americans in particular more sensitive to an implied threat of assassination than Brits, for whom such sentiments were taken merely as good humour. One of the composing techniques of both Lennon and McCartney was to use dummy lyrics as place holders until the appropriate phrasing fell into place by

---

[267] In addition, the group finished up [173] Bridge On The River Suite, which served as a B-side to Walking In The Park With Eloise when issued out as a single 'by' the Country Hams. Overdubs were also added to [100] Hey Diddle and Linda's Wide Prairie, unreleased until 1998. Send Me The Heart was not issued, Laine eventually claiming it for his 1980 solo album, *Japanese Tears*.
[268] According to Madinger and Easter (p194). Luca Perasi (p120) cites the demos, Arab Nights and Little Bass Man, as germinal – but as neither is in circulation, they are impossible to evaluate.
[269] McCartney claims a link to Maggie's Farm (1965) in the relevant entry of *The Lyrics*, and further suggests the word 'eskimo' was included in respect of The Mighty Quinn (1967). (The word is also street slang for a deliverer of 'snow' – ie, cocaine.)

automatic suggestion, and McCartney might have come up with a more incisive text had he spent time on it – although he considered meaninglessness as both stimulating to the imagination and amusing, wondering to himself how his audience would interpret it (see also [25]; [105]; [138]; [166] and so on).

Musically, Junior's Farm gallops along on a horizontal G major, its harmony line holding a steady tonic for much of it, the unchanging quality reflecting the wide open views around Putman's ranch until it leaps to a high B to *jump* the fence. Having given his band directions on how their parts should go, McCartney must have been pleased to see Geoff Britain rise to the occasion, as did Jimmy McCulloch with a set of cutting guitar spots including a main solo just a quarter of the way in. McCulloch's work on the soulful instrumental coda too is melodically adventurous, its riff stepping excitedly across the strings against McCartney's drowsy bass, recorded with the tape machine running at half speed so as to alter the frequencies.[270] At some stage, probably in October, McCartney's vocals were subjected to a hefty phasing effect, the whole thing mixed by George Martin at AIR ready for release on 45, the seventh stand-alone single of McCartney's post-Beatles career.

McCartney turned 32 in Nashville, his birthday on 18 June marked by Linda presenting him with a special gift – the upright bass which used to belong to Elvis's backing musician, Bill Black, and which McCartney would use in the studio later in the year ([287]). This event and the consolidation of Wings mark II will have put a gloss on things, but as ever there were clouds in the air, McCulloch and Britton continuing to have a strained personal relationship, and neither of them elevated to full group membership, being retained, as were Henry McCullough and Denny Seiwell before them, on a wage packet. Partly this was calculated so McCartney would not be obligated long-term to musicians he hardly knew, but there lurks a feeling that he was insensitive to their professional ambitions, treating them as hired hands while simultaneously depending on their talents to forge ahead.

At this stage there was still a possibility that Wings could coalesce into more than an anonymous backing group, Jimmy McCulloch in particular firming up his position with a new composition – Medicine Jar – which he would sing on their next album. On the other hand his erratic temperament was a cause for concern, the reported throwing of a glass bottle through the studio console window followed by a traffic stop for driving under the influence, which soon escalated into a fist fight with a police officer, resulting

---

[270] Quoted in Perasi (p121), Sound Shop engineer, Ernie Winfrey, says McCartney's bass was recorded with the tape running at double speed. However this would have resulted in playback an octave lower, which is not what we hear in the mix.

in a night in jail. Consequent of McCartney's discretionary visa, neither he nor the rest of the band had US work permits and when it became obvious McCulloch would have to appear in court, the entourage fled the States, heading back to Britain on 17 July via New York City (see also [249]).

It's a measure of McCartney's fructuous talent that having gone on holiday with no particular plans, he returned with a double hit ready to go, bar the mixing. [240] Junior's Farm / [239] Sally G was released in late autumn, once the singles from *Band On The Run* had finished their runs, amid an advertising campaign which mirrored the A-side's lyrics by presenting the surrealist image of a sea lion seated at a poker table. With no album to promote, his previous release having remained current through 1974, Junior's Farm became McCartney's last record on the Apple label.

RECORD RELEASES

[240] **Junior's Farm** / [239] **Sally G**
(UK: 25 Oct 1974, US: 4 Nov 1974)

Walls And Bridges sessions:
July 1974 to August 1974

Sessions for Nilsson's *Pussy Cats* had, by the end of week two, generated an album's worth of raw cuts including some celebrated oldies (Save The Last Dance For Me; Rock Around The Clock) and a new Lennon original, Mucho Mungo. With the tapes safely in the can, Lennon decided he'd had enough of the wild life in LA and made plans to return to New York where besides finishing production on *Pussy Cats*, he could also dry out, embarking on a period of abstinence and buckling down to serious work – his move on 19 April effectively bringing his 'lost weekend' to a close after seven months, even if he was still apart from his wife. Lennon checked into The Pierre on Fifth Avenue, a stroll across Central Park from the Dakota, significantly without May Pang who he'd unceremoniously left in LA on the vague promise that he'd send for her at some point.

In theory, Lennon's main project was the lingering *Oldies But Mouldies*, yet since Spector had the tapes locked away, plans to finish it were so forlorn that by the start of July he decided to shelve it and press on with a brand new set. For all her grievances, May Pang's main job when she finally joined him in New York was to ring around and assemble a group, as if she were still on the staff, although she and Lennon would finally move into a new home together at the start of July – a penthouse on 434 East 52nd Street in Manhattan's Sutton

Place district. The team which was organised was essentially the same as that on *Pussy Cats* – Keltner, Voormann, Jesse Ed Davis and so on – a loosely permanent crew, some of whom would also contribute to Starr's *Goodnight Vienna* and then return later in the year for *Rock 'N' Roll*. Assembling at Record Plant West on 13 July for two days' pre-practice, the decision to rehearse the material in advance was a wise one, bringing a sense of discipline and sobriety which paid dividends over the days to come, in contrast to the shambolic *Oldies But Mouldies* period.

John Lennon: [241] **MOVE OVER MS. L** (*Lennon*)
Produced by John Lennon
Recorded: 15 Jul 1974; Aug 1974, Record Plant, New York
UK: 18 Apr 1975 (single B-side)
US: 10 Mar 1975 (single B-side)
John Lennon: vocals, guitar; **Jesse Ed Davis**: guitar; **Eddie Mottau**: guitar; **Klaus Voormann**: bass; **Ken Ascher**: piano; **Jim Keltner**: drums; **Arthur Jenkins**: percussion; **Ron Aprea**: alto sax; **Bobby Keys**: tenor sax; **Frank Vicari**: tenor sax; **Howard Johnson**: baritone sax

Having rehearsed the album over the weekend, Lennon was ready to roll the tape on the Monday in a busy session which secured four tracks. Chief among them was Move Over Ms. L, seeming to point a goading finger at Ono, the real-life Ms. L, via an uncharacteristically oblique lyric. Exactly what the normally blunt Lennon was getting off his chest is not clear, his cryptic text skirting the idea that life, love and radical art – the centre of the couple's former world-view – are just a game they were playing. That being so, the hook line, 'move over', comes across as a renunciation, written as Lennon was with May Pang, and using a phrase probably derived from his past life: [147] Roll Over Beethoven.

Lennon's conflicted feelings towards Ono, who he hadn't given up on, is reflected in his uncertainty over how to approach the track. Rehearsed as a lively rockabilly he re-arranged it in a low-paced *Dylanesque* before changing tack and settling on a brassy rocker, sprightly enough that if challenged over its lyric, he could dismiss it as just a piece of fun. When the stack of *Walls And Bridges* material was subsequently assessed Lennon found he had almost 50 minutes' worth, too much for a single LP, and perhaps wary of offending his wife, pulled the song from its proposed place on side 2. Later in the year he decided he wanted it after all and during a remix session for *Rock 'N' Roll* on 15 October, tidied it up for deployment as the B-side to his final Apple single in 1975 [282], concurrent with a cover version by Keith Moon. (Its 1950s style, and association with the *Rock 'N' Roll* release, led many to wrongly assume it was fresh recording at that point.)

John Lennon: [242] SURPRISE, SURPRISE (SWEET BIRD OF PARADOX)
(*Lennon*)
Produced by John Lennon
Recorded: 15 Jul 1974; 31 Jul 1974; Aug 1974, Record Plant, New York
UK: 4 Oct 1974 (*Walls And Bridges* LP)
US: 30 Sep 1974 (*Walls And Bridges* LP)
John Lennon: vocals, guitar; **Elton John:** backing vocals; **Jesse Ed Davis:** guitar; **Eddie Mottau:** guitar; **Nicky Hopkins:** piano; **Klaus Voormann:** bass; **Ken Ascher:** clavinet; **Jim Keltner:** drums; **Arthur Jenkins:** percussion; **Steve Madaio:** trumpet; **Ron Aprea:** alto sax; **Bobby Keys:** tenor sax; **Frank Vicari:** tenor sax; **Howard Johnson:** baritone sax (the previous five musicians billed collectively as 'Little Big Horns')

Written for May Pang, Surprise, Surprise was (according to her) begun the day after she and Lennon first made love, placing it in August 1973, before they left for LA. To judge by period demos, Lennon initially had only a middle eight, a vaguely questioning couple of lines about his situation, but by the time he recorded *Walls And Bridges*, he'd fleshed it into something which he later observed resembled Harrison's Here Comes The Sun.[271]

A qualified love song, the subtext is that Pang helps Lennon avoid loneliness, his 'romantic' overtures including such offerings as that she is able to induce perspiration in him – yet with a degree of love-blindness, Pang claimed she received the song with tears in her eyes, 'the nicest present you could ever give me'.[272] The fact is, Lennon's devotion, if it existed at all, was a slender one, and when in song he finally gets to the point by using the word 'love', he promptly twists off into a humorous quote from Drive My Car, itself just a euphemism for intercourse. When Elton John showed up at Record Plant on the final day of July (see [245]) he offered to add some backing vocals to the track, for some reason mixed down so as to become unrecognisable. Six years later, Lennon gave his hindsight assessment of the song, and by extension its sentiments, to *Playboy*: 'Just a piece of garbage'.[273]

---

[271] Lennon made the comparison in an interview for San Francisco's KSAN-FM on 21 September that year, just before the album release. He probably had in mind the descending run at 0:53 ('I need her'), similar to a structure in Harrison's original. (Since Lennon demonstrated by singing the line, 'Little darling, de de de de...' he unwittingly gave rise to a misunderstanding that he was thinking of Little Darlin' by Canadian vocal quartet, the Diamonds (1957).)
[272] Pang and Edwards, p223.
[273] Golson, p183.

John Lennon: [243] **SCARED** (*Lennon*)
Produced by John Lennon
Recorded: 15 Jul 1974; Aug 1974; 22 Aug 1974; 30 Aug 1974, Record Plant, New York
UK: 4 Oct 1974 (*Walls And Bridges* LP)
US: 30 Sep 1974 (*Walls And Bridges* LP)
John Lennon: vocals, guitar, piano, wolf howl sample[274]; **Jesse Ed Davis**: guitar; **Eddie Mottau**: guitar; **Nicky Hopkins**: piano; **Ken Ascher**: electric piano; **Klaus Voormann**: bass; **Jim Keltner**: drums; **Arthur Jenkins**: percussion; **Steve Madaio**: trumpet; **Ron Aprea**: alto sax; **Bobby Keys**: tenor sax; **Frank Vicari**: tenor sax; **Howard Johnson**: baritone sax (the previous five musicians billed collectively as 'Little Big Horns'); **unknown**: string section (billed as 'The Philharmonic Orchestrange', directed by Ken Ascher)

A mid-life crisis set to music, Scared has Lennon's self-doubt imprinted on it, his personal insecurity mystifying to the world looking in, but real nonetheless. Set minor, with Voormann's leaden bass and a lyric raking over his own mortality ('as the years slip away'), the track's pessimism belies the fact that its author was only 33, a soul out of touch with himself, making it an analogue of Help!, for the 1970s. While Lennon was forever plagued by uncertainty about himself, usually masked with public shows of bravado, that this song arrived when it did is a consequence of his alienation from Ono, regular life having been cast to the winds, a deeply personal connection he revealed in an interview for radio the day after he turned 34.[275] In this context, the lonesome howl at the start is a call-out to his lost wife, an animalistic longing for the person he most needed through the final decade of his life.[276]

As a performance, Scared expresses its pessimism through a dour arrangement which plods over four and a half dejected minutes. The late removal of Lennon's confession of fatigue five additional times prior to the final verse may have avoided sapping the song's mood even more, but the

---

[274] Lennon is billed in the official credits as Mel Torment, a play on singer and musician, Mel Tormé. (Other pseudonyms he used on the album include Rev. Fred Ghurkin [244], Rev. Thumbs Ghurkin [250], Dr. Winston O'Ghurkin [246], Dr. Winston O'Reggae [249], Dr. Winston [252], Hon. John St. John Johnson [245], Dwarf McDougal [247], Kaptain Kundalini [248] and Dr. Dream [251]. We stick with 'John Lennon' throughout.)

[275] KMET-FM of Los Angeles, 10 October 1974: 'I'm not always scared. When it gets to writing down how Yoko and I feel about each other, that's how I feel about her.'

[276] The howl is sampled from the 1971 LP, *The Language And Music Of The Wolves* ('band 5'), an audio documentary narrated by actor, Robert Redford, and dubbed on by Lennon on 30 August. He had sampled the same howl for Elephant's Memory's Gypsy Wolf in 1972.

overall effect remains bleak, despite momentary fire in the middle eight and an effectively moody baritone sax solo from noted jazz musician, Howard Johnson. Even when at a personal low Lennon was capable of creating works of genuine expressive power, whether or not it made for a comfortable listening experience.

John Lennon: [244] **BLESS YOU** (*Lennon*)
 Produced by John Lennon
 Recorded: 15 July 1974; Aug 1974, Record Plant, New York
 UK: 4 Oct 1974 (*Walls And Bridges* LP)
 US: 30 Sep 1974 (*Walls And Bridges* LP)
 John Lennon: vocals, guitar; **Jesse Ed Davis**: guitar; **Eddie Mottau**: guitar; **Ken Ascher**: electric piano, Mellotron; **Klaus Voormann**: bass; **Steve Madaio**: trumpet; **Jim Keltner**: drums; **Arthur Jenkins**: percussion

In Lennon's absence, Ono had begun to invest considerable effort in cultivating a musical career on her own terms, *Feeling The Space* released in November 1973, three weeks before she began sessions for a follow-up, to be titled *A Story*, with David Spinozza as producer. Work included, on 3 December, a recording of the desolate Loneliness, the most obvious comment on her separation from Lennon, to which Spinozza added a prominent bluesy guitar, and as sessions extended into 1974 there was speculation in the press that Ono and Spinozza were a couple, something not publicly admitted but a possibility conceded by Lennon, who according to the account in Philip Norman's 2009 biography, positively encouraged her to see other men.[277] Accordingly, Bless You is Lennon's tacit acceptance, partly to reassure Ono but enclosing within itself a vicarious plea to any would-be lover to take care of her. (In this unusually selfless part of the song, Lennon can be heard over-stressing his words, 'Be warm and kind *hearted*' as if he doesn't really believe what he's saying.)

Recorded in 12 takes, Bless You exudes a jazzy sensuality, its cool acoustics and wandering bass washed over by an uncredited trumpet solo from Steve Madaio. On *Walls And Bridges* Lennon expected his session men to come up with their own contributions rather than giving them (McCartney-style) direction, and hence its most notable ingredient is Ken Ascher's electric piano, fluttering around the upper end of the keyboard and capturing the essence of contemporary Stevie Wonder, from numbers such as All In Love Is

---

[277] The relevant passage on p737 rings true. Norman states Lennon also advised Ono to maintain an active love life in his absence, 'as a precaution against cancer', a notion he will have taken from the writings of Wilhelm Reich, (eg, *The Discovery Of The Orgone* (1942)), whom he read in the late 1960s.

Fair from his highly acclaimed 1973 album, *Innervisions*.

Pregnant with personal significance, its no surprise that Lennon nominated this thoughtful ballad as his favourite on the album, having programmed it to run into the opening cry of [243] Scared. Much admired for its gently falling melody, and the most cohesive musicality of Lennon's solo career, Bless You was considered too light for the charts and lounging on *Walls And Bridges* slipped under the radar. Convinced of its potential, Lennon tried to persuade Andy Williams to cover it in 1975, before hearing the Rolling Stones' Miss You, and deciding he'd been mimicked – and so was right about its hit credentials all along.

John Lennon: [245] **WHATEVER GETS YOU THRU THE NIGHT** (*Lennon*)
Produced by John Lennon
Recorded: 16 Jul 1974; 17 Jul 1974; 23 Jul 1974; 31 Jul 1974, Record Plant, New York
UK: 4 Oct 1974 (*Walls And Bridges* LP)
US: 23 Sep 1974 (single A-side)
John Lennon: vocals, guitar; **Elton John**: organ, piano, backing vocals; **Jesse Ed Davis**: guitar; **Eddie Mottau**: guitar; **Klaus Voormann**: bass; **Ken Ascher**: clavinet; **Jim Keltner**: drums; **Arthur Jenkins**: percussion; **Bobby Keys**: tenor sax

After an exhausting first session for *Walls And Bridges*, Lennon was back the following day to start work on this, the stand-out track. The last thing written for the LP, Whatever Gets You Thru The Night was born from his habit of tuning into late-night radio, when he chanced on a sermon by New York preacher, Reverend Ike, who uttered the song's title phrase.[278] Written and demoed on acoustic guitar, the song was then subject to Lennon's familiar deliberations, initially arranged slow, its momentum achieved with an overbusy guitar *obligato*, before being transferred to keyboard but rejected. (Madinger and Easter state an electric sitar was also tried out; it's unclear who will have played it.) It wasn't until the session on 23 July that Lennon found what he wanted, a conventional band arrangement attacking the number and giving it a propulsion absent from the earlier attempts.

Take seven would get its final, decisive overdubs at the end of the month, after Elton John visited Lennon's apartment en-route to the Caribou Ranch studio in Colorado, to record *Captain Fantastic and the Brown Dirt Cowboy*.[279]

---

[278] Lennon said as much in his interview for KMET-FM on 10 October 1974. Ike was at that time well known for his weekly radio sermons in which he exhorted listeners to send him cash in return for holy blessings – hence the line, 'It's your money of your life'.
[279] In July, Lennon had invited Cynthia and Julian over for a visit (see [253]). They >

Treated to a listen of some of the *Walls And Bridges* tapes, John offered to contribute to the current track, believing it a potential hit. A few nights on he was taken to Record Plant, the 31 July session seeing him add piano, organ, and significantly, a vocal track recorded side-by-side with Lennon, providing the type of high harmony line the former Beatle would have once enjoyed from McCartney, so effective in the middle eight that Elton effectively steals it. Lennon was later modest about the results, joking that together they sounded like Patience and Prudence, but there's no missing the creative flair on show.[280]

Lennon ended up with a fairly rudimentary rocker which varies from the standard blues structure only by stepping straight from G major to A, otherwise home turf for Lennon. About nothing in particular, the song may have been another with Ono as its *raison d'être*, Lennon's shout-out around 2:40, 'Can you hear me, mother?' calling her by her code name in a phrase borrowed from the northern comedian, Sandy Powell, who Lennon remembered from his childhood. This excepted, his words are as empty as any he ever came up with, part of the reason he didn't consider the song a hit and had to be persuaded by Capitol to issue it as a single.

Once cleared for release, Elton John famously challenged Lennon that should it make number 1 they'd appear on stage together; with Harrison, McCartney and Starr all having made top spot as solo artists, Lennon was the only one of the four without a number 1 on his cv, and not believing this would be his first, accepted the wager. While by no means the best crafted among Lennon's post-Beatles work, Whatever Gets You Thru The Night, with its jangling hook lines and stop-time verses, was engaging enough that even without Elton John explicitly billed, it reached the top of *Billboard* on 16 November.[281] Honouring his pact, Lennon stepped out with Elton at Madison Square Garden 12 days after, where the two performed Whatever Gets You Thru The Night plus two Beatles songs, I Saw Her Standing There and Lucy In The Sky With Diamonds, the last of which they had meantime recorded at Caribou Ranch for Elton's next single, taking Lennon back to number 1 as a guest star in the new year.

---

travelled over on the *SS France* accompanied by Elton John, and on arrival in New York, they all checked into apartments at The Pierre where Lennon was currently living. (Elton's potted account of his visit is carried in his 2019 autobiography, p115-120.)

[280] Patience and Prudence were a child vocal duo from California who scored a couple of hits for the Liberty label in the 1950s. Lennon's comments from an interview with Michael Wale for BBC radio, 27 September 1974.

[281] The story in Britain was rather different, the song polling a miserable 26, illustrating the Beatles' wane in their home country during the 1970s; other than McCartney, no ex-Beatle would get anywhere near the UK top 10 in the second half of the decade.

John Lennon: [246] **GOING DOWN ON LOVE** (*Lennon*)
Produced by John Lennon
Recorded: 16 Jul 1974; Aug 1974, Record Plant, New York
UK: 4 Oct 1974 (*Walls And Bridges* LP)
US: 30 Sep 1974 (*Walls And Bridges* LP)
John Lennon: vocals, guitar; **Jesse Ed Davis**: guitar; **Eddie Mottau**: guitar; **Nicky Hopkins**: piano; **Ken Ascher**: electric piano; **Klaus Voormann**: bass; **Jim Keltner**: drums; **Arthur Jenkins**: percussion; **Steve Madaio**: trumpet; **Ron Aprea**: alto sax; **Bobby Keys**: tenor sax; **Frank Vicari**: tenor sax; **Howard Johnson**: baritone sax (the previous five musicians billed collectively as 'Little Big Horns')

Going Down On Love was written over the summer of 1974, demo recordings finding Lennon testing out various tempos, the mood shifting from furious to miserable. The fact that he ultimately pitched it mid-tempo, with a breezy arrangement, disguises the fact that beneath its open exterior the song dwells in the same pit of despondency as much of his post-1972 output. Taken into the studio on 16 July, Lennon's austerity is expressed in his instruction to the band to avoid adorning it with frills and decorations, as included on the rehearsal version recorded just prior to the session, which gave the track an unwanted uplift.

Lennon later characterised his lyric as 'about a love affair... some intensity that goes away', but the objectivity implied is illusory.[282] While the 'precious and rare' thing he needs can only mean Ono, his falling down to his knees is not a religious gesture, as some commentators inferred, but the action of a man begging; this passage, appended to the main song early on, is a further example of Lennon's habit of deriving vocal lines by singing over the top of electric guitar riffs ([81]; [155]). Most telling, on an album containing the desperate [243] Scared, is a restatement of the personal woes expressed as long ago as 1965, 'please, please help me', in a section forming part of the song's multi-partite structure. Shaken from its inherent malaise by animated bongos and shimmering bells, the final recording does an admirable job of hiding the fact that the clouds which had hung over *Mind Games* were not yet clear.

---

[282] Interview for RKO Radio Network, 25 September 1974.

John Lennon: [247] **NOBODY LOVES YOU (WHEN YOU'RE DOWN AND OUT)** (*Lennon*)
Produced by John Lennon
Recorded: 17 Jul 1974; 22 Aug 1974; Aug 1974, Record Plant, New York
UK: 4 Oct 1974 (*Walls And Bridges* LP)
US: 30 Sep 1974 (*Walls And Bridges* LP)
John Lennon: vocals, guitar; **Nicky Hopkins**: piano; **Ken Ascher**: organ; **Klaus Voormann**: bass; **Jim Keltner**: drums; **Steve Madaio**: trumpet; **Ron Aprea**: alto sax; **Bobby Keys**: tenor sax; **Frank Vicari**: tenor sax; **Howard Johnson**: baritone sax (the previous five musicians billed collectively as 'Little Big Horns'); **unknown**: string section (billed as 'The Philharmonic Orchestrange', directed by Ken Ascher)

Lennon's 'lost weekend' defined, Nobody Loves You (When You're Down And Out) was the first and likely only complete song he wrote during his months in LA, and therefore his first composition since separating from Ono. Drawn from the bottom of a long bottle, this depressed and depressing thing borrowed its title from the old blues standard by American vaudeville star, Jimmie Cox, obscure enough that Lennon probably only learned of it through Derek and the Dominos' electrified version on *Layla And Other Assorted Love Songs* in 1970.

Lennon's own [215] Aisumasen may have served as a model for the song's bleak mood, but a mix of familiar ingredients work their way in too. While the 'one-eyed witchdoctor leading the blind' comes straight from the lexicon of Dylan, the main chord pattern borrows from Harrison's similarly mournful [36] Isn't It A Pity, particularly the reflective Version 2. Pointedly, in an early take available on *John Lennon Anthology* a vibraphone flirts with the guitar solo from Harrison's track, part of which is retained in the finished recording, Jesse Ed Davis's solo containing at 2:58 the fingerprint 'devil's interval' tritone. (It's as if the implied presence of a few old faces felt to Lennon like supportive arm around him.)

Lennon later associated the song's self-pitying lyric with his destructive LA lifestyle, the fact it was copyrighted on 3 December 1973 indicating it was penned during the alcoholic sessions for *Oldies But Mouldies*. However a degree of calculation seems to have gone into the track, the use of the American 'hustlin' for a buck and a dime' suggesting his later description of it as a 'pension song', which would earn him lucrative royalties in cover versions, was at least part of his thought process all along.[283]

---

[283] He mentioned the 'pension song' in his RKO Radio Network interview on 25 September 1974. Six years on, interviewed for *Playboy*, he hadn't given up hope, attempting to plug it to Sinatra: 'Ya listenin', Frank? Here's one for you' (Golson, p183).

John Lennon: [248] **WHAT YOU GOT** (*Lennon*)
Produced by John Lennon
Recorded: 19 Jul 1974; Aug 1974, Record Plant, New York
UK: 4 Oct 1974 (*Walls And Bridges* LP)
US: 30 Sep 1974 (*Walls And Bridges* LP)
John Lennon: vocals, guitar; **Jesse Ed Davis**: guitar; **Eddie Mottau**: guitar; **Klaus Voormann**: bass; **Jim Keltner**: drums; **Nicky Hopkins**: piano; **Ken Ascher**: clavinet; **Arthur Jenkins**: percussion; **Steve Madaio**: trumpet; **Ron Aprea**: alto sax; **Bobby Keys**: tenor sax; **Frank Vicari**: tenor sax; **Howard Johnson**: baritone sax (the previous five musicians billed collectively as 'Little Big Horns')

After the spirit-sapping [247] Nobody Loves You (When You're Down And Out), it's pleasing to hear a revitalised Lennon tackle this new song, recorded just two days later and audibly casting off his blues. Discovered by playing with the riff from the O'Jays' spring hit, For The Love Of Money, the musical foundation of What You Got is barely recognisable in the finished recording, having by then gone through the filter of Lennon's acoustic guitar.[284] The outcome was a fiery urban number whose funky groove edges towards the then current blaxploitation genre of Curtis Mayfield, Sly Stone and Isaac Hayes – one of the most interesting diversions of style in Lennon's solo catalogue, and one he pulls off comfortably, thanks in no small measure to the versatility of his band, in particular Little Big Horns and the pulsating bass of Klaus Voormann.

Lyrically the content is nothing so bold, consisting of another expression of his post-Ono loneliness, wherein he curses the drag of the days. (So different in mood and manner are the track's music and lyrics that it's hard to believe they arrived in Lennon's mind together; that they did is proven by the sequence of demo versions now circulating on bootlegs.) Using his patent technique of spinning off beloved oldies, the source was You Don't Know What You've Got (Until You Lose It), a 1961 hit for rock and roller, Ral Donner, released in Britain on Parlophone and taken into the Beatles' repertoire. Revelling in his musical roots, he also name-drops another old favourite: Little Richard's [280] Rip It Up (1956).

---

[284] Interviewed for *The Dennis Elsas Show* (WNEW-FM) on 28 September, Lennon mistakenly named the O'Jays' song as Money Money Money. He was currently a fan, having particularly enjoyed Love Train (1973).

John Lennon: [249] **STEEL AND GLASS** (*Lennon*)
Produced by John Lennon
Recorded: 20 Jul 1974; 22 Aug 1974; Aug 1974, Record Plant, New York
UK: 4 Oct 1974 (*Walls And Bridges* LP)
US: 30 Sep 1974 (*Walls And Bridges* LP)
John Lennon: vocals, guitar; **Jesse Ed Davis**: guitar; **Eddie Mottau**: guitar; **Nicky Hopkins**: piano; **Ken Ascher**: clavinet; **Klaus Voormann**: bass; **Jim Keltner**: drums; **Arthur Jenkins**: percussion; **Steve Madaio**: trumpet; **Ron Aprea**: alto sax; **Bobby Keys**: tenor sax; **Frank Vicari**: tenor sax; **Howard Johnson**: baritone sax (the previous five musicians billed collectively as 'Little Big Horns'); **unknown**: string section (billed as 'The Philharmonic Orchestrange', directed by Ken Ascher)

The subject of Lennon's scorn in this latest recording has prompted endless debate among fans and critics, something Lennon fuelled with his evasive comments, starting with his introducing the song as about 'your friend and mine', followed by a teasing, 'who is it?'. Never coming clean, Lennon insisted it didn't concern McCartney, but also remarked with a sly wink that is wasn't aimed at Eartha Kitt either, and when asked directly if it were about Allen Klein, pointed out the opening line, 'With your LA tan', which if describing anyone specific, certainly wasn't the rough-styled New Yorker.

Lennon's denials, knowingly cryptic, have fostered an idea that having disengaged from Klein's management in 1973, the song *was* about him after all, written by way of concession to McCartney. The main evidence in support is the fact that what passes for a chorus is essentially a reprise of the corresponding part in [129] How Do You Sleep?, pointing at cross-reference – and by 1974 the two ex-Beatles were back on friendly terms, a visit by McCartney to Lennon's apartment in which they spent a couple of nights reminiscing about the past happening to fall right at the time Steel And Glass was recorded.[285] If Lennon was indeed re-writing How Do You Sleep? from an opposite perspective he wasn't about to decrypt it and preferred to let fans puzzle over the song's intent; the line, 'You wrote a song when you were just 16', featured on an early piano demo but then excised, does tend to point at McCartney, whereas 'Your mother left you when you were small' sounds confusingly autobiographical, and if literal, wouldn't have applied to either McCartney or Allen Klein.

---

[285] This little-discussed social visit is dated by Madinger and Raile as circa 21 July. Lennon mentioned it in a couple of interviews, for example for KMET-FM on 10 October, 'Paul and I were together in New York a couple of nights. We just drank wine and said, "remember this?" "remember that?" and we did all that trip.' McCartney was in New York *en route* to London, following the Nashville sessions for [239] and [240].

Recorded in eight takes, Steel And Glass finds Lennon in insinuating mood, giving *Walls And Bridges* an edge missing from *Mind Games*. The basic track, completed on 20 July, was subsequently treated to brass and string overdubs, the central contribution of Ken Ascher's 'Philharmonic Orchestrange' added during a lengthy session on 22 August, providing the song's characteristic riff and accusatory slant.

John Lennon: [250] **OLD DIRT ROAD** (*Lennon, Nilsson*)
Produced by John Lennon
Recorded: 20 Jul 1974; 8 Aug 1974; 22 Aug 1974, Record Plant, New York
UK: 4 Oct 1974 (*Walls And Bridges* LP)
US: 30 Sep 1974 (*Walls And Bridges* LP)
John Lennon: vocals, piano; **Jesse Ed Davis**: guitar; **Eddie Mottau**: guitar; **Nicky Hopkins**: piano; **Ken Ascher**: electric piano; **Klaus Voormann**: bass; **Jim Keltner**: drums; **Harry Nilsson**: backing vocals; **unknown**: string section (billed as 'The Philharmonic Orchestrange', directed by Ken Ascher)

One of Lennon's gentler creations, Old Dirt Road was written in the late spring after he and Nilsson left the heady madness of LA for the more sober surroundings of New York. Started by Lennon, the song was developed on piano (in the presence of several invasive businessmen hovering around the studio after his attention), a request for a good Americanism in verse 2 answered by Nilsson's spontaneous, 'Trying to shovel smoke with a pitchfork in the wind', which provided its most memorable line. Perhaps inevitably, given Lennon's current obsession with oldies, he proceeded to construct a third verse based on Frankie Laine's 1955 country hit, Cool Water, which he effectively distils into five lines.[286]

The casual circumstances of its birth are reflected in the listlessness of the finished track, which relies on the soulful musicianship of the group to see it though, in particular Jesse Ed Davis's soft-focus lead guitar and Nicky Hopkins' omnipresent piano. Adding to the seemingly bottomless list of musical and lyrical quotations peppering *Walls And Bridges*, Lennon's repeat fade 'keep on keeping on' could have been borrowed from one of several sources, the most likely, Bob Dylan's You Ain't Going Nowhere (1967).[287]

[286] Lewisohn makes the point in *Tune In* (2013, p764). Laine's song concerns a laboured journey across the desert sands, the narrator longing for some 'cool, clear water (water)'.
[287] Another possible contender is Jr Walker's 1966 Motown hit, (I'm A) Road Runner, which has a vaguely matching theme to Old Dirt Road. Equally Lennon might have heard Curtis Mayfield's 1971 album, *Roots*, whose second track was titled Keep On Keeping On.

Sealing his claim, Nilsson turned up at Sunset Sound Studios on 8 August, where Lennon was helping Starr with [260] All By Myself, and added a harmony vocal parked low in the mix, six years before releasing his own version on *Flash Harry*, with Starr sitting in on drums.

John Lennon: [251] **#9 DREAM** (*Lennon*)
  Produced by John Lennon
  Recorded: 23 Jul 1974; 22 Aug 1974; 24 Aug 1974, Record Plant, New York
  UK: 4 Oct 1974 (*Walls And Bridges* LP)
  US: 30 Sep 1974 (*Walls And Bridges* LP)
  John Lennon: vocals, guitar; **Jesse Ed Davis**: guitar; **Eddie Mottau**: guitar; **Nicky Hopkins**: electric piano; **Klaus Voormann**: bass; **Ken Ascher**: clavinet; **Jim Keltner**: drums; **Arthur Jenkins**: percussion; **May Pang, Lori Burton, Joey Dambra**: backing vocals (collectively billed as the 44th Street Fairies); **unknown**: string section (billed as 'The Philharmonic Orchestrange', directed by Ken Ascher)

Aside from the inconsequential [252] Beef Jerky and the disposable snippet [253] Ya Ya, the last song captured for *Walls And Bridges* was #9 Dream, likely Lennon's most popular period recording. His intent was to make something from the attractive backing melody he'd created for Nilsson's cover of Many Rivers To Cross, the opening cut on *Pussy Cats*, against which he ran some exploratory words, 'so long ago', giving it a working title. With nothing else, he supposedly played it to May Pang who, according to her memoir, cajoled him into writing more of the same, having perceptively sensed the coming of its 'beautiful melody'.[288]

The earliest recordings of the song are a couple of acoustic demos probably taped not long before the studio version. These renditions show Lennon locking onto Harrison's [34] My Sweet Lord in the then sketchy middle section, which consisted of block chords switching between F sharp minor and B, if not a straight copy then certainly making a recognisable match. (In one of these run-throughs Lennon can be heard singing notes from Harrison's guitar solo, not the first time he'd cribbed from his former colleague ([144]; [247]).) At some point Lennon awoke from a dream in which he heard two women saying his name and the meaningless incantation, 'bowakowa poussé poussé, all of which happened to marry up with the song's fantasy theme and provided lyrics for the vacant bars. Perhaps thinking again of Harrison's 'Hare Krishna' backing vocals, Lennon elected to sing his chant to almost the same melody, unashamedly emphasising the link.[289]

---

[288] Pang and Edwards, p227.
[289] At one point, May Pang's whispered 'John' is spooled backwards, fortuitously >

String overdubs and backing vocals softened the effect, and in the process transformed the song into something evoking the semi-elusive dream mood Lennon had in mind, the results gliding placidly above the rational world on close-ratio chords and somnambulistic cellos. Seeming to be a discovered effect, the sonic landscape was in fact the product of considerable planning, Lennon's vocals having been studiously processed with tape delay and double tracking, arousing a sense of having emanated from another reality. Re-named Walls And Bridges, a phrase picked up while idly watching television, a more enigmatic option was devised folding in his 'magic number' and leaving 'Walls And Bridges' available for the album title.[290] Serving the LP in the same way [213] Mind Games had for its parent album, by providing a glimpse of Lennon the dreamer-idealist, #9 Dream was an inevitable choice as a single, issued as soon as [245] Whatever Gets You Thru The Night had run its course. As if in mysterious synchronicity, it peaked at number 9 on *Billboard*.

John Lennon: [252] **BEEF JERKY** (*Lennon*)
Produced by John Lennon
Recorded: 23 Jul 1974; Aug 1974, Record Plant, New York
UK: 4 Oct 1974 (*Walls And Bridges* LP)
US: 23 Sep 1974 (single B-side)
John Lennon: guitar; **Jesse Ed Davis**: guitar; **Klaus Voormann**: bass; **Jim Keltner**: drums; **Arthur Jenkins**: percussion; **Steve Madaio**: trumpet; **Ron Aprea**: alto sax; **Bobby Keys**: tenor sax; **Frank Vicari**: tenor sax; **Howard Johnson**: baritone sax (the previous five musicians billed collectively as 'Little Big Horns'); **unknown**: chanted vocals, sound effects

Lennon discovered the basis of Beef Jerky during the compositional phase of [206] Tight A$, which makes it one of the oldest things on *Walls And Bridges*. From his subsequent remarks it seems he planned to write a lyric but couldn't play it and sing at the same time, so after several months gave up and registered it as an instrumental, on the same day as [247] Nobody Loves You (When You're Down and Out).[291] The most surprising thing about an otherwise routine guitar boogie is the inclusion of a stop-time riff essentially duplicating McCartney's signature lick in [225] Let Me Roll It, correct in pitch and tempo. That *Band On The Run* landed in American stores on 5 December, just two days after Beef Jerky was copyrighted, seems more than coincidence, Lennon no

---

sounding as if she's saying 'Krishna, George'.
[290] 'Walls separate people and bridges bring them together,' he later rationalised. (Interview with Michael Raile for BBC Radio 1, 27 September 1974.)
[291] Interview for San Francisco station, KSAN-FM on 21 September: 'I couldn't sing it and play it at the same time, so I never got any lyrics for it.'

doubt having heard an advance copy. (As a director of Apple, he would have been supplied with gratis copies of upcoming releases as a matter of routine.) It's not obvious what Lennon rated so highly about his unfinished track, but he clearly liked it, rehearsing it with the band ahead of *Walls And Bridges*, then on 23 July making this formal recording – doubly odd since even discounting [241] Move Over Ms. L, he already had 10 complete songs, the same number as *Imagine*, which collectively stretched to more than 41 minutes, making it theoretically surplus to requirements.

Unusually named, the title references a foodstuff consisting of sliced, dried meat, popular in North America but much less known in Lennon's native UK. Why he chose to call it thus is anyone's guess, one possible point of reference the similarity of the phrase to [211] Meat City, which like the current song, served as B-side to a hit single.

John Lennon: [253] **YA YA** (*Robinson, Dorsey, Lewis*)
Produced by John Lennon
Recorded: 1 Aug 1974, Record Plant, New York
UK: 4 Oct 1974 (*Walls And Bridges* LP)
US: 30 Sep 1974 (*Walls And Bridges* LP)
John Lennon: vocals, piano; **Julian Lennon**: drums

With Ono out of Lennon's day-to-day life, Cynthia had been in touch to discuss the possibility of son, Julian, paying a visit to his long-estranged father, something Lennon was open to, agreeing to schedule it for the school summer holidays.[292] Cynthia and 11-year-old Julian arrived on 25 July with Elton John in tow (see [245]), staying for a couple of weeks during which Lennon's priorities meant that at one point all of them had to travel to LA, while Cynthia often found herself left with Mal Evans or Jim Keltner for company.[293]

Understandably drawn to music from a young age, Julian took pleasure from accompanying his father to the studio, enjoying freedom to play around with the instruments, which one evening saw him sitting on his own bashing a snare drum with a single stick. Amused/impressed, Lennon joined in on piano, and spotting an opening called out to the tape op to press record, jamming with Julian on Ya Ya, a Lee Dorsey oldie from the Beatles' early days, suggested by the fact that it was one of Morris Levy's copyrights – Lennon still owing him three recordings consequent of their 1973 settlement. His decision

---

[292] In Britain, the school year ends during July, children being granted a six-week break before resuming at the start of September.
[293] In her book, *John*, Cynthia recounts an often testy period in America, describing their family visit to Disneyland as 'excruciating' (p340), and accusing Lennon of blanking her throughout.

to include this minute's worth of musical mucking around at the and of the album did nothing to assuage Levy's entitlement, but did delight Julian who was unaware it was on the record until he received a copy. (Lennon would record the song properly later in the year [284].) Thus, Lennon followed McCartney's curious lead in issuing a track featuring contributions from his child ([162]; [165]).

On the day Ya Ya was recorded, Yoko Ono started a week of rehearsals with the Plastic Ono Super Band along with David Spinozza (see [244]), preparing for a tour of Japan. Arriving there on 9 August, she kicked off with a festival appearance in Koriyama, Fukushima, and over the next 10 days played half a dozen gigs, taking in Tokyo and Hiroshima along the way.[294] It was at the conclusion of the tour that Ono travelled to London and met up with McCartney, reportedly giving him a message to pass on to her husband, to the effect that she wanted him back – provided he first court her with flowers and romantic gestures.

Walls And Bridges was wrapped up with a set of overdubs and mixing sessions running into the second half of August, its artwork recycling an idea first considered for *Oldies But Mouldies*, a painting Lennon had done when he was 11 showing George Robledo scoring the winning goal in the 1952 FA Cup Final.[295] Taking to the idea, Capitol's designer, Roy Kohara, created a package featuring a series of layered images cut into flaps which could be folded out to reveal new combinations – the top of one against the middle of another etc – and including several other paintings from Lennon's childhood in its outer sleeve and lyric book. The expense of the packaging was part of a wider drive to recover Lennon's popular standing after the poor reception for *Some Time In New York City* and the less than glowing notices for *Mind Games*. Promotion was key, the strategy centring on the slogan, 'Listen to…', which was in turn picked up from a marketing drive by A&M.[296] The plan worked, *Walls And*

---

[294] At this stage, Ono's recently recorded album, *A Story* (see [244]), was awaiting release, but wouldn't see light of day until 1997. In the interim she re-recorded most of the tracks for other projects.

[295] Lennon's painting was a copy of a photograph, although he used artistic licence in portraying goalkeeper, George Swindin, leaping with outstretched arms when in fact the ball crossed the goal line somewhere near his left ankle. According to Mark Lewisohn (2013, p761) it was likely copied from the *Daily Express* 5 May 1952 (ie, the Monday after the match) in which case Lennon was working from a black and white image, and despite his limited interest in the sport, gets the colours of the football kits correct. By happy fluke, in the foreground is footballer, Jackie Milburn, wearing Lennon's special number 9 on his jersey.

[296] In 1971-72 A&M started including inner sleeves in their LPs with the same large >

Bridges becoming the seventh solo Beatles album to top the US charts.

With the benefit of hindsight, *Walls And Bridges* sits as a partner to *Mind Games*, the two sharing a similar pace and for the record-buying public, covering off Lennon's 'lost weekend' period. Like *Mind Games*, it has several dark moments, Lennon's domestic troubles often revealed between its brighter spots, but unlike its predecessor benefits from the input of a confident, expressive group, comfortable in a range of styles which allow Lennon's vocals to shine. An all-round more satisfying listen, *Walls And Bridges* also happens to be the last real solo album Lennon would ever make, his recording career unknowingly coming to an end before the 1970s were even half done.

RECORD RELEASES

[245] **Whatever Gets You Thru The Night** / [252] **Beef Jerky**
(UK: 4 Oct 1974, US: 23 Sep 1974)

Walls And Bridges
(UK: 4 Oct 1974, US: 30 Sep 1974)
[246] Going Down On Love / [245] Whatever Gets You Thru The Night / [250] Old Dirt Road / [248] What You Got / [244] Bless You / [243] Scared / [251] #9 Dream / [242] Surprise, Surprise (Sweet Bird Of Paradox) / [249] Steel And Glass / [252] Beef Jerky / [247] Nobody Loves You (When You're Down And Out) / [253] Ya Ya

[251] **#9 Dream** / [248] **What You Got**
(UK: 24 Jan 1975, US: 16 Dec 1974)

---

lettering reading, 'Listen to your world'. Lennon might have seen such A&M albums by artists like Billy Preston, Cat Stevens, Joe Cocker etc.

PART 4: NOW THE DREAM'S OVER

'We signed all those silly pieces of paper when we were lads, which keep up together until '76'

Ringo Starr, 3 December 1973

Goodnight Vienna sessions: July 1974 to October 1974

After completing work on *Ringo* the previous July, Starr anticipated a financial windfall and so when Lennon decided to put his abandoned Tittenhurst Park estate on the market, he had an immediate offer – from his old pal, who took possession on 18 September. Along with the house and its extensive grounds came Ascot Sound Studios where Lennon had made much of *Imagine*, duly re-branded Startling Studios and advertised locally for hire. Starr's other business interests were meanwhile flourishing, his design concern, ROR, making news with innovatively designed and frighteningly expensive trinkets for several famous rock stars – backgammon sets, apple-shaped ornaments and even a commission from current Prime Minister, Edward Heath, who was supplied with a bespoke mirror bearing his own silhouette. With prestigious exhibitions in Paris and New York, the company was at its commercial zenith by the mid-1970s, moving in 1974 to a showroom close to the Tate Gallery, overlooking the River Thames.[297]

An unlikely businessman, Starr's personal circumstances betrayed a middle age creeping up on a millionaire lost for direction. Notwithstanding his new property, Starr spent much of the first part of 1974 in LA, hanging out with the same set of revellers Lennon had fled from in April, chief among them Harry Nilsson, Mal Evans and Keith Moon, who among various excesses, hired a plane to write Starr a 34th birthday greeting across the Hollywood sky – all a long way from Liverpool's Dingle.[298] One of Starr's other sidelines, his increasingly sporadic involvement in the movie industry, saw an attempt to write a script with Nilsson for *Ringo And Harry's Night Out* – its title flagging the self-indulgent nature of the project which was never finished.[299]

Irrespective of extra-curricular activities, Starr's real interest was recording and with the substantial success of *Ringo* fresh in his mind, he elected to repeat

---

[297] It was still trading into the 1980s, operating from a retail outlet in central London. Startling Studios also boomed, attracting a stream of bookings from artists including Judas Priest, Def Leppard, Split Enz, Whitesnake etc.

[298] Starr, Nilsson, Evans and Moon were members of 'The Hollywood Vampires', a hard-drinking gang formed by Alice Cooper, whose favourite haunt was the Rainbow on Sunset Strip. Other members included, variously, Lennon, Marc Bolan and Klaus Voormann.

[299] Starr revealed in an interview for BBC Radio 1, 6 February 1974 (broadcast 7 April), 'We're the only live people in it, the rest it is cartoon animation.' (Not, therefore, to be confused with the later animated Starr vehicle, *Scouse The Mouse*, which was scripted by Donald Pleasence.) Another contemporary Starr-Nilsson collaboration the public happily did without was the unissued track, I Want You To Sit On My Face.

the trick, pulling in favours from multiple famous friends and assembling a set of new recordings running to formula. In truth, *Ringo* had been born of no such calculation, coming about largely by chance, but having found a path to commercial success it's no surprise he attempted to repeat it – and the talent at his disposal justified the effort, producer duties naturally falling again to Richard Perry. Notable by their absence were both Harrison and McCartney, there being no hint of reunion about this latest album.

Ringo Starr: [254] **OCCAPELLA** (*Toussaint*)
Produced by Richard Perry
Recorded: 30 May 1974; 26 Sep 1974, Sunset Sound Studios, Los Angeles
UK: 15 Nov 1974 (*Goodnight Vienna* LP)
US: 18 Nov 1974 (*Goodnight Vienna* LP)
Ringo Starr: vocals, drums; **Lon Van Eaton**: guitar; **Jesse Ed Davis**: guitar; **Dr John**: electric piano; **Klaus Voormann**: bass; **Jim Keltner**: drums; **Trevor Lawrence**: saxophone; **Bobby Keys**: saxophone; **Steve Madaio**: trumpet; **Lou McCreery**: trombone; **Jimmy Gilstrap**: backing vocals; **Joe Greene**: backing vocals; **Clydie King**: backing vocals; **Ira Hawkins**: backing vocals

Two months prior to the album sessions, Starr went into Sunset Sound with his band and taped three tracks, one of which, Occapella, ultimately turned up on *Goodnight Vienna*. (The others, Parole and It's All Right, were never heard of again.) Whether or not it was intended for his next album, nothing further was done until late September when brass was added, indicating the decision to include it may have been a late one.

Like [253] Ya Ya, Occapella was sourced from Lee Dorsey, whose latter-day recording on his 1970 album, *Yes We Can*, was issued as a British A-side. What producer, Allen Toussaint, created for Dorsey was a sparse soul number which relied for its groove on a thumping, bass-heavy configuration provided by funk backing group, the Meters. By comparison, Starr's version fills out the mid-frequencies with Dr John's playful electric piano bubbling between lead guitars, while Voormann's bass manages a fair approximation of George Porter Jr's original basslines. (Interestingly Starr's recording is pitched in B flat, a semitone sharp of Lee Dorsey's model, suggesting the added brass was in the planning at the outset.) An interesting selection, the track pales for the fact that Starr's vocals are too stiff to carry it convincingly.

Ringo Starr: [255] **CALL ME** (*Starkey*)
   Produced by Richard Perry
   Recorded: 26 Jul 1974, Producer's Workshop, Los Angeles; unknown dates
      for overdubs: Sunset Sound Studios, Los Angeles
   UK: 15 Nov 1974 (*Goodnight Vienna* LP)
   US: 11 Nov 1974 (single B-side)
   Ringo Starr: vocals, drums; **Steve Cropper**: guitar; **David Foster**: piano;
   Klaus Voormann: bass, backing vocals; **Lon Van Eaton**: backing vocals;
   Derrek Van Eaton: backing vocals; **Vini Poncia**: backing vocals; **Richard Perry**: backing vocals; **Cynthia Webb**: backing vocals

The ninth and final Starkey-only copyright of his solo career, Call Me marked the start of sessions proper, with the backing track taped at Producer's Workshop across the evening of 26 July.[300] Typical of his writing style, the melody carries itself largely on a single note, underlined throughout by David Foster's off-beat piano, its horizontality no doubt suggesting the interest-sustaining key step for the final verses. It fell to the assembled crew to make something of this not very promising offer, which they attempted through some novel wordless backing vocal sections and the insertion of Voormann's descending bass run down the octave, which inevitably only works its way back to the tonic where it started. (He seems to have fluffed his second attempt, resorting to a face-saving *glissando* at 1:41, which was retained.) Archetypal filler, the track gained an airing on the B-side of Only You in November.

Ringo Starr: [256] **HUSBANDS AND WIVES** (*Miller*)
   Produced by Richard Perry
   Recorded: 29 Jul 1974; 30 Jul 1974; 1 Aug 1974; 14 Aug 1974; 20 Aug 1974;
      1 Oct 1974, Sunset Sound Studios, Los Angeles
   UK: 15 Nov 1974 (*Goodnight Vienna* LP)
   US: 18 Nov 1974 (*Goodnight Vienna* LP)
   Ringo Starr: vocals; **Lon Van Eaton**: guitar; **Vini Poncia**: guitar, backing
   vocals; **Richard Bennett**: guitar; **Tom Hensley**: electric piano; **Carl Fortina**:
   accordion

As 1973 slipped into 1974, the respective marriages of both Harrison and Starr were noticeably strained, both ex-Beatles lost in their opulent mansions, no

---

[300] Starr's singular efforts consist of [14]; [57]; [77]; [78]; [142]; [143]; [199]; [204] and the current track. Written but not released were Band Of Steel, covered by Guthrie Thomas in 1976, and a couple of outtakes from 1981, Wake Up and You Can't Fight Lightning, now available as CD bonus tracks.

longer feeling they had any obligations to fulfil. In Harrison's case this tended to manifest in a spiritual self-absorption in which he would often while away whole days in meditation, with no-one for company, least of all Pattie (see [187]), while Starr would frequently go away with his pals, aware that travelling with a wife and three children would only cramp his style. Maureen had been with Starr since 1962, a Liverpool sweetheart who became his wife in 1965. Six years his junior, she was still in her twenties and with her husband spending much of his time in LA, it was no great surprise she started to feel an attraction to her close friend, Harrison, someone who in the end was as alone as her.

Their subsequent affair was unknown to Starr until one night, when the four of them were having dinner together, and Harrison casually announced he was in love with Maureen, a bolt from the blue which engendered more disbelief in Starr than anger. The friendship they had enjoyed was rocked, which no doubt played a part in Harrison having nothing to do with Starr's current album, although they were eventually able to put it behind them. For Pattie's part, she had suspected something was going on for weeks, Maureen's frequent night visits to Friar Park causing her increasing annoyance in the face of Harrison's uninterested denials. When the truth came out she expressed her frustration by going up to the roof and tearing down an Om flag Harrison had flown, replacing it with a skull and crossbones, before going out and dying her hair red in an act of rebellion. How any of them truly felt about the looming end of their marriages is moot; within a year they would all have moved apart, as new relationships emerged.

A melodic cousin to Dylan's To Ramona (1964), Husbands And Wives was recorded by its writer, Roger Miller, in 1966, scoring him a hit on the US charts. Admired by Starr for its country flavour, the song's lyrics ('Two broken hearts lonely, looking like houses where nobody lives') held a particular relevance for him in 1974, making the recording a personal act, accounting for the fact that he spent a month working on it across five separate sessions, by far the most effort expended on anything on *Goodnight Vienna*. Slowed to a glum waltz, Starr's heartfelt arrangement dispenses with the drum kit, leaving him alone to sing out his sadness, the sincere mood not broken by Miller's risible rhyming of 'be-*lief pride*' with '*dee-cline*' in the song's main hook.

Featuring popular session man, Richard Bennett, on guitar, the track was recorded among a couple more lost outtakes, Lonely Weekends and Up The Tempo, the first of which can't have been far off release since it received two sets of overdubs in August before being permanently abandoned.

Ringo Starr: [257] **OO-WEE** (*Poncia, Starkey*)
   Produced by Richard Perry
   Recorded: 5 Aug 1974 (and subsequent dates for overdubs), Sunset Sound Studios, Los Angeles
   UK: 15 Nov 1974 (*Goodnight Vienna* LP)
   US: 18 Nov 1974 (*Goodnight Vienna* LP)
   Ringo Starr: vocals, drums; **Dennis Coffey**: guitar; **Dr John**: piano; **Klaus Voormann**: bass; **Jim Keltner**: drums; **Trevor Lawrence**: saxophone; **Bobby Keys**: saxophone; **Steve Madaio**: trumpet; **Lou McCreery**: trombone; **Vini Poncia**: backing vocals; **Clydie King and the Blackberries**: backing vocals

A variation on the Little Willie Green classic, Fever, made famous in Peggy Lee's 1958 hit version, this third Starkey-Poncia composition was recorded in a night session running into Tuesday 6 August. A piece of fun to blow away the blues of [256] Husbands And Wives, the song makes joking reference to 'Blonde Bombshell', Jean Harlow, and has a shout-out for Dr John, as he slips into an animated 16-bar piano solo. The assembled cast also includes one of Motown's legendary Funk Brothers, guitarist Dennis Coffey, whose recent cv included several hit recordings with the Temptations and the Jackson 5. Joining him were the Blackberries, also part of Motown's exceptional backroom staff, comprising Sherlie Matthews, Clydie King and Venetta Fields. Enjoyable but shallow, Oo-Wee was utilised as the B-side of [261] Snookeroo in the UK and [258] Goodnight Vienna in the US, earning Starr some lucrative songwriter's royalties.

Ringo Starr: [258] **GOODNIGHT VIENNA** (*Lennon*)
   Produced by Richard Perry
   Recorded: 6 Aug 1974; 18 Sep 1974, Sunset Sound Studios, Los Angeles
   UK: 15 Nov 1974 (*Goodnight Vienna* LP)
   US: 18 Nov 1974 (*Goodnight Vienna* LP)
   Ringo Starr: vocals, drums; **John Lennon**: piano; **Lon Van Eaton**: guitar, brass; **Jesse Ed Davis**: guitar; **Billy Preston**: clavinet; **Carl Fortina**: accordion; **Jim Keltner**: drums; **Trevor Lawrence**: saxophone; **Bobby Keys**: saxophone; **Steve Madaio**: trumpet; **Clydie King**: backing vocals; **the Blackberries**: backing vocals; **the Masst Alberts**: backing vocals[301]

According to May Pang, Lennon had what became Starr's title track available for some time before he offered it, having written it specifically for him. In her

---

[301] In the official credits for this 6 August session, no bass guitarist is nominated. It's likely, but not certain, to have been Klaus Voormann.

account Lennon was waiting for a suitable opportunity which came to pass when Starr called to ask for a contribution to the album, whereupon a demo version was hastily prepared.[302] All of this makes for a reasonable chronology except that the 23 May demo pre-dates [254] Occapella, indicating that track would also have been taped for the album, despite being an isolated recording which was subsequently put to use. While verifying the exact sequence of events is now impossible, there is little dispute that Goodnight Vienna was designed for Starr all along, unlike [200] I'm The Greatest, underlining the close friendship he and Lennon enjoyed, probably the tightest personal relationship among the four Beatles.

Goodnight Vienna was written around an idiom meaning something has come to an inevitable finishing point, Lennon claiming the phrase was a cockney expression often used by Starr's 'friend and advisor', by whom he probably meant his new manager, Londoner, Hilary Gerrard.[303] Pulling meaning from the rest of Lennon's outlandish lyric is speculative, there being no linearity to a series of bizarre characters pitched roughly in the style of mid-60s Dylan – although the essence is to cast Starr in the same lovable underdog role as Act Naturally or the movie, *Help!*. (Knowing Lennon, the butcher turning up to the party with some needles on show may be a drug reference.)

For the recording Lennon liaised with Starr in LA during Cynthia and Julian's summer visit (see [253]), taking them both along for the ride. Goodnight Vienna and [259] Only You were recorded at Sunset Sound in a single session running into the early hours, producer, Richard Perry, using Lennon's demo as a guide which he followed as closely as possible, so that the new recording adds little to what was already there. A piano-led rocker, the only technically tricky sections are the time-stop devices which deliver the song's title, where synchronisation was essential and which give the song its lumbering character. (The backing vocal credits include the Blackberries as well as the unidentified 'Masst Alberts' who likely added their parts during the brass overdub session on 18 September.[304])

---

[302] Pang claims Starr was desperate for songs, and that Lennon offered one 'he had been holding for him' (Pang and Edwards, p226).

[303] Lennon would not have been aware that before he was born his father, Alf, apparently knew English entertainer, Eric Maschwitz, who wrote a radio operetta called *Good-Night Vienna* which – via a 1932 film adaptation – may well have given rise to the term in the first place (see Lewisohn, 2013, p65). Lennon's comments on its cockney origins were made in an interview by Paul Drew for RKO Radio Networks, on 25 September. (Oddly, in the same interview Lennon remarked that he had yet to add his piano track to Goodnight Vienna, which so far as is known, was recorded seven weeks earlier.)

[304] The Massed Alberts was the name of a musical comedy group produced by George Martin in 1964 for their Parlophone single, Goodbye Dolly. (They also went by the >

When the album was released, a short 'reprise' version was included as a book-end, an idea harkening back to *Sgt Pepper*. Thanks to some creative editing, when the US single arrived several months later it contained an edit of the two to make for a 'long version'. Its number 31 showing on *Billboard* belied Lennon's hand in creating it and was comfortably Starr's poorest performing single since [46] Beaucoups Of Blues. It wasn't released in the UK.

Ringo Starr: [259] **ONLY YOU** (*Ram, Rand*)[305]
Produced by Richard Perry
Recorded: 6 Aug 1974 (and subsequent dates for overdubs), Sunset Sound Studios, Los Angeles
UK: 15 Nov 1974 (*Goodnight Vienna* LP)
US: 18 Nov 1974 (*Goodnight Vienna* LP)
Ringo Starr: vocals, drums; **John Lennon**: guitar; **Steve Cropper**: guitar; **Jesse Ed Davis**: guitar; **Billy Preston**: electric piano; **Jim Keltner**: drums; **Harry Nilsson**: backing vocals

With *Walls And Bridges* more or less finished by August, Lennon's thoughts were on the dormant *Oldies But Mouldies*, which he was now planning to complete, having negotiated the studio tapes from Phil Spector. On his mind was a list of additional songs to include in the project, among them Only You, the old Samuel 'Buck' Ram number recorded by Kentucky vocal group, the Hilltoppers, in 1955.[306] With Starr expressing a need for extra material, Lennon recognised Only You as suitable for him and generously abdicated it, helping record a version straight after [258] Goodnight Vienna. Consequently the session featured some of the same musicians, including Billy Preston beside the two ex-Beatles, with Steve Cropper and Harry Nilsson joining the ranks. Despite the stellar line-up, Lennon's arrangement relies mostly on his own rhythmic guitar strum, taking the song at a faster pace than the original, which necessitated the loss of its triplet rhythm, converting it into a novel 4/4. For Starr's benefit Lennon also recorded a guide vocal, unwittingly creating a version of his own which has since been rediscovered and released, and which could have passed for a *Rock 'N' Roll* outtake. Starr's own vocal, wrapped around a spoken-word section in lieu of an instrumental break is set to a high

---

name, the Alberts.) There is no known connection.
[305] Buck Ram wrote the song and sometimes used the professional name, Ande Rand. Starr's recording carries a joint credit – for the same person twice.
[306] Lennon had the Hilltoppers' recording in mind as opposed to the better-known Platters version, as confirmed in contemporary interviews such as that for Wisconsin-based WDGY-AM on 10 August. To muddy things further, Starr was under the impression the Mills Brothers had recorded it first, although they never did.

(for him) A major, unusually light in tone and leading Richard Perry to suppose he was trying to imitate Sinatra.[307]

This hasty session gave rise to another single for Starr, the first thing to see release from the *Goodnight Vienna* sessions. It was helped on its commercial way by a mock sci-fi video in which Starr and Nilsson risked life and limb by miming on the domed roof of Capitol's office building on LA's Vine Street, a landmark circular structure said to have been designed to resemble a pile of records on a spindle.

Ringo Starr: [260] **ALL BY MYSELF** (*Poncia, Starkey*)
Produced by Richard Perry
Recorded: 8 Aug 1974; 17 Sep 1974; 28 Sep 1974, Sunset Sound Studios, Los Angeles
UK: 15 Nov 1974 (*Goodnight Vienna* LP)
US: 18 Nov 1974 (*Goodnight Vienna* LP)
Ringo Starr: vocals, drums; **John Lennon**: guitar; **Alvin Robinson**: guitar; **Dr John**: piano; **Klaus Voormann**: bass; **Jim Keltner**: drums; **Trevor Lawrence**: saxophone; **Bobby Keys**: saxophone; **Lou McCreery**: trombone; **Steve Madaio**: trumpet; **Richard Perry**: backing vocals; **Vini Poncia**: backing vocals; **Clydie King**: backing vocals; **Lynda Lawrence**: backing vocals; **Joe Greene**: backing vocals

Lennon's LA sojourn lasted a few days, encompassing a testy family outing to Disneyland before a return to the studio to help with this latest Starkey-Poncia track, a buoyant affair which centres on the idea of emotional self-sufficiency. In an arrangement featuring an unusually crowded cast, familiar faces include gospel singer-songwriter and associate of Billy Preston, Joe Greene, as well as New Orleans guitarist, Al Robinson, and continuing the soulful influences, Lynda Lawrence – the 25-year-old who'd been Cindy Birdsong's replacement in the Supremes from 1972 to 1973. (She was introduced to the sessions by her husband, saxophonist Trevor Lawrence, who also appears here.) On an album infused with Motown personnel, further references surface in Richard Perry's deep comic interjections, obviously based on Melvin Franklin's similar contributions to several Temptations recordings, one of which, Hey Jude (1969), has a corresponding 'honky-tonk' piano introduction and is a likely model.

As for Lennon, his inaudible contribution consists of discreet strumming on acoustic guitar somewhere down in the mix, as if he were only there for the pleasure of being in the studio. In any respect he had more important things on the agenda, including plans to travel to Caribou two days later to work

---
[307] Perry, 2020.

again with Elton John, where the two were set to record a version of Lucy In The Sky With Diamonds (see also [245]).

Ringo Starr: [261] **SNOOKEROO** (*John, Taupin*)
   Produced by Richard Perry
   Recorded: 17 Sep 1974 (and other dates), Sunset Sound Studios,
      Los Angeles
   UK: 15 Nov 1974 (*Goodnight Vienna* LP)
   US: 18 Nov 1974 (*Goodnight Vienna* LP)
   Ringo Starr: vocals, drums; **Elton John**: piano, backing vocals; **Robbie Robertson**: guitar; **James Newton Howard**: synthesizer; **Klaus Voormann**: bass; **Jim Keltner**: drums; **Trevor Lawrence**: saxophone; **Bobby Keys**: saxophone; **Steve Madaio**: trumpet; **Chuck Findley**: brass; **Clydie King**: backing vocals; **Lynda Lawrence**: backing vocals; **Joe Greene**: backing vocals

At some point over the span of these sessions, Elton John and his lyricist, Bernie Taupin, took some time out to make Starr a custom track, an act of no mean generosity considering their standing at the time. (John was currently in the middle of a run of major hit singles, several of which were US chart-toppers.) Assuming John and Taupin followed their regular method the lyric will have been completed first, a quasi-biographical tale of an English working-class upbringing which, but for the finer detail, could have been an account of Starr's own childhood. Aiming for shameless commerciality, John set it to a gently rocking piano track, uncomplicated in form and mood, in the style of his own Honky Cat/Crocodile Rock, a formula pitched for success.

Continuing the conveyor-belt of stellar guests, the solo here is handled by the Band's Robbie Robertson, a quick-paced blues processed to sound 'distant', and sharing the available 16 bars with Elton John's piano section; there were few musicians who could casually attract such talent the way Starr did, a measure of the golden appeal the Beatles still held among their peers. (The decision to halve the solo was presumably made in deference to the stature of the two musicians, but might equally have been prompted by Harrison's decision to do similar on [189] The Light That Has Lighted The World.) Released in the US on the back of [262] No No Song, the track missed its moment in the spotlight, the decision not to release it as an A-side mystifying. Its subsequent issue in the UK, whereupon it failed to chart at all, perhaps shows Capitol's judgement to have been correct after all.

Ringo Starr: [262] **NO NO SONG** (*Axton*)
Produced by Richard Perry
Recorded: 18 Sep 1974 (and other dates), Sunset Sound Studios, Los Angeles
UK: 15 Nov 1974 (*Goodnight Vienna* LP)
US: 18 Nov 1974 (*Goodnight Vienna* LP)
Ringo Starr: vocals, drums, percussion; **Jesse Ed Davis**: guitar; **Nicky Hopkins**: electric piano; **Klaus Voormann**: bass; **Trevor Lawrence**: saxophone; **Bobby Keys**: saxophone; **Harry Nilsson**: backing vocals

One of three tracks from *Goodnight Vienna* whose recording dates are unconfirmed, No No Song was likely started in July or August then wrapped up with its brass overdubs on 18 September. A light-hearted calypso, the song was presumably written specifically for Starr since his is the first recording extant, although its writer, Hoyt Axton, would release his own version a few months later.[308] Probably Axton was thinking autobiographically, having battled substance misuse himself, although the irony of a lyric renouncing some of the very intoxicants Starr was currently freely enjoying in his quasi-bachelor lifestyle, was lost on no-one. (The song's candid mention of a ten-pound bag of cocaine, not enough in its day for a broadcasting ban, was mockingly acknowledged by Starr snorting in the second chorus.)

The 1940s drinking song, Skokiaan, by Zimbabwe musician, August Msarurgwa, was also current around now, having been recorded as a keyboard instrumental by Hot Butter for their second album in 1973. Their remake defined the song's main riff, which recurs almost exactly in the instrumental break of No No Song, leading to a claim from Skokiaan's copyright holders, Peter Morris Music, whereupon the track was officially re-titled as a medley of the two.

---

[308] Axton was credited as sole writer on initial releases, the name of his sometime collaborator, David Jackson, being added later. As a result of this recording, Starr accepted an invitation to appear alongside the writer in the NBC TV special, *The Hoyt Axton Country Western Boogie Woogie Gospel Rock And Roll Show*, in 1975. (Axton's mother, Mae Boren Axton, also has a place in pop history as co-writer of Elvis Presley's first hit, Heartbreak Hotel, a record Starr had certainly taken notice of in 1956.)

Ringo Starr: [263] **EASY FOR ME** (*Nilsson*)
Produced by Richard Perry
Recorded: 16 Oct 1974 (and other dates), Sunset Sound Studios,
   Los Angeles
UK: 15 Nov 1974 (*Goodnight Vienna* LP)
US: 18 Nov 1974 (*Goodnight Vienna* LP)
Ringo Starr: vocals; **Lincoln Mayorga**: piano; **unknown**: strings (arranged by Trevor Lawrence and Vini Poncia)

Next to the frivolity of [262] No No Song, the brief Easy For Me shows the serious side of Starr, this classically-pitched lullaby having been supplied to him by Harry Nilsson, its orchestral score added in a late evening session in October while the rest of the album was undergoing final mixing. A miniature account of a forlorn love affair, the song's gentle descent down the scale describes the philosophical melancholy of the lyric, which culminates with a conclusive if pessimistic update on Lennon [86]: 'Now the dream's over'. One of the most restrained recordings of Starr's career, Easy For Me has an unforced clarity about it, which makes it an album highlight, tastefully arranged and unobtrusively positioned at the end of side 2. Nilsson didn't let it go, recording it himself for *Duit On Mon Dei* in 1975 in a more dramatic interpretation, and with a minor change to the title. Although Starr guested on Nilsson's album, he does not contribute to Easier For Me, which required no drums.

Goodnight Vienna was wrapped up in October, its choice of title inevitable given Lennon's key contribution. History views the album, with its star contributors, as an attempt to stick to a formula established with the better known *Ringo*, yet this is to overlook the fact that unlike its predecessor only one 'Beatle' contribution is included, much of the rest coming from Starr's wider circle of friends and industry colleagues, or from his own pen. While not as strong as *Ringo* on a song-by-song count, the album stands on its own terms, Starr's inherent likeability giving it an enjoyable tone.

The main outstanding matter was one of packaging, *Goodnight Vienna* needing to create its own identity to minimise charges of repetition. In the early 1970s the 'space' gimmick was in vogue among popular artists, someone at Capitol suggesting Starr follow the trend, which planted a seed in his mind. Visiting Nilsson a short while later, he chanced upon some colour shots from the 1951 black and white sci-fi film, *The Day The Earth Stood Still*, and selected one on which to base his LP sleeve.[309] Thus, with actor, Michael Rennie's head covered up with a picture of Starr's, the album cover was completed – although what the imagery had to do with the musical content was another question.[310]

Between recording and releasing the set, information started to trickle out in the music press that Starr was plotting to launch his own record label. He'd recently explored the prospect of reviving Apple in partnership with Harrison, one idea being that they buy the label out, before both agreeing they were on a hiding to nothing.[311] Instead he made plans for his own Ring O'Records, which would see its first release in the new year, but wouldn't put out a second album for another two, by which time Starr's stature as a major recording artist

---

[309] A curious hangover of 1960s drug culture, popular music references to space and alien visitation manifested in several period hits including Starman (David Bowie, 1972); Rocket Man (Elton John, 1972); Supersonic Rocket Ship (the Kinks, 1972); Also Sprach Zarathustra (theme from *2001: A Space Odyssey*) (Deodato, 1973); Life On Mars (David Bowie, 1973); *Dark Side Of The Moon* (1973); the artwork for Electric Light Orchestra's *On The Third Day* (1973) and so on. Closer to the Beatles are Chris Hodge's Apple single, We're On Our Way (1972), Nilsson's Spaceman (from *Son Of Schmilsson*, 1973) and Billy Preston's instrumentals, Outa-Space (1972) and Space Race (1973).

[310] Rennie's original character was Klaatu, linking to one of Beatlemania's sillier reunion theories. After Canadian band, Klaatu, released their eponymous debut album on Capitol in 1976, rumours started to circulate that this 'mystery group' was none other than Lennon, McCartney, Harrison and Starr under a cloak of anonymity. The stories began when journalist, Steve Smith, published an article in the Rhode Island newspaper, *The Providence Daily Journal*, titled 'Could Klaatu be Beatles?', comparing the style of certain tracks to Beatles recordings and highlighting the album's 'magic, mystery' qualities. In an echo of the 1969 Paul Is Dead story, clues were then presented to flesh out a theory, the link to Starr's album cover exhibit A. The inclusion of a Morse code signal on the LP, apparently decoded as Starship Apple, offered further 'evidence', as did the similarity of one of the song titles, Sub Rosa Subway, to McCartney's *Red Rose Speedway*. (Another song title, Bodsworth Rubblesby, was deconstructed to reveal a hidden meaning: men of worth, born of quarrying – a supposed allusion to the Quarry Men.) Another track included the lyrics, 'Yeah, yeah, yeah'. Investigations into the group turned up little, which merely added to the rumour mill, crossing the Atlantic in 1977 when the 20 March edition of the *Sunday Telegraph* headlined with, 'Mystery record may be Beatles comeback', ahead of band sessions in London for a follow-up album. In fact, *Klaatu* turned out to be the work of three Canadian musicians, John Woloschuk, Dee Long and Terry Draper, who between them had written all the songs. (Practically forgotten, Klaatu's enduring claim to fame is the track, Calling Occupants Of Interplanetary Craft, which subsequently became a hit for the Carpenters.)

[311] In an interview with Nicky Horn in August, Harrison revealed that Lennon and McCartney 'were getting ready to sweep Apple Records underneath the carpet [ie, let it quietly fold], and Ringo and I were planning to try and keep it going'.

had waned.[312] *Goodnight Vienna* and its associated 45s were Starr's final releases on Apple (bar a 1975 hits package) and marked the last time he would trouble the upper ends of the charts in Britain or America.

RECORD RELEASES

[259] **Only You (And You Alone)** / [255] **Call Me**
  (UK: 15 Nov 1974, US: 11 Nov 1974)
Goodnight Vienna
  (UK: 15 Nov 1974, US: 18 Nov 1974)
  [258] Goodnight Vienna / [254] Occapella / [257] Oo-Wee / [256] Husbands And Wives / [261] Snookeroo / [260] All By Myself / [255] Call Me / [262] No No Song / [259] Only You / [263] Easy For Me / [258] Goodnight Vienna (Reprise)
[262] **No No Song** / [261] **Snookeroo**
  (US: 27 Jan 1975)
[261] **Snookeroo** / [257] **Oo-Wee**
  (UK: 21 Feb 1975)
[258] **It's All Down To Goodnight Vienna** / [257] **Oo-Wee**
  (US: 2 Jun 1975)

One Hand Clapping sessions: August 1974

Wings: [264] **SOILY** (*McCartney*)
  Produced by Geoff Emerick[313]
  Recorded: 27 Aug 1974; 8-9 October 1974, EMI Studios, London
  UK/US: unreleased
  Paul McCartney: vocals, bass; **Linda McCartney**: keyboards; **Denny Laine**: guitar, vocals; **Jimmy McCulloch**: guitar; **Geoff Britton**: drums

---

[312] Ring O'Records was never a commercial success, Starr soon tiring of the administrative side of running a label. Its first release, an instrumental version of *Ringo* by producer, David Hentschel (*Startling Music*, 1975), is its best known. Ring O'Records also reissued John Tavener's Apple album, *The Whale*, and put out a new single by friend and session supremo, Bobby Keys – but little else in its modest catalogue is memorable. The label shut up shop in 1978.

[313] Geoff Emerick is credited as 'sound engineer' on this and [265], there being no formal producer.

As a Beatle, McCartney was prolific in thinking up ideas to keep the group active and in the public eye. While initiatives like *Sgt Pepper's Lonely Hearts Club Band* and the Hey Jude promotional shoot proved successful, he could just as easily run into difficulties, particularly when trying to branch into full-scale films, *Magical Mystery Tour* being a notorious example alongside which we can nominate the troubled *Let It Be*. Despite an unenviable track record his ever-busy mind continued to come up with more of the same in his solo years, the unrealised *Rupert* and *Bruce McMouse* movies preceding the underwhelming *James Paul McCartney* television special [192]. Come 1974 he was at it again, setting to work on *One Hand Clapping*, a 50-minute documentary-style peek behind the scenes at Wings ostensibly practising in EMI's Studio 2, but in fact performing for the film.[314]

This curiously titled song was apparently written, or at least started, as part of the *Bruce McMouse* project, Soily being the name of one of five animated character mice. As a result it arrived at the right moment to enter Wings' 1972 European tour set lists, at a time when they were chronically short of material, being offered up as a thudding rocker. As recorded two years on for *One Hand Clapping*, it was faster, its intensity ratcheted up several notches by Jimmy McCulloch's fiercely riffing Stratocaster achieving a sound approaching that of a full-throttle Rolling Stones. That the lyrics were essentially a string of meaningless words hardly mattered, Soily succeeding through increasingly energised stage performances for the next few years, where it served as a rousing curtain closer.

This studio version was taped on day two of filming and although particulars are sketchy, appears to be one of seven attempts. According to Madinger and Easter (p196), the track was recorded again on 8-9 October, the re-make being dubbed over the footage, accounting for the discrepancies between the audio and visuals. If so, this is its last known studio attempt, the song's strength as a live number seeing it pulled from *Wings Over America* for the B-side of [29] Maybe I'm Amazed (1977). The stage rendition, recorded at the McNichols Sports Arena in Denver on 7 June 1976 is therefore definitive.

Wings: [265] **I'LL GIVE YOU A RING** (*McCartney*)
Produced by Geoff Emerick
Recorded: 28 Aug 1974, EMI Studios, London
UK/US: unreleased
Paul McCartney: vocals, piano

---

[314] The session has been said to be in preparation for a tour, although they would not actually appear on stage for another year. Elsewhere it's been asserted that McCartney was planning a 'live' studio album. If so, it's odd that very little new material was performed.

One of the more intriguing sequences in *One Hand Clapping* is the five-and-a-half minutes of McCartney running through a series of songs alone at the piano. His selections are particularly interesting, including a snippet of Let's Love, an earnest ballad he'd written for Peggy Lee, whose 1958 recording of Fever had made a lasting impression on McCartney in his teens. (Lee made Let's Love the title track of her next album.) In full flow, McCartney proceeds to improvise a short number which has gone down as Sitting At The Piano, followed by a longer piece, generally known as All Of You, which Madinger and Easter reckon to also be improvised.[315]

The sequence rounds off with the fully-formed I'll Give You A Ring, something McCartney had recently come up with and which also circulates as a home demo probably dating to early in 1974. (It was conceivably taped during sessions for *McGear* (see [238]).) A breezy dance around the keys, the song resists coming to its expected conclusion by virtue of McCartney playing a bass E against a high C chord, proceeding to roll away to a G7, giving the song a sense of perpetual movement. When the progression finally gets to a firm cadence, it does so through an emphatic three-step change probably borrowed from Stevie Wonder's I Was Made To Love Her (1967). Written in the old-time show tune style (compare [192] Gotta Sing, Gotta Dance) the song's romantic slant is accented in the dual meaning of its sly title, the lyrics revealing that McCartney is only looking to chat – as opposed to the hint of a proposal. The version captured on *One Hand Clapping* has the song essentially complete, but no other studio recording is known from the era, leaving the song unheard until McCartney was working on *Tug Of War* in 1982, whereupon it came out as the B-side to Take It Away.

Predictably, *One Hand Clapping* was another of McCartney's no-shows when fate conspired to effect a change in Wings' line-up after drummer, Geoff Britton, quit the group at the start of 1975. Thus, the film promptly became unusable, featuring as it did plentiful footage of the judo-suited Britton, including interview and drum solo spot. It's unfortunate since *One Hand Clapping* offers a more authentic impression of Wings at work than had the archly choreographed *James Paul McCartney*, which was coloured throughout by a distinct air of trying too hard to please. *One Hand Clapping* was the *real* Wings, working together regardless of the camera crew, and giving the viewer a sense of being there with them in the moment. Fans should seek out the expanded 2010 reissue of *Band On The Run* where the whole film is available as bonus material.

---

[315] p197. If it is a spur-of-the-moment invention, it's exceptional. The fact that the lyric begins, 'When I get feverish high' suggests as much, there being a spontaneous association with Peggy Lee's old hit.

Dark Horse sessions:
April 1974, August 1974 to October 1974

Harrison's slow release schedule, which had produced only one studio album since 1970, belied a musician constantly busy on a range of side projects which would continue to occupy him through 1974. A February visit to India, primarily to visit Ravi Shankar's new home (see [272]), inspired some ambitious plans for the coming year and served also as a break from his failing marriage to Pattie, which by summer would be all but over. Most significantly, like Starr, he was in the process of setting up his own label, diverting a couple of tentative Apple projects into his newly conceived Dark Horse company, much of 1973 into 1974 spent on recording an album with Splinter, a two-piece outfit featuring Bill Elliott (see [122]), and *Shankar Family & Friends* by Ravi, who was inevitably signed up. Harrison launched Dark Horse in May, naming it after a song he was about to record [274], its first product arriving on the market in late summer.[316] These and other goings on would feed into Harrison's writing and consequently colour his next set of recordings which, over the following six months, generated his most disparaged album, which across piecemeal songs, charted a hectic 12 months of his life.

George Harrison: [266] **HARI'S ON TOUR (EXPRESS)** (*Harrison*)
Produced by George Harrison
Recorded: 23 Apr 1974, Friar Park Studios, Henley-on-Thames
UK: 20 Dec 1974 (*Dark Horse* LP)
US: 9 Dec 1974 (*Dark Horse* LP)
George Harrison: guitar; **Robben Ford**: guitar; **Roger Kellaway**: piano; **Max Bennett**: bass; **John Guerin**: drums, percussion (?); **Tom Scott**: saxophone

---

[316] Dark Horse Records was run in partnership with A&M, with the expectation that Harrison would transfer to the label when his EMI contract expired in January 1976. Its logo was a depiction of Uchchaihshravas, the seven-headed flying horse of Hindu belief, said to have appeared supernaturally during the 'churning of the Ocean of Milk' (c/w Harrison's Sour Milk Sea), switched from its traditional white representation to a 'dark' black. Better received than Ring O'Records, Dark Horse was nonetheless something of a vanity project, only Splinter achieving any meaningful sales. (A few other acts were signed up over the following year including ex-Wings guitarist, Henry McCullough, plus Attitudes, a four-piece band made up of LA session men featuring drummer, Jim Keltner. None other than Splinter had a hit and Dark Horse's roster was put out to pasture in 1977.)

The April session for Hari's On Tour was a spur-of-the-moment one, Harrison chancing to see Joni Mitchell play the third of three nights at London's New Victoria Theatre in central London, and inviting her five-piece backing group, LA Express, to come to Friar Park the following day. (Harrison was on friendly terms with saxophonist, Tom Scott, having worked with him on *Shankar Family & Friends*.) Jamming in Harrison's home studio, the team found this riff-based instrumental by exploring a guitar pattern which over the course of a couple of hours consolidated into a formal structure. In the end running close to five minutes, the track has little going for it and other than the interest of Harrison's lead guitar running in unison with Scott's sax, soon drags. (Like Harrison's previous instrumental jams (see [59]), he took the copyright entirely for himself.) The track might have been better served with the addition of a lyric, had Harrison been inclined, but as it was, it worked as an overture on his North American Tour at the close of the year, in respect of which it was given its punning title.[317] Thus, although there was a certain logic to using it as the opener to *Dark Horse*, the song has a sense of filler about it which is hard to get past. (The title song [274] would have been a better choice.)

George Harrison: [267] **SIMPLY SHADY** (*Harrison*)
Produced by George Harrison
Recorded: 23 Apr 1974, Friar Park Studios, Henley-on-Thames
UK: 20 Dec 1974 (*Dark Horse* LP)
US: 9 Dec 1974 (*Dark Horse* LP)
George Harrison: vocals, guitar; **Robben Ford**: guitar; **Roger Kellaway**: piano, organ (?); **Max Bennett**: bass; **John Guerin**: drums; **Tom Scott**: saxophone

Simply Shady was written in Bombay during Harrison's February visit and records the early fall-out of his separation from Pattie, a situation he dealt with through extravagant intake of alcohol – whole bottles of brandy his preferred tipple. Decamping for India gave him the perspective he needed, this troubled account of what he'd left behind pouring out of him a safe distance from home and the attendant temptations of the music business. (He brought back a demo of the song, recorded at the tranquil Lake Palace Hotel in Udaipur.) Sober enough to take an objective view, Harrison apparently hadn't forgotten the troubles surrounding his previous Indian visit in 1968, slipping Lennon's period piece, Sexy Sadie into the lyrics, in a *White Album*-style exercise in song referencing.[318]

---

[317] Harrison Tour', with LA 'Express' appended.
[318] In 1968 Harrison dropped Ob-La-Di, Ob-La-Da into the lyric of Savoy Truffle, recorded shortly after the multi-cited Glass Onion, six months after his and Lennon's >

Recorded with LA Express before their departure for a date in Denver, Simply Shady shows Harrison revelling in the lead guitar role, including use of the volume swell pedal in each of the three verses, giving his riffs a distinctive 'backwards' feel. The condition of Harrison's voice on *Dark Horse* was the cause of much criticism when the album appeared in December, its gravel texture an unintended side-effect of his recent self-abuse. In this case it lends the track a pained sense of world-weariness, landing somewhere between soul and bar-room blues, which works to the song's advantage – and to judge by the particularly rough timbre, may have been dubbed on at some unknown point later in the year, possibly at A&M, in late October.

George Harrison: [268] **BYE BYE, LOVE** (*Bryant, Bryant, Harrison*)
Produced by George Harrison
Recorded: Aug-Sep 1974, Friar Park Studios, Henley-on-Thames
UK: 20 Dec 1974 (*Dark Horse* LP)
US: 9 Dec 1974 (*Dark Horse* LP)
George Harrison: vocals, guitar, electric piano, bass, drums, 'Rhythm Ace' drum machine

Having banked the previous two tracks in April, Harrison appears to have done little on *Dark Horse* until August, the intervening months having seen Pattie finally up and leave him, packing a case and flying to the States on 4 July.[319] A week later she was with Eric Clapton, who'd been in love with her for years [59] and was currently on a seven-week tour of North America which ended in early August, at which point Pattie returned to England to pick up her things. Right around then Harrison recorded the current song, marking the final period of his marriage and wishing both Pattie and Eric well, which to judge by his subsequent remarks, was sincere.[320]

Bye Bye Love was one of the early rock and roll classics issued in Britain in the period just prior to Harrison joining the Quarry Men, and as such held particular memories. His changes to the fatalistic lyric make it clear who he's singing about, but most telling is the dropping the key from A major to minor, an uneasy switch which implies it was more than a throwaway. (Here,

---

disillusioned return to the UK. Sexy Sadie's name was originally Harrison's suggestion, and curiously had also been mentioned in song by Starr [197].
[319] *Wonderful Tonight*, p184.
[320] Asked how he felt in a press conference in Beverly Hills on 23 October, Harrison remarked, 'I'm very happy about it. I'd rather she was with him than some dope'. Pattie and Eric would marry in March 1979, with Harrison, Starr and McCartney at the reception, where they jumped on stage and played together for the first time since January 1970.

Harrison followed both Lennon [244] and Starr [256] in recording a song lamenting his marital problems, all in the space of a few weeks.)

Musically crabby, the track was fundamentally personal, taped alone with multiple overdubs including a drum machine capable of playing a pre-set rhythm, Harrison lacking McCartney's prowess around the kit. Why he chose to issue it to the world is a matter for conjecture, the probable explanation a desire to take ownership of the situation and pre-empt speculation as to whether he was, in fact, heart-broken – which he wasn't. In a turn of events which would have made him smile, when he submitted his cover art to EMI he included among the hand-written credits, the massage, 'and Pattie + Eric Clapton' as an adjunct to the song title. Misinterpreted by company execs, a credit for Clapton's supposed participation was added after clearance was sought from his label, RSO.

George Harrison: [269] **FAR EAST MAN** (*Harrison, Wood*)
   Produced by George Harrison
   Recorded: Aug-Sep 1974, Friar Park Studios, Henley-on-Thames;
      31 Oct 1974, A&M Studios, Hollywood
   UK: 20 Dec 1974 (*Dark Horse* LP)
   US: 9 Dec 1974 (*Dark Horse* LP)
   George Harrison: vocals, guitar; **Billy Preston**: electric piano; **Willie Weeks**: bass; **Andy Newmark**: drums; **Tom Scott**: saxophone

During 1973 Harrison struck up a friendship with Faces songwriter-guitarist, Ronnie Wood, one of several British rock personalities of the day, whose paths continually crossed in and out of the studio.[321] Harrison invited Wood to stay as his guest during the autumn, and in the restful surroundings of Friar Park, with its secluded grounds, it was perhaps inevitable that Wood took a shine to Pattie with whom he had a brief fling right in front of Harrison. If Ono had a liberal view of marriage, content to provide Lennon with another lover, it was no less so with Harrison, who in the spirit of 1960s free love, returned the compliment by sleeping with Wood's wife, Krissy, none of which seemed to particularly trouble any of them, until Wood had the temerity to go public on it. (All of this of course taking place *before* Harrison's indiscretion with Mrs Starkey [256].)

Harrison and Wood jammed together in 1974, probably at Wood's home in Richmond, Surrey, where they came up with a modest instrumental, a part-song which like Harrison's other main collaborative effort [35], was built on a

---

[321] The Faces were primarily an album band, their 1971 offering, *Long Player*, including a live recording of [29] Maybe I'm Amazed, on which Wood did a fair imitation of McCartney's guitar solos.

series of warm major sevenths. It might have been forgotten but for the fact that Wood was in the process of extracting himself from the Faces for a solo career, and so wanted the track finished off with some lyrics. Harrison came up with the goods on a car journey over, basing them on a slogan he'd seen printed on one of Wood's T-shirts, before developing the song yet further with a middle eight concocted during the session. Apart from doing his mate a favour, Harrison's contributions had a beneficial effect: he got to know a couple of Wood's session guys, drummer, Andy Newmark, and bassist, Willie Weeks, who together would form the back line of Harrison's band for the rest of 1974.

Realising Far East Man was at least as good as anything else he had, Harrison opted to capture his own version with Newmark and Weeks requisitioned for the job, which consequently has much in common with Wood's recording, including Harrison's high vocal line in parallel octaves, indicating that at this stage, his voice was in decent shape.[322] Oddly, what got lost between the two recordings was the fingerprint slide guitar, which on Wood's version is endlessly riffing, carrying the melody on a bluesy breeze; in remaking the song, Harrison cedes ground to the backing group, bringing up Far East Man's jazzy elements but denying it incision, the overall effect being to lower the musical definition.

Old-time luminary, Frank Sinatra, had covered Harrison's Something in 1970, after which he heaped extravagant praise on the song before each stage performance. Ever open to a wry joke, Harrison can be heard encouraging the legendary crooner to include Far East Man on his next live album, presumably an ad-libbed gag which he decided to leave in the final mix. More relevant are Tom Scott's saxophone bars at the other end of the song, paying tribute to Jr. Walker, whose 1969 Motown hit, What Does It Take (To Win Your Love) is quoted for fun, on a recording replete with musical points of reference.

George Harrison: [270] **MAYA LOVE** (*Harrison*)
  Produced by George Harrison
  Recorded: Aug-Sep 1974, Friar Park Studios, Henley-on-Thames;
    31 Oct 1974, A&M Studios, Hollywood
  UK: 20 Dec 1974 (*Dark Horse* LP)
  US: 9 Dec 1974 (*Dark Horse* LP)
  George Harrison: vocals, guitar, percussion; **Billy Preston**: electric piano; **Willie Weeks**: bass; **Andy Newmark**: drums; **Tom Scott**: saxophone

---

[322] This novel vocal arrangement was probably suggested by the Band's circa 1970 recording, Bessie Smith, not yet in full circulation but featuring Robbie Robertson's high line locked above Rick Danko's low lead.

Another track which started life as a guitar instrumental, Maya Love may have been spun off [266] Hari's On Tour (Express), which carries a similar riff to that heard in the instrumental break here – although this could be a coincidence of the song's composition on slide guitar, which with its open tuning, naturally lends to certain melodic patterns. (Musically, Maya Love may be seen as the third part of a trilogy, starting with [179] Sue Me, Sue You Blues.) A philosophical stance on romance, Maya Love emphasises transience, an analogue to the passing of the days and drifting of the clouds which, given its timing, is so emotionally detached as to border on the heartless. Birthed by his Krishna-Hindu outlook, the song is the second in Harrison's *oeuvre* to invoke the concept of Maya (see [62]), Sanskrit for 'that which is not' and implying something lacking its own essence.[323] The curiosity is that in penning such an incorporeal text, Harrison elected to drop in a flippant link back to the human world, starting each verse by knowingly singing the title of McCartney's [178] My Love.[324] The track was a used as a B-side to This Guitar (Can't Keep From Crying) in 1975, the last 45 released on Apple which has the ignominy of being the first Beatle single to fail to chart on both sides of the Atlantic.

George Harrison: [271] **HIS NAME IS LEGS (LADIES AND GENTLEMEN)**
(*Harrison*)
Produced by George Harrison
Recorded: Aug-Sep 1974, Friar Park Studios, Henley-on-Thames
UK/US: unreleased
George Harrison: vocals, guitar, piano; **'Legs' Larry Smith**: vocals; **David Foster**: tack piano; **Billy Preston**: electric piano; **Willie Weeks**: bass; **Andy Newmark**: drums

Keen to fend off accusations that his music was over-earnest, Harrison liked to record the occasional eccentricity, reminding the world that he did, after all, retain a sense of humour. This comedy skit was written on Harrison's Steinway grand at the end of 1973, its lyric centred on the sayings and doings of musician and one-time Beatle friend, 'Legs' Larry Smith, formerly of the Bonzo Dog Doo-Dah Band and latterly reintroduced to Harrison's orbit by mutual friend, Terry Doran. Something of a private joke, the song's referential word-play went over the heads of listeners not personally acquainted with

---

[323] Which he expounded on during an interview by Levi Booker for Houston-based KLOL-FM (26 November 1974): 'Maya Love is something which is, I love you *if*... I love you *when*... I love you *but*...'
[324] Harrison's hand-written lyrics, reproduced in *I, Me, Mine* (p271) have the song structured in two halves, the first of which is titled 'My Love', intended to be sung that way before transitioning to 'Maya Love' for the second section.

Smith's whimsical personality – which in practice meant nearly everyone who heard it.

Recorded at Friar Park, the track features David Foster on a piano adapted to achieve a thinner sound by affixing metal tacks to its felt pads, and as a finishing touch, a rambling monologue by Smith himself mixed low and sent to the stereo extremes. (The experience of hearing his lengthy chatter behind the circulating chords as the song winds down is unintentionally reminiscent of the closing section of I Am The Walrus.) Overlooked when *Dark Horse* was released, His Name Is Legs was recalled and overdubbed with a brass section by Tom Scott and Chuck Findley in LA in June 1975 in readiness for *Extra Texture (Read All About It)*, where it was used to round off side 2.

George Harrison: [272] **IT IS 'HE' (JAI SRI KRISHNA)** (*Harrison*)
>Produced by George Harrison
>Recorded: Aug-Sep 1974, Friar Park Studios, Henley-on-Thames;
> 30 Oct 1974, A&M Studios, Hollywood
>UK: 20 Dec 1974 (*Dark Horse* LP)
>US: 9 Dec 1974 (*Dark Horse* LP)
>**George Harrison**: vocals, guitar, gubgubbi, Moog synthesizer; **Billy Preston**: piano; **Willie Weeks**: bass; **Chuck Findley**: flute; **Jim Horn**: flute; **Tom Scott**: flute; **Andy Newmark**: drums; **Emil Richards**: wobble board, bells (?)

Harrison's excursion to India in early 1974, as a guest of Ravi Shankar, allowed him an opportunity to visit the ancient sites and holy shrines of Vrindavan, where Krishna is said to have lived some millennia ago. Enthralled by the experience of walking unrecognised among throngs of chanting, saffron-robed devotees, Harrison was deeply moved, the more so after his guide took him to visit the local temples where he underwent something of a transcendental episode.[325]

Early next morning, Harrison participated in a group *bhajan*, which went on for several uninterrupted hours, after which the suggestion was put to him that he turn the chant into a formal song, It Is 'He' duly developed by incorporating the words of an old hymn to Radha-Krishna, the essence of which is to offer up all glories (Jai Sri Krishna translating into English as, approximately, 'Victory To Krishna'). Although Harrison's post-Beatles output is liberally infused with Hindu mystical elements, he rarely set his music in the tradition so overtly as here, only the unreleased [68] Om Hare Om (Gopala Krishna) bearing any real comparison – which perhaps explains why he elected to intersperse his *bhajan* with orthodox 'popular' verses, as if mindful

---

[325] For his impressions of Vrindavan, see *I, Me, Mine*, p296-297.

not to over-stretch his mass audience. (In this respect Harrison betrays the fact that, as with his hesitancy over whether to put out [34] My Sweet Lord, he was aware than not all of his fan-base was on the same spiritual journey.)

One of the benefits of having his own studio was that Harrison had space to work on song arrangements in a suitably relaxed setting, typically aided by window views onto his lush estate and the burning of mood-setting incense, aparajita being his preferred choice. Here, he achieved an authentic sound-mood by use of the obscure Indian gubgubbi, essentially a drum with a string attached, which can be plucked to provide a basic drone. It wasn't until Harrison left for LA later in the year that he finished the recording by adding dancing Krishna-esque flutes from three players, one of whom, Tom Scott, brought along his associate, percussionist Emil Richards – the two having worked together with Ravi Shankar as far back as 1968.[326] Richards' contribution of wobble board, and likely the shimmering bells which sound in the song's verses, completes the picture, It Is 'He' by far the most celebratory thing Harrison had yet recorded.

George Harrison: [273] **I DON'T CARE ANYMORE** (*Harrison*)
Produced by George Harrison
Recorded: Oct 1974 (?), Friar Park Studios, Henley-on-Thames
UK: 6 Dec 1974 (single B-side)
US: 18 Nov 1974 (single B-side)
George Harrison: vocals, guitar; **unknown**: Jew's harp, percussion

Recorded under time constraints, this track probably dates to the second half of October, before Harrison embarked on his North American Tour. Custom-made for deployment as a B-side, the song was knocked off in a casual manner, which Harrison claimed consisted of a single run-through.[327] Assuming this is correct, he can't have recorded the song alone since around half a minute in, he asks the studio engineer to turn up the Jew's harp in his headphones – which he couldn't simultaneously be playing, and which could scarcely have been on its own pre-recorded track. Likewise the percussion effect, sounding like someone knocking on the hollow body of an acoustic guitar, while technically possible, was probably not him either.

With its extraneous chatter and a vocal error at the start of the third verse, Harrison's commitment to this quasi-country number is betrayed by its title.[328]

---

[326] On the soundtrack to *Charly*, the Ralph Nelson-directed drama scored by Shankar.
[327] 'I did it in one take' – interview by Timothy White for *Musician* magazine, November 1987, p65.
[328] The garbled opening dialogue, 'An old cowpoke went riding out one cold December day' is a twisted quotation from Stan Jones' 1940s 'Western' song, (Ghost) Riders In >

Thrown away as intended, on the B-side of the album's first trailer single [274], the divergence of the UK and US release schedules saw it coupled with [228] Ding Dong in Britain, a waste of what might, with a little more attention, have been a meaningful addition to his period catalogue, with a lyric touching again on the complexities of extra-marital affairs.

George Harrison: [274] **DARK HORSE** (*Harrison*)
Produced by George Harrison
30 Oct 1974; 31 Oct 1974, Nov 1974 (?), A&M Studios, Hollywood
UK: 20 Dec 1974 (*Dark Horse* LP)
US: 18 Nov 1974 (single A-side)
George Harrison: vocals, guitar; **Robben Ford**: guitar; **Billy Preston**: electric piano; **Willie Weeks**: bass; **Chuck Findley**: flute; **Jim Horn**: flute; **Tom Scott**: flute; **Andy Newmark**: drums; **Emil Richards**: percussion; **Jim Keltner**: hi-hats; **Lon Van Eaton**: backing vocals; **Derrek Van Eaton**: backing vocals

The fact that the new album was completed against the clock is revealed by this, the title track, which was recorded in LA while Harrison was already in rehearsals for the tour. Conscious of time, and seeing an opportunity for the band to learn their way around the song, Harrison went for a 'live' studio version in sessions which also allowed for final touches to a number of others ([188]; [269]; [270]; [272]). Dark Horse was still incomplete just 48 hours before the tour was due to open in Vancouver, and so Harrison was forced to squeeze in one further studio date for vocal additions (including contributions from Lon and Derrek Van Eaton) with the 45 set to be issued on 18 November, the late rush of which accounts for the fact that of all the *Dark Horse* tracks, this shows his vocals at their most ragged.

Dark Horse was written at Friar Park in 1973, Harrison having stayed up all night when lyrics started to come to him from nowhere. Initially unsure of the meaning of the term 'dark horse' to say nothing of the following 'automatically written' line concerning a race track, he rationalised it the following day along the lines of, 'I'll admit my sins, but I was just born into it.'[329] Upon this premise the rest of the largely self-descriptive lyric was shaped, outlining Harrison as a character, according to Simon Leng, 'one step ahead of his detractors, triumphing with quicker feet and better gags'.[330] (The state of his vocal chords was such that the lyrics are sometimes hard to decipher, his penchant for assembling words as if to deliberately mislead the ear (eg, 'You

---

The Sky: A Cowboy Legend.
[329] Interview by Alan Freeman, 18 October 1974 for US radio.
[330] Leng, p155.

knew where I was and when') adding to its mischievous spirit.)

Extending from its opening two-chord exchange, Dark Horse proceeds around the 'Circle of Fifths' for its chorus, F through to A, a pattern Harrison had previously explored in a different key and tempo in the middle section of Here Comes The Sun. (Harrison initially pitched Dark Horse in G before raising it to A and again to B flat, then finally to B, edging his capo up the fretboard to help his struggling vocals.) Sportingly self-deprecating, this was the last track recorded in these sessions, but the first to be released, the US single landing on the day Harrison played two shows in Denver. A minor hit over Christmas, the track became – due to its associated album and tour – one of Harrison's higher profile recordings, making it an obligatory inclusion on his 1976 *Best Of* collection, where superior material such as [43] All Things Must Pass and [35] I'd Have You Anytime were considered surplus to requirements.

The first two thirds of 1974 had been a period of extremes for Harrison, who besides recording *Dark Horse* had lost a wife, launched a record label and found time to produce records for Splinter and Ravi Shankar. In this context it's astonishing that instead of taking a much-needed break before embarking on his epic North American trip, he chose to help out with a promotional tour for Ravi Shankar, bringing more than a dozen Indian musicians to England, rehearsing them, then appearing with them at an historic performance at London's Royal Albert Hall, after which Shankar headed off to Europe.[331] In truth it was a distraction Harrison could have done without, the *Dark Horse* sessions, which began way back in April having generated a sum total of seven LP tracks, a lean tally which had to be boosted by the addition of a couple of older cuts with Starr on drums ([188] and [228]). Still *Dark Horse* was so much behind schedule that Harrison was forced to finish it in LA, meaning it wouldn't be in the shops when he took to the stage.

In packaging the album, Harrison and designer, Tom Wilkes, built the cover around an April 1956 photograph of Liverpool Institute's school cohort – a photo which in its uncropped state included a 13-year-old McCartney way off to the left.[332] With a careful cut-and-paste, Harrison placed his own image top centre, face blued-out like Krishna, directly above his old headmaster, John 'Jack' Edwards, against whom Harrison continued to bear a grudge, depicting

---

[331] Recordings from Shankar's tour were released by Dark Horse Records in 1976 as *Ravi Shankar's Music Festival From India*. The opening Royal Albert Hall show was also filmed.

[332] The large, panoramic photograph also included Mike McCartney, Neil Aspinall, Ivan Vaughan and some of the future Quarry Men.

him with Capitol Records' bulls eye-like logo in the middle of his chest.[333] The resultant image was overlaid onto a painting of a lotus flower floating before the Himalayas, the effect of the crowd amassed on an open landscape resembling the design on *Sgt Pepper*. For the inner sleeve, Harrison's do-it-yourself approach was even more readily apparent, the credits being drawn out in felt pen – an idea which also has a precedent: the second disc of *Some Time In New York City*.

Like the rest of the album, the artwork was submitted at the last minute, Harrison heading to Los Angeles in the middle of October for a couple of weeks' tour rehearsal. Naturally he wasted no time visiting his Dark Horse office in LA, where for the first time he met one of its staff, the striking, 25-year-old Olivia Arias who he'd previously spoken to only on the telephone. Another turning point in a remarkable year, he fell for her instantly, their relationship starting at once and leading, come 1978, to marriage.

Harrison's plans for what become his North American Tour had been formulated through the year, his initial idea being to play eight or ten shows, travelling between cities by train. (He'd also mused, then abandoned, the thought of playing some dates in the UK.) By the time he landed, the project had mushroomed to an itinerary of some 45 concerts distributed across the width of the continent, with a coterie of 22 other musicians, plus assorted personnel along for the ride. When the tour was formally announced it was lost on no-one that this was the first time since 1966 that a Beatle had played on such a scale, and at a press conference on 24 October at the Beverly Wilshire hotel, Harrison was forced to address reporters' continual questions about the prospects of his old group re-forming, which at length tested his patience. His widely reported remark that he'd prefer Willie Weeks as his bassist over McCartney, had as much to do with supporting his current band as a repudiation of his former colleague, but flagged something of a sour tone which would surface intermittently throughout the coming two months.

The question of why Harrison undertook the tour at all, given his widely understood aversion to playing live, has never been fully answered. Having left England in mid-October he wouldn't be finished until days before Christmas – a gruelling schedule reminiscent of the Beatles' hectic tours a decade previously – except this time, there weren't four of them to help one another out, and no Brian Epstein to organise things. Escapism might have played a part, 1974 having been a particularly turbulent year. Then there was the revenue to be earned, and the chance to promote his album and label – the

---

[333] Close scrutiny shows all of the teachers similarly adorned. One has (Lennon's) Bag Productions written on his shirt, others Parlophone and Dark Horse logos, despite this being an Apple record. Harrison's old art teacher, who he liked, was allowed the Om symbol.

decision to focus on North America perhaps underlining his commercial interest. The closest Harrison came to explaining his thoughts was in the same press conference, 'I was turning into a lawyer, or an accountant. I wanted to get back to being a musician', which makes some sense after years of preoccupation with legal and contractual wrangling (see [179]). Unacknowledged but likely another factor was that Harrison had watched Dylan embark on *his* first tour in eight years at the start of 1974, which attracted strong reviews and an impressive live album.[334] Irrespective of Harrison's rationale, the project took some guts, this being the first time other than the Bangla Desh concerts that he'd gone out on his own, leading the stage as principal headliner, all eyes on him. (It's perhaps no coincidence that his co-stars here, Billy Preston and Ravi Shankar, had also appeared at Bangla Desh.) Events kicked off at the Canada Pacific Coliseum in Vancouver on 2 November, the early sequencing of the show seeing Harrison more or less alternate with his support acts, possibly a strategy to give his voice a rest between songs but making for a disjointed presentation. After some trial and error the show sequence was re-jigged into a more satisfactory arrangement which allowed Harrison to present his songs in 'sets', although the extravagant indulgence of Ravi Shankar and his troupe of Indian musicians invariably caused grumblings among the assembled audiences.[335]

The second show, 4 November, was moved to Seattle after Portland authorities refused to host it, allowing Harrison to revisit the Seattle Center Coliseum where the Beatles had played in both 1964 and 1966. Then it was south to another old haunt, Cow Palace in San Francisco for a fund-raiser for the Haight-Ashbury Medical Clinic, then another at The Forum in LA (with Dylan in attendance) in aid of the Self Realisation Fellowship, founded by Harrison's friend, Pararanz Yoga Anda, which was scheduled to be filmed by David Acomba for a proposed live movie and album.

The obvious problem with Acomba's plan was that Harrison's voice had been deteriorating, putting paid to thoughts of reprising the *Bangla Desh* film and LP. In an effort to nurse his larynx, Harrison resorted to gargling a mixture of honey, vinegar and warm water before each show, but the truth is, his voice was by now shot. Another trick he'd picked up from Dylan was the art of re-inventing his songs in different styles and tempos (see also [268] Bye Bye, Love), which helped him get around his vocal troubles but disappointed many fans hoping to hear the old hits the way they remembered them.

---

[334] *Before The Flood*, number 3 on *Billboard* and number 8 in the UK.
[335] Harrison went to great lengths to promote the Indian part of the show, prostrating himself before Shankar on stage and giving the musicians extensive coverage in the tour programme, including individual biographies, diagrams of their instruments and even a glossary of terms.

The retrospective take on the North American Tour is of failure, a view formed largely as a consequence of a hostile write-up of the first few shows by Ben Fong-Torres for *Rolling Stone* in which he quoted nothing but critical opinion and ridiculed even the Om sign.[336] In truth as the entourage made its way down the West Coast, inland to Arizona and up to Salt Lake City on 16 November, the show was attracting significantly more positive notices, a reporter from *Seattle Post Intelligencer* remarking on 'the fullest, finest explosion of rock 'n' roll that I think I have ever heard', and the *Salt Lake Tribune* commending 'one of the most interesting, most entertaining and most memorable shows ever put on in Utah'.[337]

This, to an extent, reflects the duality at the heart of Harrison's concert set which, while including four much-appreciated Beatles songs (one of which was Lennon-McCartney's In My Life) featured just two from the lauded *All Things Must Pass* ([34]; [61]) and three as-yet unknowns from *Dark Horse* ([266]; [270]; [274]). Opinion seemed to divide on whether the good outweighed the average, the media debate still in flow as the show rolled relentlessly on, city to city, drifting forever east towards it ultimate destination in New York. After Jim Keltner joined the party on 27 November, the band travelled to Atlanta, Harrison taking to the stage on Thanksgiving at the same moment Lennon was playing with Elton John, a divide of 870 miles separating them, and then it was on to Chicago for two gigs back-to-back.[338] In a sense, the tour had been running since September when Ravi and his Indian troupe first hit the road, and the strain of constant travelling was starting to tell on Shankar, now well into his 50s. On 30 November he was taken ill with a suspected heart attack, causing him to miss most of the remaining dates – a blow personally to Harrison who was forced to continue without his close friend. (Shankar was able to re-join the tour a few days before it ended.)

A brighter turn of events was the long-awaited release of *Dark Horse* on 9 December, the album landing in the shops more than a month after the tour had started, and with only 11 days left to run. Tour and album were supposed to be mutually promoting but the record didn't chart on *Billboard* until the new year – and not at all in Britain where little effort was expended on marketing,

---

[336] His notorious review was written roughly 10 shows in, and published under the title, *George Harrison: Lumbering In The Material World*. The cover date was 19 December but it had been available several weeks before. (*Rolling Stone* seemed to revel in going on the offensive, famously beginning a review of one Bob Dylan album with the words, 'What is this shit?'.)

[337] Local press reviews across the tour have been researched by Patti Murawski and Kristen Tash of the *Harrison Alliance* fanzine, and several were selectively published in Leng, p160-165.

[338] Keltner joined the band in return for a Mercedes 450SL, about which, Harrison wrote a song: It's What You Value (*Thirty Three & 1/3*, 1976).

Harrison not even present to help publicise it. Suffering further from its association with a tour of poor reputation, the album has tended to be derided but in truth, *Dark Horse* contains some creditable material, including the smooth, soulful moods of [188] So Sad, [269] Far East Man and [267] Simply Shady which point towards Harrison's stylistic development in the second half of the decade. Four days after release, Friday 13th, Harrison travelled to Landover, Maryland, where he was received by President Ford, the type of functional meeting he had so disliked in his Beatle days, but which due to the stature of his host, he readily consented to. Photographs of the occasion show Harrison joined by his father, Billy Preston, Ravi Shankar and others, in the faintly bizarre presence of a mildly awkward-looking politician who knew little of Harrison's music, and sought to 'get down with the kids' by gifting him a pin button bearing the slogan, WIN, which the guitarist proceeded to sport on stage.[339] Thus, in the midst of such Beatlemania-like nonsense, the North American Tour edged towards its conclusion. Saturday was a rest day, a welcome break before the group made their final journey to New York for the last few shows, Harrison having expended months of his life on an adventure of highs and lows which he would never look to repeat.

RECORD RELEASES

[274] **Dark Horse** / [273] **I Don't Care Anymore**
(US: 18 Nov 1974)
[228] **Ding Dong** / [273] **I Don't Care Anymore**
(UK: 6 Dec 1974)
Dark Horse
(UK: 20 Dec 1974, US: 9 Dec 1974)
[266] Hari's On Tour (Express) / [267] Simply Shady / [188] So Sad / [268] Bye Bye, Love / [270] Maya Love / [228] Ding Dong, Ding Dong / [274] Dark Horse / [269] Far East Man / [272] It Is 'He' (Jai Sri Krishna)
[228] **Ding Dong; Ding Dong** / [266] **Hari's On Tour (Express)**
(US: 23 Dec 1974)
[274] **Dark Horse** / [266] **Hari's On Tour (Express)**
(UK: 28 Feb 1975)

---

[339] Standing for Whip Inflation Now, a drive to encourage Americans to put their money into savings.

Rock 'N' Roll sessions: October 1974

Lennon's *Oldies But Mouldies* album, dormant since Phil Spector's withdrawal in February, hadn't been forgotten through 1974, negotiations taking place to acquire the tapes from the reclusive producer since there was no prospect of his completing the work. In April Spector had advised EMI through lawyers that he would graciously accept a substantial pay-off in return for the studio masters, the sum of $93,000 and a royalty deal eventually agreed on, and a large consignment of tape reels was accordingly delivered to Record Plant a few days before work commenced on *Walls And Bridges*. Lennon's reaction to hearing them in the cold light of day was one of disheartenment, a realisation dawning that much of the material, recorded in a drunken fog, was unsuitable for release. The question was, what to do with it, a problem he tried to address with some preliminary mixing and editing on 11 and 12 July before conceding defeat and turning his attention to the more pressing *Walls And Bridges*. It was a conundrum which nagged in the back of his mind throughout the month, one of his ideas to pick the best four tracks and release them on EP (or a couple of singles, to better service the US market), another to drop the project entirely – which he was talked out of when he played the tapes to some friends who managed to convince him they were worth salvaging.[340]

Two days after *Walls And Bridges* was released Stateside, Lennon went back over the tapes to see what could be made of them, mixing and overdubbing at Record Plant as best he could. Meantime an increasingly restless Levy met with Lennon to set down a plan of action, the upshot being the album had to happen and a new set of recordings would need to be made, for which Lennon hired his regular circle of session men. Perhaps mindful not to risk the opportunity slipping away, Levy had them convene under a watchful eye at his property, the opulently furnished Sunnyview Farm, not far from Albany, New York, for three days of rehearsals running into sessions proper.

---

[340] Lennon's agreement with Morris Levy that he release three of the publisher's songs on his next album was out-of-court and therefore not strictly binding – although Morris could still have sued had Lennon not delivered. Had a standard four-track EP have proved agreeable, Lennon had recordings of [231] Angel Baby and [236] You Can't Catch Me available, to add to [253] Ya Ya, all owned by Levy.

John Lennon: [275] **THAT'LL BE THE DAY** (*Holly, Allison, Petty*)
Produced by John Lennon
Recorded: 21 Oct 1974, Record Plant, New York
UK/US: unreleased
John Lennon: vocals, guitar; **Jesse Ed Davis**: guitar; **Eddie Mottau**: guitar; **Ken Ascher**: piano; **Klaus Voormann**: bass; **Jim Keltner**: drums; **Arthur Jenkins**: percussion; **unknown**: backing vocals

After two days at Sunnyview Farm, Lennon and his team moved to Record Plant for a final day of rehearsal, proceedings of which were taped for reference. The band ran through their repertoire plus one extra, the Crickets' 1957 classic, That'll Be The Day, which was never returned to. ([280] Rip It Up-Ready Teddy was not featured in the rehearsal set, suggesting it was a substitute, perhaps because Lennon also had Buddy Holly's [276] Peggy Sue ready to go.[341]) Little more than an exploratory run-through, Lennon's recording tends to weigh heavily, fuzzed electric guitar giving an unwanted grunge-like quality not helped by the low fidelity of the circulating copies. Despite Lennon typically forgetting his lines, the performance benefits from Jesse Ed Davis's authentic-styled lead solo and a successful attempt at the stuttering clomps in the final verse, one of the musicians – likely Klaus Voormann – also pitching in with a vocal harmony, which might have been developed further had the song not been dropped (see also [278]).

One of the key figures in the Beatles' musical development, Buddy Holly was the originator of many songs taken into their act, including Crying, Waiting, Hoping, included in the failed Decca audition of 1962, and Words Of Love, recorded for EMI in 1964. That'll Be The Day, one of Holly's most famous, happens to be the first thing the Beatles ever recorded in a studio, while they were still an amateur five-piece going by the name, the Quarry Men.[342] So committed a fan was McCartney that when Norman Petty's Nor-Va-Jak Music publishing company was put up for sale in 1973, the Eastmans purchased it on his behalf, bagging McCartney the copyrights to Holly's classic songs.

---

[341] The studio tape from 21 October has been widely bootlegged with Sunnyview erroneously given as the venue. Parts of Thirty Days and C'mon Everybody were also rehearsed, but were unlikely to have been contenders for the LP given their half-hearted treatment.

[342] Made at Percy Phillips' facility at 38 Kensington in Liverpool, perhaps in the summer of 1958. On the same day they also captured McCartney's original, In Spite Of All The Danger, the two tracks preserved on either side of a lone shellac disc, now reckoned to me the most valuable record in the world.

John Lennon: [276] **PEGGY SUE** (*Holly, Allison, Petty*)
Produced by John Lennon
Recorded: 22 Oct 1974, Record Plant, New York
UK: 21 Feb 1975 (*Rock 'N' Roll* LP)
US: 17 Feb 1975 (*Rock 'N' Roll* LP)
John Lennon: vocals, guitar; **Jesse Ed Davis**: guitar; **Eddie Mottau**: guitar; **Ken Ascher**: piano; **Klaus Voormann**: bass; **Jim Keltner**: drums; **Arthur Jenkins**: percussion

Lennon's love for Buddy Holly is exemplified by the fact that the first proper session at Record Plant was dedicated to capturing Peggy Sue, the 1957 song which had fascinated the teenaged Beatles, and which hadn't dimmed in Lennon's affections in the intervening years.[343] Back in the day Lennon and McCartney hadn't merely admired Peggy Sue, they *studied* it, trying to figure out how to play like the Crickets – something helped by a television broadcast of *Sunday Night At The London Palladium* in March 1958 where they got to see Holly and the group in action, poring over how he worked his fingers (answer: he used a capo), which make of guitar he used, and how drummer, Jerry Allison, effected the distinctive beat.[344]

Determined to do the song justice, Lennon asked his band to play as faithful to the original as possible, the only notable concession being to Ken Ascher, since Holly's recording does not feature a piano. Maintaining the original key of A, Lennon's vocal is pitched low in his register, something he overcomes in the third verse, when he adopts Holly's vocal style in direct imitation, his nasal hiccupping followed by a suddenly impassioned, 'look out!', running into the instrumental section. (Commenting on this two minutes of happy retro-escapism in early 1975, Lennon revealed he sang it without a lyric sheet, remembering the vocal inflections as he went, 'so I really would suddenly find myself aged 16 again.'[345])

---

[343] Holly had been in Lennon's thoughts to a greater or lesser extent throughout his career, several of his songs for example surfacing in the *Get Back* sessions. In September 1971 Lennon recorded a soundtrack to his aborted film, *Clock*, consisting of acoustic guitar versions of a dozen or so oldies, including Holly's Heartbeat, Peggy Sue, Peggy Sue Got Married, Maybe Baby, Mailman, Bring Me No More Blues, and Rave On (see [144]). As recently as 1974, he'd written a letter to *Rolling Stone* journalist, Jim Dawson, in fulsome praise of Holly, the text of which is reproduced in Davies (Ed), 2012, part 16.

[344] Allison was playing a *paradiddle*, where each main beat is echoed by a double strike from the other hand, generating a rapid pattering. In his 1974 letter, Lennon recalled the significance of the 1958 broadcast, noting, 'the "secret" of drumming on Peggy Sue was revealed… live' (*ibid*).

[345] Said in a radio 'conference call' on 21 February, with all and sundry stations linked in.

John Lennon: [277] **AIN'T THAT A SHAME** (*Domino, Bartholomew*)
Produced by John Lennon
Recorded: 22 Oct 1974; 28-29 Oct 1974, Record Plant, New York
UK: 21 Feb 1975 (*Rock 'N' Roll* LP)
US: 17 Feb 1975 (*Rock 'N' Roll* LP)
John Lennon: vocals, guitar; **Jesse Ed Davis**: guitar; **Eddie Mottau**: guitar; **Ken Ascher**: piano; **Klaus Voormann**: bass; **Jim Keltner**: drums; **Arthur Jenkins**: percussion; **Joseph Temperley**: saxophone; **Frank Vicari**: saxophone; **Dennis Morouse**: tenor saxophone

New Orleans rock and roller, Fats Domino, was 27 when he had his first crossover hit in 1955, Ain't That A Shame following a long string of R&B successes on the Imperial label. There being no comparable scene in England, black performers struggled to break through as white artists stepped up with opportunistic versions of their hits, in this case, Pat Boone's harmlessly conservative rendition which made the top 10 and is how Lennon came to know the song, via his mother's banjo tutoring. Part of the satisfaction the teenaged Lennon experienced in learning Ain't That A Shame was that he could, for the first occasion, sing and play something at the same time, making it a key moment in his musical life and a song he would lovingly cling to, performing it with the Quarry Men between 1958 and 1961, and jamming it in sessions for both *Plastic Ono Band* and *Some Time In New York City*.[346]

This, Lennon's first formal attempt at recording the song, was secured in 11 takes, a lively performance which like Boone's earlier remake, dispenses with the triplet patterning of Domino's original, jarring the transition from the juddering introductory bars. Underpinned by Ken Ascher's piano, played high up the keyboard and mixed low to make room for jeering, Domino-esque saxophones, the results are competent if not outstanding.

---

[346] McCartney was similarly enthused, going on to perform it on tour between 1989 and 1991, besides recording it for his album, *CHOBA B CCCP*, which along with versions of [233] and [278a] give some credence to the idea that *CHOBA* is his *Rock 'N' Roll*. It's not known whether McCartney or Lennon took lead vocals with the Quarry Men.

John Lennon: [278] **BRING IT ON HOME TO ME-SEND ME SOME LOVIN'**
(*Cooke, Price, Marascalco*)
Produced by John Lennon
Recorded: 22 Oct 1974; 28-29 Oct 1974, Record Plant, New York
UK: 21 Feb 1975 (*Rock 'N' Roll* LP)
US: 17 Feb 1975 (*Rock 'N' Roll* LP)
John Lennon: vocals, guitar, harmonica; **Jesse Ed Davis**: guitar; **Eddie Mottau**: guitar; **Ken Ascher**: piano; **Klaus Voormann**: bass, backing vocals; **Jim Keltner**: drums; **Joseph Temperley**: saxophone; **Frank Vicari**: saxophone; **Dennis Morouse**: tenor saxophone; **Arthur Jenkins**: percussion

Presented as a single piece, this medley brings together songs from either end of Lennon's pre-fame years, Send Me Some Lovin' dating back to 1957, just around the time he and McCartney met, with Bring It On Home To Me a hit in 1962.

Sam Cooke's Bring It On Home To Me was in the Beatles' act in late 1962, via the Atlantic recording by Carla Thomas which Lennon preferred over the original.[347] Initially uncertain whether to record it, given that both Rod Stewart and Dave Mason had included versions on their latest albums, nostalgia probably got the better of him, Lennon digging out his harmonica, recalling the one he 'slap leathered' en route to Hamburg in 1960, when songs like these were coursing through his veins. The track was not without some latter-day associations either; Lennon had to hunt down his old 7-inch copy to transcribe the lyrics, the label of which would have shown the publisher as Kags Music, one of Allen Klein's, which he may not have realised.[348] Moreover, on an album sparked by his appropriation of a line from [236] You Can't Catch Me, this was also a song Lennon had recently borrowed from, adapting its opening lyrics in 1970 for [89] Remember.

Of the two sections, Bring It On Home To Me bulks largest, benefiting from a hammy guitar solo and a rare backing vocal part from Klaus Voormann, and at just over 2:00, could have stood on its own terms. However Lennon elected to join it to Send Me Some Lovin', which was slashed to around a minute and a half and linked with a brief but awkward pause. Send

---

[347] Interviewed for WNEW-FM of New York on 13 February 1975, Lennon added that he obtained a copy of the Carla Thomas version first, and called the song one of his all-time favourites. Her version was re-styled as I'll Bring It On Home To You, narrated from the perspective of the other partner.

[348] Kags Music was set up to handle Sam Cooke's copyrights, when Klein was acting as his manager. The company name was subsequently changed to ABKCO Music Ltd, as printed on 1980s pressings of *Rock 'N' Roll*.

Me Some Lovin' was originally tucked away on the B-side of Little Richard's [238] Lucille, and as such formed part of Lennon's musical DNA. It hadn't escaped his attention that the Crickets also released a version on their 1958 LP, *The 'Chirping' Crickets*, consolidating its credentials and helping establish it as a Beatles regular over the next four years. Acknowledging both antecedents, Lennon's middle eight vocal includes an impassioned snarl mirroring the former, and some jokingly exaggerated hiccups 15 seconds on, suggesting the latter.

Since both Bring It On Home To Me and Send Me Some Lovin' share the same tempo and chord repertoire (allowing for Lennon's transposition to A major), and a corresponding lyrical theme, the fit was comfortable enough but although the medley was rehearsed as a continuous performance, the two halves here are distinct. Send Me Some Lovin' sees Voormann's vocals gone and Ken Ascher's piano suddenly more prominent in the soundscape, opening up the likelihood that these were two separate performances assembled with an edit, hence the momentary gap in the audio where the two songs meet.

John Lennon: [279] **DO YOU WANT TO DANCE** (*Freeman*)
Produced by John Lennon
Recorded: 22 Oct 1974; 25 Oct 1974; 28-29 Oct 1974, Record Plant, New York
UK: 21 Feb 1975 (*Rock 'N' Roll* LP)
US: 17 Feb 1975 (*Rock 'N' Roll* LP)
John Lennon: vocals, guitar; **Jesse Ed Davis:** guitar; **Eddie Mottau:** guitar; **Klaus Voormann:** bass; **Jim Keltner:** drums; **Arthur Jenkins:** percussion; **Joseph Temperley:** saxophone; **Frank Vicari:** saxophone; **Dennis Morouse:** tenor saxophone; **May Pang (and others?):** backing vocals

Do You Want To Dance was a 1958 American hit for teenager, Bobby Freeman, but practically unknown in Britain until Cliff Richard covered it in mid-1962 – after which it was tackled by a host of different artists. Unlikely to have been inspired by Richard's version, the filter here is probably Bette Midler's 1972 recording for *The Divine Miss M* (featuring David Spinozza on guitar), whose sensual arrangement drifts on a relaxed percussive off-beat, suggesting the reggae style, which Lennon later admitted he was also aiming for.[349] Stretching the definition of rock and roll to the limit, this re-working relies for its energy on Klaus Voormann's bubbling bass and Eddie Mottau's heavily wah-wahed electric guitar, which with accompanying saxophone blasts (approximating the

---

[349] Although Lennon never spoke of a musical interest in Bette Midler, the coincidence in name of *The Divine Miss M* to his own [241] Move Over Ms. L implies he may have taken notice.

sound of trumpets), comes closer to ska. (According to Madinger and Easter, the final arrangement was obtained by stripping down the standard take 13 and layering on a succession of overdubs.[350]) Whether or not Lennon's work tempts the listener to their feet, as the title asks, was an anomaly admitted at the end of the performance, where his off-mike answer 'I'm not quite sure' can be heard in the right channel. Regardless, the recording attracts interest by virtue of being so far from Lennon's usual style, something underscored by the fact that on *Rock 'N' Roll* it's seated between the pillars of Fats Domino and Chuck Berry.

John Lennon: [280] **RIP IT UP-READY TEDDY** (*Blackwell, Marascalco*)
Produced by John Lennon
Recorded: 23 Oct 1974; 28-29 Oct 1974, Record Plant, New York
UK: 21 Feb 1975 (*Rock 'N' Roll* LP)
US: 17 Feb 1975 (*Rock 'N' Roll* LP)
John Lennon: vocals, guitar; **Jesse Ed Davis**: guitar; **Eddie Mottau**: guitar; **Klaus Voormann**: bass; **Jim Keltner**: drums; **Joseph Temperley**: saxophone; **Frank Vicari**: saxophone; **Dennis Morouse**: tenor saxophone; **Arthur Jenkins**: percussion

Little Richard's first British release arrived in November 1956, a coupling of Rip It Up and Ready Teddy, issued on the Decca-owned London label. Richard had already delivered Tutti-Frutti, Long Tall Sally, [281] Slippin' And Slidin' and several others to the American market, tracks which Lennon had been intoxicated by as a 15-year-old, this inaugural UK single giving him the chance to get a copy and play both sides to death, forever welding the two songs together in his mind.

Given their importance in Lennon's life, it's surprising that this medley, in which he covers both at once, extends to a mere minute and a half, one of the shortest in his catalogue. Its brevity was the result of the removal of a perfectly serviceable minute's worth of Ready Teddy, heard intact on earlier takes, although Lennon's enthusiasm for the material wasn't in question; his vocal is wild and urgent, exemplified by a scream prior to the saxophone solo. Used to seamlessly connect the two sections, this sax part was dubbed onto take 6 the following week and is a match for anything on either of Richard's originals, compounding the mystery of why the medley was so drastically truncated.

---

[350] p107.

John Lennon: [281] **SLIPPIN' AND SLIDIN'** (*Penniman, Bocage, Collins, Smith*)
Produced by John Lennon
Recorded: 23 Oct 1974; 28-29 Oct 1974, Record Plant, New York
UK: 21 Feb 1975 (*Rock 'N' Roll* LP)
US: 17 Feb 1975 (*Rock 'N' Roll* LP)
John Lennon: vocals, guitar; **Jesse Ed Davis:** guitar; **Eddie Mottau:** guitar; **Ken Ascher:** piano; **Klaus Voormann:** bass; **Jim Keltner:** drums; **Joseph Temperley:** saxophone; **Frank Vicari:** saxophone; **Dennis Morouse:** tenor saxophone; **Arthur Jenkins:** percussion

Having captured two of Little Richard's oldies, Lennon went straight for one more, Slippin' And Slidin' dating back to spring of 1956, like [278] Send Me Some Lovin', a comparatively obscure choice which in this case was first issued on the B-side of the most important of the lot, so far as Lennon was concerned: Long Tall Sally. (Unlike most of the material on *Rock 'N' Roll*, Slippin' And Slidin' is not known to have been performed by the Beatles – although it's possible it was, undocumented.) Lennon came across the song when school friend, Michael Hill, brought a copy of the 78 home from Amsterdam and insisted Lennon hear it – a singular event which left him utterly speechless and which made an indelible impression.[351]

Determined to rise to the occasion, Lennon's performance blows the original out of the water, delivered at a slightly slower pace but with considerably more *chutzpah*, its boldness deriving from a switch in emphasis to the on-beat, and a 'dirty' lead vocal burning through two minutes. (The fact that this raucous piece of dive-bar R&B was made by the same band as the ethereal [251] #9 Dream, just three months earlier, is testament to their outstanding interpretative and technical abilities.) Set to be released as a single in 1975, backed with [277] Ain't That A Shame, it was pulled at the 11th hour, but would have been a more representative choice than [282] Stand By Me.

---

[351] For full documentation of Lennon's introduction to Slippin' And Slidin' and Little Richard generally, see Lewisohn, 2013, p258-260.

John Lennon: [282] **STAND BY ME** (*King, Glick*)[352]
   Produced by John Lennon
   Recorded: 23 Oct 1974; 24 Oct 1974; 28-29 Oct 1974, Record Plant,
      New York
   UK: 21 Feb 1975 (*Rock 'N' Roll* LP)
   US: 17 Feb 1975 (*Rock 'N' Roll* LP)
   John Lennon: vocals, guitar; **Jesse Ed Davis**: guitar; **Eddie Mottau**: guitar; **Klaus Voormann**: bass; **Ken Ascher**: keyboards; **Jim Keltner**: drums; **Joseph Temperley**: saxophone; **Frank Vicari**: saxophone; **Dennis Morouse**: tenor saxophone; **Arthur Jenkins**: percussion

Lennon's decision to relinquish [259] Only You to Starr may have left a hole in his provisional listing for *Rock 'N' Roll*, a substitute being found in the Ben E King number, Stand By Me, onto which he imposed the same acoustic guitar figure, based on the regular upward strum of his right hand. That the definition of rock and roll is at best vague is illustrated by the fact that the original, which most would classify as a soul cut, was remade by Lennon on the same day as three authentic ravers from Little Richard, the main thing the songs have in common that they date to the same general era.

Stand By Me was written (or at lest, started) by King as a gospel-inspired vehicle for his group the Drifters, who elected not to release it. Instead it became King's defining solo release in 1961, adopted into the Beatles' live sets until 1962, with Lennon handling lead vocal and rubbing matchboxes together on stage to imitate the distinctive sound achieved by King's percussionist, Phil Kraus (described as a being played on a gourd, meaning a guiro-like resonator). Another evergreen for Lennon, it re-surfaced on 28 March 1974 when he and McCartney jammed it together at Record Plant West (see [238]), a spontaneous selection which might have reawakened Lennon's interest in the original.

Taken up again in October, Stand By Me was recorded in five takes, formally laid out over Lennon's whole-bar chord blocks. Using an old arranging trick, the recording generates momentum by the strategic addition of instruments, Ken Ascher's keyboard riffs punctuated with lustrous piano notes before, almost a minute in, the full band comes to life. The highlight of the piece, Jesse Ed Davis's upward-yearning guitar break was taped in a separate session the following day, consisting of multiple tracks overlaid on one another, the most accomplished piece of individual musicianship on the album.

With Lennon's echo-laden vocals striding confidently, he claims full

---

[352] 1970s editions of *Rock 'N' Roll* credit Elmo Click as co-writer, this being a pseudonym used by Jerry Leiber and Mike Stoller.

ownership of the song which was selected for single release, its delay attributable to the fact that [251] #9 Dream was on chart through the start of 1975. In preparation Lennon dubbed a synthesiser onto the introductory bars in February, simulating a string section but mixed so low as to be scarcely worth the effort. Finally issued in March, by which time *Rock 'N' Roll* was old news, the single fared only modestly on chart despite the attraction of a non-album B-side, [241] Move Over Ms. L, its relative failure leading to the cancellation of a follow-up [281]. It was his last new single until 1980.

John Lennon: [283] **BE-BOP-A-LULA** (*Davis, Vincent*)
Produced by John Lennon
Recorded: 26 Oct 1974, Record Plant, New York
UK: 21 Feb 1975 (*Rock 'N' Roll* LP)
US: 17 Feb 1975 (*Rock 'N' Roll* LP)
John Lennon: vocals, guitar; **Jesse Ed Davis**: guitar; **Eddie Mottau**: guitar; **Ken Ascher**: piano; **Klaus Voormann**: bass; **Jim Keltner**: drums; **Arthur Jenkins**: percussion

After the successful recordings of 23 October, which captured the two stand-out tracks on *Rock 'N' Roll* ([281]; [282]), Lennon took two days out to concentrate on mixing and overdubbing his growing stock of tapes, no new material being started until this Saturday session in which a couple more were secured, necessary to complete the project. Yet to be recorded were [284] Ya Ya, and this, the 1956 Gene Vincent hit which was the first record Paul McCartney ever bought, and which Lennon later recalled as one he performed the day the two met.[353] Another key record for both of them, it was naturally taken into the stage act and played on countless occasions, a tape of them performing it at Hamburg's Star Club surviving – albeit with waiter, Fredi Fascher, on vocals. Accordingly, the song was high in Lennon's thinking all along, paradoxically left until the final day but programmed as the lead cut when *Rock 'N' Roll* was released.

True to Vincent's original, Lennon's re-make includes heavy echo on the vocals (particularly noticeable in the slightly off-key *'well!...'* which starts the performance), and two solos from Jesse Ed Davis which, while not slavish copies, are close enough to guitarist, Cliff Gallup's, to be recognisable – Davis

---

[353] Interview for WNEW-FM of New York City, 13 February 1975. Much is said of the influence of artists like Carl Perkins and Buddy Holly on the nascent Beatles, but Vincent looms just as large. The group's classic leather style, developed in Hamburg in 1961, had them looking, said Lennon, 'like four Gene Vincents' (unused sleeve notes for *Rock 'N' Roll*, quoted in Lewisohn, 2013, p928). They also took to wearing coloured caps, in imitation of Vincent's backing group, the Blue Caps. See also [42].

having the pre-advantage of knowing the original recording inside out. Running slightly faster than its template, Lennon's disdain for Vincent's later 'slow and heavy' treatment of the song was a factor in his decision to defer to the 1956 arrangement in a performance which is more of a tribute than any other selection on the LP.

John Lennon: [284] **YA YA** (*Robinson, Dorsey, Lewis*)
Produced by John Lennon
Recorded: 26 Oct 1974; 28-29 Oct 1974, Record Plant, New York
UK: 21 Feb 1975 (*Rock 'N' Roll* LP)
US: 17 Feb 1975 (*Rock 'N' Roll* LP)
John Lennon: vocals, guitar; **Jesse Ed Davis**: guitar; **Eddie Mottau**: guitar; **Klaus Voormann**: bass; **Jim Keltner**: drums; **Joseph Temperley**: saxophone; **Frank Vicari**: saxophone; **Dennis Morouse**: tenor saxophone; **Arthur Jenkins**: percussion

Recorded in seven takes, Ya Ya was the last thing made for the album, no doubt shoe-horned in for the purpose of completing the agreement with Morris Levy but also in view of Lennon's long-standing fondness for it. (The song, a snippet of which he'd half-jokingly appended to *Walls And Bridges* [253], had been yet another Beatles regular in the early days.[354]) Recorded in 1961 by New Orleans-born vocalist, Lee Dorsey, Ya Ya was never a hit in Britain but made a splash in America, becoming Dorsey's first and biggest hit. This re-working, forced on Lennon and presumably done with an eye on the clock, borders on satire, the slow introduction replaced with an ironic musical gag and a clichéd bass run solidified into a full-blown riff in lieu of an instrumental break.

Morris Levy's name is sometimes added to the compositional credits, a claim which others have called into question. Attribution varies on different pressings of *Rock 'N' Roll*, some US copies citing only Levy and Lewis, others, including the original UK album, giving the trio of names shown above.

Utilising the final few days of October for a further round of overdubs, mostly aimed at strengthening and tightening up the existing instrumentation, *Rock 'N' Roll* was mixed, edited and all but ready by mid-November. All told it had taken more than a year to come this far, the breakdown of the early round of sessions followed by a period of stagnation and finally a burst of activity to recover what started out as a simple plan to re-make some much-loved oldies.

---

[354] A recording of Ya Ya by Tony Sheridan and the Beat Brothers was issued in 1962, often wrongly assumed to feature the Beatles as backing group.

In concept, as well as through its torturous history, *Rock 'N' Roll* is Lennon's *Get Back*, bringing the curtain down on his recording career proper and taking him full circle to the halcyon days of the Quarry Men and Silver Beatles, back across the years to a time when he played rock and roll simply for fun. The album's final track listing reflects Lennon's musical loves, and yet there are anomalies; of the 13 tracks which made it onto vinyl, there was nothing from Elvis, Carl Perkins or Jerry Lee Lewis, all formative influences on Lennon, and of the rejects from the *Oldies But Mouldies* phase, which were hand-selected in the first place for their personal import, none were re-done in 1974.

The Beatles had now been five years gone, hopes that the four might re-unite some day sporadically growing then fading as the 1970s moved on, an increasing sense of nostalgia abroad as the second half of the decade loomed without them. An offshoot of the enduring interest in the group was the creation in 1974 of *Beatlefest*, a two-day convention celebrating all things Fab, organised by Mark Lapidos, who summoned the courage to knock on Lennon's door and request his support. Providing some promo films to be screened at the event, Lennon also donated a signed guitar for charity auction – and in a gesture surely beyond Lapidos' expectations, got in touch with McCartney, Harrison and Starr who, perhaps feeling a twinge of nostalgia themselves, all followed suit, a moment of Beatle unity expressed in support of a good cause.[355] The festival was staged in New York over the weekend of 7-8 September and although Lennon had initial plans to attend, he was put off by the prospect of bumper crowds, instead sending May Pang with instructions to pick up any Beatles bootlegs she could find, something Lennon was taking increasing interest in.[356] An unexpected turn of events was that Pang bumped into an old friend of the Beatles from Hamburg, photographer, Jurgen Vollmer, who had a stall selling some of his early group portraits. Not only did Pang take copies back, she put Vollmer in touch with Lennon, giving him the chance to pore over some of the impressive black and white photography, much of it taken in the back alleys and bustling clubs of Hamburg and seeming to represent a forgotten era. The rediscovery of Vollmer's images could scarcely have occurred at a more opportune time, Lennon finishing up an album

---

[355] McCartney also donated a signed guitar, Starr some signed drum sticks and Harrison a tabla (a type of Indian drum) which had been used on *Sgt Pepper*. See Rodriguez, 2010, p302-305 for further details of *Beatlefest*.

[356] It's not known which records Pang brought back, but among the mushrooming number of illicit discs circulating were titles like *Sweet Apple Trax*, *Telecasts*, *Yellow Matter Custard*, *LS Bumblebee*, *Abbey Road Revisited* and so on, between them mopping up assorted bits of *Get Back* detritus, barely listenable live recordings from various sources, home tapes of old BBC radio broadcasts and at least one bona fide EMI outtake, What's The New Mary Jane from 1968. Most of these, Lennon hadn't heard since they were recorded.

redolent of gruelling Hamburg nights fuelled by rock and roll, providing at once the ideal imagery for his LP cover. The shot Lennon selected was taken in early 1961 and had him centre, caught in the shadow of a Hamburg doorway, while three blurred figures cross in front of him – in order, McCartney, Sutcliffe and Harrison – this last album recorded under the Beatles' joint contracts featuring, therefore, a group photo – taken in a deserted courtyard behind Wohlwillstrasse, one of the commercial drags a few streets up from the Reeperbahn.[357]

Meantime, the other main party in the *Rock 'N' Roll* saga, Morris Levy, had managed to ingratiate himself with Lennon through the Sunnyview Farm sessions, so that a relationship which began on antagonistic terms was threatening to develop into friendship. Still awaiting product, Levy met with Lennon on 12 November at Club Cavellero on New York's East 58th Street, where he was presented with a set of tape reels, ostensibly as reassurance that the recordings had been completed and the album was in progress. It happened that Levy's business interests included running a television-advertised, mail-order record label, Adam VIII, which had issued more than a dozen albums through 1974, and therefore had the wherewithal, should Levy choose, to both advertise and issue these new recordings. All that was required was Lennon's verbal assent, which Levy claimed to have got before putting the commercial wheels in motion.

Whether Lennon understood the risk he was taking in handing out copies of his tapes like this, Levy set about issuing them as *Roots: John Lennon Sings The Great Rock And Roll Hits*, an album housed in a garish day-glo cover featuring a photo of an incongruous, limp-haired Lennon, circa 1969. Lennon claimed not to have seen this coming, and so cue another round of legal action on both sides, one of Capital's winning arguments that Lennon – whether he agreed to Levy's plan or not – had no authority to authorise it anyway, being under exclusive contract to EMI throughout. The immediate consequence of Levy's efforts was the now urgent preparation of *Rock 'N' Roll*, the official EMI version, which arrived in the second half of February but without its intended deluxe packaging.[358] In the end, *Rock 'N' Roll* contained only two of Levy's copyrights, since [231] Angel Baby had been omitted, leaving [236] You Can't Catch Me and [284] Ya Ya, something now entangled in the broader dispute

---

[357] McCartney therefore appears on the front cover of *Rock 'N' Roll* and since he now owned the publishing rights to [276] Peggy Sue, his name also appears on the back of later copies inscribed McCartney Music Inc.

[358] *Roots* contained 15 tracks, everything which would appear on *Rock 'N' Roll* plus two additional cuts from the *Oldies But Mouldies* period – [230] Be My Baby and [231] Angel Baby. (The fact that these were on the tapes Lennon handed over to Levy implies they were also in the running for the official album.)

over *Roots*, all of which rumbled on through 1975 leaving a rueful Lennon to remark that there was a jinx on *Rock 'N' Roll*.

Lennon realised that issuing an album of seasoned oldies might not go down well with his contemporary audience, and the album is often regarded as something of a curio which doesn't bear comparison with his other work. The truth is, like Starr's *Sentimental Journey* before it, the material is of primarily personal significance, an album *by* Lennon, *for* Lennon, which, if listeners didn't warm to, then too bad.[359] Reviews for what was Lennon's second studio album in less than five months were variable but often supportive, few rating it a classic but several at least commending it, *Los Angeles Times* going so far as to call it, 'one of the finest rock retrospectives ever made'.[360] Hyperbole, of course, but a measure of the approval Lennon still had.

At the end of 1974 Lennon was still living with May Pang, but knew that he was close to a reconciliation with Ono after more than a year apart. Having straightened up his act through a busy and productive recent period, Ono was increasingly receptive to his advances to the extent that in the first week of February, he moved back in to the Dakota for good. A couple of weeks before, McCartney had paid another of his flying visits, on his way to record *Venus And Mars* in New Orleans, sessions to which he invited Lennon. Initially enthused, Lennon found that once he was back in the safe arms of Ono, he no longer felt the desire to go, and so this last chance of a meaningful reunion of the two faded as each moved on with their own life, one into the dazzling spotlight of vast tour itineraries, the other into near total reclusion.

RECORD RELEASES

Rock 'N' Roll
    (UK: 21 Feb 1975, US: 17 Feb 1975)
    [283] Be-Bop-A-Lula / [282] Stand By Me / [280] Medley: Rip It Up-Ready Teddy / [236] You Can't Catch Me / [277] Ain't That A Shame / [279] Do You Want To Dance / [232] Sweet Little Sixteen / [281] Slippin' And Slidin' / [276] Peggy Sue / [278] Medley: Bring It On Home To Me-Send Me Some Lovin' / [229] Bony Moronie / [284] Ya Ya / [233] Just Because
[282] **Stand By Me** / [241] **Move Over Ms. L**
    (UK: 18 Apr 1975, US: 10 Mar 1975)

---

[359] The album has sometimes been described as a contract-fulfilling exercise, Lennon's last release under his EMI agreement. However the 1967 contract signed by the Beatles stipulated they put out 70 sides (ie songs) over the subsequent nine years, counting solo as well as group recordings. Thus, the contract was satisfied as far back as 1969 and none of the Beatles were obliged to release anything further after that point.
[360] 18 February 1975.

Wings EMI sessions:
November 1974

Wings: [285] **ROCK SHOW** (*McCartney*)
Produced by Paul McCartney
Recorded: 1 Nov 1974; 14 Nov 1974; 15 Nov 1974, EMI Studios, London
UK/US: unreleased
Paul McCartney: vocals, bass, hand bells; **Linda McCartney**: backing vocals; **Denny Laine**: guitar; **Jimmy McCulloch**: guitar; **Geoff Britton**: drums

A couple of months after the Nashville sessions for [239] Sally G and [240] Junior's Farm, McCartney attempted to get Wings off on another adventure, this time looking to New Orleans to record a new album. This would have been the first full-scale band project for Jimmy McCulloch and Geoff Britton, but seemingly dogged by travel woes, Denny Laine carelessly failed to obtain a US visa in time, and so the trip was deferred until the new year. McCartney had meantime announced that Wings were to embark on a large-scale world tour starting mid-1975, meaning he had to pull his act together and get an album ready, a year having now passed since *Band On The Run*. Consequently a handful of dates were booked at EMI where they could, at least, make a start.

Both a thematic emblem for the tour to come, and a statement of intent, Rock Show takes itself on a mini-tour of several famous concert venues including the ambiguously nominated Rainbow, likely a reference to Skull's Rainbow Room in Nashville's Printer's Alley, where McCartney had recently written [239] Sally G.[361] Doubling down on the popular references, the song, which he later confessed embarrassment over, also indulges in some topical name-dropping – Philly soul, Jimmy Page – and, so he later claimed, an allusion to New Orleans bluesman, Professor Longhair, all touch points inevitably prone to aging as time went by.[362] What he got away with was the

---

[361] An alternative theory holds that McCartney is referencing the Astoria in Finsbury Park, where the Beatles had played their 1963 Christmas shows, which re-opened as Rainbow Theatre in 1971 with the Who as its first headliner. Wings would play there in 1979.

[362] McCartney mentions the Professor Longhair connection in his sleeve notes to *Venus And Mars Deluxe Edition*, 2014. Prof Longhair was enjoying a revival in popularity in the early 1970s, and stopped by McCartney's New Orleans sessions. He subsequently recorded his album, *Live On The Queen Mary*, at the party held to mark the completion of *Venus And Mars*.

line, 'The tension mounts, you score an ounce', going down well with concert-goers but wisely cut from the single edit, thus avoiding the censors who's banned [169] Hi, Hi, Hi a couple of years earlier.

Ostensibly a straight-forward rocker, the EMI version of Rock Show ran to a bloated seven minutes. When re-made in New Orleans, it was trimmed to a more manageable five and a half, but simultaneously extended by the addition of the Venus And Mars overture, conceptually preparing the listener for the show about to start. A memorable curtain-opener for the subsequent tour, the Venus And Mars-Rock Show medley did its business in a live setting, where context was everything, a truncated 7-inch release failing to engage armchair listeners and not charting when issued in the UK in late 1975.

Wings: [286] **LETTING GO** (*McCartney*)
Produced by Paul McCartney
Recorded: 5 Nov 1974, EMI Studios, London
UK: 30 May 1975 (*Venus And Mars* LP)
US: 27 May 1975 (*Venus And Mars* LP)
Paul McCartney: vocals, guitar, electric piano, bass; **Linda McCartney**: organ, backing vocals; **Denny Laine**: backing vocals; **Jimmy McCulloch**: guitar; **Geoff Britton**: drums

In its final form, the minor Letting Go is one of McCartney's more intensely focused pieces, its fiery lead guitar riffs knowingly edging Wings into contemporary rock territory. This, though, was largely the result of the overdubs applied in February, McCartney and McCulloch adding their parts along with a brass section in New Orleans.[363] In its raw state, take 21 from EMI runs close to six minutes, the result of a collaborative session in which each instrument is indulged in the collective soundscape, self-absorbed, fuzz-toned lead and strategically prodding keys placed under a melody line carried mainly on a high-floating fifth, Wings sounding more like an integrated band with a cohesive mind than at any stage. (The irony was, even as this recording was being made, tensions continued to fester between McCulloch and Britton to the extent that within weeks, the drummer had left the group.) An accomplished piece of studio work, the track was nonetheless a poor choice for the album's second trailer single, sounding gloomy next to the uber-pop of the preceding Listen To What The Man Said, McCartney momentarily faltering in the commercial arena.

---

[363] As heard on the release: Clyde Kerr and John Longo on trumpet, Michael Pierce, Alvin Thomas and Carl Blouin on sax.

Wings: [287] **LOVE IN SONG** (*McCartney*)
Produced by Paul McCartney
Recorded: 7 Nov 1974, EMI Studios, London
UK: 16 May 1975 (single B-side)
US: 23 May 1975 (single B-side)
Paul McCartney: vocals, piano, bass, hand bells; **Linda McCartney**: Moog synthesizer, hand bells, backing vocals; **Denny Laine**: guitar, piano, backing vocals; **Jimmy McCulloch**: guitar; **Geoff Britton**: drums, milk bottles

The last product of this brief set of sessions, Love In Song was written for Linda and born of an inspired opening line discovered on McCartney's 12-string acoustic during the summer. As recorded at EMI, the track commences with a descending figure stepping softly down the chromatic scale, given an other-worldly quality by the mixing in of high, glassy notes and a percussion effect using milk bottles. The rest of the opening minute of this solemn piece contains a dialogue between the tactile, finger-picked guitar strings and the blank purity of a piano's white keys, representing a yin-yang duality of tones, the two instruments at once individual and intertwined – literally, a love expressed in the medium of song.

Credit is due to Linda for her contribution, a distinctive, angular figure on the Moog, which was likely prepared for her by Paul (he can be heard vocalising the melody under the break's second appearance, at 2:15). For this section, and the second part of the song built around a conventional band line-up, McCartney utilised the double bass Linda had bought for him in Nashville the previous summer, another sense in which Love In Song revolves around the two of them to the effective exclusion of the outside world. Taken to the States in the new year, Love In Song was treated to strings and harp overdubs in Los Angeles during the final round of work on *Venus And Mars*, set to be McCartney's first post-Apple album when released in May.[364]

---

[364] Noted harpist, Gayle Levant, added her contribution on 10 March at Sunset Sound in Hollywood, where the other three ex-Beatles had recorded together in 1973 [200]; the Sid Sharp Strings were recorded four days later at Wally Heider Studios.

PART 5: LETTING GO

'We all arrived for the big dissolution meeting in the Plaza Hotel in New York. There were green baize tables like the Geneva Conference'

Paul McCartney, December 1984

The network of inter-connected interests the Beatles were caught in during the late 1960s and early 1970s has been the subject of book-length studies attempting to untangle labyrinthine company structures, complex contractual clauses and binding agreements. McCartney's 1971 case to dissolve some of them was intended to force a separation so that all four could work and earn separately, but the case was merely left dangling, Justice Stamp effectively telling the four of them to go and work something out themselves and report back to the court when done. This, they failed to do over the next three and a half years, the matter intermittently flaring up and straining their fluctuating friendships. The main sticking point was that Lennon, Harrison and Starr had been convinced by their legal advisors (ie, Allen Klein) that to dissolve their business partnership would be to suddenly land the four individuals with lump sums of *personal* income, which would be subject to income tax and therefore attract cripplingly large demands for money already spent.

So intractable was the situation that by 1972 the four had more or less resigned themselves to the fact that not only could they not resolve affairs, they couldn't even face up to them, each content to defer to managers and lawyers while simply getting on with their professional lives. A glimmer of light appeared at the end of a long tunnel in spring of 1973 when the three former Beatles still represented by Klein severed their relationship with him, and were free to take legal guidance from more co-operative minds – although that particular parting ended up adding to the seeming futility of the situation by provoking yet further litigation, a turn of events Harrison might have predicted in his wry [179] Sue Me, Sue You Blues. (Currently on tour, Harrison was performing the song with a pointed twist in the lyric: 'Bring your lawyers, I'll bring *Klein*'.)

In principle the ex-Beatles had come to accept there was no sense in pooling their record royalties into a common pot, and moreover their obligation to EMI was due to expire in January 1976, meaning each could go off to different labels entirely separately, compounding the nonsense of being locked into a joint financial agreement. What they had to do was work out the details of *how* to separate, knowing that until they each signed on the dotted line, the partnership would remain and none of them would be truly free. Neither was it lost on any of them how much of their money had passed into the hands of lawyers over the years, an ironic consequence of trying to protect their revenues.

Efforts to settle were ongoing through 1974, a week's worth of meetings among their attorneys in February merely resulting in stalemate, reputedly due to Lennon's wanting too big a share of the spoils – although, underlining the psychological separation of business and personal life they all now observed, just six weeks later Lennon and McCartney were jamming and socialising together, as if the best of pals (see [238]). Through another six months of behind-the-scenes negotiation, a settlement continued to edge closer so that by September, a deal was imminent, Lennon reporting to a journalist that through advisors, 'an agreement for an agreement' had been put in place, although his optimistic, 'by the time this [interview] goes out it should be all over' proved unrealistic.[365]

Lennon's 'agreement for an agreement' was nonetheless a step forward, the respective teams of lawyers working through the autumn to finalise the finer terms of a possible deal. For the four Beatles, the moment was going to be historic enough that they agreed to endorse the papers together, face to face and in front of witnesses, the first time they would have all been in the same room since 1969. However there were logistical problems in that Harrison was away on tour towards the end of the year. It was noted that he was due in New York, where Lennon lived, in mid-December, and both McCartney and Starr agreed they could also be there on 19th, the date duly set down for a final signing ceremony, for which a reception room was booked in the poignant setting of the Plaza Hotel, where the Beatles had stayed on their first night in America, 7 February 1964.

Harrison's tour duly arrived in New York City on Saturday 14 December, one day ahead of two gigs at Nassau Coliseum. He at once met up with Lennon who, in the spirit of camaraderie, agreed to appear on stage with him on the tour's closing night at Madison Square Garden, six days away (it had been just 16 days since Lennon performed alongside Elton John at the same venue). Harrison, though, was frazzled from his exhausting tour, and although initially appreciative, according to May Pang became increasingly agitated and eventually lost his temper, unleashing a furious tirade at Lennon, accusing him of betraying the friendship, then at one point, tearing Lennon's glasses from his face in a moment which might have developed into a physical fight, had Lennon not kept his head.[366] Quite what had been brewing in Harrison's mind is hard to fathom, he and Lennon having ostensibly been on good terms and worked harmoniously together over the past few years ([3]; [128]; [200]), but his outburst threatened to cause a fatal late fracture which could have derailed the dissolution agreement. In the event, things calmed down and a refreshed Harrison made his peace with Lennon the following day, the latter turning up to watch the matinee performance at a distance.

Troubling for Harrison was the fact that he was being pursued through these final few tour dates by Allen Klein, whose private investigator, the burly John Loiacono, repeatedly tried to corner him to serve a summons in affairs linked to the litigious ending of Klein's management contract in 1973. Loiacono apparently tracked down Harrison's hotel room late on 18 December,

---

[365] 25 September 1974, interview with Paul Drew for RKO Radio Networks.
[366] See Pang and Edwards, p276-277.

pounding on the door before being thrown out. Unrelenting, he proceeded to show up at the Madison Square Garden concert the following day, slipping his way backstage before being ejected, then re-surfacing from the audience (having bought himself a ticket specifically to regain entry) and trying to collar Harrison before the show started. All of which seemed to spook Starr, who like Harrison, was in Klein's legal crosshairs, and it was in this context that Starr decided not to travel to the dissolution summit, and remain in the relative safety of London. It was unfortunate since it meant the four would not be coming together for this one last occasion, Starr arranging instead to sign the necessary forms and have them couriered to New York, ready for the others to add their signatures. Four were down to three.

McCartney landed in New York as planned with no such concerns, since he never instructed Klein as manager in the first place. (Although that didn't stop Klein trying to initiate speculative legal action against him, which was thrown out of court.) McCartney arrived ahead of Harrison's 41st show at Madison Square Garden, previously the scene of the Concert For Bangla Desh, and where Lennon had performed his One To One concert in 1972 – both events at which McCartney had been invited to perform. McCartney went to the gig, where surreptitious photos were taken of him and Linda sitting in the audience in comical disguises, hoping in vain not to be recognised. It so happened that the same day, 19 December, Lennon's son, Julian, arrived in New York, having arranged to spend Christmas there – only to be met with an agitated father who had begun to panic about the prospects of signing the dissolution papers.

After the night's show finished it was time for the signing ceremony, Harrison making his way back to the Plaza Hotel at around midnight. The concert tour was being filmed by David Acomba, who sought to record this historic moment for inclusion in his planned documentary movie, one of the first things he captured, footage of Harrison hurriedly escaping from Klein's investigator, John Loiacono, who was there in the lobby ready to serve his papers, Harrison ducking down a stairwell to escape – a move he'd learned in his Beatlemania years. The main room was set out with two large tables, one on either side, piled with documents awaiting the signatures which were to legally end the Beatles' partnership. Starr was connected from London by speakerphone, his signatures already in place. McCartney was present, ready to sign, Harrison turned up – but someone was conspicuously absent. Lennon's current home on East 52nd Street was only a few minutes from the Plaza, there being no practical reason why he couldn't be there. In fact he'd got cold feet during the evening and locked himself in his bedroom, according to May Pang, panicking over his coming tax liabilities and so refusing to attend.[367]

---

[367] See Pang, 2008, p98. In her 1983 memoir, she gives a different context to his stalling, >

Likely Lennon was also wrestling with the thought that once he signed, there was no going back – this act would mean the irreversible end of the group, a finality he might well have sensed the enormity of – as he had in 1969 when refusing to divulge his resignation from the Beatles for more than half a year. An irritated Harrison got on the phone to berate Lennon and tell him he couldn't join him on stage the next night as agreed, but to no avail. Lennon wasn't going to change his mind and so three were down to two.

Harrison and McCartney went ahead and signed the forms, as captured in Acomba's fascinating footage. Both look extremely uncomfortable, McCartney sporting a Wings jumper and scratching his forehead in seeming annoyance, Harrison wearing a Paramahansa Yogananda badge and chanting 'Krishna, Krishna' under his breath as he puts pen to paper. This remarkable film, less than a minute of which has been seen, also finds Harrison pensively, and tellingly remarking, 'these are more papers that I don't know what they say, that I'm signing', as various officers and advisors bustle around him, pointing to where he should apply his name.[368] Unfortunately, without Lennon the papers were meaningless, and so Harrison and McCartney were forced to sleep on it, unsure exactly where things now stood.

The following day, Friday 20th, *Dark Horse* was finally issued in Britain, on the very date that Harrison's tour was due to close with two further performances at Madison Square Garden, in aid of UNICEF – shows which Lennon wouldn't now be attending.[369] In the fall-out of the previous night's events, McCartney contacted Lennon directly to try to reassure him that dissolving the group was the right thing to do and that the tax issues could be overcome. Whatever McCartney said, Lennon's resolve softened and he consented to travel over to Park Avenue to discuss options with McCartney's advisor, John Eastman – a scene inconceivable had Allen Klein still been in the picture.

Julian had meantime been taken to see Harrison's show by Hilary Gerrard, there on Starr's behalf, a performance at which Harrison had worn a seemingly conciliatory 'Free Lennon' badge (a campaign button linked to his residency

---

claiming Lennon only left the Beatles in the first place because Ono wanted him to, and that, 'he felt inclined to take a position opposite from that of Paul McCartney' (p275). None of this rings particularly true.

[368] The footage can be seen at the start of the Martin Scorsese documentary, *Living In The Material Word* (2011). Paramahansa Yogananda was author of *Autobiography Of A Yogi* which in 1966 sparked Harrison's interest in Hindu philosophy.

[369] It's interesting to consider what Harrison and Lennon might have performed together had things not turned sour. Harrison had Lennon's In My Life in his set list, which must have been a contender. Other candidates were Harrison's Beatles songs, eg, Something. More likely they would have fallen back on some old rock and roll favourites from the Cavern days.

struggles). The 11-year-old chatted to Harrison and was told his father had been forgiven, and was welcome to attend the after-show party that night – news which was telephoned through to Lennon, interrupting his business meeting. It seems that despite everything, and quite unexpectedly, solidarity was somehow going to win the day.

The night's party was another event of historical Beatles importance. Held at the fashionable Hippopotamus discothèque on Manhattan's East 62nd Street, two minutes from the Plaza, it was the last time Harrison, Lennon and McCartney were together, the three of them reportedly sharing a group hug with the dissolution issue temporarily parked to one side. (This was likely also the last time Harrison ever saw Lennon.[370]) Although the rest of the night seems to have gone without a hitch, the spectre of Klein still lurked at the edges, another of his investigators, William Ward, trying to get to Harrison as he entered the club, meeting a physical obstruction as 'eight men formed a circle around one of the car doors from which Harrison emerged'.[371] Klein's summons never was served – at least, not that night, and by the morning he seemed to have given up the chase.

The Beatles went their separate ways on the Saturday. Lennon, Pang and Julian had been invited to stay with Morris Levy and his son, Adam, in Florida, and perhaps welcoming the breathing space it promised, they set off that same day. Lennon realised they could spend Christmas away from the pressures of New York, and that while they were there, he could take Julian to see Disney World. The break allowed him to clear his head, and over Christmas he reconciled himself to finally signing the group's dissolution papers. Accordingly they were transported down to him, and on Sunday 29 December he signed off the Beatles in a rented room at the Polynesian Village Resort Hotel in Disney World.[372] Lennon, who had started the group in late 1956 now committed the final act to end it, the conclusion of an 18-year journey from Quarry Bank High School For Boys in Liverpool, around the world to Disney, Florida.

The legal conclusion of the Beatles technically occurred on 9 January 1975, when McCartney's four-year-old case was settled, the completed paperwork having been sent back to London for the court to make its formal declaration. A cursory glance at the current edition of *Billboard* shows that on this day, Lennon was at 47 on the singles chart with [251] #9 Dream; Harrison was at 16

---

[370] It was probably this week that Harrison and Lennon did a joint radio interview for Radio KHJ, in which they discuss the Beatles and other acts. It's sometimes dated to the following day, 21 December, but is likely earlier.

[371] Soocher, p176.

[372] May Pang took photos of him in the act of signing, published in Pang, 2008, p99-101.

with [274] Dark Horse; Starr was at 7 with [259] Only You and McCartney was at 4 with [240] Junior's Farm. Appropriately, Lennon and McCartney were at number 1, courtesy of Elton John's version of Lucy In The Sky With Diamonds, on which Lennon sang and played.

They ended at the very top.

SONG LIST

Years indicate release dates. Where a track is marked as unreleased, this refers to the period until 1975. Several 'unreleased' tracks are available today, principally on CD reissues of their associated albums.

[94]   3 Legs [McCartney, 1971]
[251] #9 Dream [Lennon, 1974]
[50] $15 Draw [Starr, 1970]
[176] 1882 [McCartney, unreleased]

[277] Ain't That A Shame [Lennon, 1975]
[215] Aisumasen (I'm Sorry) [Lennon, 1973]
[260] All By Myself [Starr, 1974]
[43]   All Things Must Pass [Harrison, 1970]
[71]   Almost 12 Bar Honky Tonk [Harrison, unreleased]
[231] Angel Baby [Lennon, unreleased]
[152] Angela [Lennon, 1972]
[92]   Another Day [McCartney, 1971]
[73]   Apple Scruffs [Harrison, 1970]
[65]   Art Of Dying [Harrison, 1970]
[155] Attica State [Lennon, 1972]
[63]   Awaiting On You All [Harrison, 1970]

[143] Back Off Boogaloo [Starr, 1972]
[98]   Back Seat Of My Car, The [McCartney, 1971]
[39]   Ballad Of Sir Frankie Crisp (Let It Roll) [Harrison, 1970]
[221] Band On The Run [McCartney, 1973]
[140] Bangla-Desh [Harrison, 1971]
[182] Be Here Now [Harrison, 1973]
[46]   Beaucoups Of Blues [Starr, 1970]
[283] Be-Bop-A-Lula [Lennon, 1975]
[230] Be My Baby [Lennon, unreleased]
[252] Beef Jerky [Lennon, 1974]
[40]   Behind That Locked Door [Harrison, 1970]
[62]   Beware Of Darkness [Harrison, 1970]
[157] Big Barn Bed [McCartney, 1973]
[132] Bip Bop [McCartney, 1971]
[244] Bless You [Lennon, 1974]
[142] Blindman [Starr, 1972]
[8]   Blue, Turning Grey Over You [Starr, 1970]
[224] Bluebird [McCartney, 1973]
[229] Bony Moronie [Lennon, 1975]
[173] Bridge On The River Suite [McCartney, unreleased]
[278] Bring It On Home To Me-Send Me Some Lovin' [Lennon, 1975]

[209]	Bring On The Lucie (Freda Peeple)	[Lennon, 1973]
[17]	Bye Bye Blackbird	[Starr, 1970]
[268]	Bye Bye, Love	[Harrison, 1974]

[166]	C Moon	[McCartney, 1972]
[255]	Call Me	[Starr, 1974]
[2]	Cold Turkey	[Lennon, 1969]
[57]	Coochy-Coochy	[Starr, 1970]
[170]	Country Dreamer	[McCartney, 1973]
[128]	Crippled Inside	[Lennon, 1971]

[274]	Dark Horse	[Harrison, 1974]
[183]	Day The World Gets 'Round, The	[Harrison, 1973]
[115]	Dear Boy	[McCartney, 1971]
[135]	Dear Friend	[McCartney, 1971]
[141]	Deep Blue	[Harrison, 1971]
[31]	Dehra Dun	[Harrison, unreleased]
[197]	Devil Woman	[Starr, 1973]
[228]	Ding Dong	[Harrison, 1974]
[123]	Do The Oz	[Lennon, unreleased]
[279]	Do You Want To Dance	[Lennon, 1975]
[190]	Don't Let Me Wait Too Long	[Harrison, 1973]
[204]	Down And Out	[Starr, 1973]
[69]	Down To The River (Rocking Chair Jam)	[Harrison, unreleased]
[7]	Dream	[Starr, 1970]

[77]	Early 1970	[Starr, 1971]
[263]	Easy For Me	[Starr, 1974]
[95]	Eat At Home	[McCartney, 1971]
[28]	Every Night	[McCartney, 1970]

[269]	Far East Man	[Harrison, 1974]
[53]	Fastest Growing Heartache in the West	[Starr, 1970]

[93]	Get On The Right Thing	[McCartney, 1973]
[145]	Give Ireland Back To The Irish	[McCartney, 1972]
[184]	Give Me Love (Give Me Peace On Earth)	[Harrison, 1973]
[125]	Give Me Some Truth	[Lennon, 1971]
[1]	Give Peace A Chance	[Lennon, 1969]
[86]	God	[Lennon, 1970]
[122]	God Save Us	[Lennon, unreleased]
[246]	Going Down On Love	[Lennon, 1974]
[32]	Going Down To Golders Green	[Harrison, unreleased]
[258]	Goodnight Vienna	[Starr, 1974]
[192]	Gotta Sing, Gotta Dance	[McCartney, unreleased]
[114]	Great Cock And Seagull Race	[McCartney, unreleased]

[174]	Hands Of Love	[McCartney, 1973]
[78]	Happy Birthday John	[Starr, unreleased]
[144]	Happy Xmas (War Is Over)	[Lennon, 1971]
[266]	Hari's On Tour (Express)	[Harrison, 1974]
[11]	Have I Told You Lately That I Love You?	[Starr, 1970]
[194]	Have You Seen My Baby	[Starr, 1973]
[64]	Hear Me Lord	[Harrison, 1970]
[109]	Heart Of The Country	[McCartney, 1971]
[222]	Helen Wheels	[McCartney, 1973]
[235]	Here We Go Again	[Lennon, unreleased]
[100]	Hey Diddle	[McCartney, unreleased]
[169]	Hi, Hi, Hi	[McCartney, 1972]
[271]	His Name Is Legs (Ladies And Gentlemen)	[Harrison, unreleased]
[167]	Hold Me Tight	[McCartney, 1973]
[84]	Hold On	[Lennon, 1970]
[148]	Honey, Don't	[Lennon, unreleased]
[151]	Honey Hush	[Lennon, unreleased]
[23]	Hot As Sun-Glasses	[McCartney, 1970]
[127]	How?	[Lennon, 1971]
[129]	How Do You Sleep?	[Lennon, 1971]
[256]	Husbands And Wives	[Starr, 1974]
[134]	I Am Your Singer	[McCartney, 1971]
[37]	I Dig Love	[Harrison, 1970]
[273]	I Don't Care Anymore	[Harrison, 1974]
[121]	I Don't Want To Be A Soldier	[Lennon, 1971]
[81]	I Found Out	[Lennon, 1970]
[205]	I Know (I Know)	[Lennon, 1973]
[97]	I Lie Around	[McCartney, 1973]
[41]	I Live For You	[Harrison, unreleased]
[72]	I Remember Jeep	[Harrison, 1970]
[56]	I Wouldn't Have You Any Other Way	[Starr, 1970]
[49]	I'd Be Talking All the Time	[Starr, 1970]
[35]	I'd Have You Anytime	[Harrison, 1970]
[265]	I'll Give You A Ring	[McCartney, unreleased]
[74]	I'll Still Love You	[Harrison, unreleased]
[12]	I'm A Fool To Care	[Starr, 1970]
[119]	I'm The Greatest	[Lennon, unreleased]
[200]	I'm The Greatest	[Starr, 1973]
[38]	If Not For You	[Harrison, 1970]
[130]	Imagine	[Lennon, 1971]
[3]	Instant Karma!	[Lennon, 1970]
[208]	Intuition	[Lennon, 1973]
[36]	Isn't It A Pity	[Harrison, 1970]
[85]	Isolation	[Lennon, 1970]
[14]	It Don't Come Easy	[Starr, 1971]
[272]	It Is 'He' (Jai Sri Krishna)	[Harrison, 1974]

[258] It's All Down To Goodnight Vienna [Starr, 1974]
[75]   It's Johnny's Birthday [Harrison, 1970]
[117] It's So Hard [Lennon, 1971]

[177] Jazz Street [McCartney, unreleased]
[124] Jealous Guy [Lennon, 1971]
[226] Jet [McCartney, 1973]
[156] John Sinclair [Lennon, 1972]
[240] Junior's Farm [McCartney, 1974]
[24]   Junk [McCartney, 1970]
[233] Just Because [Lennon, 1975]

[27]   Kreen-Akrore [McCartney, 1970]

[168] Lazy Dynamite [McCartney, 1973]
[67]   Let It Down [Harrison, 1970]
[225] Let Me Roll It [McCartney, 1973]
[13]   Let The Rest Of The World Go By [Starr, 1970]
[286] Letting Go [McCartney, 1975]
[189] Light That Has Lighted The World, The [Harrison, 1973]
[111] Little Lamb Dragonfly [McCartney, 1973]
[108] Little Woman Love [McCartney, 1972]
[191] Live And Let Die [McCartney, 1973]
[186] Living In The Material World [Harrison, 1973]
[102] Long Haired Lady [McCartney, 1971]
[90]   Look At Me [Lennon, 1970]
[185] Lord Loves The One (That Loves The Lord), The [Harrison, 1973]
[55]   Loser's Lounge [Starr, 1970]
[87]   Lost John [Lennon, unreleased]
[163] Loup (1st Indian On The Moon) [McCartney, 1973]
[91]   Love [Lennon, 1970]
[47]   Love Don't Last Long [Starr, 1970]
[101] Love For You, A [McCartney, unreleased]
[287] Love In Song [McCartney, 1975]
[9]   Love Is A Many Splendoured Thing [Starr, 1970]
[133] Love Is Strange [McCartney, 1971]
[18]   Lovely Linda, The [McCartney, 1970]
[238] Lucille [Lennon/McCartney, unreleased]
[154] Luck Of The Irish, The [Lennon, 1972]

[162] Mama's Little Girl [McCartney, unreleased]
[218] Mamunia [McCartney, 1973]
[30]   Man We Was Lonely [McCartney, 1970]
[165] Mary Had A Little Lamb [McCartney, 1972]
[270] Maya Love [Harrison, 1974]
[29]   Maybe I'm Amazed [McCartney, 1970]
[211] Meat City [Lennon, 1973]

[159]	Mess, The [McCartney, unreleased]
[213]	Mind Games [Lennon, 1973]
[181]	Miss O'Dell [Harrison, 1973]
[21]	Momma Miss America [McCartney, 1970]
[105]	Monkberry Moon Delight [McCartney, 1971]
[80]	Mother [Lennon, 1970]
[241]	Move Over Ms. L [Lennon, 1975]
[219]	Mrs. Vandebilt [McCartney, 1973]
[138]	Mumbo [McCartney, 1971]
[237]	My Baby Left Me [Lennon, unreleased]
[178]	My Love [McCartney, 1973]
[79]	My Mummy's Dead [Lennon, 1970]
[34]	My Sweet Lord [Harrison, 1970]
[88]	Mystery Train [Lennon, unreleased]
[58]	Nashville Freakout [Starr, unreleased]
[153]	New York City [Lennon, 1972]
[4]	Night And Day [Starr, 1970]
[171]	Night Out [McCartney, unreleased]
[227]	Nineteen Hundred And Eighty Five [McCartney, 1973]
[262]	No No Song [Starr, 1974]
[220]	No Words [McCartney, 1973]
[247]	Nobody Loves You (When You're Down And Out) [Lennon, 1974]
[113]	Now Hear This Song Of Mine [McCartney 1971]
[217]	Nutopian International Anthem [Lennon, 1973]
[254]	Occapella [Starr, 1974]
[131]	Oh My Love [Lennon, 1971]
[196]	Oh My My [Starr, 1973]
[104]	Oh Woman, Oh Why [McCartney, 1971]
[126]	Oh Yoko! [Lennon, 1971]
[250]	Old Dirt Road [Lennon, 1974]
[68]	Om Hare Om (Gopala Krishna) [Harrison, unreleased]
[216]	One Day (At A Time) [Lennon, 1973]
[172]	One More Kiss [McCartney, 1973]
[212]	Only People [Lennon, 1973]
[259]	Only You [Starr, 1974]
[25]	Oo You [McCartney, 1970]
[257]	Oo-Wee [Starr, 1974]
[70]	Out Of The Blue [Harrison, 1970]
[214]	Out The Blue [Lennon, 1973]
[276]	Peggy Sue [Lennon, 1975]
[198]	Photograph [Starr, 1973]
[223]	Picasso's Last Words (Drink To Me) [McCartney, 1973]
[60]	Plug Me In [Harrison, 1970]
[175]	Power Cut [McCartney, 1973]

[120]   Power To The People [Lennon, 1971]

[112]   Ram On [McCartney, 1971]
[280]   Ready Teddy [Lennon, 1975]
[89]   Remember [Lennon, 1970]
[280]   Rip It Up-Ready Teddy [Lennon, 1975]
[207]   Rock & Roll People [Lennon, unreleased]
[285]   Rock Show [McCartney, 1975]
[99]   Rode All Night [McCartney, unreleased]
[147]   Roll Over Beethoven [Lennon, unreleased]
[66]   Run Of The Mill [Harrison, 1970]

[239]   Sally G [McCartney, 1974]
[243]   Scared [Lennon, 1974]
[150]   Send Me Some Lovin' [Lennon, unreleased]
[278]   Send Me Some Lovin' [Lennon, 1975]
[10]   Sentimental Journey [Starr, 1970]
[54]   Silent Homecoming [Starr, 1970]
[267]   Simply Shady [Harrison, 1974]
[24]   Singalong Junk [McCartney, 1970]
[160]   Single Pigeon [McCartney, 1973]
[203]   Six O'Clock [Starr, 1973]
[281]   Slippin' And Slidin' [Lennon, 1975]
[110]   Smile Away [McCartney, 1971]
[261]   Snookeroo [Starr, 1974]
[188]   So Sad [Harrison, 1974]
[264]   Soily [McCartney, unreleased]
[136]   Some People Never Know [McCartney, 1971]
[282]   Stand By Me [Lennon, 1975]
[6]   Stardust [Starr, 1970]
[249]   Steel And Glass [Lennon, 1974]
[199]   Step Lightly [Starr, 1973]
[5]   Stormy Weather [Starr, unreleased]
[179]   Sue Me, Sue You Blues [Harrison, 1973]
[22]   Suicide [McCartney, unreleased]
[146]   Sunday Bloody Sunday [Lennon, 1972]
[201]   Sunshine Life For Me (Sail Away Raymond) [Starr, 1973]
[103]   Sunshine Sometime [McCartney, unreleased]
[242]   Surprise, Surprise (Sweet Bird Of Paradox) [Lennon, 1974]
[232]   Sweet Little Sixteen [Lennon, 1975]

[26]   Teddy Boy [McCartney, 1970]
[164]   Thank You Darling [McCartney, unreleased]
[59]   Thanks For The Pepperoni [Harrison, 1970]
[187]   That Is All [Harrison, 1973]
[19]   That Would Be Something [McCartney, 1970]
[275]   That'll Be The Day [Lennon, unreleased]

[206]   Tight A$ [Lennon, 1973]
[234]   To Know Her, Is To Love Her [Lennon, unreleased]
[137]   Tomorrow [McCartney, 1971]
[107]   Too Many People [McCartney, 1971]
[161]   Tragedy [McCartney, unreleased]
[116]   Try Some Buy Some [Harrison, 1973]

[106]   Uncle Albert-Admiral Halsey [McCartney, 1971]

[20]   Valentine Day [McCartney, 1970]

[33]   Wah-Wah [Harrison, 1970]
[48]   Waiting [Starr, 1970]
[42]   Wedding Bells (Are Breaking Up That Old Gang Of Mine) [Harrison, unreleased]
[118]   Well! [Lennon, unreleased]
[82]   Well Well Well [Lennon, 1970]
[61]   What Is Life [Harrison, 1970]
[248]   What You Got [Lennon, 1974]
[245]   Whatever Gets You Thru The Night [Lennon, 1974]
[158]   When The Night [McCartney, 1973]
[96]   When The Wind Is Blowing [McCartney, unreleased]
[16]   Whispering Grass (Don't Tell The Trees) [Starr, 1970]
[180]   Who Can See It [Harrison, 1973]
[139]   Wild Life [McCartney, 1971]
[51]   Wine, Women And Loud Happy Songs [Starr, 1970]
[52]   Wishing Book, The [Starr, unreleased]
[45]   Without Her [Starr, 1970]
[76]   Woman Don't You Cry For Me [Harrison, unreleased]
[149]   Woman Is The Nigger Of The World [Lennon, 1972]
[44]   Woman Of The Night [Starr, 1970]
[83]   Working Class Hero [Lennon, 1970]

[253]   Ya Ya [Lennon, 1974]
[284]   Ya Ya [Lennon, 1975]
[15]   You Always Hurt The One You Love [Starr, 1970]
[202]   You And Me (Babe) [Starr, 1973]
[210]   You Are Here [Lennon, 1973]
[236]   You Can't Catch Me [Lennon, 1975]
[195]   You're Sixteen [Starr, 1973]

[193]   Zoo Gang [McCartney, 1974]

RECORD RELEASES

All releases were on the Apple label. Highest chart placings are given in parentheses, taken from the recognised official listings in the UK (*Record Retailer/Music Week*) and US (*Billboard*).

Chronological list of studio albums

1970

Starr: *Sentimental Journey*
(UK: 27 Mar 1970 (7), US: 24 Apr 1970 (22))
[10] Sentimental Journey / [4] Night And Day / [16] Whispering Grass (Don't Tell The Trees) / [17] Bye Bye Blackbird / [12] I'm A Fool To Care / [6] Stardust / [8] Blue, Turning Grey Over You / [9] Love Is A Many Splendoured Thing / [7] Dream / [15] You Always Hurt The One You Love / [11] Have I Told You Lately That I Love You? / [13] Let The Rest Of The World Go By

McCartney: *McCartney*
(UK: 17 Apr 1970 (2), US: 20 Apr 1970 (1))
[18] The Lovely Linda / [19] That Would Be Something / [20] Valentine Day / [28] Every Night / [23] Hot As Sun-Glasses / [24] Junk / [30] Man We Was Lonely / [25] Oo You / [21] Momma Miss America / [26] Teddy Boy / [24] Singalong Junk / [29] Maybe I'm Amazed / [27] Kreen-Akrore

Starr: *Beaucoups Of Blues*
(UK: 25 Sep 1970 (-), US: 28 Sep 1970 (65))
[46] Beaucoups Of Blues / [47] Love Don't Last Long / [53] Fastest Growing Heartache in the West / [45] Without Her / [44] Woman Of The Night / [49] I'd Be Talking All the Time / [50] $15 Draw / [51] Wine, Women And Loud Happy Songs / [56] I Wouldn't Have You Any Other Way / [55] Loser's Lounge / [48] Waiting / [54] Silent Homecoming

Harrison: *All Things Must Pass*
(UK: 30 Nov 1970 (4), US: 27 Nov 1970 (1))
[35] I'd Have You Anytime / [34] My Sweet Lord / [33] Wah-Wah / [36] Isn't It A Pity (Version One) / [61] What Is Life / [38] If Not For You / [40] Behind That Locked Door / [67] Let It Down / [66] Run Of The Mill / [62] Beware Of Darkness / [73] Apple Scruffs / [39] Ballad Of Sir Frankie Crisp (Let It Roll) / [63] Awaiting On You All / [43] All Things Must Pass / [37] I Dig Love / [65] Art Of Dying / [36] Isn't It A Pity (Version Two) / [64] Hear Me Lord / [70] Out Of The Blue / [75] It's Johnny's Birthday / [60] Plug Me In / [72] I Remember Jeep / [59] Thanks For The Pepperoni

Lennon: *John Lennon/Plastic Ono Band*
(UK: 11 Dec 1970 (11), US: 11 Dec 1970 (6))
    [80] Mother / [84] Hold On / [81] I Found Out / [83] Working Class Hero / [85] Isolation / [89] Remember / [91] Love / [82] Well Well Well / [90] Look At Me / [86] God / [79] My Mummy's Dead

1971

McCartney: *RAM*
(UK: 17 May 1971 (1), US: 17 May 1971 (2))
    [107] Too Many People / [94] 3 Legs / [112] Ram On / [115] Dear Boy / [106] Uncle Albert-Admiral Halsey / [110] Smile Away / [109] Heart Of The Country / [105] Monkberry Moon Delight / [95] Eat At Home / [102] Long Haired Lady / [112] Ram On (Reprise) / [98] The Back Seat Of My Car

Lennon: *Imagine*
(UK: 8 Oct 1971 (1), US: 7 Sep 1971 (1))
    [130] Imagine / [128] Crippled Inside / [124] Jealous Guy / [117] It's So Hard / [121] I Don't Want To Be A Soldier / [125] Give Me Some Truth / [131] Oh My Love / [129] How Do You Sleep? / [127] How? / [126] Oh Yoko!

McCartney [with Wings]: *Wild Life*
(UK: 7 Dec 1971 (11), US: 7 Dec 1971 (10))
    [138] Mumbo / [132] Bip Bop / [133] Love Is Strange / [139] Wild Life / [136] Some People Never Know / [134] I Am Your Singer / [137] Tomorrow / [135] Dear Friend

1972

Lennon [with Yoko Ono]: *Some Time In New York City*
(UK: 15 Sep 1972 (11), US: 12 Jun 1972 (48))
    [149] Woman Is The Nigger Of The World / [155] Attica State / [153] New York City / [146] Sunday Bloody Sunday / [154] The Luck Of The Irish / [156] John Sinclair / [152] Angela
    [Yoko Ono tracks: Sisters, O Sisters / Born In A Prison / We're All Water. Also contains a bonus disc of live recordings.]

1973

McCartney [with Wings]: *Red Rose Speedway*
(UK: 4 May 1973 (5), US: 30 Apr 1973 (1))
    [157] Big Barn Bed / [178] My Love / [93] Get On The Right Thing / [172] One More Kiss / [111] Little Lamb Dragonfly / [160] Single Pigeon / [158] When The Night / [163] Loup (1st Indian On The Moon) / Medley: [167] Hold Me Tight-[168] Lazy Dynamite-[174] Hands Of Love-[175] Power Cut

Harrison: *Living In The Material World*
(UK: 22 Jun 1973 (2), US: 30 May 1973 (1))
> [184] Give Me Love (Give Me Peace On Earth) / [179] Sue Me, Sue You Blues / [189] The Light That Has Lighted The World / [190] Don't Let Me Wait Too Long / [180] Who Can See It / [186] Living In The Material World / [185] The Lord Loves The One (That Loves The Lord) / [182] Be Here Now / [116] Try Some Buy Some / [183] The Day The World Gets 'Round / [187] That Is All

Starr: *Ringo*
(UK: 9 Nov 1973 (7), US: 31 Oct 1973 (2))
> [200] I'm The Greatest / [194] Have You Seen My Baby / [198] Photograph / [201] Sunshine Life For Me (Sail Away Raymond) / [195] You're Sixteen / [196] Oh My My / [199] Step Lightly / [203] Six O'Clock / [197] Devil Woman / [202] You And Me (Babe)

Lennon: *Mind Games*
(UK: 16 Nov 1973 (13), US: 5 Nov 1973 (9))
> [213] Mind Games / [206] Tight A$ / [215] Aisumasen (I'm Sorry) / [216] One Day (At A Time) / [209] Bring On The Lucie (Freda Peeple) / [217] Nutopian International Anthem / [208] Intuition / [214] Out The Blue / [212] Only People / [205] I Know (I Know) / [210] You Are Here / [211] Meat City

McCartney [with Wings]: *Band On The Run*
(UK: 7 Dec 1973 (1), US: 5 Dec 1973 (1))
> [221] Band On The Run / [226] Jet / [224] Bluebird / [219] Mrs. Vandebilt / [225] Let Me Roll It / [218] Mamunia / [220] No Words / [223] Picasso's Last Words (Drink To Me) / [227] Nineteen Hundred And Eighty Five
> *US copies add [222] Helen Wheels between [220] and [223].*

1974

Lennon: *Walls And Bridges*
(UK: 4 Oct 1974 (6), US: 30 Sep 1974 (1))
> [246] Going Down On Love / [245] Whatever Gets You Thru The Night / [250] Old Dirt Road / [248] What You Got / [244] Bless You / [243] Scared / [251] #9 Dream / [242] Surprise, Surprise (Sweet Bird Of Paradox) / [249] Steel And Glass / [252] Beef Jerky / [247] Nobody Loves You (When You're Down And Out) / [253] Ya Ya

Starr: *Goodnight Vienna*
(UK: 15 Nov 1974 (30), US: 18 Nov 1974 (8))
> [258] Goodnight Vienna / [254] Occapella / [257] Oo-Wee / [256] Husbands And Wives / [261] Snookeroo / [260] All By Myself / [255] Call Me / [262] No No Song / [259] Only You / [263] Easy For Me / [258] Goodnight Vienna (Reprise)

Harrison: *Dark Horse*
(UK: 20 Dec 1974 (-), US: 9 Dec 1974 (4))
   [266] Hari's On Tour (Express) / [267] Simply Shady / [188] So Sad / [268] Bye Bye, Love / [270] Maya Love / [228] Ding Dong, Ding Dong / [274] Dark Horse / [269] Far East Man / [272] It Is 'He' (Jai Sri Krishna)

1975

Lennon: *Rock 'N' Roll*
(UK: 21 Feb 1975 (6), US: 17 Feb 1975 (6))
   [283] Be-Bop-A-Lula / [282] Stand By Me / [280] Medley: Rip It Up-Ready Teddy / [236] You Can't Catch Me / [277] Ain't That A Shame / [279] Do You Want To Dance / [232] Sweet Little Sixteen / [281] Slippin' And Slidin' / [276] Peggy Sue / [278] Medley: Bring It On Home To Me-Send Me Some Lovin' / [229] Bony Moronie / [284] Ya Ya / [233] Just Because

Chronological list of singles

1969

Lennon: [1] **Give Peace A Chance** / Remember Love [B-side by Yoko Ono]
   (UK: 4 Jul 1969 (2), US: 7 Jul 1969 (14))
Lennon: [2] **Cold Turkey** / Don't Worry Kyoko (Mummy's Only Looking For A Hand In The Snow) [B-side by Yoko Ono]
   (UK: 24 Oct 1969 (14), US: 20 Oct 1969 (30))

1970

Lennon: [3] **Instant Karma!** / Who Has Seen The Wind? [B-side by Yoko Ono]
   (UK: 6 Feb 1970 (5), US: 16 Feb 1970 (3))
Starr: [46] **Beaucoups Of Blues** / [57] **Coochy-Coochy**
   (US: 5 Oct 1970 (87))
Harrison: [34] **My Sweet Lord** / [36] **Isn't It A Pity**
   (US: 23 Nov 1970 (1))
Lennon: [80] **Mother** / Why [B-side by Yoko Ono]
   (US: 28 Dec 1970 (43))

1971

Harrison: [34] **My Sweet Lord** / [61] **What Is Life**
   (UK: 15 Jan 1971 (1))
Harrison: [61] **What Is Life** / [73] **Apple Scruffs**
   (US: 15 Feb 1971 (10))
McCartney: [92] **Another Day** / [104] **Oh Woman, Oh Why**
   (UK: 19 Feb 1971 (2), US: 22 Feb 1971 (5))

Lennon: [120] **Power To The People** / Open Your Box [B-side by Yoko Ono]
   (UK: 8 Mar 1971 (7))
Lennon: [120] **Power To The People** / Touch Me [B-side by Yoko Ono]
   (US: 22 Mar 1971 (11))
Starr: [14] **It Don't Come Easy** / [77] **Early 1970**
   (UK: 9 Apr 1971 (4), US: 16 Apr 1971 (4))
Harrison: [140] **Bangla-Desh** / [141] **Deep Blue**
   (UK: 30 Jul 1971 (10), US: 28 Jul 1971 (23))
McCartney: [106] **Uncle Albert-Admiral Halsey** / [107] **Too Many People**
   (US: 2 Aug 1971 (1))
McCartney: [98] **The Back Seat Of My Car** / [109] **Heart Of The Country**
   (UK: 13 Aug 1971 (39))
Lennon: [130] **Imagine** / [117] **It's So Hard**
   (US: 11 Oct 1971 (3))
Lennon: [144] **Happy Xmas (War Is Over)** / Listen, The Snow Is Falling
   [B-side by Yoko Ono]
   (US: 6 Dec 1971 (42))

1972

McCartney [with Wings]: [145] **Give Ireland Back To The Irish** / [145] **Give Ireland Back To The Irish (Version)**
   (UK: 25 Feb 1972 (16), US: 28 Feb 1972 (21))
Starr: [143] **Back Off Boogaloo** / [142] **Blindman**
   (UK: 17 Mar 1972 (2), US: 20 Mar 1972 (9))
Lennon: [149] **Woman Is The Nigger Of The World** / Sisters, O Sisters
   [B-side by Yoko Ono]
   (US: 24 Apr 1972 (57))
McCartney [with Wings]: [165] **Mary Had A Little Lamb** / [108] **Little Woman Love**
   (UK: 12 May 1972 (9), US: 29 May 1972 (28))
Lennon: [144] **Happy Xmas (War Is Over)** / Listen, The Snow Is Falling
   [B-side by Yoko Ono]
   (UK: 24 Nov 1972 (4))
McCartney [with Wings]: [169] **Hi, Hi, Hi** / [166] **C Moon**
   (UK: 1 Dec 1972 (5), US: 4 Dec 1972 (10))

1973

McCartney [with Wings]: [178] **My Love** / [159] **The Mess**
   (UK: 23 Mar 1973 (9), US: 9 Apr 1973 (1))
Harrison: [184] **Give Me Love (Give Me Peace On Earth)** / [181] **Miss O'Dell**
   (UK: 25 May 1973 (8), US: 7 May 1973 (1))
McCartney [with Wings]: [191] **Live And Let Die** / [97] **I Lie Around**
   (UK: 1 Jun 1973 (9), US: 18 Jun 1973 (2))
Starr: [198] **Photograph** / [204] **Down And Out**
   (UK: 19 Oct 1973 (8), US: 24 Sep 1973 (1))

McCartney [with Wings]: [222] **Helen Wheels** / [170] **Country Dreamer**
 (UK: 26 Oct 1973 (12), US: 12 Nov 1973 (10))
Lennon: [213] **Mind Games** / [211] **Meat City**
 (UK: 9 Nov 1973 (26), US: 29 Oct 1973 (18))
Starr: [195] **You're Sixteen** / [197] **Devil Woman**
 (UK: 8 Feb 1974 (4), US: 3 Dec 1973 (1))

1974

McCartney [with Wings]: [226] **Jet** / [218] **Mamunia**
 (US: 28 Jan 1974 (-))
McCartney [with Wings]: [226] **Jet** / [225] **Let Me Roll It**
 (UK: 15 Feb 1974 (7), US: 18 Feb 1974 (7))
Starr: [196] **Oh My My** / [199] **Step Lightly**
 (US: 18 Feb 1974 (5))
McCartney [with Wings]: [221] **Band On The Run** / [227] **Nineteen Hundred And Eighty-Five**
 (US: 8 Apr 1974 (1))
McCartney [with Wings]: [221] **Band On The Run** / [193] **Zoo Gang**
 (UK: 28 Jun 1974 (3))
Lennon: [245] **Whatever Gets You Thru The Night** / [252] **Beef Jerky**
 (UK: 4 Oct 1974 (36), US: 23 Sep 1974 (1))
McCartney [with Wings]: [240] **Junior's Farm** / [239] **Sally G**
 (UK: 25 Oct 1974 (16), US: 4 Nov 1974 (3))
Starr: [259] **Only You (And You Alone)** / [255] **Call Me**
 (UK: 15 Nov 1974 (28), US: 11 Nov 1974 (6))
Harrison: [274] **Dark Horse** / [273] **I Don't Care Anymore**
 (US: 18 Nov 1974 (15))
Harrison: [228] **Ding Dong** / [273] **I Don't Care Anymore**
 (UK: 6 Dec 1974 (38))
Lennon: [251] **#9 Dream** / [248] **What You Got**
 (UK: 24 Jan 1975 (23), US: 16 Dec 1974 (9))
Harrison: [228] **Ding Dong; Ding Dong** / [266] **Hari's On Tour (Express)**
 (US: 23 Dec 1974 (36))

1975

Starr: [262] **No No Song** / [261] **Snookeroo**
 (US: 27 Jan 1975 (3))
Starr: [261] **Snookeroo** / [257] **Oo-Wee**
 (UK: 21 Feb 1975 (-))
Harrison: [274] **Dark Horse** / [266] **Hari's On Tour (Express)**
 (UK: 28 Feb 1975 (-))
Lennon: [282] **Stand By Me** / [241] **Move Over Ms. L**
 (UK: 18 Apr 1975 (30), US: 10 Mar 1975 (20))
Starr: [258] **It's All Down To Goodnight Vienna** / [257] **Oo-Wee**
 (US: 2 Jun 1975 (31))

BIBLIOGRAPHY

Allan, Adrian *Paul McCartney After The Beatles: A Musical Appreciation*
— Meadow Music Publishing (2019)

Badman, Keith *The Beatles Diary Volume 2: After The Break-Up 1970-2001*
— Omnibus (revised, 2001)

Badman, Keith *The Beatles – The Dream Is Over: Off The Record 2* – Omnibus (2002)

Baker, Ginger *Hellraiser – The Autobiography Of The World's Greatest Drummer*
— John Blake Publishing (2010)

Beatles, The *Anthology* – Cassell & Co (2000)

Bedford, Carol *Waiting For The Beatles: An Apple Scruff's Story* – Blandford Press (1984)

Bennahum, David *In Their Own Words: The Beatles… After The Break-Up*
— Omnibus (1991)

Black, Cilla *What's It All About?* – Ebury Press (2003)

Blake, John *All You Needed Was Love* – Hamlyn (1981)

Blaney, John *John Lennon: Listen To This Book* – Paper Jukebox (2017)

Boyd, Pattie *Wonderful Tonight: George Harrison, Eric Clapton And Me*
— Harmony Books (2007)

Clayson, Alan *Ringo Starr* – Sanctuary (1996)

Davies, Hunter *The Beatles* – first published 1968; updated edition, Cassell (2002)

Davies, Hunter (Ed) *The John Lennon Letters* – Weidenfeld & Nicolson (2012)

Doggett, Peter *You Never Give Me Your Money: The Battle For The Soul Of The Beatles*
— The Bodley Head (2009)

Emerick, Geoff *Here, There And Everywhere: My Life Recording The Music Of The Beatles*
— Gotham Books (2006)

Fawcett, Anthony *John Lennon One Day At A Time* – Grove Press (1976)

Fearon, Gary *After Abbey Road: The Solo Hits Of The Beatles* – (self-published) (2020)

Friede, Goldie; Titone, Robin; Weiner, Sue *The Beatles A To Z* – Eyre Methuen (1981)

Giuliano, Geoffrey *Dark Horse – The Private Life Of George Harrison* – Dutton (1990)

Golson, G. Barry (Ed) *The Playboy Interviews With John Lennon & Yoko Ono*
– Playboy Press (1981)

Granados, Stefan *Those Were The Days: An Unofficial History Of The Beatles Apple Organization* – Cherry Red (2002)

Harrison, George *I, Me, Mine* – Genesis (1980)

Howlett, Kevin *The Beatles: The BBC Archives 1962 To 1970* – BBC Books (2013)

Ingham, Chris *The Rough Guide To The Beatles* – Rough Guides (2006)

Jackson, Andrew Grant *Still The Greatest – The Essential Songs Of The Beatles' Solo Careers* – Scarecrow Press (2012)

Janov, Dr Arthur *The Primal Scream* – Abacus (first UK edition, 1973)

John, Elton *Me* – Henry Holt & Co (2019)

Leng, Simon *While My Guitar Gently Weeps: The Music Of George Harrison* – Hal Leonard (2006)

Lennon, Cynthia *John* – Hodder & Stoughton (2005)

Lewisohn, Mark *The Complete Beatles Chronicle* – Chancellor Press (1996)

Lewisohn, Mark *All These Years Volume 1: Tune In* [extended special edition] – Little, Brown (2013)

MacDonald, Ian *Revolution In The Head: The Beatles' Records And The Sixties* – revised edition, Vintage Books (2005)

Madinger, Chip; Easter, Mark *Eight Arms To Hold You: The Solo Beatles Compendium* – 44.1 Productions (2000)

Madinger, Chip; Raile, Scott *Lennonology Volume One: Strange Days Indeed – A Scrapbook Of Madness* – Open Your Books (2015)

Masters, Robert; Houston, Jean *Mind Games: The Guide To Inner Space* – Barnes & Noble (1972)

McCartney, Paul *The Lyrics* – Allen Lane (2021)

McCartney, Paul with Miles, Barry *Many Years From Now* – Henry Holt and Company (1997)

Mellers, Wilfred *Twilight Of The Gods* – Faber (1973)

Norman, Philip *John Lennon: The Life* – Harper Collins (2009)

Norman, Philip *Paul McCartney: The Biography* – W&N (2016)

Ono, Yoko (Ed) *Memories Of John Lennon* – Perfect Bound (2005)

Pang, May *Instamatic Karma: Photographs Of John Lennon* – St Martin's Press (2008)

Pang, May; Edwards, Henry *Loving John* – Warner Books (1983)

Perasi, Luca *Paul McCartney: Recording Sessions (1969-2013)* – L.I.L.Y. Publishing (2013)

Perry, Richard *Cloud Nine: Memoirs Of A Record Producer* – Redwood Publishing (2020)

Piepa, Jorg with MacCarthy, Ian *The Solo Beatles Film & TV Chronicle*
– (self-published) (2019)

Prescott, Rick *Save The Beatles: The Rescued Albums 1970-1982* – (self-published) (2020)

Ram Dass *Be Here Now* – Lama Foundation (1971)

Rodriguez, Robert *Fab Four FAQ 2.0 – The Beatles' Solo Years, 1970-1980*
– Backbeat (2010)

Rodriguez, Robert *Solo In The 70s John, Paul, George, Ringo: 1970-1980*
– Parading Press (2014)

Rubin, Jerry *DO IT!: Scenarios Of The Revolution* – Simon and Schuster (1970)

Schaffner, Nicholas *The Beatles Forever* – McGraw-Hill (1978)

Snow, Mat *The Beatles Solo* – Race Point Publishing (2013)

Soocher, Stan *Baby You're A Rich Man: Suing The Beatles For Fun And Profit*
– ForeEdge (2015)

Sounes, Howard *An Intimate Life Of Paul McCartney* – Harper Collins (2010)

Spector, Ronnie *Be My Baby* – Onyx (1990)

Stannard, Neville *Working Class Heroes: An Illustrated Discography* – Virgin (1983)

Sulpy, Doug with Schweighardt, Ray *Drugs, Divorce And A Slipping Image*
– The 910 (2007)

Thomson, Graeme *George Harrison: Behind That Locked Door* – Omnibus (2016)

Unterberger, Richie *The Unreleased Beatles* – Backbeat (2006)

Urish, Ben; Bielen, Ken *The Words And Music Of John Lennon* – Praeger (2007)

Wenner, Jan (Ed) *Lennon Remembers* – Straight Arrow Books (1971)

Wild, Andrew *The Solo Beatles 1969-1980* – Sonicbond (2019)

Womack, Kenneth; Kruppa, Jason *All Things Must Pass Away: Harrison, Clapton And Other Assorted Love Songs* – Chicago Review Press (2021)

INDEX

12 Songs, 245
44th Street Fairies, the, 329
100 Proof Aged In Soul, 309
200 Motels, 169
10538 Overture, 282

ABKCO, 74, 177, 274, 370
AC Bhaktivedanta Swami Prabhupada, 232, 233
Acomba, David, 363, 387, 388
Across The Great Divide, 104
Admiral Halsey, 122
Adock, Johnny, 65
Again And Again And Again, 281
Ahh Laine!, 281
Ain't She Sweet, 55
Ain't That A Shame, 369
Ali, Muhammad, 136
Ali, Tariq, 93, 138, 140, 145, 147
All Along The Watchtower, 46
All I Really Want To Do, 145
All In Love Is Fair, 322
All Things Pass, 56
Allan, Adrian, 166
Allison, Jerry, 368
Also Sprach Zarathustra (theme from *2001: A Space Odyssey*), 348
American Graffiti, 247
Anderson, Jim, 143
Apple Records, 17, 134, 159, 170, 220, 228, 248, 292, 305, 317, 348, 357
Apple Scruffs, the, 84
Apple Studios, 47, 134, 173, 174, 226, 227, 228, 229, 230, 231, 232, 233, 234, 235, 236, 237, 246, 255, 256
Applejacks, the, 19
Aprea, Ron, 318, 319, 320, 324, 325, 326, 327, 330
Armstrong, Louis, 14, 15
Aronowitz, Al, 82, 83
Ars Moriendi, 78
Ascher, Ken, 260, 261, 262, 263, 265, 266, 267, 268, 269, 270, 271, 272, 318, 319, 320, 321, 322, 324, 325, 326, 327, 328, 329, 367, 368, 369, 370, 371, 373, 374, 375
Ascot Sound Studio, 135, 136, 137, 139, 141, 142, 143, 145, 146, 147, 148, 149, 150, 151, 153, 156, 337
Asher, Peter, 228
Ashton, Gardner and Dyke, 49

Ashton, Tony, 47, 49
Aspinall, Neil, 361
Astaire, Fred, 13
Atkins, Chet, 314
Attica Correctional Facility, 193
Attitudes, 352
Autobiography Of A Yogi, 388
Autumn Leaves, 13
Axton, Hoyt, 346
Axton, Mae Boren, 346

Baby Let's Play House, 40, 305
Badfinger, 21, 40, 42, 43, 47, 72, 80, 140, 155, 170, 171, 245, 255
Baez, Joan, 172
Baker, Ginger, 83, 276, 277, 278, 282, 286, 287, 288, 313
Baldi, Ferdinando, 173
Ballad of East and West, The, 265
Band, The (album), 254
Band, the, 46, 53, 56, 57, 82, 104, 191, 201, 254, 280, 345, 356
Barham, John, 42, 44, 47, 48, 56, 72, 73, 75, 76, 77, 80, 88, 139, 143, 145, 153, 228, 234
Barrett, John, 39, 55, 65
Barrett, Richie, 10
Barrow, Len, 65
Barry, Jeff, 297, 298, 299, 300, 301, 302, 304, 305, 306
Barry, John, 240
Basement Tapes, The, 82
Basil Brush Show, The, 205
Bassey, Shirley, 240
BBC, 11, 112, 114, 137, 169, 174, 179, 181, 186, 205, 246, 251, 252, 255, 269, 284, 287, 300, 303, 311, 323, 330, 337, 377
Be Here Now (book), 229
Beatlefest, 377
Beatles & Co, 226
Beatles, the, *passim*
  1962-1966, 221, 238, 251
  1967-1970, 221, 238, 251
  Abbey Road (album), 9, 30, 35, 37, 119, 209, 216, 305
  Abbey Road Revisited, 377
  Across The Universe, 269
  Act Naturally, 342
  Alpha Omega, 221
  Anthology, 55, 325
  Back In The USSR, 35

Ballad Of John And Yoko, The, 29, 42, 124, 192
Beatles For Sale, 186
Beatles' Second Album, The, 185
Being For The Benefit Of Mr Kite, 29
Blackbird, 203, 288
Boys, 200
Can't Buy Me Love, 215
Carry That Weight, 119
Christmas Time Is Here Again, 176
Come Together, 184, 198, 226, 266, 305, 306
Dear Prudence, 191
Decca audition, 181, 303, 367
Dig A Pony, 148, 269
Dizzy Miss Lizzy, 257
Don't Pass Me By, 20, 250
Drive My Car, 319
Eleanor Rigby, 109, 110
End, The, 119, 216
Everybody's Got Something To Hide Except Me And My Monkey, 245
Fixing A Hole, 254
Fool On The Hill, The, 161
Free As A Bird, 175
Get Back, 78, 131
Get Back (album), 11, 32, 57, 112, 167, 377
Get Back (sessions), 28, 31, 33, 38, 40, 46, 48, 57, 76, 79, 81, 95, 102, 109, 115, 144, 145, 148, 250, 368, 377
Getting Better, 56, 261
Glass Onion, 353
Good Morning Good Morning, 131
Happiness Is A Warm Gun, 8, 100, 121
Hard Day's Night, A (album), 24
Hard Day's Night, A (film), 30
Help!, 320, 324
Help! (album), 161
Help! (film), 342
Helter Skelter, 64, 184
Here Comes The Sun, 253, 319, 361
Here, There And Everywhere, 56
Hey Bulldog, 100
Hey Jude, 119, 153, 294, 344, 350
Hold Me Tight, 210
Honey Pie, 30
I Am The Walrus, 14, 358
I Me Mine, 26
I Saw Her Standing There, 126, 323
I Told You Before, 95
I Want To Tell You, 78, 234
I Want You (She's So Heavy), 266
I'll Get You, 152

I'm A Loser, 67
I've Got A Feeling, 54, 261
In My Life, 364, 388
In Spite Of All The Danger, 367
Inner Light, The, 52
Julia, 105, 173
Let It Be, 35, 173
Let It Be (album), 4, 36, 38, 123, 144
Let It Be (film), 36, 41, 148, 286, 350
Like Dreamers Do, 20
Long And Winding Road, The, 41, 162, 219, 234
Long Long Long, 46
Love Me Do, 216
Lovely Rita, 50
LS Bumblebee, 377
Lucy In The Sky With Diamonds, 265, 323, 345, 390
Magical Mystery Tour (film), 102, 242, 350
Martha My Dear, 290
Mean Mr. Mustard, 137
Mother Nature's Son, 26, 115, 144, 203
Nagra tapes, 76, 77, 131
Ob-La-Di, Ob-La-Da, 353
Octopus's Garden, 20, 250, 271
Oh! Darling, 94, 121
Penny Lane, 29, 72
Please Mr Postman, 200
Please Please Me (album), 167
Polythene Pam, 114, 216
Real Love, 29
Revolution, 97, 99, 137, 138, 230
Revolver, 47, 56, 78, 166
Savoy Truffle, 353
Sgt Pepper, 24, 29, 56, 107, 150, 154, 166, 251, 253, 258, 282, 285, 293, 295, 343, 350, 362, 377
Sexy Sadie, 57, 101, 248, 270, 305, 353, 354
She Loves You, 289
She's Leaving Home, 110
Something, 104, 235, 356, 388
songs written in India, 29, 31, 39, 105, 144, 145
Strawberry Fields Forever, 14, 50, 184
Sun King, 213
Sweet Apple Trax, 377
Telecasts, 377
Thank You Girl, 204
Things We Said Today, 203
This Boy, 100
Two Of Us, 144
What's The New Mary Jane, 377

While My Guitar Gently Weeps, 41, 46, 295
White Album, 30, 31, 57, 64, 144, 265, 353
Why Don't We Do It In The Road, 211
With A Little Help From My Friends, 13, 63, 118
With The Beatles, 185, 210
Yellow Matter Custard, 181, 377
Yellow Submarine (film), 120, 122, 206, 288
Yer Blues, 262, 305
Yesterday, 60, 150, 164
You Never Give Me Your Money, 119, 284
Beatty, Warren, 301
Beaux Arts Orchestra, 281, 282, 283, 286, 290, 291, 292
Beaver, Paul, 131
Be-Bop-A-Lula, 379
Bedford, Carol, 85
Bee Gees, the, 23, 177
Before The Flood, 363
Beginnings, 249
Bell, Madeline, 174, 175
Below, Fred, 300
Bennett, Max, 352, 353
Bennett, Richard, 339, 340
Berlin, Irving, 14
Bernstein, Elmer, 18
Berry, Chuck, 62, 71, 90, 148, 149, 183, 185, 261, 295, 300, 305, 306, 372
Bessie Smith (song), 356
Bevan, Bev, 282
Bhagavad Gita, The, 84, 101, 233, 238
Bhaktivedanta Manor, 232
Big Seven Music Corp, 148, 295
Birdsong, Cindy, 344
Black Dog, 148
Black Dwarf, The, 137, 138
Black, Bill, 29, 316
Black, Cilla, 86, 174, 236, 243, 249
Blackberries, the, 341, 342
Blackburn, Robin, 138, 140
Blaine, Hal, 18, 297, 298, 299, 300, 301, 302, 304, 305, 306
Blindman, 169, 170, 173
Blonde On Blonde, 231
Bloody Sunday, 179, 183, 184, 192, 193, 198
Blossoms, the, 307
Blouin, Carl, 381
Blue Caps, the, 375
Blue Mink, 175
Blue Moon Of Kentucky, 208
Bluejean Bop!, 55

Blunstone, Colin, 281
Bodsworth Rubblesby, 348
Bolan, Marc, 174, 175, 245, 246, 249, 258, 337
Bonds, Gary U.S., 266, 305
Bonham, John, 244
Bonzo Dog Doo-Dah Band, 357
Booker T & the MGs, 251, 297
Booker, James, 245, 246
Boone, Pat, 369
Born To Boogie, 244
Boulting, Roy, 240
Bowie, David, 135, 348
Brambell, Wilfrid, 30
Bramlett, Bonnie, 42
Bramlett, Delaney, 38, 42, 87
Brecker, Michael, 263, 266, 267, 272
Brendell, Steve, 148
Bright Tunes, 44, 45
Brill Building, 297, 298
Bring It On Home To Me, 104, 370, 371, 379
Britton, Geoff, 313, 314, 315, 349, 351, 380, 381, 382
Brodie, Philip, 139
Bromberg, David, 253, 254
Bronstein, Stan, 183, 184, 185, 186, 189, 190, 191, 192, 193, 194
Brooker, Gary, 40, 80, 81, 256
Brother, 228
Brower, John, 10
Brown, James, 291
Brown, Jocelyn, 264
Brown, Melvin, 43
Bruce, Jack, 309
Bruce, Lenny, 71
Bruckner, Tim, 258
Buchanan, Jim, 59, 60
Build Me Up Buttercup, 246
Burnette, Johnny, 190, 246
Burton, Lori, 329
Butler, Joe, 181
Buttercup, 209

C'mon Everybody, 367
Calling Occupants Of Interplanetary Craft, 348
Calvert, Jim, 297, 298, 299, 300, 301, 302, 304, 305, 306
Calvert, Jimmy, 246, 247, 248, 249, 250
Candoli, Conte, 301, 302, 305, 306
Candy, 12, 170
Capp, Frank, 302, 304, 306
Captain Beefheart, 312

Captain Fantastic and the Brown Dirt Cowboy, 322
Carlton, Larry, 297
Carmichael, Hoagy, 14
Carol, 306
Carpenters, the, 213, 348
Casali, Kim, 106
Casey, Howie, 279, 280, 288, 289, 290, 291
Cattermole, Ron, 20, 21
Cavern Club, Liverpool, 185, 190, 208, 276, 313, 388
Chapman, Mark, 194
Charly, 359
Cher, 301
Chiffons, the, 44
Chinn and Chapman, 126
'Chirping' Crickets, The, 371
Christmas Gift For You, A, 177
Churchill, Winston, 101
Cicala, Roy, 267, 302
Cipriani, Stelvio, 174
Cipriano, Gene, 300
Circle of Fifths, 34, 210, 361
Clapton, Eric, v, 4, 8, 9, 10, 38, 40, 41, 42, 45, 47, 48, 49, 56, 70, 71, 72, 73, 74, 75, 76, 77, 78, 80, 81, 83, 84, 87, 169, 170, 171, 280, 295, 354, 355
Clark, Petula, 7
Clark, Tony, 165
Clayton, Merry, 247
Clements, Vassar, 314
Cliff, Jimmy, 66
Coakley, Diane, 264
Cochran, Eddie, 19, 300
Cocker, Joe, 333
Coffey, Dennis, 341
Cohen, David, 301, 302, 304, 305, 306
Cole, Nat King, 14
Coleman, Gary, 302, 304, 305
Collins, Phil, 78
Comin' Home, 41
Communist Manifesto, the, 152
Concert For George, 42, 186
Congratulations, 86
Connolly, James, 187
Conway, Gerry, 310, 313
Cooke, Sam, 104, 370
Cool Water, 328
Coolidge, Rita, 42
Cooper, Alice, 337
Cooper, Ray, 240
Coronation Street, 287
Coulson, Michael, 285

Coulter, Phil, 86
Count Basie, 13
Cousins, 'Magic' Michael, 142
Cox, Jimmie, 325
Cox, Kyoko, 10, 11, 141, 152, 168, 169, 172, 177, 272
Cox, Tony, 10, 141, 169
Coxhill, Dave, 143
Cramer, Floyd, 314
Crickets, the, 189, 367, 368, 371
Crisp, Sir Frank, 52
Crocodile Rock, 345
Cropper, Steve, 250, 251, 297, 298, 339, 343
Crosby, Bing, 13, 14, 19
Crosby, Stills, Nash & Young, 66
Crudup, Arthur 'Big Boy', 307
Cruikshank, Robin, 12, 169
Crying, Waiting, Hoping, 367
Crystals, the, 133, 177
Curtis, Dean, 67

Dakota Building, 259, 274, 317, 379
Daley, Patti, 308
Daltrey, Roger, 117
Dambra, Joey, 329
Daniels, Charlie, 59, 60
Danko, Rick, 253, 356
Dankworth, John, 21
Dark Horse Records, 87, 142, 294, 352, 361
Dark Side Of The Moon, 203, 348
David Frost Show, The, 194, 195
Davis, Andy, 145, 146
Davis, Angela, 190, 191, 194
Davis, Jesse Ed, 226, 297, 298, 299, 300, 301, 302, 304, 305, 306, 308, 309, 318, 319, 320, 321, 322, 324, 325, 326, 327, 328, 329, 330, 338, 341, 343, 346, 367, 368, 369, 370, 371, 372, 373, 374, 375, 376
Davis, Philip, 131
Day After Day, 255
Day The Earth Stood Still, The, 347
Day, Doris, 17
Dearie, Blossom, 86
Def Leppard, 337
Delaney and Bonnie, 38, 41, 42, 70, 87
Delilah, 19
Dellums, Ron, 188
Demidjuk, Stan, 142
Dennis, Felix, 143
Denny and the Diplomats, 159
Deodato, 348
Derek and the Dominos, v, 48, 49, 71, 72, 74, 77, 79, 81, 82, 83, 87, 135, 325

Derry and the Seniors, 281
Diamonds, the, 319
Dick Cavett Show, 188
Dickens, Charles, 217
Diddley, Bo, 161
Discovery Of The Orgone, The, 321
Disney World, 1, 389
Disneyland, 331, 344
Divine Miss M, The, 371
Domino, Fats, 245, 369, 372
Don't Be Cruel, 29
Donegan, Lonnie, 102, 310
Donner, Ral, 326
Donovan, 86, 253
Doran, Terry, 51, 54, 357
Dorsey, Lee, 331, 338, 376
Down By The River, 121
Dr John, 300, 301, 338, 341, 344
Drake, Pete, 40, 44, 51, 52, 53, 54, 55, 56, 57, 58, 59, 60, 61, 62, 63, 64, 65, 66, 67, 68, 69
Draper, Terry, 348
Drifters, the, 374
Driscoll, Geoff, 143
Duit On Mon Dei (album), 258, 347
Duncan, Lesley, 174
Dycus, Frank, 65
Dykins, John, 32, 92
Dylan, Bob, 40, 45, 46, 47, 50, 51, 52, 53, 54, 56, 57, 58, 65, 66, 82, 83, 93, 101, 109, 121, 145, 151, 155, 171, 172, 192, 228, 231, 237, 264, 267, 310, 315, 318, 325, 328, 340, 342, 363, 364
Dylan, Sara, 50

Eagles, the, 204
Eastman & Eastman, 367
Eastman, John, 183, 388
Eastman, Lee, 290, 313
Edmunds, Dave, 113
Edwards, Gordon, 260, 261, 262, 263, 264, 265, 266, 267, 268, 269, 271, 272
Edwards, John 'Jack', 361
Edwin Hawkins Singers, 42, 43
Elastic Oz Band, 143
Electric Light Orchestra, 282, 348
Electric String Band, 282
Elephant's Memory (album), 191
Elephant's Memory, 169, 182, 183, 184, 185, 186, 188, 189, 191, 192, 194, 195, 197, 264, 320
Elliott, Bill, 142, 352
Emerick, Geoff, 277, 279, 289, 291, 349, 350
Emerson, Gloria, 7

Encouraging Words, 43, 57
Entrapment Of John Sinclair, The, 195
Epstein, Brian, 97, 362
Estes, Alan, 305
Evans, Mal, 10, 11, 20, 84, 86, 142, 165, 252, 254, 258, 307, 331, 337
Evans, Tom, 20, 21, 40, 42, 47, 72, 80, 139, 143
Everly Brothers, 235

Faces, the, 172, 205, 356
Family Way, The, 240
Far From The Madding Crowd, 112
Fascher, Fredi, 375
feminism, 124, 138, 187, 189
Fever, 341, 351
Fields, Venetta, 341
Findley, Chuck, 245, 248, 297, 298, 299, 345, 358, 360
Fisher, Doris, 22
Fisher, Fred, 22
Flash Harry, 329
Flux Fiddlers, the, 135, 143, 144, 147, 149, 151
Fong-Torres, Ben, 364
Fontana, DJ, 60
For The Love Of Money, 326
Ford, Gerald (President), 365
Ford, Mary, 19
Ford, Robben, 352, 353, 360
Forman, Steven, 297, 298, 299, 300, 301, 302, 304, 305, 306
Fortina, Carl, 339, 341
Foster, David, 339, 357, 358
Foundations, the, 246
Four Aces, the, 16
Frampton, Peter, 50, 54, 244
Frangipane, Ron, 187, 191, 193
Frank, Richard Jr, 183, 185, 186, 189, 190, 191, 192, 193, 194
Frankie And Johnny (song), 121
Franklin, Melvin, 344
Freeman, Bobby, 371
Freeman, Ed, 308, 310
Freewheelin' Bob Dylan, 45
Fries, Bob, 176
Frosty The Snowman, 177
Fulfillingness' First Finale, 311
Funk Brothers, the, 341

Gabriel, Wayne (Tex), 183, 185, 186, 189, 190, 191, 192, 193, 194
Gaffney, Diane, 314
Gallico, Paul, 243
Gallup, Cliff, 375

Gandhi, 187
Gay Divorce, 13
Gaye, Marvin, 232
Geffen, David, 301
Gentle, Johnny, 129
Gerrard, Hilary, 258, 342, 388
Gershwin, George, 14
Get It On, 175
(Ghost) Riders In The Sky: A Cowboy Legend, 359
Gibb, Maurice, 22, 23
Gibbins, Mike, 40, 42, 47, 72
Gibbs, Terry, 306
Giddy, 117
Gilbert, Jean, 174
Gilmour, David, 271
Gilstrap, Jimmy, 338
Gimble, Johnny, 314
Ginsberg, Allen, 7
glam rock, 113, 175, 286, 295, 297
Glaub, Bob, 301, 302, 304, 305, 306
Glazier, Tom, 177
Go Now!, 115
Goat's Head Soup, 237
God Save Oz, 142
Goddess Of Fortune, 233
Goldfinger, 240
Gone Gone Gone, 96
Goodbye Dolly, 342
Good-Night Vienna (operetta), 342
Goodwin, Ron, 22, 23
Goose-Step Mama, 140
Gordon, Jim, 38, 42, 49, 56, 70, 71, 72, 73, 74, 75, 76, 77, 79, 80, 81, 82, 83, 85, 134, 135, 136, 137, 300, 301
Gordy, Berry, 100
Grade, Sir Lew, 241, 243
Graham, Leo, 129
Grant, Cornelius, 43
Grapefruit, 11, 105, 152
Grateful Dead, 171
Graves, Harry (Starr's stepfather), 13, 14, 22, 23, 64
Great White Wonder II, 82
Green, Little Willie, 341
Green, Lloyd, 314
Greene, Joe, 338, 344, 345
Gregory, Dick, 151
Grieg, Edvard, 241
Guercio, Jim, 131
Guerin, John, 352, 353
Guerrilla Art Group, 273
Gurur Bramha (song), 229

Gypsy Wolf, 320

Half Breed, 142
Half Past Ten, 161
Ham, Pete, 20, 21, 40, 42, 47, 72, 80, 173
Hamburg, 96, 183, 186, 189, 200, 281, 295, 300, 303, 370, 375, 377
Hamlin, Rosie, 299
Hammond, John P, 280
Hanratty, James, 138
Hardaway, Bob, 301
Hardy, Oliver, 315
Hardy, Thomas, 112
Hare Krishna Mantra, 44
Harlem Community Choir, 176
Harlow, Jean, 341
Harman, Buddy, 60, 62, 63, 65, 66, 67, 68, 69
Harrison, George, *passim*
    affair with Krissy Wood, 355
    affair with Maureen Starkey, 340, 355
    Beautiful Girl, 40, 87
    Best Of George Harrison, 361
    Brainwashed, 82
    break-up with Pattie, 80, 352, 353, 354
    Concert For Bangla Desh, 21, 42, 51, 76, 225, 226, 227, 230, 239, 245, 363, 387
    Concert For Bangla Desh (album), 225, 239, 363
    Concert For Bangla Desh (film), 225, 239, 363
    Crackerbox Palace, 52
    Electronic Sound, 88
    Flying Hour, 229
    Friar Park, v, 51, 52, 74, 75, 225, 228, 232, 235, 294, 295, 340, 352, 353, 354, 355, 356, 357, 358, 359, 360
    Friar Park Studios (FPSHOT), v, 52, 225, 235, 294, 352, 353, 354, 355, 356, 357, 358, 359
    George Harrison: Living in the Material World, 234, 388
    It's What You Value, 364
    North American Tour (1974), 235, 353, 360, 361, 362, 364, 365, 386,
    North American Tour reviews, 364
    Soft Touch, 80
    Sour Milk Sea, 39, 352
    Thirty Three & 1/3, 87, 364
    vocal deterioration, 354, 360, 363
    Wonderwall (film), 276
    Wonderwall Music, 49, 88, 276
Harrison, Louise (mother), 38, 70, 84, 172
Harrison, Olivia (nee Arias), 89, 295, 362

FOUR SIDES OF THE CIRCLE 415

Harrison, Pattie (nee Boyd), 51, 54, 58, 70, 73, 80, 81, 234, 235, 295, 340, 352, 353, 354, 355
Hatfield, Bobby, 244
Hawkins, Edwin, 42, 43
Hawkins, Erskine, 22
Hawkins, Ira, 338
Hayes, Isaac, 326
Haymes, Dick, 19
Hazelwood, Michael, 302, 304, 305, 306
He's So Fine, 44, 45
Heartbeat, 368
Heartbreak Hotel, 59, 305, 346
Heath, Edward, 337
Helm, Levon, 56, 253
Hendrix, Jimi, 31, 111, 121, 171, 280, 313
Henry, Clarence 'Frogman', 246
Hensley, Thomas, 305, 306
Hensley, Tom, 248, 339
Hentschel, David, 258, 349
Hewson, Richard, 133, 162, 218, 219
Hey Joe, 121
Hieronymus, Dick, 305
Hill, Jimmy, 174
Hill, Michael, 373
Hillier, Tony, 243
Hilltoppers, the, 343
Hindu belief, 44, 73, 78, 101, 173, 231, 232, 236, 352, 357, 358, 388
Hinton, Milt, 124, 125
Hitler, Adolf, 101
Hodge, Chris, 348
Hoffman, Abbie, 155, 195
Hoffman, Dustin, 286
Holland, Milt, 245, 248, 254
Holland-Dozier-Holland, 248, 309
Holley, Steve, 118
Holly, Buddy, 160, 176, 367, 368, 375
Hollywood Vampires, the, 337
Homeward Bound, 30
Honky Cat, 345
Honky Tonk Blues, 213
Honky Tonk Women, 8
Hopkin, Mary, 14
Hopkins, Nicky, 139, 142, 143, 145, 146, 147, 148, 149, 153, 154, 169, 176, 225, 226, 227, 229, 230, 231, 232, 233, 234, 235, 236, 237, 246, 249, 250, 254, 319, 320, 324, 325, 326, 327, 328, 329, 346
Horn, Jim, 142, 170, 171, 232, 233, 245, 247, 297, 298, 299, 358, 360
Horne, Ian, 277, 278, 281
Hot Butter, 346

Hot Love, 175
House Of The Rising Sun, 93
Houston, Jean, 268
Howard, Chuck, 58, 60, 62, 63
Howard, James Newton, 345
Howlin' Wolf, 244
Hoyt Axton Country Western Boogie Woogie Gospel Rock And Roll Show, The, 346
Hudson, Garth, 191, 253
Humble Pie, 54
Humperdinck, Engelbert, 107
Hurston, Zora Neale, 186
Huskey, Roy 'Junior', 59, 60, 61, 62, 63, 64, 65, 67, 69
Hussein, Zakir, 232, 233

I Am Woman, 125, 188
I Apologize, 100, 305
(I Don't Know Why) But I Do, 246
I Got To Find My Baby, 306
I Love Him Like I Love My Very Life, 134
I Love How You Love Me, 177
I Shall Be Released, 46
I Want You (Bob Dylan song), 231
I Want You To Sit On My Face, 337
I Want You, I Need You, I Love You, 307
I Was Made To Love Her, 351
I Will Always Love You, 314
I Would Only Smile, iv, 217, 220, 281
I Wrote A Simple Song, 170
I'd Like To Teach The World To Sing, 268
I'll Be Seeing You, 13
I'll Be Your Baby Tonight, 46
(I'm A) Road Runner, 328
I'm Talking About You, 306
I've Been Good To You, 305
Ike, Reverend, 322
Immigrant, The, 274
Ingham, Chris, 23
Ink Spots, the, 22
In-Laws, The, 118
Innervisions, 311, 322
Interstellar Overdrive, 204
Invisible Strings, the, 186, 190, 192, 193
Ippolito, Adam, 185, 186, 189, 190, 191, 192, 193, 194
IRA, 184, 189
Irwin, Teddy, 176
Isle of Wight Festival (1969), 53
It's All Over Now, Baby Blue, 228
It's Alright, Ma (I'm Only Bleeding), 145
It's Not Unusual, 19

Jackson 5, the, 341
Jackson, David, 346
Jagger, Bianca (nee Pérez-Mora Macias), 249
Jagger, Mick, 190, 249, 309
Jambalaya (On The Bayou), 213
James Bond, 240
James, Dick, 22
Jan and Dean, 25
Janov, Arthur, 91, 94, 95, 99, 100, 137, 146, 148, 154
Japanese Tears, 115, 281, 315
Jarry, Alfred, 212
Jefferson Airplane, 171
Jenkins, Arthur, 318, 319, 320, 321, 322, 324, 326, 327, 329, 330, 367, 368, 369, 370, 371, 372, 373, 374, 375, 376
Jerry Lewis Muscular Dystrophy Telethon, 197
John (book), 331
John Dawson Winter III, 262
John Wesley Harding, 46, 53
John, Elton, 159, 244, 275, 301, 319, 322, 323, 331, 345, 348, 364, 386, 390
Johnny B Goode, 90, 183, 306
Johns, Glyn, 32, 167, 199, 204, 206, 209
Johnson, Howard, 318, 319, 320, 321, 324, 325, 326, 327, 330
Johnson, Lee Otis, 196
Johnson, Plas, 302
Joi Bangla, 171
Jones, Mick, 294
Jones, Quincy, 16, 18
Jones, Stan, 359
Jones, Tom, 19
Jones, Trevor, 277, 278, 281
Joplin, Janis, 86
Jordanaires, the, 59, 60, 61, 62, 63, 64, 65, 66, 67
Juber, Laurence, 118
Judas Priest, 337
Jungle Juice, 243
Junior Walker, 328, 356
Justice Stamp, 132, 385

Kabaka, Remi, 288
Kass, Ron, 240
Katz, David, 292
Keep On Keeping On, 328
Keith, Ben, 60
Kellaway, Roger, 352, 353
Kelso, Jackie, 297, 298, 299, 304

Keltner, Jim, 38, 136, 139, 140, 142, 143, 169, 170, 171, 172, 176, 183, 185, 186, 189, 190, 191, 192, 193, 194, 225, 226, 227, 228, 230, 231, 232, 233, 234, 235, 236, 237, 238, 245, 246, 247, 248, 249, 260, 261, 262, 263, 264, 265, 266, 267, 268, 269, 271, 272, 275, 294, 297, 298, 299, 300, 301, 302, 304, 305, 306, 308, 309, 310, 318, 319, 320, 321, 322, 324, 325, 326, 327, 328, 329, 330, 331, 338, 341, 343, 344, 345, 352, 360, 364, 367, 368, 369, 370, 371, 372, 373, 374, 375, 376
Kendall, Albert (McCartney's uncle), 122
Kendall, Jeannie, 67
Kendall, Royce, 67
Kendalls, the, 67
Kennedy, Jerry, 59, 60, 61, 63, 64, 65, 66, 67, 68, 69
Kennedy, John F, 101
Kenzie, Phil, 143
Kerouac, Jack, 116
Kerr, Clyde, 381
Keys, Bobby, 38, 40, 72, 75, 76, 77, 79, 80, 81, 82, 83, 136, 137, 139, 142, 170, 244, 249, 305, 306, 308, 309, 311, 318, 319, 320, 322, 324, 325, 326, 327, 330, 338, 341, 344, 345, 346, 349
Killen, Buddy, 313
Kinfauns, 30, 51
King Curtis, 135, 136, 139, 140, 155
King, BB, 244
King, Ben E, 374
King, Carole, 298
King, Clydie, 338, 341, 344, 345
Kingston, Larry, 58, 63, 64, 65
Kinks, the, 348
Kintyre, 24, 112, 125, 212, 281, 285, 290
Kipling, Rudyard, 265
Kirby, Dave, 60
Kitt, Eartha, 327
Klaatu, 348
Klein, Allen, 2, 10, 45, 74, 89, 128, 132, 149, 162, 170, 172, 183, 226, 227, 230, 251, 253, 256, 258, 327, 370, 385, 386, 388
Klein, Eddie, 86
Kleinow, 'Sneaky Pete', 261, 262, 263, 264, 265, 266, 269, 271, 272
Koerner, Ray And Glover, 148
Kohara, Roy, 332
Kooper, Al, 309
Kortchmar, Danny, 308, 309
Kossajda, Ronald, 297, 298, 299, 300, 302, 305, 306
Kraus, Phil, 374

Krishna, 7, 20, 42, 43, 44, 74, 80, 81, 87, 95, 227, 229, 232, 233, 329, 330, 357, 358, 359, 361, 365, 388
Kurtz, Irma, 186
Kuti, Fela, 278

LA Express, 353, 354
Laine, Denny, iv, 114, 115, 126, 127, 159, 160, 161, 163, 164, 165, 178, 179, 199, 200, 201, 202, 203, 204, 205, 207, 208, 209, 210, 211, 212, 213, 214, 215, 216, 217, 218, 220, 240, 243, 277, 278, 279, 281, 282, 283, 284, 285, 286, 288, 289, 290, 291, 292, 310, 314, 315, 349, 380, 381, 382
Laine, Frankie, 328
Laine, Joanne 'Jo Jo' (nee LaPatrie), 207
Lamps Of Fire, 52
Lang, Michael, 301, 302
Lang, Ronnie, 305
Language And Music Of The Wolves, The, 320
Lao Tse, 56
Lapidos, Mark, 377
Last Supper, The, 238
Lavender, Grover 'Shorty', 60
Lawrence, Jack, 25
Lawrence, Lynda, 344, 345
Lawrence, Trevor, 309, 338, 341, 344, 345, 346, 347
Lay Lady Lay, 65, 267
Layla And Other Assorted Love Songs, 73, 87, 325
Le Sève, Pierre Denis, 286, 287
Leary, Timothy, 7, 56
Lee, Alvin, 235, 294
Lee, Byron and the Dragonaires, 208
Lee, Peggy, 22, 341, 351
Leiber and Stoller (Jerry Leiber and Mike Stoller), 374
Lennon, Alf 'Freddie' (father), 93, 103, 105, 151
Lennon, Cynthia (nee Powell), 118, 322, 331, 342
Lennon, James (great grandfather), 192
Lennon, John, *passim*
  Apotheosis, 249
  Bag One, 98
  Bag Productions, 362
  bagism, 8, 124
  Clock, 176, 368
  death, 98, 144, 178
  deportation campaign, 183, 196, 197, 259, 264, 272
  Fat Budgie, The, 152, 251

Fly (film), 107, 249
How I Won The War, 173, 269
In His Own Write, 152
Lennon and drugs, 8, 97, 196
Lennon-Ono joint copyright dispute, 154, 155, 178, 187, 226, 251
live appearance with Elton John, 323
Live In New York City [DVD], 198
London Air And New York Wind, 197
lost weekend, 275, 295, 317, 325, 333
Man Is Half Of Woman (Woman Is Half Of Man), 187
Mahirishi Song, 101
marital issues, 260, 270, 274, 379
Menlove Avenue, 92, 94, 263, 303, 307
Mucho Mungo, 304, 317
Nutopia, 272, 273, 274
One To One concert, 183, 188, 197, 207, 387
peace campaigns, 7, 176
peace pact with McCartney, 182
resigns from Beatles, 1, 8
returns MBE, 9
Rolling Stone interview, 107, 128
Roots: John Lennon Sings The Great Rock And Roll Hits, 298, 328, 378
Serve Yourself, 151
Shaved Fish, 153, 188
Two Virgins, 97, 106
Up Your Legs Forever, 107
You Are Here (To Yoko From John, With Love), 265
Lennon, John and the Bleechers, 129
Lennon, Julia (mother), 32, 92, 137, 369
Lennon, Julian (son), 322, 331, 342, 387, 388, 389
Lettermen, the, 107
Levant, Gayle, 382
Levy, Adam, 389
Levy, Morris, 295, 305, 331, 366, 376, 378, 389
Lewis, Jerry Lee, 377
Lewisohn, Mark, iv, 16, 47, 192, 300
Life On Mars, 348
Lindsay-Hogg, Michael, 286
Lindsey, Benny, 64
Liston, Sonny, 136
Little Big Horns, 319, 320, 324, 325, 326, 327, 330
Little Darlin', 319
Little Queenie, 306
Little Richard, 32, 150, 189, 311, 313, 326, 371, 372, 373, 374
Live Aid (1985), 172

Live And Let Die (book), 240
Live On The Queen Mary, 380
Loaded, 264
Lockwood, Sir Joseph, 179
Loesser, Frank, 14
Loiacono, John, 386, 387
Lomax, Jackie, 39
Lonely Man, 254
Long Player, 355
Long Tall Sally, 372, 373
Long, Dee, 348
Longo, John, 381
Lots More Blues, Rags And Hollers, 148
Louie Louie, 165
Love Train, 326
Love, Darlene, 307
Lovely La-De-Day, 134
Lovin' Spoonful, 181
Lower East Side, the, 182
Lucille, 189, 311, 371
Lulu, 67
Lutton, Davey, 214
Lynne, Jeff, 175
Lynton, Rod, 145, 146, 148

Mack, Ronnie, 44
Maclen Music, 110, 167, 226, 241, 251, 305
Macmillan, Ian, 178
Macon, Uncle Dave, 253
Madaio, Steve, 319, 320, 321, 324, 325, 326, 327, 330, 338, 341, 344, 345
Madison Square Garden, 171, 180, 188, 197, 207, 323, 386, 387, 388
Maeskela, Hugh, 278
Maga Dog, 208
Maggie's Farm, 315
Magic Christian, The, 10, 12, 15, 18
Maharishi Mahesh Yogi, 95, 100, 101, 144, 145, 248, 285
Mailman, Bring Me No More Blues, 368
Malcontent Music, 254
Mann, Barry, 297, 298, 299, 300, 304, 305, 306
Manuel, Richard, 254
Many Rivers To Cross, 329
Mao Zedong, 267
Marascalco, John, 189
Marotta, Rick, 264, 266
Martin, Bill, 86
Martin, Dean, 22
Martin, George, 3, 7, 12, 13, 14, 15, 16, 17, 18, 19, 21, 22, 50, 116, 119, 122, 127, 129, 131, 181, 217, 240, 241, 267, 282, 290, 310, 316, 342

Maschwitz, Eric, 342
Mason, Dave, 38, 49, 70, 71, 73, 370
Massachusetts, 177
Massed Alberts, the, 342
Masst Alberts, the, 341, 342
Masters, Robert, 268
Material World Foundation, 234
Matlock, Matty, 306
Matthews, Sherlie, 341
Maybe Baby, 368
Mayfield, Curtis, 326, 328
Mayorga, Lincoln, 347
McCartney, Heather (daughter), 24, 111, 121, 131, 203, 205, 208
McCartney, Jim (father), 13
McCartney, Linda (nee Eastman), *passim*
  Cook Of The House, 113
  Seaside Woman, iv, 207, 209, 220
  Suzy and the Red Stripes, 209
  Wide Prairie, iv, 315
McCartney, Mary (daughter), 24, 36, 113, 160, 205, 208
McCartney, Mary (mother), 290
McCartney, Mike (brother), 310, 313, 361
McCartney, Paul, *passim*
  All Of You, 351
  Beatles break-up announcement (1970), 1, 37, 41
  Best Friend, 162, 211, 220
  Blackbird Singing, 121
  Bluff City Music, 202
  Bruce McMouse Show, The, 120, 207, 350
  Brung To Ewe By, 130
  CHOBA B CCCP, 117, 369
  Cold Cuts, 114, 117, 118, 203, 213
  Country Hams, the, 215, 315
  court case (1971), 1, 2, 89, 128, 132, 149, 226, 254, 385, 389
  drug use, 198, 207, 211, 212, 220, 283, 284
  establishment of Wings, 111, 118, 168
  European tour (1972), 206, 211, 217, 218
  Give My Regards To Broad Street, 288
  James Paul McCartney (television show), 199, 241, 242, 255, 276, 286, 288, 350, 351
  Kisses On The Bottom, 24
  Let 'Em In, 294
  Listen To What The Man Said, 381
  London Town, 290
  McCartney Music, 241, 378
  McCartney-McCartney joint copyright dispute, 167, 226, 241
  Mull Of Kintyre, 281

Nor-Va-Jak Publishing, 367
One Hand Clapping, 28, 120, 209, 349, 350, 351
peace pact with Lennon, 182
Put It There, 203
Rude Studio, 160, 276
Run Devil Run, 190
Rupert and the Frog Song, 120
Rupert the Bear (film project), 108, 113, 120, 127, 207, 350
Sitting At The Piano, 351
Step Inside Love, 243
Take It Away, 351
Thingumybob, 243
Thrillington, 133
Thrillington, Percy 'Thrills', 133
Tug Of War, 351
UK tour (1973), 276
University Tour (1972), 199, 201, 211, 216, 219
Venus And Mars, iv, 290, 379, 380, 381, 382
Walking In The Park With Eloise, 215, 315
Wings Over America, 35, 211, 350
McCartney, Stella (daughter), 159, 168
McCoy, Charlie, 59, 61, 62, 63, 64, 66, 67, 68
McCracken, Hugh, 114, 115, 117, 118, 119, 120, 121, 122, 123, 124, 125, 126, 159, 176, 177
McCracklin, Jimmy, 112, 305
McCreery, Lou, 338, 341, 344
McCulloch, Jimmy, iv, 214, 310, 313, 314, 315, 316, 349, 350, 380, 381, 382
McCullough, Henry, 114, 178, 198, 199, 200, 201, 202, 203, 204, 205, 207, 208, 209, 210, 211, 212, 213, 214, 215, 216, 217, 218, 219, 220, 240, 243, 277, 316, 352
McDonald, Barry, 214
McDonald, Phil, 99
McGear, 310, 313
McGear, Mike, 310, 313, 361
Medicine Jar, iv, 316
Melvoin, Michael, 302
Memphis, Tennessee, 183, 306
Menon, Bhaskar, 257
Menza, Donald, 302, 304
Mercer, Johnny, 15
Meters, the, 338
Michael X, 138
Mickey & Sylvia, 161
Midler, Bette, 371
Midnight Special, 310

Mighty Quinn, The, 315
Mike Douglas Show, the, 183, 266, 267, 306
Milburn, Jackie, 332
Miller, Jody, 44
Miller, Roger, 340
Mills Brothers, the, 21, 343
Mind Games: The Guide To Inner Space, 268
Miracles, the, 305
Miss You, 322
Mitchell, Joni, 297, 300, 353
Mitchell, Mitch, 313
Molland, Joey, 40, 42, 47, 72, 80, 139, 143
Money (That's What I Want), 100
Monterey Pop Festival, 171
Moody Blues, the, 115, 140, 281, 282
Moon, Keith, 244, 309, 318, 337
Moondog Matinee, 254
Moore, Scotty, 59
Morning Star, the, 138
Morouse, Dennis, 369, 370, 371, 372, 373, 374, 376
Morrell, Dave, 302
Most, Mickie, 108
Motown, 100, 247, 309, 311, 328, 341, 344, 356
Mott The Hoople, 172
Mottau, Eddie, 318, 319, 320, 321, 322, 324, 326, 327, 328, 329, 367, 368, 369, 370, 371, 372, 373, 374, 375, 376
Mrs Dale's Diary, 137
Msarurgwa, August, 346
Mull, Kathy, 264
Munson, Art, 299, 300, 301, 302, 304
Murray The K, 7
Murray, Charles Shaar, 142
Museum of Modern Art, New York, 273
Music From Big Pink, 56, 57
My Friend Stan, 297

Nashville Skyline, 46, 53, 58, 59, 65
Neapolitan, Ray, 297, 298, 299, 300, 301, 302, 304, 305, 306
Nelson, Oliver, 15
Nelson, Ralph, 359
Nelson, Tracy, 69
NEMS, 23
Neville, Richard, 143
New Morning, 50, 51
New York Philharmonic, 115, 116, 119, 122, 126, 144
New York Times, 7, 196
Newman, Randy, 245
Newmark, Andy, 355, 356, 357, 358, 360

Newton-John, Olivia, 73
Nilsson Sings Newman, 245
Nilsson, Harry, 235, 244, 245, 246, 258, 265, 304, 308, 309, 310, 312, 317, 328, 329, 337, 343, 344, 346, 347, 348
Nitzsche, Jack, 245, 249, 254, 287
Nixon, Richard (President), 145, 190, 264
No Secrets, 244
Northern Songs, 110, 132, 167, 178, 226, 241, 251, 305
Nova (magazine), 186

O'Dell, Chris, 228
O'Farrill, Chico, 12, 13
O'Jays, the, 326
Ochs, Phil, 195
Oh Happy Day, 42
Ohio killings (1970), 66
Olympics, the (group), 136
Omartian, Michael, 304
On The Road, 116
On The Road To Freedom, 235
On The Third Day, 348
On Top Of Old Smokey, 176
On Top Of Spaghetti, 177
One Of The Boys, 117
Ono, Yoko, *passim*
  Approximately Infinite Universe, 220, 259
  Born In A Prison, 197
  Feeling The Space, 260, 275, 303, 321
  Fly (album), 154
  Listen, The Snow Is Falling, 177, 180
  Plastic Ono Band 1968 (artwork), 8
  Plastic Ono Super Band, 302, 332
  Remember Love, 11, 106
  She Hits Back, 260
  Sisters, O Sisters, 187, 198
  Story, A, 321, 332
  To The Wesleyan People, 191
  Unfinished Paintings, 269
  Who Has Seen The Wind?, 11
  Woman Power, 260
  Yoko Ono/Plastic Ono Band, 105, 107, 139
Orbison, Roy, 227
Orwell, George, 292
Osbourne, Chris, 176
Outa-Space, 348
Owens, Buck, 121
Oz (magazine), 142, 143, 171

Page, Elaine, 29
Page, Jimmy, 380
Palmer, Tony, 169

Pang, May, 1, 176, 177, 274, 295, 296, 297, 299, 300, 301, 303, 307, 308, 310, 312, 317, 318, 319, 329, 341, 371, 377, 379, 386, 387, 389
Papillon, 286
Paramahansa Yogananda, 388
Pararanz Yoga Anda, 363
Paris Sisters, the, 177
Parish, Mitchell, 14
Parker, Junior, 103
Parkinson, Michael, 114
Parlophone, 15, 22, 62, 326, 342, 362
Parsons, Alan, 161, 215
Parton, Dolly, 314
Pat Garrett And Billy The Kid, 237
Patience and Prudence, 323
Paul, Billy, 245
Paul, Les, 19
Peebles, Ann, 308
Peel, David, 155, 182, 191, 195
Peer Gynt Suite No. 1, 241
Peggy Sue Got Married, 368
Peggy Sue, 368
Penniman, Richard [Little Richard], 32, 150, 189, 311, 313, 326, 371, 372, 373, 374
Perkins, Carl, 96, 129, 186, 375, 377
Perkins, William, 306
Perry, André, 7
Perry, Richard, 17, 244, 245, 246, 247, 248, 249, 250, 251, 252, 253, 254, 255, 256, 257, 258, 338, 339, 341, 342, 343, 344, 345, 346, 347
Perry, William, 304, 305, 306
Peter Morris Music, 346
Peter, Paul and Mary, 177
Petty, Norman, 367
Phil Spector's Christmas Album, 96, 177
Philharmonic Orchestrange, the, 320, 325, 327, 328, 329
Philly (Philadelphia) soul, 380
Picasso, Pablo, 113, 286, 287, 293
Pickard, Sorrells, 58, 60, 61, 64, 66
Pierce, Bobby, 67
Pierce, Michael, 381
Pinder, Mike, 139, 140, 143, 144
Pink Floyd, 203, 271, 348
Piper At The Gates Of Dawn, The, 204
Place I Love, The, 294
Platters, the, 343
Plaza Hotel, 379, 386, 387
Please Mrs Henry, 82
Pleasence, Donald, 337
Poison Pressure, 208

Polak, Dick, 23
Poncia, Vini, 246, 247, 248, 249, 253, 254, 255, 339, 341, 344, 347
Pope John XXIII, 71
Pope Smokes Dope, the (song), 182
Porter, Cole, 13
Porter, George Jr, 338
Powell, Sandy, 323
Presley, Elvis, 18, 19, 29, 32, 40, 59, 101, 102, 103, 208, 305, 307, 316, 346, 377
Preston, Billy, v, 3, 10, 16, 19, 38, 40, 42, 43, 44, 45, 47, 48, 49, 50, 51, 53, 55, 57, 72, 76, 77, 83, 90, 100, 101, 170, 171, 231, 247, 251, 252, 258, 333, 341, 343, 344, 348, 355, 356, 357, 358, 360, 363, 365
Price, Jim, 38, 40, 72, 75, 76, 77, 79, 80, 82, 85
Price, Leo, 189
Price, Lloyd, 301
Primal Scream, The (book), 91, 93, 147
Primal Therapy, 91, 92, 94, 95, 97, 100, 103, 105, 137, 138, 146, 147, 148, 154, 263, 268, 272
Pritchard, Gill, 85
Procol Harum, 269
Professor Longhair, 380
Promised Land, The, 62
Psychedelic Prayers, 56
Puitt, Bill, 214
Purple Haze, 31
Purvis, Bobby, 142
Pussy Cats, 310, 317, 318, 329
Putman, Curly, 313, 315
Puttnam, David, 36

Quarry Bank High School, 97, 389
Quarry Men, the, 30, 32, 55, 103, 137, 159, 219, 296, 348, 354, 361, 367, 369, 377
Quarter To Three, 266, 305
Quatro, Suzy, 126
Queen Elizabeth, the Queen Mother, 97
Quillen, Dale, 214

Rabin, Buzz, 61
Radha Krishna Temple, 7, 44, 82
Radha Krsna Temple, The (album), 233
Radle, Carl, 38, 47, 48, 49, 70, 71, 72, 73, 75, 76, 77, 79, 80, 81, 82, 83, 85
Rag Mama Rag, 254
Raga (film), 170, 229
Rakah, Alla, 233
Ram Dass, 229
Ram You Hard, 129
Ram, Samuel 'Buck', 343

Ramone, Phil, 129
Rand, Ande, 343
Rave On, 368
Ravi Shankar's Music Festival From India, 361
Ray, Norman, 214
Reach Out I'll Be There, 248
Rebennack, Malcolm John Jr [Dr John], 300, 301, 338, 341, 344
Re-Conquest Of Ireland, The, 187
Red Mole, 93, 138, 139, 184
Redding, Otis, 171
Reddy, Helen, 125, 188
Redford, Robert, 320
Reed, Jerry, 60, 64
Reed, Les, 19
Reed, Lou, 264
Reeves, Martha, 247, 250
Reich, Wilhelm, 96, 321
Religions Inc, 71
Rennie, Michael, 348
Rice, Tim, 29
Richard, Cliff, 86, 371
Richard, Thaddeus, 214
Richards, Emil, 358, 359, 360
Richards, Keith, 190
Richey, George, 60
Ride A White Swan, 175
Ring O'Records, 258, 348, 349, 352
Ringo And Harry's Night Out, 337
Robertson, Robbie, 57, 253, 254, 345, 356
Robinson, Alvin, 344
Robinson, Smokey, 100
Robledo, George, 332
Rock And Roll Music (song), 149, 306
Rock And Roll Revival Festival, Toronto (1969), 9
Rock Around The Clock, 317
Rocket Man, 348
Rodgers, Jimmie, 82
Roll It Over, 71
Roll Over Beethoven, 185, 186, 282, 306, 318
Rolling Stones, the, 8, 82, 237, 287, 322, 350
Ronettes, the, 133, 177, 247, 298
Rosie and the Originals, 299
Ross, Diana, 242
Route 66, 285
Rowan & Martin's Laugh-In, 18
Roxy Music, 144
Rubin, Jerry, 155, 182, 183, 191, 193, 260, 267
Rudolph The Red-Nosed Reindeer, 177
Rundgren, Todd, 170
Russell, Leon, 4, 38, 170, 171, 238, 244, 297
Rutles, the, 140, 226

Sail Away Ladies, 253
Sam the Sham and the Pharaohs, 208
Save The Last Dance For Me, 317
Say You Don't Mind, 281
Scharf, Stuart, 176
Scorsese, Martin, 42, 234, 388
Scotland, Winston, 209
Scott, Tom, 245, 246, 247, 248, 250, 254, 255, 294, 352, 353, 355, 356, 358, 359, 360
Seale, Bobby, 183
Second Coming Of Suzanne, The, 108
Sedaka, Neil, 274
See, Mel, 131, 149
Seider, Harold, 1, 308
Seiwell, Denny, 109, 111, 112, 114, 115, 116, 117, 118, 119, 120, 121, 122, 123, 124, 125, 126, 127, 131, 159, 160, 161, 162, 163, 164, 165, 178, 198, 199, 200, 201, 202, 203, 204, 205, 207, 208, 209, 210, 211, 212, 213, 214, 215, 216, 217, 218, 240, 243, 277, 316
Seiwell, Monique, 127
Self Realisation Fellowship, 363
Send Me The Heart, 281, 315
Sesame Street, 99
Shankar Family & Friends, 352, 353
Shankar, Ravi, 170, 171, 172, 229, 233, 253, 352, 353, 358, 359, 361, 363, 364, 365
Shape I'm In, The, 201
Shapiro, Helen, 276
Shelton, Louie, 301
Sheridan, Tony and the Beat Brothers, 376
Sherman Brothers, the, 246
Shirelles, the, 298
Shook, Jerry, 60
Shoop Shoop Song, The, 247
Shout (song), 67
Sid Sharp Strings, the, 382
Simon & Garfunkel, 30
Simon, Carly, 244
Sinatra, Frank, 13, 28, 325, 344, 356
Sinclair, John, 193, 194, 195, 196, 198
Skilling, Raymond, 253
Skokiaan, 346
Slade, 113, 295, 297
Smith, 'Legs' Larry, 357
Smith, Ethel [Ethel Diddley], 161
Smith, George (Lennon's uncle), 92
Smith, Mimi ('Aunt Mimi'), 92, 97
Smith, Steve, 348
Smothers Brothers, the, 308
Smothers, Tom, 7
Snow, Hank, 314
So Sad (To Watch Good Love Go Bad), 235

Solitaire, 235
Some Other Guy, 10, 140
Something Different, 264, 265, 267, 268, 269, 272
Son Of Dracula, 244, 258
Son Of Schmilsson, 244, 348
Song Of Bangladesh, 172
Sounds Of Sadness, 62
Space Race, 348
Spaceman, 348
Spector, Phil, 10, 11, 38, 39, 40, 41, 42, 43, 44, 45, 47, 48, 49, 50, 51, 52, 53, 54, 55, 56, 70, 71, 72, 73, 74, 75, 76, 77, 78, 79, 80, 81, 82, 83, 85, 86, 87, 91, 93, 95, 96, 98, 99, 100, 102, 103, 105, 106, 107, 133, 134, 135, 136, 137, 139, 142, 143, 145, 146, 147, 148, 149, 151, 153, 162, 169, 170, 172, 176, 177, 183, 184, 186, 190, 191, 192, 193, 194, 225, 247, 275, 287, 288, 295, 296, 297, 298, 299, 300, 301, 302, 304, 305, 306, 308, 343, 366
Spector, Ronnie, 86, 133, 134, 170, 177
Spence, Johnnie, 15
Spinozza, David, 109, 111, 112, 113, 114, 125, 260, 261, 262, 263, 265, 266, 267, 268, 269, 271, 272, 303, 321, 332, 371
Splinter, 142, 254, 294, 352, 361
Split Enz, 337
St Paul The Apostle, 95
St Regis Hotel, New York, 169, 181, 240
Stackridge, 145
Star Club, Hamburg, 300, 306, 313, 375
Starkey, Elsie (Starr's mother), 19, 20, 23
Starkey, Lee (Starr's son), 169
Starkey, Maureen (nee Cox), 18, 169, 295, 340
Starkey, Richard 'Richy' (Starr's father), 17
Starman, 348
Starr, Ringo, *passim*
    acting career, 12, 169, 244
    Band Of Steel, 68, 339
    Blast From Your Past, 248
    break-up with Maureen, 340
    Give More Love, 250
    head of Apple Films, 244
    It's All Right, 338
    Liverpool 8, 208
    Lonely Weekends, 340
    Parole, 338
    Richoroony Ltd, 258
    Ringo Or Robin (design company), 12, 169, 337
    Ringo's Rotogravure, 86
    Scouse The Mouse, 337

Startling Studios, 337
Up The Tempo, 340
Wake Up, 339
You Can't Fight Lightning, 339
Startling Music (album), 258, 349
Steiner, Armin, 123, 279
Steptoe And Son, 29
Stevens, Cat, 333
Stewart, Rod, 370
Stewball, 177
Stills, Stephen, 20, 90, 244
Stone, Sly, 326
Stop Records, 58, 61, 62, 63, 65, 67
Storm, Rory, 55
Straight Up, 170
Streisand, Barbra, 94, 107
Strong, Barrett, 100, 305
Sub Rosa Subway, 348
Subterranean Homesick Blues, 145, 310
Sunday Night At The London Palladium, 368
Sunnyview Farm, 366, 367, 378
Supersonic Rocket Ship, 348
Supremes, the, 344
Sutcliffe, Stuart, 378
Swami Vivekananda, 44
Sweet Black Angel, 190
Sweet Jane, 264
Sweet Little Sixteen, 303, 306, 379
Sweet Music, 228
Sweet, the, 126
Swindin, George, 332

T Rex, 113, 244, 280
Talk of the Town, 17
Tandoori Chicken (song), 134
Tangled Mind, 314
Tao Te Ching, 56
Tapestry, 298
Taupin, Bernie, 345
Tavener, John, 349
Taylor, Derek, 7, 258
Teddy Bears, the, 133, 303
Telegram Sam, 246
Tell Me When, 19
Tell The Truth, 71
Temperley, Joseph, 369, 370, 371, 372, 373, 374, 376
Tempo, Nino, 298, 299, 300, 301, 302, 304, 305, 306
Temptations, the, 43, 341, 344
Ten Years After, 235
Tennyson, Lord Alfred, 294
Terran, Anthony, 300, 304

Texans, the, 55
That'll Be The Day, 367
That'll Be The Day (film), 244, 258
That's All Right, 59, 307
That's My Life (My Love And My Home), 151
That's The Way God Planned It (album), 72, 83
Their Eyes Were Watching God, 187
(There'll Be Bluebirds Over) The White Cliffs Of Dover, 288
There's One in Every Crowd, 84
Thirty Days, 367
Thomas, Alvin, 381
Thomas, Andy, 302
Thomas, Carla, 370
Thomas, Guthrie, 68, 339
through-composition, 119, 285
Thunderclap Newman, 313
Tidwell, George, 214
Time Passes Slowly, 50
Time To Hide, 281
Tin Man Was a Dreamer, The, 237
Tittenhurst Park, 10, 74, 103, 135, 138, 154, 155, 175, 250, 337
To Ramona, 340
Toche, Jean, 273
Too Many Cooks (Spoil The Soup), 309
Too Much Monkey Business, 306
Toot And A Snore In '74, A, 312
Top Of The Pops, 11, 112, 179
Tora! Tora! Tora!, 122
Tosh, Peter, 208
Townshend, Pete, 195, 206
Trade Winds, the, 248
Tree Publishing, 313
Troup, Bobby, 285
Troy, Doris, 17
Turner, 'Big' Joe, 190
Turner, Ted, 148
Tutti-Frutti, 372
Twain, Mark, 266
Twiggy, 242

Ubu Cocu, 212

Van Eaton, Derrek, 228, 244, 249, 339, 360
Van Eaton, Lon, 228, 244, 249, 338, 339, 341, 360
Van Scyoc, Gary, 183, 185, 186, 189, 190, 191, 192, 193, 194
Van Winkle, Dixon, 110
Vanderbilt, Gloria, 280
Vatican, the, 76

Vaughan, Ivan, 361
Velvet Underground, the, 264
Vicari, Frank, 318, 319, 320, 324, 325, 326, 327, 330, 369, 370, 371, 372, 373, 374, 376
Vietnam (song), 66
Vietnam war, 8, 66
Vincent, Gene, 55, 307, 375
Visconti, Tony, 280, 282, 283, 284, 287, 290, 291, 292
Vollmer, Jurgen, 377
Voormann, Klaus, v, 8, 10, 19, 20, 39, 40, 42, 45, 47, 48, 49, 50, 51, 53, 54, 55, 56, 73, 74, 75, 82, 83, 89, 90, 93, 95, 96, 98, 99, 100, 102, 103, 105, 134, 135, 136, 137, 139, 142, 143, 145, 146, 147, 148, 149, 151, 153, 169, 170, 172, 173, 174, 177, 225, 226, 227, 228, 229, 230, 231, 232, 233, 234, 235, 236, 237, 245, 246, 247, 248, 249, 250, 251, 252, 253, 254, 255, 256, 258, 294, 318, 319, 320, 321, 322, 324, 325, 326, 327, 328, 329, 330, 337, 338, 339, 341, 344, 345, 346, 367, 368, 369, 370, 371, 372, 373, 374, 375, 376

Waiting For A Train, 82
Walk, The, 112, 305
Wangberg, Eirik, 119, 130, 132
Ward, William, 389
Warhol, Andy, 155
Watergate, 264
Wayne, Delon, 202
Wayne, Thomas with the DeLons, 202
We're On Our Way, 348
Webb, Cynthia, 339
Weeks, Willie, 235, 355, 356, 357, 358, 360, 362
Weep For Love, 281
Weight, The, 56
Went To See The Gypsy, 50
Western Movies (song), 136
Whale, The, 349
What Does It Take (To Win Your Love), 356
What's Going On, 232
When Irish Eyes Are Smiling, 19
White Christmas, 176
White, Alan, v, 9, 10, 11, 18, 40, 42, 45, 50, 51, 53, 54, 55, 143, 144, 145, 146, 147, 148, 149, 151, 153
White, Bill, 43
Whiter Shade Of Pale, A, 269
Whitesnake, 337
Whitlock, Bobby, 38, 40, 47, 48, 49, 51, 54, 55, 56, 70, 71, 72, 73, 76, 77, 79, 80, 81, 82, 83, 85

Who, the, 171, 172, 205, 380
Wigg, David, 169
Wilkes, Tom, 361
Will It Go Round In Circles, 231
Will You Love Me Tomorrow, 298
Williams, Andy, 235, 322
Williams, Hank, 121, 213
Williams, Larry, 297
Williams, Taffy, 32
Wills, Bob, 314
Wiltshire, Christine, 264
Wind of Change, 244
Wind Ridge, 191
Window Music, 58, 65
Wine, Toni, 134
Winfrey, Ernie, 316
Wings At The Sound Of Denny Laine, 285
Winter Wonderland, 177
Winter, Johnny, 262
Wishbone Ash, 148
Without The Lord, 228
Without You, 245
Wizzard, 295
Wofford, Michael, 304, 305, 306
Woloschuk, John, 348
Wonder, Stevie, 195, 221, 308, 311, 321, 351
Wood, Krissy, 355
Wood, Ron, 294, 355
Woodstock Festival, 53, 195
Wooly Bully, 208
Words Of Love, 160, 367
Working On A Guru, 50
Wrecking Crew, the, 18, 245, 248, 296
Wright, Gary, 20, 42, 47, 49, 50, 51, 53, 73, 76, 77, 79, 80, 82, 134, 174, 225, 226, 227, 229, 230, 231, 232, 233, 234, 236, 237, 256, 257, 294
Wyman, Bill, 309

Yes We Can, 338
Yorke, Ritchie, 10
You Ain't Going Nowhere, 82, 328
You Can't Catch Me, 148, 295, 305, 366, 370, 378, 379
You Don't Know What You've Got (Until You Lose It), 326
You Keep Me Hanging On, 248
Young, Neil, 121, 159

Zappa, Frank, 136, 155, 169, 191, 197
Zip-A-Dee Doo-Dah, 288
Zito, Torrie, 153
Zoo Gang, The (television show), 243

Printed in Great Britain
by Amazon